Cases and Materials on Equity and Trusts

Authors

Matthew Carn
Adam Doyle
Christine Flutter
Jan Maltby
Katharine Matheson
Richard Quenby
Elena Solaro
Charlotte Bois-Pursey
John Reynolds

Editor

Matthew Carn

Seventh edition July 2017

Published ISBN 9781509714797

British Library Cataloguing-in-Publication Data
A catalogue record for this book is available from the British Library

Published by BPP Law School

Printed by
Ashford Colour Press Ltd
Unit 600, Fareham Reach
Fareham Road
Gosport, Hampshire
PO13 0FW

Your learning materials, published by BPP Law School, are printed on paper obtained from traceable sustainable sources.

Contents

A note about copyright

Dear Customer

What does the little © mean and why does it matter?

Your market-leading BPP books, course materials and e-learning materials do not write and update themselves. People write them: on their own behalf or as employees of an organisation that invests in this activity. Copyright law protects their livelihoods. It does so by creating rights over the use of the content.

Breach of copyright is a form of theft – as well as being a criminal offence in some jurisdictions, it is potentially a serious breach of professional ethics.

With current technology, things might seem a bit hazy but, basically, without the express permission of BPP:

Photocopying our materials is a breach of copyright

Scanning, ripcasting or conversion of our digital materials into different file formats, uploading them to Facebook or e-mailing them to your friends is a breach of copyright

You can, of course, sell your books, in the form in which you have bought them – once you have finished with them. (Is this fair to your fellow students? We update for a reason.) But the e-products are sold on a single user licence basis: we do not supply 'unlock' codes to people who have bought them second-hand.

And what about outside the UK? BPP strives to make our materials available at prices students can afford by local printing arrangements, pricing policies and partnerships which are clearly listed on our website. A tiny minority ignore this and indulge in criminal activity by illegally photocopying our material or supporting organisations that do. If they act illegally and unethically in one area, can you really trust them?

Index of Cases

A

B

C

D

E

F

G

H

I

J

K

L

M

N

O

P

R

S

T

U

V

W

X

Y

Z

1

Introduction to Equity and Trusts

Customs of the Rest of the Courts at Westminster, which are as a Law to those Courts, and of which the Common Law takes Notice. ...

... The Chancellor sits in Chancery according to an absolute and uncontrolable Power, and is to judge according to that which is alledged and proved; but the Judges of the Common Law are to judge according to a strict and ordinary (or limited) Power...

There was no need to make a judgment upon the specific facts of the case as the suit had been discontinued by this stage. However, the essence of Coke CJ's judgment is that whenever there is a conflict between the Common Law and Equity, then Equity will take preference over the Common Law rules.

Following the Judicature Acts 1873-1875 we now have a single High Court, Court of Appeal and (since October 2009) Supreme Court, which have replaced the various Common Law courts and the Court of Chancery. Instead each court now has the ability to resort to equity in order to do justice between the parties. However, a consequence of Equity being a separate body of rules for so long is that there are a body of rules which have enabled a more sophisticated way of dealing with property than the Common Law allowed. This body of rules has also developed over time and has culminated in the law of trusts.

The key advantage of the trust over what can be done with property at Common Law is the flexibility with what can be done with property when a trust is used. For more detail on this, please refer to Chapter 1 of your study notes. Trusts nowadays play a pivotal role in the commercial world. Indeed, they are so prominent that it is practically impossible to calculate the number of trust funds in existence worldwide, or the combined worth of all the assets held under these trusts. The importance of trusts has been even been noted outside of Common Law legal systems as far back as the 1930s by the noted French commentator Pierre Lepaulle. This is particularly noteworthy as France is a civil law system, in which traditionally it is impossible to have split ownership rights in the way that trustees and beneficiaries do.

Pierre Lepaulle, Traité théorique et pratique des trusts en droit interne, en droit fiscal et en droit international, Paris (1932), p 113.

Thus from settlement of the greatest of wars down to the simplest inheritance on death, from the most audacious Wall Street scheme down to the protection of grandchildren, the trust can see marching before it the motley procession of the whole of human endeavour: dreams of peace, commercial imperialism, attempts to strangle competition or to reach paradise, hatred or philanthropy, love of one's family or the desire to strip it of everything after one's death, all those in the procession being dressed either in robes or in rags, and either crowned in a halo or walking with a grin. The trust is the guardian angel of the Anglo-Saxon, accompanying him everywhere, impassively, from the cradle to the grave.

1

Introduction to Equity and Trusts

1.1 Why do we have 'Equity'?

Although many other legal systems have a notion of 'equity' as a process of modifying what are otherwise harsh and inflexible rules, the concept of 'Equity' as a second body of legal rules is a special anomaly of the common law world. Indeed, English law was not always structured this way, and were it not for decisions made over 700 years ago, the structure of English law would be quite different.

To understand how Equity came to exist in this way we have to go back to the reign of Henry III. At this time if you wanted to go to court you had to use a writ, or legal template, to structure your claim and bring it to court. If you could not find a suitable writ you could somehow fit your case within, then in effect you had no claim. Fortunately, new writs could be created and so if there was an obvious lacuna in the law then this could, at least theoretically, be corrected.

However, by the reign of Henry III there was a growing fear that there were too many writs and that this would lead to the undeserving obtaining legal remedies and the courts being flooded with litigation. This fear reached its zenith in 1258, when the nobles presented Henry with the Provisions of Oxford. This document stipulated that the writ system should not be expanded any further.

While this provided a temporary respite for the English legal system from a flood of claims, the rigidity of having to fit your claim within a suitable writ and the inability to create new writs quickly led to ossification and unfairness within the law. Fortunately there was a final option available to litigants denied access to the court system: they could petition the King in person as the fount of all justice. With kings having to spend their time on so many other competing issues, this duty was quickly passed on to the Chancellor, who was a senior member of the ruling council and close advisor to the King. Traditionally, the Chancellor was also a cleric and was not only concerned with the facts of the case but also with the fate of the souls of the litigants. When he heard petitions he would, therefore, give his judgment in accordance with good conscience. Nevertheless the decisions made by the Chancellor in his court of Chancery did much to ameliorate the harshness of the Common Law.

By doing this, however, the Court of Chancery was brought into conflict with the Common Law courts. Until the Judicature Acts of 1873-1875, the civil courts did not have a uniform or neatly defined structure. Instead they competed between themselves for cases as a means of funding their survival. This led to a problem in that an unsuccessful claim at Common Law might be given a remedy in the Court of Chancery. The question as to which decision should prevail was finally answered in the *Earl of Oxford's Case* 21 ER 485.

***The Earl of Oxford's Case in Chancery* 21 ER 485**

Panel: Coke CJ

Facts: In 1574 Magdalene College, Cambridge sold some land to Benedict Spinola, who then sold it to the Earl of Oxford. This land was considerably developed and 130 houses, among other things, were constructed on the land. On or about 1612 the Master of Magdalene College tried to regain the property for the college and during this time attempted to obtain possession of one of the 130 houses by undue means. The question was whether the Court of Chancery had jurisdiction to hear the claim by the Earl of Oxford. It was held that whenever there is a conflict between the rules of Common Law and Equity, the rules of Equity should always take precedence.

CHIEF JUSTICE COKE

Decipher Archaic language

First, As a Right in Law cannot die, no more can Equity in Chancery die, and therefore *nullus recedat a Cancellaria sine remedio*, 4 E. 4, 11, a. Therefore the Chancery is always open, and although the Term be adjourned the Chancery is not; for Conscience and Equity is always ready to render to every one their Due, and 9 E. 4, 11, a. The Chancery is only removable at the Will of the King and Chancellor; and by 27 E. 3, 15. The Chancellor must give Account to none but only to the King and Parliament.

The Cause why there is a Chancery is, for that Mens Actions are so divers and infinite, That it is impossible to make any general Law which may aptly meet with every particular Act, and not fail in some Circumstances. ...

But in this Case, upon the Matter there is no Judgment, but only a Discontinuance of the Suit, which gives no Possession; and altho' to prosecute Law and Equity together be a Veration; yet voluntarily to attempt the Law in a doubtful Case, and after to resort to Equity, is neither strange nor unreasonable.

But take it as a Judgment to all Intents; then I answer,

That in this Case there is no Opposition to the Judgment; neither will the Truth or Justice of the Judgment be examined in this Court, nor any Circumstance depending thereupon; but the same is justified and approv'd; and therefore a Judgment is no Let to examine it in Equity, so as all the Truth of the Judgment, &c., be (not) examin'd. ...

In Chancery upon a Recognizance, a Capias may be awarded, and the Precedents of that Court shall close up the Mouths of the Judges of the Common Law, notwithstanding the Statute of Magna Charta, cap. 29. Quod nullus liber homo capiatur aut imprisonetur nisi per legale Judicium Parium suorum vel per Legem Terræ. And so it was adjudged in Clement Parson's Case, 21 Eliz. in the Exchequer, which you may see in 8 Coke, 142, and 25 Eliz. in Martin and Bye's Case, and in 7 Jac. in Com. Banco, Higham's Case, and Kilway's Case vouched to be adjudged, 9 Co 29. Vide Doctor and Student, 306 a, and every Court at Westminster ought to take Notice of the Usages and

Customs of the Rest of the Courts at Westminster, which are as a Law to those Courts, and of which the Common Law takes Notice. ...

...The Chancellor sits in Chancery according to an absolute and uncontrolable Power, and is to judge according to that which is alledged and proved; but the Judges of the Common Law are to judge according to a strict and ordinary (or limited) Power...

There was no need to make a judgment upon the specific facts of the case as the suit had been discontinued by this stage. However, the essence of Coke CJ's judgment is that whenever there is a conflict between the Common Law and Equity, then Equity will take preference over the Common Law rules.

Following the Judicature Acts 1873-1875 we now have a single High Court, Court of Appeal and (since October 2009) Supreme Court, which have replaced the various Common Law courts and the Court of Chancery. Instead each court now has the ability to resort to equity in order to do justice between the parties. However, a consequence of Equity being a separate body of rules for so long is that there are a body of rules which have enabled a more sophisticated way of dealing with property than the Common Law allowed. This body of rules has also developed over time and has culminated in the law of trusts.

The key advantage of the trust over what can be done with property at Common Law is the flexibility with what can be done with property when a trust is used. For more detail on this, please refer to Chapter 1 of your study notes. Trusts nowadays play a pivotal role in the commercial world. Indeed, they are so prominent that it is practically impossible to calculate the number of trust funds in existence worldwide, or the combined worth of all the assets held under these trusts. The importance of trusts has been even been noted outside of Common Law legal systems as far back as the 1930s by the noted French commentator Pierre Lepaulle. This is particularly noteworthy as France is a civil law system, in which traditionally it is impossible to have split ownership rights in the way that trustees and beneficiaries do.

Pierre Lepaulle, Traité théorique et pratique des trusts en droit interne, en droit fiscal et en droit international, Paris (1932), p 113.

Thus from settlement of the greatest of wars down to the simplest inheritance on death, from the most audacious Wall Street scheme down to the protection of grandchildren, the trust can see marching before it the motley procession of the whole of human endeavour: dreams of peace, commercial imperialism, attempts to strangle competition or to reach paradise, hatred or philanthropy, love of one's family or the desire to strip it of everything after one's death, all those in the procession being dressed either in robes or in rags, and either crowned in a halo or walking with a grin. The trust is the guardian angel of the Anglo-Saxon, accompanying him everywhere, impassively, from the cradle to the grave.

1.2 The Nature of Trustee and Beneficiary Rights in a Trust

Once a trust has been created, the settlor no longer has a role to play in the trust unless they are also acting as a trustee. The legal title has been transferred to the trustee and the equitable title is held by the beneficiary. The trustee and beneficiary are therefore the only parties within the trust relationship. As the trustee has legal title to the trust assets, this means the trustee has power as to how those assets are used, such as how they are invested, or to whom they are transferred. However, the trustee cannot deal with the trust property freely. Instead, the trustee has active duties regarding what is to be done with the trust assets. The flip side of these trustee duties are the rights of the beneficiary. The beneficiary's rights not only assert the fact the trustee is not an absolute owner of the property, but also that the ultimate control of the trust assets is in the hands of the beneficiary. The clearest example of this ultimate control is the ability of the beneficiary to collapse the trust and take trust assets as an absolute owner, even in circumstances where the settlor did not want this to happen.

***Saunders v Vautier* 41 E.R. 482**

Panel: Lord Langdale MR

Facts: In his will, Richard Wright left his stock in the East India Company to be held on trust for Daniel Vautier. The income generated from the stock was to be accumulated and this income together with the stock itself to be transferred to Vautier as absolute owner when he was 25. When Vautier was 21 (the age of majority at the time) he applied to receive the stock and the income. The trustee, Saunders, contested this, stating that Vautier would only become entitled to the stock and the income according to the terms of the trust. It was held that Vautier became entitled to the property of the trust as soon as he was an adult and as long as he was of full mental capacity.

LORD LANGDALE MR

I think the principle has been repeatedly acted upon; and where a legacy is directed to accumulate for a certain period, or where the payment is postponed, the legatee, if he has an absolute indefeasible interest in the legacy, is not bound to wait until the expiration of that period, but may require payment the moment he is competent to give a valid discharge.

Vautier was therefore allowed to take the stock and the income immediately, despite wishes to the contrary in Wright's will. The rule in *Saunders v Vautier* from this case is that once the beneficiary is of full age and capacity the terms of the trust should be secondary to the law's treatment of people as autonomous individuals. The law of trusts should not, therefore, treat sane adults as if they were children. Therefore, once beneficiaries are adults they should be treated as being capable of running their own affairs, including their property rights.

The strict legal principle, however, is quite narrow; taken literally the rule in *Saunders v Vautier* will only apply where the sole beneficiary is absolutely entitled to the property, is of full age and is of full mental capacity. Subsequent case law has extended the rule to trusts where there are multiple beneficiaries. By extending the rule in this way, however, two further questions arise. First, if the trust is a fixed trust, where the beneficiary has a fixed share of the trust assets, can they take absolute ownership of that specific part of the trust assets? Second, if the trust is a discretionary trust, where it is uncertain what amount of the trust assets each beneficiary will receive, can all the beneficiaries agree to take absolute ownership of the assets under the rule in *Saunders v Vautier* despite the uncertainty?

With regard to the fixed trust question, there are two High Court decisions that give some guiding principles.

***Stephenson (Inspector of Taxes) v Barclays Bank Trust Co Ltd* [1975] 1 WLR 882**

Panel: Walton J

Statute: Finance Act 1965 s22

Facts: In his will Sir Richard Winfrey made Barclays Bank his executors and trustees. His will provided, among other things, for annuities to be given to his daughters during their widowhood. These assets were then to be held on trust in equal shares for all of his grandchildren who were alive at the testator's death that reached the age of 21.

A subsequent deed of arrangement modified this arrangement so that an extra fund was added to the assets used by the annuities. Upon these extra assets being added to the annuities the widows would not be entitled to any of the other trust assets. The trustees did not transfer any of those assets to the grandchildren. The Inland Revenue claimed that the trust was liable to capital gains tax as a consequence of this deed of arrangement. The trustees resisted this claim, stating that since the grandchildren were not capable of overriding the terms of the trust by becoming absolute owners of the property there could be no such disposal that would attract capital gains tax.

It was held that the grandchildren were together entitled to the trust assets and therefore the trust was liable to capital gains tax.

MR JUSTICE WALTON

Now it is trite law that the persons who between them hold the entirety of the beneficial interests in any particular trust fund are as a body entitled to direct the trustees how that trust fund is to be dealt with, and this is obviously the legal territory from which that definition derives. ... I think it may be desirable to state what I conceive to be certain elementary principles.

(1) In a case where the persons who between them hold the entirety of the beneficial interests in any particular trust fund are all *sui juris* and acting

together, ("the beneficial interest holders"), they are entitled to direct the trustees how the trust fund may be dealt with. (2) This does not mean, however, that they can at one and the same time override the pre-existing trusts and keep them in existence. ... (3) Nor, I think, are the beneficial interest holders entitled to direct the trustees as to the particular investment they should make of the trust fund. I think this follows for the same reasons as the above. Moreover, it appears to me that once the beneficial interest holders have determined to end the trust they are not entitled, unless by agreement, to the further services of the trustees. Those trustees can of course be compelled to hand over the entire trust assets to any person or persons selected by the beneficiaries against a proper discharge, but they cannot be compelled, unless they are in fact willing to comply with the directions, to do anything else with the trust fund which they are not in fact willing to do. (4) Of course, the rights of the beneficial interest holders are always subject to the right of the trustees to be fully protected against such matters as duty, taxes, costs or other outgoings; for example, the rent under a lease which the trustees have properly accepted as part of the trust property.

So much for the rights of the beneficial interest holders collectively. When the situation is that a single person who is sui juris has an absolutely vested beneficial interest in a share of the trust fund, his rights are not, I think, quite as extensive as those of the beneficial interest holders as a body. In general, he is entitled to have transferred to him (subject, of course, always to the same rights of the trustees as I have already mentioned above) an aliquot share of each and every asset of the trust fund which presents no difficulty so far as division is concerned. This will apply to such items as cash, money at the bank or an unsecured loan, Stock Exchange securities and the like. However, as regards land, certainly, in all cases, as regards shares in a private company in very special circumstances ... and possibly (although the logic of the addition in fact escapes me) mortgage debts ... the situation is not so simple, and even a person with a vested interest in possession in an aliquot share of the trust fund may have to wait until the land is sold, and so forth, before being able to call upon the trustees as of right to account to him for his share of the assets. ...

Thus the conclusion of the whole matter appears to me to be that when the deed of family arrangement was executed the two grandchildren became, for the purposes of capital gains tax, jointly absolutely entitled as against the trustees of their grandfather's will trusts to the remaining residue of the estate not thereby appropriated to answer their aunts' annuities within the meaning of section 22(5) of the Finance Act 1965, and paragraph 9 of Schedule 19 to the Finance Act 1969; and that, consequent thereupon, the trustees are, by virtue of section 25(3), deemed for the purposes of capital gains tax to have disposed of the whole of such remaining residue and immediately reacquired the same in their capacity as trustees for a consideration equal to its market value. I have already indicated that the figure of £10,000 is purely notional, and the actual figures will now remain to be worked out by the parties.

It must be noted, as Walton J did at the end of his judgment, that on the facts of this case the trustees were only liable to capital gains tax on a few small parcels of unquoted shares and some land. However, this case is authority for the suggestion that beneficiaries of fixed trusts are able to become absolute owners of their specific part of the trust as long as there is no problem in dividing the assets. While land is clearly a type of property that is hard to divide up, another important example is shares within a private company. Therefore, where a trust has shares in a private company and one of the beneficiaries has a fixed interest in a majority of the shares, the court will not automatically allow that beneficiary to take the shares absolutely.

***Lloyds Bank Plc v Duker and Others* [1987] 1 WLR 1324**

Panel: John Mowbray QC sitting as a deputy High Court judge

Facts: In his will Rowland Smith made Lloyds Bank his personal representative. Among his assets were 999 of 1,000 shares in a private company (Rowland Smith Hotels Ltd) that owned a hotel in Torquay. These shares were subject to a partial intestacy (some of the legatees had died without leaving any heirs to take their shares in the company) and therefore the family entered into a deed of arrangement. The testator's wife, Freda Smith, was to receive 46/80ths of the shares and the remaining amount was to be divided among the other five beneficiaries of Mr Smith's will in proportion to the amount of specified assets they were entitled to. Freda Smith wanted to become absolute owner of her shares in the company, but no transfer was made before she died. In her will she left her shares to Mr Duker, the managing director of the company controlling the hotel. Mr Duker then asked Lloyds Bank to transfer the shares to him absolutely. The other beneficiaries objected to this and so Lloyds Bank applied to the court as to whether it had to comply with Mr Duker's request or whether all of the company shares should be sold on the open market. It was held that Mr Duker was not entitled to take his shares absolutely as this would give him an unfair advantage over the other beneficiaries.

JOHN MOWBRAY QC

The whole net estate is ready for immediate distribution. I assume for the purpose of answering the question that anyone entitled to an aliquot part of such an estate as this is normally entitled to insist on a corresponding part of any easily divisible property being distributed to him as it is, rather than the whole property being sold and the money proceeds distributed. Other beneficiaries, if they like, can ask the executors to sell their parts of the property, or they can do it for themselves.

What the other beneficiaries say here is that if the shares are transferred out in the 1/80th fractions, Mr Duker will not take 46/80ths of the total value received by all the beneficiaries as a group, but much more, because a majority holding is worth more per share than a minority holding. ...

What is more, none of the minority holdings can be expected to participate in dividends for the foreseeable future, if Mr Duker takes 574 shares. That appears from a letter which his (and the company's) accountants wrote to Mrs. Arnold Smith on 13 February 1986. I shall read it. It says:

'Dear Mrs. Smith,

Palace Hotel, Torquay — Shares

"Further to our letter of 21 January, our client wishes us to provide You with further information concerning the shares in Rowland Smith Hotels Ltd. — 1. It is the opinion of the executors that the shares in the company should be allocated pro rata to the residuary legatees of the estate of Rowland Smith. 2. This opinion is supported by counsel's opinion which has been reiterated recently despite the alternative advice which has been given to some of the 'minority' beneficiaries. 3. We believe that in the light of counsel's opinion and the offer made by our client, the court would be unlikely to recommend a sale of the hotel but should it take this step there are doubts as to whether such a sale could be enforced having regard to the structure of the company. 4. Although profitability is now running at a more satisfactory level, in order to maintain the hotel in a competitive position, the directors have embarked on a number of major projects. Accordingly, profits will need to be retained in the business for the foreseeable future and shareholders are unlikely, therefore, to receive dividends during this time. 5. In view of the lack of good dividend prospects, the value of the minority shareholdings in the company is certainly substantially lower than the offer of £403 per share recently made to You by our client."

As I understand it, Mr Duker offered £403 a share to all the other beneficiaries, and has subsequently increased this offer to £510 a share. (The minority beneficiaries' counsel confirmed this on instructions.) At that price, the minority's 425 shares would be worth a total of £216750. The minority could, on any view, insist on their joint holding of 425 shares being sold as a single block, and I think that en bloc they might fetch more than that. None the less, the want of any dividends for the foreseeable future, and the inability of the buyer of any minority block to force a dividend would be bound to have a definite depressing effect on the value of the holding.

Mr Duker could not be expected to join in a winding up resolution, and he would not need dividends, because he could pay himself a salary as managing director.

So, though the state of the evidence does not enable me to make any precise finding about values, I can find this much, which is all I need for the present purpose: the value per share of a holding of 574 shares in the company is markedly higher than the value per share of a holding even of 425 shares. The result is that, if Mr Duker takes 574 shares, the value of what he takes will be markedly more than 46/80ths of the aggregate values of his and the other holdings.

Is that finding of fact enough to override what I am assuming is the normal rule by which Mr Duker would be entitled to call for a transfer of 574 of the shares? It seems clear to me that such a transfer would not be in accordance with Mr Smith's will. When he gave one half of his residuary estate to his wife and the other half to his brothers and sisters and others, he must have meant half by value. The partial intestacy does not affect the meaning of the will. No one is suggesting that the shares should be distributed otherwise than in the 1/80th fractions.

To bring about a fair division in the 1/80th fractions, according to values, it would be necessary for the bank to sell all 999 shares and distribute the money proceeds in those fractions. ...

Are the circumstances in the present case such as to require the bank to sell all 999 shares, rather than distributing 574 of them to Mr Duker? To answer this question, I need to see what kind of circumstances would exclude his normal right to have this aliquot part of the shares distributed to him. ...

...The operative reason is that, if the shares were transferred out in the 1/80th fractions, Mr Duker would get a greater value per share than the other beneficiaries and so would get more than his 46/80ths of the total value received by the beneficiaries as a body.

I have not had much help from dicta in the authorities...

I can, though, get some help from another general principle. I mean the principle that trustees are bound to hold an even hand among their beneficiaries, and not favour one as against another... Of course Mr Duker must have a larger part than the other beneficiaries. But if he takes 46/80ths of the shares he will be favoured beyond what Mr Smith intended, because his shares will each be worth more than the others. The trustees' duty to hold an even hand seems to indicate that they should sell all 999 shares instead.

Mr Harrod pointed out that if Mr Duker's shares are sold, immediate capital gains tax will be incurred on the unrealised capital appreciation which has accrued since the death of Mrs. Smith (or it may be Mr Smith) whereas if the bank transfers them to Mr Duker as a residuary legatee no capital gains tax will be immediately payable. This is something I must take into account, though I think it might be tempered to some extent by a sale of the whole company realising more per share than even a majority holding of 574 shares. ...

In all the circumstances, to prevent the unfairness which would result from a transfer of 574 of the shares to Mr Duker, and to ensure that he takes 46/80ths of the residuary estate measured by value, I consider that the bank should not transfer any of the shares to him, but should sell all 999 on the general market, Mr Duker being left free to become a buyer.

From these cases it is clear that a fixed trust beneficiary does not have an automatic right to take a share of the trust assets absolutely by using the rule in *Saunders v Vautier*. Instead, the court has to consider whether the property can easily be divided, and whether an absolute transfer would be to the detriment of the other beneficiaries.

The comments made in *Duker* indicate exceptions to the general rule rather than negating the rule absolutely. Therefore, fixed interest beneficiaries do theoretically have the right to exercise *Saunders v Vautier* rights, although these might be prevented from being used depending upon the type of property and the facts of the case.

The situation is less clear, however, with regard to beneficiaries under discretionary trusts. All that is directly relevant upon this point is conflicting *obiter* from two cases, which leaves an important and therefore unfortunate lacuna in the law.

***Re Smith* [1928] Ch 915**

Panel: Romer J

Facts: Mr Aspinall left one fourth of his residuary estate to be held on discretionary trust for his widow and any children she may have. The widow, who was well beyond child bearing age, her two surviving children and the legal personal representatives of the deceased child all joined in executing a mortgage assigning all the interests they would have taken under the will. The Public Trustee went to court to see if the property under a discretionary trust was capable of being assigned in this way. It was held that as all the discretionary beneficiaries had joined together in making the assignment, the property was capable of being assigned in this way.

MR JUSTICE ROMER

... The question I have to determine is whether the Legal and General Assurance Company are now entitled to call upon the trustees to pay the whole of the income to them. It will be observed from what I have said that the whole of this share is now held by the trustees upon trusts under which they are bound to apply the whole income and eventually pay over or apply the whole capital to Mrs Aspinall and the three children or some or one of them. So far as the income is concerned they are obliged to pay it or apply it for her benefit or to pay it or apply it for the benefit of the children. So far as regards the capital they have a discretion to pay it and to apply it for her benefit and, subject to that, they must hold it upon trust for the children. Mrs Aspinall, the two surviving children and the representatives of the deceased child are between them entitled to the whole fund. In those circumstances it appears to me, notwithstanding the discretion which is reposed in the trustees, under which discretion they could select one or more of the people I have mentioned as recipients of the income, and might apply part of the capital for the benefit of Mrs Aspinall and so take it away from the children, that the four of them, if they were all living, could come to the Court and say to the trustees: "Hand over the fund to us." It appears to me that that this is in accordance ... with principle. What is the principle? As I understand it it is this. Where there is a trust under which trustees have a discretion as to applying the whole or part of a fund to or

for the benefit of a particular person, that particular person cannot come to the trustees, and demand the fund; for the whole fund has not been given to him but only so much as the trustees think fit to let him have. But when the trustees have no discretion as to the amount of the fund to be applied, the fact that the trustees have a discretion as to the method in which the whole of the fund shall be applied for the benefit of the particular person does not prevent that particular person from coming and saying: "Hand over the fund to me." ...

There will, consequently, be a declaration that, in the events which have happened, the plaintiff is bound to pay the whole of the income of the one-fourth to the defendant society during the lifetime of Mrs Aspinall, or until the mortgage is discharged.

Note that since there was no taking of the property absolutely by any of the discretionary beneficiaries, this is not a case where the rule in *Saunders v Vautier* is directly used. This case is therefore strictly only an *obiter* comment upon how *Saunders v Vautier* might apply. What is clear though is that Romer J clearly held that the fact the trust is discretionary should not interfere with the rights of the discretionary beneficiaries if they all agree to embark on a course of action with the trust property and they are all of full age and full capacity.

However, the question of whether discretionary beneficiaries have any right to trust property before they are selected by the trustees has not been consistently answered in this way.

***Gartside and Another v Inland Revenue Commissioners* [1968] AC 553**

Panel: Lord Reid, Lord Morris of Borth-Y-Gest, Lord Hodson, Lord Guest and Lord Wilberforce

Statute: Finance Act 1940 s43

Facts: In his will Thomas Gartside left one fourth of his residuary estate to be held on discretionary trust for his son John, John's wife if he married and any grandchildren. When John died the assets were then held on trust in equal shares for any male grandchildren who reached the age of 21 or any female grandchildren who reached the age of 21 or were married. John married and he and his wife had twin sons.

Before John died the trustees advanced £23,500 to each of the grandchildren. There was clearly a passing of property when John died, as each of the grandchildren then had a fixed share in the assets. However, the Inland Revenue claimed there was also a definite interest held by the grandchildren before John died, when the trust was a discretionary trust. Therefore, when the advancement of £23,500 was made to each grandchild, this was liable to estate duty under the Finance Act 1940 s43.

The question before the court was strictly whether the interest each grandchild had was a 'measurable interest' within the specific ambit of the Finance Act.

It was held that as the amount was not measurable it was not liable to estate duty. However, Lords Reid and Wilberforce made comments in their judgments that can be considered relevant to the application of the rule in *Saunders v Vautier*.

LORD REID

... [A] right to require trustees to consider whether they will pay you something does not enable you to claim anything. If the trustees do decide to pay you something, you do not get it by reason of having the right to have your case considered: you get it only because the trustees have decided to give it to you. ...

LORD WILBERFORCE

I have said that no one of the discretionary beneficiaries had at the relevant time any right to receive any income, but this is not the whole of the matter. It is also necessary to appreciate that the discretionary beneficiaries taken together had no right to receive any or, a fortiori, all of the income. Two of them were infants but even if they had been of age they could not, with their parents, have called upon the trustees to pay them the income of any year; the reason being that the trustees had power to accumulate so much as they did not distribute, which might be the whole, for the possible benefit of persons unborn. To describe them as "the only people who could during the relevant period obtain any benefit from the property or have any beneficial enjoyment of it" may be misleading, unless one bears in mind that, singly or collectively, they had no right in any year to receive a penny. ...

The *obiter* suggestion of *Smith* is preferable to that of *Gartside*. This is because their Lordships' judgments were greatly influenced by the notion that further grandchildren might be born, whose rights in the property would be affected by those already alive if they were said to be able to use *Saunders v Vautier*. This particular point must be correct; if the number of beneficiaries can be increased in the future then it is not possible for them all to come together and agree to take the property absolutely. However, where the number of beneficiaries is fixed there is no risk of any beneficiaries losing out through use of *Saunders v Vautier*. The trustees have discretion as to the distribution of assets to beneficiaries, but they are limited to only being able to select from the list of beneficiaries. It is certain, therefore, that whenever a discretion is made it will benefit the class of beneficiaries as a whole. There is no reason to prevent the class, if they all agree and are of full age and mental capacity, from being able to bring the trust to an end and take the property absolutely.

Therefore, *Gartside* should be considered as useful *obiter* for an exceptional circumstance justifying deviation from the general availability of *Saunders v Vautier*, rather than authority for a blanket denial of availability of the rule itself.

1.3 An Important Distinction: Trusts and Powers

Since the beginning of the 20th century trusts have become more complex as a means of combating increasingly sophisticated rules of taxation. Fixed trust beneficiaries came to be seen as having a definite interest in the future, which could be taxed. Consequently, the discretionary trust was conceived to combat this. As tax law evolved to touch upon discretionary trusts, the reaction was to make those capable of benefiting objects of powers of appointment rather than beneficiaries.

Powers of appointment (sometimes called 'mere powers') have a number of extremely important differences from either fixed or discretionary trusts. The rules regarding powers were clarified by Templeman J in *Re Manisty's Settlement Trusts* [1974] Ch 17, which was endorsed and developed by Sir Robert Megarry V-C in *Re Hay's Settlement Trusts* [1982] 1 WLR 202.

***Re Hay's Settlement Trusts* [1982] 1 WLR 202**

Panel: Sir Robert Megarry V-C

Facts: In clause 4 of her deed of settlement Lady Hay settled property for people or purposes as the trustees may appoint by deed within 21 years of the date the settlement was created, with the proviso that no appointment should be made to Lady Hay, any husband of hers, or any trustee or past trustee. If no appointment was made the property was to be held on trust for Lady Hay's nieces and nephews alive at the time the settlement was created.

In clause 2 of a subsequent deed of appointment Lady Hay further authorised the trustees to hold on trust any unappointed income for the benefit of 'any person or persons whatsoever or to any charity,' with the exception of the settlor, any husband of hers and any present or past trustee.

The trustees went to court to find out whether clause 4 was valid, and whether 'any person or persons whatsoever' as allowed under clause 2 was a valid class for a discretionary trust. It was found that clause 4 was valid but clause 2 of the subsequent deed was void.

SIR ROBERT MEGARRY V-C

Two provisions of these instruments are at the centre of the dispute. They are, first, the power of appointment conferred by what I have called the first main limb of clause 4 of the settlement; and, second, the discretionary trust of income under clause 2 of the deed of appointment. Under the power of appointment the trustees were to hold the trust fund on trust for "such persons or purposes" as the trustees should appoint before May 7, 1979, subject to excluding the settlor, her husband and trustees or former trustees, by virtue of the second proviso. Such a provision raises obvious questions about the enormous class of persons who were possible objects of the power: everyone in the world is included save for a handful of persons. If that power is invalid, then of course the appointment made under it must also be invalid, and no other appointment could ever have been valid. The result would therefore be that the second main limb of clause 4 would take effect, and the nieces and nephews living at the date of the settlement would have become entitled to the trust fund in equal shares *ab initio*. ...

he starting point must be to consider whether the power created by the first limb of clause 4 of the settlement is valid. ... The essential point is whether a power for trustees to appoint to anyone in the world except a handful of specified persons is valid. Such a power will be perfectly valid if given to a person who is not in a fiduciary position: the difficulty arises when it is given to trustees, for they are under certain fiduciary duties in relation to the power, and to a limited degree they are subject to the control of the courts. ...

In *Re Manisty's Settlement* [1974] Ch 17, a settlement gave trustees a discretionary power to apply the trust fund for the benefit of a small class of the settlor's near relations, save that any member of a smaller "excepted class" was to be excluded from the class of beneficiaries. The trustees were also given power at their absolute discretion to declare that any person, corporation or charity (except a member of the excepted class or a trustee) should be included in the class of beneficiaries. Templeman J. held that this power to extend the class of beneficiaries was valid. ... In general, I respectfully agree with Templeman J.

Alert

I propose to approach the matter by stages. First, it is plain that if a power of appointment is given to a person who is not in a fiduciary position, there is nothing in the width of the power which invalidates it per se. The power may be a special power with a large class of persons as objects; the power may be what is called a "hybrid" power, or an "intermediate" power, authorising appointment to anyone save a specified number or class of persons; or the power may be a general power. Whichever it is, there is nothing in the number of persons to whom an appointment may be made which will invalidate it. The difficulty comes when the power is given to trustees as such, in that the number of objects may interact with the fiduciary duties of the trustees and their control by the court. ...

Alert

That brings me to the second point, namely, the extent of the fiduciary obligations of trustees who have a mere power vested in them, and how far the court exercises control over them in relation to that power. In the case of a trust, of course, the trustee is bound to execute it, and if he does not, the court will see to its execution. A mere power is very different. Normally the trustee is not bound to exercise it, and the court will not compel him to do so. That, however, does not mean that he can simply fold his hands and ignore it, for normally he must from time to time consider whether or not to exercise the power, and the court may direct him to do this.

When he does exercise the power, he must, of course (as in the case of all trusts and powers) confine himself to what is authorised, and not go beyond it. But that is not the only restriction. Whereas a person who is not in a fiduciary position is free to exercise the power in any way that he wishes, unhampered by any fiduciary duties, a trustee to whom, as such, a power is given is bound by the duties of his office in exercising that power to do so in a responsible manner according to its purpose. It is not enough for him to refrain from acting capriciously; he must do more. He must "make such a survey of the range of objects or possible beneficiaries ..." as will enable him to carry out his fiduciary duty. He must find out "the permissible area of selection and then consider responsibly, in individual cases, whether a contemplated beneficiary was within the power and whether, in relation to other possible claimants, a particular grant was appropriate": *Re Baden (No 1)* [1971] AC 424, 449, 457 *per* Lord Wilberforce. ...

The last proposition, relating to the survey and consideration, at first sight gives rise to some difficulty. It is now well settled that no mere power is invalidated by it being impossible to ascertain every object of the power; provided the language is clear enough to make it possible to say whether any given individual is an object of the power, it need not be possible to compile a complete list of every object... .

That brings me to the third point. How is the duty of making a responsible survey and selection to be carried out in the absence of any complete list of objects? ...[P]lainly the requirements for a mere power cannot be more stringent than those for a discretionary trust, the duty, I think, may be expressed along the following lines... . The trustee must not simply proceed to exercise the power in favour of such of the objects as happen to be at hand or claim his attention. He must first consider what persons or classes of persons are objects of the power within the definition in the settlement or will. In doing this, there is no need to compile a complete list of the objects, or even to make an accurate assessment of the number of them: what is needed is an appreciation of the width of the field, and thus whether a selection is to be made merely from a dozen or, instead, from thousands or millions... . Only when the trustee has applied his mind to the size of the problem "should he then consider in individual cases whether, in relation to other possible claimants, a particular grant is appropriate. In doing this, no doubt he should not prefer the undeserving to the deserving; but he is not required to make an exact calculation whether, as between deserving claimants, A is more deserving than B... .

If I am right in these views, the duties of a trustee which are specific to a mere power seem to be threefold. Apart from the obvious duty of obeying the trust instrument, and in particular of making no appointment that is not authorised by it, the trustee must, first, consider periodically whether or not he should exercise the power; second, consider the range of objects of the power; and third, consider the appropriateness of individual appointments. I do not assert that this list is exhaustive; but as the authorities stand it seems to me to include the essentials, so far as relevant to the case before me. ...

From what I have said it will be seen that I cannot see any ground upon which the power in question can be said to be void. Certainly it is not void for linguistic or semantic uncertainty; there is no room for doubt in the definition of those who are or are not objects of the power. Nor can I see that the power is administratively unworkable. ... Nor do I think that the power is void as being capricious. In *Re Manisty's Settlement* [1974] Ch 17, 27, Templeman J. appears to be suggesting that a power to benefit "residents of Greater London" is void as being capricious "because the terms of the power negative any sensible intention on the part of the settlor." In saying that, I do not think that the judge had in mind a case in which the settlor was, for instance, a former chairman of the Greater London Council, as subsequent words of his on that page indicate. In any case, as he pointed out earlier in the page, this consideration does not apply to intermediate powers, where no class which could be regarded as capricious has been laid down. Nor do I see how the power in the present case could be invalidated as being too vague, a possible ground of invalidity considered in *Re Manisty's Settlement*, at p. 24.

Alert

Of course, if there is some real vice in a power, and there are real problems of administration or execution, the court may have to hold the power invalid: but I think that the court should be slow to do this. Dispositions ought if possible to be upheld, and the court ought not to be astute to find grounds upon which a power can be invalidated. Naturally, if it is shown that a power offends against some rule of law or equity, then it will be held to be void: but a power should not be held void upon a peradventure. In my judgment, the power conferred by clause 4 of the settlement is valid.

With that, I turn to the discretionary trust of income under clause 2 of the deed of appointment. Apart from questions of the validity of the trust per se, there is the prior question whether the settlement enabled the trustees to create such a trust, or, for that matter, the power set out in clause 1 of the deed of appointment. The power conferred by clause 4 of the settlement provides that the trustees are to hold the trust fund on trust "for such persons or purposes for such interests and with such gifts over and (if for persons) with such provisions for their respective maintenance or advancement at the discretion of the trustees or of any other persons" as the trustees shall appoint. Clause 2 of the deed of appointment provides that the trustees are to hold the trust fund on trust to pay the income "to or for the benefit of any person or persons whatsoever ... or to any charity" in such manner and shares and proportions as the trustees think fit. I need say nothing about purposes or charities as no question on them has arisen. The basic question is whether the appointment has designated the "persons" to whom the appointment is made.

Looked at as a matter of principle, my answer would be "No." There is no such person to be found in clause 2 of the deed of appointment: instead, there is merely the mechanism whereby a person or persons may be ascertained from time to time by the exercise of the discretion given to the trustees. If that mechanism is operated, then persons may emerge who will be entitled: but they will emerge not by virtue of any exercise of the power in the settlement but by virtue of the exercise of the discretion in the deed of appointment. That seems to me to be a plain case of delegation: the power in the settlement is not being exercised by appointing the persons who are to benefit but by creating a discretionary trust under which the discretionary trustees will from time to time select those who will benefit. True, the appointor under the settlement and the trustees under the discretionary trust are the same persons: but I do not think that this affects the matter. The power in the settlement is a power to appoint to persons and not a power to nominate those (whether the appointors or anyone else) who will select persons who are to benefit; and I do not see how

> identity in the appointors and nominators can alter the fact that the mechanisms set up by the deed of appointment differs from anything authorised by the settlement. ...
>
> I do not think that the fact that the power is an intermediate power excludes it from the rule against delegation. On the contrary, the fact that the power is vested in trustees subjects it to that rule unless there is something in the settlement to exclude it. I can see nothing in the settlement which purports to authorise any such appointment or to exclude the normal rule against delegation. In my judgment, both on principle and on authority clause 2 of the deed of appointment is void as being an excessive execution of the power. ...
>
> I consider that the duties of trustees under a discretionary trust are more stringent than those of trustees under a power of appointment (see, for example, *In Re Baden (No. 1)* at p. 457), and as at present advised I think that I would, if necessary, hold that an intermediate trust such as that in the present case is void as being administratively unworkable. In my view there is a difference between a power and a trust in this respect. The essence of that difference, I think, is that beneficiaries under a trust have rights of enforcement which mere objects of a power lack. ...

Sir Robert Megarry V-C held that the discretionary trust under clause 2 was void. He therefore held that, upon the expiration of the 21-year time period as set out in clause 4, the nieces and nephews that were alive at the time the settlement was created became entitled to the trust fund.

2

The Three Certainties

Introduction

A trustee has a duty to look after trust property for the beneficiary, upon the terms set out by the settlor. It is therefore vital that the trustee knows the terms of the trust, the property subject to it and the beneficiary. These elements are known as the 'three certainties': certainty of words or intention to create a trust; certainty of subject matter; and certainty of object or beneficiary. If these are not sufficiently clear there are two serious consequences: first, the trustee may inadvertently breach the trust; second, the court may feel unable to assist it if it is unsure what it is being asked to enforce. Therefore, in order to be valid and enforceable, an express private trust must be sufficiently certain. A court, if asked to pronounce on the validity and enforceability of a trust, will construe the trust document as a whole. This is because it is hard to separate the certainties: they overlap, but for ease of analysis they are discussed individually.

2.1 Certainty of Intention

In deciding whether there is certainty of intention to create a trust, the court will look at the overall intention of the settlor, rather than at the exact wording. Words can of course be evidence of intention, but all of the circumstances will be considered.

***In re Adams and the Kensington Vestry* (1884) 27 Ch D 394**

Panel: Baggally, Cotton and Lindley LJJ

Facts: In his will, George Smith left his property 'unto and to the absolute use of my wife Harriet, in full confidence that she will do what is right as to the disposal thereof between my children either in her lifetime or by will after her decease.' The question was whether Harriet was absolutely entitled to the property and thus able to sell it, or whether she held it on trust for the children.

LORD JUSTICE COTTON

... [I]t seems to me perfectly clear what the testator intended. He leaves his wife his property absolutely, but what was in his mind was this: "I am the head of the family, and it is laid upon me to provide properly for the members of my family - my children: my widow will succeed me when I die, and I wish to put her in the position I occupied as the person who is to provide for my children." Not that he entails upon her any trust so as to bind her, but he simply says, in giving her this, I express to her, and call to her attention, the moral obligation which I myself had and which I feel that she is going to discharge. The motive of the gift is, in my opinion, not a trust imposed upon her by the gift in the will. He leaves the property to her; he knows that she will do what is right, and carry out the moral obligation which he thought lay on him, and on her if she survived him, to provide for the children.

He then looked at authority and at how the courts' attitude to interpretation of dispositions had changed:

> ...in the later cases, especially *Lambe v Eames* and *In re Hutchinson and Tenant*, both the Court of Appeal and the late Master of the Rolls shewed a desire really to find out what, upon the true construction, was the meaning of the testator, rather than to lay hold of certain words which in other wills had been held to create a trust, although on the will before them they were satisfied that that was not the intention. I have no hesitation in saying myself, that I think some of the older authorities went a great deal too far in holding that some particular words appearing in a will were sufficient to create a trust. Undoubtedly confidence, if the rest of the context shews that a trust is intended, may make a trust, but what we have to look at is the whole of the will which we have to construe, and if the confidence is that she will do what is right as regards the disposal of the property, I cannot say that that is, on the true construction of the will, a trust imposed upon her. Having regard to the later decisions, we must not extend the old cases in any way, or rely upon the mere use of any particular words, but, considering all the words which are used, we have to see what is their true effect, and what was the intention of the testator as expressed in his will. In my opinion, here he has expressed his will in such a way as not to shew an intention of imposing a trust on the wife, but on the contrary, in my opinion, he has shown an intention to leave the property, as he says he does, to her absolutely.

Alert

See also *Comiskey v Bowring-Hanbury* where the same wording was analysed but a different conclusion reached as the overall context differed.

***Comiskey and Others v Bowring-Hanbury and Another* [1905] AC 84**

Panel: The Earl of Halsbury LC, Lord Macnaghten, Lord Davey, Lord James, Lord Robertson and Lord Lindley

Facts: By his will, Mr Hanbury left all his property to his wife Ellen 'absolutely in full confidence that she will make such use of it as I should have made myself and that at her death she will devise it to such one or more of my nieces as she may think fit and in default of any disposition by her thereof by her will or testament I hereby direct that all my estate and property acquired by her under this my will shall at her death be equally divided among the surviving said nieces.'

His widow, Ellen, asked the court whether she took the property by way of absolute gift, or whether her husband had intended her to hold it on trust for his seven nieces. The Court of Appeal held, by a majority, that no trust was created and that she took the property by way of absolute gift. As the gift over to the nieces was incompatible with an absolute gift to the widow, it was invalid. The nieces appealed.

The House of Lords, by a majority, reversed this decision. Their Lordships looked at the wording in the context of the will as a whole to find that the testator intended a life interest for Ellen, and after her death his nieces were entitled to the property equally, unless Ellen selected differently.

EARL OF HALSBURY LC

... he did not contemplate that during her lifetime she would have disposed of it in any way or placed upon it such an irrevocable character, either by way of settlement or anything else, that at the time when she died herself it would have passed away from her power of disposition. ... He does contemplate that she might make a will herself, and that those words, "in default of any disposition by her thereof by her will," ought to be read with the other words, so that what he is contemplating is, first of all, that the property is to remain capable of being left by her, and, secondly, that she may have made a will, but have made no disposition of that particular property which she has come into possession of under his will.

Then, ... he gives directions. I cannot think that if it was in his mind that she was to be absolute owner and to do what she pleased with it he would, after he had given her a complete power of disposition, use such a phrase as "I hereby direct." To my mind it is clear that he is contemplating that she shall have the full use of the property during her lifetime, and that after her death one or more of his nieces is to be the object of his bounty, and if his widow does not select one or more, then they are all to share alike. That, to my mind, is the meaning of the language. I do not stop to bring in any rules of law or any canons of construction. I look at the words merely as they stand in the will, and I think the natural and ordinary meaning of those words is what I have suggested.

LORD DAVEY

The words which have been so much commented upon, "in full confidence," are, in my opinion, neutral. I think it would be impossible to regard them as technical words in any sense. They are words which may or may not create a trust, and whether they do so or not must be determined by the context of the particular will in which you find them. In the present case I do not think it necessary to determine any such question.

Link
See Adams

... Reading the will without paying any attention to legal rules, and for the purpose only of seeking the testator's intention and the meaning of the words he used, it is obvious that he did not intend that his wife should have an absolute power to dispose of the estate in her lifetime or otherwise than by her will.

Alert

... The use of the word "absolutely," as defining the amount of the estate which is given to the wife, must of course be subject to any executory limitation or any other valid limitation or exception which you find engrafted on that estate in fee simple; therefore I attach no importance, or very little importance, to the use of the word "absolutely".

Thus, the court held that the wife was not free to deal with the property as she chose: there was a trust imposed upon her.

Paul v Constance **[1977] 1 WLR 527**

Panel: Cairns, Scarman and Bridge LJJ

Facts: Mrs Paul and Mr Constance lived together in the late 1960s and early 1970s while Mr Constance was still married. He received damages for a work-related injury which, as most people did not know they were not married, he paid into a deposit account in his sole name. Other money, including joint bingo winnings, was paid in. Mrs Paul had authority to withdraw funds, and money was used for joint purchases, then the remainder was shared. Mr Constance said to Mrs Paul on several occasions, 'the money is as much mine as yours'. He died intestate and his widow was administrator of his estate. Mrs Paul claimed the money in the account, on the ground that it had been held on express trust by Mr Constance for himself and Mrs Paul. The Court of Appeal upheld the decision of the judge at first instance: Mr Constance's words were held to be a clear oral declaration of trust, for the benefit of himself and Mrs Paul.

LORD JUSTICE SCARMAN

...we are dealing with simple people, unaware of the subtleties of equity, but understanding very well indeed their own domestic situation. It is, of course, right that one should consider the various things that were said and done by the plaintiff and the deceased during their time together against their own background and in their own circumstances.

He said that technical language was not needed, but all of the facts and circumstances must be considered:

When one bears in mind the unsophisticated character of the deceased and his relationship with the plaintiff during the last few years of his life, Mr. Wilson submits that the words that he did use on more than one occasion, "This money is as much yours as mine," convey clearly a present declaration that the existing fund was as much the plaintiff's as his own. The judge accepted that conclusion. I think that he was well justified in doing so and, indeed, I think that he was right to do so. There are, as Mr. Wilson reminded us, other features in the history of the relationship between the plaintiff and the deceased which support the interpretation of those words as an express declaration of trust. I have already described the interview with the bank manager when the account was opened. I have mentioned also the putting of the "bingo" winnings into the account and the one withdrawal for the benefit of both of them.

He did, however, acknowledge that it is difficult to pinpoint a specific moment of declaration.

These principles are not confined to personal and family arrangements.

***In re Kayford Limited (in liquidation)* [1975] 1 WLR 279**

Panel: Megarry J

Facts: A mail order company sold soft furnishings. Customers paid in advance for goods ordered. The company had financial problems and wanted to protect the customers' money. It was paid into a dormant deposit account in the company's name, which was changed to a Customers' Trust Deposit account shortly before the company went into liquidation. The liquidators wanted to know whether the money in the account was part of the company's assets, or whether it was held on trust for the customers in proportion to their contributions.

MR JUSTICE MEGARRY

There is no doubt about the so-called 'three certainties' of a trust. The subject-matter to be held on trust is clear, and so are the beneficial interests therein, as well as the beneficiaries. As for the requisite certainty of words, it is well settled that a trust can be created without using the words 'trust' or 'confidence' or the like: the question is whether in substance a sufficient intention to create a trust has been manifested. ... I feel no doubt that here a trust was created. From the outset the advice (which was accepted) was to establish a trust account at the bank. The whole purpose of what was done was to ensure that the moneys remained in the beneficial ownership of those who sent them, and a trust is the obvious means of achieving this. No doubt the general rule is that if you send money to a company for goods which are not delivered, you are merely a creditor of the company unless a trust has been created. The sender may create a trust by using appropriate words when he sends the money (though I wonder how many do this, even if they are equity lawyers), or the company may do it by taking suitable steps on or before receiving the money. If either is done, the obligations in respect of the money are transformed from contract to property, from debt to trust. Payment into a separate bank account is a useful (though by no means conclusive) indication of an intention to create a trust, but of course there is nothing to prevent the company from binding itself by a trust even if there are no effective banking arrangements.

Alert

Although in this case the judge concluded that there was a trust, he did say, *obiter*, different considerations might apply where trade creditors were involved.

2.2 Certainty of Subject Matter

Trusts can be declared over all types of property, but the specific property to be subject to the trust must be certain.

Sprange v Barnard (1789) 2 Bro CC 585

Panel: Lord Arden MR

Facts: Susannah Sprange made a valid will: '... for my husband Thomas Sprange, to bewill to him the sum of £300, ...for his sole use; and, at his death, the remaining part of what is left, that he does not want for his own wants and use, to be divided between ...[my brother and sisters].'

Thomas Sprange applied for a declaration that he was absolutely entitled to the £300. The court held that the property subject to the purported trust was not sufficiently certain to create a valid trust, and that therefore Thomas took the money absolutely.

LORD ARDEN MR

It is contended for the persons to whom it is given in remainder, that he shall only have it for his life, and that the words are strictly mandatory on him to dispose of it in a certain way; but it is only to dispose of what he has no occasion for; therefore, the question is, whether he may not call for the whole; and it seems to me perfectly clear on all the authorities, that he may. ...The property, and the person to whom it is to be given, must be certain, in order to raise a trust. Now here, the property ... is only what shall remain at his death.... it appears to me to be a trust which would be impossible to be executed. I must, therefore, declare him to be absolutely entitled to the £300, and decree it to be transferred to him.

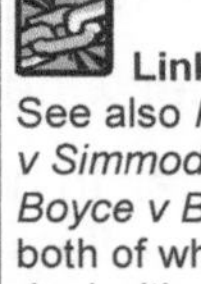

Link
See also *Palmer v Simmods* and *Boyce v Boyce* both of which deal with property which is not sufficiently certain to be the subject matter of a trust.

Palmer v Simmonds (1854) 2 Drew 221

Panel: R T Kindersley V-C

Facts: Henrietta Roscoe made a will leaving the residue of her estate to Thomas Harrison'... for his own use and benefit, as I have full confidence in him, that if he should die without lawful issue he will, after providing for his widow during her life, leave the bulk of my said residuary estate unto...[four named people] equally.'

The executors asked whether the property to be subject to the trust was sufficiently certain. The Vice Chancellor found that there was the requisite intention (an expression of 'confidence' being sufficient at the time) and certain objects. However there was no certainty of subject-matter.

R T KINDERSLEY V-C

If she had said "my residuary estate," I must, according to the cases, have held that there was a trust. But the question is whether the words "the bulk of my residuary estate" mean the same thing as "my residuary estate," or anything precise and definite. The testatrix has here used a term which is not a legal term; a term which has not in law any appropriate meaning. ...

Then there is another instance of the use of legal terms... when she wishes to describe persons to take in remainder, whether the gift over is absolute or only in certain events, she uses appropriate terms. Still more when she gives her residuary estate does she use appropriate legal terms. But when we come to the clause in question, we find her using this language: she expresses her confidence that Harrison will give "the bulk of my said residuary estate". Now what she there meant could not be her residuary estate, which she had already in clear terms given; but the bulk of it. ... Its popular meaning we all know. When a person is said to have given the bulk of his property, what is meant is not the whole but the greater part, and that is in fact consistent with its classical meaning. When, therefore, the testatrix uses that term, can I say she has used a term expressing a definite, clear, certain part of her estate, or the whole of her estate? I am bound to say she has not designated the subject as to which she expresses her confidence; and I am therefore of opinion that there is no trust created; that Harrison took absolutely, and those claiming under him now take.

Link
Refer back to *Sprange v Barnard*

In re Golay's Will Trusts [1965] 1 WLR 969

Panel: Ungoed-Thomas J

Facts: In his will, Golay directed his executors to let his housekeeper enjoy one of his flats for her life and to receive a 'reasonable income' from his other properties. Although they had no difficulty choosing which flat was subject to the trust, the executors asked the court whether the direction as to 'reasonable income' was void for uncertainty. The court found that the trust was valid, because what was a reasonable income for a housekeeper can be objectively identified and is therefore certain.

MR JUSTICE UNGOED-THOMAS

It is ... submitted that what the court is concerned with in the interpretation of this will is not to ascertain what is "reasonable income" in the opinion of the court but to ascertain the testator's intention in using the words "reasonable income". The question therefore comes to this: whether the testator by the words "reasonable income" has given a sufficient indication of his intention to provide an effective determinant of what he intends so that the court in applying that determinant can give effect to the testator's intention.

Alert

Whether the yardstick of "reasonable income" were applied by trustees under a discretion given to them by a testator or applied by a court in course of interpreting and applying the words "reasonable income" in a will, the yardstick sought to be applied by the trustees in the one case and the court in the other case would be identical. The trustees might be other than the original trustees named by the testator and the trustees could even surrender their discretion to the court. It would seem to me to be drawing too fine a distinction to conclude that an objective yardstick which different persons sought to apply would be too uncertain, not because of uncertainty in the yardstick but as between those who seek to apply it.

In this case, however, the yardstick indicated by the testator is not what he or any other specified person subjectively considers to be reasonable but what he identifies objectively as "reasonable income". The court is constantly involved in making such objective assessments of what is reasonable and it is not to be deterred from doing so because subjective influences can never be wholly excluded. In my view the testator intended by "reasonable income" the yardstick which the court could and would apply in quantifying the amount so that the direction in the will is not in my view defeated by uncertainty.

***Boyce v Boyce* (1849) 16 Sim 476**

Panel: Wigram V-C

Facts: The testator left his several houses in trust for his wife for her life. After the wife's death, his daughter Maria was to choose one of the houses to be conveyed to her. The will then stated that 'all the other of my freehold houses which my daughter Maria shall not choose and elect' were to be conveyed to the testator's other daughter Charlotte. Maria died before her father, so did not choose any house. The court held that there was no trust in favour of Charlotte as the property to be subject to the trust was uncertain. The houses therefore formed part of the testator's residuary estate. The case report explained the testator's reasoning thus, without quoting him directly:

WIGRAM V-C

[T]he gift in favour of Charlotte was a gift, not of all the testator's freehold houses situate on the North Cliff in Southwold, but of all *the other* of his freehold houses which Maria should not choose; and, therefore, it was only a gift of the houses that should remain, provided Maria should choose one of them: that no choice had been, or, indeed, could have been made by Maria, and, therefore, the gift in favour of Charlotte had failed.

Link
Sprange v Barnard

***Hunter v Moss* [1994] 1 WLR 452**

Panel: Dillon, Mann and Hirst LJJ

Facts: Moss held 490 ordinary shares in Moss Electrical Company Limited. Moss said to Hunter, the financial director, that he intended to give him 50 shares to put him on an equal footing with the managing director, who had bought 50 shares with bonus money. Moss had said he would hold 50 shares for Hunter and would account for all dividends. The company was sold and the question was whether the trust was void for uncertainty of subject matter. The Court of Appeal upheld the trust.

Lord Justice Dillon rejected the analogy with *Re London Wine Co (Shippers) Ltd* [1986] PCC 121 where tangible chattels were not segregated and therefore there was no certainty of subject matter.

LORD JUSTICE DILLON

That was a case in which the business of the company was that of dealers in wine and over a period it had acquired stocks of wine which were deposited in various warehouses in England. Quantities were then sold to customers by the company, but in many instances the wine remained at the warehouse. There was no appropriation – on the ground, as it were — from bulk, of any wine, to answer particular contracts. But the customer received from the company a certificate of title for wine for which he had paid which described him as the sole and beneficial owner of such-and-such wine of such-and-such a vintage. The customer was charged for storage and insurance, but specific cases were not segregated or identified. Subsequently, at a stage when large stocks of wine were held in various warehouses to the order of the company and its customers, a receiver was appointed by a debenture holder. The question that arose was whether the customers who had received these certificates of title had a good title to the quantity of wine referred to in the certificate as against the receiver appointed under a floating charge. The judge held that it could not be said that the legal title to the wine had passed to individual customers and the description of the wine did not adequately link it with any given consignment or warehouse. And, furthermore, it appeared that there was a lack of comparison at the time the certificates were issued in that, in some cases, the certificates were issued before the wine which had been ordered by the company had actually been received by the company. It seems to me that that case is a long way from the present. It is concerned with the appropriation of chattels and when the property in chattels passes. We are concerned with a declaration of trust, accepting that the legal title remained in the defendant and was not intended, at the time the trust was declared, to pass immediately to the plaintiff.

Link
See the comments on *re Wait* in the judgment of Neuberger J in *re Harvard Securities Ltd.*

Link
See *re Harvard Securities Ltd* which was another case concerning shares on one class in one company.

He said it was crucial that the case concerned the shares of one class in one company, and that this was relevant whether that company was large, such as ICI, or small. Such gifts will not fail simply because the Testator or Donor has not indicated which of the identical shares the beneficiary is to have. Just as a person can give, by will, a specified number of his shares of a certain class in a certain company, so equally, in my judgment, he can declare himself trustee of 50 of his ordinary shares in M.E.L. or whatever the company may be and that is effective to give a beneficial proprietary interest to the beneficiary under the trust.

Alert

Re Harvard Securities Ltd (in liquidation) **[1997] BCLC 369**

Panel: Neuberger J

Facts: This case concerned a number of unidentified and unsegregated shares of one particular class in one particular company. Until 1988 Harvard Securities was a stockbroking investment business. It purchased shares in a US company and sold them to clients in parcels of shares. For costs and time saving reasons it did not register these parcels in the names of individual clients, but held the legal title under a nominee name. Harvard wrote to clients referring to 'your shares' being 'held to your order' by the nominee.

The liquidator of Harvard Securities wanted to know whether the shares were held by the nominee for Harvard Securities beneficially or for their clients beneficially.

In his judgment, Neuberger J surveyed the authorities on certainty of subject matter, beginning with Atkins LJ in the case of *Re Wait* [1927] 1 Ch 606. Wait bought 1,000 tons of wheat and by a sub-contract he sold 500 tons to sub-purchasers. He went bankrupt without delivering the wheat to the sub-purchasers, although they had paid for it. By a majority the Court of Appeal held that there was no trust and that the sub-purchasers were merely ordinary creditors.

MR JUSTICE NEUBERGER:

"He [Atkin LJ] said ([1927] 1 Ch 606 at 629-630:

'no 500 tons of wheat have ever been ear-marked, identified or appropriated as the wheat to be delivered to the claimants under the contract. The claimants have never received any bill of loading, warrant, delivery order or any document of title representing the goods.'

Link
See the similar facts and comments in *Hunter v Moss*.

He then turned to the decision of Oliver J in *Re London Wine Co*:

"In that case, a company had substantial stocks of wine in a number of warehouses. Most of these stocks had been sold to customers, who received from the company a 'Certificate of Title' in respect of the wine for which they had paid, and each such certificate described the customer as 'the sole and beneficial owner' of the wine in question. There was no appropriation from the bulk of any wine to answer any particular contracts. When receivers were appointed in respect of the company, it had sufficient stocks of wine to answer the claims of all of its customers. Oliver J held that the company did not hold any of the wine in trust for its customers, he further held that the customers had no proprietary right in respect of any of the wine, even though they had paid for the wine. He reached this conclusion even where the customer had purchased the company's total stock of a particular wine. Mirroring similar observations of Atkin LJ in *Re Wait*, Oliver J said (at 137):

'I cannot see how, for instance, a farmer who declares himself to be a trustee of two sheep (without identifying them) can be said to have created a perfect and complete trust whatever rights he may confer by such declaration as a matter of contract. And it would seem to me to be immaterial that at the time he has a flock of sheep out of which he could satisfy the interest. Of course, he could by appropriate words, declare himself to be a trustee of the specified proportion of his whole flock and thus create an equitable tenancy in common between himself and the named beneficiary ... But the *mere* declaration that a given number of animals would be held upon trust could not ... without very clear words pointing to such an intention, result in the creation of an interest ...

at the time of the declaration. And where the mass from which the numerical interest is to take effect is not itself ascertainable at the date of the declaration such conclusion becomes impossible.' (Oliver J's emphasis.)

Then he considers *Re Goldcorp Exchange Ltd (in receivership)* [1995] 1 AC 74, a decision of the Privy Council where the same principle was applied to gold bullion:

In that case, the company, which dealt in bullion, sold to its customers bullion which it stored for them. Each customer received an invoice certificate verifying his ownership, and had the right to require physical delivery to his order on seven days' notice and payment of delivery charges. Although the company assured customers that it would maintain sufficient stock of bullion to meet all their demands, it failed to do so. The question which fell to be considered was whether or not the customers had any interests in the bullion owned and stored by the company.

In giving the judgment of the Privy Council, Lord Mustill began with the following observations ([1995] 1 AC 74 at 89-90):

'It is common ground that the contracts in question were for the sale of unascertained goods. For present purposes, two species of unascertained goods may be distinguished. First, there are "generic goods". These are sold on terms which preserve the seller's freedom to decide for himself how and from what source he will obtain goods answering the contractual description. Secondly, there are "goods sold ex-bulk". By this expression their Lordships denote goods which are by express stipulation to be supplied from a fixed and a pre-determined source, from within which the seller may make his own choice ... Approaching these situations a priori common sense dictates that the buyer cannot acquire title until it is known to what goods the title relates. Whether the property then passes will depend upon the intention of the parties and in particular on whether there has been a consensual appropriation of particular goods to the contract ... Their Lordships have laboured this point, about which there has been no dispute, simply to show that any attempt by the non-allocated claimant to assert that a legal title passed by virtue of the sale would have been defeated, not by some arid legal technicality but by what Lord Blackburn called "the very nature of things". The same conclusion applies, and for the same reason, to any argument that a title in equity was created by the sale, taken in isolation from the collateral promises.'

Having explained that it was strictly unnecessary to consider *Re Wait*, because that case involved a contract for a sale ex-bulk, Lord Mustill suggested that the reasoning in the whole of the judgment of Atkin LJ was 'irresistible' (see [1995] 1 AC 74 at 91).

Therefore in *Re Goldcorp* there was no trust for the customers.

Mr Justice Neuberger then turned to *Hunter v Moss,* where the supposedly indistinguishable nature of the property was crucial to the decision that there was a valid trust of the shares. He acknowledged that as he is sitting in the

High Court, he was bound by the decision in *Hunter v Moss* and refused to follow *Re Wait, Re London Wine* and *Re Goldcorp*.

> Should I refuse to follow *Hunter*? In Underhill and Hayton *Law Relating to Trusts and Trustees* (15th edition, 1995) there is strong adverse criticism of the decision and reasoning in *Hunter*. It is said that Dillon LJ's reliance on the analogy of testamentary dispositions was inappropriate... .
>
> In addition, ... the reliance by Dillon LJ on the decision in *Re Rose* appears to overlook the fact that, in the relevant document, Mr Rose had specifically identified the shares which were intended to be the subject matter of the gift...
>
> I see the force of these points. However, the decision in *Hunter* is binding on me, unless I am satisfied that it is *per incuriam* or that it has been overruled by a subsequent decision.

He explained why he could not find the decision in *Hunter v Moss* to be *per incuriam*, and why he could not find that it has been overruled. He then referred to the distinction between tangible and intangible property:

> While I am not particularly convinced by the distinction, it appears to me that a more satisfactory way of distinguishing Hunter from the other cases is that it was concerned with shares, and not with chattels. First, that is a ground which is consistent with Dillon LJ's reliance on *Re Rose* (a case concerned with shares) and his ground for distinguishing *Re London Wine Co (Shippers) Ltd* (and, by implication, *Re Wait*) which, it will be remembered, he described as being 'concerned with the appropriation of chattels and when property in chattels passes'. Second, it is on this basis that the editors of *Underhill and Hayton* believe that *Hunter* is explained (although they regard it on an unsatisfactory basis). Third, the observations of Atkin LJ in *Re Wait* [1927] 1 Ch 606 at 630, referring to the 'ordinary operations of buying and selling goods' could be said to provide a policy ground for there being one rule for chattels and another for shares.
>
> Fourth, as the editors of Meagher Gummow & Lehane *Equity Doctrines & Remedies* (3rd edition) paras 679-682 point out, the need for appropriation before any equitable interest can exist in relation to chattels can be contrasted with the absence of any such need before there can be an effective equitable assignment of an unascertained part of a whole debt or fund. This distinction is described by the editors as 'very difficult to see'; none the less, they accept that, despite the criticism to which cases such as *Re Wait* have been subjected, it is unlikely that they will be overruled. ...
>
> The description of the sub-contracted grain in *Re Wait*, the client's wine in *Re London Wine Co (Shippers) Ltd,* and the customer's bullion in *Goldcorp* as 'an unascertained part of a mass of goods' is quite apt. It would not, however, be a sensible description of the 50 shares in *Hunter* or, indeed, the shares in the present case. Mr Halpern pointed out that it is not really possible to identify, whether physically or by words, a proportion of a debt, whereas it is possible to identify chattels (by labelling or segregation) or shares (by reference to their

> number); he also pointed out that part of a debt or fund is fungible with the balance. For those two reasons, he submitted that the inconsistency suggested in *Meagher Gummow & Lehane* is not valid. There is obvious force in that point, but, in the end, it seems to me that, given that the distinction exists between an assignment of part of a holding of chattels and an assignment of part of a debt or fund, the effect of the decision in *Hunter* is that, in this context, shares fall to be treated in this context in the same way as a debt or fund rather than chattels.
>
> In all the circumstances, therefore, it seems to me that the correct way for me, at first instance, to explain the difference between the result in *Hunter*, and that in *Re Wait*, *Re London Wine Co (Shippers) Ltd* and *Goldcorp*, is on the ground that *Hunter* was concerned with shares as opposed to chattels."

Thus, having surveyed the authorities on unsegregated property in depth, Neuberger J concluded that, although he found it unsatisfactory that different rules apply to tangible and intangible property, he was bound by the authorities which make such a distinction. He therefore applied *Hunter v Moss*, which also concerned intangible property, and held that although the shares were identical and unsegregated, there was nevertheless certainty of subject matter and thus a valid trust.

2.3 Certainty of Objects

The 'objects' of a trust are the beneficiaries. The beneficiaries of any particular trust must be ascertainable, otherwise a court would not be able to enforce it in their favour, or prevent benefits being given to the wrong people. The test to be applied to check whether the objects are certain differs according to the type of arrangement in question. A more stringent test is applied to fixed trusts than to discretionary trusts, powers of appointment and gifts subject to conditions precedent.

2.3.1 Powers of Appointment

***Re Gulbenkian's Settlement Trusts* [1970] AC 508**

Panel: Lord Reid, Lord Hodson, Lord Guest, Lord Upjohn and Lord Donovan

Facts: A 1929 Settlement contained a power to appoint property 'for the maintenance and personal support or benefit of all or any one or more to the exclusion of the other or others of the following persons, namely, the said Nubar Sarkis Gulbenkian and any wife and his children or remoter issue for the time being in existence whether minors or adults and any person or persons in whose house or apartments or in whose company or under whose care or control or by or with whom the said Nubar Sarkis Gulbenkian may from time to time be employed or residing.'

The House of Lords held, unanimously, that the power was valid as it could be said with certainty that any given individual is or is not a member of the class.

LORD REID

It may be true that when a mere power is given to an individual he is under no duty to exercise it or even to consider whether he should exercise it. But when a power is given to trustees as such, it appears to me that the situation must be different. A settlor [sic] or testator who entrusts a power to his trustees must be relying on them in their fiduciary capacity so they cannot simply push aside the power and refuse to consider whether it ought in their judgment to be exercised and they cannot give money to a person who is not within the classes of persons designated by the settlor: the construction of the power is for the court.

If the classes of beneficiaries are not defined with sufficient particularity to enable the court to determine whether a particular person is or is not, on the facts at a particular time, within one of the classes of beneficiaries, then the power must be bad for uncertainty. If the donee of the power (whether or not he has any duty) desires to exercise it in favour of a particular person it must be possible to determine whether that particular person is or is not within the class of objects of the power, and it must be possible to determine the validity of the power immediately it comes into operation. ...

Alert

The appellants submitted a further argument, that a power is bad for uncertainty unless it is possible to make a complete list of the possible beneficiaries at the time when it falls to be exercised. It is said that trustees cannot properly exercise their discretion unless they can survey the whole field: otherwise there might be in existence potential beneficiaries whom they might regard as more deserving than those who are known to them. In my view that cannot be right.

Lord Upjohn first of all set out the test proposed by Lord Denning MR in the same case in the Court of Appeal:

LORD UPJOHN

The Master of the Rolls ([1968] Ch. 126, 134E) propounded a test in the case of powers collateral, namely, that if you can say of one particular person meaning thereby, apparently, any one person only that he is clearly within the category the whole power is good though it may be difficult to say in other cases whether a person is or is not within the category, and he supported that view by reference to authority. ... Moreover, the Master of the Rolls (at p. 133B) expressed the view that the different doctrine with regard to trust powers should be brought into line with the rule with regard to conditions precedent and powers collateral.

However Lord Upjohn rejected this broad test:

But with respect to mere powers, while the court cannot compel the trustees to exercise their powers, yet those entitled to the fund in default must clearly be entitled to restrain the trustees from exercising it save among those within the power. So the trustees or the court must be able to say with certainty who is

Alert

within and who is without the power. It is for this reason that I find myself unable to accept the broader proposition advanced by Lord Denning M.R.

Instead, Lord Upjohn gave his own, narrower, interpretation:

If a donor (be he a settlor or testator) directs trustees to make some specified provision for "John Smith", then to give legal effect to that provision it must be possible to identify "John Smith". If the donor knows three John Smiths then by the most elementary principles of !aw neither the trustees nor the court in their place can give effect to that provision; neither the trustees nor the court can guess at it. It must fail for uncertainty unless of course admissible evidence is available to point to a particular John Smith as the object of the donor's bounty.

Then, taking it one stage further, suppose the donor directs that a fund or the income of a fund should be equally divided between members of a class. That class must be as defined as the individual; the court cannot guess at it. Suppose the donor directs that a fund be divided equally between "my old friends," then unless there is some admissible evidence that the donor has given some special "dictionary" meaning to that phrase which enables the trustees to identify the class with sufficient certainty, it is plainly bad as being too uncertain. Suppose that there appeared before the trustees (or the court) two or three individuals who plainly satisfied the test of being among "my old friends," the trustees could not consistently with the donor's intentions accept them as claiming the whole or any defined part of the fund. They cannot claim the whole fund for they can show no title to it unless they prove they are the only members of the class, which of course they cannot do, and so, too, by parity of reasoning they cannot claim any defined part of the fund and there is no authority in the trustees or the court to make any distribution among a smaller class than that pointed out by the donor. The principle is, in my opinion, that the donor must make his intentions sufficiently plain as to the objects of his trust and the court cannot give effect to it by misinterpreting his intentions by dividing the fund merely among those present. Secondly, and perhaps it is the more hallowed principle, the Court of Chancery, which acts in default of trustees, must know with sufficient certainty the objects of the beneficence of the donor so as to execute the trust. Then, suppose the donor does not direct an equal division of his property among the class but gives a power of selection to his trustees among the class; exactly the same principles must apply. The trustees have a duty to select the donees of the donor's bounty from among the class designated by the donor; he has not entrusted them with any power to select the donees merely from among known claimants who are within the class, for that is constituting a narrower class and the donor has given them no power to do this.

Decipher Lord Upjohn seems to endorse the 'complete list' test, which appears contrary to what he stated earlier. However, see Lord Wilberforce in *McPhail v Doulton* who interprets the passage as *not* requiring a complete list of all possible beneficiaries.

LORD DONOVAN

My Lords, where trustees are given power to make payments out of a trust fund to members of a designated class, then if the trustees have a complete discretion as to whom they shall pay the money, or as to whether they shall make any payment at all, I see no reason why the whole clause should be regarded by the law as void for uncertainty simply because some members of the designated class might be unascertainable. It is true that this means that such members will never even get considered as possible objects of the trustees' discretion, but I regard that result as less unfortunate than depriving all the ascertainable members of any chance of benefit. I find myself therefore in complete sympathy with the rule that provided one can say with certainty whether a given individual is or is not a member of the class, the power collateral (as it is called) does not fail altogether simply because a complete list of every member cannot be drawn up.

2.3.2 Fixed Trusts

***Inland Revenue Commissioners v Broadway Cottages Trust* [1955] Ch 20**

Panel: Singleton, Jenkins and Hodson LJJ

Facts: The settlor settled £80,000 upon trust and directed the trustees to apply the income for the benefit of all or any of the objects set out in the trust deed. Broadway Cottages Trust was a charity mentioned in the deed, which received income and paid tax on it. The tax could only be reclaimed if it could be shown that there was a valid trust. The court held that there was not. This was a fixed trust, and to be valid, the objects had to be certain. The test for certainty of objects for a fixed trust is whether it is possible to make a complete list of the beneficiaries. In this particular case, it was not possible and the trust failed.

LORD JUSTICE JENKINS

It must, we think, follow from the appellants' concession to the effect that the class of "beneficiaries" is incapable of ascertainment, ... that the trust of the capital of the settled fund for all the beneficiaries living or existing at the termination of the appointed period, and if more than one in equal shares, must be void for uncertainty, inasmuch as there can be no division in equal shares amongst a class of persons unless all the members of the class are known.

2.3.3 Discretionary Trusts

***McPhail v Doulton* [1971] AC 424**

Panel: Lord Reid, Lord Hodson, Lord Guest, Viscount Dilhorne and Lord Wilberforce

Facts: In 1941, Mr Baden executed a deed setting up a trust in favour of the staff of Matthew Hall & Co Limited and their 'relatives and dependants'. Clause 9(a) of the deed said:

'9.(a) The trustees shall apply the net income of the fund in making at their absolute discretion grants to or for the benefit of any of the officers and employees or ex-officers or ex-employees of the company or to any relatives or dependants of any such persons in such amounts at such times and on such conditions (if any) as they think fit'

The House of Lords, by a majority, held that Clause 9(a) constituted a trust and not a power; and that the test for determining the validity of a discretionary trust in terms of certainty of objects was that in *re Gulbenkian*: the trust would be valid if it could be said with certainty that any individual was or was not a member of the class.

The 'complete list' test in *IRC v Broadway Cottages Trust* [1955] Ch 20 was overruled.

LORD WILBERFORCE

In this House, the appellants contend, and this is the first question for consideration, that the provisions of clause 9(a) constitute a trust and not a power. If that is held to be the correct result, both sides agree that the case must return to the Chancery Division for consideration, on this footing, whether this trust is valid. But here comes a complication. In the present state of authority, the decision as to validity would turn on the question whether a complete list (or on another view a list complete for practical purposes) can be drawn up of all possible beneficiaries. This follows from the Court of Appeal's decision in *Inland Revenue Commissioners v Broadway Cottages Trust* [1955] Ch 20 as applied in later cases by which, unless this House decides otherwise, the Court of Chancery would be bound. The respondents invite your Lordships to review this decision and challenge its correctness. So the second issue which arises, if clause 9 (a) amounts to a trust, is whether the existing test for its validity is right in law and, if not, what the test ought to be.

Lord Wilberforce concluded that the arrangement was a trust:

Naturally read, the intention of the deed seems to me clear: clause 9(a), whose language is mandatory ('shall'), creates, together with a power of selection, a trust for distribution of the income...

He then considered whether the *Broadway Cottages* 'complete list' test is the correct test, or whether it is the 'is/is not' test for powers in *Re Gulbenkian*. He started by considering whether the complete list test is appropriate, and decided that it is not:

The basis for the *Broadway Cottages* principle is stated to be that a trust cannot be valid unless, if need be, it can be executed by the court, and (though it is not quite clear from the judgment where argument ends and decision begins) that the court can only execute it by ordering an equal distribution in which every beneficiary shares. So it is necessary to examine the authority and reason for this supposed rule as to the execution of trusts by the court.

Assuming, as I am prepared to do for present purposes, that the test of validity is whether the trust can be executed by the court, it does not follow that execution is impossible unless there can be equal division.

As a matter of reason, to hold that a principle of equal division applies to trusts such as the present is certainly paradoxical. Equal division is surely the last thing the settlor ever intended: equal division among all may, probably would, produce a result beneficial to none. Why suppose that the court would lend itself to a whimsical execution? And as regards authority, I do not find that the nature of the trust, and of the court's powers over trusts, calls for any such rigid rule. Equal division may be sensible and has been decreed, in cases of family trusts, for a limited class, here there is life in the maxim 'equality is equity,' but the cases provide numerous examples where this has not been so, and a different type of execution has been ordered, appropriate to the circumstances.

Having decided that the 'complete list' test is not appropriate for a discretionary trust, he cited early examples of discretionary trusts, family or other trusts where equal division was not ordered. He then looked at modern authorities, in particular *IRC v Broadway Cottages Trust* where the 'complete list' test was applied not only to a fixed trust of capital, which necessarily involved equal division, but also to a discretionary trust of income. The Court of Appeal in that case reasoned that the trust of income could only be executed on the basis of equal division. Lord Wilberforce did not agree with this.

Lord Wilberforce rejected any arguments which sought to suggest that the speeches in *Re Gulbenkian* (and in particular the speech of Lord Upjohn) can be interpreted as an endorsement of the complete list test in *Broadway Cottages* for a discretionary trust. He examined the pertinent passage from Lord Upjohn's speech, and commented on it:

'The trustees have a duty to select the donees of the donor's bounty from among the class designated by the donor; he has not entrusted them with any power to select the donees merely from among known claimants who are within the class, for that is constituting a narrower class and the donor has given them no power to do this' ([1970] A.C. 508 , 524).

Link
See *Re Gulbenkian's Settlements*

What this does say, and I respectfully agree, is that, in the case of a trust, the trustees must select from the class. What it does not say, as I read it, or imply, is that in order to carry out their duty of selection they must have before them, or be able to get, a complete list of all possible objects.

So I think that we are free to review the *Broadway Cottages* case [1955] Ch. 20. The conclusion which I would reach, implicit in the previous discussion, is that the wide distinction between the validity test for powers and that for trust powers is unfortunate and wrong, that the rule recently fastened upon the courts by *Inland Revenue Commissioners v Broadway Cottages Trust* ought to be discarded, and that the test for the validity of trust powers ought to be similar to that accepted by this House in *In re Gulbenkian's Settlements* [1970] AC 508 for powers, namely, that the trust is valid if it can be said with certainty that any given individual is or is not a member of the class.

Assimilation of the validity test does not involve the complete assimilation of trust powers with powers. As to powers, I agree with my noble and learned friend Lord Upjohn in *In re Gulbenkian's Settlements* that although the trustees may, and normally will, be under a fiduciary duty to consider whether or in what way they should exercise their power, the court will not normally compel its exercise. It will intervene if the trustees exceed their powers, and possibly if they are proved to have exercised it capriciously. But in the case of a trust power, if the trustees do not exercise it, the court will: I respectfully adopt as to this the statement in Lord Upjohn's opinion [sic] (p. 525). I would venture to amplify this by saying that the court, if called upon to execute the trust power, will do so in the manner best calculated to give effect to the settlor's or testator's intentions... .

Then, as to the trustees' duty of inquiry or ascertainment, in each case the trustees ought to make such a survey of the range of objects or possible beneficiaries as will enable them to carry out their fiduciary duty... .

Two final points: first, as to the question of certainty. I desire to emphasise the distinction clearly made and explained by Lord Upjohn ([1970] AC 508, 524) between linguistic or semantic uncertainty which, if unresolved by the court, renders the gift void, and the difficulty of ascertaining the existence or whereabouts of members of the class, a matter with which the court can appropriately deal on an application for directions. There may be a third case where the meaning of the words used is clear but the definition of beneficiaries is so hopelessly wide as not to form 'anything like a class' so that the trust is administratively unworkable or in Lord Eldon's words one that cannot be executed (*Morice v Bishop of Durham*, 10 Ves.Jr. 522, 527). I hesitate to give examples for they may prejudice future cases, but perhaps 'all the residents of Greater London' will serve. I do not think that a discretionary trust for 'relatives' even of a living person falls within this category.

In the final part of his speech, above, Lord Wilberforce said that even where the three certainties are present, the trust may still fail for 'administrative unworkability'. This was the point at issue in *R v District Auditor, ex p. West Yorkshire Metropolitan Count Council* [1986] RVR 24 where a purported discretionary trust for the inhabitants of West Yorkshire, although certain, was impossible to execute simply because of the sheer numbers involved. This point has caused much academic debate.

Link
See Further Reading

***Re Baden's Deed Trusts (No 2)* [1973] Ch 9**

Panel: Sachs, Megaw and Stamp LJJ

Facts: Following the House of Lords decision in *McPhail v Doulton*, the case was sent back to the Chancery Division for the 'is/is not' test to be applied to find whether the discretionary trust for 'relatives and dependants' was valid or void for uncertainty of objects.

Mr Justice Brightman in the Chancery Division found that the test was satisfied for 'relatives and dependants'. So did all three judges in the Court of Appeal, but they all interpreted and applied the test differently in coming to the same conclusion.

LORD JUSTICE SACHS

His general approach was that in order to be valid, there had to be conceptual certainty. To assess whether this is present, the court must have a practical common-sense approach. Once the class *as a concept* is certain, it is merely a matter of evidence as to whether someone is or is not within it. He remarked on Lord Wilberforce's speech in *McPhail v Doulton*, saying that it does *not* say that a trust is invalid simply because it is impossible to bring evidence that someone *is not* within the class. When Lord Wilberforce said that the trustees need to survey the range of possible objects/beneficiaries as to enable them to carry out their fiduciary duty, he did *not* mean that the trustees have to survey everyone – they simply need to know the size of the possible class.

The test to be applied to each of these words is: "can it be said with certainty that any given individual is or is not a member of the class?" *per* Lord Wilberforce [1971] AC 424, 450, 454 and 456, words which reflect those of Lord Reid and Lord Upjohn in *In re Gulbenkian's Settlements* [1970] AC 508, 518, 521 and 525. ...

It is first to be noted that the deed must be looked at through the eyes of a businessman seeking to advance the welfare of the employees of his firm and those so connected with the employees that a benevolent employer would wish to help them. He would not necessarily be looking at the words he uses with the same eyes as those of a man making a will. Accordingly, whether a court is considering the concept implicit in relevant words, or whether it is exercising the function of a court of construction, it should adopt that same practical and common-sense approach which was enjoined by Upjohn J. in *In re Sayer* [1957] Ch 423 , 436, and by Lord Wilberforce in the *Baden* case [1971] AC 424 , 452, and which would be used by an employer setting up such a fund.

The next point as regards approach that requires consideration is the contention, strongly pressed by Mr. Vinelott, that the court must always be able to say whether any given postulant is not within the relevant class as well as being able to say whether he is within it. In construing the words already cited from the speech of Lord Wilberforce in the *Baden* case (as well as those of Lord Reid and Lord Upjohn in the *Gulbenkian* case), it is essential to bear in mind the difference between conceptual uncertainty and evidential difficulties. That distinction is explicitly referred to by Lord Wilberforce in *In re Baden's Deed Trusts* [1971] AC 424, 457 when he said:

"... as to the question of certainty. I desire to emphasise the distinction clearly made and explained by Lord Upjohn [1970] AC 508, 524 between linguistic or semantic uncertainty which, if unresolved by the court, renders the gift void, and the difficulty of ascertaining the existence or whereabouts of members of the class, a matter with which the court can appropriately deal on an application for directions."

As Mr. Vinelott himself rightly observed, "the court is never defeated by evidential uncertainty," and it is in my judgment clear that it is conceptual

> certainty to which reference was made when the "is or is not a member of the class" test was enunciated. ... Once the class of persons to be benefited is conceptually certain it then becomes a question of fact to be determined on evidence whether any postulant has on inquiry been proved to be within it: if he is not so proved, then he is not in it. That position remains the same whether the class to be benefited happens to be small (such as "first cousins") or large (such as "members of the X Trade Union" or "those who have served in the Royal Navy"). The suggestion that such trusts could be invalid because it might be impossible to prove of a given individual that he was not in the relevant class is wholly fallacious – and only Mr. Vinelott's persuasiveness has prevented me from saying that the contention is almost unarguable.
>
> It was suggested that some difficulty arises from the passage in the speech of Lord Wilberforce in the *Baden* case [1971] AC 424, 457 where he referred to the need of trustees "to make such a survey of the range of objects or possible beneficiaries as will enable them to carry out their fiduciary duty." The word "range," however, in that context has an inbuilt and obvious element of considerable elasticity, and thus provides for an almost infinitely variable range of vision suitable to the particular trust to be considered. In modern trusts of the category now under consideration it may be sufficient to know whether the range of potential postulants runs into respectively dozens, hundreds, thousands, tens of thousands or even hundreds of thousands. I cannot imagine that the above-quoted passage was intended to cast doubt, for instance, on the validity of wide-ranging discretionary trusts such as those of the Army Benevolent Fund. When looked at in the context of the rest of the speech this particular passage does not seem to me to cause any difficulty. In my judgment it refers to something quite different, to a need to provide a list of individuals or to provide a closely accurate enumeration of the numbers in the class: it relates to that width of the field from which beneficiaries may be drawn and which the trustees should have in mind so that they can adapt to it their methods of discretionary selection. Assessing in a businesslike way "the size of the problem" is what the trustees are called on to do.

Having set these principles out he then looked at whether the words 'dependants' and 'relatives' are certain, while acknowledging that it is not the function of the court to provide an exhaustive definition of the words. As regards 'dependants', he agreed with Brightman J in the Chancery Division:

> I consider that the trustees, or if necessary the court, are quite capable of coming to a conclusion in any given case as to whether or not a particular candidate could properly be described as a dependant – a word that, as the judge said, "conjures up a sufficiently distinct picture". I agree, too, that any one wholly or partly dependent on the means of another is a "dependant". There is thus no conceptual uncertainty inherent in that word and the executors' contentions as to the effect of its use fail.

As regards the term 'relatives' he also agreed that this term was certain:

As regards "relatives" Brightman J., after stating, at p. 625, "It is not in dispute that a person is a relative of an ... employee ..., if both trace legal descent from a common ancestor:" a little later said: "In practice, the use of the expression 'relatives' cannot cause the slightest difficulty." With that view I agree for the reasons he gave when he correctly set out the evidential position. As regards the suggested uncertain numerative range of that concept of the word "relative" (a matter which strictly would only be relevant to the abandoned "administratively unworkable" point) and also when considering the practical side of the functions of the trustees, it is germane to note that in *In re Scarisbrick* [1951] Ch 622, Lord Evershed M.R. observed, with regard to a class of "relations," at p. 632: "That class is, in theory, capable of almost infinite expansion, but proof of relationship soon becomes extremely difficult in fact." That factor automatically narrows the field within which the trustees select. Further, a settlor using the word "relatives" in the context of this deed (which is not the same context as that of a will) would assume that the trustees would, in the exercise of their discretion, make their selection in a sensible way from the field, however wide. ...

As a footnote to this conclusion it is interesting to observe that no case was cited to us in which a court has actually decided that a trust was invalid on account of the use of that word, whatever may have been said obiter. If this is due to a tendency to construe deeds and wills so as to give effect to them rather than to invalidate trusts, that is an approach which is certainly in accord with modern thought. I would accordingly dismiss this appeal.

LORD JUSTICE MEGAW

He rejected the executors' close and narrow interpretation of the test. They had argued that the words 'or is not' had special importance, and had been included for a reason. It followed that the trust would be void if it was not possible to say with certainty that someone was not a relative of an employee. Lord Justice Megaw rejected this as completely impractical because although it may be possible to say that there is no proof that someone is a relative, it may still not be certain that he is not. He said that the trust is valid if a substantial number could be said to fall within the class. This of course raises another question as to what 'substantial' means.

The main argument of Mr. Vinelott was founded upon a strict and literal interpretation of the words in which the decision of the House of Lords in *In re Gulbenkian's Settlements* [1970] AC 508 was expressed. That decision laid down the test for the validity of powers of selection. It is relevant for the present case, because in the previous excursion of this case to the House of Lords [1971] AC 424 it was held that there is no relevant difference in the test of validity, whether the trustees are given a power of selection or, as was held by their Lordships to be the case in this trust deed, a trust for selection. The test in either case is what may be called the *Gulbenkian* test. The *Gulbenkian* test, as expressed by Lord Wilberforce at p. 450, and again in almost identical words at p. 454 is this:

"... the power is valid if it can be said with certainty whether any given individual is or is not a member of the class and does not fail simply because it is impossible to ascertain every member of the class."

The executors' argument concentrates on the words "or is not" in the first of the two limbs of the sentence quoted above: "if it can be said with certainty whether any given individual is *or is not* a member of the class." It is said that those words have been used deliberately, and have only one possible meaning; and that, however startling or drastic or unsatisfactory the result may be – and Mr. Vinelott does not shrink from saying that the consequence is drastic – this court is bound to give effect to the words used in the House of Lords' definition of the test. It would be quite impracticable for the trustees to ascertain in many cases whether a particular person was *not* a relative of an employee. The most that could be said is: "There is no proof that he is a relative." But there would still be no "certainty" that such a person was not a relative. Hence, so it is said, the test laid down by the House of Lords is not satisfied, and the trust is void. For it cannot be said with certainty, in relation to any individual, that he is not a relative.

I do not think it was contemplated that the words "or is not" would produce that result. It would, as I see it, involve an inconsistency with the latter part of the same sentence: "does not fail simply because it is impossible to ascertain every member of the class". The executors' contention, in substance and reality, is that it does fail "simply because it is impossible to ascertain every member of the class."

...

In my judgment, much too great emphasis is placed in the executors' argument on the words "or is not." To my mind, the test is satisfied if, as regards at least a substantial number of objects, it can be said with certainty that they fall within the trust; even though, as regards a substantial number of other persons, if they ever for some fanciful reason fell to be considered, the answer would have to be, not "they are outside the trust," but "it is not proven whether they are in or out." What is a "substantial number" may well be a question of common sense and of degree in relation to the particular trust: particularly where, as here, it would be fantasy, to use a mild word, to suggest that any practical difficulty would arise in the fair, proper and sensible administration of this trust in respect of relatives and dependants.

Alert

Lord Justice Megaw, like Sachs LJ, agreed with Brightman J's definition of 'relatives' as people who can trace their legal descent through a common ancestor. He thus found that the class was conceptually certain and upheld the trust.

LORD JUSTICE STAMP

He said that for the class to be conceptually certain, its size must be known. He felt that it is not possible to know the boundaries of a class of 'relatives' as defined by Sachs LJ and Megaw LJ. Instead, he defined 'relatives' more narrowly as 'next of kin'. Having done that, he decided that the class was then conceptually certain. He said that the true application of the is/is not test is to show that a given individual is or is not within the class. He said that it was possible in this case to do that if relatives was defined as 'next of kin' and on that basis upheld the trust.

Clearly Lord Wilberforce in expressing the view that the test of validity of a discretionary trust ought to be similar to that accepted by the House of Lords in the *Gulbenkian* case did not take the view that it was sufficient that you could find individuals who were clearly members of the class; for he himself remarked, towards the end of his speech as to the trustees' duty of inquiring or ascertaining, that in each case the trustees ought to make such a survey of the range of objects or possible beneficiaries as will enable them to carry out their fiduciary duty. It is not enough that trustees should do nothing but distribute the fund among those objects of the trust who happen to be at hand or present themselves. ... the trustees ought to make such a survey of the range of objects or possible beneficiaries as will enable them to carry out their fiduciary duty... But, as I understand it, having made the appropriate survey, it matters not that it is not complete or fails to yield a result enabling you to lay out a list or particulars of every single beneficiary. Having done the best they can, the trustees may proceed upon the basis similar to that adopted by the court where all the beneficiaries cannot be ascertained and distribute upon the footing that they have been... .

Validity or invalidity is to depend upon whether you can say of any individual - and the accent must be upon that word "any," for it is not simply the individual whose claim you are considering who is spoken of - "is or is not a member of the class," for only thus can you make a survey of the range of objects or possible beneficiaries.

If the matter rested there, it would in my judgment follow that, treating the word "relatives" as meaning descendants from a common ancestor, a trust for distribution such as is here in question would not be valid. Any "survey of the range of the objects or possible beneficiaries" would certainly be incomplete, and I am able to discern no principle upon which such a survey could be conducted or where it should start or finish. The most you could do, so far as regards relatives, would be to find individuals who are clearly members of the class – the test which was accepted in the Court of Appeal, but rejected in the House of Lords, in the *Gulbenkian* case.

However, if the narrower meaning of relatives, as 'next of kin' is adopted, it *is* possible to make a survey of the class:

> The class of beneficiaries thus becomes a clearly defined class and there is no difficulty in determining whether a given individual is within it or without it.

Finally, he looked at whether 'dependants' as a concept is certain, and found that it is:

> The only other challenge to the validity of the trust is directed against the use of the word "dependants" which it is said introduces a linguistic or semantic uncertainty. That in the context the word connotes financial dependence I do not doubt, and although in a given case there may be a doubt whether there be a sufficient degree of dependence to satisfy the qualification of being a "dependant," that is a question which can be determined by the court and does not introduce linguistic uncertainty.

2.3.4 Gifts Subject to a Condition Precedent

***Re Allen* [1953] Ch 810**

Panel: Evershed MR, Birkett and Romer LJJ

Facts: This case involved a gift subject to a condition precedent. The testator, Allen, left certain property to the eldest of the sons of his nephew Francis, 'who shall be a member of the Church of England and an adherent to the doctrine of that Church.' There was a gift over. The question for the Court of Appeal was whether the gift was void for uncertainty of objects.

EVERSHED MR

The Master of the Rolls discussed the appropriate test to be applied and drew a distinction between conditions subsequent and conditions precedent. Conditions subsequent are conditions which may bring to an end an interest which has already vested in a donee. For gifts subject to such conditions, the object or class of objects must be capable of exact description. However, the test is different for gifts subject to a condition precedent. These are gifts where the condition must be performed before the gift can vest. Here, it is not necessary to have a complete list of possible donees: the class should not necessarily be capable of exact description.

> All that the claiming devisee has to do is at the relevant date to establish, if he can, that he satisfies the condition or qualification whatever be the appropriate test. If the formula is such as to involve questions of degree (as, prima facie, is implicit in any requirement of "adherence" or "attachment" to a particular faith or creed), the uncertainty of the test contemplated may well invalidate the formula as a condition subsequent but will not, in my judgment, necessarily do so in the case of a condition precedent; for if the claimant he [sic] able to satisfy any, or at least any reasonable test, is he disentitled to the benefit of the gift? The essential difference which, I think, exists, and to which I have alluded, was well illustrated by Mr. Hunter-Brown in the course of argument. A condition subsequent divesting an estate vested in A if A at some relevant date should

> not be a tall man would, as it seems to me, be held void for uncertainty. For tallness being a matter of degree, by what standard is it, for the supposed purposes, to be judged? If "tallness" is achieved by being above the "average" height, then what average is contemplated? The average of A's town or neighbourhood, the average of Englishmen, the average of all mankind? and would a man in height above the average, say of all Englishmen, by however small a fraction of an inch, be called "tall" in any ordinary sense? But questions of this kind, which might be fatal to the supposed formula as a condition subsequent, might have no application in the case of a condition precedent or qualification; for a claimant who was 6ft. 6ins. tall might fairly say that he satisfied the testator's requirement judged by any reasonable standard.
>
> It may well be that, in a case such as I have supposed, very difficult questions might arise, for example, if the claimant proved that he was a man very slightly above the average height of Englishmen. The court would then have to decide on the facts and on the construction of the bequest (for example, that by "tall" the testator had meant "lofty") whether the claimant satisfied the requirements of the testator and had established his claim to the gift. But I am not persuaded that where a formula constitutes a condition precedent or a qualification it is right for the court to declare the condition or qualification void for uncertainty so as thereby to defeat all possible claimants to the gift unless the terms of the condition or qualification are such that it is impossible to give them any meaning at all, or such that they involve repugnancies or inconsistencies in the possible tests which they postulate, as distinct, for example, from mere problems of degree.

He concluded:

> ... in the case of a will it is in general the function and duty of a court to construe the testator's language with reasonable liberality and to try, if it can, to give sensible effect to the intention he has expressed. To this general rule conditions subsequent seem to me to be an exception. The requirement that it must be known with certainty from the outset what are the exact events which will cause a forfeiture or divesting (to borrow once again the language of Lord Russell) seems to me to be founded on principles well established by authority but peculiarly applicable to provisions for forfeiting or divesting an estate or interest previously conferred.

Having stated these principles he concluded that the two parts of the formula set out in the will were valid, although he acknowledged that the second part was more problematic.

***Re Barlow's Will Trust* [1979] 1 All ER 296**

Panel: Browne-Wilkinson J

Facts: Helen Barlow had a large collection of pictures, some of which she bequeathed to specific people in her will. Her executors were directed to allow any of her family and friends who wished to do so to buy one of the remaining pictures. The executors asked the court whether this direction was void for uncertainty.

MR JUSTICE BROWNE-WILKINSON

First of all, the judge drew attention to the arguments on either side:

Those arguing against the validity of the gift in favour of the friends contend that, in the absence of any guidance from the testatrix, the question "Who were her friends?" is incapable of being answered. The word is said to be "conceptually uncertain" since there are so many different degrees of friendship and it is impossible to say which degree the testatrix had in mind. In support of this argument they rely on Lord Upjohn's remarks in *In re Gulbenkian's Settlements* [1970] AC 508, and the decision of the House of Lords in *In re Baden's Deed Trusts* [1971] AC 424, to the effect that it must be possible to say who is within and who without the class of friends. They say that since the testatrix intended all her friends to have the opportunity to acquire a picture, it is necessary to be able to ascertain with certainty all the members of that class.

Mr. Shillingford, who argued in favour of the validity of the gift, contended that the test laid down in the *Gulbenkian* and *Baden* cases was not applicable to this case; the test, he says, is that laid down by the Court of Appeal in *In re Allen, decd.* [1953]

Ch 810, as appropriate in cases where the validity of a condition precedent or description is in issue, namely, that the gift is valid if it is possible to say of one or more persons that he or they undoubtedly qualify even though it may be difficult to say of others whether or not they qualify.

He stressed that this case was not the type of case where it is necessary to decide all the members of the class:

The distinction between the Gulbenkian test and the In re Allen test is, in my judgment, well exemplified by the word "friends". The word has a great range of meanings; indeed, its exact meaning probably varies slightly from person to person. Some would include only those with whom they had been on intimate terms over a long period; others would include acquaintances whom they liked. Some would include people with whom their relationship was primarily one of business; others would not. Indeed, many people, if asked to draw up a complete list of their friends, would probably have some difficulty in deciding whether certain of the people they knew were really "friends" as opposed to "acquaintances". Therefore, if the nature of the gift was such that it was legally necessary to draw up a complete list of "friends" of the testatrix, or to be able to say of any person that "he is not a friend", the whole gift would probably fail even as to those who, by any conceivable test, were friends.

But in the case of a gift of a kind which does not require one to establish all the members of the class (e.g. "a gift of £10 to each of my friends"), it may be possible to say of some people that on any test, they qualify. Thus in In re Allen, dec'd, at p. 817, Sir Raymond Evershed M.R. took the example of a gift to X "if he is a tall man"; a man 6 ft. 6 ins. tall could be said on any reasonable basis to satisfy the test, although it might be impossible to say whether a man, say, 5 ft. 10 ins. high satisfied the requirement.

He decided that the case before him was not a gift to a particular class, but a series of possible gifts to individuals who answered the description of friend by any reasonable test. The judge helpfully set out some ideas as to how one determines who is a friend.

The effect of clause 5(a) is to confer on friends of the testatrix a series of options to purchase. Although it is obviously desirable as a practical matter that steps should be taken to inform those entitled to the options of their rights, it is common ground that there is no legal necessity to do so. Therefore, each person coming forward to exercise the option has to prove that he is a friend; it is not legally necessary, in my judgment, to discover who all the friends are. In order to decide whether an individual is entitled to purchase, all that is required is that the executors should be able to say of that individual whether he has proved that he is a friend. The word "friend," therefore, is a description or qualification of the option holder.

It was suggested that by allowing undoubted friends to take I would be altering the testatrix's intentions. It is said that she intended all her friends to have a chance to buy any given picture, and since some people she might have regarded as friends will not be able to apply, the number of competitors for that picture will be reduced. This may be so; but I cannot regard this factor as making it legally necessary to establish the whole class of friends. The testatrix's intention was that a friend should acquire a picture. My decision gives effect to that intention.

I therefore hold that the disposition does not fail for uncertainty, but that anyone who can prove that by any reasonable test he or she must have been a friend of the testatrix is entitled to exercise the option. Without seeking to lay down any exhaustive definition of such test, it may be helpful if I indicate certain minimum requirements: (a) the relationship must have been a long-standing one. (b) The relationship must have been a social relationship as opposed to a business or professional relationship. (c) Although there may have been long periods when circumstances prevented the testatrix and the applicant from meeting, when circumstances did permit they must have met frequently. If in any case the executors entertain any real doubt whether an applicant qualifies, they can apply to the court to decide the issue.

He then cited authority to show ‘friends’ is an uncertain concept in a trust context:

Secondly, in *In re Lloyd's Trust Instruments* (unreported), June 24, 1970 , but extracts from which are to be found in *Brown v Gould* [1972] Ch.53 Megarry J. stated, at p. 57:

"If there is a trust for 'my old friends,' all concerned are faced with uncertainty as to the concept or idea enshrined in those words. It may not be difficult to resolve that 'old' means not 'aged' but 'of long standing'; but then there is the question of how long is 'long'. Friendship, too, is a concept with almost infinite shades of meaning. Where the concept is uncertain, the gift is void. Where the concept is certain, then mere difficulty in tracing and discovering those who are entitled normally does not invalidate the gift."

3

Formalities

Introduction

When discussing formalities within the law in general, we are describing a set of rules required for a transaction to have legal effect. Within equity and trusts, however, the word takes on a more specific definition. In this context, formalities are the rules that must be followed before a party can either acquire rights as a beneficiary, or transfer an equitable interest on to another party. This definition is therefore beneficiary focussed and should be contrasted with the transfer of legal title from one party to another (which is covered in the chapter on Constitution).

To fully appreciate how the rules on formalities work, it is necessary to understand the background behind why they were created. The various statutory sections concerning formalities are there to rectify potential specific legal problems, which is why the requirements of each section are not exactly the same. The four main reasons for formalities and rules of constitution have been stated in an academic article, which has been universally praised.

Informal trusts and third parties, J.D. Feltham, Conv. 1987, July-August, 246-252, at 248-249

Such requirements have been analysed to have (a) a ritual or cautionary function, requiring a donor to pause and give due consideration to the transfer, (b) a protective function, safeguarding against undue influence and impositions, (c) an evidentiary function, providing reliable evidence of the creation of the trust as a guard against false claims, a guide to the location of beneficial ownership which constitutes a link in the chain of beneficial entitlement and a source of knowledge of the details of the trust, and (d) a channelling function, standardising transactions in an effective way. The purpose of such requirements, particularly (a) and (c), is defeated if equity treats the transaction as effective notwithstanding that the formalities are not complied with. Moreover there is no longer a sanction to ensure an impetus to comply with the relevant formal requirements.

These requirements highlighted by Feltham, especially (c), are important for considering the application of the Law of Property Act 1925 s53(1)(c) to dispositions of an equitable interest.

3.1 Creation of Trusts of Land

The general rule for creation of trusts is that they do not have to comply with any formalities; so long as the three certainties are present this will suffice. However, to create an enforceable trust of land the requirements in s53(1)(b) the Law of Property Act 1925 have to be complied with. This section specifically requires that a declaration of a trust of land has to be evidenced in writing that is signed by the settlor or the settlor's authorised agent. If this written document does not exist, the trust is valid but unenforceable. However, since the requirement is only for *evidence* of the existence of the trust, a document that is subsequently written and signed will make a trust of land enforceable from the date the trust was created.

Re Vandervell's Trusts (No 2) **[1974] Ch 269**

Panel: Lord Denning MR, Stephenson and Lawton LJJ

Statute: Law of Property Act 1925 s53(1)(b)

Facts: The facts of this case are not directly relevant to the application of s53(1)(b). However, it is submitted that the judgment by Lord Denning MR makes the clearest distinction between declarations of trusts generally and declarations of trusts of land.

LORD DENNING MR

But, as soon as the option was exercised and the shares registered in the trustees' name, there was created a valid trust of the shares in favour of the children's settlement. Not being a trust of land, it could be created without any writing. A trust of personalty can be created without writing. Both Mr. Vandervell and the trustee company had done everything which needed to be done to make the settlement of these shares binding on them. So there was a valid trust...

The entire panel of the Court of Appeal allowed the appeal as this was a creation of a trust of shares, which fell outside of the ambit of s53(1)(b).

Trusts of land can be created without writing where they come within the ambit of s53(2), which exempts resulting or constructive trusts from the writing requirements of s53(1)(b).

Hodgson v Marks **[1971] Ch 892**

Panel: Russell, Buckley and Cairns LJJ

Statute: Law of Property Act 1925 s53(1)(b)

Facts: Mrs Hodgson was an elderly widow, who had taken in Mr Evans as her lodger. Mrs Hodgson transferred legal title of her house to Mr Evans to prevent her nephew from turning Mr Evans out of the house. Mr Evans then sold the house to Mr Marks, who had acquired a registered mortgage from a building society to finance the purchase. Mrs Hodgson knew nothing of the sale or of the existence of Mr Marks. When she found out what had happened, Mrs Hodgson sued Mr Marks and the building society and asked the court to convey the house to her free of the mortgage. It was held that Mrs Hodgson had a beneficial interest in the house under a resulting trust, which fell within s53(2) LPA 1925 and, therefore, did not need to be evidenced in writing.

LORD JUSTICE RUSSELL

I turn next to the question whether section 53(1) of the Law of Property Act 1925 prevents the assertion by the plaintiff of her entitlement in equity to the house. Let me first assume that, contrary to the view expressed by the judge, Mr. Marks is not debarred from relying upon the section, and the express oral arrangement or declaration of trust between the plaintiff and Mr. Evans found by the judge was not effective as such. Nevertheless, the evidence is clear that the transfer was not intended to operate as a gift, and, in those circumstances, I do not see why there was not a resulting trust of the beneficial interest to the plaintiff, which would not, of course, be affected by section 53 (1). ... If an attempted express trust fails, that seems to me just the occasion for implication of a resulting trust, whether the failure be due to uncertainty, or perpetuity, or lack of form. It would be a strange outcome if the plaintiff were to lose her beneficial interest because her evidence had not been confined to negativing a gift but had additionally moved into a field forbidden by section 53 (1) for lack of writing.

The decision in Hodgson was rooted in the judgment of the Court of Appeal in the much earlier case of *Rochefoucauld v Boustead*. In that case, the court enforced a trust of land notwithstanding there was no compliance with the requirements of the forerunner to s53(1)(b) LPA 1925. The court's conclusion was based on the idea that, in some circumstances, strict enforcement of formality rules may actually promote the fraud which these rules are intended to prevent.

Rochefoucauld v Boustead [1897] 1 Ch 196

Panel: Lindley LJ, Smith LJ, Lord Halsbury LC

Statute: Statute of Frauds 1677, s7

Facts: The claimant, the Comtesse de la Rochefoucauld, was the registered owner of certain coffee estates, which were subject to a mortgage in favour of a Dutch lender. The lender sought to call in the mortgage but the Comtesse was unable to repay the debt. She therefore entered into an agreement with Boustead by which he agreed to purchase the estates and hold them on trust for her. The arrangement was not documented in writing. Boustead repeatedly mortgaged the estates without the Comtesse's knowledge and eventually sold them. The court held that Boustead could not invoke s7 of the statute of Frauds (the forerunner to s53(1)(b) LPA 1925) in order to deny the Comtesse's interest in the land. To do so would contravene the maxim that 'equity will not allow a statute to act as an instrument of fraud.'

Link

See Chapter 5 on secret trusts

LORD JUSTICE LINDLEY

It is further established... that the Statute of Frauds does not prevent the proof of a fraud; and it is a fraud on the part of a person to whom land is conveyed as a trustee, and who knows it was so conveyed, to deny the trust and claim the land himself. Consequently, notwithstanding the statute, it is competent for a person claiming land conveyed to another to prove by parol evidence that it was so conveyed upon trust for the claimant, and that the grantee, knowing the facts, is denying the trust and relying upon the form of conveyance and statute, in order to keep the land himself.

3.2 Disposition of an Equitable Interest

It is extremely important to note that s53(1)(b) only applies to the creation of trusts, while s53(1)(c) applies to the disposition of equitable interests. In other words, s53(1)(c) only applies to situations where a trust has *already* been created. Therefore, the two paragraphs are mutually exclusive; you cannot use both paragraphs for the same specific transfer.

***Grey v Inland Revenue Commissioners* [1960] AC 1**

Panel: Viscount Simonds, Lord Radcliffe, Lord Cohen and Lord Keith of Avonholm. Lord Reid was present at the hearing in the Appellate Committee.

Statutes: Law of Property Act 1925 s53(1)(c); Statute of Frauds 1677 s9

Facts: In an attempt to avoid paying stamp duty on the transfer of 18,000 shares from himself to his grandchildren, Mr Hunter entered into a convoluted scheme of transfer. He arranged for trustees (one of whom was Mr Grey) to hold the 18,000 shares with him as the beneficiary, as follows:

Trustees (*Legal Title*)

↓

Mr Hunter (Beneficiary – *Equitable Title*)

Mr Hunter then orally instructed the trustees to hold the 18,000 shares on trust for his grandchildren, so that the trust could be represented diagrammatically as follows.

Trustees (*Legal Title*)

~~Mr Hunter (Beneficiary – Equitable Title)~~ → Grandchildren (Beneficiaries – *Equitable Title*)

Finally, five weeks after this oral instruction, Mr Hunter and the trustees executed six deeds in which the oral instruction was evidenced as having transferred the equitable interest from Mr Hunter to his grandchildren.

The issue before the House of Lords was whether this type of transfer came within the meaning of 'disposition' in s53(1)(c) Law of Property Act 1925. It was agreed by the parties before the hearing that if the oral instruction had been ineffective then the shares had been transferred by the deed, and as such their Lordships did not consider this specific issue at length in their judgments. It was held there was an effective disposition of the equitable interest that was liable to be taxed.

VISCOUNT SIMONDS

These facts give rise to the plain question whether the oral directions given by Mr. Hunter, which are recited in each of the instruments, were effective or were, having regard to section 53(1)(c) of the Law of Property Act, 1925 , wholly ineffective. In the former event the instruments would not, and in the latter would, be chargeable with a valorem duty.

Section 53(1) of the Act is as follows "Subject to the provisions hereinafter contained with respect to the creation of interest in land by parol, ... (c) a disposition of an equitable interest or trust subsisting at the time of the disposition, must be in writing signed by the person disposing of the same, or by his agent thereunto lawfully authorised in writing or by will."

Briefly, then, were the several oral directions given by Mr. Hunter dispositions by him of the equitable interest in the shares held by the appellants as nominees for him?

Alert

If the word "disposition" is given its natural meaning, it cannot, I think, be denied that a direction given by Mr. Hunter, whereby the beneficial interest in the shares theretofore vested in him became vested in another or others, is a disposition. But it is contended by the appellants that the word "disposition" is to be given a narrower meaning and (so far as relates to *inter vivos* transactions) be read as if it were synonymous with "grants and assignments" and that, given this meaning, it does not cover such a direction as was given in this case. As I am clearly of the opinion, which I understand to be shared by your Lordships, that there is no justification for giving the word "disposition" a narrower meaning than it ordinarily bears, it will be unnecessary to discuss the interesting problem that would otherwise arise. ...

LORD RADCLIFFE

My Lords, if there is nothing more in this appeal than the short question whether the oral direction that Mr. Hunter gave to his trustees on February 18, 1955, amounted in any ordinary sense of the words to a "disposition of an equitable interest or trust subsisting at the time of the disposition," I do not feel any doubt as to my answer. I think that it did. Whether we describe what happened in technical or in more general terms the full equitable interest in the 18,000 shares concerned, which at that time was his, was (subject to any statutory invalidity) diverted by his direction from his ownership into the beneficial ownership of the various equitable owners, present and future, entitled under his six existing settlements. ...

> In my opinion, it is a very nice question whether a parol declaration of trust of this kind was or was not within the mischief of section 9 of the Statute of Frauds. The point has never, I believe, been decided and perhaps it never will be. Certainly it was long established as law that while a declaration of trust respecting land or any interest therein required writing to be effective, a declaration of trust respecting personalty did not. Moreover, there is warrant for saying that a direction to his trustee by the equitable owner of trust property prescribing new trusts of that property was a declaration of trust. But it does not necessarily follow from that that such a direction, if the effect of it was to determine completely or *pro tanto* the subsisting equitable interest of the maker of the direction, was not also a grant or assignment for the purposes of section 9 and therefore required writing for its validity. Something had to happen to that equitable interest in order to displace it in favour of the new interests created by the direction: and it would be at any rate logical to treat the direction as being an assignment of the subsisting interest to the new beneficiary or beneficiaries or, in other cases, a release or surrender of it to the trustee. ...
>
> For these reasons I think that there is no direct link between section 53(1)(c) of the Act of 1925 and section 9 of the Statute of Frauds. The link was broken by the changes introduced by the amending Act of 1924, and it was those changes, not the original statute, that section 53 must be taken as consolidating. If so, it is inadmissible to allow the construction of the word "disposition" in the new Act to be limited or controlled by any meaning attributed to the words "grant" or "assignment" in section 9 of the old Act.

Their Lordships were all in agreement that the appeal should be dismissed. The Court of Appeal decision ([1958] Ch 690), in which it was held that the deed evidencing the oral instruction was sufficient signed writing for the transaction, was therefore upheld. Since this was a written document, it was subject to stamp duty that Mr Hunter was liable to pay.

Consequently, it would appear that this decision is *ratio* for the proposition that writing evidencing an earlier void oral disposition of an equitable interest will make the disposition valid. It is respectfully submitted that this reasoning is flawed. A strict reading of s53(1)(c) reveals that signed writing is required to dispose of an equitable interest at the time of disposition, not later. Furthermore, the consequence of not having this signed writing is that the disposition is void; it is automatically of no legal effect. Unlike s53(1)(b), where the result of not fulfilling the formalities is that the trust is unenforceable but still exists, failing to fulfil s53(1)(c) strictly means we should say there has been no disposition at all. Subsequent writing is therefore not sufficient.

The outcome of *Grey*, therefore, should have been that the deed evidencing the oral transfer should not have been treated as signed writing fulfilling s53(1)(c). This would have meant that Mr Hunter was still the beneficiary of the shares, but it would also have meant that Mr Hunter would not have been liable to pay stamp duty.

***Vandervell v Inland Revenue Commissioners* [1967] 2 AC 291**

Panel: Lord Reid, Lord Pearce, Lord Upjohn, Lord Donovan and Lord Wilberforce

Statutes: Law of Property Act 1925 s53(1)(c); Statute of Frauds 1677 s9

Facts: Mr Vandervell was a successful engineer and had, amongst other things, his own private company, Vandervell Products Limited ('VPL'). He had nearly all the shares (100,000) in VPL, which were held on bare trust with him as beneficiary and the National Provincial Bank as the trustee. Mr Vandervell wanted to use dividends from the VPL shares in order to fund a professorship of Pharmacology with the Royal College of Surgeons ('RCS'). Mr Vandervell's interest in the VPL shares at the outset may be represented diagrammatically as follows:

National Provincial Bank (Trustee – *Legal Title*)

↓

Mr Vandervell (Beneficiary – *Equitable Title*)

Following negotiations with the RCS, Mr Vandervell orally instructed the National Provincial Bank to transfer legal title of the shares to the RCS, as follows:

National Provincial Bank ⟶ Legal Title ⟶ Royal College of Surgeons

The RCS were intended to be absolute owners of the shares, so that when Mr Vandervell declared dividends of the shares they could be retained by the RCS to fund the professorship.

The argument before the House of Lords was whether this type of transfer counted as a 'disposition' under s53(1)(c). If the transfer made when Mr Vandervell instructed the National Provincial Bank to transfer legal title of the shares to the RCS came within s53(1)(c) then it was a taxable disposition. If it did not come within the ambit of s53(1)(c) then there was no tax liability on that specific transfer.

It was held that the transfer of the shares was not a transfer coming within the ambit of s53(1)(c).

LORD UPJOHN

There are two points to be considered, completely different, each in a watertight compartment. ...

Alert

...[T]he object of the section, as was the object of the old Statute of Frauds, is to prevent hidden oral transactions in equitable interests in fraud of those truly entitled, and making it difficult, if not impossible, for the trustees to ascertain who are in truth his beneficiaries. But when the beneficial owner owns the whole beneficial estate and is in a position to give directions to his bare trustee with regard to the legal as well as the equitable estate there can be no possible ground for invoking the section where the beneficial owner wants to deal with the legal estate as well as the equitable estate.

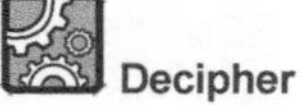
Decipher

I cannot agree with Diplock L.J. that prima facie a transfer of the legal estate carries with it the absolute beneficial interest in the property transferred; this plainly is not so, e.g., the transfer may be on a change of trustee; it is a matter of intention in each case. But if the intention of the beneficial owner in directing the trustee to transfer the legal estate to X is that X should be the beneficial owner I can see no reason for any further document or further words in the document assigning the legal estate also expressly transferring the beneficial interest; the greater includes the less. X may be wise to secure some evidence that the beneficial owner intended him to take the beneficial interest in case his beneficial title is challenged at a later date but it certainly cannot, in my opinion, be a statutory requirement that to effect its passing there must be some writing under section 53(1)(c).

Counsel for the Crown admitted that where the legal and beneficial estate was vested in the legal owner and he desired to transfer the whole legal and beneficial estate to another he did not have to do more than transfer the legal estate and he did not have to comply with section 53(1)(c); and I can see no relevant difference between that case and this.

As I have said, that section is, in my opinion, directed to cases where dealings with the equitable estate are divorced from the legal estate and I do not think any of their Lordships in Grey ... had in mind the case before your Lordships. To hold the contrary would make assignments unnecessarily complicated; if there had to be assignments in express terms of both legal and equitable interests that would make the section more productive of injustice than the supposed evils it was intended to prevent. ...

I think the Court Of Appeal reached a correct conclusion on this point, which was not raised before Plowman J.

LORD WILBERFORCE

There remains the alternative point taken by the Crown that in any event, by virtue of section 53(1)(c) of the Law of Property Act, 1925, the appellant never effectively disposed of the beneficial interest in the shares to the Royal College of Surgeons. This argument I cannot accept. Section 53(1)(c), a successor to the dormant section 9 of the Statute of Frauds, has recently received a new lease of life as an instrument in the hands of the Revenue. The subsection, which has twice recently brought litigants to this House (*Grey v Inland Revenue Commissioners*; *Oughtred v Inland Revenue Commissioners*), is certainly not easy to apply to the varied transactions in equitable interests which now occur. However, in this case no problem arises. The shares in question, the 100,000 "A" shares in Vandervell Products Ltd., were, prior to November 14, 1958, registered in the name of the National Provincial Bank Ltd. upon trust for the appellant absolutely. On November 14, 1958, the appellant's solicitor received from the bank a blank transfer of the shares, executed by the bank, and the share certificate. So at this stage the appellant was the absolute master of the shares and only needed to insert his name as transferee in the transfer and to register it to become the full legal owner. He was also the owner in equity. On November 19, 1958, the solicitor ... handed the transfer to the college which, in due course, sealed it and obtained registration of the shares in the college's name. The case should then be regarded as one in which the appellant himself has, with the intention to make a gift, put the college in a position to become the legal owner of the shares, which the college in fact became. ... No separate transfer, therefore, of the equitable interest ever came to or needed to be made and there is no room for the operation of the subsection. What the position would have been had there simply been an oral direction to the legal owner (viz. the bank) to transfer the shares to the college, followed by such a transfer, but without any document in writing signed by Mr. Vandervell as equitable owner, is not a matter which calls for consideration here. The Crown's argument on this point fails but, for the reasons earlier given, I would dismiss the appeal.

Mr Vandervell therefore succeeded, as it was held that s 53(1)(c) did not apply to a situation where an absolutely entitled beneficiary instructs the trustee to make a third party the absolute owner of the property. In effect, Mr Vandervell's instruction to the National Provincial Bank had the effect of transferring both the Bank's legal title and Mr Vandervell's own equitable title to RCS, as follow:

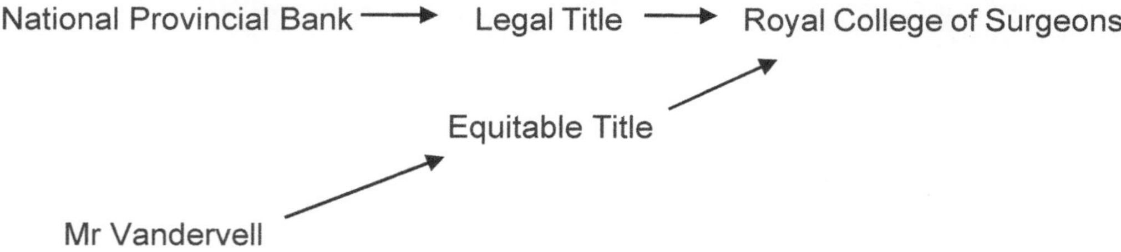

The decision in *Vandervell* has traditionally been seen by many academics as controversial and contradictory to *Grey*. However, it is submitted that the judgments of Lords Upjohn and Wilberforce are sound. Lord Upjohn (with whom Lords Pearce and Donovan agreed) has clearly taken a purposive interpretation of s53(1)(c) in looking at the reasons behind why the paragraph is there, rather than merely looking at the words. If his analysis that the paragraph is to prevent fraud is accepted, then there clearly is no risk of fraud on any beneficiaries in a situation like *Vandervell*; when the RCS received the shares, they did so as absolute owners and therefore there was no beneficiary.

Link
See Chapter 1

Alternatively, Lord Wilberforce's reasoning is that Mr Vandervell had effectively collapsed the trust by using his rights under *Saunders v Vautier* 49 ER 282 (which he was perfectly entitled to do as the absolutely entitled beneficiary). This is because Mr Vandervell's solicitor received a blank share transfer form from the National Provincial Bank. Completion of this form is one of the requirements for transferring legal title of shares. Since Mr Vandervell had equitable title to the shares and the solicitor was his agent, in essence at this point both equitable and legal interests in the shares had been combined before the share transfer form was completed in favour of the RCS. It is absolutely correct to say that, if Vandervell had exercised his *Saunders v Vautier* rights and then transferred absolute title of the shares to the RCS, this would not come within s53(1)(c). If that is the case, following Lord Wilberforce's judgment it is a logical step that s53(1)(c) does not apply in *Vandervell* type situations either.

It is submitted that either interpretation is perfectly valid and therefore there is good justification for why s53(1)(c) is not applicable in this situation.

3.2.1 Other situations where s53(1)(c) of the Law of Property Act 1925 will not apply

It is important to note that pursuant to s53(2) of the Law of Property Act 1925, neither s53(1)(b) nor s53(1)(c) apply to resulting, implied or constructive trusts. A common scenario where a constructive trust arises is when there is a contract for a type of property of which equity will grant specific performance if there is a breach. A type of property that is frequently subject to this type of contract is shares in a private company.

***Neville v Wilson* [1997] Ch 144**

Panel: Nourse, Rose and Aldous LJJ

Statute: Law of Property Act 1925 s53(1)(c)

Facts: Before he died, Mr Neville had a private company, J E Neville Ltd ('J.E.N'). During Mr Neville's lifetime J.E.N acquired the shares of another company, Universal Engineering Co (Ellesmere Port) Ltd ('U.E.C.'). After Mr Neville's death J.E.N. was informally liquidated and treated as defunct. U.E.C. meanwhile continued to be profitably run. Two of Mr Neville's children, Joseph Neville and Eileen Hill, were shareholders of J.E.N. with another of Mr Neville's children, Lillian Wilson, and two members of her family, Courtney Wilson and Jonathan Wilson. The two factions of the family fell out. Joseph and Eileen sued the other faction as to whether the informal dissolution of J.E.N. led to a disposal of J.E.N.'s equitable interest in U.E.C. If there had been a valid disposal of the equitable interest, then all of the family members shared the interest in U.E.C. as shareholders of J.E.N. when it existed. If there had not been a valid disposal, then the shares would go to the Crown as *bona vacantia* when J.E.N. was informally dissolved.

It was held that as this was a contract to sell property that was subject to the remedy of specific performance, a constructive trust was created regarding the shares. As the shares were subject to a constructive trust, they came within the ambit of s53(2). The requirements of s53(1)(c) were not necessary and therefore no signed writing was required for the transfer to be valid. Consequently, the shares went to the family members, not the Crown.

LORD JUSTICE NOURSE

Here again we think that common sense comes into play. It is an undisputed fact that after 1969 J.E.N. was treated by all concerned as being defunct. From that it is reasonable to infer that its shareholders, in making their agreement, intended that it should not be left with any assets. To put it in another way, it is reasonable to infer that they would have given an affirmative answer to the question whether they intended their agreement to apply to all assets whether known or unknown. ...

We are therefore of the opinion that in about April 1969 the shareholders of J.E.N. entered into an agreement with one another for the informal liquidation of J.E.N. as contended for by Mr. Jacob and thus, as part of it, for the division of J.E.N.'s equitable interest in the 120 ordinary shares in U.E.C. registered in the names of the widow and Mr. Wilson amongst themselves, as Mr. Hyde put it, "on a shareholding basis," in other words, in proportions corresponding to their existing shareholdings. ... In consequence J.E.N.'s equitable interest in the shares would, as the plaintiffs now claim, be divided amongst the shareholders in the proportions 104 for the trustees of the will of the testator and four each for the widow, Mr. Neville, Mrs. Hill and Mrs. Wilson.

Alert

The effect of the agreement, more closely analysed, was that each shareholder agreed to assign his interest in the other shares of J.E.N.'s equitable interest in exchange for the assignment by the other shareholders of their interests in his own aliquot share. Each individual agreement having been a disposition of a subsisting equitable interest not made in writing, there then arises the question whether it was rendered ineffectual by section 53 of the Law of Property Act 1925...

The simple view of the present case is that the effect of each individual agreement was to constitute the shareholder an implied or constructive trustee for the other shareholders, so that the requirement for writing contained in subsection (1)(c) of section 53 was dispensed with by subsection (2). That was the view taken by Upjohn J. [1958] Ch. 383 at first instance and by Lord Radcliffe in the House of Lords in *Oughtred v Inland Revenue Commissioners* [1960] A.C. 206 . In order to see whether it is open to us to adopt it in this court, we must give careful consideration to those views and to the other speeches in the House of Lords.

Lord Justice Nourse then proceeded to give a thorough analysis of *Oughtred*, a case that does not give a clear conclusion as to whether s53(1)(c) applies to this situation or not. He therefore felt able to adopt the reasoning of Lord Radcliffe in his dissenting judgment in *Oughtred*.

The views of their Lordships as to the effect of section 53 can be summarised as follows. Lord Radcliffe, agreeing with Upjohn J., thought that subsection (2) applied. He gave reasons for that view. Lord Cohen and Lord Denning thought that it did not. Although neither of them gave reasons... Keith and Lord Jenkins expressed no view either way. ...

Alert

We do not think that there is anything in the speeches in the House of Lords which prevents us from holding that the effect of each individual agreement was to constitute the shareholder an implied or constructive trustee for the other shareholders. In this respect we are of the opinion that the analysis of Lord Radcliffe, based on the proposition that a specifically enforceable agreement to assign an interest in property creates an equitable interest in the assignee, was unquestionably correct... A greater difficulty is caused by Lord Denning's outright rejection of the application of section 53(2), with which Lord Cohen appears to have agreed.

So far as it is material to the present case, what subsection (2) says is that subsection (1)(c) does not affect the creation or operation of implied or constructive trusts. Just as in *Oughtred v Inland Revenue Commissioners* [1960] A.C. 206 the son's oral agreement created a constructive trust in favour of the mother, so here each shareholder's oral or implied agreement created an implied or constructive trust in favour of the other shareholders. Why then should subsection (2) not apply? No convincing reason was suggested in argument and none has occurred to us since. Moreover, to deny its application in this case would be to restrict the effect of general words when no restriction is called for, and to lay the ground for fine distinctions in the future. With all the respect which is due to those who have thought to the contrary, we hold that subsection (2) applies to an agreement such as we have in this case.

For these reasons we have come to the conclusion that the agreement entered into by the shareholders of J.E.N. in about April 1969 was not rendered ineffectual by section 53 of the Act of 1925. The plaintiffs' alternative claim succeeds and they are entitled to relief accordingly. That means that J.E.N.'s equitable interest in the 120 shares did not vest in the Crown as *bona vacantia* in 1970.

3.3 Application of s53(1)(c) to Sub-Trusts

A former area of considerable debate within formalities was the application of s53(1)(c) to sub-trusts. A sub-trust occurs when a beneficiary becomes a trustee of their equitable interest for another person, who becomes the sub-beneficiary.

Note that a distinction can be drawn between the scenario in which a beneficiary attempts to create a sub-trust of the whole of his equitable interest for a sub-beneficiary (sometimes referred to as a 'bare sub-trust') and the scenario in which a beneficiary attempts to create a sub-trust of only part of his equitable interest (sometimes referred to as a 'non-bare sub-trust').

***Nelson v Greening & Sykes (Builders) Ltd* [2007] EWCA Civ 1358, [2008] 1 EGLR 59**

Panel: Ward, Wall and Lawrence Collins LJJ

Statute: Law of Property Act 1925 s53(1)(c)

Facts: This case focusses upon the application of s2 the Charging Orders Act 1979 to a contract for the sale of land. A side effect of creation of the contract of the land between Greening & Sykes and Mr Nelson was that a constructive trust was created in favour of Mr Nelson. Mr Nelson in turn passed the benefit of this contract on to his associate Ms Hanley, for whom he was a nominee. In essence, Mr Nelson held his interest under the contract on trust for Ms Hanley. One of the questions before the court was whether Mr Nelson holding his interest on trust for Ms Hanley was a disposition of an equitable interest. It was held that there was no disposition of Mr Nelson's interest.

LORD JUSTICE LAWRENCE COLLINS

Lord Justice Lawrence Collins first considered the traditional case-law distinction before going on to consider the rules in regard to the facts of the case before him.

These authorities do not bind this court to hold that as a matter of law an intermediate trustee ceases to be a trustee. I accept the submission for G&S that saying... that the practical effect [of Mr Nelson holding the property on sub-trust for Ms Hanley] would seem to amount to or be capable of amounting to the "getting rid" of the trust of the equitable interest then subsisting, is not the same as saying that as a matter of law it does get rid of the intermediate trust. What he was saying was that in the case of a trust and sub-trust of personal property the trustees may decide that as a matter of practicality it is more convenient to deal directly with the beneficiary of the sub-trust.

But in any event it seems to me that the authorities have no application to a case where the trust property is the purchaser's interest in land created by the existence of an executory contract for sale and purchase. ...

In summary Lawrence Collins LJ is stating that even if all the property of a trust has been placed on a sub-trust, this does not mean that the original trust has come to an end. The trustee of the original trust still has duties regarding that trust to the beneficiary; even though the sub-trust has been created these duties continue to exist. The argument therefore is that despite the sub-trust being declared over all of the trust assets, this does not destroy the original trustee-beneficiary relationship and therefore there has been no 'disposition' of trust assets.

It must be noted, however, that the comments by Lawrence Collins LJ were considered to have no general effect upon the rules of sub-trusts generally. Instead the statements made were in the context of a commercial relationship. These comments, in regard to the general law, are therefore *obiter*.

The court's approach in *Nelson* appears to have been followed in the below case. This lends further support to the proposition that s53(1)(c) compliance is not necessary for a sub-trust.

***Sheffield v Sheffield* [2013] EWHC 3927 (Ch), [2014] WTLR 1039**

Panel: Judge Penning QC

Facts: The facts are complicated but, in essence involved a number of trust settlements set up for tax planning purposes. In 1968 the claimant's grandfather, Mr John Vincent Sheffield ('JVS') and grandmother purchased farmland, which they held under a settlement as tenants in common with JVS holding a quarter share. In 1983, JVS made a declaration of trust under which he held his quarter-share beneficial interest in the land on trust for the claimant. In 2005 the claimant claimed that he was owed, inter alia, a quarter of the trust income since 1983. The defendants (who were the executors of JVS's will and trustees of the 1968 settlement) argued that the 1983 declaration was subject to a separate, informal arrangement whereby JVS would continue to keep all the income attributable to the quarter interest while he was alive, as if he was still the owner of the share.

One of the key legal issues for the judge was whether the 1983 declaration had in fact made JVS a sub-trustee, so that the claimant's claims for income should be made against JVS's estate and not against the 'head' trustees i.e. the trustees of the 1968 settlement. Applying *Nelson and Greening v Sykes*, Judge Penning QC found for the claimant. He held that JVS had disposed of the equitable interest by declaring himself to be a trustee of it for the claimant. Furthermore, whilst the trustees of the 1968 settlement could have paid income to the claimant rather than JVS they were not obliged to do so because, in effect, the original trust does not come to an end on creation of a sub-trust. Therefore, the failure to pay was a breach of trust by JVS and not on the part of the trustees of the 1968 settlement.

JUDGE PENNING QC

The Defendants submit that an equitable interest in the hands of a trustee can be disposed of by the beneficiary in favour of a third party in one of but only in one of four ways (a) assignment, (b) a direction to the trustees to hold the property on trust for the third party (c) entering into a contract to assign with the third party or (d) declaring himself to be a trustee of the interest in favour of the third party – see *Timpson's Executors v. Yerbury* [1936] 1 KB 645 per Romer LJ at 664. I agree with that submission. I also agree that by executing the 1983 Declaration JVS chose the fourth of these options.

...The Defendants then rely on a statement of principle by Turner LJ in the earlier Court of Appeal case of *Milroy v. Lord* (1862) 4 D F & J 264 at 274 (cited by Romer LJ in *Timpson's Executors v. Yerbury* (ante) at 664-5) that "... if the settlement is intended to be effectuated by one of the modes to which I have referred, the Court will not give effect to it by applying another of those modes ..." The modes being considered in that case were assignment and declaration of trust. It was submitted that the approach adopted by Upjohn J in *Grey v. IRC* contradicts this principle because it involves the court giving effect to mode (d) by treating it as if it were mode (a), which is precisely what Turner LJ suggested could not be done. There is significant force in this point.

The Defendants submit that this issue was put beyond doubt by the decision of the Court of Appeal in *Nelson v. Greening & Sykes (Builders) Limited* (ante) where it was held that *Grey v. IRC* (ante) did not establish that an intermediate trustee ceased to be a trustee as a matter of law but only that in the case of a trust and sub-trust of personal property the trustees may decide, as a matter of practicality that it is more convenient to deal directly with the beneficiary of the sub-trust – see Lawrence Collins LJ at [57]. The Claimant submits however that this decision was reached per incuriam *Burgess v. White*, *Grainge v. Wilberforce* and in *Re Lashmar* (ante). In my judgment this submission is mistaken because there is nothing in these authorities that is necessarily inconsistent with the conclusion of the Court of Appeal in *Nelson*.

4

Constitution

4.1 Constitution

To constitute a trust, legal title must be vested in the trustee(s). If the settlor intends to make themselves the sole trustee, there is no need for a transfer of legal title and the trust is perfected once they have made a valid self-declaration of trust (which can be informal except in the case of land – see Chapter 3 on formalities).

If the settlor intends to use another/others as trustee(s), they must transfer legal title to them, using the correct method for the type of property being transferred. Until legal title vests in the trustee(s), the trust is incompletely constituted and, as the cases below demonstrate, the intended beneficiary is unable to enforce the trust if, as is usual, they are a volunteer – equity will not assist a volunteer.

Similar principles apply to making outright gifts: until legal title is correctly vested in the intended donee(s), the gift is incomplete and equity will not perfect an imperfect gift or assist the donee as a volunteer. Some of the cases extracted in this chapter involve incompletely constituted trusts and some involve incomplete gifts. The leading case is *Milroy v Lord*, which we will discuss first.

Milroy v Lord **(1862) 4 De Gex, Fisher & Jones 264, 45 ER 1185**

Panel: Knight Bruce and Turner LJJ

Facts: Thomas Medley executed a deed purporting to transfer shares in a certain bank to Samuel Lord to hold on trust for the plaintiffs. No transfer of the shares into Lord's name was ever made in the books of the bank, as required by the bank's constitution, and they remained in Medley's name until his death. The judge held that the shares were bound by the trusts. Medley's personal representative (one of the defendants) appealed. It was held that there was no valid trust of the shares.

LORD JUSTICE TURNER

...Under the circumstances of this case it would be difficult not to feel a strong disposition to give effect to this settlement to the fullest extent, and certainly I have spared no pains to find the means of doing so, consistently with what I apprehend to be the law of the Court; but, after full and anxious consideration, I find myself unable to do so. I take the law of this Court to be well settled, that, in order to render a voluntary settlement valid and effectual, the settler must have done everything which, according to the nature of the property comprised in the settlement, was necessary to be done in order to transfer the property and render the settlement binding upon him. He may of course do this by actually transferring the property to the persons for whom he intends to provide, and the provision will then be effectual, and it will be equally effectual if he transfers the property to a trustee for the purposes of the settlement, or declares that he himself holds it in trust for those purposes; and if the property be personal, the trust may, as I apprehend, be declared either in writing or by parol; but, in order to render the settlement binding, one or other of these

Alert

modes must, as I understand the law of this Court, be resorted to, for there is no equity in this Court to perfect an imperfect gift. The cases I think go further to this extent, that if the settlement is intended to be effectuated by one of the modes to which I have referred, the Court will not give effect to it by applying another of those modes. If it is intended to take effect by transfer, the Court will not hold the intended transfer to operate as a declaration of trust, for then every imperfect instrument would be made effectual by being converted into a perfect trust. ...

Alert

Alert

...Now it is plain that it was not the purpose of this settlement, or the intention of the settlor, to constitute himself a trustee of the bank shares. The intention was that the trust should be vested in the Defendant Samuel Lord, and I think therefore that we should not be justified in holding that by the settlement, or by any parol declaration made by the settlor, he himself became a trustee of these shares for the purposes of the settlement. By doing so we should be converting the settlement or the parol declaration to a purpose wholly different from that which was intended to be effected by it, and, as I have said, creating a perfect trust out of an imperfect transaction.

...The decree must be altered accordingly... .

This case illustrates the vital importance of correctly transferring legal title. It also shows that, if legal title is not correctly transferred, equity will not rescue the failed trust (or gift) by holding that the settlor has made himself a trustee, as that was never his intention. This point is also illustrated by the next two cases, which show how harshly the rule can operate. While *Milroy v Lord* related to an intended trust, the following case related to a failed gift.

Jones v Lock **(1865-66) LR 1 Ch App 25**

Panel: Lord Cranworth LC

Facts: Robert Jones had received a cheque for £900 (payable to him) in payment of a mortgage and had told his solicitor that he intended to add £100 to it and invest it for the benefit of his nine-month old son. On being asked if he had brought his son a gift on his return from a business trip, he fetched the £900 cheque and put it in his son's hands saying 'I give this to baby'. He then put the cheque in a safe stating that he was going to put it away for his son. Robert Jones died a few days later, having told his solicitor that he intended to alter his will to provide for his son. His will (made before the son's birth) left most of his estate to his children from a previous marriage. The son's mother brought a claim for £900 on his behalf against the estate. The judge held that there was a valid declaration of trust for the son. The other children appealed. It was held that there was no valid gift or declaration of trust.

LORD CRANWORTH LC

...I regret to say that I cannot bring myself to think that, either on principle or on authority, there has been any gift or any valid declaration of trust. ... If I give any chattel that, of course, passes by delivery, and if I say, expressly or impliedly, that I constitute myself a trustee of personality, that is a trust executed, and capable of being enforced without consideration. ...[T]he authorities cited before me ... all turn upon the question, whether what has been said was a declaration of trust or an imperfect gift. In the latter case the parties would receive no aid from a Court of equity if they claimed as volunteers. But when there has been a declaration of trust, then it will be enforced, whether there has been consideration or not. Therefore the question in each case is one of fact; has there been a gift or not, or has there been a declaration of trust or not?

I should have every inclination to sustain this gift, but unfortunately I am unable to do so; the case turns on the very short question whether Jones intended to make a declaration that he held the property in trust for the child; and I cannot come to any other conclusion than that he did not. I think it would be of very dangerous example if loose conversations of this sort, in important transactions of this kind, should have the effect of declarations of trust.

...[T]he testator would have been very much surprised if he had been told that he had parted with the £900, and could no longer dispose of it. It all turns upon the facts, which do not lead me to the conclusion that the testator meant to deprive himself of all property in the note, or to declare himself a trustee of the money for the child. I extremely regret this result, because it is obvious that, by the act of God, this unfortunate child has been deprived of a provision which his father meant to make for him.

Richards v Delbridge (1874) LR 18 Eq 11

Panel: Sir George Jessel MR

Facts: A grandfather was the leaseholder of business premises and endorsed a memorandum on the lease to the effect that he gave the lease and his business stock-in-trade to his grandson, who was under the age of majority. He then arranged for the lease to be delivered to the grandson's mother. The grandfather died soon afterwards and an action was brought on behalf of the grandson claiming that there was a valid declaration of trust in his favour of the lease and stock-in-trade. It was held that the ineffectual transfer could not be upheld as a declaration of trust, as the grandfather had not intended to declare himself a trustee.

SIR GEORGE JESSEL MR

...The principle is a very simple one. A man may transfer his property, without valuable consideration, in one of two ways: he may either do such acts as amount is (sic) law to a conveyance or assignment of the property, and thus completely divest himself of the legal ownership, in which case the person who by those acts acquires the property takes it beneficially, or on trust, as the case may be; or the legal owner of the property may, by one or other of the modes recognised as amounting to a valid declaration of trust, constitute himself a trustee, and, without an actual transfer of the legal title, may so deal with the property as to deprive himself of its beneficial ownership, and declare that he will hold it from that time forward on trust for the other person. It is true he need not use the words, "I declare myself a trustee", but he must do something which is equivalent to it, and use expressions which have that meaning; for, however anxious the Court may be to carry out a man's intention, it is not at liberty to construe words otherwise than according to their proper meaning. ...

The true distinction appears to me to be plain, and beyond dispute: for a man to make himself a trustee there must be an expression of intention to become a trustee, whereas words of present gift shew an intention to give over property to another, and not retain it in the donor's own hands for any purpose, fiduciary or otherwise.

Alert

In *Milroy v Lord*, Lord Justice Turner, after referring to the two modes of making a voluntary settlement valid and effectual, adds these words:

"The cases, I think, go further, to this extent, that if the settlement is intended to be effectuated by one of the modes to which I have referred, the Court will not give effect to it by applying another of those modes. If it is intended to take effect by transfer, the Court will not hold the intended transfer to operate as a declaration of trust, for then every imperfect instrument would be made effectual by being converted into a perfect trust."

It appears to me that that sentence contains the whole law on the subject. ...

I must, therefore, [find for the defendants]... .

These three cases can be contrasted with the case of *T Choithram International SA and others v Pagarani and others* [2001] 1 WLR 1, where the Privy Council felt able, on the somewhat unusual facts, to find a valid trust from a seemingly imperfect gift. In contrast to the three cases extracted above, the settlor in this case *did* intend to make himself a trustee.

***T Choithram International SA and others v Pagarani and others* [2001] 1 WLR 1**

Panel: Lord Browne-Wilkinson, Lord Jauncey of Tullichettle, Lord Clyde, Lord Hobhouse of Woodborough and Lord Millett

Facts: Thakurdas Choithram Pagarani (TCP) was the majority shareholder in a number of companies. Rather than drawing profits from the companies, he built up credits on accounts with them. Having made generous provision for his family, he intended to leave much of his remaining wealth to charity and, after being diagnosed with cancer, he executed a trust deed setting up a charitable Foundation with himself as one of the trustees. After signing the trust deed, he said words to the effect that he was giving his shares and wealth in the companies to the Foundation and he instructed the accountant to the companies to make the transfers. TCP then held meetings of the Boards of Directors of the companies and of the Trustees of the Foundation at which he confirmed that he had gifted his wealth to the Foundation. The accountant altered some entries in the company books to show the Foundation as creditor in place of TCP; he gave instructions for his assistant to make similar alterations in respect of other credit balances but this was not done until after TCP's death. TCP did not execute any share transfer forms but, after his death, the Trustees of the Foundation were registered as shareholders in his place.

His first wife and their children challenged the validity of those gifts to the Foundation which had not been completed before TCP's death. The Court of Appeal of the British Virgin Islands upheld the judge's decision to the effect that TCP's actions were insufficient to constitute a completed gift to the Foundation. The defendants appealed to the Privy Council.

It was held that TCP's words of gift were essentially words of gift on trust and so the deposit balances and shares were held on the trusts of the Foundation trust deed.

LORD BROWNE-WILKINSON

...The case again raises, but with a new twist, the question "when is a gift completed". ...

In order to have made an effective gift of his shares and deposit balances to the foundation TCP must have intended to make an immediate gift... .

...[T]heir Lordships are satisfied that that was TCP's intention. Perhaps the most telling evidence of all is the minutes of the companies' meetings... . ... They record that the directors of each of the four companies, who in each case included TCP, "acknowledge and confirm that the trustees of the [foundation] are henceforth the holders of the shares and assets in the company gifted to the [foundation] by Mr T C Pagarani". Those minutes were signed by TCP. It is hard to imagine a clearer statement of what TCP understood to be the position, ie that he had already given outright to the foundation all his interests in the company balances and the shares.

...[T]he judge ... founded his decision on the ground that the requirements laid down in *Milroy v Lord* (1862) 4 De GF & J 264 had not been satisfied. ...

Their Lordships ... turn to the central and most important question: on the basis that TCP intended to make an immediate absolute gift "to the foundation" but had not vested the gifted property in all the trustees of the foundation, are the trusts of the foundation trust deed enforceable against the deposits and the shares or is this (as the judge and the Court of Appeal held) a case where there has been an imperfect gift which cannot be enforced against TCP's estate whatever TCP's intentions.

The judge and the Court of Appeal understandably took the view that a perfect gift could only be made in one of two ways, viz (a) by a transfer of the gifted asset to the donee, accompanied by an intention in the donor to make a gift; or (b) by the donor declaring himself to be a trustee of the gifted property for the donee. In case (a), the donor has to have done everything necessary to be done which is within his own power to do in order to transfer the gifted asset to the donee. If the donor has not done so, the gift is incomplete since the donee has no equity to perfect an imperfect gift: *Milroy v Lord* 4 De GF & J 264;

Richards v Delbridge (1874) LR 18 Eq 11; *In re Rose; Midland Bank Executor and Trustee Co Ltd v Rose* [1949] Ch 78; *In re Rose; Rose v Inland Revenue Comrs* [1952] Ch 499. Moreover, the court will not give a benevolent construction so as to treat ineffective words of outright gift as taking effect as if the donor had declared himself a trustee for the donee: *Milroy v Lord* 4 De GF & J 264. So, it is said, in this case TCP used words of gift to the foundation (not words declaring himself a trustee): unless he transferred the shares and deposits so as to vest title in all the trustees, he had not done all that he could in order to effect the gift. It therefore fails. Further it is said that it is not possible to treat TCP's words of gift as a declaration of trust because they make no reference to trusts. Therefore the case does not fall within either of the possible methods by which a complete gift can be made and the gift fails.

Though it is understandable that the courts below should have reached this conclusion since the case does not fall squarely within either of the methods normally stated as being the only possible ways of making a gift, their Lordships do not agree with that conclusion. The facts of this case are novel and raise a new point. It is necessary to make an analysis of the rules of equity as to complete gifts. Although equity will not aid a volunteer, it will not strive officiously to defeat a gift. This case falls between the two common form situations mentioned above. Although the words used by TCP are those normally appropriate to an outright gift—"I give to X"—in the present context there is no breach of the principle in Milroy v Lord if the words of TCP's gift (i.e. to the foundation) are given their only possible meaning in this context. The foundation has no legal existence apart from the trust declared by the foundation trust deed. Therefore the words "I give to the foundation" can only mean "I give to the trustees of the foundation trust deed to be held by them on the trusts of foundation trust deed". Although the words are apparently words of outright gift they are essentially words of gift on trust.

But, it is said, TCP vested the properties not in all the trustees of the foundation but only in one, i.e. TCP. Since equity will not aid a volunteer, how can a court order be obtained vesting the gifted property in the whole body of trustees on the trusts of the foundation. Again, this represents an over-simplified view of the rules of equity. ...[B]eneficiaries under a trust, although volunteers, can enforce the trust against the trustees. Once a trust relationship is established between trustee and beneficiary, the fact that a beneficiary has given no value is irrelevant. It is for this reason that the type of perfected gift referred to in class (b) above is effective since the donor has constituted himself a trustee for the donee who can as a matter of trust law enforce that trust.

What then is the position here where the trust property is vested in one of the body of trustees, *viz.* TCP? In their Lordship's view there should be no question. TCP has, in the most solemn circumstances, declared that he is giving (and later that he has given) property to a trust which he himself has established and of which he has appointed himself to be a trustee. All this occurs at one composite transaction taking place on 17 February. There can in principle be no distinction between the case where the donor declares himself to be sole

trustee for a donee or a purpose and the case where he declares himself to be one of the trustees for that donee or purpose. In both cases his conscience is affected and it would be unconscionable and contrary to the principles of equity to allow such a donor to resile from his gift. Say, in the present case, that TCP had survived and tried to change his mind by denying the gift. In their Lordship's view it is impossible to believe that he could validly deny that he was a trustee for the purposes of the foundation in the light of all the steps that he had taken to assert that position and to assert his trusteeship. In their Lordship's judgment in the absence of special factors where one out of a larger body of trustees has the trust property vested in him he is bound by the trust and must give effect to it by transferring the trust property into the name of all the trustees. ...

Alert

Their Lordships will therefore humbly advise Her Majesty that the appeal ought to be allowed and the action dismissed on the grounds that at TCP's death the deposit balances and the shares in the companies were held on the trusts of the foundation trust deed and the same are now validly vested in the trustees of the foundation.

Link
See also the case of *Pennington v Waine* (below) where the Court of Appeal referred to the concept of unconscionability.

It could be argued that this case is confined to the particular facts – TCP was treated as declaring himself to be a trustee, albeit one of several trustees, and therefore bound by his declaration. However, the idea of it being unconscionable for the donor to change his mind and resile from the gift is arguably a wider concept and this was picked up by the Court of Appeal in the case of *Pennington and another v Waine and others* [2002] 1 WLR 2075.

A number of principles have emerged to mitigate the harshness of the rules laid down in *Milroy v Lord*. One is the principle from *Re Rose, Rose v Inland Revenue Commissioners* [1952] Ch 499. It will be recalled that, in *Milroy v Lord,* it was said that the settlor must have done *everything necessary* in order to transfer the property and make the settlement binding on them. The precise meaning of this was explored in *Re Rose*, where it was held to mean only that the settlor must have done *everything that he himself could do* to transfer legal title. This prevents trusts or gifts from failing merely because something remains to be done by a third party.

The case involved both an attempted outright gift and an attempted transfer on trust and Lord Evershed MR stated that he would confine himself to discussing the gift, as a decision on that would necessarily involve a similar decision in relation to the trust.

***In re Rose, Rose v Inland Revenue Commissioners* [1952] Ch 499**

Panel: Lord Evershed MR, Jenkins and Morris LJJ

Facts: On 30 March 1943, Mr Rose executed two transfers of shares in a private company. One transferred shares to his wife by way of gift. The other transferred shares to his wife and another person as trustees for Mr Rose's wife and son. The transfers and share certificates were delivered to the transferees but were only registered by the company on 30 June 1943. Mr Rose died in 1947 and it was vital that the transfers were effective before 10 April 1943 if estate duty on the shares was to be avoided. The judge held that estate duty was not payable. The Crown appealed. It was held that once the settlor had done everything in his power to transfer the shares, he was a trustee of the shares for the transferees and so no estate duty was payable in respect of them.

LORD EVERSHED MR

...[The transfer] was in form in exact correspondence with the requirements of the company's regulations; ... On its execution the deed of transfer was, beyond question, delivered to the transferee, together with the certificate relative to those shares. It follows, therefore, that so far as lay in his power, the deceased did all that he could – he followed carefully and precisely the obligations imposed on a proposing transferor ... – to divest himself then and there ... of all his interest, legal and equitable, in the ... shares. ...

...I will now go to the case of *Milroy v Lord*, which is in truth the foundation of the Crown's argument; since it is on that case that depends the proposition that, if this document was intended to operate as a transfer, effect cannot be given to what may be thought to have been the intention behind it by treating it as operating as a declaration of trust. It is necessary to examine the case with a little care because, being a decision of this court, it is binding on us. ...

Mr. Pennycuick has mostly founded his argument on the passage in the judgment of Turner L.J.

The Master of the Rolls then cited a passage, extracted above.

Those last few sentences form the gist of the Crown's argument and on it is founded the broad, general proposition that if a document is expressed as, and on the face of it intended to operate as, a transfer, it cannot in any respect take effect by way of trust... In my judgment, that statement is too broad and involves too great a simplification of the problem; and is not warranted by authority. I agree that if a man purporting to transfer property executes documents which are not apt to effect that purpose, the court cannot then extract from those documents some quite different transaction and say that they were intended merely to operate as a declaration of trust, which ex facie they were not; but if a document is apt and proper to transfer the property – is in truth the appropriate way in which the property must be transferred – then it does not seem to me to follow from the statement of Turner L.J. that, as a result, either during some limited period or otherwise, a trust may not arise, for the purpose of giving effect to the transfer. ... And, for my part, I do not think that the case of *Milroy v Lord* is an authority which compels this court to hold that in this case – where, in the terms of Turner L.J.'s judgment, the settlor did everything which, according to the nature of the property comprised in the settlement, was necessary to be done by him in order to transfer the property – the result necessarily negatives the conclusion that, pending registration, the settlor was a trustee of the legal interest for the transferee.

The view of the limitations of *Milroy v Lord*, which I have tried to express, was much better expressed by Jenkins J. in the recent case which also bears the same name of *In re Rose* (though that is a coincidence). ...[I]n that case, Rose ... had executed (as had this Mr. Rose) a transfer in appropriate form and handed the transfer and the certificate to Hook; but, at the time of his death, the transfer had not been registered. ... [M]y brother considered the case of *Milroy v Lord*, and in regard to it he used this language; "I was referred on that to the well-known case of *Milroy v Lord*, and also to the recent case of *In re Fry*. Those cases, as I understand them, turn on the fact that the deceased donor had not done all in his power, according to the nature of the property given, to vest the legal interest in the property in the donee. In such circumstances it is, of course, well settled that there is no equity to complete the imperfect gift. If any act remained to be done by the donor to complete the gift at the date of the donor's death the court will not compel his personal representatives to do that act and the gift remains incomplete and fails. In *Milroy v Lord* the imperfection was due to the fact that the wrong form of transfer was used for the purpose of transferring certain bank shares. The document was not the appropriate document to pass any interest in the property at all." Then he refers to *In re Fry*, which is another illustration. "In this case, as I understand it, the testator had done everything in his power to divest himself of the shares in question to Mr. Hook. He had executed a transfer. It is not suggested that the transfer was not in accordance with the company's regulations. He had handed that transfer together with the certificate to Mr. Hook. There was nothing else the testator could do." I venture respectfully to adopt the whole of the passage I have read which, in my judgment, is a correct statement of the law. If that be so, then it seems to me that it cannot be asserted on the authority of *Milroy v Lord*, and I venture to think it also cannot be asserted as a matter of logic and good sense or principle, that because, by the regulations of the company, there had to be a gap before Mrs. Rose could, as between herself and the company, claim the rights which the shares gave her vis-à-vis the company, the deceased was not in the meantime a trustee for her of all his rights and benefits under the shares ... and if the deceased had received a dividend between execution and registration and Mrs. Rose had claimed to have that dividend handed to her, what would have been the the deceased's answer? ... How could he, in the face of his own statement under seal, deny the proposition that he had, on March 30, 1943, transferred the shares to his wife? – and by the phrase "transfer the shares" surely must be meant transfer to her "the shares and all my right title and interest thereunder."...

...If, as I have said, the phrase "transfer the shares" is taken to be and to mean a transfer of all rights and interests in them, then I can see nothing contrary to the law in a man saying that so long as, pending registration, the legal estate remains in the donor, he was, by the necessary effect of his own deed, a trustee of that legal estate. ... I would dismiss the appeals.

LORD JUSTICE JENKINS

...On the deceased executing the transfers and handing them over, together with the relative share certificates, to the transferees or their agent, the matter, then, stood thus: The deceased had done all in his power to divest himself of and to transfer to the transferees the whole of his right, title and interest, legal and equitable, in the shares in question. He had ... done all he could, in appropriate form, to transfer the whole of his interest, but so far as the legal title was concerned, it was not in his power himself to effect the actual transfer of that, inasmuch as it could only be conferred on the transferees in its perfect form by registration of the transfers. But he had, in my judgment, transferred to the transferees the right to be placed on the register in his stead as the owners of the shares, subject to the directors' power to refuse registration.

...[I]t seems to me plain enough that this gift or disposition must have been made on the date when the deceased executed instruments of transfer and delivered them, with the certificates, to the transferees.

...I can understand that in given circumstances a gift might, rightly or wrongly, be claimed to be incomplete because it could be recalled by the donor. If here it could be said that the deceased, had he changed his mind at any moment before registration, could, by the taking of appropriate proceedings, recall the transfers and recover the certificates and restrain the directors of the company from registering the transfers, then I would understand the proposition that the gift was incomplete, inasmuch as the property had never passed irrevocably to the donees. ... It seems to me impossible to suppose that any such action could have been brought by the deceased in this case with any prospect of success. ...

I agree with my Lord that the case of *Milroy v Lord* by no means covers the question with which we have to deal in the present case. If the deceased had in truth transferred the whole of his interest in these shares so far as he could transfer the same, ... in my view, ... his only remaining interest consisted in the fact that his name still stood on the register as holder of the shares; but having parted in fact with the whole of his beneficial interest, ... in my view the effect ... must be that, pending registration, the deceased was in the position of a trustee of the legal title in the shares for the transferees. ...

In my view, in order to arrive at a right conclusion in this case, it is necessary to keep clear and distinct the position as between transferor and transferee and the position as between transferee and the company. It is, no doubt, true that the rights conferred by shares are all rights against the company, and it is no doubt true that, in the case of a company with ordinary regulations, no person can exercise his rights as a shareholder vis-à-vis the company or be recognized by the company as member unless and until he is placed on the register of members. But in my view it is a fallacy to adduce from that the conclusion that there can be no complete gift of shares as between transferor and transferee unless and until the transferee is placed on the register. In my view, a transfer ... in the form appropriate under the company's regulations, coupled with

 Alert

delivery of the transfer and certificate to the transferee, does suffice, as between transferor and transferee, to constitute the transferee the beneficial owner of the shares, and the circumstance that the transferee must do a further act in the form of applying for and obtaining registration in order to get in and perfect his legal title, having been equipped by the transferor with all that is necessary to enable him to do so, does not prevent the transfer from operating, in accordance with its terms as between the transferor and transferee, and making the transferee the beneficial owner. ...

For these reasons, as well as those given by my Lord, I am of the opinion that the learned judge came to a right conclusion in this case, and that the shares ... did not attract duty... .

LORD JUSTICE MORRIS

I am in agreement with the judgments which my Lords have delivered.

The case of *Re Rose, Rose v IRC* is authority for treating both gifts and transfers on trust as complete in equity where the settlor has done all in his power to transfer title. The case was subjected to some criticism. There were suggestions that it was inconsistent with *Milroy v Lord* in treating the settlor as a trustee for the intervening period, when it was not his intention to be a trustee. However, the principle is now well established and was applied to a gift of registered land in the following case, which rejected the idea of any inconsistency with *Milroy v Lord*.

Mascall v Mascall **(1985) 50 P & CR 119**

Panel: Lawton, Browne-Wilkinson LJJ and Sir Denys Buckley

Facts: A father executed a transfer of a house to his son by way of gift. He handed the transfer to the son and also handed him the land certificate relating to the house. The son's solicitors sent the transfer to the Stamp Office and, while it was there, the father and son had a very serious quarrel and the father decided that he did not want to go through with the transfer of the house. The father applied for a declaration that the transfer was void. The deputy judge held that there had been a gift of the house to the (defendant) son. The (plaintiff) father appealed. It was held that the gift was complete as the plaintiff had done everything in his power to transfer the house and it was for the defendant to ask the Land Registry to register him as owner.

LORD JUSTICE LAWTON

...[I]t seems to me that ... in *Milroy v Lord* the Chancery Court of Appeal proceeded on the basis that the settlor had not done everything that was necessary to give the legal title to Mr. Lord.

The first person to appreciate that *Milroy v Lord* did not have the effect which it was often thought to have had, namely that everything had to be done before a gift could be perfected, was Jenkins J. in *Re Rose, Midland Bank Executor and Trustee Co Ltd v Rose...*

His Lordship then cited extracts from the judgment of Jenkins J in that case and explained:

It was on that principle as to whether the donor had done everything in his power to effect the transfer of the legal interest to the donee that Jenkins J. decided in favour of the donee.

The same problem arose in *Re Rose, Rose v Inland Revenue Commissioners...* Jenkins L.J. pointed out that the statement that a failed transfer cannot be construed in any circumstances as a trust was a statement which was much too wide. He qualified the proposition by saying that, if the effect in law is that the donor holds the legal interest for the benefit of the donee, in those circumstances there is a trust to which the court will give effect.

In my judgment, that is the situation here. The plaintiff had done everything in his power to transfer the house to the defendant. He had intended to do it. He had handed over the land certificate. He had executed the transfer and all that remained was for the defendant, in the ordinary way of conveyancing, to submit the transfer for stamping and then to ask the Land Registry to register his title. Mr. Pearson sought to say that, in relation to registered land, if not to unregistered land, the plaintiff could have done more because he himself ... could have asked the Land Registry to register the transfer and he had not done so; therefore he had not done everything within his power. In my judgment, that is a fallacious argument. He had done everything in his power in the ordinary way of the transfer of registered property and, in the ordinary way, it was for the defendant to get the Land Registry to register him as the proprietor of the property. In those circumstances, it seems to me that the deputy judge's judgment was correct and I would dismiss the appeal.

LORD JUSTICE BROWNE-WILKINSON

...Gifts can be made by a donor either direct to the donee or to a trustee for donees. In either case the property, the subject-matter of the gift, has to be vested in the donee or the trustee for the donee. The settlor can achieve that broadly in two different ways. First, he can transfer the gifted property itself. Secondly, he can declare himself a trustee of the gifted property for the benefit of the donee. In the present case, a declaration of trust of that kind by the plaintiff for the benefit of the defendant simply does not arise. The only question is: Has there been a sufficient transfer of the land to the defendant?

The basic principle underlying all the cases is that equity will not come to the aid of a volunteer. Therefore, if a donee needs to get an order from a court of equity in order to complete his title, he will not get it. If, on the other hand, the donee has under his control everything necessary to constitute his title completely without any further assistance from the donor, the donee needs no

Alert

assistance from equity and the gift is complete. It is on that principle, which is laid down in *Re Rose*, that in equity it is held that a gift is complete as soon as the settlor or donor has done everything that the donor has to do, that is to say, as soon as the donee has within his control all those things necessary to enable him, the donee, to complete his title.

...[I]n my judgment, *Milroy v Lord* is entirely consistent with *Re Rose*. ... The principle set out by Turner L.J. in his judgment is often treated as being a general proposition that everything must have been done which was necessary to complete the legal transfer of property. But ... I can see nothing in that [judgment] requiring that all formalities necessary to complete a legal transfer have to be carried through. Turner L.J. is saying the settlor must have done everything it is necessary for him to do. For those reasons, I can see no inconsistency in the authorities.

In this case, the plaintiff executed a transfer and put it within the control of the defendant together with the land certificate. He had done everything necessary to complete the transaction so far as he, the plaintiff, was concerned. The gift was in equity complete. ...

...I too, would dismiss the appeal.

SIR DENYS BUCKLEY

I agree with both the judgments... .

It can be seen that Browne-Wilkinson LJ regarded *Re Rose* and *Milroy v Lord* as consistent with each other. The second paragraph in the extract from his judgment suggests that the donee must have under his control everything necessary to complete his title. Following *Re Rose* and *Mascall,* it was generally assumed that, for a gift or trust to be regarded as complete in equity, the settlor must have parted with the documents so that there was nothing further he could do and it was out of his power to change his mind. However, in the case of *Pennington and another v Waine and others* [2002] 1 WLR 2075, the Court of Appeal held that handing over the documents was not always necessary. Picking up on comments in *Choithram v Pagarani*, the Court of Appeal held that in some circumstances it might be unconscionable for the settlor to change his mind.

Pennington and another v Waine and others **[2002] 1 WLR 2075**

Panel: Schiemann, Clarke and Arden LJJ

Facts: Ada Crampton owned 75% of the shares in Crampton Bros. Ltd (the company). In 1998, just over a month before her death, she executed a transfer form transferring 400 shares by way of gift to her nephew Harold Crampton. She handed the completed form to Mr Pennington, who was a partner in the company's auditors and the form was placed on the file of the company. Ada told Harold that she was giving him some shares and that she wanted him to become a director of the company. The company's articles required directors to hold at least one share. In October, Mr Pennington sent Harold a form to sign, consenting to act as a director, and his accompanying letter explained that Ada had instructed him to arrange the transfer of 400 shares to Harold and stated that this required no action on Harold's part. Harold signed the consent form and Ada countersigned it. In November 1998, Ada executed a will making gifts of the rest of her shareholding and making no reference to the 400 shares. No further action was taken regarding the stock transfer form before Ada's death in November. Ada's executors brought an action against a number of defendants including Harold. The judge held that the gift was effective and Ada had transferred the beneficial interest in the shares to Harold. Some of the other defendants appealed.

It was held that, although the transfer form had not been handed to Harold, a stage had been reached where it would have been unconscionable for Ada to recall the gift, so the beneficial interest had passed to Harold.

LADY JUSTICE ARDEN

...The judge held that Mr Pennington was not the company's agent when he received the form of transfer signed by Ada.

[In other words, the form was not treated as having been delivered to the company. Mr Pennington was, in effect, holding it as Ada's agent.]

...I will refer to the decision of Jenkins J in In *re Rose* [1949] Ch 78 as *Midland Bank Executor and Trustee Co Ltd v Rose* and to the decision of this court in the (unconnected) case of *In re Rose* [1952] Ch 499 as *Rose v Inland Revenue Comrs*.

...[T]he principle that equity will not assist a volunteer at first sight looks like a hard-edged rule of law not permitting much argument or exception. Historically the emergence of the principle may have been due to the need for equity to follow the law rather than an intuitive development of equity. The principle against imperfectly constituted gifts led to harsh and seemingly paradoxical results. Before long, equity had tempered the wind to the shorn lamb (i e the donee). It did so on more than one occasion and in more than one way.

First it was held that an incompletely constituted gift could be upheld if the gift had been completed to such an extent that the donee could enforce his right to the shares as against third parties without forcing the donor to take any further step. Accordingly, if a share transfer has been executed by the donor and duly presented to the company for registration, the donee would be entitled, if necessary, to apply to the court for an order for rectification of the share register...

That exception was extended in *Rose v Inland Revenue Commissioners* [1952] Ch 499 and other cases by holding that for this exception to apply it was not necessary that the donor should have done all that it was necessary to be done to complete the gift, short of registration of the transfer. On the contrary it was sufficient if the donor had done all that it was necessary for him or her to do.

There is a logical difficulty with this particular exception because it assumes that there is a clear answer to the question, when does an equitable assignment of a share take place? ... The equitable assignment clearly occurs at some stage before the shares are registered. But does it occur when the share transfer is executed, or when the share transfer is delivered to the transferee, or when the transfer is lodged for registration ... or the directors resolve that the transfer should be registered? I return to this point below.

According to counsel's researches, the situation in the present case has not arisen in any reported cases before. I note that in her recent work, *Personal Property Law, Text, Cases and Materials* (2000), p 241 Professor Sarah Worthington takes it as at (sic) axiomatic that:

"notwithstanding any demonstrable intention to make a gift, there will be no effective gift in equity if the donor simply places matters (such as completed transfer forms accompanied by the relevant share certificates) in the hands of the donor's agents. In those circumstances the donor remains at liberty to recall the gift simply by revoking the instructions previously given to the agent. The donor has not done all that is necessary, and the donee is not in a position to control completion of the transfer. It follows that the intended gift will not be regarded as complete either at law or in equity."

Secondly equity has tempered the wind (of the principle that equity will not assist a volunteer) to the shorn lamb (the donee) by utilising the constructive trust. This does not constitute a declaration of trust and thus does not fall foul of the principle (see *Milroy v Lord* 4 De GF & J 264 and *Jones v Lock* LR 1 Ch App 25) that an imperfectly constituted gift is not saved by being treated as a declaration of trust. Thus, for example, in *T Choithram International SA v Pagarini* (sic) [2001] 1 WLR 1 the Privy Council held that the assets which the donor gave to the foundation of which he was one of the trustees were held upon trust to vest the same in all the trustees of the foundation on the terms of the trusts of the foundation. This particular trust obligation was not a term of the express trust constituting the foundation but a constructive trust adjunct to it. So, too, in *Rose v Inland Revenue Comrs.* [1952] Ch 499, the Court of Appeal held that the beneficial interest in the shares passed when the share transfers were delivered to the transferee, and that consequently the transferor was a trustee of the legal estate in the shares from that date. ...

I will need to return to this point below.

Thirdly equity has tempered the wind to the shorn lamb by applying a benevolent construction to words of gift. As explained above an imperfect gift is not saved by being treated as a declaration of trust. But where a court of equity is satisfied that the donor had an intention to make an immediate gift, the court will construe the words which the donor used as words effecting a gift or declaring a trust if they can fairly bear that meaning and otherwise the gift will fail. This point can also be illustrated by reference to *T Choithram International SA v Pagarini* (sic) [2001] 1 WLR 1. ... The Privy Council held that the gift to "the foundation" could only properly be construed as a gift to the

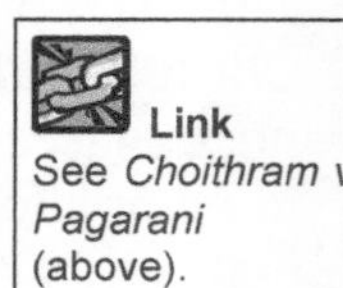
Link
See *Choithram v Pagarani* (above).

purposes declared by the trust deed and administered by the trustees. Lord Browne-Wilkinson giving the judgment of the Privy Council [stated]: [Her Ladyship cited a passage from *Choithram v Pagarani*, extracted above]

Accordingly the principle that, where a gift is imperfectly constituted, the court will not hold it to operate as a declaration of trust, does not prevent the court from construing it to be a trust if that interpretation is permissible as a matter of construction, which may be a benevolent construction. ...

The cases to which counsel have referred us do not reveal any, or any consistent single policy consideration behind the rule that the court will not perfect an imperfect gift. The objectives of the rule obviously include ensuring that donors do not by acting voluntarily act unwisely in a way that they may subsequently regret. This objective is furthered by permitting donors to change their minds at any time before it becomes completely constituted. This is a paternalistic objective, which can outweigh the respect to be given to the donor's original intention as gifts are often held by the courts to be incompletely constituted despite the clearest intention of the donor to make the gift. ... There must also be, in the interests of legal certainty, a clearly ascertainable point in time at which it can be said that the gift was completed, and this point in time must be arrived at on a principled basis.

There are countervailing policy considerations which would militate in favour of holding a gift to be completely constituted. These would include effectuating, rather than frustrating, the clear and continuing intention of the donor, and preventing the donor from acting in a manner which is unconscionable. ...[B]oth these policy considerations are evident in *T Choithram International SA v Pagarini* (sic) [2001] 1 WLR 1. It does not seem to me that this consideration is inconsistent with what Jenkins LJ said in *In re McArdle*, decd [1951] Ch 669. His point was that there is nothing unconscionable in simply (without more) changing your mind. That is also the point which Professor Worthington makes in the passage I have cited.

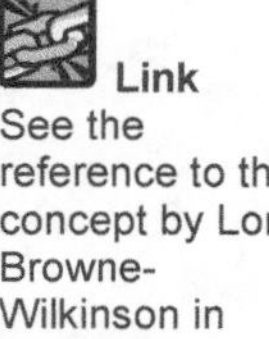
Link
See the reference to this concept by Lord Browne-Wilkinson in *Choithram v Pagarani* (above).

If one proceeds on the basis that a principle which animates the answer to the question whether an apparently incomplete gift is to be treated as completely constituted is that a donor will not be permitted to change his or her mind if it would be unconscionable, in the eyes of equity, vis-a-vis the donee to do so, what is the position here? There can be no comprehensive list of factors which makes it unconscionable for the donor to change his or her mind: it must depend on the court's evaluation of all the relevant considerations. What then are the relevant facts here? Ada made the gift of her own free will: there is no finding that she was not competent to do this. She not only told Harold about the gift and signed a form of transfer which she delivered to Mr Pennington for him to secure registration: her agent also told Harold that he need take no action. In addition Harold agreed to become a director of the company ..., which he could not do without shares being transferred to him. If Ada had changed her mind on (say) 10 November 1998, in my judgment the court could properly have concluded that it was too late for her to do this as by that date Harold

Alert

signed the form ...[agreeing to become a director], the last of the events identified above, to occur.

There is next the pure question of law: was it necessary for Ada deliver (sic) the form of transfer to Harold? ... In *Rose v Inland Revenue Comrs.* [1952] Ch 499 the issue was whether the gift was perfected by 10 April 1943, by which date the donor had executed the declarations of gift and delivered the share transfers to reflect the gifts to the transferees. Argument was not therefore directed to the question whether a beneficial interest in the shares passed on the dates of the declarations of trust or on the date on which the share transfers were handed over. For my own part I do not consider that it was necessary to the conclusions of Sir Raymond Evershed MR that the gift should have taken effect before the transfers were delivered to the transferees. ... [I]f this were the view of Sir Raymond Evershed MR it seems to me that it would not ... be possible to reconcile it with *Milroy v Lord* 4 De GF & J 264, and in particular with the principle that the court will not convert an imperfect gift into a declaration of trust. There could not be a constructive trust until the gift was perfected. The conclusion of Jenkins LJ was predicated on the basis that delivery of the transfer to the donee was necessary and had occurred. Likewise the decision of this court in *Mascall v Mascall* 50 P & CR 119 ... [was] predicated on the same basis. ... Accordingly the ratio of *Rose v Inland Revenue Comrs.* [1952] Ch 499 was as I read it that the gifts of shares in that case were completely constituted when the donor executed share transfers and delivered them to the transferees even though they were not registered in the register of members of the company until a later date.

However, that conclusion as to the ratio in *Rose v Inland Revenue Comrs.* does not mean that this appeal must be decided in the appellant's favour. Even if I am correct in my view that the Court of Appeal took the view in Rose v Inland Revenue Comrs that delivery of the share transfers was there required, it does not follow that delivery cannot in some circumstances be dispensed with. Here, there was a clear finding that Ada intended to make an immediate gift. Harold was informed of it. Moreover, I have already expressed the view that a stage was reached when it would have been unconscionable for Ada to recall the gift. It follows that it would also have been unconscionable for her personal representatives to refuse to hand over the share transfer to Harold after her death. In those circumstances, in my judgment, delivery of the share transfer before her death was unnecessary so far as perfection of the gift was concerned.

Alert

It is not necessary to decide the case simply on that basis. After the share transfers were executed Mr Pennington wrote to Harold on Ada's instructions informing him of the gift and stating that there was no action that he needed to take. I would also decide this appeal in favour of the respondent on this further basis. If I am wrong in the view that delivery of the share transfers to the company or the donee is required and is not dispensed with by reason of the fact that it would be unconscionable for Ada's personal representatives to refuse to hand the transfers over to Harold, the words used by Mr Pennington should be construed as meaning that Ada and, through her, Mr Pennington became agent for Harold for the purpose of submitting the share transfer to the company. This is an application of the principle of benevolent construction to give effect to Ada's clear wishes. Only in that way could the result "This requires no action on your part" and an effective gift be achieved. Harold did not question this assurance and must be taken to have proceeded to act on the basis that it would be honoured.

...Nothing in this judgment is intended to detract from the requirement that a donor should comply with any formalities required by the law to be complied with by him or her, such as, in the case of a gift of shares, the completion of an instrument of transfer or, in the case of a gift of land, the requirements of ... the Law of Property (Miscellaneous Provisions) Act 1989 or, in the case of a gift of a chattel, delivery of the chattel. ...

In the circumstances I would dismiss the appeal.

Lord Justice Schiemann, in dismissing the appeal, agreed with the reasons given by Arden LJ. Lord Justice Clarke decided the case the same way but on a slightly different basis. However, he also expressed agreement with the majority view in the following terms.

LORD JUSTICE CLARKE

...It is certainly true that Ada could have done more. She could have delivered the transfer form to Harold or to the company. She could indeed have applied to the company to enter Harold's name in its register of members...

[A]lthough I know that hard cases make bad law, I would have expected Harold to be entitled ... to the 400 shares apparently transferred by stock transfer form... I should add that, if unconscionability is the test, I agree with Arden LJ that it would have been unconscionable of Ada, as at the time of her death (if not earlier), to assert that the beneficial interest in the 400 shares had not passed to Harold. It would certainly be unconscionable of the estate to seek to resile from the transfer after Ada's death because, as at her death, she plainly intended Harold to own the shares. ...

Later in his judgment, he said:

As Arden LJ has observed, Lord Browne-Wilkinson [in *Choithram v Pagarani*]... highlighted the contrast between the maxim that equity will not aid a volunteer and the maxim that it will not strive officiously to defeat a gift. It seems to me that if equity refuses to aid Harold on the facts of this case, it will prefer the former maxim to the latter, whereas all the circumstances of the case lead to the conclusion that it should give effect to the gift which Ada intended. ...

In her judgment, Arden LJ refers to conflicting policy considerations.

Although the outcome of this case seems to accord with the settlor's intentions, there are difficulties with the decision. It is not easy to predict when a court might consider it unconscionable for a settlor to change his mind.

There is also a question as to how the idea of it being unconscionable for a donor to change his mind relates to the more established doctrine of proprietary estoppel, where a person may be prevented from going back on a promise or assurance, relating to property, which has been relied on by another to his detriment as, for example, in the case of *Gillett v Holt* [2001] Ch 210.The limitations of both *Re Rose* and *Pennington v Waine* can be seen in the following case, in which the purported donee of company shares attempted to argue both exceptions in order perfect the imperfect transfer of the equitable (as opposed to the legal interest) in those shares.

***Zeital v Kaye* [2010] EWCA Civ 159**

Panel: Dyson, Maurice Kay and Rimer LJJ

Facts: The facts are complicated, but essentially relate to the ownership of a company called Dalmar Limited ('Dalmar') set up by Raymond Zeital. Raymond died intestate in 2004 and there was a dispute as to who owned the shares in Dalmar and, consequently, an apartment purchased by Dalmar. Dalmar had only two issued shares, the legal title to which was held by a Mr and Mrs Kumar, the agents that Raymond had used to incorporate the company. Beneficial ownership of the shares was vested in Raymond. The Kumars had each signed and given Raymond a stock transfer form. The forms were undated and blank, in that the transferee boxes were not filled in. Raymond's widow, Giselle Zeital, had separated from him approximately 20 years before his death and his more recent partner, Stefka Appostolova, asserted that the shares in Dalmar had been gifted to her. Raymond had given the blank stock transfer forms to Stefka, dating and filling in her name on the first but only handing over the second, in respect of the share legally owned by Mrs Kumar. After Raymond's death, Stefka purported to appoint herself as sole director of the company (which had in the meantime gone into liquidation and been removed from the register of companies) and to have it restored to the register of companies.

At first instance, Knowles J found that the steps taken by Raymond had been sufficient to give Stefka his beneficial interest in the shares. Mrs Zeital appealed the decision in respect of one of the shares (the "second share" referred to below) and the Court of Appeal allowed the appeal.

LORD JUSTICE RIMER

The appellants do not dispute the judge's findings in relation to Raymond's donative intent with regard to the second share. Their submission is that Raymond's method of purportedly transferring that share to Stefka fell so far short of the formalities required for a transfer of a share that the gift failed as an imperfect one.

In my judgment that submission is correct. I consider, with respect, that the judge was wrong to find that Raymond's actions of August 2003 operated to transfer the beneficial interest in the second share to Stefka. Such interest remained in Raymond. My reasons are these.

It is common ground that immediately before the handing of the stock transfer form to Stefka in August 2003 Mrs Kumar was the legal owner of the second share and Raymond was its beneficial owner. Raymond had, therefore, no more than an equitable interest in the share. Accepting that his actions and words of August 2003 evinced a donative intent in respect of the second share, he could on one view do no more than transfer or assign that equitable interest. Moreover, it is no part of Mr Banks' argument for Stefka that Raymond did transfer to Stefka more than that equitable interest.

There are, however, difficulties in the way of the case that he did transfer that interest to her. Subject to Mr Banks' point based on the authorities to which I come below, so far as I am aware the only way in which he could do so was by (i) declaring himself a trustee for Stefka of his equitable interest, thus creating a sub-trust; (ii) assigning his interest to her by 'writing signed by [him], or by his agent thereunto lawfully authorised in writing ...' so as to comply with section 53(1)(c) of the Law of Property Act 1925 ; or (iii) making a like written assignment of his interest to a trustee for Stefka. He did none of these things.

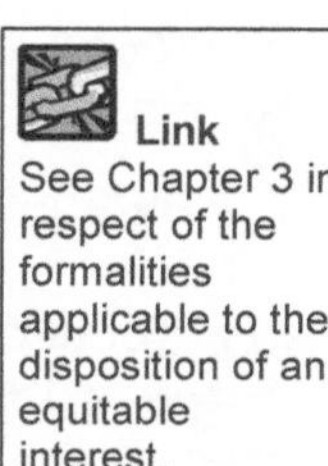

Link
See Chapter 3 in respect of the formalities applicable to the disposition of an equitable interest.

He did not purport to declare a trust (which, had he wanted to, he could have done orally). Nor did he effect a written assignment either to Stefka or to a trustee for her. I would not regard the stock transfer form signed by Mrs Kumar as constituting such an assignment. That was a document she had signed for the purpose of enabling a future transfer of the legal title to the second share. It did not purport to assign Raymond's equitable interest in the share. Even if, however, such a construction of it is possible, I am unaware of any evidence to the effect that she was Raymond's agent for such purpose or that she had been 'thereunto lawfully authorised in writing' for the purposes of section 53(1)(c) . It follows in my view that Raymond's actions of August 2003 were ineffective to divest him of his equitable interest in the second share.

In respect of the attempts by Stefka's counsel to invoke the rule in Re Rose and the principle in Pennington v Waine, Rimer LJ said the following:

I do not, however, regard those cases as providing the help that Stefka claims to derive from them. The cases all concerned the question of whether the legal owner of shares had made a valid gift of them.

...In broad terms, what the two Rose cases decided was that once the legal owner of shares hands to his donee a properly completed share transfer form relating to such shares and the relative share certificate, he will thereby have done all within his own power to transfer the shares to the donee. The donee will only become their legal owner upon being later registered as a member, a matter commonly outside the donor's control; and until such registration, the donor will remain the legal owner. But once the donor has done all in his own power to transfer the shares, he will be regarded as holding the legal title to them upon trust for the donee, who will thereupon become their beneficial owner.

...In the Pennington case (which raised special facts relating to the delivery of the stock transfer form not in point in this case) the gift of the beneficial interest was regarded as complete even though no share certificate was handed over, a point to which I infer the court was sensitive. But Arden LJ explained in paragraph [5] that '[n]othing turns on the absence of the share certificates as Ada's [the donor's] share certificates were held by the company.' The point Arden LJ was implicitly making was, I consider, that in those particular circumstances no question arose on the donor's omission to deliver the certificates to the donee. The court in Pennington did not speak with one voice as to why the appeal in that case should be dismissed, but the majority comprised Arden and Schiemann LJJ.

Rimer LJ went on to highlight the factual differences between the Re Rose case and the facts of the present case, reiterating the fact that, unlike the Rose donors, Raymond was not the legal owner of the second share. As to whether Raymond had done all in his power to transfer the second share to Stefka, Rimer LJ's view was as follows:

...Raymond did not do all in his power to transfer the second share to Stefka. To become registered as a member, Stefka also needed the share certificate in respect of that share. The evidence was that its whereabouts were unknown. If it was lost, it was open to Mrs Kumar, as the legal owner, to procure the creation of a duplicate; and Raymond could have asked her to do so. He might perhaps first have had to procure Dalmar's restoration, but as the beneficial owner of the second share he could have asked Mrs Kumar to lend him her name for that purpose, upon giving her appropriate indemnities as to costs. But Stefka herself would not, I consider, have had any right to obtain a duplicate. Company registrars or secretaries do not ordinarily provide duplicates for lost shares to putative transferees so as to enable them to apply to be registered as members: they require such a transferee already to have a share certificate as part of his title to a claim to be registered. Raymond had not therefore equipped Stefka with the title documentation that she needed in order to be registered as a member of Dalmar, whereas he could have done. Unlike the donors in the Rose cases he had not, therefore, done all in his own power to transfer to her, or to procure the transfer to her, of the second share. For this further reason, his actions of August 2003 did not constitute her the beneficial owner of that share.

Mr Banks' second responsive argument was unsupported by evidence, was not the subject of any finding by the judge and was not raised in a respondents' notice. It was that Stefka had changed her position to her detriment in reliance on Raymond's actions of August 2003 with regard to the second share, with the consequence that Raymond should be regarded as having at some point become a constructive trustee of the second share. That was to tread the path that is now well trodden by those presented with a section 53(1)(c) problem (see section 53(2)). Mr Banks relied on the fact that Stefka incurred expense in applying for the restoration of Dalmar to the register and had guaranteed all Mr Kaye's costs as Dalmar's liquidator.

I have difficulty in seeing how those considerations turned Raymond into a constructive trustee for Stefka of the second share. The basis on which she applied for the restoration of the company was her claimed ownership merely of the first share; and I have explained how it was only when giving evidence at the trial that Stefka advanced the claim that she had also been given the second share. The inference is thus that it was only very late in the day that the 'gift' claim occurred to her and so it is also difficult to see how she had earlier changed her position in reliance on a belief that Raymond had made such a gift. If, however, there is anything in the 'change of position' point, I regard it as one that required a factual investigation at the trial, whereas I understand that there was none: and, in the circumstances that this part of Stefka's case emerged so late, that is perhaps not surprising. I propose to say no more about this part of Mr Banks' argument than that I regard it as one that, for the reasons given at the beginning of this paragraph, is not open to Stefka in this court.

For these reasons, I consider that the judge was wrong to declare that the Zeitals have no beneficial interest Dalmar. He should have held that any purported gift by Raymond to Stefka of the second share, or of his beneficial interest in it, failed as having been imperfect; and he should have declared that the Zeitals are entitled, as administratrices of Raymond's estate, to that beneficial interest. He should not have declared that Dalmar 2004 was to be treated as a member of Dalmar for the purposes of the latter's liquidation. I would allow the appeal.

Whilst Rimer LJ did not overtly criticise the decision in Pennington, his judgment that the case "raised special facts" does seem to indicate a reluctance to apply the case other than to a substantially similar factual scenario.

The decision in *Zeital v Kaye* must also now be considered in light of the case of *Curtis v Pulbrook*.

***Curtis v Pulbrook* [2011] EWHC 167 (Ch)**

Panel: Briggs J

Facts: The case involved a dispute in respect of the ownership of 314 shares in a company called Farnham Royal Nurseries Limited ('FRN'). The claimants were the children of the late Mr and Mrs Towns. The defendant (Henry Pulbrook) was a cousin of Mrs Towns. Henry Pulbrook became a director of FRN in 1991 and also acted as a trustee of three family trusts. Following a number of complex claims and disputes amongst family members, in 2009 the beneficiaries of the family trusts successfully sued Pulbrook for breach of trust and were awarded an interim charging order over 445 shares in FRN, which they believed to be owned by Pulbrook. In his defence, Pulbrook stated that he had gifted 300 of the shares to his wife and 14 of the shares to his daughter in 2007.In his judgment, Briggs J considered whether transfer of title to the shares had been perfected. After carefully reviewing the authorities, he concluded that not only were the transfers ineffective at law, but they were also ineffective in equity. Again, Briggs J seems to take the view that the decision in Pennington should be limited to its facts.

MR JUSTICE BRIGGS

Miss Angus very properly treated me to a full citation of the two most recent authorities bearing upon this question, namely *Pennington v. Waine* [2002] 1 WLR 2075 and *Zeital & anr v. David Norman Kaye & ors* [2010] EWCA Civ 159 . In *Pennington v. Waine*, Arden LJ (with whom Schiemann LJ agreed) identified three routes by which, in the context of a defective voluntarily transfer of shares, the court might avoid the rigorous application of the principle that equity will not compel the completion of an imperfect gift, in the absence of a valid declaration of trust. She described all three as methods whereby a court of equity might temper the wind to the shorn lamb. The first is where the donor has done everything necessary to enable the donee to enforce a beneficial claim without further assistance from the donor: see paragraphs 55 to 56 and *Rose v. Inland Revenue Commissioners* [1952] Ch 499 . The second is where some detrimental reliance by the donee upon an apparent although ineffective gift may so bind the conscience of the donor to justify the imposition of a constructive trust: see paragraph 59. The third is where by a benevolent construction an effective gift or implied declaration of trust may be teased out of the words used: see paragraphs 60 to 61, apparently based upon *Choithram International SA v. Pagarani* [2001] 1 WLR 1 .

On its facts, *Pennington v Waine* appears to have been an example of a sufficient detrimental reliance by the donee, who had agreed to become a director of the subject company upon an assumption that he had received an effective gift of qualifying shares in it: see paragraphs 64 and 66.

In the present case, as in *Zeital v Kaye*, no amount of benevolence in construction would lead to the conclusion that Mr Pulbrook intended to declare himself a trustee. On the contrary he did his incompetent best to transfer both legal and beneficial title to the shares. Nor do the difficulties in identifying a perfect gift stem from any lack of clarity of intention that there should be an immediate gift, capable of being resolved by a benevolent construction. Again, on the contrary, Mr Pulbrook did his best, but without success, to effect an immediate and outright transfer of his beneficial interest.

As in *Zeital v. Kaye* , the difficulty arises from Henry Pulbrook's failure to take the necessary steps sufficient to enable his wife and daughter to obtain a transfer of the 300 and the 14 shares without further recourse to assistance from him. In fact, he failed to send either of them the share certificate of his own from which he intended that the gifts should be carved out, and he failed to send either of them the executed stock transfer forms. While it appears that he did send his relevant share certificates to the company, in the sense that they duly turned up among the documents which he sent to solicitors for safekeeping in October, he did not send the stock transfer forms to the company, but kept them himself. All that his wife and daughter received were documents purporting to be new share certificates in their names which Mr Pulbrook had created without FRN's authority. The result was that, without his assistance in making available the duly completed stock transfer forms, neither his wife nor his daughter could perfect the intended gifts without further assistance from Mr Pulbrook.

The evidence does not show any acts or omissions by either Anucha or Alice Pulbrook in reliance (let alone detrimental reliance) upon having received an apparent gift of shares, so that there is no basis upon which Mr Pulbrook could be treated as a constructive trustee. It follows that none of the methods of tempering the wind to the shorn lamb identified by Arden LJ in *Pennington v. Waine* avail either of them.

I reach that conclusion without any great comfort that the existing rules about the circumstances when equity will and will not perfect an apparently imperfect gift of shares serve any clearly identifiable or rational policy objective.

...It follows that there was not an effective gift of Mr Pulbrook's beneficial interest either in the 14 or in the 300 shares which he attempted to give respectively to his daughter and to his wife so that, in the result, there is nothing to prevent the charging order being made final in relation to all of them.

In addition to the cases above which illustrate ways in which the strict rule from *Milroy v Lord* may be mitigated, the rule in *Strong v Bird* (1874) LR 18 Eq 315 and the concept of *donatio mortis causa* are two well-established exceptions to the general rule that equity will not perfect an imperfect gift.

The rule in *Strong v Bird* stems from the case of that name and has been developed in a number of cases. The key point is that a failure to perfect legal title may be cured if the intended recipient becomes the personal representative because, as such, the legal title vests in him.

***Strong v Bird* (1874) LR 18 Eq 315**

Panel: Sir George Jessel MR

Facts: Mrs Bird lived with her step-son (the defendant) and paid him a quarterly sum for her board and lodging. The step-son borrowed a sum of money from her and it was agreed that it would be repaid by her deducting £100 a quarter from her quarterly payments. She deducted £100 from each of her next two payments but then said that she forgave the debt and made no further deductions. She died four years later, having appointed the step-son as her sole executor. One of her next of kin claimed that the step-son owed the balance of the debt to the estate. It was held that the debt was released at law by the debtor becoming executor and the debtor was not liable in equity because of the continuing intention to forgive the debt.

SIR GEORGE JESSEL MR

...Upon these facts, I consider it to be clear that whether Mrs. Bird did or did not give in law, she intended to do so. The question is, Did the law allow her to make this a complete gift without doing more than she actually did?

First of all, it is said, and said quite accurately, that the mere saying by a creditor to a debtor, "I forgive you the debt," will not operate as a release at law. ... [I]n a case where the thing which is the subject of donation is transferable or releasable at law, the legal transfer or release shall take place. The gift is not perfect until what has been generally called a change of the property at law has taken place. Allowing that rule to operate to its full extent, what occurred was this. The donor, or the alleged donor, had made her will, and by that will had appointed Mr. Bird, the alleged donee, executor. After her death he proved the will, and the legal effect of that was to release the debt in law, and therefore the condition which is required, namely, that the release shall be perfect at law, was complied with by the testatrix making him executor. It is not necessary that the legal change shall knowingly be made by the donor with a view to carry out the gift. It may be made for another purpose; but if the gift is clear, and there is to be no recall of the gift, and no intention to recall it, ... there is no reason why the legal instrument should not have its legal effect. ...[W]hen a testator makes his debtor executor, and thereby releases the debt at law, he is no longer liable at law. It is said that he would be liable in this Court: and so he would, unless he could shew some reason for not being made liable. Then what does he shew here? Why he proves to the satisfaction of the Court a continuing intention to give; and it appears to me that there being the continuing intention to give, and there being a legal act which transferred the ownership or released the obligation – for it is the same thing – the transaction is perfected, and he does not want the aid of a Court of Equity to carry it out, or to make it complete, because it is complete already, and there is no equity against him to take the property away from him.

On that ground I shall hold that this gentleman had a perfect title to the £900...

The case related to perfecting the release of a debt, and also discussed the perfecting of gifts, where the debtor or donee is executor to the creditor or donor. As executor, he acquires legal title which puts right the previous defect. Providing the intention to forgive the debt or make the gift continued until the creditor or donor's death, the debtor cannot be required to pay the debt and the donee can keep the gift. The principle was applied to perfecting a gift in the case described below.

***In re Stewart, Stewart v McLaughlin* [1908] 2 Ch 251**

Panel: Neville J

Facts: Dr Stewart informed his wife that he had bought bonds for her and handed her an envelope which contained a letter from his brokers confirming the purchase. However, the gift was not completed prior to Dr Stewart's death. The wife was appointed an executrix. It was held that the wife was entitled to the bonds, as the principle of *Strong v Bird* could be used to perfect imperfect gifts and applied whether or not the donee was the sole executor.

MR JUSTICE NEVILLE

...The intention of the testator to give the bonds being ... proved, does the fact that the wife was appointed executrix give validity to what, unless it can be supported as a declaration of trust, would be an imperfect and invalid gift? I think it does, the case, in my opinion, being within the principle of *Strong v Bird*, which is a decision of the late Sir George Jessel that has remained unchallenged for upwards of thirty years and has been followed in several cases. It purports to lay down a principle of general application, and I think I am bound to apply that principle to the present case. The decision is, as I understand it, to the following effect: that where a testator has expressed the intention of making a gift of personal estate belonging to him to one who upon his death becomes his executor, the intention continuing unchanged, the executor is entitled to hold the property for his own benefit. The reasoning by which the conclusion is reached is of a double character – first, that the vesting of the property in the executor at the testator's death completes the imperfect gift made in the lifetime, and, secondly, that the intention of the testator to give the beneficial interest to the executor is sufficient to countervail the equity of beneficiaries under the will, the testator having vested the legal estate in the executor. The whole of the property in the personal estate in the eye of the law vesting in each executor, it seems to me immaterial whether the donee is the only executor or one of several; nor do I think the rule is confined to cases of the release of a debt owing by the donee. The intention to give, however, must not be an intention of testamentary benefaction, although the intended donee is the executor, for in that case the rule cannot apply, the prescribed formalities for testamentary disposition not having been observed... I think, therefore, that the plaintiff is entitled ... to the ... bonds... .

Alert

Alert

The above case shows that the rule can apply even where the donee is not the sole executor. The case of *Re James* [1935] Ch 449 applied the rule to a donee acquiring title as administrator, although this was regarded, *obiter dicta*, as doubtful in *Re Gonin* [1979] Ch 16.

The next case examines in more detail the requirements of the rule in *Strong v Bird* as to the donor's intention, and stresses the need for an intention to make an immediate gift, which must continue unchanged until death.

In re Freeland, Jackson v Rodgers [1952] Ch 110

Panel: Lord Evershed MR, Jenkins and Morris LJJ

Facts: The plaintiff, Mrs Jackson, claimed that in the spring of 1949 her friend Mrs Freeland had given her a Hillman motor car. The car was not handed over to the plaintiff and was not then in running order. The plaintiff's evidence was that Mrs Freeland had said she would let her have the car as soon as she could get it on the road. Several months later, Mrs Freeland wrote to the plaintiff explaining that another friend's car had broken down and that she was lending the car to this other friend (Mrs Rodgers) for a few months, but that she was not going back on her word to let the plaintiff have it if she would like it. Mrs Freeland lent the car to Mrs Rodgers after having it put in order. Mrs Freeland died in April 1950, having appointed Mrs Jackson and Mrs Rodgers as executrices of her will, executed in June 1949. The plaintiff (Mrs Jackson) sought a declaration that she owned the car and that the defendant (Mrs

Rodgers) be ordered to deliver it to her. The judge held that the gift to the plaintiff had been perfected and the defendant appealed. It was held that the rule in *Strong v Bird* does not apply where the intention is to make a gift in the future, rather than a present intention to make an immediate gift.

LORD EVERSHED MR

...[T]he transactions with which we are concerned took place in the spring of 1949. The plaintiff's allegation is that in that spring the testatrix gave to her the Hillman motor car, that is to say, "gave" it in the popular sense of the term, meaning to make then and there a gift of it, such gift being, however, in the eye of the law imperfect, because it was not accompanied by actual manual delivery or its equivalent; and the plaintiff says that that imperfection is, by reason of the so-called rule in *Strong v Bird*, cured by the circumstance that the plaintiff was appointed personal representative of the testatrix.

...The bare and simple proposition which is associated with the case of *Strong v Bird*, namely, that an imperfect gift may be perfected by the subsequent appointment of the donee as personal representative, disguises an important distinction. In the headnote to the case of *In re Stewart* the principle is stated thus: "The principle laid down by Jessel M.R. in *Strong v Bird* – that where a testator has expressed in his lifetime an intention to give personal estate belonging to him to one who becomes his executor, the intention to give continuing, the donee is entitled to hold the property for his own benefit - is not confined to the release of a debt; and it is immaterial whether the donee is the only executor or one of several."

That summary of the decision of Jessel M.R. seems to me to be equivocal; for the words "an intention to give" may mean either one of two things: they may mean an intention of giving, that is to say, an intention to do that which at the time of doing it was meant to be a gift out and out; or they may mean an intention to make a gift in the future, which is in effect a promise, not enforceable in the eyes of the law, to make a gift thereafter.

Alert

I am quite satisfied that the doctrine enunciated in Strong v Bird does not apply to the latter of the two types of case. There must, for the application of this doctrine, be an intention of giving, as distinct from an intention to give. ...

The question, then, is whether it is established that the testatrix, at the relevant date, intended to make an absolute gift to the plaintiff of this motor car, a gift which was only imperfect in the eye of the law because of the technicality of the absence of the transfer of possession, manual delivery or its equivalent, which the law requires to perfect such a gift. ...

In relation to the letter written to Mrs Jackson, which the judge had treated as favourable to her claim, his Lordship said:

It is all in the future.

It may be that you could have a case in which a gift might be absolute, though immediate possession by the donee might be postponed. I need not discuss to what extent the two conceptions are possible as a matter of broad general theory, but prima facie, if I make an absolute gift, or purport to do so, of some chattel, and then assert a right to use it, not merely to keep it for custody, but to use it for such purposes as I think fit, on such terms as I think fit, and for such time as I think fit, it seems to me that the assertion of that right is not consistent with an absolute gift, though it may well be consistent with a promise to give at some future date. ...

LORD JUSTICE JENKINS

I agree. In order to succeed in this case the plaintiff had to prove that there was on the part of the testatrix a present intention to make an immediate gift to her, the plaintiff, of the motor car in question, and that that intention survived until the date of the testatrix's death. ...

It seems to me that th[e] conversation as reported by the plaintiff ... is consistent with a promise by the testatrix to give the car to the plaintiff when the car had been put into running order, and if that were the true construction of this conversation it would not, in my view, suffice to satisfy the requirements for the application of the rule in *Strong v Bird*.

...[T]he car was put in running order, and it was lent to the defendant...

In my view, the lending of the car to the defendant, albeit with the consent of the plaintiff, is really fatal to the plaintiff's claim that there was a continuing intention to make an immediate gift. ...[T]he principle of *Strong v Bird* ... is confined, in my view, to cases where nothing remains to be done but the mere formality of transfer, in order to perfect what was intended by the testator or testatrix to be an immediate gift, inter vivos, and surely there can be no room for its application in a case where there is an intention to give, but the gift is not completed because the intending donor desires first of all to apply the subject-matter of the contemplated or promised gift to some other purpose. ...

Accordingly, for the reasons I have endeavoured to express, as well as those stated by my Lord, I agree that this appeal should be allowed.

Lord Justice Morris also reached the conclusion that the appeal should be allowed on the basis that there was an intention to give in the future.

As has been seen above, the rule in *Strong v Bird* can apply to perfect a gift as well as to perfect the release of a debt. There seems no reason why it should not also apply to perfectly constitute a trust if the intended trustee acquires legal title as executor. The following case related to the constitution of a trust where the trustee acquired legal title indirectly. The rule in *Strong v Bird* was mentioned but the situation was not precisely the same, as the trustee obtained legal title as trustee of another family trust, rather than as executor.

***In re Ralli's Will Trusts, Calvocoressi v Rodocanachi and Another, In Re Ralli's Marriage Settlement* [1964] Ch 288**

Panel: Buckley J

Facts: A.P. Ralli left his residuary estate on trust for his wife for life, the remainder to his two daughters, Irene and Helen, in equal shares. Some years later, Helen executed a marriage settlement, settling her existing and after-acquired property on trust for herself for life with remainder (if, as happened, she died without issue) to Irene's children. Helen also covenanted that she would transfer existing and after-acquired property to the trustees of the marriage settlement. Helen never assigned to the trustees her remainder interest under her father's will trust and she died several years before her mother, i.e. before her remainder interest fell into possession. The plaintiff had at some point become a trustee of the father's (A.P. Ralli's) will trust and, as the sole surviving trustee both of that trust and of Helen's marriage settlement, he brought an action to ascertain whether he should hold Helen's remainder interest for Irene's children, under the marriage settlement.

It was held that he held it on the trust of the marriage settlement. As legal title had come (without impropriety) into his hands, the trust became completely constituted and the means by which he acquired title were irrelevant.

MR JUSTICE BUCKLEY

In this case I have to consider whether certain investments which are now standing in the plaintiff's name, representing one-half of the residuary estate of the late Ambrose Pandia Ralli (whom I will call "the testator"), form in the events which have happened part of the estate of the testator's daughter Helen ... or are held upon the trusts of Helen's marriage settlement.

In the argument before me the plaintiff has supported the view that in the events which have happened Helen's half of the testator's residue is held on the trusts of the settlement. The defendants have contended that, the covenant to settle the property in question being executory and unenforceable for the benefit of Irene's children as mere volunteers outside the marriage consideration, the share of residue belongs by operation of the trusts of the will to Helen's estate. ...

The plaintiff, on the other hand, contends that, as he already holds the fund, no question of his having to enforce the covenant arises. The fund, having come without impropriety into his hands, is now, he says, impressed in his hands with the trusts upon which he ought to hold it under the settlement; and because of the covenant it does not lie in the mouth of the defendants to say that he should hold the fund in trust for Helen's estate. ...

Sir Milner Holland, for the plaintiff, says that the capacity in which the trustee has become possessed of the fund is irrelevant. Thus in *Strong v Bird* an imperfect gift was held to be completed by the donee obtaining probate of the donor's will of which he was executor. ... Similarly in *In re James* a grant of administration to two administrators was held to perfect an imperfect gift by the intestate to one of them... .

Alert

In my judgment the circumstance that the plaintiff holds the fund because he was appointed a trustee of the will is irrelevant. He is at law the owner of the fund, and the means by which he became so have no effect upon the quality of his legal ownership. The question is: For whom, if anyone, does he hold the fund in equity? In other words, who can successfully assert an equity against him disentitling him to stand upon his legal right? It seems to me to be indisputable that Helen, if she were alive, could not do so, for she has solemnly covenanted under seal to assign the fund to the plaintiff, and the defendants can stand in no better position. It is, of course, true that the object of the covenant was not that the plaintiff should retain the property for his own benefit, but that he should hold it on the trusts of the settlement. It is also true that, if it were necessary to enforce performance of the covenant, equity would not assist the beneficiaries under the settlement, because they are mere volunteers; and that for the same reason the plaintiff, as trustee of the settlement, would not be bound to enforce the covenant and would not be constrained by the court to do so, and indeed, it seems, might be constrained by the court not to do so. As matters stand, however, there is no occasion to invoke the assistance of equity to enforce the performance of the covenant. It is for the defendants to invoke the assistance of equity to make good their claim to the fund. To do so successfully they must show that the plaintiff cannot conscientiously withhold it from them. When they seek to do this, he can point to the covenant which, in my judgment, relieves him from any fiduciary obligation he would otherwise owe to the defendants as Helen's representatives. ...

Had someone other than the plaintiff been the trustee of the will and held the fund, the result of this part of the case would, in my judgment, have been different; and it may seem strange that the rights of the parties should depend upon the appointment of the plaintiff as a trustee of the will in 1946, which for present purposes may have been a quite fortuitous event. The result, however, in my judgment, flows – and flows, I think, quite rationally – from the consideration that the rules of equity derive from the tenderness of a court of equity for the consciences of the parties. ... In the circumstances of the present case ... it is not unconscientious in the plaintiff to withhold from Helen's estate the fund which Helen covenanted that he should receive: on the contrary, it would have been unconscientious in Helen to seek to deprive the plaintiff of that fund, and her personal representatives can be in no better position. The inadequacy of the volunteers' equity against Helen and her estate consequently is irrelevant, for that equity does not come into play... .

For these reasons I am of opinion that in the events which have happened the plaintiff now holds the fund in question on the trusts of the marriage settlement, and I will so declare.

The effect of this judgment is that a trust can become constituted if the legal title to the intended trust property vests in the trustee by any legitimate means. In the case itself, it vested in the trustee in his capacity as trustee of a different family trust. However, the case has been subjected to some criticism. The judge referred to the rule in *Strong v Bird* by way of analogy but did not allude to the requirements regarding intention that apply to that rule.

A further exception by which gifts can be perfected is by way of *donatio mortis causa* (plural: *donationes mortis causa*). The next case is often cited as setting out the essential requirements for this.

***Cain v Moon* [1896] 2 QB 283**

Panel: Lord Russell of Killowen CJ and Wills J

Facts: The deceased deposited money at a bank and received a deposit note, which she handed to her mother (the defendant) in 1893. Five days before her death in 1895, she told her mother that, if she died, the deposit note was for her. The deceased's husband, as administrator, sued to recover the deposit note. The judge held that there was a valid *donatio mortis causa*. The plaintiff appealed. It was held that all the conditions for a valid *donatio mortis causa* had been complied with.

LORD RUSSELL OF KILLOWEN CJ

 Alert

...[F]or an effectual *donatio mortis causâ*, three things must combine: first, the gift or donation must have been made in contemplation, though not necessarily in expectation, of death; secondly, there must have been delivery to the donee of the subject-matter of the gift; and, thirdly, the gift must be made under such circumstances as shew that the thing is to revert to the donor in case he should recover. This last requirement is sometimes put somewhat differently, and it is said that the gift must be made under circumstances shewing that it is to take effect only if the death of the donor follows; it is not necessary to say which way of putting it is the better. ...

...Now, two of the three conditions of a good *donatio mortis causâ* existed here, for the gift was made in contemplation of death, and with the intention that it should revert to the donor in case of her recovery; but it is said that the third essential condition of such a gift was not satisfied, because there was no delivery. ... If, when the defendant visited her daughter in her last illness, she had had the note in her purse, and, when her daughter expressed her intention of benefiting her, she had handed the note to her, and the latter had handed it back accompanied with the language which she did in fact use, the case would be unarguable: because this form was not gone through, is the transaction to be deprived of the character of a *donatio mortis causâ* which it would otherwise have borne? I think not. I concede that there must be a delivery to the person to be benefited of the subject of the *donatio mortis causâ*; but, in my judgment, there s no reason why an antecedent delivery should not be effective. ... I think, therefore, that in the present case all the conditions legally necessary for an

 Alert

effective *donatio mortis causâ* were complied with, and this appeal must, consequently, be dismissed.

MR JUSTICE WILLS

I am of the same opinion. ...

In the next case, the Court of Appeal examined the issue of what needs to be 'delivered'.

***Birch v Treasury Solicitor* [1951] Ch 298**

Panel: Lord Evershed MR, Asquith and Jenkins LJJ

Facts: The deceased had a serious accident, was admitted to hospital and died just over a month later. Shortly before her death, she instructed one of the plaintiffs to go to her home and find a handbag containing her bank books, saying she wanted the two plaintiffs (husband and wife) to have the money at the banks if anything happened to her. The plaintiffs claimed the money in the banks by way of *donatio mortis causa*. The judge dismissed the claim and the plaintiffs appealed. It was held that there was a valid *donatio mortis causa* of the money in the accounts by delivery of the deposit books.

LORD EVERSHED MR

The judgment which I am about to read is that of the court...

Th[e] evidence establishes beyond question that certain prerequisites of a valid *donatio mortis causa* were fulfilled. The gift, if otherwise valid, was made in contemplation of death; and was to take effect conditionally on death occurring and in that event only. ...

The English Law in regard to *donationes mortis causa* ... is in many respects anomalous. It was indeed questioned at one time whether the old decisions supporting *donationes mortis causa* were consistent with the Wills Act, 1837, on the ground that they are in a sense testamentary in that full effect is not given to them until the donor's death. Being before that date incomplete, the gifts are then (unlike other gifts or trusts) rendered perfect and complete by the law. "A *donatio mortis causa*", said Buckley, J., in *In re Beaumont*, "is a singular form of gift. It may be said to be of an amphibious nature being a gift which is neither entirely *inter vivos* nor testamentary. It is an act *inter vivos* by which the donee is to have the absolute title to the subject of the gift not at once but if the donor dies. If the donor dies the title becomes absolute not under but as against his executor. ..."

Because of these peculiar characteristics the courts will examine any case of alleged *donatio mortis causa* and reject it if in truth what is alleged as a *donatio* is an attempt to make ... a will ... not complying with the forms required by the Wills Act. Such, as we read it, was the case of *Reddel v Dobree*, where the donor stipulated that the box delivered to the claimant should be returned to him, the donor, every three months, thereby preserving to the donor an effective dominion over the contents which he could change from time to time. For the same reasons it is of the essence of a valid donatio that there should be ... delivery in fact of the thing given to the donee. As Lord Hardwicke observed in the course of his judgment in *Ward v Turner*, mere symbolic delivery will not suffice. It might, therefore, be supposed that there could be a valid *donatio* only of such subject matters as were capable of actual manual delivery. But this is clearly not the law. Thus (as Lord Hardwicke himself noted) where the thing given is of a bulky nature, the handing to the donee of the key of the box or place where the thing is kept will be sufficient and is not to be regarded as merely symbolic. So Lord Hardwicke summed the matter up by stating that it is impossible to make a *donatio mortis causa* "without a transfer or something amounting to that".

Alert

Alert

The question then is, where actual transfer does not or cannot take place, what will "amount to that"? As a matter of principle the indicia of title, as distinct from mere evidence of title, the document or thing the possession or production of which entitles the possessor to the money or property purported to be given, should satisfy Lord Hardwicke's condition. On this ground, in our judgment, the validity of a donation of money standing to the donor's credit in a Post Office Savings Bank deposit, or a mortgage debt, should be sustained; and it appears to us irrelevant in such cases whether all the terms of the contract out of which a chose in action arises are stated in the document of title.

Alert

...As Buckley J., stated in *In re Beaumont*: "in order that the gift may be valid it must, I think, be shown that the donor handed over either property or the indicia of title to property which belonged to him. His own cheque is not property; it is only a revocable order, such that if the banker acts on it, the donee will have the money to which it relates".

...[I]n *In re Dillon*... Cotton, L.J. [said]: "The case of *Duffield v Elwes* shows that there may be a good *donatio mortis causa* of an instrument which does not pass by delivery, and that the executors of the donor are trustees for the donee for the purpose of giving effect to the gift. ..."

Alert

...[W]e think that the real test is whether the instrument "amounts to a transfer" as being the essential indicia or evidence of title, possession or production of which entitles the possessor to the money or property purported to be given.

We must not, however, be taken to be casting any doubt upon the correctness of the decision in *Delgoffe v Fader*, for, as the judge observed upon the evidence before him, the deposit book there in question "was in no way essential to be produced if the depositor had required to withdraw her money". ...

What, then, is the evidence in this case as to the necessity for production of the books upon any withdrawal - for this, in the view we take, is the essential matter? In each case upon the face of the deposit book such production was beyond doubt made a term or condition of the deposit. ...

...We think accordingly that the book[s were] and [are] the essential indicia of title and that delivery of the book[s] "amounted to transfer" of the chose[s] in action.

The result is that, in our judgment, the plaintiffs are entitled to succeed... .

In the case which follows, the doctrine of *donatio mortis causa* was, for the first time, applied to a gift of land. (In an older House of Lords case, there had been *dicta* to the effect that the doctrine did not apply to land.) The judgment in this case explains how the established requirements for a valid *donatio mortis causa* can be applied in the case of land.

***Sen v Headley* [1991] Ch 425**

Panel: Purchas, Nourse and Leggatt LJJ

Facts: Mr Hewett owned an unregistered freehold house. He and Mrs Sen had lived together for about 10 years from 1954 to 1964 and had remained close friends from then until Mr Hewett's death in December 1986. In November 1986, Mr Hewett was admitted to hospital suffering from terminal cancer and Mrs Sen visited him daily and looked after his house, to which she had always had a set of keys. At his request, she took him a bunch of keys from the sideboard drawer. Three days before he died, he told her 'The house is yours, Margaret. You have the keys. They are in your bag. The deeds are in the steel box'. After he died, Mrs Sen found in her bag the bunch of keys she had taken to him in hospital. One key was the only key to the locked steel box containing the house deeds and she found this box shortly after he died. Mrs Sen, as plaintiff, claimed that there had been a valid gift of the house. The judged dismissed her claim and the plaintiff appealed. Lord Justice Nourse gave the judgment of the Court of Appeal, holding that land is capable of passing by way of *donatio mortis causa* and that the three general requirements for such a gift had been met.

LORD JUSTICE NOURSE

Donationes mortis causa may be said to have been an anomaly in our law, both for their immunity to ... the Wills Act 1837 (7 Will. 4 & 1 Vict. c. 26) and as exceptions to the rule that there is no equity to perfect an imperfect gift. ...

There have been several judicial statements of what, in general terms, is necessary to constitute a *donatio mortis causa*: *Cain v Moon* [1896] 2 QB 283, 286 (Lord Russell of Killowen C.J.); *In re Craven's Estate* [1937] Ch 423, 426 (Farwell J.); and *Delgoffe v Fader* [1939] Ch 922, 927 (Luxmoore L.J.). Regard must also be had to what was said by this court in *Birch v Treasury Solicitor* [1951] Ch 298, the most authoritative of the modern decisions. If the question whether the subject matter is capable of passing by way of *donatio mortis causa* is put on one side, the three general requirements for such a gift may be stated very much as they are stated in Snell's Equity, 29th ed.(1990), pp. 380-383. First, the gift must be made in contemplation, although not necessarily in expectation, of impending death. Secondly, the gift must be made upon the

condition that it is to be absolute and perfected only on the donor's death, being revocable until that event occurs and ineffective if it does not. Thirdly, there must be a delivery of the subject matter of the gift, or the essential indicia of title thereto, which amounts to a parting with dominion and not mere physical possession over the subject matter of the gift.

...Mummery J. [at the trial] ... found no difficulty in holding that the first and second requirements were satisfied on the evidence and that part of his decision has not been questioned. He said [1990] Ch. 728, 736:

"The real difficulty in this case is caused by the third requirement which raises acutely the question whether it can ever be complied with in the case of real property when all that has occurred is an informal delivery of title deeds, or the means of access to the title deeds, accompanied by oral words of gift."

...The sufficiency of delivery in the case of a chose in action was considered at length in the judgment of this court ... in *Birch v Treasury Solicitor* [1951] Ch. 298, where it was held that there had been *donationes mortis causa* of the money standing in four accounts, by the delivery of a Post Office Savings Bank book and three other bank books of various descriptions. ...

...This court held ... that there had to be a transfer "or something amounting to that," that delivery must be made of "the essential indicia... of title, possession or production of which entitles the possessor to the money or property purported to be given;" see [1951] Ch 298, 308 and 311.

It cannot be doubted that title deeds are the essential indicia of title to unregistered land. Moreover, on the facts found by the judge, there was here a constructive delivery of the title deeds ... equivalent to an actual handing of them by Mr. Hewett to Mrs. Sen and it could not be suggested that Mr. Hewett did not part with dominion over the deeds. The two questions which remain to be decided are, first, whether Mr. Hewett parted with dominion over the house; secondly, if he did, whether land is capable of passing by way of a *donatio mortis causa*.

We have traced the need for there to be a parting with dominion over the subject matter of the gift, i.e. with the ability to control it, to the judgment of Lord Kenyon C.J. in *Hawkins v Blewitt* (1798) 2 Esp. 663, where he said:

"In the case of a *donatio mortis causa*, possession must be immediately given. That has been done here; a delivery has taken place; but it is also necessary that by parting with the possession, the deceased should also part with the dominion over it. That has not been done here."

A similar view was taken in *Reddel v Dobree* (1839) 10 Sim. 244 and *In re Johnson* (1905) 92 LT 357. In each of those three cases the alleged donor delivered a locked box to the alleged donee and either retained or took back the key to it; in *Reddel v Dobree* he also reserved and exercised a right to take back the box. In each of them it was held that the alleged donor had retained dominion over the box and that there had been no *donatio mortis causa*.

It appears therefore that the need for there to be a parting with dominion was first identified in cases where the subject matter of the gift was a locked box and its contents. In *Birch v Treasury Solicitor* [1951] Ch 298 as we have seen, a similar need was recognised where the subject matter of the gift was a chose in action. Without in any way questioning that need, we think it appropriate to observe that a parting with dominion over an intangible thing such as a chose in action is necessarily different from a parting with dominion over a tangible thing such as a locked box and its contents. We think that in the former case a parting with dominion over the essential indicia of title will *ex hypothesi* usually be enough. ...

...We therefore respectfully disagree with the judge's view ... that a delivery of title deeds can never amount to a parting with dominion over the land. As appears from *Birch v Treasury Solicitor* [1951] Ch 298, the question is one to be decided on the facts of the individual case.

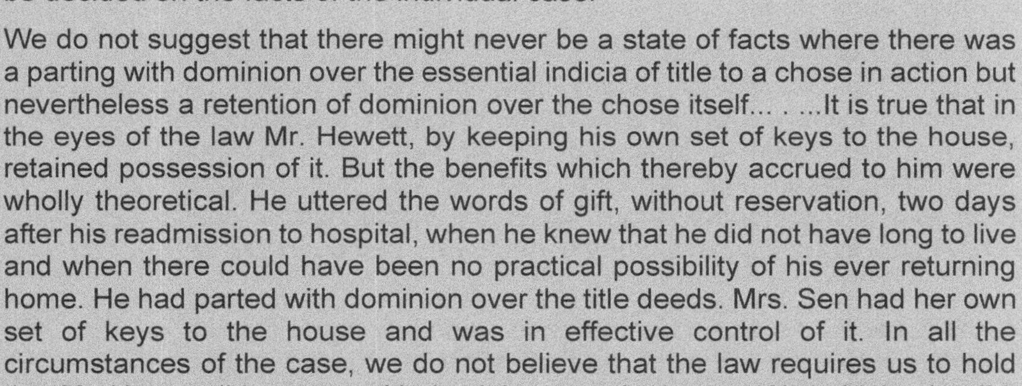

We do not suggest that there might never be a state of facts where there was a parting with dominion over the essential indicia of title to a chose in action but nevertheless a retention of dominion over the chose itself... . ...It is true that in the eyes of the law Mr. Hewett, by keeping his own set of keys to the house, retained possession of it. But the benefits which thereby accrued to him were wholly theoretical. He uttered the words of gift, without reservation, two days after his readmission to hospital, when he knew that he did not have long to live and when there could have been no practical possibility of his ever returning home. He had parted with dominion over the title deeds. Mrs. Sen had her own set of keys to the house and was in effective control of it. In all the circumstances of the case, we do not believe that the law requires us to hold that Mr. Hewett did not part with dominion over the house. We hold that he did.

Having now decided that the third of the general requirements for a *donatio mortis causa* was satisfied in this case, we come to the more general question whether land is capable of passing by way of such a gift. ...

His Lordship referred to the formalities for declaring trusts of land contained in s53(1)(b) the Law of Property Act 1925 and continued:

Section 53(2) is in these terms: "This section does not affect the creation or operation of resulting, implied or constructive trusts."

...In general it may be said that the constructive trust has been a ready means of developing our property law in modern times and that the process is a continuing one.

Let it be agreed that the doctrine is anomalous. Anomalies do not justify anomalous exceptions. ... [I]t is apparent that to make a distinction in the case of land would be to make just such an exception. A *donatio mortis causa* of land is neither more nor less anomalous than any other. Every such gift is a circumvention of the Wills Act 1837. Why should the additional statutory formalities for the creation and transmission of interests in land be regarded as some larger obstacle? The only step which has to be taken is to extend the application of the implied or constructive trust arising on the donor's death... .

...

We hold that land is capable of passing by way of a *donatio mortis causa* and that the three general requirements for such a gift were satisfied in this case. We therefore allow Mrs. Sen's appeal.

The court noted the very exceptional nature of the doctrine of *donatio mortis causa* in the following case, In their judgment, the Court of Appeal conducted a thorough review of the case law relating to the doctrine, highlighting the very strict parameters within which the doctrine may operate. In particular, the court emphasised that the doctrine should not be relied upon as a substitute for making a will.

King v The Chiltern Dog Rescue and Others **[2015] EWCA Civ 581**

Panel: Jackson, Patten and Sale LJJ

Facts: The claimant lived with and cared for his elderly aunt, June Margaret Fairbrother. In March 1998, June made a valid will in which she left the bulk of her estate to a number of animal welfare charities. After her death, the claimant contended that June had made a deathbed gift of her home to him approximately 4-6 months before she had died. She had also attempted to make a number of wills in the months before her death, indicating that she wanted to leave her home to the claimant. None of these wills had been validly executed.

At first instance, the judge held that, on the evidence, June had made a valid *donatio mortis causa* and ordered that her entire estate be passed to the claimant. The charities appealed.

The Court of Appeal overturned the first instance decision. It was held that June had no reason to anticipate dying imminently, thereby failing to satisfy first requirement for a valid deathbed gift. Furthermore, the fact that she had tried to make subsequent wills was inconsistent with the idea that she had already disposed of her property. These wills demonstrated that June did not intend to make a gift that was conditional on her death within a limited period of time (thus failing the second requirement for a valid death bed gift).

In his judgment, Jackson LJ helpfully set out and clarified the three requirements for a valid *donatio mortis causa*. He also stressed the limitations of the doctrine and the importance of a valid will, which cannot be easily overridden.

LORD JUSTICE JACKSON

Let me now stand back and summarise the legal principles which emerge from the case law. I have enumerated all the authorities which counsel have cited. I have also taken into account the numerous other authorities which are discussed in those judgments. It is clear that there are three requirements to constitute a valid DMC. They are:

i) D contemplates his impending death.

ii) D makes a gift which will only take effect if and when his contemplated death occurs. Until then D has the right to revoke the gift.

iii) D delivers dominion over the subject matter of the gift to R.

As many judges have observed, the doctrine of DMC in the context of English law is an anomaly. It enables D to transfer property upon his death without complying with any of the formalities of section 9 of the Wills Act or section 52 of the Law of Property Act. Thus the doctrine paves the way for all of the abuses which those statutes are intended to prevent.

...In my view therefore it is important to keep DMC within its proper bounds.

Let me now consider what those proper bounds are. The first requirement is that D should be contemplating his impending death. That means D should be contemplating death in the near future for a specific reason: see the dictum of Farwell J in *Craven. Beaumont, Wilkes v Allington, Craven's Estate, Birch* and *Sen* are all good illustrations of such contemplation. In *Beaumont* D was in hospital and seriously ill. In *Wilkes v Allington* D had an incurable disease and knew that he could not live long. In *Craven* D was about to undergo an operation which might (and in the event did) prove fatal. In *Birch* D was a frail elderly woman, who was in hospital after suffering a serious accident. In *Sen* D was in hospital suffering from pancreatic cancer. His condition was inoperable and he knew that he was dying. I do not say that DMC is only available when D is on his deathbed, even though that is the situation in which the doctrine might be said to serve a useful social purpose (provided that no-one is taking advantage of D's dire situation). Nevertheless it is clear on the authorities that D must have good reason to anticipate death in the near future from an identified cause. It is also clear on the authorities that the death which D is anticipating need not be inevitable. The illness or event which D faces can be one which D may survive. In *Craven*, for example, if the operation had been successful D would have recovered.

It is an essential feature of DMC, articulated in Justinian and later sources, that the gift lapses if D recovers or survives. Obviously D will die at some later date, but the DMC does not run on until that happens. It comes to an end if D fails to succumb to the death which was anticipated when he made the DMC.

I turn now to the second requirement. This is that D should make an unusual form of gift. It will only take effect if his contemplated death occurs. D reserves the right to revoke the gift at will. In any event the gift will lapse automatically if D does not die soon enough. Of course it is possible to make a conditional gift of that nature. Craven is a good example. The monies and shares would have reverted to D, if she had survived the operation. In cases where early death is inevitable the law relaxes the requirement that D should specifically require the property back if he survives. As Lord Tomlin said in *Wilkes* at 111:

"Of course, the line is rather fine, because when a man is smitten with a mortal disease, he may know, in fact, that there cannot be any recovery; yet I apprehend that a man in that situation in point of law, is capable of creating a good *donatio mortis causa*."

In my view, subject to that qualification, the Court should treat proper compliance with the second requirement as an essential element of DMC.

I turn now to the third requirement. This is that D should deliver "dominion" over the subject matter. Since property will not pass until a future date (if ever) and D has the right to recover the property whenever he chooses, it is not easy to understand what "dominion" actually means. I take comfort from the fact that even chancery lawyers find the concept difficult. Buckley J in *Beaumont* said that it was "amphibious". The deputy judge in *Vallee* said that the concept was "slippery". I agree. From a review of the cases I conclude that "dominion" means physical possession of (a) the subject matter or (b) some means of accessing the subject matter (such as the key to a box) or (c) documents evidencing entitlement to possession of the subject matter.

Let me now draw the threads together. The doctrine of DMC is only applicable if the three requirements set out above are met. Because the doctrine is open to abuse, courts should require strict proof of compliance with those requirements. The courts should not permit any further expansion of the doctrine.

He went on to explain why the requirements for a valid DMC were not met on the facts:

In my view, it cannot be said that June was contemplating her impending death (in the sense in which that phrase is used in the authorities) at the relevant time. She was not suffering from a fatal illness. Nor was she about to undergo a dangerous operation or to undertake a dangerous journey. If June was dissatisfied with her existing will and suddenly wished to leave everything to the claimant, the obvious thing for her to do was to go to her solicitors and make a new will. June was an intelligent retired police officer. There is not the slightest reason why she should not have taken that course.

If June had taken that course, the solicitors would have talked to her in the absence of the claimant. They would have ensured that June understood the new will which she was making and that she intended the consequences. One of those consequences was that the animal charities, which June had supported for many years, would inherit nothing on her death. If the DMC claim is upheld, the effect will be that June's will is largely superseded and the bulk of her estate will pass to the claimant, who is not even named as a beneficiary in the will. This would bypass all of the safeguards provided by the Wills Act and the Law of Property Act.

5

Secret Trusts

Introduction

Generally, anyone who wishes to create a trust to take effect on his or her death must make sure that the trust is sufficiently certain: a clear intention to create a trust must be expressed in the will, and there must be certainty of object and subject-matter. The testator must also comply with the rules on formalities and constitution. The formalities to be followed are set out in s9 Wills Act 1837: in writing, signed by the testator and witnessed correctly. Constitution of the trust happens on death, when the legal title to all of the property vests in the trustees by operation of law.

There are, however, some situations in which a person may wish to set up a trust upon death without revealing the details in his or her will. For example, historically, a testator may have wished to provide for his mistress and illegitimate children without anyone else knowing.

The courts have recognised the validity of certain trusts which do not comply with the formalities in s9 Wills Act. Some trusts are known as fully secret trusts, because their existence and terms are not obvious from reading the will: it appears that there is an absolute gift to the secret trustee. Other trusts are mentioned in the will but the terms of the trust are not fully disclosed. These are known as half secret trusts.

There are stringent rules which must be obeyed before these trusts are valid, and there are differences in the rules applicable to fully secret trusts and to half secret trusts.

5.1 Essential Characteristics of a Secret Trust

The following case highlights both the essential characteristics of secret trusts and the fact that secret trusts, like any other form of express trust, must satisfy the three certainties. In particular, clear intention to create a binding legal obligation on the trustee must be shown.

***Kasperbauer and another v Griffith and others* [2000] 1 WTLR 333**

Panel: Peter Gibson, Aldous LJJ and Harman J

Facts: In his will, Mr Griffith left a freehold property, Lower Hazel House, to his widow Rosemary. At a family meeting prior to his death, Mr Griffith explained that he wanted to benefit his two children, and that in order to avoid inheritance tax, he did not intend to write his wishes down. He said that Rosemary 'knew what she had to do' with the house. After his death, his son and daughter claimed that Rosemary held the house on secret trust for them. The Court of Appeal agreed with the judge at first instance that there was no intention to create a trust. Rosemary took the house absolutely.

LORD JUSTICE PETER GIBSON

First, he quoted the explanation of the doctrine of secret trusts by Nourse J in *In re Cleaver, decd*, [1981] 1 WLR 939.

"The principle of all these cases is that a court of equity will not permit a person to whom property is transferred by way of gift, but on the faith of an agreement or clear understanding that it is to be dealt with in a particular way for the benefit of a third person, to deal with that property inconsistently with that agreement or understanding. If he attempts to do so after having received the benefit of the gift equity will intervene by imposing a constructive trust on the property which is the subject matter of the agreement or understanding...

Alert

I would emphasise that the agreement or understanding must be such as to impose on the donee a legally binding obligation to deal with the property in the particular way and that the other two certainties, namely, those as to the subject matter of the trust and the persons intended to benefit under it are as essential to this species of trust as they are to any other."

He then set out the requirements for a valid fully secret trust:

... the authorities make plain that what is needed is (i) an intention by the testator to create a trust, satisfying the traditional requirement of three certainties (that is to say certain language in imperative form, certain subject-matter and certain objects or beneficiaries); (ii) the communication of the trust to the legatee, and (iii) acceptance of the trust by the legatee, which acceptance can take the form of silent acquiescence. The crucial question in the present case is whether there was that intention and, as Mr Justice Brightman said in *Ottaway v Norman* [1972] Ch 698, ... it is an essential element that the testator must intend to subject the legatee to an obligation in favour of the intended beneficiary. That will be evidenced by appropriately imperative, as distinct from precatory, language. Similarly in *In re Snowden*, decd [1979] Ch 528, ... Sir Robert Megarry V.-C., in considering whether a secret trust was imposed on a legatee by an arrangement, raised the question at page 534:

"In particular, did it impose a trust, or did it amount to a mere moral or family obligation?"

The judge emphasised that once the appropriate elements are found, a secret trust will be imposed by the court by way of constructive trust:

Whilst I of course accept that, once the essential elements of a secret trust are found to be present, equity acts to prevent fraud or other unconscionable conduct by imposing a constructive trust, I emphasise the need to fulfil those essential requirements.

Link
See also the Express / Constructive trusts section in this chapter

After surveying the evidence, including the solicitor's attendance notes, he concluded:

To my mind the phrase which the testator repeated, that the widow knew what she had to do, is equivocal and is at least consistent with the belief and intention on the part of the testator that his expressed intentions imposed only a moral obligation on her. Plainly there was evidence on which the judge could reach that conclusion. It is to my mind strongly supported by Dr Burrows' [the solicitor's] attendance notes and her oral evidence. True it is that Dr Burrows was never told of the meeting on 14 February. Nevertheless the words used by the testator, recorded in the attendance note of 9 March 1993, of an outright gift coupled with the testator's realisation that it was up to the widow whether to pass a share back to Rhodri and Sian after the testator's death and his feeling that she would do so, are plainly indicative of the fact that the testator regarded the obligation on the widow to be only a moral one. It is supported too by the language used by the testator to Mr Havens [a friend] that there had to be a certain amount of trust. There was ample evidence before the judge on which he could reach his conclusion that the testator did not intend to impose an enforceable obligation on the widow.

5.2 Fully Secret Trusts

As stated above, not only must there be an intention to create a trust but the trust must be communicated to the intended trustee and accepted by them. Unless this is done, the trustee's conscience is not affected by trusteeship and they take the property as an absolute gift. In the case of a fully secret trust, the existence of, terms of, and property subject to the trust must be communicated before death, generally to all trustees.

5.2.1 Communication

Wallgrave v Tebbs **(1855) 2 K&J 313**

Panel: Sir W Page Wood V-C

Facts: In his will, William Coles left £12,000 and some freehold property to Tebbs and Martin. Coles had thought about whether these gifts should be applied for charitable purposes, and he had had a letter drawn up setting out his ideas, but had never signed it. Tebbs and Martin knew nothing about this letter until after Coles' death, nor had they promised to carry out his wishes. Wallgrave, Coles' executor, wanted the money to be applied for the charitable purposes, but Tebbs and Martin claimed that they took it absolutely because no trust had been created. The court agreed: there was no trust as there had been no communication of its existence during the testator's lifetime.

SIR W PAGE-WOOD V-C

Where a person, knowing that a testator in making a disposition in his favour intends it to be applied for purposes other than his own benefit, either expressly promises, or by silence implies, that he will carry the testator's intention into effect, and the property is left to him upon the faith of that promise or undertaking, it is in effect a case of trust; and, in such a case, the Court will not allow the devisee to set up the Statute of Frauds, or rather the Statute of Wills, by which the Statute of Frauds is now, in this respect, superseded; and for this reason: the devisee by his conduct has induced the testator to leave him the property; and, as Lord Justice Turner says in *Russell v Jackson*, (10 Hare, 211) no one can doubt that, if the devisee had stated that he would not carry into effect the intentions of the testator, the disposition in his favour would not have been found in the will. But in this the Court does not violate the spirit of the statute: but for the same end, namely, prevention of fraud, it engrafts the trust on the devise, by admitting evidence which the statute would in terms exclude, in order to prevent a party from applying property to a purpose foreign to that for which he undertook to hold it.

But the question here is totally different. Here there has been no such promise or undertaking on the part of the devisees. Here the devisees knew nothing of the testator's intention until after his death. That the testator desired, and was most anxious, to have his intentions carried out is clear. But it is equally clear that he has suppressed everything illegal. He has abstained from creating, either by his will or otherwise, any trust upon which this Court can possibly fix. Upon the face of the will the parties take indisputably for their own benefit. Can I possibly hold that the gift is void? If I knew perfectly well that a testator in making me a bequest, absolute on the face of the will, intended it to be applied for the benefit of a natural child, of whom he was not known to be the father, provided that intention had not been communicated to me during the testator's life, the validity of the bequest as an absolute bequest to me could not be questioned.

He applied that reasoning to the facts before him:

In the present case there is no trust created. It is impossible for the Court to look upon a document which is excluded by the statute; and, such evidence being excluded, the case is reduced to one in which the testator has relied solely on the honour of the devisees, who, as far as this Court is concerned, are left perfectly at liberty to apply the property to their own purposes.

***In re Maddock* [1902] 2 Ch 220**

Panel: Collins MR; Stirling and Cozens-Hardy LJJ

Facts: Sarah Maddock made a will in which she left the residue of her estate to Susan Washington absolutely. A few days afterwards, Maddock executed a memorandum, which did not comply with the relevant formalities so as to be a valid codicil to the will. The memorandum instructed the trustees to hold part of the residue on trust. Maddock communicated the contents of the memorandum to Washington before her death and Washington accepted that she held the residue on trust. It was held that there was a binding trust, and that the property subject to the trust could not be used to pay the debts of the estate.

The Master of the Rolls applied *Wallgrave v Tebbs*.

COLLINS MR

The obligation ... has, it would seem, as between the legatee, who under such circumstances accepts the legacy, and the persons designated by the testator as beneficiaries, the character of a trust. But the right of the latter is wholly dependent on whether the legatee accepts the legacy with knowledge of the mandate, and no right for them arises at all unless and until the legatee has, with notice, accepted the legacy. A personal relation is then established between these two parties, without reference to others, and, as between them, would seem to have the incidents of a trust.

LORD JUSTICE STIRLING:

...as between Miss Washington and the beneficiaries under the memorandum, the savings have been separated in favour of those beneficiaries from the general mass of the testator's estate, and made subject to the disposition expressed in the memorandum. *Primâ facie*, therefore, it seems to me that, as between Miss Washington and those beneficiaries, ... that the savings ought (as between that property and the other property given to Miss Washington) to be held exempted from the charges which fall primarily on the personal estate not specifically bequeathed.

The memorandum itself when carefully examined seems to me to contain much which serves to indicate that this was the meaning of the testatrix. She states that she leaves the document "with her will": she desires the fund to be invested by her trustees. In my opinion, this indicates her meaning to be that the memorandum should (as between the beneficiaries thereunder and Miss Washington) be taken as forming part of her testamentary disposition, and that (as between the same parties) the memorandum should take effect as if it had been a duly executed codicil, and the like consequences as regards the administration of the estate must follow.

Lord Justice Cozens-Hardy agreed that there was a secret trust:

LORD JUSTICE COZENS-HARDY

It is clear that no unattested document can be admitted to probate or treated as part of the will. It is established that a devisee or legatee, who is entitled absolutely upon the terms of the will, is in no way affected by the existence of a document shewing that he was not intended to enjoy beneficially, if he had no knowledge of the document until after the death of the testator. Such a memorandum may or may not influence him as a man of honour, but no legal effect can be given to it. If, however, the devisee or legatee is informed of the testator's intention, either before the will in his favour is made or at any time afterwards before the testator's death, different considerations arise. It is sometimes said that under such circumstances a trust is created in favour of the beneficiaries under the memorandum.

[He makes some obiter comments on what would happen to the trust if the secret trustee were to predecease the testator, or disclaim:]

Now, the so-called trust does not affect the property except by reason of a personal obligation binding the individual devisee or legatee. If he renounces and disclaims, or dies in the lifetime of the testator, the persons claiming under

Link
See *Blackwell v Blackwell*

the memorandum can take nothing against the heir-at-law or next of kin or residuary devisee or legatee.

Thus, a secret trust may fail if the secret trustee predeceases the testator or disclaims the gift, in exactly the same way that an absolute gift will fail in the same circumstances. The opposite view was taken by Lord Buckmaster in *Blackwell v Blackwell,* which is set out later in this chapter. He suggested, obiter, that a trustee in a fully secret trust will not be permitted to renounce the gift and thereby defeat the trust. He did not, however, say what would happen in the event of the trustee predeceasing the testator.

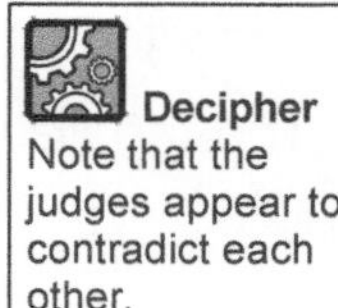

Decipher
Note that the judges appear to contradict each other.

It is unclear what happens in the case of a half secret trust, although the general equitable principle that a court will not permit a trust to fail for want of a trustee may operate.

***Re Boyes* (1884) 26 Ch D 531**

Panel: Kay J

Facts: Boyes wished to provide for Nell Brown (his lover), and their child. He instructed his solicitor, Carritt, to prepare a will in which he left his estate to Carritt absolutely. Carritt was to hold the estate subject to directions which Boyes would give him later. After Boyes' death, two letters were found, leaving £25 to Carritt and the rest to Nell. At no time did Carritt argue that this was an absolute gift to him: he always acknowledged that he held the property on trust. Boyes' legitimate next of kin argued that because Carritt did not know the terms of the trust during Boyes' lifetime, he held the estate on resulting trust for them. The court reluctantly agreed.

MR JUSTICE KAY

There is another well-known class of cases where no trust appears on the face of the will, but the testator has been induced to make the will, or, having made it, has been induced not to revoke it by a promise on the part of the devisee or legatee to deal with the property, or some part of it in a specified manner. In these cases the Court has compelled discovery and performance of the promise, treating it as a trust binding the conscience of the donee, on the ground that otherwise a fraud would be committed, because it is to be presumed that if it had not been for such promise the testator would not have made or would have revoked the gift. ...

But no case has ever yet decided that a testator can by imposing a trust upon his devisee or legatee, the objects of which he does not communicate to him, enable himself to evade the Statute of Wills by declaring those objects in an unattested paper found after his death.

The essence of all those decisions is that the devisee or legatee accepts a particular trust which thereupon becomes binding upon him, and which it would be a fraud in him not to carry into effect.

If the trust was not declared when the will was made, it is essential in order to make it binding, that it should be communicated to the devisee or legatee in the testator's lifetime and that he should accept that particular trust. It may possibly be that he would be bound if the trust had been put in writing and placed in his hands in a sealed envelope, and he had engaged that he would hold the property given to him by the will upon the trust so declared although he did not know the actual terms of the trust: *McCormick v Grogan* . ...

The legatee might be a trustee, but the trust declared by such an unattested paper would not be good. For this purpose there is no difference whether the devisee or legatee is declared to be a trustee on the face of the will, or by an engagement with the testator not appearing on the will. The devisee or legatee cannot by accepting an indefinite trust enable the testator to make an unattested codicil.

I cannot help regretting that the testator's intention of bounty should fail by reason of an informality of this kind, but in my opinion it would be a serious innovation upon the law relating to testamentary instruments if this were to be established as a trust in her favour.

Re Stead [1900] 1 Ch 237

Panel: Farwell J

Facts: Maria Stead made a will leaving the residue of her estate to Mrs Witham and Mrs Andrew as joint tenants absolutely. Mrs Witham alleged that Maria had, after executing her will, told her that she and Mrs Andrew would hold the residue subject to a trust in favour of Maria's nephew and charities. Maria left her will unchanged, on the basis that Mrs Witham had consented to carry out the trust, and in confidence that Mrs Andrew would also carry out her obligations under the trust. Mrs Andrew denied that she was bound by the secret trust as she did not know about it until after Maria's death. The judge surveyed the authorities and found the state of the law to be unsatisfactory and difficult to justify. The general rule is that only those to whom the trust is communicated are bound by the trust. The exception is that if the gift is to joint tenants, both are bound if the communication took place prior to the execution of the will. In this case, as the communication took place after the execution of the will to joint tenants, Mrs Andrew was not bound by the trust and took a half share absolutely.

MR JUSTICE FARWELL

If A. induces B. either to make, or to leave unrevoked, a will leaving property to A. and C. as tenants in common, by expressly promising, or tacitly consenting, that he and C. will carry out the testator's wishes, and C. knows nothing of the matter until after A.'s death, A. is bound, but C. is not bound: *Tee v Ferris* 2 K&J 357; the reason stated being, that to hold otherwise would enable one beneficiary to deprive the rest of their benefits by setting up a secret trust. If, however, the gift were to A. and C. as joint tenants, the authorities have established a distinction between those cases in which the will is made on the faith of an antecedent promise by A. and those in which the will is left unrevoked on the faith of a subsequent promise. In the former case, the trust binds both A. and C.: *Russell v Jackson* 10 Hare 204; *Jones v Badley* LR 3 Ch 362; the reason stated being that no person can claim an interest under a fraud committed by another; in the latter case A. and not C. is bound: *Burney v Macdonald* 15 Sim 6 and *Moss v Cooper* 1 J&H 352, the reason stated being that the gift is not tainted with any fraud in procuring the execution of the will. Personally I am unable to see any difference between a gift made on the faith of an antecedent promise and a gift left unrevoked on the faith of a subsequent promise to carry out the testator's wishes; but apparently a distinction has been made by the various judges who have had to consider the question. I am bound, therefore, to decide in accordance with these authorities, and accordingly I hold that the defendant Mrs. Andrew is not bound by any trust.

It is unclear whether the principle in *Re Stead* applies to secret trusts of land, and to half secret trusts of any type of property. Trustees must hold the legal title in a trust of land as joint tenants (s1(6) Law of Property Act 1925). Therefore, it appears that there is no scope for the application of the principle, as there is no possibility of the trustees holding land as tenants in common. Further, in *Re Stead* communication took place after the execution of the will. Where there is a half secret trust, communication must take place before the execution of the will so it is doubtful whether the principle can apply.

5.2.2 Acceptance

In addition to communication of the trust, the secret trustee must accept the trust; either expressly, or impliedly by conduct or silence.

***Moss v Cooper* (1861) 1 J&H 352**

Panel: Sir W Page Wood V-C

Facts: The testator wanted to give the residue of his estate to charity. He made a will giving it to Mr Gawthorn, Mr Sedman and Mr Owen absolutely, with a memorandum containing the testator's suggestions for dividing it in favour of various charities. The will and memorandum were communicated by Gawthorn to the others without any express acceptance or refusal of the trust. Sedman later said he would try to carry out the testator's wishes as far as he could; Owen did not say anything; Gawthorn predeceased the testator. It was argued that as Sedman and Owen had not accepted the trust and their consciences had therefore not been affected, they could take absolutely. The court disagreed. Sedman had specifically accepted; Owen's acceptance could be inferred from his silence.

SIR W PAGE WOOD V-C

...To fasten any trust upon an absolute bequest of property, it is necessary to prove knowledge on the part of the legatee of the intended trust, and

acquiescence, either by words of consent or by silence, when the intention is communicated to him. ...

Here it is said that the testator intended to give the legatees full and complete control over the property. On the face of the will he did; but the question is whether, behind that intention, he had not a further desire to secure as far as possible their obedience to his wishes. ...

If, immediately after making his will (for a bargain before the will is not at all essential), the testator had invited Gawthorn, Owen and Sedman to his house, and had said to them, "Here is my will, made in this form, because I am told that the property must be put entirely at your disposal; but I want a promise from you to dispose of it in a particular way:" and if they, by their silence, led him to believe they would so apply it, I apprehend it is quite clear that a trust would be created, and that it is altogether immaterial whether the promise is made before or after the execution of the will, that being a revocable instrument. The legatees, as soon as they learned the intention of the testator, would be bound to elect whether they would undertake the trust or not. If they are silent, the trust, if legal, must be executed, and if not, the gift will altogether fail.

Once the trust has been communicated and accepted, and the testator relies on that acceptance by making the will accordingly, or by changing it, or by not making a will at all, the secret trust is valid and the trustee is bound. Usually, the secret trustee is obliged to deal with the relevant property in accordance with the testator's wishes, during their lifetimes. However, the obligation may be for the trustee to make a will in a particular way.

***Ottaway v Norman* [1972] Ch 698**

Panel: Brightman J

Facts: Ottaway left his house and contents to Eva Hodges by his will. There was ample evidence of conversations during which Ottaway communicated his intention that she dispose of the property by will in favour of Ottaway's son and his wife. She agreed and made a will in appropriate terms, but some years afterwards made a new one leaving it to Norman. The son and wife sought a declaration that there had been an intention to create a trust, communication, acceptance and reliance, and therefore Eva was not at liberty to gift the property elsewhere in her will. The court held that there was a valid secret trust and Eva's conscience was bound. It did not matter that there was no deliberate fraud on Eva's part, nor was it relevant how Ottaway's intention was to be carried out: there was no distinction to be drawn between an obligation to transfer property *inter vivos* or by will.

MR JUSTICE BRIGHTMAN

The general principle can, for present purposes, be sufficiently explained by reference to two cases. In *In re Gardner* [1920] 2 Ch 523 a testatrix had given all her estate to her husband for his use and benefit during his life "knowing that he will carry out my wishes". Four days later she signed a memorandum

> expressing the wish that what she described as "the money I leave to my husband" should on his death be equally divided among certain named beneficiaries. She died in 1919 possessed of a personal estate only, and her husband died four days later. After his death his wife's will and the memorandum were found in his safe, and there was parol evidence that shortly after the execution of the will the testatrix had said in his presence that her property after his death was to be equally divided between the named beneficiaries, and that he assented thereto. ...
>
> Warrington L.J. said, at p. 530:
>
> "The question is really this: can the husband, who, as a result of the particular form in which the testamentary disposition of the wife is made, takes at law for his own benefit the corpus of her personal estate, properly refuse to carry into effect a wish as to the disposition of that property expressed to him by the wife before her death and assented to and accepted by him? The principle upon which the jurisdiction of the court is based is stated, in extremely clear language, by Lord Davey in *French v French* [1902] 1 IR 172: 'The basis of the jurisdiction' – that is the jurisdiction to which I have referred- 'is of course that the testator has died, leaving the property by his will in a particular manner on the faith and in reliance upon an express or implied promise by the legatee to fulfil his wishes, and your Lordships will at once see that it makes no difference whatever whether the will be made before the communication to the legatee or afterwards, because, as was said, I think, by Vice-Chancellor Turner in one of the cases which were cited, the presumption is that the testator would have revoked his will and made another disposition if he had not relied upon the promise, express or implied, made by the legatee to fulfil his wishes.

The second case referred to by Brightman J is *Blackwell v Blackwell* [1929] AC 318. He refers to a passage from the speech of Viscount Sumner, set out below.

He also quotes Lord Warrington of Clyffe, also set out below.

He then concludes:

> It will be convenient to call the person upon whom such a trust is imposed the "primary donee" and the beneficiary under that trust the "secondary donee." The essential elements which must be proved to exist are: (i) the intention of the testator to subject the primary donee to an obligation in favour of the secondary donee; (ii) communication of that intention to the primary donee; and (iii) the acceptance of that obligation by the primary donee either expressly or by acquiescence. It is immaterial whether these elements precede or succeed the will of the donor. I am informed that there is no recent reported case where the obligation imposed on the primary donee is an obligation to make a will in favour of the secondary donee as distinct from some form of inter vivos transfer. But it does not seem to me that there can really be any distinction which can validly be taken on behalf of the defendant in the present case. The basis of the doctrine of a secret trust is the obligation imposed on the conscience of the

Link
See the section in this chapter on Express / Constructive trusts

> primary donee and it does not seem to me that there is any materiality in the machinery by which the donor intends that that obligation shall be carried out.

5.3 Half Secret Trusts

Half secret trusts differ from fully secret trusts in that it is clear on the face of the will that a trust exists, but the terms of that trust are kept secret. The rules have developed in a piecemeal fashion, with the rules on timing of communication differing from those for fully secret trusts.

***Blackwell v Blackwell* [1929] AC 318**

Panel: Lord Hailsham LC, Viscount Sumner, Lord Buckmaster, Lord Carson and Lord Warrington of Clyffe

Facts: John Blackwell validly executed a codicil to his will, giving £12,000 to five people to apply the income and pay the capital 'for the purposes indicated by me to them'. He told the trustees, before the execution of the codicil, that the objects of the trust were a lady and her son, but the exact details were not put in writing until afterwards. Blackwell's widow and son, the residuary legatees, brought an action to test whether the trust was valid. The House of Lords recognised the concept of the half secret trust, and held that the trust was valid, justifying it on two grounds: first, that 'fraud' included failure to carry out the testator's wishes; and second, that the trust did not arise under the will, but outside or '*dehors*', and that therefore the provisions of the Wills Act were irrelevant.

LORD BUCKMASTER

His lordship made some *obiter* comments on whether a fully secret trustee can renounce the gift and defeat the trust:

> ... In the case where no trusts are mentioned the legatee might defeat the whole purpose by renouncing the legacy and the breach of trust would not in that case enure to his own benefit, but I entertain no doubt that the Court, having once admitted the evidence of the trust, would interfere to prevent its defeat.

He then gave judicial recognition to the half secret trust as a concept for the first time:

> ... a testator having been induced to make a gift on trust in his will in reliance on the clear promise by the trustee that such trust will be executed in favour of certain named persons, the trustee is not at liberty to suppress the evidence of the trust and thus destroy the whole object of its creation, in fraud of the beneficiaries.

He surveyed the authorities culminating in an examination of *In re Fleetwood* (15 Ch D 594):

I omit the detailed examination of other cases, for they are all carefully considered and dealt with by Hall V.-C. in the case of *In re Fleetwood*, an authority which indisputably covers the present case if it be accurately decided. In that case the testatrix left to a named person all her personalty, "to be applied as I have requested him to do." The request was made out and the named trustee jotted down in the presence of the testatrix the names of the persons and the amounts which the testatrix

desired to give and, after this, the codicil was executed. The point raised was the same as in the present case – namely, that when the trusteeship appears upon the instrument the trust must be for the next of kin or residuary legatees and that the Wills Act prevented effect being given to a trust to be effected by parol evidence. The learned Vice-Chancellor went through all the cases, including the case of *McCormick v Grogan*, and decided that the trusts should be executed. That decision has never been definitely disapproved in any decided case, for the statements in *Le Page v Gardom* 84 LJ Ch 749 and *In re Gardner* are mere dicta in cases where the point raised here was not material, and, in my opinion, it was in fact followed in *In re Huxtable* [1902] 2 Ch 793. In that case a testatrix bequeathed a sum of £4000 [to her trustee] "for the charitable purposes agreed upon between us". The testatrix had, in fact, verbally communicated to the legatee her intention to leave him the sum of £4000, the income of which he was to apply during his life for the relief of sick and necessitous persons being members of the Church of England and that he was to dispose of the principal as his own property. Farwell J. admitted the evidence, including that which conferred upon the trustee power of disposing of the principal after his death. The Court of Appeal held that the evidence was admissible as to the trusts of the £4000, which, upon the face of the will, was wholly given for charitable purposes but was not admissible for the purpose of providing for the £4000 after the death of the trustee, since the will had given the whole £4000, and such evidence would contradict the will. All the learned Lords Justice agreed that the affidavit of the trustee was admissible for the purpose of showing what were the charitable purposes but for no further purpose. There is nothing in the judgments that shows that this decision was affected by the fact that the gift was a charitable gift, nor on principle can I see that such distinction could be maintained, for, if a general charitable purpose only were disclosed by the will, a scheme might be prepared for carrying it into effect, and unless evidence were admitted the testatrix's specific instructions could have been disregarded; but they were not, they were distinctly carried out.

I agree with the Court of Appeal in thinking that this also is an authority in support of the doctrine laid down in *In re Fleetwood*. In these circumstances, even if the antecedent decisions had been less definite, it would require a very clear conviction that *In re Fleetwood* was wrongly decided to render it right and proper that it should now be overruled.

... In my opinion, however, *In re Fleetwood* was not wrongly decided. It was decided in accordance with the series of authorities by which the law was established and which it is now too late to question or to overrule.

Decipher
Note that Dankwerts J in *re Young* takes the opposite view.

VISCOUNT SUMNER

In itself the doctrine of equity, by which parol evidence is admissible to prove what is called "fraud" in connection with secret trusts, and effect is given to such trusts when established, would not seem to conflict with any of the Acts under which from time to time the Legislature has regulated the right of testamentary disposition. A Court of conscience finds a man in the position of an absolute legal owner of a sum of money, which has been bequeathed to him under a valid will, and it declares that, on proof of certain facts relating to the motives and actions of the testator, it will not allow the legal owner to exercise his legal right to do what he will with his own. This seems to be a perfectly normal exercise of general equitable jurisdiction. The facts commonly but not necessarily involve some immoral and selfish conduct on the part of the legal owner. The necessary elements, on which the question turns, are intention, communication, and acquiescence. The testator intends his absolute gift to be employed as he and not as the donee desires; he tells the proposed donee of this intention and, either by express promise or by the tacit promise, which is signified by acquiescence, the proposed donee encourages him to bequeath the money in the faith that his intentions will be carried out. The special circumstance, that the gift is by bequest only makes this rule a special case of the exercise of a general jurisdiction, but in its application to a bequest the doctrine must in principle rest on the assumption that the will has first operated according to its terms. It is because there is no one to whom the law can give relief in the premises, that relief, if any, must be sought in equity. So far, and in the bare case of a legacy absolute on the face of it, I do not see how the statute-law relating to the form of a valid will is concerned at all, and the expressions, in which the doctrine has been habitually described, seem to bear this out. For the prevention of fraud equity fastens on the conscience of the legatee a trust, a trust, that is, which otherwise would be inoperative; in other words it makes him do what the will in itself has nothing to do with; it lets him take what the will gives him and then makes him apply it, as the Court of conscience directs, and it does so in order to give effect to wishes of the testator, which would not otherwise be effectual.

Link
See *Ottaway v Norman*

To this two circumstances must be added to bring the present case to the test of the general doctrine, first, that the will states on its face that the legacy is given on trust but does not state what the trusts are, and further contains a residuary bequest, and, second, that the legatees are acting with perfect honesty, seek no advantage to themselves, and only desire, if the Court will permit them, to do what in other circumstances the Court would have fastened it on their conscience to perform.

Since the current of decisions down to *In re Fleetwood* and *In re Huxtable* has established that the principles of equity apply equally when these circumstances are present as in cases where they are not, the material question is whether and how the Wills Act affects this case. It seems to me that, apart from legislation, the application of the principle of equity, which was made in Fleetwood's and Huxtable's cases, was logical, and was justified by the same considerations as in the cases of fraud and absolute gifts. Why should equity forbid an honest trustee to give effect to his promise, made to a deceased testator, and compel him to pay another legatee, about whom it is quite certain that the testator did not mean to make him the object of this bounty? In both cases the testator's wishes are incompletely expressed in his will. Why should equity, over a mere matter of words, give effect to them in one case and frustrate them in the other? No doubt the words "in trust" prevent the legatee from taking beneficially, whether they have simply been declared in conversation or written in the will, but the fraud, when the trustee, so called in the will, is also the residuary legatee, is the same as when he is only declared a trustee by word of mouth accepted by him. I recoil from interfering with decisions of long standing, which reject this anomaly, unless constrained by statute.

LORD WARRINGTON OF CLYFFE

It has long been settled that if a gift be made to a person or persons in terms absolutely but in fact upon a trust communicated to the legatee and accepted by him, the legatee would be bound to give effect to the trust, on the principle that the gift may be presumed to have been made on the faith of his acceptance of the trust, and a refusal after the death of the testator to give effect to it would be a fraud on the part of the legatee. Of course in these cases the trust is proved by parol evidence, and such evidence is clearly admissible. It is also settled that in such cases it is immaterial whether the trust is communicated and accepted before or after the execution of the will, inasmuch as in the latter case the testator, if it had not been accepted, might have revoked the will.

Further in *Moss v Cooper* Wood V.-C. said: "If, on the faith of a promise by A., a gift is made in favour of A. and B., the promise is fastened on to the gift to both, for B. cannot profit by A.'s fraud".

I think the principle on which this doctrine is founded is that the parol evidence is not adduced for the purpose of altering or affecting the will itself, the legatee still takes under the will, but is under a personal obligation the breach of which would be a fraud on the testator: *Cullen v Attorney-General for Ireland* (1866) LR 1 HL 190.

The question is whether the same principle applies where, as in the present case, the fact that the gift is upon trust is mentioned in the will, though the terms of the trust can only be established by parol.

Eve J. and the Court of Appeal (the Master of the Rolls and Lawrence and Russell L.JJ.) have answered the question in the affirmative, basing their decisions on the judgment of Hall V.-C. in *In re Fleetwood*, the Court of Appeal also expressing the view that that judgment was followed by the Court of Appeal in *In re Huxtable*.

I confess to having felt considerable doubt during the argument whether to apply the principle in such a case as the present would not be to give validity to a parol will in spite of the provisions first of the Statute of Frauds and secondly of the Wills Act. Subsequent reflection however and a careful perusal of the judgment of Hall V.-C.

In re Fleetwood, wherein the earlier authorities under both statutes are cited and discussed, have satisfied me that that case and, in consequence, the present case in the Courts below were rightly decided. I think the solution is to be found by bearing in mind that what is enforced is not a trust imposed by the will, but one arising from the acceptance by the legatee of a trust, communicated to him by the testator, on the faith of which acceptance the will was made or left unrevoked, as the case might be. If the evidence had merely established who were the persons and what were the purposes indicated it would in my opinion have been inadmissible, as to admit it would be to allow the making of a will by parol. It is the fact of the acceptance of the personal obligation which is the essential feature, and the rest of the evidence is merely for the purpose of ascertaining the nature of that obligation.

***Re Colin Cooper* [1939] Ch 811**

Panel: Sir Wilfred Greene MR; Clauson and Goddard LJJ

Facts: Cooper made a will leaving £5000 to two trustees 'upon trusts which I have already communicated to them'. He had in fact communicated the trusts. He fell ill while on a game shoot in Africa and two days before his death made a new will, which included the following wording: 'The sum of £5000 bequeathed to my trustees in the will now cancelled is to be increased to £10,000, they knowing my wishes regarding this sum'. The trustees did not know about this increase until after Cooper's death. The court had to decide how much money was held subject to the trust. It said that the trust of £5000 was valid as it had been communicated during the testator's lifetime (and before the will was executed, which is an additional requirement for a half secret trust).

SIR WILFRED GREENE MR

In this case it is not possible to give effect to what the testator obviously desired, because he has not taken the steps which the law requires to enable that desire to become effective. He was minded to make a disposition by means of what is commonly called a secret trust, as he was not disposed to set out upon the face of his will or upon the face of some identifiable document described in his will the dispositions which he desired to make; accordingly he adopted the familiar device of bequeathing a legacy in favour of named persons which they were to hold as trustees, but the actual trusts upon which they were to hold it had been communicated by him to them and accepted by them in his lifetime. In order that a disposition which it is desired to make by that process can be effective it is necessary that the intention of the testator be communicated to the trustees, that the trustees accept the instructions of the testator, and that acting on the faith of that acceptance, he makes the gift or, if it is a gift which has been already made, leaves it unrevoked.

He applied *Blackwell v Blackwell* (above):

It seems to me that upon the facts of this case it is impossible to say that the acceptance by the trustees of the onus of trusteeship in relation to the first and earlier legacy is something which must be treated as having been repeated in reference to the second legacy or the increased legacy, whichever way one chooses to describe it. In order that a secret trust might be made effective with regard to that added sum in my opinion precisely the same factors were necessary as were required to validate the original trusts, namely, communication, acceptance or acquiescence, and the making of the will on the faith of such acceptance or acquiescence. None of these elements, as I have said, were present. It is not possible, in my opinion, to treat the figure of £5000 in relation to which the consent of the trustees was originally obtained as something of no essential importance. I cannot myself see that the arrangement between the testator and the trustees can be construed as though it had meant "£5000 or whatever sum I may hereafter choose to bequeath". That is not what was said and it was not with regard to any sum other than the £5000 that the consciences of the trustees (to use a technical phrase) were burdened.

***Re Keen* [1937] Ch 236**

Panel: Lord Wright MR; Romer and Greene LJJ

Facts: By clause 5 of his will, Keen gave £10,000 to his trustees to be held 'upon trust and disposed of by them ... as may be notified by me ... during my lifetime'. He did not execute the will until August 1932. Before that, in March 1932, he had handed over a sealed envelope containing instructions to be opened on his death, that the money was to be used to benefit a lady, G. The court had to decide whether there was a valid half-secret trust. The Court of Appeal found that although it was acceptable to communicate the terms of the trust in a sealed envelope, in this instance the communication had been before the will was executed and was therefore inconsistent with the wording of the will and the trust therefore failed.

Link

See the comments of Kay J in *re Boyes*.

LORD WRIGHT MR

The judge at first instance had said that the identity of the lady should have been disclosed to the trustees during Keen's lifetime. Lord Wright disagreed and said:

The summons came before Farwell J., who decided adversely to the claims of the lady on the short ground that she could not prove that she was a person notified to the trustees by the testator during his lifetime within the words of clause 5. His opinion seems to be that the clause required the name and identity of the lady to be expressly disclosed to the trustees during the testator's lifetime so that it was not sufficient to place these particulars in the physical

> possession of the trustees or one of them in the form of a memorandum which they were not to read till the testator's death.
>
> I am unable to accept this conclusion, which appears to me to put too narrow a construction on the word "notified" as used in clause 5 in all the circumstances of the case. To take a parallel, a ship which sails under sealed orders, is sailing under orders though the exact terms are not ascertained by the captain till later. I note that the case of a trust put into writing which is placed in the trustees' hands in a sealed envelope, was hypothetically treated by Kay J. as possibly constituting a communication in a case of this nature: *In re Boyes*. This, so far as it goes, seems to support my conclusion. The trustees had the means of knowledge available whenever it became necessary and proper to open the envelope.

Alert

Having decided that the communication by that means was in principle valid, his Lordship went on to consider whether it was admissible in this particular case. He decided that it was not, for two reasons: first, that the will referred to future communication, and the communication in question had already been made, so there was inconsistency. Second, it is not permissible in half secret trust arrangements, to refer to future communications. Communication of the terms of the trust must take place before or contemporaneously with the will.

He distinguished *Blackwell v Blackwell*:

> There was in that case a bequest to trustees to apply the income "for the purposes indicated by me and at any time to pay part of the corpus to such person or persons indicated by me as they think fit, the balance to fall into the residuary estate". The testator had by parol at or before the execution of the will indicated or defined the nature of the trust and the beneficiaries and the trustees had accepted the trust on those terms. It was held that parol evidence was admissible to explain the trusts and to prove that the trustees had accepted the legacy on the condition of fulfilling them. The trusts were accordingly, when thus established, proper to be enforced by the Court. There was, it was held, in such a case no conflict between the express terms of the will and the actual trusts intended...

He went on to consider the judgment of Lord Sumner in *Blackwell v Blackwell*:

> But he goes on to add qualifications which are essentially relevant for the determination of the present case. These are qualifications which flow from the circumstance that the will is not completely silent as to the trust, as is the case in wills of the type discussed in *McCormick v Grogan*, but does in express terms indicate that there is a trust. The qualifications are thus stated by Lord Sumner: "The limits, beyond which the rules as to unspecified trusts must not be carried, have often been discussed. A testator cannot reserve to himself a power of making future unwitnessed dispositions by merely naming a trustee and leaving the purposes of the trust to be supplied afterwards, nor can a legatee give testamentary validity to an unexecuted codicil by accepting an indefinite trust, never communicated to him in the testator's lifetime... *In re Boyes* ... To hold

Alert

otherwise would indeed be to enable the testator to 'give the go-by' to the requirements of the Wills Act, because he did not choose to comply with them."

As in my judgment, clause 5 should be considered as contemplating future dispositions and as reserving to the testator the power of making such dispositions without a duly attested codicil simply by notifying them during his lifetime, the principles laid down by Lord Sumner must be fatal to the appellant's claim.

There has been criticism of the difference in the rules on communication for secret and half secret trusts, but *Re Keen* has been followed in *Re Bateman's Will Trust* [1970] 1 WLR 1463.

***Re Bateman's Will Trusts* [1970] 1 WLR 1463**

Panel: Pennycuick V-C

Facts: By clause 7 of his will, Bateman left £24,000 to his trustees and directed them to pay the income to 'such persons and in such proportions as shall be stated by me in a sealed letter on my own handwriting addressed to my trustees'. The question was whether the trusts were valid. The court applied *re Keen* and held that there was no trust as it was clearly envisaged, by the wording of the will, that Bateman would give the trustees a letter in the future.

PENNYCUICK V-C

It will be remembered that the direction in that clause is to set aside a sum of £24,000 and pay the income "to such persons and in such proportions as shall be stated by me in a sealed letter ... to my trustees". Now those words are, on their plain meaning, future. There is no evidence as to whether a sealed letter had been written and addressed to the trustees by the testator at the date that he made his will. The only thing that does appear clear is that after his death some sealed letter, or at any rate some document, was in existence upon which the trustees acted. However, whatever the facts, the terms of the direction in clause 7 are plainly future. The direction is to pay the income "to such persons and in such proportions as shall be stated by me in a sealed letter." Those words clearly, I think, import that the testator may, in the future, after the date of the will, give a sealed letter to his trustees. It is impossible to confine the words to a sealed letter already so given. If that is the true construction of the wording it is not in dispute that the direction is invalid.

Wilde, D., 'Secret and semi-secret trusts: justifying distinctions between the two', 1995 Conv. 366

In this article, Wilde argues against those who criticise the differences in the rules on the validity of secret and half secret trusts. He says that the reason that both types of trust are enforced is prevention of fraud. The differences in the rules can, he argues, be justified on the basis that a solicitor is less likely to be involved in the creation of a fully secret trust, and therefore extensive protections should be given to those dispositions:

Link
See further the "Justification for Upholding Secret Trusts" section of this chapter, below

... a fully secret trust is typically liable to arise where a benefactor is, understandably, only dimly aware of the need for formality in desired arrangements, and where, accordingly, no recourse to legal advice is made. A fully secret trust can be set up without a solicitor ever being instructed to draw up any will; and even where a solicitor is instructed to draw up a will, it might easily be that the solicitor is kept completely ignorant of the secret trust to operate in conjunction with it, which trust might be put in place before or after the making of the will. This is not necessarily the case with a fully secret trust. It may be that a fully secret trust is used as a conveyancing device with the benefit of full legal advice. But, it is a common situation that the law must allow for in its regulation of fully secret trusts that, quite understandably, no legal advice is taken. However, a semi-secret trust always appears on the face of a will. It is difficult to imagine how one might obtain empirical proof, but it seems reasonable to assume that the overwhelming majority of wills are drawn up by solicitors; and, insofar as some people make wills without instructing a solicitor, that they are aware they are drawing up a formal legal document with a complex of law affecting its operation, and that they are consequently taking a risk in not consulting a solicitor. Accordingly, semi-secret trusts always arise in a situation where a solicitor is consulted and is made aware by the terms of the will that the trust is being set up; or, at least, in a very few cases, where the risk of not consulting a solicitor is deliberately taken.

Thus, the introduction of substantive legal rules whose observance was to be necessary to the validity of fully secret trusts would operate harshly on the benefactor operating in the dark with respect to their existence. There would not necessarily be any solicitor to advise the benefactor to observe them. Testamentary intentions would be liable to be defeated by such rules, when it is a major function of the secret trust doctrine to rescue a benefactor who has acted in understandable ignorance of rules. This would not be true where a fully secret trust was used as a conveyancing device on legal advice, but it would be unworkable to set up a separate set of legal rules for this situation, operating when some unspecifiable degree of legal advice had been obtained. So, minimal regulation of fully secret trusts generally is desirable. However, in the case of semi-secret trusts, there always is – or, at the very least, there is a realisation that there ought to be – a solicitor consulted, so that it is appropriate to lay down legal rules substantively limiting the recognition of semi-secret trusts, which the solicitor is in a position to advise the benefactor to observe, provided those rules serve some legally valuable purpose. ...

Where there is a failure to observe these special rules limiting the recognition of semi-secret trusts, the courts are able to say that the proximate cause of the failure of the trust is not the fraud of the trustee, but rather the disregard of legal rules in a context where legal advice was taken or where the taking of proper legal advice was known to be appropriate. Should a solicitor fail to advise observance, the redress of the intended beneficiary on the failure of the trust – admittedly not perfect redress, since it depends upon awareness of the right (but then so do many other legal remedies) – is an action in negligence for damages against the solicitor.

Turning, then, to an attempted justification, one by one, of the distinctions drawn by the courts between secret and semi-secret trusts.

Declaration prior to or contemporaneously with will

In the case of a fully secret trust, the courts require only that the trust be declared at any time before the death of the benefactor. In the case of a semi-secret trust, however, the courts require that the trust must be declared before or contemporaneously with the execution of the will by the terms of which the property is left upon the unspecified trust; and, moreover, the terms of the will must not contemplate the possibility of any later new declaration (even where the only actual declaration was a prior or contemporaneous one); otherwise the trust fails, and there is a resulting trust for the residuary beneficiary or successor upon intestacy. This is the most widely criticised of the distinctions drawn between secret and semi-secret trusts. Certainly it cannot be supported upon the ground stated by the courts. However, it is suggested that the rule does have a value. A solicitor is obliged to advise the settlor that the terms of the trust must be finalised at the date of the will, and that they cannot be varied thereafter without a new will. Unless, unusually, the settlor wishes to keep the terms of the trust secret even from the solicitor, there is then no risk of a declaration of trust being made which is not under the supervision of a solicitor, as could easily happen were the settlor instead left free to declare or vary the trust at will at any time later. The scrutiny of a solicitor should ensure that the trust is valid in all respects, not just in terms of the rules relating to semi-secret trusts, that it is sufficiently certain and so on; that a suitable record is made to evidence the terms of the trust; and that the trust is drawn up with the benefit of general advice as to the prudence of the provision made which a solicitor should be peculiarly competent to give, as to such matters as tax implications. In these respects, the rule is in the interests of the settlor: securing the general validity of the trust, facilitating its proof, and ensuring that it is the most desirable provision the settlor can make for the intended beneficiary generally.

This rule should not, therefore, be viewed simply as an arbitrary trap liable to frustrate the intentions of a benefactor. It should operate towards the fullest achievement of those intentions, provided a competent solicitor is instructed; and where a solicitor fails to observe this rule, the intended beneficiary can sue for compensation.

It is true that the rule inhibits the benefactor who is not so much interested in secrecy, but rather in flexibility, wishing to make frequent informal changes of mind. But there is much to be said for the view that while a desire for secrecy is a legitimate motive for setting up a semi-secret trust, a desire for such flexibility is not a motive the law should indulge.

5.4 The Justification for Upholding Secret Trusts: The Fraud and *Dehors* Will Theories

The justification for recognising the fully secret trust was the prevention of fraud on the part of the secret trustee. As the existence of the trust was not apparent on the face of the will, it was open to the secret trustee to use the Wills Act 1837 to say that, as the testator had not complied with the statutory provisions, the secret trustee took the property absolutely.

***McCormick v Grogan* (1869) LR 4 HL 82**

Panel: Lord Hatherley LC, Lord Westbury, Lord Colonsay and Lord Cairns

Facts: The testator made a will leaving his estate to Grogan. After he had made the will, the testator told Grogan this. Grogan was surprised, but the testator told him he would have it no other way. He told him where to find the will and that there was a letter with it. After the death, Grogan found the letter which contained the names of many people and stated 'I do not wish you to act strictly on the foregoing instructions, but leave it to your own good judgement to do as you think I would, if living…'. Grogan paid many of the gifts itemised in the letter, but not all of them. McCormick, who had not received anything although he was mentioned in the letter, sought a declaration that there was a secret trust in his favour.

The House of Lords said that a secret trust could be enforced where the alleged trustee is perpetuating a fraud on the testator and the intended beneficiary. The fraud arises when he refuses to carry out his obligations on the basis that the formalities in s9 the Wills Act had not been complied with and that therefore the trust had not been properly set up. However, the House of Lords in this case held that there was no secret trust: the testator had not intended to impose a trust on Grogan. Further, Grogan had genuinely believed that he had good reason to exclude McCormick and therefore there was no bad conscience on his part.

LORD HATHERLEY LC

Now this doctrine has been established, no doubt, a long time since upon a sound foundation with reference to the jurisdiction of Courts of Equity to interpose in all cases of fraud; and therefore if, for example, an heir said to a person who was competent to dispose of his property by will, "Do not dispose of it by will, I undertake to carry into effect all such wishes as you may communicate to me." And if the testator, acting on that representation, did not dispose of his property by will, and the heir has kept the property for himself, without carrying those instructions into effect, the Court of Equity has interposed on the ground of the fraud thus committed by the heir in inducing the testator to die intestate, upon the faith of the heir's representations that he would carry all such wishes as were confided to him into effect. …

So again, if a legatee states to the testator that upon the testator's confiding his property, apparently disposing of it, to him, the legatee, by a regular and formal

> instrument, he will carry into effect all such intentions as the testator shall confide to him, then that legatee, although he apparently may be held in law to take the whole interest, shall have fastened upon his conscience the trust of carrying into full effect those instructions which he received upon such representations as I have described. ... Such an undertaking or promise on the part of the legatee has been held, in some cases, to be capable of being inferred from the conduct of the person when secret instructions have been communicated to him by the testator, which conduct has been held by the Court to be equivalent to an undertaking or promise on his part that he will abide by the instructions so communicated to him.
>
> But this doctrine evidently requires to be carefully restricted within proper limits. It is in itself a doctrine which involves a wide departure from the policy which induced the Legislature to pass the Statute of Frauds, and it is only in clear cases of fraud that this doctrine has been applied—cases in which the Court has been persuaded that there has been a fraudulent inducement held out on the part of the apparent beneficiary in order to lead the testator to confide to him the duty which he so undertook to perform.

His Lordship then reviewed the evidence and found that there was no trust, and no fraud on the testator's intention:

> ...this gentleman did, to a certain extent, carry into effect the arrangements described in this letter of instructions. ... Finding himself thus placed in a position which was in no way of his own seeking, and finding this letter of his friend, he has, to the best of his judgment, carried those instructions into effect, with the desire, doubtless, of doing that which he would think it right and reasonable to do, though under no possible legal obligation to effectuate intentions which were not properly and legally conveyed to him.

Lord Westbury also emphasised the rationale for upholding secret trusts: The prevention of fraud on the intentions of the testator. Like Lord Hatherley LC, he found that there was no fraud in this particular case.

> **LORD WESTBURY**
>
> ...if an individual on his deathbed, or at any other time, is persuaded by his heir-at-law, or his next of kin, to abstain from making a will, or if the same individual, having made a will, communicates the disposition to the person on the face of the will benefited by that disposition, but, at the same time, says to that individual that he has a purpose to answer which he has not expressed in the will, but which he depends on the disponee to carry into effect, and the disponee assents to it, either expressly, or by any mode of action which the disponee knows must give to the testator the impression and belief that he fully assents to the request, then, undoubtedly, the heir-at-law in the one case, and the disponee in the other, will be converted into trustees, simply on the principle that an individual shall not be benefited by his own personal fraud.

This justification had been used before in *Wallgrave v Tebbs* (1855) 2 K&J 313. It was subsequently reiterated for fully secret trusts in *Blackwell v Blackwell* [1929] AC 318, although the remarks are *obiter*, as the case concerned a half secret trust (it is discussed fully later in this chapter in the section on half secret trusts). With half secret trusts, the existence of the trust was clear, so fraud was an insufficient reason to uphold them. The justification in these cases was that the trust arose outside or '*dehors*' the will, and did not therefore have to comply with s9 the Wills Act 1837.

Link
See *Blackwell v Blackwell*

Re Gardner (No. 2) **[1923] 2 Ch 230**

Panel: Romer J

Facts: The testatrix in her will gave property to her husband 'knowing he will carry out my wishes'. At that time, those words were sufficient to show an intention to create a trust. The testatrix then signed a memorandum, setting out what she wanted her husband to do, but she did not execute it formally, so it did not operate as a valid codicil. The question was whether there was a valid trust. If there was, one third of the property went to the estate of a beneficiary who had predeceased the testatrix. The judge held that a trust arose when there was communication and acceptance during the testatrix's lifetime: it therefore arose *dehors* or 'outside of' the will.

MR JUSTICE ROMER

I cannot see why a trust for the benefit of individuals engrafted upon property given to the donee by a will or by means of an intestacy should be treated as a gift made to those individuals by the will of the donor any more than it should be so treated where the property has been given to the donee by the donor in his lifetime. The principle has nothing to do with the fact that the gift has been made by one method rather than by another. Apart from authority I should without hesitation say that in the present case the husband held the corpus of the property upon trust for the two nieces and the nephew, notwithstanding the fact that the niece predeceased the testatrix. The rights of the parties appear to me to be exactly the same as though the husband, after the memorandum had been communicated to him by the testatrix in the year 1909, had executed a declaration of trust binding himself to hold any property that should come to him upon his wife's partial intestacy upon trust as specified in the memorandum.

Alert

This reasoning creates a difficulty in that the trust was not in fact completely constituted until the death of the testatrix as the legal title to the property did not vest in the trustee until the death had occurred. This however did not seem to worry the courts and the '*dehors* the will' theory was discussed again in *Blackwell v Blackwell* and in the following case.

Link
to *Blackwell v Blackwell,* passage marked C

Re Young [1951] Ch 344

Panel: Danckwerts J

Facts: The testator made a will containing a half secret trust. The testator's chauffeur was one of the beneficiaries under that trust. He was also one of the witnesses to the will. Under s15 the Wills Act 1837, a gift to a beneficiary who witnesses the will fails. The question here was whether the gift given by way of secret trust failed. The court upheld the trust on the basis that it arose outside of the will, so it was irrelevant that the chauffeur witnessed the will.

MR JUSTICE DANCKWERTS

The widow has testified that the testator's intention, as communicated to her, was that the man who had been employed by the testator for many years as chauffeur and general factotum should receive a legacy of £2,000. The chauffeur was one of the two attesting witnesses to the will, and if he takes the legacy under the terms of the will the result of s.15 of the Wills Act, 1837, is to make his legacy ineffective. The question is whether he takes the legacy under the will. Mr. Christie, on behalf of the next-of-kin, referred to In re Fleetwood (15 Ch D 594), a case of a secret trust, decided by Hall, V.-C., where it was held that, as a woman intended to be a beneficiary was one of the attesting witnesses to the fourth codicil, the trust for her failed as to her beneficial interest, as it would have done, Hall, V.-C., said, had it been declared in the codicil. It appears that the point was not argued in that particular case, which was concerned with a number of other points; and it seems to me that that particular decision is contrary to principle. The whole theory of the formation of a secret trust is that the Wills Act has nothing to do with the matter because the forms required by the Wills Act are entirely disregarded, since the persons do not take by virtue of the gift in the will, but by virtue of the secret trusts imposed upon the beneficiary, who does in fact take under the will.

Having explained why he thinks that the decision in *In re Fleetwood* was *per incuriam*, Danckwerts J continued:

It seems to me that according to ... *In re Gardner*, every consideration connected with this principle requires me to reach the conclusion that a beneficiary under a secret trust does not take under the will, and that he is not, therefore, affected by s.15 of the Wills Act, 1837. Accordingly, the legacy intended for Thomas Cobb, though given in an indirect manner, is effective and he has not forfeited it.

Upholding secret and half secret trusts has thus been justified by case law. There has however been much academic debate and the practice has been criticised as being outmoded.

Challinor, E., 'Debunking the myth of secret trusts?' 2005 LQR 492

On analysing the '*dehors* the will' theory she says:

> I submit that a closer analysis of this temptingly neat theory reveals it to be flawed. The theory claims that secret trusts are governed by the law of trusts and not that of probate, and yet these trusts involve a departure from the usual rules pertaining to trusts. For in upholding secret trusts, the courts are allowing trusts to bind after-acquired property, and under the normal rules of trusts it is impossible to declare an immediate trust of future property, or a trust which binds such property as and when it is received.

On the fraud theory, she comments:

> In fully-secret trusts, unless evidence of the trust is admitted contrary to the provisions of the Wills Act, the intended trustee will be able to take the property beneficially and will profit from his own misconduct, so this justification for the enforcement of these trusts on this basis does seem valid. Here equity would be acting in a way with which we are familiar in other areas of the law, such as in *Rochefouchauld v Boustead*.
>
> However, this original and narrow conception of the "fraud theory" does not explain the existence of half-secret trusts. In such a trust, the intended trustee takes the property as trustee on the face of the will, and there is no possibility of him taking beneficially even if the court declined to admit evidence of the terms of the trust. He would hold the property on resulting trust for residue or next of kin. Moreover, even in cases of fully-secret trusts, the case law exhibits examples of where any justification on the basis of a "*malus animus*" is no longer valid. The "fraud theory" has been extended in an attempt to encompass a justification of half-secret trusts and the modern case law. Hodge argues that it is not the personal fraud of the purported legatee, but a general fraud committed upon the testator and the beneficiaries by reason of the failure to observe the intentions of the former and of the destruction of the beneficial interests of the latter, which secret trusts seek to avoid.
>
> ...
>
> In *Blackwell v Blackwell*, Lord Buckmaster also adopted this wider version of the fraud argument (Lord Hailsham L.C. concurring), claiming that "the personal benefit of the legatee cannot be the sole determining factor in considering the admissibility of the evidence" that if a clear promise is made by the intended trustee, inducing a gift to be made in his will, "the trustee is not at liberty to suppress the evidence of the trust and thus destroy the whole object of its creation, in fraud on the beneficiaries." While *Blackwell v Blackwell* was a case concerning a half-secret trust, it is clear that this reasoning was intended to apply equally to fully-secret trusts.
>
> However, there does exist a huge flaw in extending the theory this far; it amounts to no more than a bald assertion that a testator's wishes should be respected even if he has put them into effect in a manner that is not acceptable

> (that is, not in compliance with s.9 of the Wills Act). In many cases the true intention of the testator cannot be put into place, and purported beneficiaries under ineffective wills are routinely deprived of property which testators or settlors would desire them to have, simply because trusts and wills have not been put into effect in the proper manner. The tradition equitable maxim that "equity will not permit a statute to be used as an instrument of fraud" must be adapted to something more like "equity will not allow a statute to be used so as to renege on a promise" if it is to fit with the situations envisaged in *Blackwell v Blackwell*. As Critchley has pointed out, this widening of the fraud theory focuses "on potential, rather than actual, wrongdoing ... the policy aim underlying (it) is thus proactive (or preventative) rather than reactive (or curative)". The very mild form of fraud which it envisages does not justify equitable intervention in the face of strict statutory provisions in the same way that a *malus animus* does.
>
> In order to recap, the two principal arguments which have been advanced in order to justify and explain the existence of secret trusts do not seem to give the all-embracing and logical explanations which they purport to provide. It seems that the doctrine developed organically, changing on a case to case basis in order to suit the particular situations which arose.

Link
See Critchley's article in Further Reading

Concluding that the doctrine is difficult to justify, she says:

> Here, the continued existence of secret trusts seems to be divorced from the initial contexts in which it first operated. Changes in society have rendered the need for secrecy largely obsolete. Gifts for charity no longer require it, and a desire to provide for objects which someone would not wish to reveal can be achieved more efficiently by other means. [*Challinor* suggests that a bank account could be opened in the beneficiary's name.]
>
> We must admit, with Moffatt, that: "today it is more likely that a secret trust will be used by the indecisive rather than secretive testator" such as was with the testatrix in *Snowden, Re*; allowing such testators to avoid the expensive and tiresome process required under the Wills Act. However, as Watkin has pointed out, this is obviously no valid justification for the departure from a clear legislative intent. The role of equity seems, in this area, to have been expanded too far. The present situation is much more like that described in the contention made in this question; the trusts are used as a covert device to avoid formalities. Secret trusts, then, are a relic of older days and their continued existence seems an anomaly. Even commentators who argue that there are no sound justifications for the existence of secret trusts, tend to argue that the doctrine is "too well established to be disturbed" or they reassure us that "we should not be too alarmed" for, "the probability is that few testators wish to rely on them and hence they do not constitute a serious threat to the practice of formal will making".

Link
See article by Meager which is extracted at the end of the chapter

Conclusion

I would disagree, arguing that these reasons are not sufficient to demand the continued existence of secret trusts. There is much to be said for an abolition, or at least a fundamental revision, of the law relating to them, as the law is confused, and justifications for the distinctions between the two types of secret trusts are difficult to find. They serve a very limited social purpose and fraud would be better prevented by an insistence upon compliance with the requirements of the Wills Act.

5.5 Secret Trusts: Express or Constructive?

There is no clear answer as to whether secret trusts are express or constructive. If express, there are difficulties for secret trusts of land as, to be valid, express trusts of land must be evidenced in signed writing (Law of Property Act 1925 s53(1)(b)). It would, however, seem logical for half secret trusts, which are evident on the face of the will, to be treated as express trusts. This seems to be the interpretation in *Re Baillie* (1886) 2 TLR 660 where a half secret trust of land was unenforceable without written evidence. It must be noted, however, that this case was decided before the concept of a half secret trust had been fully recognised.

If the justification for upholding fully secret trusts is prevention of fraud, it follows that the trust is constructive, as it is imposed by the court. Constructive trusts do not need to comply with any formalities to be valid (Law of Property Act 1925 s53(2)). There is judicial support for this interpretation in *Ottaway v Norman* and *Kasperbauer v Griffith*. *Ottaway v Norman*, upheld a fully secret trust of land even though it was not evidenced in signed writing. Section 53(1)(b) was, however, not considered by the court.

5.6 Secret Trusts in the Modern World

Despite the seminal cases on this topic being decided in a very different social era, when skeletons were kept very firmly in cupboards, the secret trust does have relevance in today's world.

***Gold v Hill* [1999] 1 FLR 54**

Panel: Carnwath J

Facts: Mr Gilbert had left his wife and was living with another woman, Carol, and her two children. In his will, he left everything to his wife, but he took out life insurance intending to benefit Carol and the children in the event of his death. He nominated Mr Gold, his solicitor, as beneficiary to receive the policy proceeds. He later had informal conversations with Mr Gold in which he told him of the insurance arrangement and urged Mr Gold to 'look after Carol and the kids'. At no time did Mr Gold seek to take the proceeds for himself: he sought a declaration that he did in fact hold the proceeds on trust for Carol.

MR JUSTICE CARNWATH

The judge dismissed arguments to the effect that Mr Gold held on resulting trust for the wife as beneficiary under the will. Those arguments he set out as follows:

> ...there is no reason to doubt that Mr Gilbert intended to nominate Mr Gold. The question is in what capacity, and for what purposes, he intended Mr Gold to receive the money, and whether what he did is effective to achieve that intention. He submits that the natural interpretation of the document is that Mr Gilbert intended Mr Gold to take in his capacity as executor of a will that he intended to make, but never did. There are two possible consequences: either the nomination fails because the condition to which it was subject was never fulfilled; or it is effective, but Mr Gold holds the proceeds on resulting trust for the deceased. In either event the funds would become part of his estate to be dealt with in accordance with his will.

The judge dismissed these arguments and agreed with the arguments presented on behalf of Mr Gold, that he held the funds for Carol by way of an arrangement analogous to a secret trust:

> The nomination, like a testamentary disposition, does not transfer or create any interest until death. It is consistent with the principle of *Blackwell v Blackwell* that the nominee should take under the rules of the policy, but then be required to 'apply it as the court of conscience directs' and so 'to give effect to the wishes of the testator'. Such doubts as there may be, in the case of testamentary dispositions, as to the effectiveness of an intention communicated after the execution of the will, appear to be derived from the particular rules applying to wills. There is no reason why they should create similar difficulties in the case of nominations. Since the nomination has no effect until the time of death, it should be sufficient that the nature of the trust is sufficiently communicated prior to that time.

Link
See the article by Challinor where it is argued that these trusts are outmoded.

Meager, R., 'Secret trusts – do they have a future?', 2003 Conveyancer and Property Lawyer, 203

This article analyses the findings of a survey of practitioners to ascertain attitudes to and the levels of use of fully-secret and half-secret trusts in November 2001.

> Respondents were first required to indicate whether their clients had ever asked them about making a secret testamentary bequest and 35 per cent of the respondents stated that they had. This is a substantial proportion and the finding indicates that there is a genuine requirement amongst testators to be able to effect a bequest secretly, although it is not singularly demonstrative that secret trusts are required as there are of course other means by which to make a discreet bequest, depending upon the level of secrecy required.
>
> Respondents were then asked whether they had been involved in the creation of fully secret or half-secret trusts and 16 per cent had been involved in the

> creation of the former and 20 per cent in the latter. The respondents were not required to state on how many occasions they had been involved in the creation of secret trusts but some clearly indicated that it had been on multiple occasions….
>
> The information derived from the next question is more indicative of the respondents' own perceptions of secret trusts as they were asked whether they had ever advised a client that a secret trust would be a suitable "instrument" to fulfil their clients' requirements. Thirteen per cent of the respondents had advised clients that a fully secret trust would be appropriate and 23 per cent that a half-secret trust would be. Interestingly, fewer practitioners had advocated the use of a fully secret trust than had assisted in the creation of one, but more had advised clients about the appropriateness of half-secret trusts than had created one.
>
> Whilst the responses to this question offer some insight into the legal practitioners' perception of the appropriateness of secret trusts for the purpose of facilitating secret bequests, it is not conclusive. One respondent wrote that "he has never used or come across such a trust but would be prepared to use one if the right circumstances arose". This response automatically raises the possibility, or some might even argue probability, that whilst some respondents stated that they had neither advised clients as to the suitability of secret trusts nor assisted in the creation of one, this is not necessarily indicative that those responding in the negative would not be prepared to advocate their use. Furthermore, it may be suggestive that secret trusts are used more rarely in every day practice not because they are deemed unreliable or potentially problematic, but because too little is understood about their construction and possible use, reflecting a lack of education of the practitioners themselves.
>
> The questionnaire then asked for information about whether respondents, advising clients about means by which to effect secret bequests, had suggested devices other than secret trusts, and 27 per cent had. This response further supports earlier findings in which it had been concluded that there is clearly a genuine requirement among testators to make secret bequests. …
>
> The final question in the purely quantitative section of the survey asked, in response to the preceding question, which option their clients chose. Twenty-nine per cent chose a secret trust, 52 per cent chose another device and 19 per cent chose none of the options.10 This finding reinforces previously drawn conclusions that there is a genuine requirement among testators to make secret bequests and that both varieties of secret trust, as well as other means, are being used to achieve this end.

The article then discusses the perceptions of secret trusts within the targeted section of the legal profession. Meager concludes:

> There is clearly a demand for an instrument which enables testators to make bequests secretly. A substantial proportion of the survey sample of legal

practitioners were also of the opinion that there are many circumstances in which the use of a secret trust may be appropriate.

Secret trusts appear to be viewed with cynicism because of the insurmountable problems which can potentially arise should the trustee choose to fraudulently deny the existence of the trust. What has perhaps been largely overlooked is the power that legal practitioners have to ensure that this situation does not arise. There appears to be very little reason why they should not advise their clients to construct a document attesting to the existence and the terms of the trust and lodging it with the solicitor who holds the will.

Whilst this would inevitably result in there being a limited amount of publicity, it would be less public than any ensuing litigation to establish the existence of the trust. ...

On reflection, the secret trust is perhaps potentially more useful than it has ever been given credit for, particularly given the diverse variety of circumstances in which respondents considered their use may be appropriate. With a limited amount of administration, which would pose no real threat to the secret nature of the trust, it could be constructed in such a way as to make it no less secure and dependable than any other form of trust instrument. By constructing fully secret trusts in such a way as to make it impossible for a secret trustee to avoid the duty which he has accepted, it would perhaps be no longer necessary for half-secret trusts to exist.

The greatest hurdle to overcome, it would seem, is to assure legal practitioners of the potential reliability of such a device, carefully constructed. Perhaps it would be appropriate to review the education of potential legal practitioners to advise them on ways of avoiding the problems most commonly associated with the use of secret trusts, thus equipping them to better cater for their clients' requirements. ...

6

Private Purpose Trusts and Unincorporated Associations

Introduction

Ordinarily, a trust must be for the benefit of a legal person (i.e. an individual or a company), not for a purpose. This is known as 'the beneficiary principle'. A trust for a purpose will be invalid unless:

(a) The purpose is charitable (charitable trusts are covered in Chapter 7);

or

(b)

(i) The purpose falls within one of anomalous *Re Endacott* exceptions; or

(ii) The purpose falls within the *Re Denley* principle.

Trusts which fall within (b) are known as private purpose trusts. For a private purpose trust to be valid it must also:

- Comply with the perpetuity period; and
- Be sufficiently certain and not be purely capricious.

In some instances, even though it may appear that a trust for a purpose has been created, it may be possible to interpret the expression of purpose as a mere indication of motive for what is in fact an absolute gift, to which the rules regarding private purposes trusts do not therefore apply.

Link
See the discussion of motive cases below.

6.1 The Beneficiary Principle

The beneficiary principle derives from the first-instance decision in *Morice v Bishop of Durham* (1804) 9 Ves JR 399, where Sir William Grant MR held that the trust was void because it was a non-charitable purpose trust.

***Morice v Bishop of Durham* (1804) 9 Ves JR 399**

Panel: Sir William Grant MR

Facts: By her will the testatrix left her entire personal estate to the Bishop of Durham on trust to pay her debts and certain legacies and then to use what remained for '... such objects of benevolence and liberality as [he] in his own discretion should most approve of ...'

SIR WILLIAM GRANT MR

The only question is whether the trust upon which the residue of the personal estate is bequeathed be a trust for charitable purposes. That the residue is left on some trust and not for the personal benefit of the bishop is clear from the words of the will, and is admitted by his lordship who expressly disclaims any beneficial interest. That it is a trust, unless it be of a charitable nature, too indefinite to be executed by this court, has not been, and cannot be, denied. There can be no trust over the exercise of which this court will not assume a control, for an uncontrollable power of disposition would be ownership and not trust. If there be a clear trust, but for uncertain objects, the property that is the subject of the trust is undisposed of, and the benefit of such trust must result to those to whom the law gives the ownership in default of disposition by the former owner. But this doctrine does not hold good with regard to trusts for charity. Every other trust must have a definite object. There must be somebody in whose favour the court can decree performance. But it is now settled upon authority which it is too late to controvert that, where a charitable purpose is expressed, however general, the bequest shall not fail on account of the uncertainty of the object. The particular mode of application will be directed by the King in some cases, in others by this court.

Is this a trust for charity? Do purposes of liberality and benevolence mean the same as objects of charity? That word in its widest sense denotes all the good affections men ought to bear towards each other; in its most restricted and common sense relief of the poor. In neither of these senses is it employed in this court. Here its signification is derived chiefly from the statute 43 Eliz, c 4 [relating to charitable gifts]. Those purposes are considered charitable which that statute enumerates or which by analogies are deemed within its spirit and intendment, and to some such purpose every bequest to charity generally shall be applied. But, it is clear, liberality and benevolence can find numberless objects not included in that statute in the largest construction of it. The use of the word "charitable" seems to have been purposely avoided in this will in order to leave the bishop the most unrestrained discretion. Supposing the uncertainty of the trust no objection to its validity, could it be contended to be an abuse of the trust to employ this fund upon objects which all mankind would allow to be objects of liberality and benevolence though not to be said, in the language of this court, to be objects also of charity? By what rule of construction could it be said that all objects of liberality and benevolence are excluded which do not fall within the statute of Elizabeth? The question is not whether he may not apply it upon purposes strictly charitable, but whether he is bound so to apply it? I am not aware of any case in which the bequest has been held charitable where the testator has not either used that word to denote his general purpose or specified some particular purpose, which this court has determined to be charitable in its nature. All the cases upon that subject are to be found in the report of *Moggridge v Thackwell* (1807) 13 Ves 416. *Browne v Yeall* 7 Ves 47 I should have thought a much more doubtful case. There was ground for contending that the particular purpose specified was charitable in itself, according the decisions of this court, and it was described by the testator as a charitable design. But here there is no specific purpose pointed out to which the residue is to be applied. The words "charity" and "charitable" do not occur: the words used are not synonymous: the trusts may be completely executed without bestowing any part of this residue upon purposes strictly charitable. The residue, therefore, cannot be said to be given to charitable purposes, and, as the trust is too indefinite to be disposed of to any other purpose, it follows that the residue remains undisposed of and must be distributed among the next of kin of the testatrix.

Once it had been decided that the trust created by the bequest was not charitable, it could only be valid if it had a 'definite object', ie 'somebody in whose favour the court can decree specific performance'. As no such person could be identified, the gift failed.

A further illustration of the beneficiary principle is to be found in the case of *Re Astor's Settlement Trusts* [1952] Ch 534, in which Astor J held that various purpose trusts were void as not being for the benefit of individuals.

***Re Astor's Settlement Trusts, Astor v Schofield & Ors* [1952] Ch 534**

Panel: Roxburgh J

Facts: The settlor established a discretionary trust under which the trust income was to be used for a variety of purposes, including the 'establishment maintenance and improvement of good understanding sympathy and co-operation between nations, especially the nations of the English speaking world and also between different sections of people in any nation or community', ... 'preservation of the independence and integrity of newspapers ...[and]... the Press', ... 'the protection of newspapers ... from being absorbed or controlled by combines' ... [and] ... 'the restoration ... of the independence of ... writers in newspapers.'

MR JUSTICE ROXBURGH

The question upon which I [have to decide] is whether the non-charitable trusts of income ... are void ... on two grounds: (1) that they are not trusts for the benefit of individuals; (2) that they are void for uncertainty.

Lord Parker considered the first of these two questions in his speech in *Bowman v Secular Society Ltd* [1917] AC 406 and I will cite two important passages. The first is: "The question whether a trust be legal or illegal or be in accordance with or contrary to the policy of the law, only arises when it has been determined that a trust has been created, and is then only part of the larger question whether the trust is enforceable. For, as will presently appear, trusts may be unenforceable and therefore void, not only because they are illegal or contrary to the policy of the law, but for other reasons." The second is: "A trust to be valid must be for the benefit of individuals, which this is certainly not, or must be in that class of gifts for the benefit of the public which the courts in this country recognize as charitable in the legal as opposed to the popular sense of that term." ...

The typical case of a trust is one in which the legal owner of property is constrained by a court of equity so to deal with it as to give effect to the equitable rights of another. These equitable rights have been hammered out in the process of litigation in which a claimant on equitable grounds has successfully asserted rights against a legal owner or other person in control of property. Prima facie, therefore, a trustee would not be expected to be subject to an equitable obligation unless there was somebody who could enforce a correlative equitable right, and the nature and extent of that obligation would be worked out in proceedings for enforcement. At an early stage, however, the courts were confronted with attempts to create trusts for charitable purposes which there was no equitable owner to enforce. Lord Eldon explained in *Attorney-General v Brown* (1818) 1 Swans 265, 290 how this difficulty was dealt with: "It is the duty of a court of equity, a main part, originally almost the whole, of its jurisdiction, to administer trusts; to protect not the visible owner, who alone can proceed at law, but the individual equitably, though not legally, entitled. From this principle has arisen the practice of administering the trust of a public charity: persons possessed of funds appropriated to such purposes are within the general rule; but no one being entitled by an immediate and peculiar interest to prefer a complaint, who is to compel the performance of their obligations, and to enforce their responsibility? It is the duty of the King, as *parens patriae*, to protect property devoted to charitable uses; and that duty is executed by the officer who represents the Crown for all forensic purposes. On this foundation rests the right of the Attorney-General in such cases to obtain by information the interposition of a court of equity. ..." But if the purposes are not charitable, great difficulties arise both in theory and in practice. In theory, because having regard to the historical origins of equity it is difficult to visualize the growth of equitable obligations which nobody can enforce, and in practice, because it is not possible to contemplate with equanimity the creation of large funds devoted to non-charitable purposes which no court and no department of state can control, or in the case of maladministration reform. Therefore, Lord Parker's second proposition would prima facie appear to be well founded. Moreover, it gains no little support from the practical considerations that no officer has ever been constituted to take, in the case of non-charitable purposes, the position held by the Attorney-General in connexion with charitable purposes, and no case has been found in the reports in which the court has ever directly enforced a non-charitable purpose against a trustee. Indeed where, as in the present case, the only beneficiaries are purposes and an at present unascertainable person, it is difficult to see who could initiate such proceedings. If the purposes are valid trusts, the settlors have retained no beneficial interest and could not initiate them. It was suggested that the trustees might proceed ex parte to enforce the trusts against themselves. I doubt that, but at any rate nobody could enforce the trusts against them. ... Lord Parker's two propositions ... [are not new] but merely re-echoed what Sir William Grant had said as Master of the Rolls in *Morice v The Bishop of Durham* as long ago as 1804: "There must be somebody, in whose favour the court can decree performance." The position was recently restated by Harman J in *In re Wood* [1949] Ch 498, 501: "A gift on trust must have a *cestui que* trust," and this seems to be in accord with principle. ... [There is nothing to] justify the conclusion that a Court of Equity will recognize as an equitable obligation affecting the income of large funds in the hands of trustees a direction to apply it in furtherance of enumerated non-charitable purposes in a manner which no court or department can control or enforce.

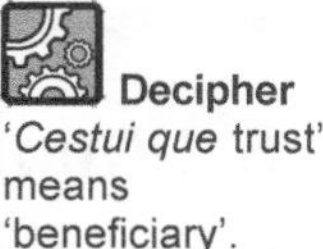

Decipher
'*Cestui que* trust' means 'beneficiary'.

The second ground on which the relevant trusts are challenged is uncertainty. If (contrary to my view) an enumeration of purposes outside the realm of charities can take the place of an enumeration of beneficiaries, the purposes must, in my judgment, be stated in phrases which embody definite concepts, and the means by which the trustees are to try to attain them must also be prescribed with a sufficient degree of certainty. The test to be applied is stated by Lord Eldon LC in *Morice v Bishop of Durham* as follows (10 Ves 539):

"As it is a maxim, that the execution of a trust shall be under the control of the court, it must be of such a nature, that it can be under that control; so that the administration of it can be reviewed by the court; or, if the trustee dies, the court itself can execute the trust: a trust therefore, which, in case of maladministration could be reformed; and a due administration directed; and then, unless the subject and the objects can be ascertained, upon principles, familiar in other cases, it must be decided, that the court can neither reform maladministration, nor direct a due administration." ...

Applying this test, I find many uncertain phrases in the enumeration of [these] purposes ... eg, "different sections of people in any nation or community", ... "integrity of the Press", ... "combines" ... [and] "the restoration ... of the independence of ... writers in newspapers ..." . The purposes must be so defined that, if the trustees surrendered their discretion, the court could carry out the purposes declared... . But how ... could I decree in what manner the trusts ... were to be performed? The settlement gives no guidance at all. ... Accordingly, in my judgment, the trusts ... are void also for uncertainty.

Alert

But while I have reached my decision on two separate grounds, both, I think, have their origin in a single principle, namely, that a court of equity does not recognize as valid a trust which it cannot both enforce and control. This seems to me to be good equity and good sense.

This decision re-affirmed the principle first enunciated in *Morice* that a trust for a non-charitable purpose which does not have someone who is capable of enforcing it *must* be invalid – 'a gift on trust must have a *cestui que trust*' – because the law will not countenance a private purpose trust that cannot be controlled or enforced by a beneficiary in the same way that a charitable trust can be controlled and enforced by the Attorney-General.

Link
See Uncertain or Capricious Trusts below.

It can also be seen that even if the beneficiary principle had been satisfied, Roxburgh J would have decided that the trusts still failed for lack of certainty as to the purposes for which they had been established, which in turn would have made it impossible for the court to determine whether the trustees had sufficiently complied with their obligations under the trusts.

6.2 Anomalous Exceptions

Despite the decision in *Morice*, many private purpose trusts were subsequently upheld by the courts, including the House of Lords, even though they quite clearly failed to comply with the beneficiary principle.

6.2.1 Trusts for the Erection and Maintenance of Monuments and Graves

In *Musset v Bingle* [1876] WN 170 a testator gave £300 for the erection of a monument. This purpose trust was upheld.

The discussion in this case assumed without adverse comment that a trust for the *erection* of a monument was a valid purpose trust. The only issue was as to perpetuity, which the judge resolved on the basis that he was simply prepared to assume that the work needed to erect the monument would inevitably be completed within the perpetuity period.

In Musset the will also contained a bequest of £200 to be held upon trust and used for the maintenance of the monument. This was held to be void for perpetuity, since the trust might endure for longer than the perpetuity period.

Link
See Perpetuity below

In *Re Hooper* [1932] 1 Ch 38, a trust for the maintenance of family graves, vaults and monuments was also upheld.

***In re Hooper, Parker v Ward* [1932] 1 Ch 38**

Panel: Maugham J

Facts: The testator left a sum of money to trustees upon trust 'so far as they legally can do so ... [to] ... provide for the care and upkeep of' various family graves, vaults and monuments.

MR JUSTICE MAUGHAM

This point is one to my mind of doubt, and I should have felt some difficulty in deciding it if it were not for *Pirbright v Salwey* [1896] WN 86, a decision of Stirling J, which unfortunately is reported, as far as I know, only in the Weekly Notes. The report is as follows: "A testator, after expressing his wish to be buried in the inclosure in which his child lay in the churchyard of E, bequeathed to the rector and churchwardens for the time being of the parish church 800*l*. Consols, to be invested in their joint names, the interest and dividends to be derived therefrom to be applied, so long as the law for the time being permitted, in keeping up the inclosure and decorating the same with flowers: *Held*, that the gift was valid for at least a period of 21 years from the testator's death, and semble that it was not charitable."

That was a decision arrived at by Stirling J, after argument by very eminent counsel. The case does not appear to have attracted much attention in text-books, but it does not appear to have been commented upon adversely, and I shall follow it.

The trustees here have the sum of 1000*l*. which they have to hold upon trust to "invest the same and to the intent that so far as they legally can do so and in any manner that they may in their discretion arrange they will out of the annual income thereof" ... [for the stated purposes] ... which have to be done expressly according to an arrangement made in the discretion of the trustees and so far as they legally can do so. I do not think that is distinguishable from the phrase "so long as the law for the time being permits" and the conclusion at which I arrive, following the decision I have mentioned, is that this trust is valid for a period of twenty-one years from the testator's death so far as regards the ... upkeep of graves or vaults or monuments in the churchyard or in the cemetery.

Alert

Again, as with *Musset v Bingle*, the discussion in this case assumed that a trust for the maintenance of family graves, vaults and monuments was a valid purpose trust. The debate centred primarily upon whether the trust was void for perpetuity.

6.2.2 Trusts for the Saying of Private Masses

In *Bourne and Another v Kean and Others* [1919] AC 815, the House of Lords upheld a purpose trust for the saying of private masses.

***Bourne and Another v Kean and Others* [1919] AC 815**

Panel: Lord Birkenhead LC, Lord Buckmaster, Lord Atkinson, Lord Parmoor, and Lord Wrenbury

Facts: The testator left the bulk of his estate to various Roman Catholic orders for the saying of private masses for the repose of his soul. The principal issues for determination were: (i) whether the saying of private masses in accordance with the Roman Catholic faith was illegal under statute, following the Reformation, as a 'superstitious use'; and (ii) if not, whether there was any reason at common law why a trust for the saying of such masses might not be upheld.

LORD BIRKENHEAD LC

My Lords, ... after the most anxious consideration, [I have come] to several conclusions:

(1) That at common law masses for the dead were not illegal, but on the contrary that dispositions of property to be devoted to procuring masses to be said or sung were recognized both by common law and by statute.

(2) That at the date of the passing of 1 Edw.6, c.14, no Act or provision having the force of an Act had made masses illegal.

(3) That 1 Edw.6, c.14, did not itself make masses illegal, or provide that property might not thereafter be given for the purpose of procuring masses to be said or sung. It merely confiscated property then held for such and similar purposes. Subsequent legislation was passed to confiscate property afterwards settled to such uses. This is certainly true of 1 Eliz. c.24, and may be true of 1 Geo.1, c.50.

(4) That, as a result of the Acts of Uniformity, 1549 and 1559, masses became illegal. The saying or singing of masses was a penal offence from 1581 to 1791, and no Court could enforce uses or trusts intended to be devoted to such uses.

(5) That neither contemporaneous exposition of the statute 1 Edw.6, c.14, nor any doctrine closely related to it in point of date, placed upon it the construction adopted in *West v Shuttleworth*. ...

(6) That the substratum of the decisions which held such uses and trusts invalid perished as a consequence of the passing of the Catholic Relief Act 1829, and thereafter your Lordships may give free play to the principle cessante ratione legis cessat lex ipsa.

(7) That the current of decisions which held that such uses and trusts are ipso facto superstitious and void begins with *West v Shuttleworth*, and is due to a misunderstanding of the old cases. ...

The conclusion therefore, so far as I am concerned, is that a gift for masses for the souls of the dead ceased to be impressed with the stamp of superstitious use when Roman Catholicism was again permitted to be openly professed in this country, and that thenceforth it could not be deemed illegal.

The conclusion therefore, was that trusts for the saying of masses had always been lawful at common law, and had only been prohibited by statute for a period between the Uniformity Act 1559 (or possibly the Uniformity Act 1549) and the Catholic Relief Act 1829. It therefore followed, in the opinion of a majority of the House, that the gift in the present case was valid. Their Lordships do not appear to have discussed the possibility that the gift was invalid for non-compliance with the beneficiary principle.

6.2.3 Trusts for the Maintenance of Particular Animals

In *Re Dean, Cooper-Dean v Stevens* [1889] 41 Ch D 552, a trust for the future upkeep of the testator's horses and hounds was held to be valid.

***Re Dean, Cooper-Dean v Stevens* [1889] 41 Ch D 552**

Panel: North J

Facts: The testator gave an annuity of £750 per year to his trustees for a period of 50 years to allow them to maintain such of his horses and hounds as were living at his death.

MR JUSTICE NORTH

The first question is as to the validity of the provision made by the testator in favour of his horses and dogs. It is said that it is not valid; because (for this is the principal ground upon which it is put) neither a horse nor a dog could enforce the trust; and there is no person who could enforce it. It is obviously not a charity, because it is intended for the benefit of the particular animals mentioned and not for the benefit of animals generally, and it is quite distinguishable from the gift made in a subsequent part of the will to the Royal Society for the Prevention of Cruelty to Animals, which may well be a charity. In my opinion this provision for the particular horses and hounds referred to in the will is not, in any sense, a charity, and, if it were, of course the whole gift would fail, because it is a gift of an annuity arising out of land alone. But, in my opinion, as it is not a charity, there is nothing in the fact that the annuity arises out of land to prevent its being a good gift.

> Then it is said, that there is no *cestui que trust* who can enforce the trust, and, that the Court will not recognise a trust unless it is capable of being enforced by some one. I do not assent to that view. There is not the least doubt that a man may if he pleases, give a legacy to trustees, upon trust to apply it in erecting a monument to himself, either in a church or in a churchyard, or even in unconsecrated ground, and I am not aware that such a trust is in any way invalid, although it is difficult to say who would be the *cestui que trust* of the monument. In the same way I know of nothing to prevent a gift of a sum of money to trustees, upon trust to apply it for the repair of such a monument. In my opinion such a trust would be good, although the testator must be careful to limit the time for which it is to last, because, as it is not a charitable trust, unless it is to come to an end within the limits fixed by the rule against perpetuities, it would be illegal. But a trust to lay out a certain sum in building a monument, and the gift of another sum in trust to apply the same to keeping that monument in repair, say, for ten years, is, in my opinion, a perfectly good trust, although I do not see who could ask the Court to enforce it. If persons beneficially interested in the estate could do so, then the present Plaintiff can do so; but, if such persons could not enforce the trust, still it cannot be said that the trust must fail because there is no one who can actively enforce it.
>
> Is there then anything illegal or obnoxious to the law in the nature of the provision, that is, in the fact that it is not for human beings, but for horses and dogs? ... It is clearly settled by authority that a charity may be established for the benefit of horses and dogs, and, therefore, the making of a provision for horses and dogs, which is not a charity, cannot of itself be obnoxious to the law, provided, of course, that it is not to last for too long a period. ... There is nothing, therefore, in my opinion, to make the provision for the testator's horses and dogs void.

Mr Justice North was clearly of the view that a trust for the maintenance of particular animals was not capable of being a charitable trust but was nonetheless a valid private purpose trust. Although he expressly referred to the fact that such a trust must not 'last for too long a period', the judgment does not reveal on what basis the judge thought that this requirement was satisfied.

Link
See Perpetuity below

In the case of Re Haines, which was heard many years later in 1952, Danckwerts J similarly upheld a trust of income for an indefinite period for the maintenance of a testator's two cats, taking note of the fact that a cat could not live for more than 21 years. This is a questionable decision, which is inconsistent with the preferred earlier judgment in the Irish case of Re Kelly.

***Re Kelly* [1932] IR 255**

Panel: Meredith J

Facts: By his will the testator sought to leave £100 to his trustees to be used to support each of his four dogs. The testator specified that the money was to be spent at a rate of £4 per year per dog, until such time as they should die. One of the questions to be considered in the case was whether the money left for this purpose should be void for remoteness.

MR JUSTICE MEREDITH

The...question concerns the validity of the following bequest: "I leave one hundred pounds sterling to my executors and trustees for the purpose of expending four pounds sterling on the support of each of my dogs per year...Should any balance remain in the hands of my trustees on the death of the last of my dogs I leave same to the Parish Priest for the time being of the Parish of Tullaroan for masses for the repose of my soul and the souls of my parents, brothers and stepfather."

Mr Michael Comyn, for the plaintiff, contended that both the gift for the support of the dogs and the gift over, which is to take effect on the death of the last of the dogs, are void.

It will be more convenient to deal first with the gift of any possible surplus remaining over on the death of the last of the dogs. Here the question, so far as there can be any question, is strictly one of remoteness. If the lives of the dogs or other animals could be taken into account in reckoning the maximum period of "lives in being and twenty-one years afterwards" any contingent or executory interest might be properly limited, so as only to vest within the lives of specified carp, or tortoises, or other animals that might live for over a hundred years, and for twenty-one years afterwards, which, of course, is absurd. 'Lives' means human lives. It was suggested that the last of the dogs could in fact not outlive the testator by more than twenty-one years.. I know nothing of that. The Court does not enter into the question of a dog's expectation of life. In point of fact neighbour's dogs and cats are unpleasantly long-lived; but I have no knowledge of their precise expectation of life.

Alert

Mr Justice Meredith was therefore very clear in his view that animals cannot be considered as lives in being and that it is not for the court to speculate as to an animal's likely life span in order to find that a trust complies with the rules of perpetuity. However, on the specific facts of the case, he determined that there was, nonetheless, a valid trust for 21 years succeeding the death of the testator on the basis that the total annual expenditure of £16 per year (based on an amount of £4 per dog per year) meant that the £100 sum would be exhausted in relatively few years in any event.

Link
See Perpetuity below

6.2.4 Miscellaneous Cases – Foxhunting

In *Re Thompson, Public Trustee v Lloyd* [1934] Ch 342, Clauson J upheld a trust for 'the promotion and furthering of fox-hunting'.

***Re Thompson, Public Trustee v Lloyd* [1934] Ch 342**

Panel: Clauson J

Facts: The testator bequeathed a legacy to a friend to be applied by him in such manner as he should in his absolute discretion think fit towards the promotion and furthering of fox-hunting.

MR JUSTICE CLAUSON

The testator ... bequeathed a legacy of 1000*l*. to his friend ... to be applied by him in such manner as he should in his absolute discretion think fit towards the promotion and furthering of fox-hunting. In the first place, it is clear that Mr Lloyd [the friend] is not entitled to the legacy for his own benefit nor indeed does he so claim it, but he is anxious to carry out the testator's expressed wishes, if and so far as he lawfully may do so. No argument has been put forward which could justify the Court in holding this gift to be a gift in favour of charity, although it may well be that a gift for the benefit of animals generally is a charitable gift: but it seems to me plain that I cannot construe the object for which this legacy was given as being for the benefit of animals generally. In my judgment the object of the gift has been defined with sufficient clearness and is of a nature to which effect can be given. The proper way for me to deal with the matter will be, not to make, as it is asked by the summons, a general declaration, but, following the example of Knight Bruce V-C in *Pettingall v Pettingall*, to order that, upon the defendant Mr Lloyd giving an undertaking (which I understand he is willing to give) to apply the legacy when received by him towards the object expressed in the testator's will, the plaintiffs do pay to the defendant Mr Lloyd the legacy of 1000*l*.; and that, in case the legacy should be applied by him otherwise than towards the promotion and furthering of fox-hunting, the residuary legatees are to be at liberty to apply.

Alert

This judgment illustrates a number of points:

(a) A trust for the promotion and furtherance of fox-hunting is a valid private purpose trust.

(b) A private purpose trust is dependent for its fulfilment – given that there is no beneficiary who can enforce it – upon the willingness of the trustee to carry out the purpose, hence the reference to the undertaking which the trustee (Mr Lloyd) was willing to give. (Because of this dependence upon the trustee for performance of the trust, private purpose trusts are also referred to as 'trusts of imperfect obligation'.)

(c) Although there would be no beneficiary of the purpose trust who could ensure that the trust was performed correctly, the due performance by the trustee of his obligations would always be monitored by the residuary legatees, who would be entitled have the trust 'terminated' (and as a result receive the balance of the legacy of £1,000 which remained unspent) in the event of any breach. The judge therefore granted them the opportunity of bringing such a breach to the court's attention by giving them liberty to apply.

Such a trust, if established today, might well be void for illegality, given the provisions of the Hunting Act 2004.

6.2.5 The validity of the anomalous exceptions

In *Re Astor* (above), Roxburgh J considered the validity of the anomalous exceptions which had been allowed by the courts over the course of the previous 148 years. The case serves as a helpful summary of some of the key 'exceptions' cases over that period of time following *Morice*.

MR JUSTICE ROXBURGH

...These cases I must now consider. First of all, there is a group relating to horses, dogs, graves and monuments, among which I was referred to *Pettingall v Pettingall* 11 LJ Ch 176; ... *In re Dean* 41 Ch D 552; *Pirbright v Salwey* [1896] WN 86; and *In re Hooper* [1932] 1 Ch 38.

In *Pettingall v Pettingall* a testator made the following bequest by his will: "'Having a favourite black mare, I hereby bequeath, that at my death, £50 per annum be paid for her keep in some park in England or Wales; her shoes to be taken off, and she never to be ridden or put in harness; and that my executor consider himself in honour bound to fulfil my wish, and see that she will be well provided for, and removable at his will. At her death all payment to cease.' It being admitted that a bequest in favour of an animal was valid, two questions were made: first, as to the form of the decree on this point; and secondly, as to the disposition of the surplus not required for the mare. Knight Bruce V-C said, that so much of the £50 as would be required to keep the mare comfortably, should be applied by the executor, and that he was entitled to the surplus. He must give full information, whenever required, respecting the mare; and if the mare were not properly attended to, any of the parties interested in the residue might apply to the court. The decree on this point ought to be, that £50 a year should be paid to the executor during the life of the mare, or until further order; he undertaking to maintain her comfortably; with liberty for all parties to apply." The points which I wish to make are (1) that it was there admitted that a bequest in favour of an animal was valid, and (2) that there were persons interested in residue who having regard to the decree made would have had no difficulty in getting the terms of the "bequest" enforced. ...

In *In re Dean* a testator ... charged his said freehold estates with the payment to his trustees, for the term of 50 years, if any of [his] horses and hounds should so long live, of an annual sum of £750. And he declared that his trustees should apply the said annual sum in the maintenance of the horses and hounds for the time being living, and in maintaining the stables, kennels and buildings inhabited by the said animals in such condition of repair as his trustees might deem fit ... . North J said: "Then it is said, that there is no *cestui que trust* who can enforce the trust, and that the court will not recognize a trust unless it is capable of being enforced by someone. I do not assent to that view. There is not the least doubt that a man may if he pleases, give a legacy to trustees, upon trust to apply it in erecting a monument to himself, either in a church or in a churchyard, or even in unconsecrated ground, and I am not aware that such a trust is in any way invalid, although it is difficult to say who would be the *cestui que trust* of the monument. In the same way I know of nothing to prevent a gift of a sum of money to trustees, upon trust to apply it for the repair of such a monument. In my opinion such a trust would be good, although the testator must be careful to limit the time for which it is to last, because, as it is not a charitable trust, unless it is to come to an end within the limits fixed by the rule against perpetuities, it would be illegal. But a trust to lay out a certain sum in building a monument, and the gift of another sum in trust to apply the same to keeping that monument in repair, say, for ten years, is, in my opinion, a perfectly good trust, although I do not see who could ask the court to enforce it. If persons beneficially interested in the estate could do so, then the present plaintiff can do so; but, if such persons could not enforce the trust, still it cannot be said that the trust must fail because there is no one who can actively enforce it." ... North J did undoubtedly uphold the particular directions, whether or not they could be "actively enforced." But putting it at its highest, he merely held that there were certain classes of trusts, of which this was one, in which that objection was not fatal. He did not suggest that it was not generally fatal outside the realms of charity.

In *Pirbright v Salwey* a testator ... bequeathed to the rector and churchwardens of the parish church £800 Consols, the interest and dividends to be derived therefrom to be applied, so long as the law for the time being permitted, in keeping up the inclosure and decorating the same with flowers. It was held that the gift was valid for at least a period of 21 years from the testator's death, and semble that it was not charitable.

In *In re Hooper* a testator bequeathed to his executors and trustees money out of the income of which to provide, so far as they legally could do so, for the care and upkeep of certain graves, a vault and certain monuments. Maugham J said: "This point is one to my mind of doubt, and I should have felt some difficulty in deciding it if it were not for *Pirbright v Salwey*. ... That was a decision arrived at by Stirling J, after argument by very eminent counsel. The case does not appear to have attracted much attention in textbooks, but it does not appear to have been commented upon adversely, and I shall follow it." In this case, and probably also in *Pirbright v Salwey*, there was a residuary legatee to bring before the court any failure to comply with the directions. But I think that Maugham J regarded them both as exceptions from general principle.

Last in this group is *In re Thompson*. I have included it in this group because, although it relates to the furtherance of foxhunting and thus moves away from the subject-matter of the group and much nearer to the present case, it is expressly founded on *Pettingall v Pettingall*, and it is indeed a most instructive case. The testator bequeathed a legacy of £1,000 to a friend to be applied by him in such manner as he should think fit towards the promotion and furthering of foxhunting, and devised and bequeathed his residuary estate to Trinity Hall in the University of Cambridge. ... When counsel, during the course of the argument, observed, "True, there is no *cestui que trust* who can enforce the application of the legacy, but that is immaterial: *In re Dean*. The object to which the legacy is to be applied is sufficiently defined to be enforced," Clauson J interposed: "The college, as residuary legatees, seem to have an interest in the legacy, as, but for the trust for its application, they would be entitled to it. The procedure adopted by Knight Bruce V-C in *Pettingall v Pettingall* ... might be followed in this case." And in his judgment he said: "In my judgment the object of the gift has been defined with sufficient clearness and is of a nature to which effect can be given. The proper way for me to deal with the matter will be, not to make, as it is asked by the summons, a general declaration, but following the example of Knight Bruce V-C in *Pettingall v Pettingall*, to order that, upon the defendant Mr Lloyd ... giving an undertaking (which I understand he is willing to give) to apply the legacy when received by him towards the object expressed in the testator's will, the plaintiffs do pay to the defendant Mr Lloyd the legacy of £1,000; and that, in case the legacy should be applied by him otherwise than towards the promotion and furthering of foxhunting, the residuary legatees are to be at liberty to apply." I understand Clauson J to have held in effect that there was somebody who could enforce the purpose indicated because the college, as residuary legatees, would be entitled to the legacy but for the trust for its application and they could apply to the court to prevent any misapplication or breach of the undertaking given by Mr Lloyd. I infer from what he said that he would not have upheld the validity of this non-charitable purpose if there had been no residuary legatee, and no possibility of making such an order as was made in *Pettingall v Pettingall*.

Let me then sum up the position so far. On the one side there are Lord Parker's two propositions with which I began. These were not new, but merely re-echoed what Sir William Grant had said as Master of the Rolls in *Morice v The Bishop of Durham* as long ago as 1804: "There must be somebody, in whose favour the court can decree performance." The position was recently restated by Harman J in *In re Wood* [1949] Ch 498: "A gift on trust must have a cestui que trust," and this seems to be in accord with principle. On the other side is a group of cases relating to horses and dogs, graves and monuments - matters arising under wills and intimately connected with the deceased - in which the courts have found means of escape from these general propositions and also *In re Thompson* ... which I have endeavoured to explain. ... [They] may, I think, properly be regarded as anomalous and exceptional and in no way destructive of the proposition which traces descent from or through Sir William Grant through Lord Parker to Harman J. Perhaps the late Sir Arthur Underhill was right in suggesting that they may be concessions to human weakness or sentiment (see Law of Trusts, 8th ed., p 79). They cannot, in my judgment, of themselves (and no other justification has been suggested to me) justify the conclusion that a Court of Equity will recognize as an equitable obligation

Alert

affecting the income of large funds in the hands of trustees a direction to apply it in furtherance of enumerated non-charitable purposes in a manner which no court or department can control or enforce. I hold that the trusts here in question are void ... .

Having reviewed the many cases since *Morice* which did not accord with the beneficiary principle, Roxburgh J concluded that they were 'anomalous and exceptional'. In his view the correct position in law, which he traced from *Morice* through to *In re Wood*, was that a non-charitable purpose trust could not be valid in the absence of 'somebody, in whose favour the court can decree performance'.

In *Re Endacott, deceased* [1960] Ch 262, the Court of Appeal had the opportunity to consider the rule in *Morice*, the many anomalous exceptions which had been sanctioned over the intervening years, and the 'return to orthodoxy' represented by the decision of Roxburgh J in *Re Astor*. The Court of Appeal affirmed the orthodox view and held that a trust 'for the purpose of providing some useful memorial to myself' was void as a non-charitable purpose trust.

***Re Endacott, deceased, Corpe v Endacott* [1960] Ch 262**

Panel: Lord Evershed MR, Sellers and Harman LJJ

Facts: A testator gave his residuary estate to the North Tawton Parish Council 'for the purpose of providing some useful memorial to myself ...'.

LORD EVERSHED MR

By his will ... the testator ... made ... the following residuary gift: "Everything else I leave to North Tawton Devon Parish Council for the purpose of providing some useful memorial to myself ... ."

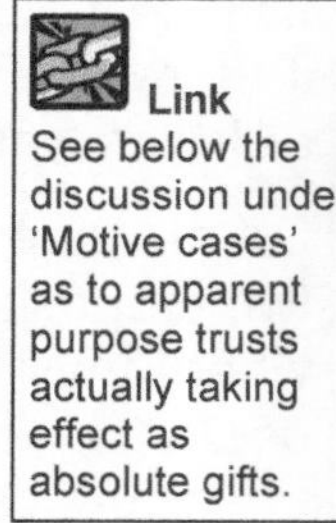

Link

See below the discussion under 'Motive cases' as to apparent purpose trusts actually taking effect as absolute gifts.

Mr Arnold, for the parish council, has put his case on two broad distinct grounds. He has first said that the words "for the purpose of providing some useful memorial to myself" merely indicated the reason why the testator had made this gift, but did not, and were not intended to, impose any obligation upon the parish council, with the result that the gift should be treated as a gift out and out to the parish council.

Alternatively, Mr Arnold has argued on the footing that the words (contrary to his first contention) do impose a trust or obligation of some kind, though it is to be noted that it has not been suggested that such a trust would offend the rule against perpetuities. But, on this alternative basis, the argument has diverged thus: First, if the trust be not (upon its true interpretation) a charitable trust, still it is said to be of a public nature and valid and effective, on the ground that it falls within a class of cases which have been referred to as "anomalous," and which were recited by Roxburgh J conveniently in his recent decision in the case of *In re Astor's Settlement Trusts* [1952] Ch 534 ...

The contention is that this case, falling within that so-called anomalous class, must be treated as effective, being of a public character and being also such that, by appropriate machinery, it can be properly controlled by the court. ...

Then, alternatively, it is said the trusts are in truth charitable, and the argument on this alternative again diverges. First of all, it has been submitted that a parish council (and, of course, this particular parish council) is, according to its statutory constitution, limited, at any rate quoad any gifts of this kind which it receives, to charitable functions and activities. If that is right, then it is said that the gift to such a body stamps (and, if necessary, qualifies) the nature of the trusts which are declared, and that they should, accordingly, be taken as being and intended to be within the scope of the (charitable) statutory activities or powers. Secondly (and this was a point particularly put to us by Mr Buckley for the Attorney-General), it is said that, whether the parish council be or be not a body confined in activity to charitable purposes, the true view of the meaning of these vital words "for the purpose of providing some useful memorial to myself" is that they are, as a matter of language, equivalent to a trust for the benefit of the local inhabitants of North Tawton Parish and therefore, according to authority, charitable.

Those, broadly, are the contentions; and I will deal at once and briefly with the first point, namely: Was the language which I have quoted intended to impose an obligation, or was it merely expository? That matter I can deal with briefly, because it is, after all, a matter of mere construction. It will, therefore, be convenient if I state at once what my view is of the meaning of these words "for the purpose of providing some useful memorial to myself"; and ... I do not think that these words were merely expository. In my judgment, they were intended to impose an obligation in the nature of a trust. In my judgment, the object of these words, the trust, the obligation, which the testator intended them to impose was this: that the council were, with his money (and subject, of course, to the obligation about the widow), to create a memorial to himself. His first idea was (and I am not saying that it was either foolish or ignoble) that there should thereafter be in North Tawton, Devon, a memorial to himself; but that the memorial was to have this quality, that it was to be useful; and that I take to mean that it was intended that it should have the quality of utility rather than ornament. Though I do not think aesthetic or ornamental considerations were excluded, still his purpose was that the memorial, whatever form it took and whether material or not, should be useful; and, by way again of anticipation of my answer to Mr Buckley, I cannot see that it was necessarily to be useful only to the inhabitants of North Tawton.

I have stated my view of the construction and that view answers the first point. It follows that this was not a gift out and out to the North Tawton Parish Council. My view of the intention of those words also carries with it the answer to many of the other points that have arisen. I go further and say that, in the end of all, this case should be decided on the grounds ... that here was a specific obligation sought to be imposed, specific in this sense, that it was to be for the purpose of providing a memorial for this testator having the quality of utility, something obviously that could not be confined to charitable purposes, but no doubt having the quality also that it served a public purpose of some kind. In my judgment this view of the words does carry with it the result, with all respect to the learning which has been put before us, that to hold it valid would be for this court to go beyond (and appreciably beyond) the tenor of the decided cases on these difficult subjects.

I come then to Mr. Arnold's alternative ground. ... It is convenient and perhaps logical to take first the point that the parish council being, it is said, confined to charitable activities so far as is relevant, then this gift must take its character by reflection of that fact. I am unable to accept that argument. The cases, of which *In re Rumball, decd* [1956] Ch 105 ... in this court is the most recent, illustrate at any rate this proposition that gifts to persons holding a particular office, and particularly an ecclesiastical office, if they are not to be treated as gifts to the holder of that office in his personal capacity, are taken to be gifts to be applied for the purposes for which the office is held. The vicar or the cardinal archbishop (to take references from two cases) receives the gift and disposes of it (as it is said) virtute officii, and the nature of the officium is such that the duties, the trusts, must be ecclesiastical and therefore charitable. If that is accepted, then general words which follow may be regarded either as merely emphasising the fact that the gift is to the ecclesiastical officer virtute officii or possibly, as intended, not only to do that but also to limit to some extent the scope of his possible disposition, within the scope of his office, of those funds. No decided case, so far as we are aware, has applied that principle to such a body as a parish council. If it were shown perfectly clearly that every activity of a parish council, at any rate so far as gifts were concerned, must be of a charitable character, it might follow that a similar reasoning would apply; but I am not satisfied that it is true to say of a parish council that it is confined in its activities to charitable activities, or that it is so confined as regards any gifts it may receive. I do not forget the argument that you might give something to a vicar not personally, but having attached to it an obligation to apply it for purposes which were outside his ecclesiastical duties, but I cannot find in this case any true analogy to that kind of illustration. There is here a gift to this parish council for the purpose which I have stated, and the relevance of the matter must be (the purpose being a very wide one and not on the face of it charitable): Is the nature of a parish council's activities so clearly defined as being of a charitable character as to impose an essential limitation on the words which I have already tried to construe?

We were referred to section 268 of the Local Government Act, 1933. That deals with acceptance of gifts by local authorities and (so far as relevant) provides: "Subject to the provisions of this section, a local authority may accept, hold and administer any gift ... for any local public purpose, or for the benefit of the inhabitants of the area," etc. I have no doubt (and I do not think Mr Arnold really contended to the contrary) that the words "for any local public purpose" cannot be confined in that context to charitable purposes. ... The words "local public purposes" are not, according to our law, regarded as being exclusively charitable; and, even against the background of the Local Government Act of

1894, I think it is plain that local public purposes in section 268 of the Act of 1933 are not only charitable purposes. But I do not forget the point that this section deals with acceptance of gifts and would not necessarily colour the general activities of a parish council, though I venture for my part to think that if, in the case of gifts, it is made plain that a parish council can apply them to non-charitable as well as charitable purposes, it is a severe obstacle in Mr Arnold's way. ...

I now turn to Mr Arnold's alternative argument based on the view that there is here a trust and a trust of a public character, but not a charitable trust. What he says is, that the trust is in line with the trusts which were rendered effective in those cases which I have called "anomalous," and many of which are referred to in Roxburgh J's decision, beginning with *Pettingall v Pettingall* (1842) 11 LJ Ch 176. I include in that list cases such as the three to which we have had our attention particularly drawn today. The argument is that assuming the non-charitable but public nature of this trust, still it is of a character which the court can efficiently, and will, enforce. It must be said that these cases are of a somewhat anomalous kind. They are classified in the recent book written by Mr J H C Morris and Professor Barton Leach, The Rule Against Perpetuities (1956) (p 298). "We proceed," say the authors, "to examine these 'anomalous' exceptions. It will "be found that they fall into the following groups: (1) trusts for the erection or maintenance of monuments or graves; (2) trusts for the saying of masses, in jurisdictions where such trusts are not regarded as charitable; (3) trusts for the maintenance of particular animals; (4) trusts for the benefit of unincorporated associations (though this group is more doubtful); (5) miscellaneous cases." I am prepared to accept, for the purposes of the argument, that it does not matter that the trusts here are attached to residue and not to a legacy; that is to say, it does not matter that the persons who would come to the court and either complain if the trusts were not being carried out, or claim the money on the footing that they had not been carried out, are next-of-kin rather than residuary legatees. Still, in my judgment, the scope of these cases (and I can call them anomalous because they have been so called both in the book of Mr Morris and Professor Barton Leach and in the course of the argument) ought not to be extended. So to do would be to validate almost limitless heads of non-charitable trusts, even though they were not (strictly speaking) public trusts, so long only as the question of perpetuities did not arise; and, in my judgment, that result would be out of harmony with the principles of our law. No principle perhaps has greater sanction or authority behind it than the general proposition that a trust by English law, not being a charitable trust, in order to be effective, must have ascertained or ascertainable beneficiaries. These cases constitute an exception to that general rule. The general rule, having such authority as that of Lord Eldon, Lord Parker and my predecessor, Lord Greene MR, behind it, was most recently referred to in the Privy Council in *Leahy v Attorney-General for New South Wales* [1959] AC 457 ... .

Alert

Alert

I therefore, so far as this case is concerned, conclude (having already stated my view of the meaning of the words) that, though this trust is specific, in the sense that it indicates a purpose capable of expression, yet it is of far too wide and uncertain a nature to qualify within the class of cases cited. It would go far beyond any fair analogy to any of those decisions. I do not wish to take time by much example, particularly because I am not unmindful of having already said that I do not wish to add to the future burden of citation; but, merely by way of example, take trusts for the maintenance of memorials, I refer to *In re Hooper* [1932] 1 Ch 38. That was a case where the purpose of the bequest was to provide for the care and upkeep of certain graves, a vault and monuments. Maugham J said: "This point is one, to my mind, of doubt, and I should have felt some difficulty in deciding it if it were not for *Pirbright v Salwey* [1896] WN 86. That was a decision arrived at by Stirling J after argument by very eminent counsel. The case does not appear to have attracted much attention in textbooks, but it does not appear to have been commented upon adversely, and I shall follow it." It may be said that other cases in regard to monuments, which were closely on the facts in line, might similarly follow the decision of Stirling J, but this case, as I construe the purposes of the gift, is very different from *In re Hooper*. ...

Those, then, are my reasons for the conclusion which I stated at the beginning of this judgment, that in my view Danckwerts J rightly decided the case, and I therefore would dismiss the appeal.

LORD JUSTICE HARMAN

I agree. At first sight, my mind recoiled from the possibility of this gift being held valid, and I have not seen any cause in the course of the hearing to resile from that view. One must first construe the will; and my view of that is that this testator, as my Lord has said, intended by his will to provide himself with a memorial in his native town. He added that the memorial to himself should also be useful. ... So read, it seems to me apparent that the law cannot uphold the will, unless connected with the fabric of a church, without throwing over every kind of authority on this subject. A gift for public purposes in the parish of North Tawton, a gift for patriotic purposes, a gift for benevolent purposes, are all, as we all know, universally now held to be bad. How, then, shall it be held that a gift for useful purposes is good without upsetting the whole structure so elaborately built up and ... so firmly established? I cannot think that charity has anything to do with this bequest. As for establishing it without the crutch of charity, I applaud the orthodox sentiments expressed by Roxburgh J in the *Astor* case, and I think, as I think he did, that though one knows there have been decisions at times which are not really to be satisfactorily classified, but are perhaps merely occasions when Homer has nodded, at any rate these cases stand by themselves and ought not to be increased in number, nor indeed followed, except where the one is exactly like another. Whether it would be better that some authority now should say those cases were wrong, this perhaps is not the moment to consider. At any rate, I cannot think a case of this kind, the case of providing outside a church an unspecified and unidentified memorial, is the kind of instance which should be allowed to add to those troublesome, anomalous and aberrant cases.

In my judgment, Danckwerts J came to the right conclusion, and this appeal ought to be dismissed.

In *Re Endacott* the Court of Appeal therefore:

(a) re-affirmed the necessity for a private purpose trust to comply with the beneficiary principle in order for it to be valid;

(b) identified five categories of 'anomalous' private purpose trust which had been upheld in the years since Morice and which it would not be right to overrule given the length of time for which they had stood unchallenged, namely:

   a. Trusts for the erection and maintenance of monuments and graves (e.g. Re Hooper [1932] 1 Ch 38);

   b. Trusts for the saying of private masses (e.g. Bourne v Keane [1919] AC 815);

   c. Trusts for the maintenance of particular animals (e.g. Pettingall v Pettingall (1842) 11 LJ Ch 176; Re Dean [1889] 41 Ch D 552);

   d. Trusts for the benefit of unincorporated associations (see Chapter 7); and

   e. Miscellaneous cases – of which the one most frequently cited is Re Thompson.

(c) made clear that no further exceptions were to be allowed.

The result is that any trust (whenever created) which falls fairly and squarely within one of the anomalous purposes sanctioned in *Re Endacott* will be valid. However, any other private purpose trust will not be valid unless it falls within the Re Denley exception.

See Re Denley - Trusts for Persons below.

6.3 Perpetuity

Even if a private purpose trust falls within one of the *Re Endacott* exceptions (see above), nonetheless it will still be invalid if it infringes the rule against perpetuity.

The rule against perpetuity (also known as the rule against inalienability) is a common law rule which exists to prevent property from being held for a non-charitable purpose which may never end. The rule requires that it must be possible to say, at the moment that the trust is created, that it will definitely come to an end before the expiry of the 'perpetuity period'. This is achieved by stating that the purpose is to be carried on for the duration of the perpetuity period, but then the trust fund is to be distributed elsewhere.

Under common law, 'the perpetuity period' is defined as the lifetime of any relevant life (or lives) in being plus 21 years. 'Life in being' simply means any person now born or in the womb. Case law has now clarified that a 'life' for these purposes means a human life (see *Re Kelly* above).

The person establishing the trust may nominate a life in being of their own choosing. They may choose a named individual or (which is quite common) they may identify the person simply as a member of a particular class – eg 'the last survivor of the issue of Queen Victoria living at my death' (if the trust is created by a will). This is known as a 'royal lives' clause. (Queen Victoria is often chosen because she had nine children, who themselves had a further 40 children; so over the ensuing years the class of relevant lives in being has become very large, thereby optimising the chances that the applicable perpetuity period will last for many years.)

If at the date of the testator's death the youngest living descendant of Queen Victoria is 10 years old, and that person lives to the age of 90, the relevant perpetuity period is calculated as follows:

Lifetime of relevant life in being (90 years – 10 years)		= 80	years
Plus			
Additional period of 21 years		= 21	years
	Total:	101	years

If no relevant life in being is specified, then the common law applies a 'default' perpetuity period of 21 years. The trust must expressly limit the duration to this period.

Of course, it is in the very nature of the anomalous purpose trusts discussed above that they do not have an ascertainable beneficiary and so, in the absence of a nominated 'relevant life in being' the applicable perpetuity period in relation to them will usually be 21 years.

This time constraint can present problems where the purpose trust is for an ongoing activity such as the maintenance of monuments and graves or the maintenance of animals. In *Re Hooper* (above) the testator had not nominated a relevant life in being, but had stated that the trustees were only to carry out the purpose '... so far as they legally can do so ...'. Mr Justice Maugham felt able to treat that phrase as being indistinguishable from the phrase 'so long as the law for the time being permits' which had been upheld in *Pirbright v Salwey*, and therefore sufficient to import a perpetuity period of 21 years, per Maugham J:

> This point is one to my mind of doubt, and I should have felt some difficulty in deciding it if it were not for *Pirbright v Salwey* [1896] WN 86, a decision of Stirling J ... The case does not appear to have attracted much attention in text-books, but it does not appear to have been commented upon adversely, and I shall follow it.
>
> The trustees ... [may only act] ... so far as they legally can do so. I do not think that is distinguishable from the phrase "so long as the law for the time being permits" and the conclusion at which I arrive, following the decision I have

> mentioned, is that this trust is valid for a period of twenty-one years from the testator's death so far as regards the ... upkeep of graves or vaults or monuments in the churchyard or in the cemetery.

But in the absence of such 'saving' words, any such trust will fail for perpetuity. So in *Musset v Bingle* (above), the trust for maintenance of the monument was void for perpetuity as no perpetuity period was specified. But the trust for the erection of the monument was valid, because it was assumed that the monument would be erected within the perpetuity period.

Note that it is in fact possible to ensure that a monument or grave is maintained for a period considerably in excess of 21 years under the Parish Councils and Burial Authorities (Miscellaneous Provisions) Act s1, which provides that a burial authority may agree, upon payment of a sum, to maintain a monument or grave for a period not exceeding 99 years.

The decision in *Re Dean* (above), however, is more difficult to reconcile with the need for compliance with the perpetuity period. This is particularly so given that the life of the animal in question cannot be a 'relevant life in being' (only human lives qualify as 'relevant' lives), nor is regard to be taken of the fact that many animals do not have a natural lifespan of more than 21 years: see the Irish case of *Re Kelly* [1932] IR 255.

6.4 Uncertain or Capricious Trusts

Even though a purpose trust may be allowed as an exception to the beneficiary principle and the rule against perpetuity, the law will not uphold a purpose trust if it is too vague or if it is too capricious, (i.e. if it is devoid of any beneficial use or purpose).

As stated above, in *Re Astor*, for example, Roxburgh J would have declined to enforce the trusts in issue on the additional ground that the trust obligations were too vague.

An example of a trust which was considered to be too capricious to be worthy of enforcement is to be found in *Brown v Burdett* (1882) 21 Ch D 667.

***Brown v Burdett* (1882) 21 Ch D 667**

Panel: Bacon V-C

Facts: The testatrix devised a freehold house, yard, garden, and outbuildings, to trustees and their heirs, upon trust to block up all the rooms of the house (except four rooms in which she directed that a housekeeper and his wife should be placed in occupation), and the coach-house, for twenty years; and subject thereto upon trust for a named beneficiary. She directed her trustees to visit the house and premises once in every three months to see that the trusts were effectually carried out, and declared that if any trustee should neglect or refuse to carry out the trusts aforesaid, any real or personal estate given or intended to be given to him by the will should go elsewhere.

BACON V-C

I think I must "unseal" this useless, undisposed of property.

There will be a declaration that the house and premises were undisposed of by the will ...

The court refused to give effect to a trust whose purpose was useless, and so declared that the property had not been disposed of by the will.

Note that a purpose trust of this kind would be void today, notwithstanding its capricious nature, on the basis that it does not fall within one of the exceptions recognised in *Re Endacott* (see above). Capriciousness of itself can, however, be sufficient to render a trust void even where it falls within a valid *Re Endacott* exception, as demonstrated in the case of *M'Caig v University of Glasgow (No. 2)* [1907] S.C. 231, which was subsequently followed in the case of *M'Caig's Trustees v Kirk-Session of United Free Church of Lismore* [1915] S.C. 426.

M'Caig v University of Glasgow (No. 2) 1907 S.C. 231

Panel: Lords Dundas, Justice-Clerk, Kyllachy, Stormonth-Darling and Low.

Facts: The testator, John M'Caig, left property to be used (amongst other things) for the purposes of erecting: (1) monuments and statues of himself and his immediate family on his estate; and (2) artistic towers, to be built at prominent points on his estate. The towers were to be made by Scottish sculptors. The testator explained that he wished to encourage young artists and so declared that prizes should be given to the best plans for the statues and towers before they were built. The University of Glasgow was appointed as Trustee. John's sister, Catharine M'Caig, was his only surviving heir at law, and claimed that she ought to be able to take the estate free of these purpose trusts.

Whilst arguably the trust fit within the *Endacott* exception of erection and maintenance of monuments and graves, the court refused to uphold the trust, setting aside the portion of the estate which referred to the statues and towers. The court held that the trust was not for a charitable purpose and that it conferred no beneficial interest upon any person(s).

LORD JUSTICE CLERK

Now, what was it that Mr M'Caig expressed in the deed? What was his desire and intention? He seems to have been possessed of an inordinate vanity as regards himself and his relatives, so extreme as to amount almost to a moral disease, though quite consistent with sanity. Accordingly his desire was that towers—artistic towers he calls them—similar to one which he had during life erected on his property overlooking Oban, should be built on all prominent places, and that his own likeness and that of his brothers and sisters should be perpetuated in colossal statuary in stone or bronze placed on these towers. That was the only real purpose to be served by the establishment of the trust.

Alert

It was no gift to anyone. It was solely a scheme for setting up so much stone building and statuary, and nothing else. Up to this point therefore there was no beneficiary for whom he disinherited his heir. It could hardly be held that these towers and statues could be a benefit to Oban, although I do not doubt that he thought so, but certainly no beneficial enjoyment could result to anyone.

I do not think that in setting aside this deed as not substituting any beneficiary in place of the heir the Court will be in any way narrowing the powers of a testator to deal with his estate as he will. A testator who desires to confer a benefit on an individual or a class can have no difficulty in doing so. But in this case I cannot hold that this has been done by this eccentric testator, and I am of opinion that the heir is entitled to prevail.

LORD STORMONTH-DARLING

One way of testing the real nature of the trust purposes is to ask, who would have any title or interest to enforce them? Not the pursuer, for, although she is the last survivor and representative of the family which is to be handed down to posterity in stone or bronze, she naturally disclaims any wish to have them made ridiculous in this manner. Can it be suggested that any member of the public, merely as such, would have the right? And if not, could any "young and rising artist" come forward with a claim founded on the hope that he would win a prize, if prizes were offered for the best designs of the statues and towers? Or would he be in any better position than a quarry master or mason who insisted that he should have the opportunity of tendering for the erection of the statues and towers? To each and all of these persons I apprehend that the answer of the law would be, "You are not a beneficiary for whom this trust was called into being"…. it is really in the interests of public policy that testators should not be allowed to exclude their heirs-at-law, unless they take the trouble to provide some beneficial substitute.

LORD LOW

I think that it is clear that the trust cannot be regarded as one for charitable purposes. The object of the trust was to perpetuate the memory of the M'Caig family, and of the testator in particular, and his desire to encourage young and rising artists was entirely subsidiary to that leading purpose. It seems to me to have amounted to no more than this, that as statues and towers were to be erected at any rate, it was desirable to take advantage of the opportunity thereby afforded of encouraging young and rising artists. If the testator had been told that his idea of erecting statues and towers could not be carried out, there is no reason to suppose that he would have devoted his means to any such purpose.

Interestingly, eight years after John M'Caig's death, Catherine M'Caig (John's sister and heir-at-law) sought to create a trust of an almost identical nature – providing for the erection and maintenance of statues for her family members. The validity of this trust was considered in the case of *M'Caig's Trustees v Kirk-Session of United Free Church of Lismore* 1915 S.C. 426.

***M'Caig's Trustees v Kirk-Session of United Free Church of Lismore* 1915 S.C. 426.**

Panel: Lords Salvesen, Guthrie and Justice-Clerk

Facts: Catherine M'Caig left her estate to a trustee in trust for, amongst other things, the erection and maintenance of statutes of herself and her immediate family members on one of her properties. Whilst Catherine had no heir-at-law to raise issue with this, there were a number of other beneficiaries of the estate (including the United Free Church of Lismore) who sought to claim that this trust should not be upheld – relying on the earlier decision of *M'Caig v University of Glasgow (No. 2)*.

LORD SALVESEN

It is noteworthy that no beneficial interests are created by this bequest in favour of third parties... There is, so far as I can see, no person who has a title to enforce the erection of the statues; and there are no descendants of any member of the family alive who might take pleasure in contemplating (if he were permitted to do so) the proposed representations of the forms and features of his relatives. The trustees indeed have been unable to trace the heir-at-law if any such person exists... For my own part, I desire to say that I entirely concur in the view indicated by Lord Kyllachy in the previous case of *M'Caig* , that there is nothing in our common law "against the validity of a testamentary disposition directed to the providing, on a customary and rational scale, a burial place for a testator or a suitable monument to his memory"...[however] The expenditure of this large sum on statues, which was directed apparently from motives of personal and family vanity, will serve no purpose, all the less seeing that the family has virtually become extinct. It can be of no benefit to the public, because the enclosure in which the statues are to be erected is one to which they will have no right of access. But it is unnecessary to pursue the subject further, because the question appears to me to be decided by the unanimous decision of this Division in the previous case of M'Caig . I am unable to find any substantial distinction between the bequests in the two cases...

Alert

For myself I am prepared to hold that the bequest is contrary to public policy on more than one ground. In the first place, I think it is so because it involves a sheer waste of money, and not the less so that the expenditure would give employment to a number of sculptors and workmen, for it must be assumed that their labour could be usefully employed in other ways. I think, further, that it would be a dangerous thing to support a bequest of this kind which can only gratify the vanity of testators, who have no claim to be immortalised, but who possess the means by which they can provide for more substantial monuments to themselves than many that are erected to famous persons by public subscription. A man may, of course, do with his money what he pleases while he is alive, but he is generally restrained from wasteful expenditure by a desire to enjoy his property, or to accumulate it, during his lifetime. The actings of the two M'Caigs form an excellent illustration of this principle of human conduct. For many years they had apparently contemplated the erection of similar statues, but they could not bring themselves to part with the money during their own lifetimes. Such considerations do not restrain extravagance or eccentricity in testamentary dispositions, on which there is no check except by the Courts of law. A testator may still leave his means to be expended in stone and lime which will form a monument to his memory, provided the bequest he makes serves some useful public purpose and is not merely for his own glorification. The prospect of Scotland being dotted with monuments to obscure persons who happened to have amassed a sufficiency of means, and cumbered with trusts for the purpose of maintaining these monuments in all time coming, appears to me to be little less than appalling. What a man does in his own lifetime with his own property may be removed by his successor, and no doubt will be as soon as it has ceased to serve a useful purpose. But, if a bequest such as that in Miss M'Caig's codicil were held good, money would require to be expended in perpetuity merely to gratify an absurd whim which has neither reason nor public sentiment in its favour.

LORD GUTHRIE

Whether the act is sufficiently contrary to public policy to warrant the Court's interference must depend on the degree to which it is against public policy. In this case, it seems to me that to give effect to the part of Miss M'Caig's codicil concerned with the erection of eleven statues would be of no benefit to anyone except those connected with the carrying out of the work, for whose interest she expresses no concern. If anybody went to see the statues, supposing they represented faithfully the persons to be commemorated, it would not be to admire them but to laugh at them, and perhaps to philosophise on the length to which morbid family pride may drive an otherwise sensible person. These statues would not, in fact, achieve Miss M'Caig's object of perpetuating an honourable memory. They would turn a respectable and creditable family into a laughing stock to succeeding generations. On the other hand, the benefactions in Miss M'Caig's settlement, which are not questioned, will associate the family and their name in the future with useful objects.

6.5 *Re Denley* – Trusts for Persons

The decision of Goff J in *Re Denley's Trust Deed* [1969] 1 Ch 373 suggests that there may be a category of purpose trust which will be valid even though it does not satisfy the beneficiary principle or fall within one of the *Re Endacott* exceptions: a purpose trust which is expressed to be for the benefit of ascertainable individuals.

***Re Denley's Trust Deed, Holman & Ors v H H Martyn & Co Ltd & Ors* [1969] 1 Ch 373**

Panel: Goff J

Facts: The settlor settled certain land upon trustees to be used as a sports ground 'primarily for the benefit of the employees of the company and secondarily for the benefit of such other person or persons (if any) as the trustees may allow to use the same ...'. The use of the land as a sports ground was expressly limited to the perpetuity period. Mr Justice Goff upheld the trust.

MR JUSTICE GOFF

Alert

[Counsel] has argued that the trust ... in the present case is ... a purpose trust, that is, a trust for providing recreation, which he submits is void on the beneficiary principle... . [I]n my judgment the beneficiary principle of In re Astor's Settlement Trusts which was approved in In re Endacott, decd ... is confined to purpose or object trusts which are abstract or impersonal. The objection is not that the trust is for a purpose or object per se, but that there is no beneficiary or cestui que trust. ... Where, then, the trust, though expressed as a purpose, is directly or indirectly for the benefit of an individual or individuals, it seems to me that it is in general outside the mischief of the beneficiary principle. The trust in the present case is limited in point of time so as to avoid any infringement of the rule against perpetuities and, for the reasons I have given, it does not offend against the beneficiary principle; and unless, therefore, it be void for uncertainty, it is a valid trust. ... As it is a private trust and not a charitable one, it is clear that, however it be regarded, the individuals for whose benefit it is designed must be ascertained or capable of ascertainment at any given time: see *Inland Revenue Commissioners v Broadway Cottages Trust* [1955] Ch 20. It is conceded that "the employees of the company"..., which must mean for the time being, are so ascertained or ascertainable, but [counsel] submits that the inclusion in the class of "such other person or persons (if any) as the trustees may allow" is fatal, and that the qualification "secondarily" in relation to such persons does not help. In my judgment, however, this is not so. ...[T]he provision as to "other persons" is not a trust but a power operating in partial defeasance of the trust in favour of the employees which it does not therefore make uncertain. Moreover, as it is a power, it is not necessary that the trustees should know all possible objects in whose favour it is exercisable: see *In re Gulbenkian's Settlements* [1968] Ch 126. Therefore, in my judgment, it is a valid power. ... Another question, perhaps of difficulty, might arise, if the trustees purported to admit not to a given individual or individuals but a class which they failed to specify with certainty, whether in such a case this would import uncertainty into and invalidate the whole trust or would be merely an invalid exercise of the power; but, as that has not in fact occurred, I need not consider it. There is, however, one other aspect of uncertainty which has caused me some concern; that is, whether this is in its nature a trust which the court can control, for, as Lord Eldon LC said in *Morice v Bishop of Durham* (1805) 10 Ves 522:

"As it is a maxim, that the execution of a trust shall be under the control of the court, it must be of such a nature, that it can be under that control; so that the administration of it can be reviewed by the court; or, if the trustee dies, the court itself can execute the trust: a trust therefore, which, in case of mal-administration could be reformed; and a due administration directed; and then, unless the subject and the objects can be ascertained, upon principles, familiar

> *in other cases, it must be decided, that the court can neither reform maladministration, nor direct a due administration."*
>
> The difficulty I have felt is that there may well be times when some of the employees wish to use the sports club for one purpose while others desire to use it at the same time for some other purpose of such natures that the two cannot be carried on together. The trustees could, of course, control this by making rules and regulations ..., but they might not. In any case, the employees would probably agree amongst themselves, but I cannot assume that they would. If there were an impasse, the court could not resolve it, because it clearly could not either exercise the trustees' power to make rules or settle a scheme, this being a non-charitable trust: see *In re Astor's Settlement Trusts* [1952] Ch 534. In my judgment, however, it would not be right to hold the trust void on this ground. The court can, as it seems to me, execute the trust both negatively by restraining any improper disposition or use of the land, and positively by ordering the trustees to allow the employees and such other persons (if any) as they may admit to use the land for the purpose of a recreation or sports ground. Any difficulty there might be in practice in the beneficial enjoyment of the land by those entitled to use it is, I think, really beside the point. The same kind of problem is equally capable of arising in the case of a trust to permit a number of persons - for example, all the unmarried children of a testator or settlor - to use or occupy a house or to have the use of certain chattels; nor can I assume that in such cases agreement between the parties concerned would be more likely, even if that be a sufficient distinction, yet no one would suggest, I fancy, that such a trust would be void. In my judgment, therefore, the [trust is] valid ...

The essence of Goff J's decision is that even if a purpose trust does not have a beneficiary, it may nonetheless still be valid provided that it is directly or indirectly for the benefit of an ascertained or ascertainable individual or individuals. On this reasoning, *In Re Astor's Settlement Trusts* and *Re Endacott* could be distinguished on the ground that they had involved trusts which were purely for purposes which were 'abstract or impersonal'.

Applying the judge's test, it could readily be ascertained whether an individual was or was not an employee of the relevant company. However, there was a further complication, in that the terms of the trust allowed the trustees to permit 'such other person or persons (if any) as the trustees may allow' to use the sports ground. This appeared to mean that the sports ground might be used by persons who were not ascertained or ascertainable – their identity would never be known until they were actually selected by the trustees. The judge dealt with this problem by saying that the trustees were not under a trust obligation to allow use by such third parties, but merely had a *power* to do so, and that such a power, even if implemented, did not affect the validity of the trust.

This decision has been the subject of debate and criticism, and its correctness is open to question. It was accepted as correct by Sir Robert Megarry V-C in *Re Northern Developments (Holdings)* (1978), unreported (but referred to by Sir Peter Millett in 'Quistclose Trusts' (1985) 101 LQR 280). However, in *Re*

Grant's Will Trusts [1980] 1 WLR 361, Vinelott J characterised the facts of *Re Denley* as not being concerned with a purpose trust at all, but involving simply a discretionary trust under which the trustees had a discretion to apply property for use by a defined class of beneficiaries, namely the employees of the company, per Vinelott J:

> I can see no distinction in principle between a trust to permit a class defined by reference to employment to use and enjoy land in accordance with rules to be made at the discretion of trustees on the one hand, and, on the other hand, a trust to distribute income at the discretion of trustees amongst a class, defined by reference to, for example, relationship to the settlor. In both cases the benefit to be taken by any member of the class is at the discretion of the trustees, but any member of the class can apply to the court to compel the trustees to administer the trust in accordance with its terms.

And in *Re Horley Town Football Club* [2006] All ER (D) 34, Lawrence Collins J observed (by way of implicit criticism) that:

> Goff J appears to have equated the beneficiary principle with the question of enforceability and not with the issue of equitable ownership ... there are difficulties with regard to [the] termination of such a trust which make [*Re Denley*] an unsafe basis for decision: see Thomas and Hudson, The Law of Trusts (2004), para 6.21.

6.6 Motive Cases

As stated above, it is sometimes the case that what appears at first sight to be a purpose trust is in fact an absolute gift, with the 'purpose' being no more than a mere expression of non-binding motive on the part of the testator as to the reason for making the gift. This is a matter of construction of the particular disposition and requires consideration of certainty of intention (see Chapter 2, section 2.1.). This issue was considered in the cases of *Re Sanderson's Trust* [1857] 69 E.R. 1206 and *Re Bowes* [1896] 1 Ch. 507, resulting in very different outcomes.

***Re Sanderson's Trust* [1857] 69 E.R. 1206**

Panel: Sir W. Page Wood V-C

Facts: By his will in 1836 the testator gave all of his real and personal estate to the trustees, upon trust. The trustees were instructed to apply the whole or any part of the income of the estate for the trustee's brother, John's, 'maintenance, attendance, and comfort' (John being mentally incapacitated and therefore unable to manage his own affairs). The trustees did so, however, after John's death in 1856 a question arose as to whom had a right to the savings and accumulations of the income which had not been so applied during John's lifetime.

It was held that this was not a gift to John of the whole income, and therefore his personal estate had no claim to any remaining property. The testator had created a trust for his benefit, which had been discharged, and any surplus property must therefore be passed to the residuary legatee and testator's heir-at-law, following where the capital was directed to go.

SIR W. PAGE WOOD V-C

The question that arises is, what is the interest of the testator's brother in the rents and profits of the real estate and the income of the personal estate under the trusts contained in the will?

It is contended, on the one hand, that the brother is only entitled to so much of the rents and profits of the real estate, and of the income of the personal estate, as would be, in the judgment of the trustees, sufficient for his "maintenance, attendance and comfort;" and that, inasmuch as he is now dead, and the trustees have adequately applied the rents and income for those purposes, the surplus passes to the residuary devisees of the real estate and the residuary legatees of the personal estate.

On the other hand, it is asserted that the bequest must be read as, in effect, a bequest entirely for the benefit of the brother; that the brother being, as it is admitted, not altogether in a sound state of mind, and not competent to direct his own affairs, the testator left his property in the hands of the trustees to apply the income for his brother's benefit; that there is, in effect, a trust extending to the whole yearly proceeds as well of the real as of the personal property for the brother's benefit; and that those who represent the brother are now entitled to the whole of the savings arising from what was his estate.

In reference to gifts of this description, there are two classes of cases between which the general distinction is sufficiently clear, although the precise line of demarcation is occasionally somewhat difficult to ascertain. If a gross sum be given, or if the whole income of the property be given, and a special purpose be assigned for that gift, this Court always regards the gift as absolute, and the purpose merely as the motive of the gift, and therefore holds that the gift takes effect as to the whole sum or the whole income, as the case may be.

Alert

Thus, where there is a gift of a sum to apprentice a child, or to buy a commission for a son, the Court gives effect to the entire gift; and, whether the sum can or cannot be applied for the purpose of buying the commission or apprenticing the child, the Court holds that the child is entitled to the whole of it... In the present case the trust is plainly very different. It is a trust to apply "the whole or any part" for the purposes specified, namely, for the maintenance, attendance and comfort of the testator's brother... The trust he has created is an absolute trust for his brother to have everything necessary for his maintenance, attendance and comfort. And, looking to that very large word "comfort", it appears to me that, if a bill had been filed on his behalf to have the whole fund applied according to this trust, it is extremely probably the Court would have directed it to be so applied. At the same time, I do not think it confers on him an absolute right to have the whole income applied, except in the event of a case being made, that the whole was wanted for the specific purposes directed by the will.

It is not the whole income that is given. It is "the whole or any part"... I do not think, therefore, that the present case is within the class of cases where an entire fund is given, and a purpose is assigned as the motive of the gift...

***Re Bowes* [1896] 1 Ch. 507**

Panel: North J

Facts: The testator died in 1885 having made a trust in his will to spend £5,000 planting trees for shelter on the Wemmergill estate. The trust was held to be a trust for the then owners of the estate to enjoy absolutely, with the planting of trees being considered a mere motive for the trust. The owners were therefore free to spend the £5,000 as they wished.

MR JUSTICE NORTH

The case is shortly this. Mr. Bowes, being tenant for life, but nothing more, speaks of this estate as part of his settled estates, which in a sense it was. His interest ceased at his death, and then the estate went to the Earl of Strathmore for life, with remainder to his issue in tail; and that course of limitation is still subsisting, though under a resettlement.

That being so, the will of Mr. Bowes contains this gift: "I bequeath to my trustees the sum of 5000l. sterling upon trust to expend the same in planting trees for shelter on the Wemmergill estate being part of my settled estates." Pausing there, I think there is as clear a trust as well can be. The will does not give them an option or choice about the matter; it directs that that sum is to be spent by them in planting trees upon the estate. I can entertain no doubt about the intention. It is common ground that the estate would hold far more trees than could possibly be put upon it for that sum, though, on the other hand, it is said it would be a very disadvantageous mode of spending that sum to apply it in planting trees even upon any part of the estate; for some reasons applicable to one part, and some to another, it is not the interest of any one that trees should be planted to so great an extent upon that estate. Still, there is a direct trust to plant. Then the testator says: "If I shall have designated in my lifetime the places where such trees should be planted then I desire my trustees and trustee to plant the same in the places which I have designated; but if I shall not have designated the places then I desire my trustees and trustee"—not for all purposes, but—"in the place and manner of planting such trees to have regard to the wishes of the person for the time being entitled to the possession of the said Wemmergill estate"; so that he considered that, though the estate was not his after his death, yet he still would have some power of control over it in giving a direction as to the places where trees should be planted by his trustees after his death; but, if he had not done so, regard should be had to the wishes of the person for the time being entitled in possession. Of course, it was not the testator's own estate; nothing could be done at all without consulting the person who was in possession of the estate, and who would have the opportunity of saying that unless the trees were planted where he liked they should not be planted at all. The 5069l. New Consols is the amount representing the fund. The question is to whom is it to belong...

Then, the sole question is where this money is to go to. Of course, it is a perfectly good legacy. There is nothing illegal in the matter, and the direction to plant might easily be carried out; but it is not necessarily capable of being performed, because the owner of the estate might say he would not have any trees planted upon it at all....

Therefore, there is nothing illegal in the gift itself; but the owners of the estate now say: "It is a very disadvantageous way of spending this money; the money is to be spent for our benefit, and that of no one else; it was not intended for any purpose other than our benefit and that of the estate. That is no reason why it should be thrown away by doing what is not for our benefit, instead of being given to us, who want to have the enjoyment of it." I think their contention is right. I think the fund is devoted to improving the estate, and improving the estate for the benefit of the persons who are absolutely entitled to it. If it had been for the benefit of or improving the estate by way of making it part of a public park or something of that sort, the case might possibly have been different... Here it is to be planted, not as part of a public trust, but for the benefit of the owners of the estate, the owner in possession being the person whose wishes are to be considered, not merely saying whether he will give leave for the planting or not, but in considering where the trees shall be planted. I consider it was for the benefit of the estate, and the persons who, for the time being, are entitled to the estate...

In *Re Andrew's Trust* [1905] 2 Ch 48, the court applied this construction to a trust fund which had been established by friends of the deceased in order to pay for the education of his infant children. The court upheld the trust as being for the children absolutely.

***Re Andrew's Trust* [1905] 2 Ch 48**

Panel: Kekewich J

Facts: A fund was subscribed by the friends of a deceased clergyman for the education of his children, all of whom were then infants. The trust deed stated that the money was not intended for the exclusive use of any one of them in particular, nor for equal division among them, but as deemed necessary to defray the expenses of all, and solely in the matter of education. The education of the children was paid for partly out of the trust fund and partly out of monies respectively coming to them under their father's will. When all the children had grown up there remained a portion of the trust fund which was unapplied, and an issue arose as to whether it belonged to the friends upon resulting trust or to the children.

MR JUSTICE KEKEWICH

The Court is asked to determine how these shares and dividends ought to be dealt with, all the children being still alive and of full age. ...

I have been referred by counsel for the applicants to *In re Trusts of the Abbott Fund* [1900] 2 Ch 326, but it is absolutely different from the case now before the Court. There a fund had been raised for the maintenance and support of two distressed ladies, and on the death of the survivor there was still money in the hands of the trustees. Stirling J held that there was a resulting trust of this balance for the subscribers. He did not think that the ladies ever became absolute owners of the fund, and probably no one reading the case is likely to differ from that conclusion. Here I am dealing with different facts, including the fact that the children are still alive, and I do not think myself much guided, and certainly not in the slightest degree bound, by the authority of that case.

It seems to me that the guiding principle is to be found in several authorities examined by Wood V-C in ... *In re Sanderson's Trust* 3 K & J 497 – and the judgment of the Vice-Chancellor in that case. One passage may be usefully cited: "There are two classes of cases between which the general distinction is sufficiently clear, although the precise line of demarcation is occasionally somewhat difficult to ascertain. If a gross sum be given, or if the whole income of the property be given, and a special purpose be assigned for that gift, this Court always regards the gift as absolute, and the purpose merely as the motive of the gift, and therefore holds that the gift takes effect as to the whole sum or the whole income, as the case may be." Here the only specified object was the education of the children. But I deem myself entitled to construe "education" in the broadest possible sense, and not to consider the purpose exhausted because the children have attained such ages that education in the vulgar sense is no longer necessary. Even if it be construed in the narrower sense it is, in Wood V-C's language, merely the motive of the gift, and the intention must be taken to have been to provide for the children in the manner (they all being then infants) most useful.

Alert

Therefore ... I am prepared to hold that the shares and accumulated dividends belong to the children, and the only remaining question is in what proportions do they take. The [trust deed] states that the fund was not subscribed for equal division, but was intended to defray the expenses of all as deemed necessary, and apparently the trustees of the fund exercised their discretion in dividing the money so far as it was divided at all. But there is no longer room for discretion, and I think the only safe course is to hold that the children are entitled to what remains in equal shares.

Mr Justice Kekewich referred to well-established authority for the proposition that an absolute gift to which an expression of purpose had been attached does not lose its true character as a gift so as to become a trust for a purpose instead. The advantage of this construction, of course, is that such a gift is not then subject at all to the rules governing purpose trusts.

The decision in *Re Andrew's Trust* was approved in more recent times by the High Court and, subsequently, the Court of Appeal in *Re Osoba (deceased), Osoba v Osoba and others* [1979] 1 WLR 247 where the Court of Appeal felt able to construe an apparent purpose trust as an absolute gift. The below extracts from both the High Court and Court of Appeal judgments give some insight into the rationale behind this.

Re Osoba (deceased), Osoba v Osoba and others **[1979] 1 WLR 791**

Panel: Megarry V-C

Facts: The testator gave a fund to his wife upon trust for her maintenance, for the training of his daughter, Abiola, up to University grade and for the maintenance of his aged mother. The testator died in 1965, having been predeceased by his mother. After his widow had died (in 1970) and Abiola had completed her University education (in 1975), the question arose as to who was entitled to the fund.

Although the purposes of maintaining the mother and widow, and of training the daughter, could no longer be carried out, the court construed these expressions of purpose as merely indicating the motive for making an absolute gift, and not as restricting the gift to those purposes only. Abiola and the personal representatives of the widow were, therefore, beneficially entitled to the residue in equal shares absolutely.

MEGARRY V-C

The central question [concerns], namely, the beneficial ownership of the residue today. The testator's wife is now dead, and Abiola's university education has finished. The residue can therefore no longer be used for any of the purposes specified in clause 5 by incorporation from clause 3. I have a formal, effective, will to construe, and not, as in *In re Abbott* and *In re Andrew's Trust,* a trust to be spelled out of informal documents. With the end of the specified purposes, ought I to hold that the residue of the beneficial interest remains undisposed of, and so passes as on intestacy, or ought I to hold that, despite the specifying of the purposes, and their determination, the widow and Abiola took the whole beneficial interest between them?

Now there are plainly some relevant distinctions between the present case and *In re Abbott* and *In re Andrew's Trust.* First, the latter cases were both what I may call "subscription" cases. The money was subscribed by living well-wishers, and so at least some were likely to be still living and able to take when the trusts failed. Here, on the other hand, I have a residuary gift made by a testator, so that if the gift fails or there is a resulting trust, there is no question of anything reverting to the testator himself. I would not place any great weight on the so-called presumption against intestacy; but I would lean towards construing a testamentary gift of residue as being wholly effective and not as leaving some part of the property given to pass as on intestacy. Second, in *In re Abbott* and *In re Andrew's Trust,* as I have indicated. the terms on which the money had been subscribed were ill-defined, and had to be collected from informal documents. In such cases I think that the court has a somewhat greater liberty of action in producing a sensible result, in the sense that the court has greater room for drawing inferences in holding what the terms of the trust are. Where, as in the present case, the court has before it a formal and operative document such as a will, then the duty of the court is merely that of construing the words used, and there is less scope for drawing inferences.

On the contrast between the two authorities I should say this. In *In re Abbott* every possible purpose for which the trust existed was at an end. The trust was for the benefit of the two ladies, and once they were dead it became impossible to use the funds for their benefit. No subscriber, touched by their plight, could very well be expected to have intended any surplus to pass under the wills or intestacies of the ladies to people who might well be totally unknown to the subscribers. In *In re Andrew's Trust,* on the other hand, the objects of the benefaction were still living. The immediate need had been to provide for their education, and that is what had prompted the subscriptions. But quite apart from "education" having an extended meaning, it seems improbable that any subscriber would have recoiled from the thought of any of the money being used for the benefit of the children after their formal education had ceased. I think that you have to look at the persons intended to benefit, and be ready, if they still can benefit, to treat the stated method of benefit as merely indicating purpose, and, no doubt, as indicating the means of benefit which are to be in the forefront. In short, if a trust is constituted for the assistance of certain persons by certain stated means there is a sharp distinction between cases where the beneficiaries have died and cases where they are still living. If they are dead, the court is ready to hold that there is a resulting trust for the donors; for the major purpose of the trust, that of providing help and benefit for the beneficiaries, comes to an end when the beneficiaries are all dead and so are beyond earthly help, whether by the stated means or otherwise. But if the beneficiaries are still living, the major purpose of providing help and benefit for the beneficiaries can still be carried out even after the stated means have all been accomplished, and so the court will be ready to treat the stated means as being merely indicative and not restrictive...

Alert

In the case before me the testator plainly intended to provide for his wife and daughter. The maintenance of his wife and the education of his daughter were obviously in the forefront of his mind; but plainly the overriding purpose was to provide for his immediate dependants. In those circumstances I should be reluctant to read his will as showing an intention that once his daughter's training up to university level was at an end she was to have nothing more, and there should be no further testamentary provision for her. I do not think that the words relating to using the residue for Abiola's training and the maintenance of the widow show that any residue not required for these purposes was to be withheld from Abiola and the widow. If the trusts had been similar to those for the ladies in In re Abbott, I would not consider that the case was appropriate for treating the expression of purposes as a mere indication of motive. Inter vivos benevolence towards those in distress is very different from testamentary provision for one's immediate family.

It accordingly seems to me that the wife and daughter became entitled to the whole of the residue between them, and, to echo Kekewich J. in In re Andrew's

Trust [1905] 2 Ch. 48, 53, I think the only safe course is to hold that they became entitled in equal shares.

This decision was subsequently appealed however Megarry V.C's judgment was upheld by the Court of Appeal (please see the extracts below from the Court of Appeal's judgment). However, the Court of Appeal held that the three named beneficiaries took the whole of the residuary estate as joint tenants. Consequently, the daughter was entitled to the whole of the residue, being the only surviving joint tenant.

***Re Osoba (deceased), Osoba v Osoba and others* [1979] 1 WLR 247**

Panel: Buckley, Goff, Eveleigh LJJ

LORD JUSTICE GOFF

...Sir Robert Megarry V-C devoted a not inconsiderable part of his judgment to an attempt to reconcile *Re Abbott Fund Trusts* [1900] 2 Ch 326 with *Re Andrew's Trust* [1905] 2 Ch 48 and to seeing which more nearly approximates to the present case. But I do not think it was really necessary for him, nor do I consider it necessary for us, to embark on any such exercise. Both cases may well have been right on their particular facts, but as Sir Robert Megarry V-C himself correctly pointed out, what has to be done in this case is to construe the will of the testator and endeavour to ascertain his intention from the words he has used, of course, in the light of such knowledge of relevant facts as we know he must have had. Those cases are relevant for present purposes so far only as they lay down any principle of construction which is applicable to the testator's will. *Re Abbott* does not, I think, do this at all. ...

Re Andrew's Trust [1905] 2 Ch 48, on the other hand, did establish a principle of construction, or rather applied one then already long established in these terms:

'There are two classes of cases between which the general distinction is sufficiently clear, although the precise line of demarcation is occasionally somewhat difficult to ascertain. If a gross sum be given, or if the whole income of the property be given, and a special purpose be assigned for that gift, this Court always regards the gift as absolute, and the purpose merely as the motive of the gift, and therefore holds that the gift takes effect as to the whole sum or the whole income as the case may be.'

Kekewich J was there himself citing from the judgment of Page Wood V-C in *Re Sanderson's Trust* ((1857) 3 K & J 497 at 503).

In my judgment the decision in the case depends on the ambit of that principle and of another one similar thereto, of which *Barlow v Grant* (1684) 1 Vern 255 is an early example, and their applicability to the testator's language in the present case. Page Wood V-C said in *Re Sanderson* ... that the principle is always applied. That, I think, was putting it too high as it is not a rule of law, but, in the absence of context, to which of course it must yield, or perhaps very special circumstances, it is a long established and oft applied principle which I would not seek to whittle away. Of course, it is possible to imagine examples where the application of the principle would appear to be ridiculous, and a number were suggested in argument. If and when such a case does in fact arise it can be argued and decided, for as I have said, the principle in *Re Sanderson* ... is not a rule of law, but in all ordinary circumstances and in the absence of a contrary context, it must in my view be applied.

The initial question of construction is, then, whether the words in this residuary clause do indicate an intention to make a gift with a superadded expression of purpose, and I start with this, that where there is but one beneficiary and the purpose is that of maintenance or education, that is tantamount to a gift to the beneficiary and the purpose is accordingly disregarded: see, for example, *Webb v Kelly* ((1839) 9 Sim 469 at 472), where Shadwell V-C said: 'I think that a gift for the maintenance and education of the legatee is an absolute gift ...'; and *Lewes v Lewes* ((1848) 16 Sim 266 at 267), where Shadwell V-C said: 'I think that there is no sensible way of dealing with this case except by taking the words "for the maintenance, clothing and education" to be equivalent to "for the benefit of the children".' If, therefore, the trust had been simply to be used for her, that is the widow's, maintenance, it seems to me that the principle of *Re Sanderson's Trust* ... , and *Barlow v Grant*, must be applied, and she would have taken the whole residue absolutely.

Then it seems to me that as a matter of construction it can make no difference that the trust was to use the property for the maintenance of the aged mother as well, for the intention to make an absolute gift is the same, albeit it is made to two people, not one only. Thus in *Presant and Presant v Goodwin*, the principle was applied to a bequest of 'all my remaining property to be invested and appropriated to the education of my sister Juliana's children as shall seem most meet and beneficial to them by the executor and executrix of this my will, recommending to them that the boys receive a classical education to fit them for the learned professions, and the girls to fit them for the purpose of teaching in respectable private families, or in schools of the first respectability'. See also per Lord Macnaghten, giving the judgment of the Privy Council in *Williams v Papworth*.

So the crux of the matter is the inclusion of 'the training of my daughter Abiola up to University grade'. ...

So in the end the primary question is short and straightforward, namely whether ... because the purpose in Abiola's case is different from that in the other two, and unlike maintenance is definitely finite though the beneficiary be still alive, the *Re Sanderson* principle is excluded, or whether ... the trust creates an absolute gift to the three named beneficiaries. ...

Having regard to Abiola's age at the date of the will, the purpose in her case is one which the testator could well have contemplated would, or might, exhaust a fair proportion of the fund. It is, moreover, one conferring an extensive and continuing benefit on Abiola, and it seems to me it is at least as much a provision for her benefit which ought to be treated as a gift with a superadded

purpose which should be disregarded, as the provision for placing out the beneficiary as an apprentice: see *Barlow v Grant* which I have already mentioned, and *Barton v Cooke*, or that of purchasing a commission in *Cope v Wilmot* ((1772); see 1 Coll 381 at 396. ...

Sir Robert Megarry V-C ... said:

'In those circumstances I should be reluctant to read his will as showing an intention that once his daughter's training up to university level was at an end she was to have nothing more, and there should be no further testamentary provision for her. I do not think that the words relating to using the residue for Abiola's training and the maintenance of the widow show that any residue not required for these purposes was to be withheld from Abiola and the widow.'

Subject to the observation that the will also provided for the mother, I would respectfully agree with that view. ...

In my judgment, therefore, on its true construction ... the will created a trust for the benefit of the widow, the daughter and the mother absolutely. ... [The] fact that the gift is to the widow in trust does not, as it seems to me, in any way prevent the named beneficiaries, including herself, from taking an absolute beneficial interest as joint tenants, or tenants in common, under the trust.

LORD JUSTICE BUCKLEY

...Had the trust for the daughter's benefit been the only trust declared in respect of the testator's residue, she would in my judgment have become entitled to the whole residue beneficially on the testator's death.

The principle of construction which applies in such cases is explained in Roper on Legacies 4th Edn (1847), p 646, where I find this:

'Where a legacy is given to a person to answer a particular purpose to which it becomes impossible to appropriate it, but from no fault of the legatee, he would be entitled to the money; as in instances of a sum of money being left for the benefit of an infant as an apprentice fee and he is never placed in the situation or character of an apprentice; or where a legacy is given to a person to assist him in defraying the expenses necessary to secure priest's orders and he becomes a lunatic—in each case the legacy will vest at the testator's death, and upon this principle: it is considered that the property was intended for the legatee at all events, and that the mode directed for its application was merely a secondary consideration and independent of the gift.'

If a testator has given the whole of a fund, whether of capital or income, to a beneficiary, whether directly or through the medium of a trustee, he is regarded, in the absence of any contra-indication, as having manifested an intention to benefit that person to the full extent of the subject-matter, notwithstanding that he may have expressly stated that the gift is made for a particular purpose, which may prove to be impossible of performance or which may not exhaust the subject-matter. This is because the testator has given the whole fund; he has not given so much of the fund as will suffice or be required to achieve the purpose, nor so much of the fund as a trustee or anyone else should determine, but the whole fund. This must be reconciled with the testator's having specified the purpose for which the gift is made. This reconciliation is achieved by treating the reference to the purpose as merely a statement of the testator's motive in making the gift. Any other interpretation of the gift would frustrate the testator's expressed intention that the whole subject-matter shall be applied for the benefit of the beneficiary. These considerations have, I think, added force where the subject-matter is the testator's residue, so that any failure of the gift would result in intestacy. The specified purpose is regarded as of less significance than the dispositive act of the testator, which sets the measure of the extent to which the testator intends to benefit the beneficiary. ...

Accordingly, in my judgment, the trust declared by ... the testator's will must take effect as a trust for all the three ladies absolutely.

Both Goff and Buckley LJJ construed the will as making an absolute gift of the property in question to the three named beneficiaries. They felt able to do this because it was entirely possible that the whole of the fund might have been needed to meet the needs of the three beneficiaries, which was inconsistent with the notion that the fund was to be used for a limited purpose and then applied elsewhere. The statement that the fund was to be used for maintenance or training (as the case might be), did not alter the position – those words were to be construed as a non-binding explanation of the testator's motive for making the gift.

Unincorporated Associations

Introduction

The law recognises individuals and companies as having separate legal personalities. Amongst other things, the concept of separate legal personality invests the 'person' in question with the ability to own property or to hold it on trust.

However, legal persons (both individual and corporate) often join together in the pursuit of common purposes, such as sporting, political or other activities. They often form clubs or other organisations in order to do so. Collectively, these are known as unincorporated associations.

6.7 What is an Unincorporated Association?

The essential characteristics of an unincorporated association were explained by Lawton LJ in *Conservative and Unionist Central Office v Burrell (Inspector of Taxes)* [1982] 1 WLR 522.

***Conservative and Unionist Central Office v Burrell (Inspector of Taxes)* [1982] 1 WLR 522**

Panel: Lawton, Brightman and Fox LJJ

Facts: For many years the Conservative and Unionist Party (the Party) has consisted of three elements, namely (i) the Parliamentary Party, i.e. the members of both Houses of Parliament who take the Conservative whip, (ii) the individual members of numerous constituency associations, the umbrella organisation for which is the National Union of Conservative and Unionist Associations, and (iii) the party headquarters, known as Central Office, which administers the party's affairs, including receiving all moneys raised by the constituency associations, investing and managing the party's funds and then distributing those funds in accordance with the directions of the party leader. Central Office was assessed to corporation tax in relation to the income which it received from the Party's funds on the basis that it was an 'unincorporated association' and so fell within the extended definition of 'company' contained in Income and Corporation Taxes Act 1970 s526(5). Central Office contended that (i) it was not itself an unincorporated association, but simply an administrative unit of the Party, (ii) even if the national union were an unincorporated association the funds did not belong to it because they were administered by Central Office, and so the national union could not be a taxable person, and (iii) the Party itself was an amorphous combination of various elements which lacked the characteristics of an unincorporated association, with the result that if the funds were owned by the Party the income arising from those funds was not assessable to corporation tax. The Court of Appeal held that the Party was not an unincorporated association.

LORD JUSTICE LAWTON

It was agreed before us that the Central Office was nothing more than an administrative unit of the [Party]. ... Both parties to this appeal asked the court to consider the legal nature of the [Party]. If it is an unincorporated association, corporation tax has to be paid on the income identified in the Party income and expenditure accounts for the relevant years as 'investment income and interest'. If it is not such an association, income tax will have to be paid on this income. ... The reason why the [Party] is contesting the assessments to corporation tax which have been made on it is that for the relevant years the rates at which corporation tax was charged were much higher than the rates for income tax. ...

I infer that by 'unincorporated association' in this context Parliament meant two or more persons bound together for one or more common purposes, not being business purposes, by mutual undertakings, each having mutual duties and obligations, in an organisation which has rules which identify in whom control of it and its funds rests and on what terms and which can be joined or left at will. ...

The Crown's main argument, however, was based on the proposition that the [Party's] unquestioned, valid control of funds could only be possible in law if it were an unincorporated association. The officers of the [Party] who receive donations, legacies and constituency association quota subscriptions for [Party] purposes could not hold them as trustees since the law does not recognise trusts for non-charitable purposes. Clearly they could not use the funds for their own purposes. The only form of holding which made legal sense, so it was submitted, was that they held the funds for the benefit of the members of the party, being an unincorporated association, to be used by them for the [Party's] purposes. I reject this argument for three reasons: first, because I find this working back kind of argument a most unsatisfactory way of establishing the existence of an association which could only have come into existence as the result of an agreement between two or more persons; second, because it disregards the history of the central funds; and, third, because it ignores what most people intend when they make donations to central funds. I have had the benefit of reading in draft Brightman LJ's analysis of the legal nature of a donation to Central Office central funds. I agree with what he will say.

LORD JUSTICE BRIGHTMAN

... So in the present case it seems to me that the status of a contribution to the Conservative Party central funds is this. The contributor draws a cheque (for example) in favour of, or hands it to, the [constituency association] treasurers. The treasurers are impliedly authorised by the contributor to present the cheque for encashment and to add the contribution to Central Office funds. Central Office funds are the subject matter of a mandate which permits them to be used for the purposes of the Conservative Party as directed by the leader of the party. The contributor cannot demand his money back once it has been added to Central Office funds. He could object if Central Office funds were used or threatened to be use otherwise than in accordance with their declared purposes, unless it is correct to say, on ordinary accounting principles, that his contribution has already passed out of Central Office funds.

This discussion of mandates, and complaining contributors, is all very remote and theoretical. No contributor to Central Office funds will view his contribution in this way, or contemplate even the remotest prospect of legal action on his part. He believes he is making an out and out contribution or gift to a political party. And so he is in practical terms. The only justification for embarking on a close analysis of the situation is the challenge, which was thrown down by counsel for the Crown ... to suggest ... [that the only] legal framework which fits the undoubted fact that funds are held by the Central Office and are administered for the use and benefit of the Conservative Party, [is] that the Conservative Party is an unincorporated association.

I see no legal difficulty in the mandate theory. It is not necessary to invent an unincorporated association in order to explain the situation.

6.8 Different Interpretations of Gifts to Unincorporated Associations

Property is often gifted to unincorporated associations. This presents two distinct sets of problems:

(a) If the gift is regarded as an attempt to transfer ownership to the unincorporated association in its own name, the gift must fail because an unincorporated association has no separate legal personality and so cannot own property in its own name; but

(b) If the gift is construed as a trust for the purposes of the association, then unless the unincorporated association is charitable, the gift may well fail for the reasons identified above on private purpose trusts, namely breach of the beneficiary principle, breach of the rule against perpetuity, or uncertainty.

To enable such gifts to be upheld, the courts have developed a number of differing ways of interpreting gifts to unincorporated associations.

***Neville Estates Ltd. v* Madden [1962] Ch. 832**

Panel: Cross J

Facts: The case concerned the sale of land which had been bought for a synagogue. In his judgment, Cross J helpfully summarised three ways in which a gift to an unincorporated association may be interpreted.

MR JUSTICE CROSS

The question of the construction and effect of gifts to or in trust for unincorporated associations was recently considered by the Privy Council in *Leahy v. Attorney-General for New South Wales*. The position, as I understand it, is as follows. Such a gift may take effect in one or other of three quite different ways. In the first place, it may, on its true construction, be a gift to the members of the association at the relevant date as joint tenants, so that any member can sever his share and claim it whether or not he continues to be a member of the association. Secondly, it may be a gift to the existing members not as joint tenants, but subject to their respective contractual rights and liabilities towards one another as members of the association. In such a ease [SIC] a member cannot sever his share. It will accrue to the other members on his death or resignation, even though such members include persons who became members after the gift took effect. If this is the effect of the gift, it will not be open to objection on the score of perpetuity or uncertainty unless there is something in its terms or circumstances or in the rules of the association which precludes the members at any given time from dividing the subject of the gift between them on the footing that they are solely entitled to it in equity.

Alert

Thirdly, the terms or circumstances of the gift or the rules of the association may show that the property in question is not to be at the disposal of the members for the time being, but is to be held in trust for or applied for the purposes of the association as a quasi-corporate entity. In this case the gift will fail unless the association is a charitable body. If the gift is of the second class, i.e., one which the members of the association for the time being are entitled to divide among themselves, then, even if the objects of the association are in themselves charitable, the gift would not, I think, be a charitable gift. If, for example, a number of persons formed themselves into an association with a charitable object - say the relief of poverty in some district - but it was part of the contract between them that, if a majority of the members so desired, the association should be dissolved and its property divided between the members at the date of dissolution, a gift to the association as part of its general funds would not, I conceive, be a charitable gift.

This summary was referred to and adopted in the later case of *Re Recher's Wills Trust* in 1972.

6.8.1 Gift for present members beneficially

This is one of the oldest bases for upholding a gift to unincorporated association. On this interpretation, a gift to an unincorporated association is treated as a gift to each of the individual members of the association.

However, this interpretation is only appropriate where the circumstances, and in particular the subject matter of the property, lend themselves to it. In *Leahy v A-G for New South Wales* [1959] AC 457 the Privy Council considered this interpretation but held that it did not apply on the facts.

Leahy v A-G for New South Wales **[1959] AC 457**

Panel: Viscount Simonds, Lord Morton of Henryton, Lord Cohen, Lord Somervell of Harrow and Lord Denning

Facts: The testator left a property, which consisted of a 730 acre farm, upon trust for the nuns or brothers of various non-charitable religious orders. One of the issues which fell to be decided was whether the gift under the will took effect as an immediate gift of the property to the nuns and brothers in those orders. The Privy Council advised that it did not.

VISCOUNT SIMONDS

The ... difficulty of solving ... [this question] ... arises out of the artificial and anomalous conception of an unincorporated society which, though it is not a separate entity in law, is yet for many purposes regarded as a continuing entity and, however inaccurately, as something other than an aggregate of its members. In law a gift to such a society simpliciter (i.e., where, to use the words of Lord Parker in *Bowman v Secular Society Ltd* [1917] AC 406, neither the circumstances of the gift nor the directions given nor the objects expressed impose on the donee the character of a trustee) is nothing else than a gift to its members at the date of the gift as joint tenants or tenants in common. ... If it is a gift to individuals, each of them is entitled to his distributive share (unless he has previously bound himself by the rules of the society that it shall be devoted to some other purpose).

The question then appears to be whether, even if the gift to a selected Order ... is prima facie a gift to the individual members of that Order, there are other considerations arising out of the terms of the will, or the nature of the society, its organisation and rules, or the subject-matter of the gift which should lead the court to conclude that, though prima facie the gift is an absolute one (absolute both in quality of estate and in freedom from restriction) to individual nuns, yet it is invalid because it is in the nature of an endowment and tends to a perpetuity or for any other reason. ...

The prima facie validity of such a gift (by which term their Lordships intend a bequest or demise) is a convenient starting point for the examination of the relevant law. For as Lord Tomlin (sitting at first instance in the Chancery Division) said in *In re Ogden* [1933] Ch 678, a gift to a voluntary association of persons for the general purposes of the association is an absolute gift and prima facie a good gift. He was echoing the words of Lord Parker in *Bowman's* case that a gift to an unincorporated association for the attainment of its purposes "may ... be upheld as an absolute gift to its members." These words must receive careful consideration, for it is to be noted that it is because the gift can be upheld as a gift to the individual members that it is valid, even though it is given for the general purposes of the association. If the words "for the general purposes of the association" were held to import a trust, the question would have to be asked, what is the trust and who are the beneficiaries? A gift can be made to persons (including a corporation) but it cannot be made to a purpose or to an object: so also, a trust may be created for the benefit of persons as *cestuis que trust* but not for a purpose or object unless the purpose or object be charitable. For a purpose or object cannot sue, but, if it be charitable, the Attorney-General can sue to enforce it. ... It is therefore by disregarding the words "for the general purposes of the association" (which are assumed not to be charitable purposes) and treating the gift as an absolute gift to individuals that it can be sustained. The same conclusion had been reached 50 years before in *Cocks v Manners* (1871) LR 12 Eq 574, where a bequest of a share of residue to the "Dominican Convent at Carisbrooke (payable to the Superior for the time being)" was held a valid gift to the individual members of that society. In that case no difficulty was created by the addition of words which might suggest that the community as a whole, not its members individually, should be the beneficiary. ...

See 'Trusts for the general purposes of the association' below

The cases that have been referred to (and many others might have been referred to in the courts of Australia, England and Ireland) are all cases in which gifts have been upheld as valid either on the ground that, where a society has been named as legatee, its members could demand that the gift should be dealt with as they should together think fit; or on the ground that a trust had been established (as in *In re Drummond*) which did not create a perpetuity. It will be sufficient to mention one only of the cases in which a different conclusion has been reached, before coming to a recent decision of the House of Lords which must be regarded as of paramount authority. In *Carne v Long* (1860) 2 De GF & J 75 the testator devised his mansion-house after the death of his wife to the trustees of the Penzance Public Library to hold to them and their successors for ever for the use, benefit, maintenance and support of the said library. It appeared that the library was established and kept on foot by the subscriptions of certain inhabitants of Penzance, that the subscribers were elected by ballot and the library managed by officers chosen from amongst themselves by the subscribers, that the property in the books and everything else belonging to the library was vested in trustees for the subscribers and that it was provided that the institution should not be broken up so long as 10 members remained. It was urged that the gift was to a number of private persons and there were in truth no other beneficiaries. But Campbell LC rejected the plea in words which, often though they have been cited, will bear repetition: "If the devise had been in favour of the existing members of the society, and they had been at liberty to dispose of the property as they might think fit, then it might, I think, have been a lawful disposition and not tending to a perpetuity. But looking to the language of the rules of this society, it is clear that the library was intended to be a perpetual institution, and the testator must be presumed to have known what the regulations were." This was perhaps a clear case where both from the terms of the gift and the nature of the society a perpetuity was indicated.

[I] must now turn to the recent case of *In re Macaulay's Estate*, which appears to be reported only in a footnote to *In re Price* [1943] Ch 422. There the gift was to the Folkestone Lodge of the Theosophical Society absolutely for the maintenance and improvement of the Theosophical Lodge at Folkestone. It was assumed that the donee, "the Lodge," was a body of persons. The decision of the House of Lords ... was that the gift was invalid. ... A passage from the judgment of Lord Hanworth MR (which has been obtained from the records) may usefully be cited. He said: "The problem may be stated in this way. If the gift is in truth to the present members of the society described by their society name so that they have the beneficial use of the property and can, if they please, alienate and put the proceeds in their own pocket, then there is a present gift to individuals which is good: but if the gift is intended for the good not only of the present but of future members so that the present members are in the position of trustees and have no right to appropriate the property or its proceeds for their personal benefit then the gift is invalid. ..."

... At the risk of repetition their Lordships would point out that, if a gift is made to individuals, whether under their own names or in the name of their society, and the conclusion is reached that they are not intended to take beneficially, then they take as trustees. If so, it must be ascertained who are the beneficiaries. If at the death of the testator the class of beneficiaries is fixed and ascertained or ascertainable within the limit of the rule against perpetuities, all is well. If it is not so fixed and not so ascertainable the trust must fail. Of such a trust no better example could be found than a gift to an Order for the benefit of a community of nuns, once it is established that the community is not confined to living and ascertained persons. A wider question is opened if it appears that the trust is not for persons but for a non-charitable purpose. As has been pointed out, no one can enforce such a trust.

Alert

It must now be asked, then, whether in the present case there are sufficient indications to displace the prima facie conclusion that the gift ... is to the individual members of the selected Order ... at the date of the testator's death so that they can together dispose of it as they think fit. It appears to their Lordships that such indications are ample.

In the first place, it is not altogether irrelevant that the gift is in terms upon trust for a selected Order. It is true that this can in law be regarded as a trust in favour of each and every member of the Order. But at least the form of the gift is not to the members, and it may be questioned whether the testator understood the niceties of the law. In the second place, the members of the selected Order may be numerous, very numerous perhaps, and they may be spread over the world. If the gift is to the individuals it is to all the members who were living at the death of the testator, but only to them. It is not easy to believe that the testator intended an "immediate beneficial legacy" ... to such a body of beneficiaries. ... In the third place, the subject-matter of the gift cannot be ignored. It appears from the evidence filed in the suit that Elmslea is a grazing property of about 730 acres, with a furnished homestead containing 20 rooms and a number of outbuildings. With the greatest respect to those judges who have taken a different view, their Lordships do not find it possible to regard all the individual members of an Order as intended to become the beneficial owners of such a property. Little or no evidence has been given about the organisation and rules of the several Orders, but it is at least permissible to doubt whether it is a common feature of them, that all their members regard themselves or are to be regarded as having the capacity of (say) the Corps of Commissionaires (see *In re Clarke*) to put an end to their association and distribute its assets. On the contrary, it seems reasonably clear that, however little the testator understood the effect in law of a gift to an unincorporated body of persons by their society name, his intention was to create a trust, not merely for the benefit of the existing members of the selected Order, but for its benefit as a continuing society and for the furtherance of its work. ... "

6.8.2 Gift to members subject to the rules of the association

This interpretation, known as the 'contractual analysis' represents the 'prevailing view' under which gifts in favour of an unincorporated association may be upheld. On this interpretation, a gift to an unincorporated association is treated as a gift to each of the individual members of the association, *but* (and in contrast to the previous interpretation) the members do not 'pocket' their share immediately. Instead, they take the gift subject to their mutual duties and obligations under the membership rules of the association.

***Artistic Upholstery Ltd v Art Forma (Furniture) Ltd* [1999] 4 All ER 277**

Panel: Lawrence Collins QC sitting as a deputy judge of the High Court

Facts: The claimant (Artistic) was one of the members of an unincorporated association (the Guild). For many years the Guild had organised trade exhibitions on behalf of its members under the name 'Long Point'. The defendant (Art Forma) was a former member of the Guild. Following its expulsion from the Guild, it had registered the name 'Long Point' as a trade mark. Artistic brought proceedings on behalf of itself and all the other members of the Guild to restrain Art Forma from using the name 'Long Point' in connection with its business. This raised the question as to whether an unincorporated association could own intellectual property, which required a consideration of the nature of an unincorporated association and the legal basis (if any) on which it could hold property of any kind. The judge endorsed the contractual analysis and held that intellectual property was capable of being owned by an unincorporated association.

LAWRENCE COLLINS QC sitting as a deputy judge of the High Court

... An unincorporated association is not, of course, a legal person. In *Currie v Barton* (1988) Times, 12 February, O'Connor LJ said, in relation to unincorporated associations, the law ... 'does not recognise that those bodies have any corporate or separate legal existence. They cannot be sued or sue in their own names. You cannot make a contract with the body, because in law it does not exist. It consists of all its members.'

The rights of members as between themselves are contractual. In *Re Bucks Constabulary Widows' and Orphans' Fund Friendly Society, Thompson v Holdsworth (No 2)* [1979] 1 WLR 936, Walton J said that judicial opinion ... 'is now firmly set along the lines that the interests and rights of persons who are members of any type of unincorporated association are governed exclusively by contract, that is to say rights between themselves and their rights to any surplus assets.'

Walton J had followed *Re Recher's Will Trusts, National Westminster Bank Ltd v National Anti-Vivisection Society Ltd* [1972] Ch 526, where Brightman J said, in the context of an association formed for a non-charitable purposes:

Link
See the extract from *Re Recher* below.

'Such an association of persons is bound ... to have some sort of constitution; ie the rights and liabilities of the members of the association will inevitably depend on some form of contract inter se, usually evidenced by a set of rules.'

Since there are substantial associations with a large (and changing) membership, holding property in the form of subscriptions or donations or association premises, it has been necessary to develop a legal analysis which will provide a practical solution to the problem that an unincorporated association, as such, has no capacity to hold property. Several solutions have been developed, including treating the members as holding as joint tenants, or having trustees holding on trust for the members or for the purposes of the

association. But the prevailing view is that, at least where there are no appointed trustees to hold the property of the association, or where a transfer of property has not been accompanied by a valid declaration of trust, personal property will be held under the express or implied terms of the contract of the members inter se. Thus, in *Re Recher's Will Trusts*, when the association received a donation which was not accompanied by words which purported to impose a trust, the gift took effect 'in favour of the existing members of the association as an accretion to the funds which are the subject-matter of the contract which such members have made inter se' ... . Brightman J followed the decision of Cross J in *Neville Estates Ltd v Madden* [1962] Ch 832 ... , who had analysed the proprietary effects of a gift to an unincorporated association; one of the ways in which it could take effect was as a gift to the members not as joint tenants, but subject to their rights and liabilities towards one another as members of the association: in such a case the member could not sever his share.

In the *Bucks Constabulary case* ... Walton J applied *Re Recher's Will Trusts* in the context of a friendly society and said:

'... all unincorporated societies rest in contract to this extent, that there is an implied contract between all the members inter se governed by the rules of the society. In default of any rule to the contrary, and it will seldom if ever be that there is such a rule, when a member ceases to be a member of the association he ipso facto ceases to have any interest in its funds.'

Consequently, even though an unincorporated association as such cannot hold property because it is not a legal person, property can be held by the members subject to the express or implied terms of the contract into which they enter with one another upon becoming members. ...

It follows from the authorities to which I have referred, and from the constitution and rules of the guild, that if the goodwill which is the foundation of a claim in passing off is to be regarded as property (as it plainly is ...), then an unincorporated association, such as the guild, through its members, may own goodwill which could found an action in passing off. The goodwill is held by the members as their property in that capacity in accordance with the constitution and rules.

So, in the absence of any evidence that the property is intended to be held upon trust, a gift to an unincorporated association should ordinarily be interpreted as a gift to the members subject to the rules of the association.

However, there will be circumstances where such an interpretation is not possible, for example where:

- The association has ceased to exist: see *In re Recher's Will Trusts National Westminster Bank Ltd v National Anti-Vivisection Society Ltd and Others* [1972] Ch 526.

- The association has no identifiable rules – in *Leahy*, for example, there was little or no evidence as to the rules of the relevant Orders.

- The rules of the association do not give it a sufficient degree of control over its assets: see *Re Grant's Will Trusts* [1980] 1 WLR 360 below.

In re Recher's Will Trusts National Westminster Bank Ltd v National Anti-Vivisection Society Ltd and Others **[1972] Ch 526**

Panel: Brightman J

Facts: By her will, the testatrix left a portion of her residuary estate to an unincorporated association ('the London & Provincial Anti-Vivisection Society') which had ceased to exist by the time of her death because its affairs had been transferred to a larger association ('the National Anti-Vivisection Society'). The issue for determination was whether the gift was held for the surviving association or whether it failed. The court held that the gift failed.

MR JUSTICE BRIGHTMAN

Having reached the conclusion that the gift in question is not a gift to the members of the London & Provincial society at the date of death, as joint tenants or tenants in common, so as to entitle a member as of right to a distributive share, nor an attempted gift to present and future members beneficially, and is not a gift in trust for the purposes of the society, I must now consider how otherwise, if at all, it is capable of taking effect. ...

A trust for non-charitable purposes, as distinct from a trust for individuals, is clearly void because there is no beneficiary. It does not, however, follow that persons cannot band themselves together as an association or society, pay subscriptions and validly devote their funds in pursuit of some lawful non-charitable purpose. An obvious example is a members' social club. But it is not essential that the members should only intend to secure direct personal advantages to themselves. The association may be one in which personal advantages to the members are combined with the pursuit of some outside purpose. Or the association may be one which offers no personal benefit at all to the members, the funds of the association being applied exclusively to the pursuit of some outside purpose. Such an association of persons is bound, I would think, to have some sort of constitution; that is to say, the rights and liabilities of the members of the association will inevitably depend on some form of contract inter se, usually evidenced by a set of rules. In the present case it appears to me clear that the life members, the ordinary members and the associate members of the London & Provincial society were bound together by a contract inter se. Any such member was entitled to the rights and subject to the liabilities defined by the rules. If the committee acted contrary to the rules, an individual member would be entitled to take proceedings in the courts to compel observance of the rules or to recover damages for any loss he had suffered as a result of the breach of contract. As and when a member paid his subscription to the association, he would be subjecting his money to the disposition and expenditure thereof laid down by the rules. That is to say, the member would be bound to permit, and entitled to require, the honorary trustees and other members of the society to deal with that subscription in accordance with the lawful directions of the committee. Those directions would include the expenditure of that subscription, as part of the general funds of the association, in furthering the objects of the association. The resultant situation, on analysis, is that the London & Provincial society represented an organisation of individuals bound together by a contract under which their subscriptions became, as it were, mandated towards a certain type of expenditure ... . Just as the two parties to a bi-partite bargain can vary or terminate their contract by mutual assent, so it must follow that the life members, ordinary members and associate members of the London & Provincial society could, at any moment of time, by unanimous agreement (or by majority vote, if the rules so prescribe), vary or terminate their multi-partite contract. There would be no limit to the type of variation or termination to which all might agree. There is no private trust or trust for charitable purposes or other trust to hinder the process. It follows that if all members agreed, they could decide to wind up the London & Provincial society and divide the net assets among themselves beneficially. No one would have any locus standi to stop them so doing. The contract is the same as any other contract and concerns only those who are parties to it, that is to say, the members of the society.

The funds of such an association may, of course, be derived not only from the subscriptions of the contracting parties but also from donations from non-contracting parties and legacies from persons who have died. In the case of a donation which is not accompanied by any words which purport to impose a trust, it seems to me that the gift takes effect in favour of the existing members of the association as an accretion to the funds which are the subject-matter of the contract which such members have made inter se, and falls to be dealt with in precisely the same way as the funds which the members themselves have subscribed. So, in the case of a legacy. In the absence of words which purport to impose a trust, the legacy is a gift to the members beneficially, not as joint tenants or as tenants in common so as to entitle each member to an immediate distributive share, but as an accretion to the funds which are the subject-matter of the contract which the members have made inter se.

In my judgment the legacy in the present case to the London & Provincial society ought to be construed as a legacy of that type, that is to say, a legacy to the members beneficially as an accretion to the funds subject to the contract which they had made inter se. Of course, the testatrix did not intend the members of the society to divide her bounty between themselves, and doubtless she was ignorant of that remote but theoretical possibility. Her knowledge or absence of knowledge of the true legal analysis of the gift is irrelevant. The legacy is accordingly in my view valid, subject only to the effect of the [dissolution of the London & Provincial society]. ...

In my judgment the London & Provincial society was dissolved on January 1, 1957, and the contract theretofore binding persons together, under the name and according to the rules of the London & Provincial society, was terminated. The position after 1956 was that all the members of the London & Provincial society lost their rights and shed their obligations under that contract, and some of such persons, namely, the life and ordinary members of the London & Provincial society (or those who wished) automatically acceded to another association of persons who were then bound together by another contract, namely, the National society, and assumed the rights and obligations attaching to members of that association. What I find in the will is a gift to the members of the London & Provincial society as an accretion to the funds subject to the contract between such members. In my judgment, I am not entitled to construe that gift as a gift to the members of a different association as an accretion to the funds subject to a different contract. ...

***Re Grant's Will Trusts* [1980] 1 WLR 360**

Panel: Vinelott J

Facts: By his will, the testator made a gift of a property to the Chertsey and Walton Constituency Labour Party (CLP) for use as its headquarters. The rules governing CLP were in the model form issued by the national Labour Party (NLP). Those rules could be changed at any time by NLP and CLP was obliged to conform to any changes. One of the rules provided that a constituency party could not deal with any property, nor make any changes to its rules, without the approval of NLP. Mr Justice Vinelott held that in those circumstances CLP lacked the necessary degree of control over its own assets to permit the contractual analysis to be applied. Reference to the 'first', 'second' and 'third' categories are to the categories outlined by Cross J in *Neville Estates Ltd v Madden* (see above).

MR JUSTICE VINELOTT

The question raised by the summons is whether the gift in the will of the testator's real and personal estate is a valid gift, or is void for uncertainty or for perpetuity or otherwise; and if it is a valid gift who are the persons entitled to benefit thereunder...

In a case in the first category, that is a gift which, on its true construction, is a gift to members of an association who take as joint tenants, any member being able to sever his share, the association is used in effect as a convenient label or definition of the class which is intended to take; but, the class being ascertained, each member takes as joint tenant free from any contractual fetter. So, for instance, a testator might give a legacy or share of residue to a dining or social club of which he had been a member with the intention of giving to each of the other members an interest as joint tenant, capable of being severed, in the subject-matter of the gift. Cases within this category are relatively uncommon. A gift to an association will be more frequently found to fall within the second category. There the gift is to members of an association, but the property is given as an accretion to the funds of the association so that the property becomes subject to the contract (normally evidenced by the rules of the association) which governs the rights of the members inter se. Each member is thus in a position to ensure that the subject matter of the gift is applied in accordance with the rules of the association, in the same way as any other funds of the association. This category is well illustrated by the decision of Brightman J in *Re Recher's Will Trusts*. ...

Alert

It must, as I see it, be a necessary characteristic of any gift within the second category that the members of the association can by an appropriate majority (if the rules so provide), or acting unanimously if they do not, alter their rules so as to provide that the funds, or part of them, shall be applied for some new purpose, or even distributed amongst the members for their own benefit. For the validity of a gift within this category rests essentially on the fact that the testator has set out to further a purpose by making a gift to the members of an association formed for the furtherance of that purpose in the expectation that, although the members at the date when the gift takes effect will be free, by a majority if the rules so provide or acting unanimously if they do not, to dispose of the fund in any way they may think fit, they and any future members of the association will not in fact do so but will employ the property in the furtherance of the purpose of the association and will honour any special condition attached to the gift.

Turning to the third category, the testator may seek to further the purpose by giving a legacy to an association as a quasi-corporate entity, that is to present and future members indefinitely, or by purporting to impose a trust. In the former case the gift will fail for perpetuity, unless confined within an appropriate period; though if it is so confined and if the members for the time being within the perpetuity period are free to alter the purposes for which the property is to be used and to distribute the income amongst themselves it will not, as I see it, fail on any other ground. In the latter case, the gift will fail on the ground that the court cannot compel the use of the property in furtherance of a stated purpose unless, of course, the purpose is a charitable one. ...

I have also been referred to the recent decision of Goff J in *Re Denley's Trust Deed*. There by clause 2 of a trust deed trustees were given powers of sale over land held by them and were directed to hold the land while unsold during a defined perpetuity period on trust ...

Goff J, having held that the words '... secondarily for the benefit of such other person or persons (if any) as the trustees may allow to use the same' conferred on the trustees a power operating in partial defeasance of a trust in favour of the employees, held that the trust deed created a valid trust for the benefit of the employees, the benefit being the right to use the land subject to and in accordance with the rules made by the trustees. That case on a proper analysis, in my judgment, falls altogether outside the categories of gifts to unincorporated associations and purpose trusts. I can see no distinction in principle between a trust to permit a class defined by reference to employment to use and enjoy land in accordance with rules to be made at the discretion of trustees on the one hand, and, on the other hand, a trust to distribute income at the discretion of trustees amongst a class, defined by reference to, for example, relationship to the settlor. In both cases the benefit to be taken by any member of the class is at the discretion of the trustees, but any member of the class can apply to the court to compel the trustees to administer the trust in accordance with its terms. As Goff J pointed out ([1968] 3 All ER 65 at 72, [1969] 1 Ch 373 at 388):

'The same kind of problem is equally capable of arising in the case of a trust to permit a number of persons - for example, all the unmarried children of a testator or settlor - to use or occupy a house, or to have the use of certain chattels; nor can I assume that in such cases agreement between the parties concerned would be more likely, even if that be a sufficient distinction, yet no one would suggest, I fancy, that such a trust would be void.' ...

Reading the gift in the will in the light of the rules governing the Chertsey and Walton Constituency Labour Party, it is in my judgment impossible to construe the gift as a gift made to the members of the Chertsey and Walton Constituency Labour Party at the date of the testator's death with the intention that it should belong to them as a collection of individuals, though in the expectation that they and any other members subsequently admitted would ensure that it was in fact used for what in broad terms has been labelled 'headquarters' purposes' of the Chertsey and Walton Constituency Labour Party.

I base this conclusion on two grounds. First, the members of [the Chertsey and Walton Constituency Labour Party] do not control the property, given by subscription or otherwise, to ... [it]. The rules which govern [the Chertsey and Walton Constituency Labour Party] are capable of being altered by an outside body which could direct an alteration under which the general committee of [the Chertsey and Walton Constituency Labour Party] would be bound to transfer any property for the time being held for the benefit of [the Chertsey and Walton Constituency Labour Party] to [the national Labour Party] for national purposes. The members of [the Chertsey and Walton Constituency Labour Party] could not alter the rules so as to make the property bequeathed by the testator applicable for some purpose other than that provided by the rules; nor could they direct that property to be divided amongst themselves beneficially.

Brightman J observed in *Re Recher's Will Trusts* ([1971] 3 All ER 401 at 405, [1972] Ch 526 at 536) that: 'It would astonish a layman to be told there was a difficulty in his giving a legacy to an unincorporated non-charitable society which he had or could have supported without trouble during his lifetime.' The answer to this apparent paradox is, it seems to me, that subscriptions by members of the Chertsey and Walton CLP must be taken as made on terms that they will be applied by the general committee in accordance with the rules for the time being, including any modifications imposed by the annual party conference or the NEC. In the event of the dissolution of the Chertsey and Walton CLP any remaining fund representing subscriptions would (as the rules now stand) be held on a resulting trust for the original subscribers. Thus although the members of the CLP may not be able themselves to alter the purposes for which a fund representing subscriptions is to be used or to alter the rules so as to make such a fund divisible amongst themselves the ultimate proprietary right of the original subscribers remains. There is, therefore, no perpetuity and no non-charitable purpose trust. But if that analysis of the terms on which subscriptions are held is correct, it is fatal to the argument that the gift in the testator's will should be construed as a gift to the members of the Chertsey and Walton CLP at the testator's death, subject to a direction not amounting to a trust that it be used for headquarters' purposes. Equally it is in my judgment impossible, in particular having regard to the gift over to the national Labour Party, to read the gift as a gift to the members of the national Labour Party at the testator's death, with a direction not amounting to a trust, that the national party permit it to be used by the Chertsey and Walton CLP for headquarters' purposes.

That first ground is of itself conclusive, but there is another ground which reinforces this conclusion. The gift is not in terms a gift to the Chertsey and Walton CLP, but to the Labour Party Property Committee, who are to hold the property for the benefit of, that is in trust for, the Chertsey headquarters of the Chertsey and Walton CLP. The fact that a gift is a gift to trustees and not in terms to an unincorporated association militates against construing it as a gift to the members of the association at the date when the gift takes effect, and against construing the words indicating the purposes for which the property is to be used as expressing the testator's intention or motive in making the gift and not as imposing any trust. This was, indeed, one of the considerations which led the Privy Council in Leahy's case to hold that the gift '... upon trust for such Order of Nuns of the Catholic Church or the Christian Brothers as my Executors and Trustees should select' would, apart from the Australian equivalent of the Charitable Trusts (Validation) Act 1954, have been invalid.

I am, therefore, compelled to the conclusion that the gift of the testator's estate fails, and that his estate accordingly devolves as on intestacy."

The contractual analysis presupposes that the members of an unincorporated association are bound together by rules which they are able to determine and which allow them to 'own' or 'share in' the association's property in whatever manner they choose. This essential element of internal control or self-determination was clearly absent in *Re Grant*, because the facts established that the constituency party did not have control over its rules nor, as a consequence, over any property which it owned. As a result, the contractual analysis could not be invoked to uphold the validity of the gift.

***Re Horley Town Football Club, Hunt and another v McLaren and others* [2006] EWHC 2386 (Ch), [2006] WTLR 1817**

Panel: Lawrence Collins J

Facts: Horley Town FC (the Club) was an unincorporated association. The Club's trustees held its ground, clubhouse and other assets upon trust for the Club for a defined perpetuity period. The membership was divided into full members, temporary members and associate members. Guests and visitors were entitled to temporary membership, whereas associate membership was available to anyone who was a member 'of any independently constituted club invited to use the facilities' of the Club. The various categories of membership appeared to have been created to ensure compliance with the then licensing laws. Full members were each entitled to one vote at annual general meetings, whereas associate members were restricted to one vote per independently constituted club. The court was required to determine to whom the Club's assets would belong upon expiry of the perpetuity period. The judge held that the assets belonged to the full members alone.

MR JUSTICE LAWRENCE COLLINS

I am satisfied that the Deed should be construed as a gift to the Club, as a "contract-holding" gift to the Club and its members for the time being within category (2) in *Neville Estates v Madden*.

If the gift is construed in this way, perpetuity is not a problem, because the gift to the members is not, on a true construction, contingent, under the rule in *Boraston's* case: Hawkins and Ryder, Construction of Wills, paras 20-40 et seq. The interests of the members of the Club under cl 3 nevertheless vest immediately. Their interests as members devolve with the other Club property under the Club rules. Nor can the gift be characterised as uncertain.

As Vinelott J said in *Re Grant's Will Trusts* ... it is a necessary characteristic of any [such] gift ... that the members of the association can, in accordance with the rules, direct that the funds should be applied to some new purpose or distributed among the members for their own benefit.

Alert

I do not consider that it matters that the Rules were changed in 2000 to confer a right to vote on a body which is not itself a member, namely the club of which Associate Members are members. This is far from the case of Re Grant's Will Trusts, where Vinelott J held that the influence of a body (not itself a member) on the rules and the destination of Club property was fatal to the argument that a gift should be analysed as one within the second class identified in Neville Estates v Madden. ...

Link
See Distribution of assets below.

The next question is the identity of the persons who hold the beneficial interest. I am satisfied that the beneficial ownership is in the current full members (and not the temporary or associate members), and is held on bare trust for them. The members hold subject to the current rules, and could unanimously or by AGM call for the assets to be transferred. Adult and senior members are entitled to share in distribution on per capita basis.

In my judgment I should adopt the same approach as Sir Robert Megarry in taking a "broad sword" and applying fairness and common sense. In my judgment it does not make a difference that in the present case the Rules say in r 4 that the Club shall consist of "members and temporary members"; or in r 5 provide that Associate Members will enjoy the same rights as full members except those relating to voting rights; or that r 15 gives a right to vote to "independently constituted clubs enjoying Associate Membership". I would accept that a mere inequality in voting rights would not mean that a category of members is excluded altogether from any entitlement to the surplus assets of the association upon its dissolution. But the associate members in the present case have no effective rights and it would be wholly unrealistic to treat the introduction of associate members by amendment of the Rules as a transfer of the Club's property to them.

The consequence would be that the beneficial ownership is held on bare trust for the members, who could either unanimously or at an AGM call for the assets to be transferred.

All the sets of Rules, including the 2004 Rules, provide for amendment of the Rules by AGM. The members may agree to dissolve the Club and to distribute the assets amongst themselves or the association may be wound up by the court: *Re Lead Co's Workmen's Fund Society* [1904] 2 Ch 196; *Neville Estates v Madden* [1962] Ch 832, 849; *Re Recher* [1972] Ch 526, 538-539. The Rules do not specify how the Club's assets are to be distributed following dissolution. In the absence of any rule to the contrary, there is to be implied into the rules of the Club a rule to the effect that the surplus funds of the Club should be divided on a dissolution amongst the members of the Club, and this distribution will normally be per capita among the members (irrespective of length of membership or the amount of subscriptions paid) but may reflect different classes of membership: *Re Sick and Funeral Society of St John's Sunday School, Golcar* [1973] Ch 51, at 60, [1972] 2 All ER 439, [1972] 2 WLR 962; *Re Bucks Constabulary Widows' and Orphans' Fund Friendly Society (No 2)* [1979] 1 WLR 936, at 952; *Re GKN Bolts & Nuts Ltd etc Sports & Social Club* [1982] 1 WLR 774, at 778.

In the light of these decisions and in the light of my conclusion on temporary and associate members, the persons entitled to share in a distribution would be the adult and senior members of the Club on a per capita basis.

It is not necessary to consider whether the gift took effect as a *Re Denley* trust for the benefit of the members for the time being of the Club. The existence of the Associate Members and temporary members would not in itself prevent the adoption of such a construction: the existence of those members could properly be overlooked on the basis that they are not within the class of persons for whose benefit the property is held upon trust. But there are difficulties with regard to termination of such a trust which make it an unsafe basis for decision: see Thomas and Hudson, The Law of Trusts (2004), para 6.21."

Although the judge deals with the point rather briefly, and does not offer any specific reasons for his decision on this point, his conclusion is clear enough: the mere fact that the membership of the Club included other clubs, each with their own rules and members, did not breach the 'control' requirement set out in *Re Grant*. It seems probable that the judge recognised that in this case the full members retained effective voting power over the association's property because the number of associate members was very small compared to the number of full members, whereas in *Re Grant* the members of the constituency Labour party (who were the equivalent of the full members in this case) had *no* effective voting rights at all over constituency property.

6.9 *Re Denley* Purpose Trust

However, as also discussed above, there is one species of private purpose trust which may not fall foul of the beneficiary principle, namely a Re Denley purpose trust, i.e. a purpose trust which is directly or indirectly for the benefit of an ascertainable individual or individuals.

Link
See *Re Denley* in Chapter 6

The *Re Denley* approach was applied to unincorporated associations in *Re Lipinski's Will Trusts, Gosschalk v Levy* [1976] Ch 235.

***Re Lipinski's Will Trusts, Gosschalk v Levy* [1976] Ch 235**

Panel: Oliver J

Facts: By his will, the testator bequeathed part of his residuary estate to trustees on trust as to one half for the Hull Judeans (Maccabi) Association, which provided social, cultural and sporting activities for Jewish youth in Hull, to be used in constructing and/or improving new buildings for the association. The gift was valid.

JUSTICE OLIVER MR

... [T]his is a gift to an unincorporated non-charitable association. Such a gift, if it is an absolute and beneficial one, is of course perfectly good see, for instance, the gift to the Corps of Commissionaires in *In re Clarke* [1901] 2 Ch 110. What I have to consider, however, is the effect of the specification by the testator of the purposes for which the legacy was to be applied. ...

The principles applicable to this type of case were stated by Cross J in *Neville Estates Ltd v Madden* [1962] Ch 832, 849, and they are conveniently summarised in Tudor, Charities, 6th ed. (1967), p 150, where it is said:

"In *Neville Estates Ltd v Madden* Cross J expressed the opinion (which is respectfully accepted as correct) that every such gift might, according to the actual words used, be construed in one of three quite different ways: (a) As a gift to the members of the association at the date of the gift as joint tenants so that any member could sever his share and claim it whether or not he continued to be a member. (b) As a gift to the members of the association at the date of the gift not as joint tenants, but subject to their contractual rights and liabilities towards one another as members of the association. In such a case a member cannot sever his share. It will accrue to the other members on his death or resignation, even though such members include persons who become members after the gift took effect. If this is the effect of the gift, it will not be open to objection on the score of perpetuity or uncertainty unless there is something in its terms or circumstances or in the rules of the association which precludes the members at any given time from dividing the subject of the gift between them on the footing that they are solely entitled to it in equity. (c) The terms or circumstances of the gift or the rules of the association may show that the property in question - i.e., the subject of the gift - is not to be at the disposal of the members for the time being but is to be held in trust for or applied for the purposes of the association as a quasi-corporate entity. In this case the gift will fail unless the association is a charitable body."

That summary may require, I think, a certain amount of qualification in the light of subsequent authority, but for present purposes I can adopt it as a working guide. Mr Blackburne, for the next-of-kin, argues that the gift in the present case clearly does not fall within the first category, and that the addition of the specific direction as to its employment by the association prevents it from falling into the second category. This is, therefore, he says, a purpose trust and fails both for that reason and because the purpose is perpetuitous. He relies upon this passage from the judgment of the Board in *Leahy v Attorney-General for New South Wales* [1959] AC 457, 478:

"If the words 'for the general purposes of the association' were held to import a trust, the question would have to be asked, what is the trust and who are the beneficiaries? A gift can be made to persons (including a corporation) but it cannot be made to a purpose or to an object: so also, a trust may be created for the benefit of persons as *cestuis que trust* but not for a purpose or object unless the purpose or object be charitable. For a purpose or object cannot sue, but, if it be charitable, the Attorney-General can sue to enforce it."

Mr Blackburne points out, first, that the gift is in memory of the testator's late wife (which, he says, suggests an intention to create a permanent memorial or endowment); secondly, that the gift is solely for a particular purpose (which would militate strongly against any suggestion that the donees could wind up and pocket the money themselves, even though their constitution may enable them to do so); and, thirdly, that the gift contemplates expenditure on "improvements," which connotes a degree of continuity or permanence. All this, he says, shows that what the testator had in mind was a permanent endowment in memory of his late wife.

For my part, I think that very little turns upon the testator's having expressed the gift as being in memory of his late wife. I see nothing in this expression which suggests any intention to create a permanent endowment. It indicates merely, I think, a tribute which the testator wished to pay, and it is not without significance that this self-same tribute appeared in the earlier will in which he made an absolute and outright gift to the association. The evidential value of this in the context of a construction summons may be open to doubt, and I place no reliance upon it. It does, however, seem to me that nothing is to be derived from these words beyond the fact that the testator wished the association to know that his bounty was a tribute to his late wife.

I accept, however, Mr Blackburne's submission that the designation of the sole purpose of the gift makes it impossible to construe the gift as one falling into the first of Cross J's categories, even if that were otherwise possible. But I am not impressed by the argument that the gift shows an intention of continuity. Mr Blackburne prays in aid *In re Macaulay's Estate* [1943] Ch 435 which is reported as a note to *In re Price* [1943] Ch 422, where the gift was for the "maintenance and improvement of the Theosophical Lodge at Folkestone." The House of

Lords held that it failed for perpetuity, the donee being a non-charitable body. But it is clear from the speeches of both Lord Buckmaster and Lord Tomlin that their Lordships derived the intention of continuity from the reference to "maintenance." Here it is quite evident that the association was to be free to spend the capital of the legacy. ...

But that is not the end of the matter. If the gift were to the association simpliciter, it would, I think, clearly fall within the second category of Cross J's categories. At first sight, however, there appears to be a difficulty in arguing that the gift is to members of the association subject to their contractual rights inter se when there is a specific direction or limitation sought to be imposed upon those contractual rights as to the manner in which the subject matter of the gift is to be dealt with. This, says Mr Blackburne, is a pure "purpose trust" and is invalid on that ground, quite apart from any question of perpetuity. I am not sure, however, that it is sufficient merely to demonstrate that a trust is a "purpose" trust. ...

There would seem to me to be, as a matter of common sense, a clear distinction between the case where a purpose is prescribed which is clearly intended for the benefit of ascertained or ascertainable beneficiaries, particularly where those beneficiaries have the power to make the capital their own, and the case where no beneficiary at all is intended (for instance, a memorial to a favourite pet) or where the beneficiaries are unascertainable: as in the case, for instance, of *In re Price* [1943] Ch 422. If a valid gift may be made to an unincorporated body as a simple accretion to the funds which are the subject matter of the contract which the members have made inter se – and *Neville Estates Ltd v Madden* [1962] Ch 832 and *In re Recher's Will Trusts* [1972] Ch 526 show that it may - I do not really see why such a gift, which specifies a purpose which is within the powers of the association and of which the members of the association are the beneficiaries, should fail. Why are not the beneficiaries able to enforce the trust or, indeed, in the exercise of their contractual rights, to terminate the trust for their own benefit? Where the donee association is itself the beneficiary of the prescribed purpose, there seems to me to be the strongest argument in common sense for saying that the gift should be construed as an absolute one within the second category - the more so where, if the purpose is carried out, the members can by appropriate action vest the resulting property in themselves, for here the trustees and the beneficiaries are the same persons.

Is such a distinction as I have suggested borne out by the authorities? The answer is, I think, "not in terms," until recently. But the cases appear to me to be at least consistent with this. For instance, *In re Clarke* [1901] 2 Ch 110 (the case of the Corps of Commissionaires); *In re Drummond* [1914] 2 Ch 90 (the case of the Old Bradfordians) and *In re Taylor* [1940] Ch 481 (the case of the Midland Bank Staff Association), in all of which the testator had prescribed purposes for which the gifts were to be used, and in all of which the gifts were upheld, were all cases where there were ascertainable beneficiaries; whereas in *In re Wood* [1949] Ch 498 and *Leahy's* case (where the gifts failed) there were none. *In re Price* is perhaps out of line, because there, there was no ascertained beneficiary and yet Cohen J was prepared to uphold the gift even on the supposition that (contrary to his own conclusion) the purpose was non-charitable. But, as I have mentioned, the point about the trust being a purpose trust was not argued before him.

A striking case which seems to be not far from the present is *In re Turkington* [1937] 4 All ER 501, where the gift was to a masonic lodge "as a fund to build a suitable temple in Stafford." The members of the lodge being both the trustees and the beneficiaries of the temple, Luxmoore J construed the gift as an absolute one to the members of the lodge for the time being.

Directly in point is the more recent decision of Goff J in *In re Denley's Trust Deed* [1969] 1 Ch 373 where the question arose as to the validity of a deed under which land was held by trustees as a sports ground:

"primary for the benefit of employees of [a particular company] and secondarily for the benefit of such other person or persons ... as the trustees may allow to use the same..."

The latter provision was construed by Goff J as a power and not a trust. The same deed conferred on the employees a right to use and enjoy the land subject to regulations made by the trustees. Goff J held that the rule against enforceability of non-charitable "purpose or object" trusts was confined to those which were abstract or impersonal in nature where there was no beneficiary or *cestui que trust*. A trust which, though expressed as a purpose, was directly or indirectly for the benefit of an individual or individuals was valid provided that those individuals were ascertainable at any one time and the trust was not otherwise void for uncertainty. Goff J said, at p 382:

"I think there may be a purpose or object trust, the carrying out of which would benefit an individual or individuals, where that benefit is so indirect or intangible or which is otherwise so framed as not to give those persons any locus standi to apply to the court to enforce the trust, in which case the beneficiary principle would, as it seems to me, apply to invalidate the trust, quite apart from any question of uncertainty or perpetuity. Such cases can be considered if and when they arise. The present is not, in my judgment, of that character, and it will be seen that clause 2 (d) of the trust deed expressly states that, subject to any rules and regulations made by the trustees, the employees of the company shall be entitled to the use and enjoyment of the land. Apart from this possible exception, in my judgment the beneficiary principle of *In re Astor's Settlement Trusts* [1952] Ch 534, which was approved in *In re Endacott, decd* [1960] Ch 232 – see particularly by Harman LJ, at p. 250 – is confined to purpose or object trusts which are abstract or impersonal. The objection is not that the trust is for a purpose or object per se, but that there is no beneficiary or cestui que trust.... Where, then, the trust, though expressed as a purpose, is directly or indirectly for the benefit of an individual or individuals, it seems to me that it is in general outside the mischief of the beneficiary principle."

I respectfully adopt this, as it seems to me to accord both with authority and with common sense. ...

I have already said that, in my judgment, no question of perpetuity arises here ... . There is an additional factor. This is a case in which, under the constitution of the association, the members could, by the appropriate majority, alter their constitution so as to provide, if they wished, for the division of the association's assets among themselves. This has, I think, a significance. I have considered whether anything turns in this case upon the testator's direction that the legacy shall be used "solely" for one or other of the specified purposes. Mr Rossdale has referred me to a number of cases where legacies have been bequeathed for particular purposes and in which the beneficiaries have been held entitled to override the purpose, even though expressed in mandatory terms.

Perhaps the most striking in the present context is *In re Bowes* [1896] 1 Ch 507, where money was directed to be laid out in the planting of trees on a settled estate. That was a "purpose" trust, but there were ascertainable beneficiaries, the owners for the time being of the estate; and North J. held that the persons entitled to the settled estate were entitled to have the money whether or not it was laid out as directed by the testator. He says, at p 510:

"Then, the sole question is where this money is to go to. Of course, it is a perfectly good legacy. There is nothing illegal in the matter, and the direction to plant might easily be carried out; but it is not necessarily capable of being performed, because the owner of the estate might say he would not have any trees planted upon it at all. If that were the line he took, and he did not contend for anything more than that, the legacy would fail; but he says he does not refuse to have trees planted upon it; he is content that trees should be planted upon some part of it; but the legacy has not failed. If it were necessary to uphold it, the trees can be planted upon the whole of it until the fund is exhausted. Therefore, there is nothing illegal in the gift itself; but the owners of the estate now say: 'It is a very disadvantageous way of spending this money; the money is to be spent for our benefit, and that of no one else; it was not intended for any purpose other than our benefit and that of the estate. That is no reason why it should be thrown away by doing what is not for our benefit, instead of being given to us, who want to have the enjoyment of it.' I think their contention is right. I think the fund is devoted to improving the estate, and improving the estate for the benefit of the persons who are absolutely entitled to it."

I can see no reason why the same reasoning should not apply in the present case simply because the beneficiary is an unincorporated non-charitable association. I do not think the fact that the testator has directed the application "solely" for the specified purpose adds any legal force to the direction. The beneficiaries, the members of the association for the time being, are the persons who could enforce the purpose and they must, as it seems to me, be entitled not to enforce it or, indeed, to vary it.

Alert

Thus, it seems to me that whether one treats the gift as a "purpose" trust or as an absolute gift with a superadded direction or, on the analogy of *In re*

> *Turkington* [1937] 4 All ER 501 as a gift where the trustees and the beneficiaries are the same persons, all roads lead to the same conclusion.
>
> In my judgment, the gift is a valid gift ...

In the opinion of Oliver J, the gift was valid because the trust which it imposed was for the benefit of ascertainable individuals, namely the members of the association. The direction that the gift was to be used "solely" for building or improvement works could be ignored because it had no legal force, thus leaving the members of the association free to use the gift for any other purpose in accordance with the rules of the association.

Many commentators would agree that the reasoning of Oliver J is perhaps difficult to follow. In particular, in various passages of his judgment he appears to equate a purpose trust for the benefit of ascertainable individual members of an unincorporated association as being the equivalent of a gift to those members subject to the rules of the association. The better view, it is suggested, is to treat the *Re Denley* approach and the contractual analysis as separate interpretations.

7

Charitable Trusts

Introduction

Charitable purpose trusts enjoy several advantages which give them a special status not accorded to non-charitable purpose trusts. Trusts for purposes are generally void as they do not satisfy the 'beneficiary principle'. This rule does not apply to charities because the Attorney-General can enforce them. Provided that a general charitable intention can be shown, the purposes need not be certain as the Charity Commissioners or the court can draw up a scheme for the application of the funds. Charities are exempt from the perpetuity rules against inalienability and, to an extent, the rule against remoteness of vesting. An initial gift to charity *is* subject to that rule, but a gift over from one charity to another is exempt. Charities also enjoy huge tax advantages. Not surprisingly, therefore, there are strict rules which must be complied with before an organisation can be registered as a charity, or a trust upheld as a charitable trust. In brief, these are:

(a) The purpose must be charitable. The 'Heads of Charity' referred to in the next section are relevant here;

(b) There must be an identifiable benefit to the public or a sufficient section of the public;

(c) The objects must be wholly and exclusively charitable.

7.1 The Heads of Charity

Before the enactment of the Charities Act 2011 ('the CA 2011'), in order to be charitable, a trust had to fall within the spirit of the preamble to the Charitable Uses Act 1601, often referred to as the Statute of Elizabeth. The purposes set out there were classified by Lord Macnaghten in *Commissioners for Special Purposes of Income Tax v Pemsel* [1891] AC 531 into four 'heads of charity' namely: trusts for the relief of poverty; trusts for the advancement of education; trusts for the advancement of religion; and trusts for other purposes beneficial to the community. The CA 2011 sets out twelve charitable purposes together with 'other purposes' under s3(1)(m).

The following are extracts of some leading case examples of charitable purposes.

7.1.1 Trusts for the Advancement of Education

The advancement of education was recognised as a charitable purpose by the Statue of Elizabeth, by Lord Macnaghten's classification, and now under the CA 2011 s3(1)(b). It has been interpreted much more widely than education in its formal, conventional sense, to include arts and culture. In 1972 it was extended in *Incorporated Council of Law Reporting for England and Wales v AG* [1972] Ch 73 to incorporate improving any useful branch of human knowledge and its public dissemination. Now, as it has been given its own separate category under the CA 2011, it is unclear how widely 'education' will be interpreted in future.

***In re Hopkins' Will Trusts* [1965] Ch 669**

Panel: Wilberforce J

Facts: By her will, Evelyn Hopkins left one-third of her estate to the Francis Bacon Society, whose objects were to encourage study of the life, works and influence of Bacon, and to encourage the study of evidence in favour of him being the true author of some of the plays ascribed to Shakespeare. The gift was to be applied towards the finding of the Bacon/Shakespeare manuscripts, or, if they had been found by the date of the testatrix's death, for the general work and propaganda of the Society. This was held to be a valid educational charitable trust. Mr Justice Wilberforce first examined the wording of the will closely and concluded that the purpose was certain. He then looked at the evidence as to whether the purpose was futile as, if it were, the court would be justified in declaring the trust invalid. Only then did he turn to the question of whether the purpose was charitable.

MR JUSTICE WILBERFORCE

On this evidence, should the conclusion be reached that the search for the Bacon-Shakespeare manuscripts is so manifestly futile that the court should not allow this bequest to be spent upon it as upon an object devoid of the possibility of any result? I think not. The evidence shows that the discovery of any manuscript of the plays is unlikely; but so are many discoveries before they are made (one may think of the Codex Sinaiticus, or the Tomb of Tutankhamen, or the Dead Sea Scrolls); I do not think that that degree of improbability has been reached which justifies the court in placing an initial interdict on the testatrix's benefaction.

I come, then, to the only question of law: is the gift of a charitable character? The society has put its case in the alternative under the two headings of education and of general benefit to the community and has argued separately for each. This compartmentalisation is derived from the accepted classification into four groups of the miscellany found in the Statute of Elizabeth... but the somewhat ossificatory classification to which it gave rise survives in the decided cases. It is unsatisfactory because the frontiers of "educational purposes" (as of the other divisions) have been extended and are not easy to trace with precision, and because, under the fourth head, it has been held necessary for the court to find a benefit to the public within the spirit and intendment of the obsolete Elizabethan statute. The difficulty of achieving that, while at the same time keeping the law's view of what is charitable reasonably in line with modern requirements, explains what Lord Simonds accepted as the case-to-case approach of the courts: see *National Anti-Vivisection Society v. Inland* Revenue Commissioners. There are, in fact, examples of accepted charities which do not decisively fit into one rather than the other category. Examples are institutes for scientific research (see the *National Anti-Vivisection* case, *per* Lord Wright),

Link
See Political Trusts section below

museums (see *In re Pinion*), the preservation of ancient cottages *(In re Cranstoun,)* and even the promotion of Shakespearian drama *(In re Shakespeare Memorial Theatre Trust).* The present may be such a case.

Accepting, as I have the authority of Lord Simonds for so doing, that the court must decide each case as best it can, on the evidence available to it, as to benefit, and within the moving spirit of decided cases, it would seem to me that a bequest for the purpose of search, or research, for the original manuscripts of England's greatest dramatist (whoever he was) would be well within the law's conception of charitable purposes. The discovery of such manuscripts, or of one such manuscript, would be of the highest value to history and to literature. It is objected, against this, that as we already have the text of the plays, from an almost contemporary date, the discovery of a manuscript would add nothing worth while. This I utterly decline to accept. Without any undue exercise of the imagination, it would surely be a reasonable expectation that the revelation of a manuscript would contribute, probably decisively, to a solution of the authorship problem, and this alone is benefit enough. It might also lead to improvements in the text. It might lead to more accurate dating.

He then turned to the arguments for the next of kin, relying on *In re Shaw* [1957] 1 WLR 729, where it was held that a gift was not educational if it simply added to knowledge without being 'combined with teaching or education'.

The words "combined with teaching or education," though well explaining what the judge had in mind when he rejected the gift in *Shaw's* case, are not easy to interpret in relation to other facts. I should be unwilling to treat them as meaning that the promotion of academic research is not a charitable purpose unless the researcher were engaged in teaching or education in the conventional meaning; and I am encouraged in this view by some words of Lord Greene M.R. in *In re Compton*. The testatrix there had forbidden the income of the bequest to be used for research, and Lord Greene M.R. treated this as a negative definition of the education to be provided. It would, he said, exclude a grant to enable a beneficiary to conduct research on some point of history or science. This shows that Lord Greene M.R. considered that historic research might fall within the description of "education." I think, therefore, that the word "education" as used by Harman J. in *In re Shaw, decd.; Public Trustee v. Day* must be used in a wide sense, certainly extending beyond teaching, and that the requirement is that, in order to be charitable, research must either be of educational value to the researcher or must be so directed as to lead to something which will pass into the store of educational material, or so as to improve the sum of communicable knowledge in an area which education may cover - education in this last context extending to the formation of literary taste and appreciation (compare *Royal Choral Society v. Inland Revenue Commissioners*). Whether or not the test is wider than this, it is, as I have stated it, amply wide enough to include the purposes of the gift in this case. ... I accept that research of a private character, for the benefit only of the members of a society, would not normally be educational - or otherwise charitable – ... but I do not think that the research in the present case can be said to be of a private character, for it is inherently inevitable, and manifestly intended, that the result of any discovery should be published to the world.

7.1.2 Trusts for the Advancement of Religion

***In re South Place Ethical Society* [1980] 1 WLR 1565**

Panel: Dillon J

Facts: The South Place Religious Society held land and a chapel on the trusts declared by an 1825 deed for use, 'for the public worship of one God'. In 1887, using powers conferred by the 1825 deed, the society abandoned prayer, changed its name to South Place Ethical Society and changed the objects to 'the study and dissemination of ethical principles and the cultivation of a rational religious sentiment'. The trustees sought a declaration as to whether the objects were charitable, or whether the trustees had a duty to apply the assets cy-près because the current objects were no longer charitable. It was held that the objects were not for the advancement of religion. Beginning his judgment, Dillon J explained that the society members were sincere people of integrity, agnostic rather than atheist. He explained that the society's beliefs were an aspect of Humanism, idealising the ethical principles of truth, beauty and love rather than believing in anything supernatural. The objects of the society involved the study and dissemination of these principles through public meetings, lectures, musical and social activities.

MR JUSTICE DILLON

Of course it has long been established that a trust can be valid and charitable as for the advancement of religion, although the religion which is sought to be advanced is not the Christian religion. In *Bowman v Secular Society Ltd* [1917] AC 406, Lord Parker of Waddington gave a very clear and valuable summary of the history of the approach of the law to religious charitable trusts at pp. 448 to 450. He said, at p. 449: "It would seem to follow that a trust for the purpose of any kind of monotheistic theism would be a good charitable trust."...

The Society argued that religion does not have to be dependent on the belief in any god: sincere belief in ethical qualities is equally sacred and the advancement of such beliefs advances religion. The judge surveyed the American authorities which suggested that the society would be accepted as a body established for the advancement of religion and concluded:

In a free country – and I have no reason to suppose that this country is less free than the United States of America – it is natural that the court should desire not to discriminate between beliefs deeply and sincerely held, whether they are beliefs in a god or in the excellence of man or in ethical principles or in Platonism or some other scheme of philosophy. But I do not see that that warrants extending the meaning of the word "religion" so as to embrace all other beliefs and philosophies. Religion, as I see it, is concerned with man's relations with God, and ethics are concerned with man's relations with man.

Alert

The two are not the same, and are not made the same by sincere inquiry into the question: what is God? If reason leads people not to accept Christianity or any known religion, but they do believe in the excellence of qualities such as truth, beauty and love, or believe in the platonic concept of the ideal, their beliefs may be to them the equivalent of a religion, but viewed objectively they are not religion. The ground of the opinion of the court, in the United States Supreme Court, that any belief occupying in the life of its possessor a place parallel to that occupied by belief in God in the minds of theists prompts the comment that parallels, by definition, never meet.

In *Bowman v Secular Society Ltd* [1917] AC 406, 445 Lord Parker of Waddington in commenting on one of the objects of the society in that case, namely to promote the principle that human conduct should be based upon natural knowledge and not upon supernatural belief, and that human welfare in this world is the proper end of all thought and action, said of that object, at p. 445:

"It is not a religious trust, for it relegates religion to a region in which it is to have no influence on human conduct."

That comment seems to me to be equally applicable to the objects of the society in the present case, and it is not to be answered in my judgment by attempting to extend the meaning of religion. Lord Parker of Waddington has used the word "in its natural and accustomed sense." Again, in *United Grand Lodge of Ancient Free and Accepted Masons of England v Holborn Borough Council* [1957] 1 WLR 1080, Donovan J. in delivering the judgment of the Divisional Court, after commenting that freemasonary held out certain standards of truth and justice by which masons were urged to regulate their conduct, and commenting that, in particular, masons were urged to be reverent, honest, compassionate, loyal, temperate, benevolent and chaste, said, at p. 1090: "Admirable though these objects are it seems to us impossible to say that they add up to the advancement of religion." Therefore I take the view that the objects of this society are not for the advancement of religion.

There is a further point. It seems to me that two of the essential attributes of religion are faith and worship; faith in a god and worship of that god. This is supported by the definitions of religion given in the *Oxford English Dictionary* (1914), ...

Alert

In *Reg. v Registrar General, Ex parte Segerdal* [1970] 2 QB 697, which was concerned with the so-called Church of Scientology, Buckley L.J. said, at p. 709:

"Worship I take to be something which must have some at least of the following characteristics: submission to the object worshipped, veneration of that object, praise, thanksgiving, prayer or intercession."

He went on to say that, looking at the wedding ceremony of the scientologists, he could find nothing in the form of ceremony which would not be appropriate in a purely civil, non-religious ceremony such as is conducted in a register office, and that it contained none of the elements which he has suggested are necessary elements of worship. He then said:

"I do not say that you would need to find every element in every act which could properly be described as worship, but when you find an act which contains none of those elements it cannot, in my judgment, answer to the description of an act of worship."

The society really accepts that worship by that definition, which in my view is the correct definition in considering whether a body is charitable for the advancement of religion, is not practised by the society, because, indeed, it is not possible to worship in that way a mere ethical or philosophical ideal.

He rejected the society's concept of 'natural' worship, which consisted of appreciating and finding emotional and spiritual fulfilment in nature, music and any kind of aesthetic experience. Although the trust was not a charitable trust for the advancement of religion, it was upheld as being for the advancement of education and for the public benefit.

***Church of Scientology's Application for Registration as a Charity* [2005] WTLR 1151**

Panel: The Charity Commissioners for England and Wales

Facts: In considering an application for registration as a charity by the Church of Scientology, the Board of Commissioners considered, amongst other things, whether it was established for the advancement of religion and if so, whether it was for the public benefit. They took into account the principles of the European Convention on Human Rights Articles 9 and 14. Scientology is based exclusively on the research, writing and lectures of L. Ron Hubbard, which include fundamental principles through which people can realise their natural spiritual potential. The path outlined by Hubbard must be followed closely if this is to be achieved. The core practices of Scientology are auditing and training. Auditing involves addressing past painful experiences, thereby attaining increased awareness, capability and spiritual transformation. Training is intensive study through which a person learns to be an auditor.

The Commissioners decided that the Church of Scientology was not registrable because it was not a religion for the purposes of charity law. Although Scientology acknowledges a supreme being, its nature is not fully developed. Further, as auditing and training involve private counselling and study, they are more like education and training than religious practice, as they lack essential veneration and reverence. The Commissioners elaborated on what would be classed as a religion within charity law.

The Commissioners noted that English charity law has developed empirically, within the context of the traditional Western monotheistic religions, although it has long embraced monotheistic religions other than Christianity and Judaism. Within that context, the following general principles are firmly established:

(i) Trusts for the advancement of religion take effect as charities without assessment by the court of the worth or value of the beliefs in question, unless the tenets of a particular sect inculcate doctrines adverse to the very foundations of all religion and/or subversive of all morality.

(ii) The law does not prefer one religion to another and as between religions the law stands neutral, but it assumes that any religion is at least likely to be better than none.

(iii) In deciding whether a gift is for the advancement of religion, the court does not concern itself with the truth of the religion, a matter which is not susceptible of proof. This does not mean that the court will recognise as a religion everything that chooses to call itself a religion. But when once the religion is recognised by the court as a religion, the beneficial nature of a gift for its advancement will prima facie be assumed.

(iv) In addition, in order to be charitable, the trust must not only be for the advancement of religion, it must also be of public benefit. This is a question of fact which must be answered by the court in the same manner as any other question of fact, i.e. by means of evidence cognizable by the court. In the absence of evidence to the contrary, public benefit is presumed.

Given these judicial principles, the Commissioners found it understandable that the English courts have resisted closely defining what it is that makes some belief systems religious and other not. However, the Commissioners accepted that there are some characteristics of religion which can be discerned from the legal authorities:

1. Belief in a god or a deity or supreme being – *R v Registrar General ex parte Segerdal* (Lord Denning).
2. Reverence and recognition of the dominant power and control of any entity or being outside their own body and life (i.e. outside the body and life of the follower of that religion) – *Segerdal* (Wian LJ).
3. Two of the essential attributes of religion are faith and worship: faith in a god and worship of that god – *South Place Ethical Society* (Dillon J). The Commissioners noted that Hubert Picarda QC writes that religion involves not merely faith of a particular kind, but also worship, and states that the essential ingredient of worship is found in the definition of Webster's New International dictionary which defines religion as "service and adoration of God or a god as expressed in a form of worship."
4. A trust for the purpose of any kind of monotheistic theism would be a good charitable trust – *Bowman v Secular Society* (Lord Parker of Waddington)
5. Worship must have at least some of the following characteristics: submission to the object worshipped, veneration of that object, praise, thanksgiving, prayer or intercession – *Segerdal* (Buckley LJ).

6. It would not seem to be possible to worship in this way (ie with reverence) a mere ethical or philosophical ideal – *South Place Ethical Society* (Dillon J)

7. Promotion of religion includes "the observances that serve to promote and manifest it." – *Keren Kayemeth Le Jisroel v IRC* (Lord Hanworth MR).

8. There must be a promotion of the religion, meaning "the promotion of spiritual teaching in a wide sense, and the maintenance of the doctrines on which it rests, and the observances that serve to promote and manifest it." – *Keren Kayemeth Le Jisroel v IRC* (Lord Hanworth MR). This would include observance of particular common standards, practices or codes of conduct as stipulated in particular scriptures or teachings.

9. To advance religion means "to promote it, to spread the message ever wider among mankind; to take some positive steps to sustain and increase religious belief and these things are done in a variety of ways which may be comprehensively described as pastoral and missionary" – *United Grand Lodge v Holborn BC* (Donovan J).

10. Promotion of religion includes a missionary element or other charitable work through which the beliefs of the religion are advanced – *United Grand Lodge v Holborn BC* (Donovan J).

11. Public benefit is a necessary element in religious trusts as it is in other charitable trusts – *Coats v Gilmour* (Lord Greene MR).

Having *considered* these characteristics, the Commissioners concluded that the definition of a religion in English charity law was characterised by a belief in a supreme being and an expression of that belief through worship. The cases also make clear that there must be advancement or promotion of the religion. …

Alert
see also Dillon J's comments in *South Place Ethical* case

The Commissioners noted that the *Segerdal* and *South Place Ethical Society* cases in particular, referring to the requirement of a god or deity have traditionally been regarded as decisive of the principle that theism (belief in a god) is a necessary criterion of religion for the purposes of charity law. Both cases suggest that religion in charity law is characterised by:

- Faith in the personal, creator god of the traditional monotheistic religions, having existence outside the body and life of the votary, and
- Worship of that deity in the form of formalised expressions of supplication, veneration, praise and intercession, as traditionally practised in monotheistic religions.

Against those criteria, the Commissioners noted that Scientology claims to acknowledge a supreme being which may have created the world. This supreme being ("infinity", the Eighth dynamic, the "allness of all"), is according to the expert opinion submitted by CoS in support of its application, a thoroughly impersonal abstract conception, more analogous to eastern enlightenment and realisation, which Scientologists recognise as the ultimate ground of being but of which they are reluctant to claim complete understanding.

Whilst the Commissioners noted that CoS's application stated that Scientology acknowledges a supreme being, the Commissioners concluded that the supreme being did not appear to be of kind indicated by the decided cases.

The Commissioners also noted CoS's submission that the activities of auditing and training constitute its worship, this argument being supported by the expert opinion submitted by CoS. However, the Commissioners were unable to accept that the practices of auditing and training were akin to or comparable with the acts of worship indicated by the English cases – praise, veneration, prayer, thanksgiving, intercession, submission to the object worshipped.

As the Commissioners had concluded that Scientology was not charitable they had no need to consider whether it was for the public benefit. They did however do so, and stated that 'public benefit' is an essential element of charity law, and is presumed where the purpose is for the advancement of religion. This presumption has now been abolished by the CA 2011.

7.1.3 Trusts for sports and games

***In re Dupree's Deed Trusts* [1945] Ch 16**

Panel: Vaisey J

Facts: A trust fund of £5,000 was established with the income to be used to promote an annual chess tournament for boys under 21 living in Portsmouth. The trustees sought a declaration as to whether this was a valid charitable trust on the basis that it was for the advancement of education. It was upheld, although the judge expressed unease at laying down any hard and fast rules as to where the line should be drawn on the educational value of sports and games.

MR JUSTICE VAISEY

The game of chess (which, by those who follow it, as well, perhaps, as by those who do not follow it, is regarded as something rather more than a mere game) is an institution with a very long history behind it, and it possesses the somewhat notable feature that it is essentially a game of skill into which elements of chance enter, if at all, only to a negligible extent. It is a game which, I suppose, is played all over the civilized world. I have some evidence which enables me to say – and, indeed, I think I might have said it even without that evidence – that the nature of the game is such as to encourage the qualities of foresight, concentration, memory and ingenuity. Even unguided by actual evidence, I should not have been surprised if the conclusion could have been reached that the game is essentially one which does possess an educational value.

There are many pursuits possessing an educational value which may be followed to excess, and the matter is in no way concluded by any such

> consideration. Chess players may become so obsessed by the interest of their pursuit that they may neglect other duties, but the same thing may be said of those who range the mysterious country of the higher mathematics or indulge in the study of classical authors. I am not surprised to learn from the evidence that there are schoolmasters and persons actually concerned with the business of education who regard the playing of chess as something of so much value educationally that in some places it is actually a part of a school curriculum. ...
>
> I think that the case before me may be a little near the line, and I decide it without attempting to lay down any general propositions. One feels, perhaps, that one is on rather a slippery slope. If chess, why not draughts? If draughts, why not bezique, and so on, through to bridge and whist, and, by another route, to stamp collecting and the acquisition of birds' eggs? Those pursuits will have to be dealt with if and when they come up for consideration in connexion with the problem whether or no [sic] there is in existence an educational charitable trust. Nor do I say whether, if this trust had been without a geographical limitation, if it had been for the promotion of chess playing *in vacuo* or at large, the area of what is regarded as charitable would or would not have been overstepped. Having regard to the evidence before me and to what is known about the game of chess by everybody, and, in particular, to the fact that the encouragement of chess playing here is for the benefit of young persons living within a well-defined area, and also that it is of the essence of the constitution of the trusteeship that two of the trustees should be persons closely connected with educational activities in the borough, I think I am bound, in the present case, to hold that there is a good charitable trust, and answer the question by declaring that the trusts constituted by the deed of June 30, 1932, are valid charitable trusts.

The Recreational Charities Act 1958 ('the RCA 1958') sets out the circumstances in which trusts for the provision of recreational facilities are deemed to be charitable. Amateur sports are now a charitable purpose under the CA 2011 s3(1)(g).

***Guild v Inland Revenue Commissioners* [1992] AC 310**

Panel: Lord Keith of Kinkel, Lord Roskill, Lord Griffiths, Lord Jauncey of Tullichettle and Lord Lowry

Facts: James Russell left the residue of his estate to the town council of North Berwick, 'for the use in connection with the sports centre in North Berwick or some similar purpose in connection with sport'. The Inland Revenue claimed tax on the transfer, but the executor argued that it was exempt from tax under the Finance Acts as it was charitable within the meaning of the RCA 1958. The House of Lords held that it was charitable and thus exempt from tax: no element of deprivation was required to be shown in order for a purpose to be charitable under the RCA 1958.

LORD KEITH OF KINKEL

In the course of his argument in relation to the first branch of the bequest counsel for the commissioners accepted that it assisted in the provision of facilities for recreation or other leisure time occupation within the meaning of subsection (1) of section 1 of the Act, and also that the requirement of public benefit in the proviso to the subsection was satisfied. It was further accepted that the facilities of the sports centre were available to the public at large so that the condition of subsection (2)(b)(ii) was satisfied. It was maintained, however, that these facilities were not provided "in the interests of social welfare" as required by subsection (1), because they did not meet the condition laid down in subsection (2)(a), namely that they should be "provided with the object of improving the conditions of life for the persons for whom the facilities are primarily intended." The reason why it was said that this condition was not met was that on a proper construction it involved that the facilities should be provided with the object of meeting a need for such facilities in people who suffered from a position of relative social disadvantage. Reliance was placed on a passage from the judgment of Walton J. in *Inland Revenue Commissioners v McMullen* [1978] 1 WLR 664. That was a case where the Football Association had set up a trust to provide facilities to encourage pupils of schools and universities in the United Kingdom to play association football and other games and sports. Walton J. held that the trust was not valid as one for the advancement of education nor did it satisfy section 1 of the Act of 1958. He said, at p.675, in relation to the words "social welfare" in subsection (1):

"In my view, however, these words in themselves indicate that there is some kind of deprivation - not, of course, by any means necessarily of money - which falls to be alleviated; and I think that this is made even clearer by the terms of subsection (2)(a). The facilities must be provided with the object of improving the conditions of life for persons for whom the facilities are primarily intended. In other words, they must be to some extent and in some way deprived persons."

When the case went to the Court of Appeal [1979] 1 W.L.R. 130 the majority (Stamp and Orr L.JJ.) affirmed the judgment of Walton J. on both points, but Bridge L.J. dissented. As regards the Recreational Charities Act 1958 point he said, "...Save in the sense that the interests of social welfare can only be served by the meeting of some social need, I cannot accept the judge's view that the interests of social welfare can only be served in relation to some 'deprived' class. The judge found this view reinforced by the requirement of subsection (2)(a) of section 1 that the facilities must be provided 'with the object of improving the conditions of life for the persons for whom the facilities are primarily intended; ...' Here again I can see no reason to conclude that only the deprived can have their conditions of life improved. Hyde Park improves the conditions of life for residents in Mayfair and Belgravia as much as for those in Pimlico or the Portobello Road, and the village hall may improve the conditions of life for the squire and his family as well as for the cottagers. The persons for whom the facilities here are primarily intended are pupils of schools and

> universities, as defined in the trust deed, and these facilities are in my judgment unquestionably to be provided with the object of improving their conditions of life. ... There cannot surely be any doubt that young persons as part of their education do need facilities for organised games and sports both by reason of their youth and by reason of their social and economic circumstances. They cannot provide such facilities for themselves but are dependent on what is provided for them."
>
> In the House of Lords [1981] A.C. 1 [*IRC v* McMullen] the case was decided against the Crown upon the ground that the trust was one for the advancement of education, opinion being reserved on the point under the Recreational Charities Act 1958.

Although the House of Lords did not decide *IRC v McMullen* on the RCA 1958 point, in *Guild v IRC* Lord Keith of Kinkel specifically addressed the issue:

> The fact is that persons in all walks of life and all kinds of social circumstances may have their conditions of life improved by the provision of recreational facilities of suitable character. The proviso requiring public benefit excludes facilities of an undesirable nature. In my opinion the view expressed by Bridge L.J. in *Inland Revenue Commissioners v McMullen* is clearly correct...
>
> I would therefore reject the argument that the facilities are not provided in the interests of social welfare unless they are provided with the object of improving the conditions of life for persons who suffer from some form of social disadvantage. It suffices if they are provided with the object of improving the conditions of life for members of the community generally.

7.2 Public Benefit

As well as being for a recognised charitable purpose within CA 2011 s3(1), there must be an element of public benefit: s4. Before the enactment of CA 2011, there was a presumption of public benefit where the trust was for the relief of poverty, advancement of education or advancement of religion. This presumption has been abolished by s4(2). However, existing law, particularly the cases on the 4th head of charity ('other purposes beneficial to the community'), may assist by giving an example of what the public benefit of a particular trust might be. The benefits must be capable of being identified, defined or described. The leading case in this area is *Gilmour v Coats* [1949] AC 426.

***Gilmour v Coats* [1949] AC 426**

Panel: Lord Simonds, Lord du Parcq, Lord Normand, Lord Morton of Henryton and Lord Reid

Facts: £500 was given on trust for the purposes of a Carmelite Priory in Notting Hill, London, if those purposes were charitable. The Priory was a community of cloistered nuns who spent all of their time in prayer, penance and contemplation and took no part in outside works. It was argued that this conferred a benefit on the public both through intercessionary prayers and through edification by the example of lives devoted to prayer. The trustees asked how they should apply the trust fund. The House of Lords held that the purposes of the Priory were not charitable as there was no element of public benefit shown. In his leading opinion, Lord Simonds turned first to the question whether there is any proof that intercessionary prayer benefits the public. He acknowledged that cloistered communities, though they have existed for a long time, have never been upheld as charitable, so looking back over early law is not a useful exercise.

LORD SIMONDS

... There may be circumstances in which the court will in a later age hold an object not to be charitable which has in earlier ages been held to possess that virtue. and the converse case may be possible. That degree of uncertainty in the law must be admitted. But I would ask your Lordships to say that it is only a radical change of circumstances, established by sufficient evidence, that should compel the court to accept a new view of this matter. Let me then examine briefly the law as it is to-day and, having done so, ask what are the compelling reasons for a change. I need not go beyond the case of *Cocks v Manners* which was decided nearly eighty years ago by Wickens V.-C. In that case the testatrix left her residuary estate between a number of religious institutions, one of them being the Dominican Convent at Carisbrooke, a community not differing in any material respect from the community of nuns now under consideration. The learned judge who was, I suppose, as deeply versed in this branch of the law as any judge before or since (for he had been for many years junior counsel to the Attorney-General in equity cases), used these words, which I venture to repeat, though they have already been cited in the courts below:

Link
see Chapter 7, *Leahy v A-G for New South Wales*

"On the Act [sc. the Statute of Elizabeth] unaffected by authority I should certainly hold that the gift to the Dominican Convent is neither within the letter nor the spirit of it; and no decision has been referred to which compels me to adopt a different conclusion. A voluntary association of women for the purpose of working out their own salvation by religious exercises and self-denial seems to me to have none of the requisites of a charitable institution, whether the word 'charitable' is used in its popular sense or in its legal sense. It is said, in some of the cases, that religious purposes are charitable, but that can only be true as to religious services tending directly or indirectly towards the instruction or the edification of the public; an annuity to an individual, so long as he spent his time in retirement and constant devotion, would not be charitable, nor would a gift to ten persons, so long as they lived together in retirement and performed acts of devotion, be charitable. Therefore the gift to the Dominican Convent is not, in my opinion, a gift on a charitable trust."

No case, said the learned Vice-Chancellor, had been cited to compel him to come to a contrary conclusion, nor has any such case been cited to your Lordships. Nor have my own researches discovered one. ...

Although evidence was given by the Archbishop of Westminster that the doctrine of the Roman Catholic Church was that intercessionary prayers conferred a benefit on the public, Lord Simonds refused to give it more than negligible weight as the benefit was incapable of proof.

> My Lords, I would speak with all respect and reverence of those who spend their lives in cloistered piety, and in this House of Lords Spiritual and Temporal, which daily commences its proceedings with intercessory prayers, how can I deny that the Divine Being may in His wisdom think fit to answer them? But, my Lords, whether I affirm or deny, whether I believe or disbelieve, what has that to do with the proof which the court demands that a particular purpose satisfies the test of benefit to the community? Here is something which is manifestly not susceptible of proof. But, then it is said, this is a matter not of proof but of belief: for the value of intercessory prayer is a tenet of the Catholic faith, therefore in such prayer there is benefit to the community. But it is just at this "therefore" that I must pause. It is, no doubt, true that the advancement of religion is, generally speaking, one of the heads of charity. But it does not follow from this that the court must accept as proved whatever a particular church believes. The faithful must embrace their faith believing where they cannot prove: the court can act only on proof. A gift to two or ten or a hundred cloistered nuns in the belief that their prayers will benefit the world at large does not from that belief alone derive validity any more than does the belief of any other donor for any other purpose.

He then considered the second argument in favour of public benefit: edification by example.

> It is in my opinion sufficient to say that this is something too vague and intangible to satisfy the prescribed test. The test of public benefit has, I think, been developed in the last two centuries. To-day it is beyond doubt that that element must be present. No court would be rash enough to attempt to define precisely or exhaustively what its content must be. But it would assume a burden which it could not discharge if now for the first time it admitted into the category of public benefit something so indirect, remote, imponderable and, I would add, controversial as the benefit which may be derived by others from the example of pious lives. ...

It was also argued that the element of public benefit was satisfied as qualification for membership of the community was open to any woman in the world. Lord Simonds applied established case law to reject this argument.

Questions arise as to whether the element of public benefit is satisfied where a trust is restricted to certain sections of society. This was considered in *Inland Revenue Commissioners v Baddeley* [1955] AC 572. The key considerations appear to be who is capable of benefiting, rather than who is actually benefiting, and whether the restriction to a section of society is reasonable. This in turn depends on the purpose of the charity. So the public benefit requirement can differ according to differing charitable aims.

Link
See The Charity Commissioners Guidance on Public Benefit in Further Reading.

Inland Revenue Commissioners v Baddeley [1955] AC 572

Panel: Lord Tucker, Viscount Simonds, Lord Porter, Lord Reid and Lord Somervell of Harrow

Facts: Two pieces of land were conveyed to the trustees of the Newtown Mission Church on similar terms. The first was to be used 'for the promotion of the religious social and physical well-being of persons resident in the County Boroughs of West Ham and Leyton... by the provision of facilities for religious services and instruction and for the social and physical training and recreation' of members of the church, or people likely to become members and of insufficient means otherwise to enjoy them. The second was playing fields to be used for the 'moral' rather than 'religious' well-being of the same people. The question was whether the purposes were charitable because if they were, the transfer deeds attracted a much lower rate of duty than would otherwise have been the case. The court (Lord Reid dissenting) first decided that the purposes of the trusts were not 'wholly and exclusively charitable', and that they failed on this basis. The judges then considered the element of 'public benefit' and sought to clarify exactly what this meant.

VISCOUNT SIMONDS

Suppose that, contrary to the view that I have expressed, the trust would be a valid charitable trust, if the beneficiaries were the community at large or a section of the community defined by some geographical limits, is it the less a valid trust if it is confined to members or potential members of a particular church within a limited geographical area?

The starting point of the argument must be, that this charity (if it be a charity) falls within the fourth class in Lord Macnaghten's classification. It must therefore be a trust which is, to use the words of Sir Samuel Romilly in *Morice v Bishop of Durham*, of "general public utility," and the question is what these words mean. ...But it is said that if a charity falls within the fourth class, it must be for the benefit of the whole community or at least of all the inhabitants of a sufficient area. and it has been urged with much force that, if, as Lord Greene said in *In re Strakosch*, this fourth class is represented in the preamble to the Statute of Elizabeth by the repair of bridges, etc., and possibly by the maintenance of Houses of Correction, the class of beneficiaries or potential beneficiaries cannot be further narrowed down. Some confusion has arisen from the fact that a trust of general public utility, however general and however public, cannot be of equal utility to all and may be of immediate utility to few. A sea wall, the prototype of this class in the preamble, is of remote, if any, utility to those who live in the heart of the Midlands. But there is no doubt that a trust for the maintenance of sea walls generally or along a particular stretch of coast is a good charitable trust. Nor, as it appears to me, is the validity of a trust affected by the fact that by its very nature only a limited number of people are likely to avail themselves, or are perhaps even capable of availing themselves, of its benefits. It is easy, for instance, to imagine a charity which has for its object some form of child welfare, of which the immediate beneficiaries could only be persons of tender age. Yet this would satisfy any test of general public utility. It may be said that it would satisfy the test because the indirect benefit of such a charity would extend far beyond its direct beneficiaries, and that aspect of the matter has probably not been out of sight. Indirect benefit is certainly an aspect which must have influenced the decision of the "cruelty to animal" cases. But, I doubt whether this sort of rationalization helps to explain a branch of the law which has developed empirically and by analogy upon analogy.

It is, however, in my opinion, particularly important in cases falling within the fourth category to keep firmly in mind the necessity of the element of general public utility, and I would not relax this rule. For here is a slippery slope. In the case under appeal the intended beneficiaries are a class within a class; they are those of the inhabitants of a particular area who are members of a particular church: the area is comparatively large and populous and the members may be numerous. But, if this trust is charitable for them, does it cease to be charitable as the area narrows down and the numbers diminish? Suppose the area is confined to a single street and the beneficiaries to those whose creed commands few adherents: or suppose the class is one that is determined not by religious belief but by membership of a particular profession or by pursuit of a particular trade. These were considerations which influenced the House in the recent case of *Oppenheim*. That was a case of an educational trust, but I think that they have even greater weight in the case of trusts which by their nominal classification depend for their validity upon general public utility.

It is pertinent, then, to ask how far your Lordships might regard yourselves bound by authority to hold the trusts now under review valid charitable trusts, if the only question in issue was the sufficiency of the public element. ... Relevant [on this point] is the case of *Verge v Somerville*. In that case, in which the issue was as to the validity of a gift "to the trustees of the Repatriation Fund or other similar fund for the benefit of New South Wales returned soldiers," Lord Wrenbury, delivering the judgment of the Judicial Committee, said that, to be a charity, a trust must be "for the benefit of the community or of an appreciably important class of the community. The inhabitants," he said, "of a parish or town or any particular class of such inhabitants, may, for instance, be the objects of such a gift, but private individuals, or a fluctuating body of private individuals, cannot." Here, my Lords, are two expressions: "an appreciably important class of the community" and "any particular class of such inhabitants," to which in any case it is not easy to give a precise quantitative or qualitative meaning. But I think that in the consideration of them the difficulty has sometimes been increased by failing to observe the distinction, at which I hinted earlier in this opinion, between a form of relief extended to the whole community yet by its very nature advantageous only to the few and a form of relief accorded to a selected few out of a larger number equally willing and able to take advantage of it. Of the former type repatriated New South Wales soldiers would serve as a clear example. To me it would not seem arguable that they did not form an adequate class of the community for the purpose of the particular charity that

was being established. It was with this type of case that Lord Wrenbury was dealing, and his words are apt to deal with it. Somewhat different considerations arise if the form, which the purporting charity takes, is something of general utility which is nevertheless made available not to the whole public but only to a selected body of the public - an important class of the public it may be. For example, a bridge which is available for all the public may undoubtedly be a charity and it is indifferent how many people use it. But confine its use to a selected number of persons, however numerous and important: it is then clearly not a charity. It is not of general public utility: for it does not serve the public purpose which its nature qualifies it to serve.

Alert

Oppenheim v Tobacco Securities **[1951] AC 297**

Panel: Lord Simonds, Lord Normand, Lord Oaksey, Lord Morton of Henryton and Lord Macdermott

Facts: A trust fund was established with the income and capital to be used for, 'the education of children of employees or former employees of British-American Tobacco Company Limited ... or any of its subsidiary or allied companies in such manner and according to such schemes or rules or regulations as the acting trustees shall in their absolute discretion from time to time think fit...'. There were over 100,000 employees and former employees who were potential beneficiaries of the trust find. The question was whether the trust benefited a sufficient section of the public to make it charitable. The court (Lord MacDermott dissenting) held that it did not. In the leading opinion, Lord Simonds began by acknowledging that no clear answer as to what constitutes 'public benefit' could be given, but that there must be an element of public benefit in trusts for educational purposes.

LORD SIMONDS

If I may begin at the bottom of the scale, a trust established by a father for the education of his son is not a charity. The public element, as I will call it, is not supplied by the fact that from that son's education all may benefit. At the other end of the scale the establishment of a college or university is beyond doubt a charity. "Schools of learning and free schools and scholars of universities" are the very words of the preamble to the Statute of Elizabeth. So also the endowment of a college, university or school by the creation of scholarships or bursaries is a charity and none the less because competition may be limited to a particular class of persons. It is upon this ground, as Lord Greene, M.R., pointed out in *In re Compton*, that the so-called Founder's Kin cases can be rested. The difficulty arises where the trust is not for the benefit of any institution either then existing or by the terms of the trust to be brought into existence, but for the benefit of a class of persons at large. Then the question is whether that class of persons can be regarded as such a "section of the community" as to satisfy the test of public benefit. These words "section of the community" have no special sanctity, but they conveniently indicate first, that the possible (I emphasize the word "possible") beneficiaries must not be numerically

Alert

negligible, and secondly, that the quality which distinguishes them from other members of the community, so that they form by themselves a section of it, must be a quality which does not depend on their relationship to a particular individual. It is for this reason that a trust for the education of members of a family or, as in *In re Compton*, of a number of families cannot be regarded as charitable. A group of persons may be numerous but, if the nexus between them is their personal relationship to a single propositus or to several propositi, they are neither the community nor a section of the community for charitable purposes.

I come, then, to the present case where the class of beneficiaries is numerous but the difficulty arises in regard to their common and distinguishing quality. That quality is being children of employees of one or other of a group of companies. I can make no distinction between children of employees and the employees themselves. In both cases the common quality is found in employment by particular employers. The latter of the two cases by which the Court of Appeal held itself to be bound, *In re Hobourn Aero Components Ltd.'s Air Raid Distress Fund*, is a direct authority for saying that such a common quality does not constitute its possessors a section of the public for charitable purposes. In the former case, *In re Compton*, Lord Greene, M.R., had by way of illustration placed members of a family and employees of a particular employer on the same footing, finding neither in common kinship nor in common employment the sort of nexus which is sufficient. ... It appears to me that it would be an extension, for which there is no justification in principle or authority, to regard common employment as a quality which constitutes those employed a section of the community. It must not, I think, be forgotten that charitable institutions enjoy rare and increasing privileges, and that the claim to come within that privileged class should be clearly established. ...

Learned counsel for the appellant sought to fortify his case by pointing to the anomalies that would ensue from the rejection of his argument. For, he said, admittedly those who follow a profession or calling, clergymen, lawyers, colliers, tobacco-workers and so on, are a section of the public; how strange then it would be if, as in the case of railwaymen, those who follow a particular calling are all employed by one employer. Would a trust for the education of railwaymen be charitable, but a trust for the education of men employed on the railways by the Transport Board not be charitable? and what of service of the Crown whether in the civil service or the armed forces? Is there a difference between soldiers and soldiers of the King? My Lords, I am not impressed by this sort of argument and will consider on its merits, if the occasion should arise, the case where the description of the occupation and the employment is in effect the same, where in a word, if you know what a man does, you know who employs him to do it. It is to me a far more cogent argument, as it was to my noble and learned friend in the *Hobourn* case, that if a section of the public is constituted by the personal relation of employment, it is impossible to say that it is not constituted by 1,000 as by 100,000 employees, and, if by 1,000, then by 100, and, if by 100, then by 10.

Lord Simonds refused to harmonise the law on educational purpose trusts with the 'poor relations' cases where public benefit is presumed to be present. The 'poor relations' cases are a separate line of the law which has developed independently and are beyond the scope of this Chapter.

LORD NORMAND

... The fact that the children of the employees and not the employees themselves are the beneficiaries does not help the appellants, for there is no public element in the relationship of parent and child. The common attribute that each parent has a contract of service with the same employer remains for consideration. A contract of service is in a high degree personal, and it constitutes a personal and private relationship between the parties. Whatever the number of the employees in the service of the same employer each still stands independently in this personal and private relationship to the employer. ...

In principle I am unable to say that any public element can be born out of the several private contracts between a particular employer and his employees. The appellant would not boldly submit that when the common employer employed two servants the public element at once emerged. He said it was a question of degree and the courts must take account of the number of employees, the magnitude of the sum settled by the truster, the size of the employers' undertaking, the non-contractual personal relationships (or their absence) between the employer and his employees, and other circumstances. I am unable to find any logical principles in these submissions. ...The appellant's argument would lead to a degree of uncertainty in this branch of the law which only compelling authority or logical necessity would induce me to accept.

7.3 Wholly and Exclusively Charitable

The purpose of the trust must not only be charitable: it must be wholly and exclusively charitable. This causes problems where the testator has given a fund for purposes which are charitable *or* for purposes which are not, as the trustees might apply the fund wholly for purposes other than purely charitable ones. If they could, the trust will be void unless it can be said to be a valid non-charitable purpose trust. But if the testator leaves a fund for 'charitable *and* benevolent' purposes, those purposes are exclusively charitable, as the purposes must not only be benevolent: they must *also* be charitable. If the language of the trust permits, it may be possible to sever the charitable from the non-charitable gift and apply part of the fund to the charitable purpose, as in *Salusbury v Denton* (1857) 3 K&J 529.

***Chichester Diocesan Fund and Board of Finance v Simpson* [1944] AC 341**

Panel: Viscount Simon LC, Lord Macmillan, Lord Wright, Lord Porter and Lord Simonds

Facts: Caleb Diplock left the residue of his estate to his executors and directed them to apply it 'for such charitable institution or institutions or benevolent objects' as they in their absolute discretion select. After the estate had been distributed among 139 benevolent institutions, the next of kin claimed to be entitled to the residue on the basis that the charitable trusts were void and the money was therefore held on resulting trust for them on intestacy. The House of Lords held that the gift of the residue was void for uncertainty and did not fall within the 'charitable' exception as it was not exclusively for charitable purposes.

LORD SIMONDS

... I approach this will, as I approach any other will, with the resolve to find the testator's intention from the language that he has used. When I have found it, I consider its effect. If there is an ambiguity, it may be that I am at liberty to choose that construction which will give legal effect to the instrument rather than that which will invalidate it. Where the testator's words would, if no question of invalidity arose, leave no doubt in my mind, I am not at liberty to create an ambiguity in order then to place what is sometimes called a benignant construction on the will.

My Lords, the words for your consideration are "charitable or benevolent." The question is whether, in the context in which they are found in this will, these words give to the executors a choice of objects extending beyond that which the law recognizes as charitable. If they do not, that is the end of the matter. The trust is a good charitable trust. If they do, it appears to be conceded by counsel for the appellant institution that the trust is invalid, but, in deference to the argument of the Attorney-General, who invited your Lordships to take a different view, I must say a few words at a later stage. My Lords, of those three words your Lordships will have no doubt what the first, "charitable," means. It is a term of art with a technical meaning and that is the meaning which the testator must be assumed to have intended. If it were not so, if in this will "charitable" were to be given, not its legal, but some popular, meaning, it would not be possible to establish the validity of the bequest. The last of the three words "benevolent" is not a term of art. In its ordinary meaning it has a range in some respects far less wide than legal charity, in others somewhat wider. It is, at least, clear that the two words, the one here used in its technical meaning, the other having only, and, accordingly, here used in, a popular meaning, are by no means coterminous. These two words are joined or separated by the word "or," a particle, of which the primary function is to co-ordinate two or more words between which there is an alternative. It is, I think, the only word in our language apt to have this effect. Its primary and ordinary meaning is the same, whether or not the first alternative is preceded by the word "either."

My Lords, averting my mind from the possible ill effects of an alternative choice between objects "charitable" and objects "benevolent," I cannot doubt that the plain meaning of the testator's words is that he has given this choice, and that, if he intended to give it, he could have used no words more apt to do so. Is there, then, anything in the context which narrows the area of choice by giving to the words "or benevolent" some other meaning than that which they primarily and naturally have? And if so, what is the other meaning which is to be given to them?

He examined the contention that 'or' was not to be used in its ordinary meaning, but as an explanatory word, equivalent to 'otherwise called'. This interpretation would mean that 'benevolent' means the same as charitable so the trust could be interpreted as being wholly charitable. His Lordship refused to accept this interpretation.

Then it was suggested that the words "or benevolent" should be construed as equivalent to "provided such objects are also of a benevolent character" that is to say, the objects must be charitable but of that order of charity which is commonly called benevolent. I think that this is only a roundabout way of saying that "or" should be read as "and," that the objects of choice must have the two characteristics of charitable and benevolent. It is possible that a context may justify so drastic a change as that involved in reading the disjunctive as conjunctive. I turn then to the context to see what justification it affords for reading the relevant words in any but their natural meaning. Reading and re-reading them, as your Lordships have so often done in the course of this case, I can find nothing which justifies such a departure. ... On the plain reading of this will I could only come to the conclusion that the testator intended exclusively to benefit charitable objects if I excised the words "or benevolent" which he has used. That I cannot do.

Coming to the conclusion that, on the true construction of this will, the executors may, if they think fit, distribute the testator's estate among objects which are benevolent but not charitable, I then ask what is in law the effect of such a disposition. My Lords, it may not have come as so rude a shock to some of your Lordships as it did to me to hear it suggested that there could be any doubt but that it is utterly invalid, but, in fact, the learned Attorney-General, if I understood his argument, categorically invited your Lordships to hold that a bequest for charitable or benevolent objects simpliciter is in English law a good and effective bequest, and urged that *In re Jarman's Estate* which decided the contrary should be over-ruled. In other words, his contention was that to enlarge the executors' area of choice so as to include benevolent objects which are not charitable with objects which are charitable does not make the whole gift fail for uncertainty. I do not see how, if his proposition is a sound one, it could be limited to the introduction of benevolent objects. Philanthropic objects, liberal objects, perhaps patriotic or public objects, must come within the scope of this new doctrine. Nor, if a gift for charitable or benevolent objects is valid, could it be any longer contended with any show of logic that a gift for benevolent objects alone is invalid. My Lords, I suggest that this proposition runs counter to authority and principle.

Salusbury v Denton **(1857) 3 K&J 529**

Panel: Sir Page Wood V-C

Facts: Mr Burroughs left part of the proceeds of an insurance policy upon trust for his wife, directing that she was to apply part either during her life or by her will, 'to the foundation of a charity school or such other charitable endowment for the benefit of the poor of Offley as she may prefer…'. The remainder was to be held for the benefit of relatives. Mr Burroughs directed his wife to choose how the fund should be split between these charitable and non-charitable purposes. She died without appointing, and without making a will. The question for the court was whether the fund could be severed and the charitable purpose upheld. It was held that it was possible to sever the gift and uphold the charitable purpose where the words show an intention to create separate funds, as here. The fund was divided into two equal parts, on the basis that equality is equity.

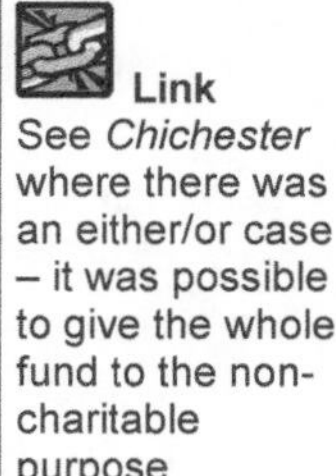
Link
See *Chichester* where there was an either/or case – it was possible to give the whole fund to the non-charitable purpose

SIR PAGE WOOD V-C

The first question that was argued was whether, as to the part intended by the testator for charitable purposes, the gift was or was not void; and as to this part of the case I have no doubt, as I said at the close of the argument, that it was not void, because under the terms of the will the widow had an option — she was at liberty to apply that part "to the foundation of a charity school, *or* such other charitable endowment," as in the will mentioned. And whatever may be the effect of the words "foundation of a charity school" occurring in the first branch of that alternative it is clear as to the second — the foundation of a charitable endowment — that a bequest for such a purpose would be a lawful bequest…

The judge then turned to the question whether the bequest was void for uncertainty on the basis that the testator had not specified which part should be applied for charitable purposes and which for private purposes, referring to two apparently conflicting cases:

The first of these — the case of *Doyley* v *The Attorney-General* — was very similar to the present. There the property in question was bequeathed in trust for certain purposes, and, subject thereto, the trustees and the survivor of them, and the heirs and executors of the survivor, were to dispose of it to such of his relations of his mother's side who were most deserving, and in such manner as they thought fit, *and* for such charitable uses and purposes as they should also think most proper and convenient; and the Master of the Rolls (Sir Joseph Jekyll) directed that one-half of the estate should go to the testator's relatives on the mother's side, and the other half to charitable uses; the known rule that equality is equity being, as he said, the best measure to go by.

It appears to me that there is no possibility of distinguishing that case from the present; for there can be no substantial difference between a direction to dispose of property to such relations and for such charitable purposes as the trustees should think most proper, and a direction like the present, to apply "a part" to such charitable purposes "and the remainder" among relatives with a like discretion. The two cases cannot be distinguished.

The case of *Down* v *Worrall* (1 My. & Kee. 561) will be found on examination not to conflict with that to which I have last referred. In *Down* v *Worrall* the testator left part of his residuary personal estate to his trustees to settle it either to or for charitable or pious purposes, at their discretion, or otherwise for the separate benefit of his sister and all or any of her children, in such manner as his trustees should think fit. And there it was held that a sum which remained at the decease of the surviving trustee, and which had not been applied either to charitable purposes or for the benefit of the testator's sister and her children, was undisposed of, and belonged to the testator's next of kin.

Now, whether that case can or cannot be reconciled with all the others on this subject, it is very clearly distinguished from the present: for it is one thing to direct a trustee to give *a part* of a fund to one set of objects *and the remainder* to another, and it is a distinct thing to direct him to give "either" to one set of objects "*or*" to another. *Down* v *Worrall* was a case of the latter description. There the trustees could give all to either of the objects. This is a case of the former description. Here the trustee was bound to give a part to each.

Link
see *Chichester*

I am therefore of opinion that, even if the case of *Down* v *Worrall* can be reconciled with the other authorities on this subject, it cannot affect my decision in the case before me. Here there is a plain direction to the widow to give a part to the charitable purposes referred to in the will as she may think fit, and the remainder among the testator's relatives as she may direct. And the widow having died without exercising that discretion, the moiety in question must be divided equally.

7.4 Trusts for Political Purposes

If the main object of an organisation is political, it cannot be said to be for charitable purposes. The following cases consider what 'counts' as political. Both cases contain lengthy dicta on 'public benefit' but these extracts focus on the issue of whether political purposes can be charitable.

***National Anti-Vivisection Society v Inland Revenue Commissioners* [1948] AC 31**

Panel: Viscount Simon, Lord Wright, Lord Porter, Lord Simonds and Lord Normand

Facts: The National Anti-Vivisection Society had the main aim of changing the law to ban vivisection, campaigning for the repeal of the Cruelty to Animals Act 1876 which allowed experiments on live animals without anaesthetic in certain circumstances. The Society claimed exemption from income tax on the basis that it was established for charitable purposes only, which gave it exemption under the Income Tax Act 1918. The court held that the society was not charitable for two reasons: first, the main object was political in that it campaigned for a change in the law; second, because any benefit to public morals was outweighed by the detriment to medical science and public health.

LORD SIMONDS

The first and shorter point is whether a main purpose of the society is of such a political character that the court cannot regard it as charitable. To this point little attention was directed in the courts below. It is mentioned only in the judgment of the learned Master of the Rolls. As will appear in the course of this opinion, it is worthy of more serious debate. ...

My Lords, on the first point the learned Master of the Rolls cites in his judgment a passage from the speech of Lord Parker in *Bowman v Secular Society, Ld*:

"A trust for the attainment of political objects has always been held invalid, not because it is illegal .... but because the court has no means of judging whether a proposed change in the law will or will not be for the public benefit."

Alert

Lord Parker is here considering the possibility of a valid charitable trust and nothing else and when he says "has always been held invalid" he means "has always been held not to be a valid charitable trust." The learned Master of the Rolls found this authoritative statement upon a branch of the law, with which no one was more familiar than Lord Parker, to be inapplicable to the present case for two reasons, first, because he felt difficulty in applying the words to "a change in the law which is in common parlance a 'non-political' question," and secondly, because he thought they could not in any case apply, when the desired legislation is "merely ancillary to the attainment of what is ex hypothesi a good charitable object."

My Lords, if I may deal with this second reason first, I cannot agree that in this case an alteration in the law is merely ancillary to the attainment of a good charitable object. In a sense no doubt, since legislation is not an end in itself, every law may be regarded as ancillary to the object which its provisions are intended to achieve. But that is not the sense in which it is said that a society has a political object. Here the finding of the commissioners is itself conclusive. "We are satisfied," they say, "that the main object of the society is the total abolition of vivisection .... and (for that purpose) the repeal of the Cruelty to Animals Act, 1876 , and the substitution of a new enactment prohibiting vivisection altogether." This is a finding that the main purpose of the society is the compulsory abolition of vivisection by Act of Parliament. What else can it mean? and how else can it be supposed that vivisection is to be abolished? Abolition and suppression are words that connote some form of compulsion. It can only be by Act of Parliament that that element can be supplied. ...

My Lords, I see no reason for supposing that Lord Parker in the cited passage used the expression "political objects" in any narrow sense or was confining it to objects of acute political controversy. On the contrary he was, I think, propounding familiar doctrine, nowhere better stated than in a text-book, [*Tyssen on Charitable Bequests*] …

Lord Parker uses slightly different language but means the same thing, when he says that the court has no means of judging whether a proposed change in the law will or will not be for the public benefit. It is not for the court to judge and the court has no means of judging. The same question may be looked at from a slightly different angle. One of the tests, and a crucial test, whether a trust is charitable, lies in the competence of the court to control and reform it. …But, my Lords, is it for a moment to be supposed that it is the function of the Attorney-General on behalf of the Crown to intervene and demand that a trust shall be established and administered by the court, the object of which is to alter the law in a manner highly prejudicial, as he and His Majesty's Government may think, to the welfare of the state? This very case would serve as an example, if upon the footing that it was a charitable trust it became the duty of the Attorney-General on account of its maladministration to intervene. There is undoubtedly a paucity of judicial authority on this point. …But in truth the reason of the thing appears to me so clear that I neither expect nor require much authority. I conclude upon this part of the case that a main object of the society is political and for that reason the society is not established for charitable purposes only.

***McGovern v Attorney General* [1982] Ch 321**

Panel: Slade J

Facts: The human rights organisation Amnesty International was advised that certain of its purposes were charitable and in 1977 the Amnesty International Trust Declaration was executed. The purposes were stated to be the relief of needy people who had recently been prisoners of conscience, and their families; attempting to secure the release of others; and procuring the abolition of torture. They applied to register the trust as a charity. The Charity Commissioners refused this as the main object of the trust was political: to procure a change in government policy and alter the law both in the UK and abroad.

MR JUSTICE SLADE

…[T]he court will not regard as charitable a trust of which a main object is to procure an alteration of the law of the United Kingdom for one or both of two reasons: first, the court will ordinarily have no sufficient means of judging as a matter of evidence whether the proposed change will or will not be for the public benefit. Secondly, even if the evidence suffices to enable it to form a prima facie opinion that a change in the law is desirable, it must still decide the case on the principle that the law is right as it stands, since to do otherwise would usurp the functions of the legislature. …

Thus far, the only types of political trust to which I have directed specific attention have been those of which a main object is to procure a change in the law of this country. The principles established by *Bowman's case* [1917] AC 406 and the *National Anti-Vivisection Society* case [1948] AC 31 will render such trusts non-charitable whether or not they are of a party-political nature. Conversely, however, several cases cited to me illustrate that trusts of which a main object is to promote the interests of a particular political party in this country fail to achieve charitable status, even though they are not directed towards any particular change in English law: see, for example, *Bonar Law Memorial Trust v Inland Revenue Commissioners* (1933) 17 TC 508, and *In re Hopkinson, decd.* [1949] 1 All ER 346. In my judgment any such trusts are plainly "political trusts" within the spirit, if not the letter, of Lord Parker of Waddington's pronouncement, and the same reasons for the court's refusing to enforce them would apply, but a fortiori. Since their nature would ex hypothesi be very controversial, the court could be faced with even greater difficulties in determining whether the objects of the trust would be for the public benefit; correspondingly, it would be at even greater risk of encroaching on the functions of the legislature and prejudicing its reputation for political impartiality, if it were to promote such objects by enforcing the trust.

I now turn to consider the status of a trust of which a main object is to secure the alteration of the laws of a *foreign* country. The mere fact that the trust was intended to be carried out abroad would not by itself necessarily deprive it of charitable status. ... The point with which I am at present concerned is whether a trust of which a direct and main object is to secure a change in the laws of a foreign country can *ever* be regarded as charitable under English law. Though I do not think that any authority cited to me precisely covers the point, I have come to the clear conclusion that it cannot.

... There is no obligation on the court to decide on the principle that any foreign law is ex hypothesi right as it stands; it is not obliged for all purposes to blind itself to what it may regard as the injustice of a particular foreign law.

In my judgment, however, there remain overwhelming reasons why such a trust still cannot be regarded as charitable. All the reasoning of Lord Parker of Waddington in *Bowman v Secular Society Ltd* [1917] AC 406 seems to me to apply a fortiori in such a case. A fortiori the court will have no adequate means of judging whether a proposed change in the law of a foreign country will or will not be for the public benefit. ...[T]he community which has to be considered in this context, even in the case of a trust to be executed abroad, is the community of the United Kingdom. Assuming that this is the right test, the court in applying it would still be bound to take account of the probable effects of attempts to procure the proposed legislation, or of its actual enactment, on the inhabitants of the country concerned, which would doubtless have a history and social structure quite different from that of the United Kingdom. Whatever might be its view as to the content of the relevant law from the standpoint of an English lawyer, it would, I think, have no satisfactory means of judging such probable effects upon the local community.

Furthermore, before ascribing charitable status to an English trust of which a main object was to secure the alteration of a foreign law, the court would also,

I conceive, be bound to consider the consequences for this country as a matter of public policy. In a number of such cases there would arise a substantial prima facie risk that such a trust, if enforced, could prejudice the relations of this country with the foreign country concerned: ... For all these reasons, I conclude that a trust of which a main purpose is to procure a change in the laws of a foreign country is a trust for the attainment of political objects within the spirit of Lord Parker of Waddington's pronouncement and, as such, is non-charitable.

... If a principal purpose of a trust is to procure a reversal of government policy or of particular administrative decisions of governmental authorities, does it constitute a trust for political purposes falling within the spirit of Lord Parker's pronouncement? In my judgment it does. If a trust of this nature is to be executed in England, the court will ordinarily have no sufficient means of determining whether the desired reversal would be beneficial to the public, and in any event could not properly encroach on the functions of the executive, acting intra vires, by holding that it should be acting in some other manner. If it is a trust which is to be executed abroad, the court will not have sufficient means of satisfactorily judging, as a matter of evidence, whether the proposed reversal would be beneficial to the community in the relevant sense, after all its consequences, local and international, had been taken into account. ...

I think one is again driven to the conclusion that trusts of the nature now under discussion, which are to be executed abroad, cannot qualify as charities any more than if they are to be executed in this country. The court, in considering whether particular methods of carrying out or reforming them would be for the public benefit, would be faced with an inescapable dilemma, of which a hypothetical example may be given. It appears from the Amnesty International Report 1978, p. 270, that Islamic law sanctions the death penalty for certain well-defined offences, namely, murder, adultery and brigandage. Let it be supposed that a trust were created of which the object was to secure the abolition of the death penalty for adultery in those countries where Islamic law applies, and to secure a reprieve for those persons who have been sentenced to death for this offence. The court, when invited to enforce or to reform such a trust, would either have to apply English standards as to public benefit, which would not necessarily be at all appropriate in the local conditions, or would have to attempt to apply local standards, of which it knew little or nothing. An English court would not, it seems to me, be competent either to control or reform a trust of this nature, and it would not be appropriate that it should attempt to do so.

This is limited to trusts of which the *purposes* are political. The fact that the trustees may employ political *means* in furthering the non-political purposes will not necessarily render it non-charitable.

8

Fiduciary Duties

8.1 What is a Fiduciary Duty?

A fiduciary duty is a legal obligation on the part of one person (the fiduciary) to act in the best interests of another person (the principal).

Fiduciary duties exist independently of any other form of duty which the fiduciary may owe to the principal. A trustee, for example, will owe the following duties to a beneficiary:

- **Trust duties** – these are duties which relate to the management and administration of the trust's affairs, e.g. the duty to keep accurate records, or to act even-handedly as between beneficiaries.
- **Statutory duties** – these are duties which statute imposes upon a trustee, e.g. the duty of care which is imposed by s1 Trustee Act 2000.
- **Fiduciary duties** – these are so-called 'overarching' duties which equity imposes upon the fiduciary because of the special relationship of trust which he occupies as regards the principal.

Equally, a fiduciary may owe contractual duties to his principal in addition to fiduciary duties, according to the nature of the particular relationship between the fiduciary and the principal.

8.2 The Relationships Which Give Rise to a Fiduciary Duty

A fiduciary duty arises where a relationship of 'trust and confidence', sometimes also characterised as a relationship of 'good faith' or 'loyalty', exists between the principal and the fiduciary.

There is no comprehensive list of the relationships which give rise to the existence of fiduciary duties under common law. Some relationships are automatically fiduciary, eg:

- Trustee and beneficiary
- Solicitor and client
- Agent and principal
- Company director and company (although this duty has now been codified by s170(1) Companies Act 2000)
- Business partner and co-partners

Other relationships, e.g. between a family member and an elderly relative, or between a company director and the company's shareholders, or between co-venturers in a joint property venture, will be characterised as fiduciary if the particular circumstances of the case establish that the relationship in question possesses the requisite characteristics of trust and confidence, good faith or loyalty. Each case turns upon its own facts.

8.3 The Duties of a Fiduciary

Although the duties of a fiduciary have been differently articulated on a number of occasions, there are two themes which consistently emerge from the cases, the classic exposition of which appears from *Bray v Ford* [1896] AC 44.

***Bray v Ford* [1896] AC 44**

Panel: Lord Halsbury LC, Lord Watson, Lord Herschell and Lord Shand

Facts: The respondent (Ford) was a governor of the Yorkshire College. He also acted as solicitor to the College, in which capacity he received payment for his services. The appellant (Bray) circulated a letter in which he alleged that in receiving payment Ford had 'illegally and improperly' taken advantage of his position as a fiduciary. Ford brought a libel action against Bray. A critical issue in the case was whether Bray's accusation was justified, i.e. was he correct in saying that, as a fiduciary, Ford was not entitled to charge for his services.

LORD HERSCHELL

It is an inflexible rule of a Court of Equity that a person in a fiduciary position, such as the respondent's, is not, unless otherwise expressly provided, entitled to make a profit; he is not allowed to put himself in a position where his interest and duty conflict. It does not appear to me that this rule is, as has been said, founded upon principles of morality. I regard it rather as based on the consideration that, human nature being what it is, there is danger, in such circumstances, of the person holding a fiduciary position being swayed by interest rather than by duty, and thus prejudicing those whom he was bound to protect.

Link
See also Authorised Remuneration, Section 6.

So:

- A fiduciary must not put himself in a position of actual or potential conflict with the interests of the principal. Potential conflict arises where there is a realistic possibility of a potential conflict rather than a mere theoretical prospect.
- A fiduciary must not derive personal profit from his position as a fiduciary.

Link
See the extract from Imageview Management v Jack below.

A more modern, and possibly wider, formulation of the duties of a fiduciary was given by Millett LJ in *Bristol and West Building Society v Mothew* [1998] Ch 1.

***Bristol and West Building Society v Mothew* [1998] Ch 1**

Panel: Staughton, Millett and Otton LJJ

Facts: The defendant solicitor acted for the claimant in relation to a mortgage advance on a property which the claimant subsequently repossessed and sold for less than the amount outstanding under the mortgage. Prior to completion of the mortgage, the defendant had failed to inform the claimant that the borrowers were funding part of the balance of the purchase price by way of a second mortgage. The claimant alleged that this failure amounted to a breach of fiduciary duty (as well as a breach of the defendant's contractual and tortious duties to it) with the result that the defendant was liable for the whole of the claimant's loss, without the claimant having to prove that it would not have proceeded with the advance if it had been told the true position. The Court of Appeal held that, although the solicitor had acted in breach of his contractual and tortuous duties to the claimant, he had not acted in breach of any fiduciary duty.

LORD JUSTICE MILLETT

The expression "fiduciary duty" is properly confined to those duties which are peculiar to fiduciaries and the breach of which attracts legal consequences differing from those consequent upon the breach of other duties. Unless the expression is so limited it is lacking in practical utility. In this sense it is obvious that not every breach of duty by a fiduciary is a breach of fiduciary duty. I would endorse the observations of Southin J in *Girardet v Crease & Co* (1987) 11 BCLR (2d) 361, 362:

"The word 'fiduciary' is flung around now as if it applied to all breaches of duty by solicitors, directors of companies and so forth. ...That a lawyer can commit a breach of the special duty [of a fiduciary] ... by entering into a contract with the client without full disclosure ...and so forth is clear. But to say that simple carelessness in giving advice is such a breach is a perversion of words. ...It is similarly inappropriate to apply the expression to the obligation of a trustee or other fiduciary to use proper skill and care in the discharge of his duties. If it is confined to cases where the fiduciary nature of the duty has special legal consequences, then the fact that the source of the duty is to be found in equity rather than the common law does not make it a fiduciary duty. ..."

I respectfully agree, and endorse the comment of Ipp J in *Permanent Building Society v Wheeler* (1994) 14 ACSR 109, 157:

"It is essential to bear in mind that the existence of a fiduciary relationship does not mean that every duty owed by a fiduciary to the beneficiary is a fiduciary duty. In particular, a trustee's duty to exercise reasonable care, though equitable, is not specifically a fiduciary duty. ... The director's duty to exercise care and skill has nothing to do with any position of disadvantage or vulnerability on the part of the company. It is not a duty that stems from the requirements of trust and confidence imposed on a fiduciary. In my opinion, that duty is not a fiduciary duty, although it is a duty actionable in the equitable jurisdiction of this court. ..."

... This leaves those duties which are special to fiduciaries and which attract those remedies which are peculiar to the equitable jurisdiction and are primarily restitutionary or restorative rather than compensatory. A fiduciary is someone who has undertaken to act for or on behalf of another in a particular matter in circumstances which give rise to a relationship of trust and confidence. The distinguishing obligation of a fiduciary is the obligation of loyalty. The principal is entitled to the single-minded loyalty of his fiduciary. This core liability has

several facets. A fiduciary must act in good faith; he must not make a profit out of his trust; he must not place himself in a position where his duty and his interest may conflict; he may not act for his own benefit or the benefit of a third person without the informed consent of his principal. This is not intended to be an exhaustive list, but it is sufficient to indicate the nature of fiduciary obligations. They are the defining characteristics of the fiduciary. As Dr Finn pointed out in his classic work Fiduciary Obligations (1977), p 2, he is not subject to fiduciary obligations because he is a fiduciary; it is because he is subject to them that he is a fiduciary.

The nature of the obligation determines the nature of the breach. The various obligations of a fiduciary merely reflect different aspects of his core duties of loyalty and fidelity. Breach of fiduciary obligation, therefore, connotes disloyalty or infidelity. Mere incompetence is not enough. A servant who loyally does his incompetent best for his master is not unfaithful and is not guilty of a breach of fiduciary duty."

8.3.1 The 'No Conflict' Rule

The 'no conflict' rule has given rise to a number of sub-rules, including the 'self-dealing rule' and the 'fair dealing' rule.

***Right Reverend Hollis (Bishop of Portsmouth) and others v Rolfe and others* [2008] All ER (D) 295 (Jul)**

Panel: Evans-Lombe J

Facts: The claimants alleged that the defendants had sold a property which had been held on charitable trusts to some of their number in circumstances which amounted to a breach of the 'no-conflict' rule.

MR JUSTICE EVANS-LOMBE

There are in fact three rules. There is what one may call the "primitive self-dealing rule" which does not require any trust or fiduciary relationship but results from the fact that no-one can contract with himself and any attempt to do so is ineffective.

The second rule, usually referred to as the "self-dealing rule", is "that if a trustee sells the trust property to himself, the sale is voidable by any beneficiary ex debito justitiae, however fair the transaction." See *Tito v Waddell (No 2)* [1977] Ch 106 at 241.

The third rule, commonly known as the "fair dealing rule", is "that if a trustee purchases the beneficial interest of any of his beneficiaries, the transaction is not voidable *ex debito justitiae*, but can be set aside by the beneficiary unless the trustee can show that he has taken no advantage of his position and has made full disclosure to the beneficiary, and that the transaction is fair and honest." See *Tito v Waddell* ibid at 241.

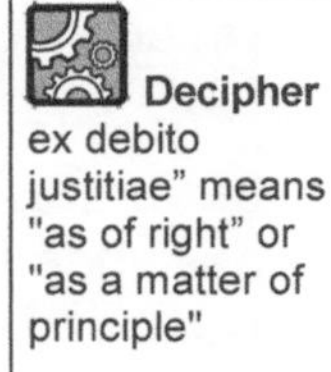

Decipher
ex debito justitiae" means "as of right" or "as a matter of principle"

The relationship between the self-dealing rule and the fair-dealing rule, and also the applicability of those rules to an acquisition of trust property by a company in which a trustee holds a controlling interest, was considered by Vinelott J in *Re Thompson's Settlement, Thompson v Thompson* [1986] Ch 99.

***Re Thompson's Settlement, Thompson v Thompson* [1986] Ch 99**

Panel: Vinelott J

Facts: The settlor had created a settlement under which two farms, one in England and the other in Scotland, were held upon trust for his two sons (Wilfrid and Jack), who were two of the three trustees of the settlement. The two farms were let to a company ('the old company'), of which the settlor's wife and his two sons were the directors. Following the settlor's death it was agreed that each son should take one of the farms. The proposal was that the farm in England would be transferred to a partnership between Wilfrid and his two children, while the farm in Scotland would be transferred to a farming company ('the new company') which was controlled by Jack and his wife. In anticipation of the formal transfer of the land to the partnership and the new company respectively, which had to await the outcome of various valuation issues, the leases of the two farms were assigned to or vested in the partnership and the new company. It was held that those transactions were unlawful.

MR JUSTICE VINELOTT

The scope of the self-dealing rule and the relationship between that rule and the fair-dealing rule were explained by Sir Robert Megarry V-C in *Tito v Waddell (No 2)* [1977] Ch 106, 240:

"Self-dealing and fair-dealing. Let me revert briefly to the subject of the rules about self-dealing and fair-dealing, though on the view I take I doubt if much turns on this. ... The self-dealing rule is (to put it very shortly) that if a trustee sells the trust property to himself, the sale is voidable by any beneficiary ex debito justitiae, however fair the transaction. The fair-dealing rule is (again putting it very shortly) that if a trustee purchases the beneficial interest of any of his beneficiaries, the transaction is not voidable ex debito justitiae but can be set aside by the beneficiary unless the trustee can show that he has taken no advantage of his position and has made full disclosure to the beneficiary, and that the transaction is fair and honest. ... I can well see that both rules ... have a common origin in that equity is astute to prevent a trustee from abusing his position or profiting from his trust: the shepherd must not become a wolf. But subject to that, it seems to me that for all practical purposes there are two rules: the consequences are different, and the property and the transactions which invoke the rules are different."

...The classic statement of the [self-dealing] rule is to be found in the judgment of Lord Eldon LC in *Ex parte Lacey* (1802) 6 Ves Jun 625, a case where the assignee in bankruptcy of a bankrupt's estate purchased a part of the estate. Having stated the rule that a trustee undertakes to manage the trust property for his beneficiaries and not for the benefit and advantage of himself he explained the reason for the rule, at p 626a:

Decipher
'Cestui que trusts' means 'beneficiary

"I disavow that interpretation of Lord Rosslyn's doctrine, that the trustee must make advantage. I say, whether he makes advantage, or not, if the connection does not satisfactorily appear to have been dissolved, it is in the choice of the *cestui que trusts* whether they will take back the property, or not; if the trustee has made no advantage. It is founded upon this; that though you may see in a particular case, that he has not made advantage, it is utterly impossible to examine upon satisfactory evidence in the power of the court, by which I mean, in the power of the parties, in ninety-nine cases out of a hundred, whether he has made advantage or not."

The only other case to which I need refer is *Holder v Holder* [1968] Ch 353. ...The relevant facts are that the third defendant, Victor Holder, was appointed one of the executors of his father's will. He was already tenant of two farms owned by the testator. After the death of the testator Victor performed some acts which it was later conceded were acts of administration which precluded him from renouncing office as executor. Later he executed a purported renunciation. Probate was granted to two of the other executors named in the will. They put the two farms of which he was tenant up for sale by auction. At the auction, which was attended by most of the members of the family, Victor, through an agent, bid successfully for the farms. The farms were conveyed to him after some delay. The plaintiff, another son of the testator, started an action to set aside the conveyance to Victor. Cross J, after referring to the rule that an executor who renounces probate before he has done any acts of administration may buy any part of the testator's property from the proving executors, declined to apply the rule to the purchase by Victor. His decision was reversed by the Court of Appeal. Harman LJ said, at p 391:

"The judge decided in favour of the plaintiff on this point because Victor at the time of the sale was himself still in a fiduciary position and like any other trustee could not purchase the trust property. I feel the force of this argument, but doubt its validity in the very special circumstances of this case. The reason for the rule is that a man may not be both vendor and purchaser; but Victor was never in that position here. He took no part in instructing the valuer who fixed the reserves or in the preparations for the auction. Everyone in the family knew that he was not a seller but a buyer. In this case Victor never assumed the duties of an executor. It is true that he concurred in 'signing a few cheques for trivial sums and endorsing a few insurance policies, but he never, so far as appears, interfered in any way with the administration of the estate. It is true he managed the farms, but he did that as tenant and not as executor. He acquired no special knowledge as executor. What he knew he knew as tenant of the farms. Another reason lying behind the rule is that there must never be a conflict of duty and interest, but in fact there was none here in the case of Victor, who made no secret throughout that he intended to buy. ... [The] acts were only technically acts of intermeddling and I find no case where the circumstances are parallel. Of course, I feel the force of the judge's reasoning that if Victor remained an executor he is within the rule, but in a case where the reasons behind the rule do not exist I do not feel bound to apply it. ..."

[The] first submission [is] that the self-dealing rule has no application to a sale by trustees to a company, although if any of the trustees has an interest in the company, the transaction falls within the fair-dealing rule. [Counsel] founded this submission on the well-known case of *Farrar v Farrars Ltd* (1888) 40 Ch D 395. In that case three mortgagees were in possession of the mortgaged property. One of them, J R Farrar, was also solicitor to the mortgagees. The property was sold to a company which was to some extent promoted by J R Farrar and in which he took a small shareholding and for which he also acted as solicitor. He took no part in the negotiations. An action to set aside the transaction failed. Lindley LJ said, at pp. 409-410:

Link
For the significance of this fact see the commentary below.

"A sale by a person to a corporation of which he is a member is not, either in form or in substance, a sale by a person to himself. To hold that it is, would be to ignore the principle which lies at the root of the legal idea of a corporate body, and that idea is that the corporate body is distinct from the persons composing it. A sale by a member of a corporation to the corporation itself is in every sense a sale valid in equity as well as at law. There is no authority for saying that such a sale is not warranted by an ordinary power of sale, and in our opinion, such a sale is warranted by such a power, and does not fall within the rule to which we have at present referred. But although this is true, it is obvious that a sale by a person to an incorporated company of which he is a member may be invalid upon various grounds, although it may not be reached by the rule which prevents a man from selling to himself or to a trustee for himself. Such a sale may, for example, be fraudulent and at an undervalue or it may be made under circumstances which throw upon the purchasing company the burden of proving the validity of the transaction, and the company may be unable to prove it."

Later he observed, at p. 410:

"But the sale cannot be set aside on the simple ground that Mr Farrar was a trustee for sale, and was a promoter of and shareholder in the company which purchased from him. It is necessary to see what his duties to his mortgagors were, and what he really did."

Then at the end of his judgment he said, at p 415:

"Mr Farrar was not a trustee selling to himself, or to others for him, nor was he buying directly or indirectly for himself, and although a sale by a mortgagee to a company promoted by himself, of which he is the solicitor, and in which he has shares, is one which the company must prove to have been bona fide, and at a price at which the mortgagees could properly sell, yet if such proves to be the fact, there is no rule of law which compels the court to set aside the sale. *Ex parte Lacey* does not require the court to hold the sale invalid, however fair and honest it may be, although the judgment in that case does throw upon the company the burden of shewing that the sale was fair and honest."

I do not think that this case assists Mr Price. [Jack] was not at the material time simply a shareholder of the new company. He and his wife were directors of the new company and he was its managing director. Their duty as directors was to further the interests of the new company in which, as it happened, they held a majority of the shares at the time of the purported assignment of the lease of the [Scottish farm]. The position as between the trustees ... and the directors of the new company is the same as it would have been if [Jack] had been a trustee of a settlement instead of a director of a company. ...[Wilfrid], of course, as a partner in a farming partnership was clearly precluded from dealing with himself as one of the trustees ... .

[The] other and more radical submission [which is] founded upon *Holder v Holder* [1968] Ch 353 [is] that the self-dealing rule only applies to a sale by trustees to one of their number, alone or jointly with others, or to a purchase by trustees from one of their number, alone or jointly with others, and to analogous dealings with trust property or trust moneys such as the grant of a lease by or to trustees. He founded that submission upon the statement by Harman LJ, at p 391, that "The reason for the rule is that a man may not be both vendor and purchaser..." He submitted that in the instant case the only dealings analogous to the sale of property were the assignments or purported assignments of the leases which were never themselves trust property. He submitted that in such a case the fair-dealing rule applies (because it is founded on the principle that a man must not put himself in a position where his duty and interest conflict and because in relation to the trustees it was their duty to consider whether to consent to the assignments) but not the self-dealing rule which only applies if there is a sale or purchase by trustees or something analogous to it. I do not think that the self-dealing rule can be so confined. It is clear that the self-dealing rule is an application of the wider principle that a man must not put himself in a position where duty and interest conflict or where his duty to one conflicts with his duty to another ... . The principle is applied stringently in cases where a trustee concurs in a transaction which cannot be carried into effect without his concurrence and who also has an interest in or owes a fiduciary duty to another in relation to the same transaction. The transaction cannot stand if challenged by a beneficiary because in the absence of an express provision in the trust instrument the beneficiaries are entitled to require that the trustees act unanimously and that each brings to bear a mind unclouded by any contrary interest or duty in deciding whether it is in the interest of the beneficiaries that the trustees concur in it.

The same principle also applies, but less stringently, in a case within the fair-dealing rule, such as the purchase by a trustee of a beneficiary's beneficial interest. There, there are genuinely two parties to the transaction and it will be allowed to stand if freely entered into and if the trustee took no advantage from his position or from any knowledge acquired from it.

In the instant case the concurrence of the trustees ... was required if the leases were to be assigned to or new tenancies created in favour of the new company and the partnership. The beneficiaries were entitled to ask that the trustees should give unprejudiced consideration to the question whether they should refuse to concur in the assignments in the expectation that a surrender of the

> leases might be negotiated from the old company and the estates sold or let on the open market.
>
> The decision of the Court of Appeal in *Holder v Holder* [1968] Ch 353 does not in my judgment assist [the trustees]. The reason why, in the words of Harman LJ, the rule did not apply was that Victor, though he might technically have been made an executor notwithstanding the purported renunciation, had never acted as executor in a way which could be taken to amount to acceptance of a duty to act in the interests of the beneficiaries under his father's will.

The following points emerge from this decision:

(a) The 'self-dealing' rule and the 'fair dealing' rule are distinct, though they both derive from the 'no conflict' rule.

(b) A fiduciary will, it appears, not infringe the self-dealing rule if, as in *Holder*, his acts as fiduciary have been so inconsequential that it is not right in all the circumstances to treat him as being a fiduciary for the purposes of the rule.

(c) A sale to a company in which the fiduciary holds a controlling interest amounts to a sale to the fiduciary.

(d) The position will be different where the fiduciary has only a small or minority shareholding: *Farrar*. However, where the fiduciary holds only a minority interest it will still be for the company to show that the fiduciary took all reasonable steps to obtain the best price.

8.4 The 'No Profit' Rule

This rule is applied very strictly. It applies to any form of payment or advantage which a fiduciary receives as a result of the position which he holds.

8.4.1 Bribes and secret commissions received by a trustee

***Williams v Barton* [1927] 2 Ch 9**

Panel: Russell J

Facts: The defendant, one of two trustees of a will, was employed as a clerk by a firm of stockbrokers on the terms that his salary should consist of half the commission earned by the firm on business introduced by him. On the defendant's recommendation, the firm was employed to value the testator's securities. The firm's charges were paid out of the testator's estate and, in accordance with its contract with the defendant, the firm paid him half the fees received. The defendant took no part in making the valuations or in fixing the fees to be charged. His co-trustee brought an action claiming that the defendant was bound to treat the fees paid to him as part of the testator's estate. It was held that the defendant had acted in breach of fiduciary duty and was liable to account for the fee.

MR JUSTICE RUSSELL

It is a well-established and salutary rule of equity that a trustee may not make a profit out of his trust. A person who has the management of property as a trustee is not permitted to gain any profit by availing himself of his position, and will be a constructive trustee of any such profit for the benefit of the persons equitably entitled to the property. On the same principle a trustee has no right to charge for his time and trouble. The rule is thus stated by Lord Herschell in *Bray v Ford* [1896] AC 44: "It is an inflexible rule of a Court of Equity that a person in a fiduciary position .... is not, unless otherwise expressly provided, entitled to make a profit; he is not allowed to put himself in a position where his interest and duty conflict." It was argued on behalf of the defendant that the case was altogether outside that rule of equity, because the sums received by the defendant were merely parts of his salary paid to him by his employers under the contract of service and were not of a character for which he was liable to account.

The point is not an easy one and there is little, if any, authority to assist in its determination. The situation is an unusual one and the contract of service presents the following peculiar features. The remuneration has no relation to the services, which the defendant has to render to his employers. The defendant, while bound to render the services, might get no remuneration at all if he introduced no work, or introduced none which was acceptable to his employers. The amount of his remuneration depends (subject to his employers' acceptance of orders) upon his own efforts, but upon efforts not in relation to the work which he is engaged to do. Any increase of his remuneration rests with him.

From this it seems to me evident that the case falls within the mischief which is sought to be prevented by the rule. The case is clearly one where his duty as trustee and his interest in an increased remuneration are in direct conflict. As a trustee it is his duty to give the estate the benefit of his unfettered advice in choosing the stockbrokers to act for the estate; as the recipient of half the fees to be earned by [the firm] on work introduced by him his obvious interest is to choose or recommend them for the job.

In the event that has happened they have been chosen, and chosen because the defendant was a trustee, with the result that half of what the estate pays must necessarily pass through them to the defendant as part of his remuneration for other services rendered, but as an addition to the remuneration which he would otherwise have received for those self-same services. The services rendered remain unchanged, but the remuneration for them has been increased. He has increased his remuneration by virtue of his trusteeship. In my opinion this increase of remuneration is a profit made by the defendant out of and by reason of his trusteeship, which he would not have made but for his position as trustee.

Alert

8.4.2 Directors' fees

Where the property of a trust includes shares in a company, the ownership of which entitles the trustees to appoint the directors of that company, the trustees cannot appoint themselves as directors and draw fees or salary as a consequence, although they may recover out-of-pocket expenses.

***In re Macadam, Dallow v Codd* [1946] Ch 73**

Panel: Cohen J

Facts: A trust fund consisted of shares in a limited company which had been formed by the testator. The company's articles of association empowered the trustees, as holders of all the shares in the company, to appoint two directors. The trustees appointed themselves as directors and received directors' fees. They were held to have acted in breach of fiduciary duty in receiving those fees.

MR JUSTICE COHEN

The question has been raised whether the [trustees] are entitled to retain the directors' fees received by them from the company or whether they are accountable to the trust estate for the sums received by them as remuneration in respect of the office of director. I desire to say at once that nobody suggested any impropriety on their part in regard to this remuneration. The question was asked purely as one of law whether, having regard to all the provisions of the material documents, on general principles of law, they are accountable or not. .... The principle, I think, is well stated in a passage from the speech of Lord Herschell in *Bray v Ford* ... as follows: "It is an inflexible rule of a court of equity that a person in a fiduciary position .... is not, unless otherwise expressly provided, entitled to make a profit; he is not allowed to put himself in a position where his interest and duty conflict. ...

The ... nearest ... case to the present - although it is a much stronger case than the one I have to decide – is *Williams v Barton* ... .

That case is ... much stronger than the present case, because, first, the profit in a sense came directly out of the estate, and, secondly, because it was a profit earned in a sense without any work done by him. I think that the root of the matter really is: Did [the trustee] acquire the position in respect of which he drew the remuneration by virtue of his position as trustee? In the present case there can be no doubt that the only way in which the [trustees] became directors was by exercise of the powers vested in the trustees of the will under ... the articles of association of the company. The principle is one which has always been regarded as of the greatest importance in these courts, and I do not think I ought to do anything to weaken it. As I have said, although the remuneration was remuneration for services as director of the company, the opportunity to receive that remuneration was gained as a result of the exercise of a discretion vested in the trustees, and they had put themselves in a position where their interest and duty conflicted. In those circumstances, I do not think this court can allow them to make a profit out of doing so, and I do not think the liability to

> account for a profit can be confined to cases where the profit is derived directly from the trust estate. I leave over the matter of the exact wording of the order, because I do not want to do anything to prejudice the question whether, in the circumstances, I ought not to allow the plaintiffs to retain the whole or a part of the remuneration. If I can be satisfied (and that is the point I had not considered) that they were the best persons to be directors, I do not think it would be right for me to expect them to do the extra work for nothing.

Link
See Authorised Remuneration below.

Mr Justice Cohen decided that:

(a) The 'no profit' rule is engaged whenever a trustee derives a benefit or advantage by virtue of his position as trustee;

(b) It is irrelevant that the 'profit' does not come at the expense of the trust but is derived from elsewhere; and

(c) It is may nonetheless be appropriate (see the discussion of 'Authorised remuneration') to allow a trustee who has made a profit to receive some reward for his services.

8.4.3 Exploiting opportunities

A fiduciary must not make a profit from an opportunity which only comes his way because of his fiduciary position. The prohibition applies regardless of whether the fiduciary's exploitation of the opportunity also benefits his principal, and also regardless of the fact that the principal could not have exploited the opportunity so as to make the profit.

***Boardman v Phipps* [1967] 2 AC 46**

Panel: Viscount Dilhorne, Lord Cohen, Lord Hodson, Lord Guest and Lord Upjohn

Facts: A trust fund owned 8,000 of the 30,000 shares in a private company. One of the appellants (B) was the solicitor to the trust. As the result of an inquiry by the company as to whether the trustees would be willing to sell the trust shares to the company, B made various enquires into the company's affairs. Those enquiries enabled B to obtain a considerable amount of information regarding the financial position of the company. B, along with one of the other beneficiaries (P), also an appellant, formed the view that a re-organisation of the company's business would substantially improve the position of its shareholders. Having been unable to persuade the board to accept their proposals for re-organisation, B and P set about acquiring the remaining 22,000 shares for themselves (at no time did the trust have sufficient funds to acquire the shares). Having bought the vast majority of those shares, B and P were able to take control of the company and secure the re-organisation which they had proposed. This significantly improved the dividend and capital value of the shares, to the benefit of the trust as much as to B and P. Following the sale by B and P of their shares at a very substantial profit, the other beneficiaries brought proceedings in which they called upon B and P to account to the trust for the profit which they had made. It was held that B and P had acted in breach of fiduciary duty and were therefore liable to account for that profit.

LORD COHEN

Wilberforce J and, in the Court of Appeal, both Lord Denning MR and Pearson LJ, based their decision in favour of the respondent on the decision of your Lordships' House in *Regal (Hastings) Ltd v Gulliver* [1967] 2 AC 134. I turn, therefore, to consider that case ... in particular ... a passage in the speech of Lord Russell of Killowen where he says:

"The rule of equity which insists on those, who by use of a fiduciary position make a profit, being liable to account for that profit, in no way depends on fraud, or absence of bona fides, or upon such questions or considerations as whether the profit would or should otherwise have gone to the plaintiff, or whether the profiteer was under a duty to obtain the source of the profit for the plaintiff, or whether he took a risk or acted as he did for the benefit of the plaintiff, or whether the plaintiff has in fact been damaged or benefited by his action. The liability arises from the mere fact of a profit having, in the stated circumstances, been made."

[and also] a passage in the speech of Lord Wright, where he says:

"That question can be briefly stated to be whether an agent, a director, a trustee or other person in an analogous fiduciary position, when a demand is made upon him by the person to whom he stands in the fiduciary relationship to account for profits acquired by him by reason of his fiduciary position, and by reason of the opportunity and the knowledge, or either, resulting from it, is entitled to defeat the claim upon any ground save that he made profits with the knowledge and assent of the other person. The most usual and typical case of this nature is that of principal and agent. The rule in such cases is compendiously expressed to be that an agent must account for net profits secretly (that is, without the knowledge of his principal) acquired by him in the course of his agency. The authorities show how manifold and various are the applications of the rule. It does not depend on fraud or corruption."

...In that case the profit arose through the application by four of the directors of Regal for shares in a subsidiary company which it had been the original intention of the board should be subscribed for by Regal. Regal had not the requisite money available but there was no question of it being ultra vires Regal to subscribe for the shares. In the circumstances Lord Russell of Killowen said:

"I have no hesitation in coming to the conclusion, upon the facts of this case, that these shares, when acquired by the directors, were acquired by reason, and only by reason of the fact that they were directors of Regal, and in the course of their execution of that office."

He goes on to consider whether the four directors were in a fiduciary relationship to Regal and concludes that they were. Accordingly, they were held accountable.

Alert

In the case before your Lordships it seems to me clear that the appellants throughout were obtaining information from the company [on behalf of the trustees] for the purpose [of extracting information as to the company's business] but it does not necessarily follow that the appellants were thereby debarred from acquiring shares in the company for themselves. They were bound to give the information to the trustees but they could not exclude it from their own minds. ...[The] mere use of any knowledge or opportunity which comes to the trustee or agent in the course of his trusteeship or agency does not necessarily make him liable to account. In the present case had the company been a public company and had the appellants bought the shares on the market, they would not, I think, have been accountable. But the company is a private company and not only the information but the opportunity to purchase these shares came to them through the introduction which [B was given] to the board of the company and ... when the discussions [moved on] to the proposed split-up of the company's undertaking it was solely on behalf of the trustees that [B] was purporting to negotiate with the board of the company. ...

[The] fact [is] that the appellants obtained both the information which satisfied them that the purchase of the shares would be a good investment and the opportunity of acquiring them as a result of acting for certain purposes on behalf of the trustees. Information is, of course, not property in the strict sense of that word and, as I have already stated, it does not necessarily follow that because an agent acquired information and opportunity while acting in a fiduciary capacity he is accountable to his principals for any profit that comes his way as the result of the use he makes of that information and opportunity. His liability to account must depend on the facts of the case. In the present case much of the information came the appellants' way when [B] was acting on behalf of the trustees ... and the opportunity of bidding for the shares came because he purported for all purposes except for making the bid to be acting on behalf of the owners of the 8,000 shares in the company. In these circumstances it seems to me that the principle of the *Regal* case applies and that the courts below came to the right conclusion.

Link
See the discussion of remedies (below).

That is enough to dispose of the case but I would add that an agent is, in my opinion, liable to account for profits he makes out of trust property if there is a possibility of conflict between his interest and his duty to his principal. [B and P] were not general agents of the trustees but they were their agents for certain limited purposes. The information they had obtained and the opportunity to purchase the 21,986 shares afforded them by their relations with the directors of the company ... were not property in the strict sense but that information and that opportunity they owed to their representing themselves as agents for the holders of the 8,000 shares held by the trustees. In these circumstances they could not, I think, use that information and that opportunity to purchase the shares for themselves if there was any possibility that the trustees might wish to acquire them for the trust. [B] was the solicitor whom the trustees were in the habit of consulting if they wanted legal advice ... [and he] would not have been able to give unprejudiced advice if he had been consulted by the trustees and

> was at the same time negotiating for the purchase of the shares on behalf of himself and [P]. In other words, there was, in my opinion, at the crucial date ... a possibility of a conflict between his interest and his duty.
>
> In making these observations I have referred to the fact that [B] was the solicitor to the trust. [P] was only a beneficiary and was not as such debarred from bidding for the shares, but no attempt was made in the courts below to differentiate between them. Had such an attempt been made it would very likely have failed as [P] left the negotiations largely to [B] and it might well be held that if [B] was disqualified from bidding [P] could not be in a better position. ...
>
> I desire to repeat that the integrity of the appellants is not in doubt. They acted with complete honesty throughout and the respondent is a fortunate man in that the rigour of equity enables him to participate in the profits which have accrued as the result of the action taken by the appellants ... in purchasing the shares at their own risk. As the last paragraph of his judgment clearly shows, the trial judge evidently shared this view. He directed an inquiry as to what sum is proper to be allowed to the appellants or either of them in respect of his work and skill in obtaining the said shares and the profits in respect thereof. The trial judge concluded by expressing the opinion that payment should be on a liberal scale. With that observation I respectfully agree."

Link
See Authorised Remuneration below.

Although the defendants were ordered to account for the profits which they had made, they were, however, allowed payment for their services on a liberal scale.

Lord Cohen's speech illustrates the following propositions:

(a) A fiduciary's liability to account for profit has nothing to do with fraud, dishonesty or bad faith; it flows from the very nature of the fiduciary relationship.

(b) A fiduciary can use knowledge which he has obtained *by virtue of* his fiduciary position *only* for the benefit of his principal. Hence Lord Cohen's reference to the fact that if the company had been publicly listed, such that Boardman had obtained all the relevant information from its publicly-filed accounts, then no liability to account would have arisen.

(c) Where the fiduciary's actions yield a profit both for his principal as well as himself, he may be entitled to be paid for his skill and effort in achieving the profit for the principal, notwithstanding his breach of fiduciary duty. see Authorised remuneration.

8.5 Authorised Remuneration

8.5.1 The inherent jurisdiction

The court has an inherent jurisdiction to authorise the payment of remuneration to express trustees, constructive trustees and other fiduciaries. However, the power to authorise remuneration is to be exercised sparingly. In particular, it should not offer any encouragement to trustees to act in breach of duty

***Guinness plc v Saunders* [1990] 2 AC 663**

Panel: Lord Keith of Kinkel, Lord Brandon of Oakbrook, Lord Templeman, Lord Griffiths and Lord Goff of Chieveley

Facts: The plaintiff company had made a takeover bid for one of its competitors. The two defendants and a third person, who were directors of the plaintiff and the only members of its remuneration committee, agreed to pay the second defendant (W) 0.2 per cent of the ultimate value of the bid for his services in providing advice and services in connection with the bid. That decision was not authorised by the plaintiff's board of directors. Following successful completion of the bid, in relation to which W carried out a significant amount of work, W received the agreed payment, which amounted to £5.2m. On discovering the facts, the plaintiff claimed recovery of the money on the ground that W had received the payment in breach of his fiduciary duty as a director, in that he had not disclosed his interest in the agreement to the plaintiffs' directors as required by Companies Act 1985 s317(1). W claimed that he should be allowed remuneration for the work which he had performed, but his claim was rejected.

LORD GOFF DF CHIEVELEY

The leading authorities ... demonstrate that the directors of a company, like other fiduciaries, must not put themselves in a position where there is a conflict between their personal interests and their duties as fiduciaries, and are for that reason precluded from contracting with the company for their services except in circumstances authorised by the articles of association. Similarly, just as trustees are not entitled, in the absence of an appropriate provision in the trust deed, to remuneration for their services as trustees, so directors are not entitled to remuneration for their services as directors except as provided by the articles of association.

...But the principle does not altogether exclude the possibility that an equitable allowance might be made in respect of services rendered. That such an allowance may be made to a trustee for work performed by him for the benefit of the trust, even though he was not in the circumstances entitled to remuneration under the terms of the trust deed, is now well established ... [see *Boardman v Phipps*]. Wilberforce J directed that, when accounting for such profits, not merely should a deduction be made for expenditure which was necessary to enable the profit to be realised, but also a liberal allowance or credit should be made for their work and skill. His reasoning was ...

"Moreover, account must naturally be taken of the expenditure which was necessary to enable the profit to be realised. But, in addition to expenditure, should not the defendants be given an allowance or credit for their work and skill? This is a subject on which authority is scanty; but Cohen J, in *In re Macadam* [1946] Ch 73, gave his support to an allowance of this kind to trustees for their services in acting as directors of a company. It seems to me that this transaction, ie, the acquisition of a controlling interest in the company, was one of a special character calling for the exercise of a particular kind of professional skill. If Boardman had not assumed the role of seeing it through, the beneficiaries would have had to employ (and would, had they been well advised, have employed) an expert to do it for them. If the trustees had come to the court asking for liberty to employ such a person, they would in all probability have been authorised to do so, and to remunerate the person in question. It seems to me that it would be inequitable now for the beneficiaries to step in and take the profit without paying for the skill and labour which has produced it." ...

It will be observed that the decision to make the allowance was founded upon the simple proposition that "it would be inequitable now for the beneficiaries to step in and take the profit without paying for the skill and labour which has produced it." *Ex hypothesi*, such an allowance was not in the circumstances authorised by the terms of the trust deed; furthermore it was held that there had not been full and proper disclosure by the two defendants to the successful plaintiff beneficiary. The inequity was found in the simple proposition that the beneficiaries were taking the profit although, if Mr Boardman (the solicitor) had not done the work, they would have had to employ an expert to do the work for them in order to earn that profit.

The decision has to be reconciled with the fundamental principle that a trustee is not entitled to remuneration for services rendered by him to the trust except as expressly provided in the trust deed. Strictly speaking, it is irreconcilable with the rule as so stated. It seems to me therefore that it can only be reconciled with it to the extent that the exercise of the equitable jurisdiction does not conflict with the policy underlying the rule. And, as I see it, such a conflict will only be avoided if the exercise of the jurisdiction is restricted to those cases where it cannot have the effect of encouraging trustees in any way to put themselves in a position where their interests conflict with their duties as trustees.

Alert

Not only was the equity underlying Mr Boardman's claim ... clear and, indeed, overwhelming; but the exercise of the jurisdiction to award an allowance in the unusual circumstances of that case could not provide any encouragement to trustees to put themselves in a position where their duties as trustees conflicted with their interests. The present case is, however, very different. Whether any such an allowance might ever be granted by a court of equity in the case of a director of a company, as opposed to a trustee, is a point which has yet to be decided; and I must reserve the question whether the jurisdiction could be exercised in such a case, which may be said to involve interference by the court in the administration of a company's affairs when the company is not being wound up. In any event, however, like my noble and learned friend, Lord Templeman, I cannot see any possibility of such jurisdiction being exercised in the present case. I proceed, of course, on the basis that ... [W] acted throughout in complete good faith. But the simple fact remains that, by agreeing to provide his services in return for a substantial fee the size of which was dependent

> upon the amount of a successful bid by Guinness, ... [he] was most plainly putting himself in a position in which his interests were in stark conflict with his duty as a director. Furthermore, for such services as he rendered, it is still open to the board of Guinness (if it thinks fit, having had a full opportunity to investigate the circumstances of the case) to award ... [him] appropriate remuneration. In all the circumstances of the case, I cannot think that this is a case in which a court of equity (assuming that it has jurisdiction to do so in the case of a director of a company) would order ... that an equitable allowance be made to ... [W] for his services.

8.6 Remedies for Breach of Fiduciary Duty

A fiduciary who acts in breach of the 'no profit' rule can be required to 'disgorge' that profit to his principal, who may pursue either a personal or a proprietary remedy in order to recover it.

8.6.1 Account

The personal remedy of an account entitles the principal to require the fiduciary to pay over an amount equal to the profit which the fiduciary has received.

Equity defines 'profit' as including *all* the benefit which the fiduciary has received during the course of the fiduciary relationship, and not merely the benefit which flows directly from the breach of fiduciary duty. The extent as well as the rigour of this rule are illustrated by the recent decisions of the Court of Appeal in *Murad v Al-Saraj* [2005] All ER (D) 503 (Jul) and *Imageview Management Ltd v Jack* [2009] 2 All ER 666.

***Murad v Al-Saraj* [2005] All ER (D) 503 (Jul)**

Panel: Clarke, Jonathan Parker and Arden LJJ

Facts: The first defendant persuaded the claimants to enter into a joint venture with him for the purchase of a hotel, under which they would divide any capital profit from the resale of the hotel as to 50 per cent for him and 50 per cent for the claimants. It was common ground on the hearing of this appeal that (i) the first defendant had owed a fiduciary duty to the claimants in relation to that venture, (ii) he had acted in breach of that duty by, amongst other things, procuring the payment to himself of a commission of £369,000 from the seller of the hotel and (iii) had he made full disclosure, the claimants would still have participated in the joint venture but would have negotiated a greater share of the capital profit for themselves. At trial, the judge held that the consequence of the first defendant's breach of duty was that he was liable to account for the whole of his share of any capital profit which might be made when the hotel was sold. The first defendant appealed on the ground that his liability should be limited to the difference between the 50 per cent share which had actually been agreed and the lower share which he would have been forced to agree if he had made full disclosure. The majority (Parker and Arden LJJ) took the traditional approach, which was that Mr Al-Saraj had to account for any 'profit' (or benefit) which he derived from his position as a fiduciary as a consequence of his breach of fiduciary duty.

LORD JUSTICE JONATHAN PARKER

...Mr Al-Saraj contends that ... the judge was wrong in law to hold him liable to account for all the profits which he made from the joint venture, but rather that he should be held accountable only for the difference between his agreed 50 per cent share of the capital profits and such lesser share as he would have had if he had made full disclosure (that is to say, the share he had would have had but for his deliberate breach of his fiduciary obligations).

In my judgment, that contention is directly contrary to long-standing authority in this jurisdiction.

I start with the well-known passage in the judgment of Sir W M James LJ in *Parker v McKenna* (1874) LR 10 Ch App 96, where he said this:

"I do not think it is necessary, but it appears to me very important, that we should concur in laying down again and again the general principle that in this Court no agent in the course of his agency, in the matter of his agency, can be allowed to make any profit without the knowledge and consent of his principal; that that rule is an inflexible rule, and must be applied inexorably by this Court, which is not entitled, in my judgment, to receive evidence, or suggestion, or argument as to whether the principal did or did not suffer any injury in fact by reason of the dealing of the agent; for the safety of mankind requires that no agent shall be able to put his principal to the danger of such an inquiry as that."

In the same case, Lord Cairns LC said this (at p118):

"Now, the rule of this Court, as I understand it, as to agents, is not a technical or arbitrary rule. It is a rule founded upon the highest and truest principles of morality. No man can in this Court, acting as agent, be allowed to put himself in a position in which his interest and his duty will be in conflict. .... The Court will not inquire, and is not in a position to ascertain, whether the bank has lost or not lost by the acts of its directors. All that the Court has to do is examine whether a profit has been made by an agent, without the knowledge of his principal, in the course and execution of his agency, and the Court finds, in my opinion, that these agents in the course of their agency have made a profit, and for that profit they must, in my opinion, account to their principal."

To similar effect is the following passage from the speech of Lord Russell of Killowen *Regal (Hastings) Ltd v Gulliver* [1967] 2 AC 134 at 144G-145A:

"The rule of equity which insists on those, who by use of a fiduciary position make a profit, being liable to account for that profit, in no way depends on fraud, or absence of bona fides; or upon such questions or considerations as whether the profits would or should otherwise have gone to the plaintiff, or whether the profiteer was under a duty to obtain the source of the profit for the plaintiff, or whether he took a risk and acted as he did for the benefit of the plaintiff, or whether the plaintiff has in fact been damaged or benefited by his action. The liability arises from the mere fact of a profit having, in the stated circumstances, been made. The profiteer, however honest and well-intentioned, cannot escape the risk of being called upon to account." ...

In ... [*Gwembe Valley Development Co Ltd & Anor v Koshy* [2004] BCLC 131] ... Mummery LJ, giving the judgment of the Court of Appeal, said this (at paragraph 145):

"In considering ... whether the director should account for unauthorised profits, what would have happened, if the required disclosure had been made, is irrelevant."

As Lord Eldon made clear in *Ex parte James* (1803) 8 Ves 337 at 345, one of the policy reasons behind equity's "inflexible rule" (for convenience I will refer to it hereafter as "the 'no conflict' rule") is the perceived difficulty in determining what might have happened but for the fact that the fiduciary had placed himself in a position of conflict (a point also made by Lord Wright in the passage in his speech in *Boardman v Phipps* referred to above). Another policy reason for the 'no conflict' rule is the need to deter fiduciaries from placing themselves in positions of conflict (see, eg, *Bray v Ford* [1896] AC 44 at 51 per Lord Herschell).

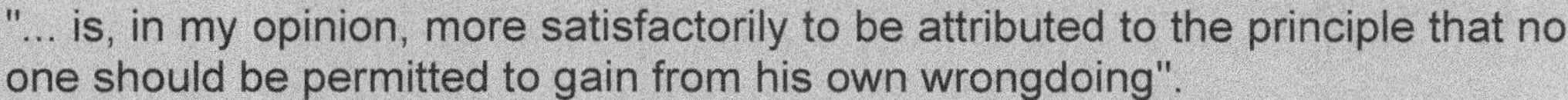

It is thus clear on authority, in my judgment, that the 'no conflict' rule is neither compensatory nor restitutionary: rather, it is designed to strip the fiduciary of the unauthorised profits he has made whilst he is in a position of conflict. As Lord Keith observed in *Attorney-General v Guardian Newspapers Ltd (No 2)* [1990] 1 AC 109, at 262E-F, the remedy of an account of profits:

"... is, in my opinion, more satisfactorily to be attributed to the principle that no one should be permitted to gain from his own wrongdoing".

I therefore conclude, on the basis of long-standing authority, that Mr Al-Saraj's liability to account extends to the entirety of the profits which he made from the joint venture."

***Imageview Management Ltd v Jack* [2009] 2 All ER 666**

Panel: Mummery, Dyson and Jacob LJJ

Facts: The defendant (J) was a professional footballer and an international for Trinidad and Tobago. He wished to play professionally in Britain and appointed the claimant (IML) as his agent to negotiate terms with interested clubs. The agency contract entitled IML to a percentage of J's salary if such a contract was secured. IML found a club who were interested in giving J a contract, but would only do so once he had obtained a work permit. IML entered into a secret deal with the club, under which the club paid IML a fee of £3,000 for obtaining that work permit. The 'true cost' to IML of obtaining the work permit was only £750. Once the work permit had been obtained by IML, J signed for the club. For several months, J paid fees to IML under the agency contract, but stopped doing so when he found out about the work permit contract. IML brought proceedings against J for unpaid agency fees and J counterclaimed both for the agency fees he had already paid as well as the full £3,000 received by IML from the club or, in the alternative, the 'excess' of £2,250 which represented the difference between £3,000 and the real value of the work done. The Court of Appeal held that J was entitled both to the £3,000 received by IML and also to repayment of all the agency fees which he had paid to date.

LORD JUSTICE JACOB

Unless there was a breach of duty ... Mr Jack is liable for the unpaid balance of the fees. Was the undisclosed side deal [in relation to the work permit] 'none of Mr Jack's business'? [The courts below have] held that it was indeed Mr Jack's business: it was not [IML's] private and separate arrangement.

The basis for such a finding was that IML in negotiating a deal for itself had a clear conflict of interest. Put shortly, it is possible that the more it got for itself, the less there would or could be for Mr Jack. Moreover it gave IML an interest in Mr Jack signing for [the club] as opposed to some other club where no side deal for IML was possible.

There is no answer to this. The law imposes on agents high standards. Footballers' agents are not exempt from these. An agent's own personal interests come entirely second to the interest of his client. If you undertake to act for a man you must act 100%, body and soul, for him. You must act as if you were him. You must not allow your own interest to get in the way without telling him. An undisclosed but realistic possibility of a conflict of interest is a breach of your duty of good faith to your client. That duty should not cause an agent any problem. All he or she has to do to avoid being in breach of duty is to make full disclosure. Any agent who is doubtful about his position would do well to do just that – the mere fact that he has doubts will generally be a message from his conscience. ...

Alert

This is a case of a secret profit obtained because [IML] was Mr Jack's agent. And there was a breach of a fiduciary duty because of a real conflict of interest. That in itself would be enough, but there is more: the profit was not only greater than the work done [in relation to the work permit] but was related to the very contract which was being negotiated for Mr Jack [with the club]. Once a conflict of interest is shown ... the right to remuneration goes.

It flies in the face of reality to say that once the terms of Mr Jack's contract [with the club] had been negotiated in principle they could not be reopened. Suppose, for instance, IML had, after negotiating [the] £3,000 fee, said to [the club]: 'Well that shows you are willing to pay more to get Mr Jack playing for you. How about reducing my fee and giving it to my client, Mr Jack?' As Mr Jack's agent [IML] had an interest in saying just that; [its] own interest was in saying nothing. He had 'a temptation not faithfully to perform his duty to his employer' (see per Cotton LJ in *Boston Deep Sea Fishing and Ice Co v Ansell* (1888) 39 Ch D 339 at 357. Of course, since he never said anything, we shall never know what [the club] would have done. Nor do we need to ('[i]t is impossible to gauge ... what the plaintiff has lost', per Lord Alverstone CJ in *Andrews v Ramsay & Co* [1903] 2 KB 635 at 637-638).

Finally in relation to this point and indeed the further points about the appropriate remedies I should mention what was something of a constant refrain from [counsel for IML]. It was this: Mr Jack got the benefit of the contract negotiated for him. Why should he not have to pay for it? Why should he have the benefit of the agent's work for nothing at all?

The answer is twofold. First, it has already been given in the cases, and second, there are sound policy reasons as to why.

As far as the cases are concerned, I have already cited enough to show that the principle is established, see for instance Atkin LJ in *Keppel v Wheeler* [1927] 1 KB 577 at 592 ('forfeit any right to remuneration at all'), Lord Alverstone CJ in *Andrews v Ramsay & Co* [1903] 2 KB 635 at 637 ('not entitled to recover any commission'), *Wills J in Andrews v Ramsay & Co* at 638 ('[t]he case ought to be the same whether the commission has already been paid or whether the agent has to sue for it') and Scrutton LJ in *Rhodes v Macalister* (1924) 29 Com Cas 19 at 28 ('The result may actually be that the employer makes money out of the fact that the agent has taken commission').

The policy reason runs as follows. We are here concerned not with merely damages such as those for a tort or breach of contract but with what the remedy should be when the agent has betrayed the trust reposed in him - notions of equity and conscience are brought into play. Necessarily such a betrayal may not come to light. If all the agent has to pay if and when he is found out are damages the temptation to betray the trust reposed in him is all the greater. So the strict rule is there as a real deterrent to betrayal. As Scrutton LJ said in *Rhodes v Macalister* at 28: 'The more that principle is enforced, the better for the honesty of commercial transactions.'

Alert

Accordingly, as the courts below held, there was a breach of fiduciary duty here. The cases I have cited make it plain that where there is such a breach commission is forfeit – so Mr Jack need pay no more agency fees and is entitled to repayment of the fees paid by him.

The £3,000 was a secret profit made by a fiduciary. On normal equitable principles it is recoverable, subject to the possibility ... of a reasonable remuneration deduction. ...

What then are the principles which govern a deduction when a fiduciary has received a secret profit in breach of his duty of fidelity?

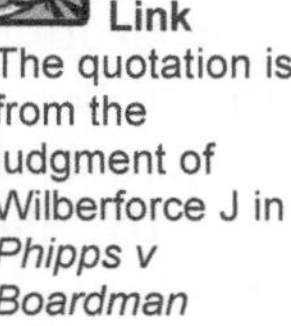
Link
The quotation is from the judgment of Wilberforce J in *Phipps v Boardman* [1964] 1 WLR 993 at 1018.

The basic principle is beyond dispute ... 'A fiduciary is bound to account for any profit that he or she has received in breach of fiduciary duty.'

Snell's Equity (31st edn, 2005, para 7-131) ... sets out the general rules about when an allowance for skill and effort will be made:

'A fiduciary who has acted in breach of fiduciary duty and against whom an account of profits is ordered, may nevertheless be given an allowance for skill and effort employed in obtaining the profit which he has to disgorge where "it would be inequitable now for the beneficiaries to step in and take the profit without paying for the skill and labour which has produced it." This power is exercised sparingly, out of concern not to encourage fiduciaries to act in breach of fiduciary duty. It will not likely be used where the fiduciary has been involved in surreptitious dealing ... although strictly speaking, it is not ruled out simply because the fiduciary can be criticised in the circumstances. The fiduciary bears the onus of convincing the court that an accounting of his or her entire profits is inappropriate in the circumstances ... .'

[Counsel for IML] did not contest any of this. ... [He] took us to *O'Sullivan v Management Agency and Music Ltd* [1985] QB 428 at 468 where Fox LJ said: 'Nor do I think that the principle [of making an allowance] is only applicable in cases where the conduct of the fiduciary cannot be criticised. I think that the justice of the individual case must be considered on the facts of that case.' ... But Fox LJ went on to say: 'Accordingly, where there has been dishonesty or surreptitious dealing or other improper conduct ... it might be appropriate to refuse relief; but that will depend on the circumstances.' The present case is, of course, one of surreptitious dealing.

Murad v Al-Saraj [2005] EWCA Civ 959, [2005] 32 LS Gaz R 31 [contains] the warning of the High Court of Australia in *Warman International Ltd v Dwyer* (1995) 182 CLR 544 that the remedy of an account should not be allowed to become a vehicle for the unjust enrichment of the plaintiff.

But ... the work involved [in obtaining the work permit] was never anything Mr Jack was expecting to pay for. It was something which he surely knew had to be done before he could play. But it was not a benefit which accrued to him financially. How [the club] arranged for the permit was simply a matter for [the club].

So ... I cannot see any reason for exercising the power – one to be exercised sparingly – to make an allowance. The onus of justifying the allowance is far from discharged. So I would dismiss this appeal in its entirety."

This decision sets out the legal and policy reasons why a fiduciary will be stripped of all profit if he commits a breach of fiduciary duty. Not only does the rule reflect the fact that it is impossible to know what deal might have been struck between the principal and the fiduciary if the principal had known of all the facts, but it also serves 'pour encourager les autres'.

8.6.2 Constructive Trust

The proprietary remedy of a constructive trust entitles the principal to claim that the fiduciary holds the profit on constructive trust for him. In accordance with established principles, this remedy: (a) survives the insolvency of the fiduciary; and (b) allows the principal to trace the profit if it is applied by the fiduciary in the acquisition of other property. Tracing is covered in Chapter 11.

A proprietary remedy is the preferred claim where the fiduciary still holds the profit or any substitute property.

***A-G for Hong Kong v Reid* [1994] 1 AC 324**

Panel: Lord Templeman, Lord Goff of Chieveley, Lord Lowry, Lord Lloyd of Berwick and Sir Thomas Eichelbaum

Facts: The defendant (R), the former Acting Director of Public Prosecutions in Hong Kong, had been found guilty of accepting bribes and was ordered to repay the amount of those bribes to the Crown. The Crown's case was that R had used the bribes to buy three properties in New Zealand. The Attorney-General for Hong Kong lodged temporary caveats in New Zealand against the titles to the properties as a prelude to forcing the sale of them. He subsequently applied to the High Court of New Zealand to renew those caveats, but the application was refused on the ground that the Crown had no equitable interest in the properties. The Court of Appeal of New Zealand dismissed the Attorney-General's appeal. The Privy Council held that the money received by R was subject to a constructive trust in favour of the Crown, with the result that any property acquired by the use of that money was similarly held on trust for the Crown.

LORD TEMPLEMAN delivering the advice of the Board

When a bribe is offered and accepted in money or in kind, the money or property constituting the bribe belongs in law to the recipient. Money paid to the false fiduciary belongs to him. The legal estate in freehold property conveyed to the false fiduciary by way of bribe vests in him. Equity, however, which acts in personam, insists that it is unconscionable for a fiduciary to obtain and retain a benefit in breach of duty. The provider of a bribe cannot recover it because he committed a criminal offence when he paid the bribe. The false fiduciary who received the bribe in breach of duty must pay and account for the bribe to the person to whom that duty was owed. In the present case, as soon as the first respondent received a bribe in breach of the duties he owed to the Government of Hong Kong, he became a debtor in equity to the Crown for the amount of that bribe. So much is admitted. But if the bribe consists of property which increases in value or if a cash bribe is invested advantageously, the false fiduciary will receive a benefit from his breach of duty unless he is accountable not only for the original amount or value of the bribe but also for the increased value of the property representing the bribe. As soon as the bribe was received it should have been paid or transferred instanter to the person who suffered from the breach of duty. Equity considers as done that which ought to have been done. As soon as the bribe was received, whether in cash or in kind, the false fiduciary held the bribe on a constructive trust for the person injured. Two objections have been raised to this analysis. First it is said that if the fiduciary is in equity a debtor to the person injured, he cannot also be a trustee of the bribe. But there is no reason why equity should not provide two remedies, so long as they do not result in double recovery. If the property representing the bribe exceeds the original bribe in value, the fiduciary cannot retain the benefit

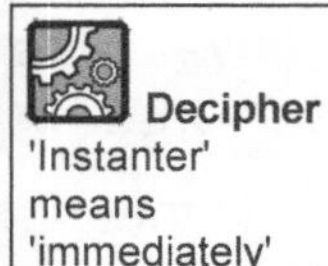

Decipher
'Instanter' means 'immediately'

of the increase in value which he obtained solely as a result of his breach of duty. Secondly, it is said that if the false fiduciary holds property representing the bribe in trust for the person injured, and if the false fiduciary is or becomes insolvent, the unsecured creditors of the false fiduciary will be deprived of their right to share in the proceeds of that property. But the unsecured creditors cannot be in a better position than their debtor. The authorities show that property acquired by a trustee innocently but in breach of trust and the property from time to time representing the same belong in equity to the cestui que trust and not to the trustee personally whether he is solvent or insolvent. Property acquired by a trustee as a result of a criminal breach of trust and the property from time to time representing the same must also belong in equity to his cestui que trust and not to the trustee whether he is solvent or insolvent.

When a bribe is accepted by a fiduciary in breach of his duty then he holds that bribe in trust for the person to whom the duty was owed. If the property representing the bribe decreases in value the fiduciary must pay the difference between that value and the initial amount of the bribe because he should not have accepted the bribe or incurred the risk of loss. If the property increases in value, the fiduciary is not entitled to any surplus in excess of the initial value of the bribe because he is not allowed by any means to make a profit out of a breach of duty. ...

[However, it] has always been assumed and asserted that the law on the subject of bribes was definitively settled by the decision of the Court of Appeal in *Lister & Co v Stubbs* (1890) 45 Ch D 1.

In that case the plaintiffs, Lister & Co, employed the defendant, Stubbs, as their servant to purchase goods for the firm. Stubbs, on behalf of the firm, bought goods from Varley & Co and received from Varley & Co bribes amounting to £5,541. The bribes were invested by Stubbs in freehold properties and investments. His masters, the firm Lister & Co, sought and failed to obtain an interlocutory injunction restraining Stubbs from disposing of these assets pending the trial of the action in which they sought, inter alia, £5,541 and damages. In the Court of Appeal the first judgment was given by Cotton LJ who had been party to the decision in *Metropolitan Bank v Heiron*, 5 Ex D 319. He was powerfully supported by the judgment of Lindley LJ and by the equally powerful concurrence of Bowen LJ. Cotton LJ said, at p 12, that the bribe could not be said to be the money of the plaintiffs. He seemed to be reluctant to grant an interlocutory judgment which would provide security for a debt before that debt had been established. Lindley LJ said, at p 15, that the relationship between the plaintiffs, Lister & Co, as masters and the defendant, Stubbs, as servant who had betrayed his trust and received a bribe:

"... is that of debtor and creditor; it is not that of trustee and cestui que trust. We are asked to hold that it is - which would involve consequences which, I confess, startle me. One consequence, of course, would be that, if Stubbs were to become bankrupt, this property acquired by him with the money paid to him by Messrs Varley would be withdrawn from the mass of his creditors and be handed over bodily to Lister & Co. Can that be right? Another consequence would be that, if the appellants are right, Lister & Co could compel Stubbs to account to them, not only for the money with interest, but for all the profits which he might have made by embarking in trade with it. Can that be right?"

For the reasons which have already been advanced their Lordships would respectfully answer both these questions in the affirmative. If a trustee mistakenly invests moneys which he ought to pay over to his *cestui que trust* and then becomes bankrupt, the moneys together with any profit which has accrued from the investment are withdrawn from the unsecured creditors as soon as the mistake is discovered. A fortiori if a trustee commits a crime by accepting a bribe which he ought to pay over to his *cestui que trust*, the bribe and any profit made therefrom should be withdrawn from the unsecured creditors as soon as the crime is discovered.

The decision in Lister & Co v Stubbs is not consistent with the principles that a fiduciary must not be allowed to benefit from his own breach of duty, that the fiduciary should account for the bribe as soon as he receives it and that equity regards as done that which ought to be done. From these principles it would appear to follow that the bribe and the property from time to time representing the bribe are held on a constructive trust for the person injured. A fiduciary remains personally liable for the amount of the bribe if, in the event, the value of the property then recovered by the injured person proved to be less than that amount.

Lord Templeman gave the only speech. He gave short shrift to the argument, which formed the basis of the decision in *Lister*, that the recipient of a bribe is only under a personal obligation to repay the bribe. It was clear, in his view, that where a fiduciary owns property which has been acquired by using the profit which the fiduciary has unlawfully acquired by virtue of his breach of duty, that property is held upon constructive trust for the principal.

***Sinclair Investments (UK) Ltd v Versailles Trade Finance Ltd (in administrative receivership) and others* [2012] Ch. 453**

Panel: Lord Neuberger of Abbotsbury MR; Richards, Hughes LJJ

Facts: Sinclair Investments (UK) Ltd paid money to Trading Partners Ltd (TPL) to carry out trades in goods. The director was a Mr Cushnie, who transferred these funds to a subsidiary company called Versailles Trade Finance Ltd (VTFL). Rather than engage in factoring, however, VTF fraudulently used the funds to pay profits to wealthy investors in TPL; the funds were also circulated around other subsidiary companies of Mr Cushnie so that they appeared extremely profitable. As a result of the frauds, the share prices of Mr Cushnie's companies rose significantly. Mr Cushnie subsequently sold his shares in TPL for £28.69m. Of this money, £9.19m went to VTFL and £11.47m to Royal Bank of Scotland. £9.98m of this money was repayment of a loan secured on a property purchased by Mr Cushnie in Kensington. Eventually, this fraud was discovered and VTFL was put into receivership. TPL also lost value as a result of VTFL's activities, and was also put into liquidation in July 2000.

LORD NEUBERGER OF ABBOTSBURY MR

The next case in time is a decision of the House of Lords, *Tyrrell v Bank of London* (1862) 10 HL Cas 26... The view of all three members of the Committee in the *Tyrrell* case was that a solicitor who bought a piece of land (which he knew that his client was interested in acquiring) (i) held that part of the land which his client then purchased on trust for his client (so that his client beneficially owned the profit which the solicitor made on that part), but (ii) did not hold the remainder of the land on trust for his client. In *Attorney General for Hong Kong v Reid* [1994] 1 AC 324 , 333 Lord Templeman seems to have thought that his conclusion that a bribe accepted by an agent was beneficially owned by his principal was inconsistent only with Lord Chelmsford's view. I find it hard to see how it is not also inconsistent with the view of all three members of the Committee in the *Tyrrell* case on point (ii)...

Lewison J followed the approach of the Court of Appeal in the *Heiron* 5 Ex D 319 and *Lister* 45 Ch D 1 cases, and accordingly held that TPL had no proprietary interest in the proceeds of sale of the shares. For TPL, Mr Miles (legal counsel) contends that this was wrong and that we should follow the decision of the Privy Council in the Reid case [1994] 1 AC 324.

I would reject that contention. We should not follow the Privy Council decision in the Reid case in preference to decisions of this court, unless there are domestic authorities which show that the decisions of this court were per incuriam or at least of doubtful reliability. Save where there are powerful reasons to the contrary, the Court of Appeal should follow its own previous decisions, and in this instance there are five such previous decisions. It is true that there is a powerful subsequent decision of the Privy Council which goes the other way, but that of itself is not enough to justify departing from the earlier decisions of this court: see In *re Spectrum Plus Ltd* [2004] Ch 337 , para 58, per Lord Phillips of Worth Matravers MR and [2005] 2 AC 680, para 153, per Lord Walker of Gestingthorpe.

I do not suggest that it would always be wrong for this court to refuse to follow a decision of the Privy Council in preference to one of its own previous decisions, but the general rule is that we follow our previous decisions, leaving it to the Supreme Court to overrule those decisions if it is appropriate to do so. Two recent cases where this court preferred to follow a decision of the Privy Council rather than an earlier domestic decision which would normally be regarded as binding (in each case a decision of the House of Lords are *R v James* [2006] QB 588 and *Abou-Rahmah v Abacha* [2007] Bus LR 220 . In each case the decision was justified, based as it was on the proposition that it was a foregone conclusion that, if the case had gone to the House of Lords, they would have followed the Privy Council decision.

In the present instance Mr Miles invited us to take the view that it was a foregone conclusion that the Supreme Court would follow the Privy Council in the Reid case [1994] 1 AC 324 rather than the Court of Appeal in the *Heiron* 5

Ex D 319 and Lister 45 Ch D 1 cases, and therefore to follow the Privy Council approach rather than that of this court.

Although it is possible that the Supreme Court would follow the Reid case rather than the *Heiron* and *Lister* cases, I am far from satisfied that they would do so. In any event it does not seem to me right to follow the Reid case.

First, there are five decisions of this court (*Metropolitan Bank v Heiron* 5 Ex D 319, *Lister & Co v Stubbs* 45 Ch D 1, Archer's Case [1892] 1 Ch 322 , *Powell & Thomas v Evan Jones & Co* [1905] 1 KB 11 and *Attorney General's Reference* (No 1 of 1985) [1986] QB 491) spread over 95 years, all of which have reached the same conclusion on the point, and there is the reasoning of the House of Lords in *Tyrrell v Bank of London* 10 HL Cas 26 . Although it may be true that the reasoning in Pearson's Case 5 Ch D 336, which was not cited to the courts in the *Heiron* 5 Ex D 319 and Lister 45 Ch D 1 cases, is inconsistent with those cases, I am not persuaded that the point has any force: (i) the point does not appear to have been argued in Pearson's Case 5 Ch D 336, (ii) the *Tyrrell* case 10 HL Cas 26 was not cited in *Pearson's* Case, (iii) *Pearson's* Case and the *Lister* case 45 Ch D 1 were both cited in *Archer's* Case [1892] 1 Ch 322 and the latter authority was preferred, and (iv) in subsequent cases this court followed the *Lister* case.

Secondly, much of the reasoning of Lord Templeman in *Attorney General for Hong Kong v Reid* [1994] 1 AC 324 seems to me to beg the question, or to assume what it asserts (although I suppose that the same can be said about the views expressed in the *Heiron* 5 Ex D 319 and Lister 45 Ch D 1 cases). Thus before setting out to explain his reasoning, Lord Templeman asserts [1994] 1 AC 324, 331B–C that a bribe paid to a "false fiduciary" vests in him and he must pay and account for it to "the person to whom [the] duty is owed". But that is the very issue he then purports to decide.

Thirdly, the concern which Lord Templeman expressed at the end of the passage I have quoted in para 71 above might well be met by ordering an equitable account: there was apparently no argument before the Privy Council to that effect.

80 Fourthly, it seems to me that there is a real case for saying that the decision in the *Reid* case [1994] 1 AC 324 is unsound. In cases where a fiduciary takes for himself an asset which, if he chose to take, he was under a duty to take for the beneficiary, it is easy to see why the asset should be treated as the property of the beneficiary. However, a bribe paid to a fiduciary could not possibly be said to be an asset which the fiduciary was under a duty to take for the beneficiary. There can thus be said to be a fundamental distinction between (i) a fiduciary enriching himself by depriving a claimant of an asset and (ii) a fiduciary enriching himself by doing a wrong to the claimant. Having said that, I can see a real policy reason in its favour (if equitable accounting is not available), but the fact that it may not accord with principle is obviously a good reason for not following it in preference to decisions of this court.

Fifthly, not only has there been much academic commentary since the Reid case [1994] 1 AC 324 which supports the approach in the *Heiron* 5 Ex D 319 and Lister 45 Ch D 1 cases, but, at least from what I have seen, there is significantly more support for the approach for those cases in scholarly articles than there is for the *Reid* case...

Sixthly, it seems to me that Lord Templeman may have given insufficient weight to the potentially unfair consequences to the interests of other creditors, if his conclusion was right. His dismissal of their concerns on the basis that they should be in no better position than the defaulting fiduciary [1994] 1 AC 324, 331F–H stands in rather stark contrast with what was said in the Lister case 45 Ch D 1, 15, and in Archer's Case [1892] 1 Ch 322 , 338, as well as more recently in *Westdeutsche Landesbank Girozentrale v Islington London Borough Council* [1996] AC 669 , 716 E. In that case Lord Browne-Wilkinson disapproved of extending the reach of resulting trusts as it could produce "most unjust results", namely conferring "on the plaintiff a right to recover property from, or at the expense of [for example] the lender whose debt is secured by a floating charge and all other parties who have purchased an equitable interest only".

Seventhly, there are some relevant domestic decisions subsequent to the *Reid* case. In *Daraydan Holdings Ltd v Solland International Ltd* [2005] Ch 119 , para 86 Lawrence Collins J (after referring, at para 81, to some other post-Reid first instance decisions which seemed to have gone in different ways) preferred to follow the Reid case, but (i) that was before the guidance given in In *re Spectrum Plus Ltd* [2004] Ch 337; [2005] 2 AC 680, referred to in para 73 above, (ii) as Lawrence Collins J pointed out [2005] Ch 119, paras 87–88, on the facts of that case the decision was not inconsistent with the reasoning in the Lister case 45 Ch D 1, and (iii) it was a first instance judgment and neither *Tyrrell v Bank of London* 10 HL Cas 26 nor *Archer's* Case [1892] 1 Ch 322 was cited to him...

In my view, Lewison J was right to reject TPL's proprietary claim to the proceeds of sale of the shares. It is true that the decisions in the *Reid* case [1994] 1 AC 324, Sugden v Crossland 3 Sm & G 192 and (at least arguably), *Pearson's* Case 5 Ch D 336 go the other way. However, there is a consistent line of reasoned decisions of this court (two of which were decided within the last ten years) stretching back into the late 19th century, and one decision of the House of Lords 150 years ago, which appear to establish that a beneficiary of a fiduciary's duties cannot claim a proprietary interest, but is entitled to an equitable account, in respect of any money or asset acquired by a fiduciary in breach of his duties to the beneficiary, unless the asset or money is or has been beneficially the property of the beneficiary or the trustee acquired the asset or money by taking advantage of an opportunity or right which was properly that of the beneficiary.

For the reasons I have given, previous decisions of this court establish that a claimant cannot claim proprietary ownership of an asset purchased by the defaulting fiduciary with funds which, although they could not have been obtained if he had not enjoyed his fiduciary status, were not beneficially owned by the claimant or derived from opportunities beneficially owned by the claimant. However, those cases also establish that in such a case a claimant does have a personal claim in equity to the funds. There is no case which appears to support the notion that such a personal claim entitles the claimant to claim the value of the asset (if it is greater than the amount of the funds together with interest), and there are judicial indications which tend to militate against that notion...

In these circumstances I cannot improve on Lewison J's conclusion on this part of the case [2011] 1 BCLC 202, para 81:

Lord Neuberger and the Court of Appeal left no doubt about their opinion of *Attorney General for Hong Kong v Reid* [1994] 1 AC 324 and its applicability to cases involving bribes or secret commissions. For various reasons, any such payments were not to be subject to a proprietary constructive trust remedy, but only a personal liability to account on the part of the fiduciary to their principal. Nevertheless, the Master of the Rolls was open to the issue being revisited by the Supreme Court.

***FHR European Ventures LLP and others v Mankarious and others* [2014] Ch. 1**

Panel: Sir Terence Etherton C, Pill, Lewison LJJ

Facts: Cedar Capital Partners LLC (CCPL) had been established by the defendant, Ramsey Neil Mankarious, to provide consultancy services to the hotel industry. In this capacity, it entered into an agreement with the Monegasque owners of the Monte Carlo Grand Hotel to sell the property for them. In exchange, CCPL would receive a commission from Monte Carlo Grand Hotel Ltd; this arrangement was to be disclosed by CCPL to prospective purchasers. In breach, CCPL failed to disclose the arrangement to the eventual purchaser of the hotel, Fairmont Hotels and Resorts European Ventures LLP (FHR). Subsequently, FHR sought to recover the €10 million commission paid to CCPL by Monte Carlo Grand Hotel Ltd.

LEWISON LJ

Accordingly, the argument that [FHR] advances in this court is that the judge ought to have held that the investor group was entitled to a proprietary remedy against Cedar on one or both of the following bases. (i) Cedar received the commission in substance out of the sale proceeds. The money paid by the investor group was money that the investor group had beneficially owned. It does not matter that the money was not paid directly to Cedar. Thus the payment of the commission falls within the first of the two exceptions referred to in the *Sinclair* case. (ii) As the agent of the investor group Cedar had a duty to negotiate the lowest price that the vendors were willing to accept. In practical terms the vendors were willing to accept €10m less than the nominal purchase price. Accordingly the receipt by Cedar of the €10m commission was a benefit that Cedar ought to have acquired on behalf of its principal but instead diverted to itself. Thus the receipt of the €10m falls within the second of the two exceptions referred to in the *Sinclair* case.

I have no difficulty in accepting Mr Pymont's (legal counsel for FHR) submission that this case is factually different from the facts considered in the *Sinclair* case. In that case the connection between the breach of fiduciary duty and the profit was relatively remote. Mr Cushnie (the defaulting fiduciary in that case) made a profit by selling shares that he already owned before any question of relevant fiduciary duties arose. It was their value that was increased by reason of breaches of fiduciary duties. As Lord Neuberger of Abbotsbury MR pointed out the proprietary claim in that case was not a claim to funds in respect of which Mr Cushnie owed any relevant fiduciary duty, nor to any asset of the proceeds of any asset bought with those funds, nor to the proceeds of any right or opportunity which belonged to the principal. In our case the connection is much closer. But in the *Sinclair* case the principal legal debate was whether this court should follow on the one hand its own previous decisions in *Metropolitan Bank v Heiron* (1880) 5 Ex D 319 and *Lister & Co v Stubbs* 45 Ch D 1 or, on the other hand, the decision of the Privy Council in *Attorney General for Hong Kong v Reid* [1994] 1 AC 324... Accordingly this court affirmed the correctness (or at least the binding nature unless overruled by the Supreme Court) of the *Metropolitan Bank* and *Lister* cases...

Mr Collings (legal counsel for CCPL) submitted that: (i) the *Sinclair* case [2012] Ch 453 clearly equates bribes and secret commissions and treats them in precisely the same way; (ii) it also holds that there is a "fundamental difference" between (a) a fiduciary enriching himself by depriving the principal of an asset and (b) a fiduciary enriching himself by doing a wrong to the principal; (iii) since there is a fundamental difference between the two it is not possible for a single breach of duty to count as both; and the taking of a secret commission is plainly in the second of the two categories; (iv) the "lost" or "diverted" opportunity cases are equally clearly in the first of the two categories. It follows that the taking of a secret commission or bribe cannot fall within that category; (v) thus in the case of a bribe or secret commission the principal can only claim a proprietary interest if he can show that the payment of the bribe or secret commission was made out of his own money. Mr Collings thus accepted that in a case in which the principal could show that the fiduciary had acquired the principal's own money or property he could properly be described as a constructive trustee of that property or money...

Given that in the *Sinclair* case [2012] Ch 453 this court approved and followed the *Metropolitan Bank* case 5 Ex D 319 and the Lister case, we must do so too. Accordingly, in my judgment Mr Pymont's appeal must fail unless he can successfully distinguish those two cases as well as the *Sinclair* case...

In my judgment this group of cases shows that the principal can acquire a proprietary interest in an asset acquired by his agent, even though the principal had no pre-existing proprietary interest in the asset, and the asset was, in the first instance, acquired by the agent with his own money...

In my judgment there is no need to inquire whether the opportunity to acquire the hotel at a lower price can be characterised as an opportunity separate from the opportunity to acquire the hotel at all. I do not, therefore, agree with Newey J in *Cadogan Petroleum plc v Tolley* [2011] EWHC 2286 (Ch) that it is necessary to isolate the opportunity to acquire an asset at a lower price from the opportunity to acquire an asset at all. Nor is there any need to inquire whether the investor group can be said to have a proprietary interest, in the strict sense, in that opportunity. In my judgment the principle we must apply is that stated by Jonathan Parker LJ in *Bhullar v Bhullar* [2003] 2 BCLC 241: is the fiduciary's exploitation of the opportunity such as to attract the application of the rule? In the present case the exclusive brokerage agreement was part of the overall arrangement surrounding the purchase of the hotel. I cannot see that it is different in principle from the contract between Tyrrell and Read in so far as it concerned the target property (see the *Tyrrell* case 10 HL Cas 26) or the contract between Green and Smith: *Whaley Bridge Calico Printing Co v Green* 5 QBD 109. In my judgment the exploitation of the opportunity by Cedar was such as to attract the operation of the rule with the consequence that Cedar held the benefit of the contract on a constructive trust for the investor group. Thence it is possible to trace into the money paid under that contract which Cedar likewise held on a constructive trust for the investor group.

I would allow the appeal.

SIR TERENCE ETHERTON C

The constructive trust is a feature of equity which arises in many different areas of the law. They include, among others, contracts for the sale of land, the perfection of imperfect gifts, gifts in contemplation of death (*donatio mortis causa*), testamentary secret trusts, mutual wills, common intention constructive trusts, fraud and undue influence, estoppel, specific performance, joint ventures, breach of trust, and breach of fiduciary duty. Although it may be said at the most general level that the constructive trust is a feature of equity to prevent or remedy unconscionable conduct, there is no generally accepted set of principles governing the existence of a constructive trust across all the different areas of the law where it is to be found. Moreover, in some cases the constructive trust is a true institutional trust arising by operation of law at a particular moment and creating a property interest in the beneficiary from that time. In other cases, it simply connotes an obligation in equity of wrongdoers, who were not or are not in fact trustees, to account as though they were.

The present case is about the existence of a constructive trust, which is a true trust, of a benefit acquired by a fiduciary in breach of fiduciary duty. Short of a decision of the Supreme Court that the law of England and Wales recognises a remedial constructive trust, as is to be found in other common law countries, such as Australia, New Zealand and Canada, this court must proceed on the basis that in this jurisdiction the constructive trust of a benefit wrongly obtained by the fiduciary in breach of duty is an institutional trust arising at the moment the benefit is received and under which the principal obtains an immediate beneficial interest. Similarly, short of an express decision of the Supreme Court to the contrary, I do not consider it would be right to view the constructive trust in this area, as at least one leading academic commentator has urged, as a mere fiction for making orders of the court that the defendant pay a sum of money to the claimant or transfer a particular right to the claimant.

The issue in the present case arises because the decision of the *Court of Appeal in Sinclair Investments (UK) Ltd v Versailles Trade Finance Ltd* [2012] Ch 453, to follow Lister & Co v Stubbs 45 Ch D 1, in the Court of Appeal, rather than *Attorney General for Hong Kong v Reid* [1994] 1 AC 324, in the Privy Council, confirms that not all benefits wrongly obtained by a fiduciary in breach of fiduciary duty are subject to a constructive trust even though the fiduciary is still under a duty to account in equity. The problem is to identify when such a situation arises and specifically whether, as Simon J thought below [2011] EWHC 2999 (Ch), the facts of the present case are such a situation...

I entirely agree with Lewison LJ that it is not the function of this court to enter into the debate about whether or not the *Lister* case 45 Ch D 1 or the *Reid* case [1994] 1 AC 324 or the *Sinclair* case [2012] Ch 453 was correctly or incorrectly decided. At this level of the judicial hierarchy we are bound to accept the decision in the Sinclair case on its facts and also the conclusion in that case that the *Lister* case was correctly decided and should be followed by the courts of England and Wales in preference to the *Reid* case.

That leaves this court with the task of applying the decision and the analysis in the *Sinclair* case, and the case law which has not been overturned by or is not inconsistent with the *Sinclair* case, to the facts of this case. In order to do so, it is necessary to provide some coherence to the large body of relevant case law, not all of which was considered or even mentioned in the *Sinclair* case.

Lord Neuberger MR's analysis in paras 88 and 89 of the *Sinclair* case divides into three broad categories the situations in which a fiduciary obtains a benefit in breach of fiduciary duty. The first category ("category 1") is where the benefit is or was an asset belonging beneficially to the principal (most obviously where the fiduciary has gained the benefit by misappropriating or misapplying the principal's property). The second category ("category 2") is where the benefit has been obtained by the fiduciary by taking an advantage of an opportunity which was properly that of the principal. The third category ("category 3") is all other cases. According to the analysis and conclusion of Lord Neuberger MR, the situations in categories 1 and 2 give rise to a constructive trust, but those in category 3 do not. The issue in the present case arises out of the difficulty of ascertaining the borderline between category 2 and category 3.

The problem can be expressed in quite simple terms. It follows from the decision in the *Sinclair* case that the facts of that case and the bribe and secret commission situations exemplified by the facts in the Lister and Reid decisions fall within category 3. As a matter of ordinary language those were "opportunity" cases in the sense that the defendants in those cases wrongly obtained a benefit through the opportunity presented by their relationship to their principal. The cases, however, fall within category 3 rather than category 2 because the opportunity, in Lord Neuberger MR's words, was not "properly that of the beneficiary" (para 88) and was not "beneficially owned by the claimant": para 89. The question is what "opportunity" situations, apart from the precise factual situations in the decisions in *Sinclair* , *Lister* and *Reid* and those precisely analogous, fall within category 3 rather than category 2? The difficulty arises because the expressions "properly that of the beneficiary" and "beneficially owned by the claimant" are not to be found as legal expressions or tests in any of the reported cases. That is not surprising because opportunities are not a species of property capable of being held on trust. Moreover, in *Bhullar v Bhullar* [2003] 2 BCLC 241 , which was not cited in the *Sinclair* case [2012] Ch 453, Jonathan Parker LJ, with whom the other members of the Court of Appeal agreed, expressly disapproved of those types of expressions and concepts. He said the following in relation to the rule, as formulated by Lord Cranworth LC in *Aberdeen Railway Co v Blaikie Bros* (1854) 1 Macq 461, 471, that "no one, having such [fiduciary] duties to discharge, shall be allowed to enter into engagements in which he has, or can have, a personal interest conflicting, or which may possibly conflict, with the interests of those whom he is bound to protect" ("the no conflict rule") [2003] 2 BCLC 241...

Lord Neuberger MR referred in the *Sinclair* case [2012] Ch 453, para 70, to the observation of the trial judge, Lewison J, that it was unclear whether the remedy granted in the *Phipps* case [1967] 2 AC 46 was proprietary or personal. Lord Neuberger MR also expressed his agreement with Lewison J that the question whether it should be proprietary or personal was never argued in the *Phipps* case and apparently did not matter. We have had the benefit of research by Mr Pymont, which demonstrates that Wilberforce J did indeed make a formal declaration of a constructive trust. Wilberforce J's judgment is reported [1964] 1 WLR 993; [1964] 2 All ER 187 . Both reports state that the writ claimed: (1) a declaration that first and second defendants held 5/18ths of 21,986 ordinary shares of £1 each in the company, or alternatively 5/18ths of the following holdings in the company, namely, 2,925 shares, 14,567 shares or 4,494 shares (or some one or more of such holdings) as constructive trustees for the plaintiff; (2) an account of the profits made by them from those holdings; and (3) an order that they should transfer to the plaintiff the shares which they held as constructive trustees for him and should pay to him 5/18ths of the profit. The report in the All England Law Reports records, at p 208H, that Wilberforce J made the declaration in (1) and ordered the account of profits in (2). That Wilberforce J made the declaration is supported by the express statements in the House of Lords to that effect by Lord Cohen [1967] 2 AC 46, 99C and Lord Guest at p 112G.

The misunderstanding in the *Sinclair* case about the declaration appears to have arisen as a result of the abbreviated record of Wilberforce J's order in the report in the Weekly Law Reports [1964] 1 WLR 993, 1018. It is misleading because it omitted reference to the declaration made by Wilberforce J, corresponding to the first head of the claim in the writ, but included reference to adjournment of the third head of relief, presumably until it had been worked out precisely how many shares should be transferred (corresponding to the percentages in the declaration) and after the taking of the account.

The declaration of a constructive trust was made in the *Phipps* case even though, as I have said, the shares could not have been purchased for the will trust without the sanction of the court since they were not an authorised investment under the testator's will. Furthermore, one of the trustees said in evidence that he would not consider the trustees buying the shares under any circumstances. Wilberforce J said [1964] 1 WLR 993, 1017 that, as was clear from the *Keech* case Sel Cas Ch 61 and *Regal (Hastings) Ltd v Guilliver* (Note) [1967] 2 AC 134, those impediments to any purchase of the shares by the trustees made no difference. The same point was made in the House of Lords [1967] 2 AC 46, per Lord Cohen at p 95G, and per Lord Guest at p 117G.

The *Phipps* case was plainly an "opportunity" case within Lord Neuberger MR's category 2. Indeed, in the House of Lords both Lord Cohen and Lord Hodson emphasised the misuse of "the opportunity" which presented itself to the first and second defendants...

The facts of the present case are in some important respects materially different from those in the *Sinclair* and *Lister* cases. Clause 3 of the exclusive brokerage agreement ("the commission agreement") provided that Cedar's €10m fee was to be paid within five working days of the vendor's receipt of the purchase price for the hotel. Mr Collings said that the commission paid to Cedar could not be identified as the claimants' money since, as a matter of law, their money ceased to be identifiable as their property the moment it was paid into the vendor's bank account. In a practical sense, however, it is plain that in reality the claimants' money funded the commission paid to Cedar. Unlike the *Sinclair* case [2012] Ch 453 and, possibly, the *Lister* case 45 Ch D 1, in both temporal and causative terms Cedar's receipt of the commission was the direct and immediate consequence of its breach of fiduciary duty.

Furthermore, as Simon J found in para 102 of his first judgment [2012] 2 BCLC 39 , the obligation of Cedar, which was the exclusive negotiator for the claimants, was to negotiate the best purchase price for them, that is to say the lowest possible price. In that context, it was material that the vendor was in fact prepared to receive a net sum of €201·5m from the sale (i.e. allowing for Cedar's €10m commission). That fact was not, however, made known to the claimants. Critically, Simon J made a finding of fact in para 106 of his first judgment that: "at the very least it is likely that they could have used the information to their financial advantage in the course of their negotiations."

If the claimants had known of the commission agreement, they might have deferred contracting to purchase the hotel until the commission agreement lapsed under the terms of clause 1 after 31 December 2005 and then negotiated the price with the vendor on the basis that the vendor was by that time free of an obligation to meet an expense of €10m. Furthermore, there was direct evidence that, if the claimants had known of the commission agreement, they would have changed their own fee arrangements with Cedar...

Do those facts bring the present case within category 2 rather than category 3? In my judgment, on the findings of the judge in the light of the evidence, they bring the case within category 2. On the basis of existing case law, that conclusion reflects both principle and precedent. It reflects principle because the commission agreement, and the fact that it was not disclosed by Cedar to the claimants, diverted from the claimants the opportunity to purchase the hotel at the lowest possible price, that is to say a price lower than the price they ultimately agreed to pay. That point remains a good one even if the claimants cannot show that the vendor would in fact have been willing to accept an amount precisely €10m less or indeed any specific amount less than the price actually paid by the claimants...

For those reasons, this case falls within category 2, and so I would allow the appeal. It throws into clear relief, however, the very considerable difficulties inherent in the analysis in the *Sinclair* case [2012] Ch 453 and the decision in *Lister* 45 Ch D 1 in marking the borderline between cases in category 2 and those in category 3. This has made the law more complex and uncertain and dependent on very fine factual distinctions. If the law is to be made simpler and more coherent, but the *Sinclair* case and the *Lister* case correctly represent the law, then that suggests a need to revisit the very many longstanding decisions in category 2 cases and to provide an overhaul of this entire area of the law of constructive trusts in order to provide a coherent and logical legal framework. If that can be done at all by the courts, rather than Parliament, it can only be accomplished by the Supreme Court. That indicates a need for informed debate and ultimately determination by the Supreme Court: (1) whether the Sinclair case was right to decide that the Lister case is to be preferred to the *Reid* case [1994] 1 AC 324 ; (2) in terms of constructive trusts and proprietary relief for breach of fiduciary duty, what are the principles to distinguish opportunity cases within category 2 and those within category 3; (3) what is the true jurisprudential nature of the constructive trust in this (and by necessity other) areas of the law, including whether it is—or should be—an institutional trust at all or something else. In considering those matters, there are important issues of policy, and the relative importance of different policies, to assess, including deterring fraud and corruption; the ability to strip the fiduciary of all benefits, including increases in the value of benefits, acquired by breach of duty, and vehicles or third parties through which those benefits have been channelled; the importance attached to the protection of those to whom fiduciary duties are owed; and the position of other creditors on the fiduciary's insolvency who may be prejudiced by a constructive trust or proprietary relief in favour of the fiduciary's principal but who, in the absence of such a trust and relief, would benefit from increases in value of assets acquired by the fiduciary's fraud, corruption or wrongdoing. It will also be necessary to bear in mind the international perspective applying to this area of trust law and equity, to which I have referred earlier in this judgment.

For the reasons I have given, I would allow this appeal.

The Court of Appeal, therefore, felt that there was enough justification in their case facts to distinguish the earlier authority of *Sinclair v Versailles*.

***FHR European Ventures LLP and others v Cedar Capital Partners LLC* [2014] UKSC 45**

Panel: Lord Neuberger, Lord Mance, Lord Sumption, Lord Carnwath, Lord Toulson, Lord Hodge, Lord Collins

Facts: Cedar Capital Partners LLC (CCPL) had been established by the defendant, Ramsey Neil Mankarious, to provide consultancy services to the hotel industry. In this capacity, it entered into an agreement with the Monegasque owners of the Monte Carlo Grand Hotel to sell the property for them. In exchange, CCPL would receive a commission from Monte Carlo Grand Hotel Ltd; this arrangement was to be disclosed by CCPL to prospective purchasers. In breach, CCPL failed to disclose the arrangement to the eventual purchaser of the hotel, Fairmont Hotels and Resorts European Ventures LLP (FHR). Subsequently, FHR sought to recover the €10 million commission paid to CCPL by Monte Carlo Grand Hotel Ltd.

LORD NEUBERGER

This is the judgment of the Court on the issue of whether a bribe or secret commission received by an agent is held by the agent on trust for his principal, or whether the principal merely has a claim for equitable compensation in a sum equal to the value of the bribe or commission. The answer to this rather technical sounding question, which has produced inconsistent judicial decisions over the past 200 years, as well as a great deal of more recent academic controversy, is important in practical terms. If the bribe or commission is held on trust, the principal has a proprietary claim to it, whereas if the principal merely has a claim for equitable compensation, the claim is not proprietary. The distinction is significant for two main reasons. First, if the agent becomes insolvent, a proprietary claim would effectively give the principal priority over the agent's unsecured creditors, whereas the principal would rank pari passu, i.e. equally, with other unsecured creditors if he only has a claim for compensation. Secondly, if the principal has a proprietary claim to the bribe or commission, he can trace and follow it in equity, whereas (unless we develop the law of equitable tracing beyond its current boundaries) a principal with a right only to equitable compensation would have no such equitable right to trace or follow...

The following three principles are not in doubt, and they are taken from the classic summary of the law in the judgment of Millett LJ in Bristol and West Building Society v Mothew [1998] Ch 1 , 18. First, an agent owes a fiduciary duty to his principal because he is "someone who has undertaken to act for or on behalf of [his principal] in a particular matter in circumstances which give rise to a relationship of trust and confidence". Secondly, as a result, an agent "must not make a profit out of his trust" and "must not place himself in a position in which his duty and his interest may conflict" and, as Lord Upjohn pointed out in Boardman v Phipps [1967] 2 AC 46, 123, the former proposition is "part of the [latter] wider rule". Thirdly, "[a] fiduciary who acts for two principals with potentially conflicting interests without the informed consent of both is in breach of the obligation of undivided loyalty; he puts himself in a position where his duty to one principal may conflict with his duty to the other". Because of the importance which equity attaches to fiduciary duties, such "informed consent" is only effective if it is given after "full disclosure", to quote Sir George Jessel MR in Dunne v English (1874) LR 18 Eq 524, 533.

Another well-established principle, which applies where an agent receives a benefit in breach of his fiduciary duty, is that the agent is obliged to account to the principal for such a benefit, and to pay, in effect, a sum equal to the profit by way of equitable compensation. The law on this topic was clearly stated in Regal (Hastings) Ltd v Gulliver (Note) (1942) [1967] 2 AC 134. The principal's right to seek an account undoubtedly gives him a right to equitable compensation in respect of the bribe or secret commission, which is the quantum of that bribe or commission (subject to any permissible deduction in favour of the agent, e.g. for expenses incurred). That is because where an agent acquires a benefit in breach of his fiduciary duty, the relief accorded by equity is, again to quote Millett LJ in Mothew at p 18, "primarily restitutionary or restorative rather than compensatory". The agent's duty to account for the bribe or secret commission represents a personal remedy for the principal against the agent. However, the centrally relevant point for present purposes is that, at least in some cases where an agent acquires a benefit which came to his notice as a result of his fiduciary position, or pursuant to an opportunity which results from his fiduciary position, the equitable rule ("the Rule") is that he is to be treated as having acquired the benefit on behalf of his principal, so that it is beneficially owned by the principal. In such cases, the principal has a proprietary remedy in addition to his personal remedy against the agent, and the principal can elect between the two remedies.

Where the facts of a particular case are within the ambit of the Rule, it is strictly applied. The strict application of the Rule can be traced back to the well- known decision in Keech v Sandford (1726) Sel Cas Ch 61, where a trustee held a lease of a market on trust for an infant, and, having failed to negotiate a new lease on behalf of the infant because the landlord was dissatisfied with the proposed security for the rent, the trustee negotiated a new lease for himself. Lord King LC concluded at p 62 that, "though I do not say there is a fraud in this case" and though it "may seem hard", the infant was entitled to an assignment of the new lease and an account of the profits made in the meantime – a conclusion which could only be justified on the basis that the new lease had been beneficially acquired for the infant beneficiary.

Since then, the Rule has been applied in a great many cases. The question on this appeal is not so much concerned with the application of the Rule, as with its limits or boundaries. Specifically, what is in dispute is the extent to which the Rule applies where the benefit is a bribe or secret commission obtained by an agent in breach of his fiduciary duty to his principal...

The cases summarised in paras 13-17 above and the observations set out in paras 19-20 above are all consistent with the notion that the Rule should apply to bribes or secret commissions paid to an agent, so that the agent holds them on trust for his principal, rather than simply having an equitable duty to account to his principal. It is true that in many of those cases there was apparently no argument as to whether the benefit obtained by the fiduciary was actually held on trust for the principal. However, in some of the cases there was a dispute on the nature of the relief; in any event, the fact that it was assumed time and again by eminent barristers and judges must carry great weight.

However, there is one decision of the House of Lords which appears to go the other way, and several decisions of the Court of Appeal which do go the other way, in that they hold that, while a principal has a claim for equitable compensation in respect of a bribe or secret commission received by his agent, he has no proprietary interest in it. The House of Lords decision is Tyrrell v Bank of London (1862) 10 HL Cas 26...

Although there have been suggestions that, with the exception of Lord Chelmsford's obiter dicta about bribes, the decision of the House of Lords in Tyrrell was not inconsistent with the respondents' case on this appeal, it appears clear that it was. If, as the House held, the solicitor was liable to account to the client for the profit which he had made on the adjoining land, that can only have been because it was a benefit which he had received in breach of his fiduciary duty; and, once that is established, then, on the respondents' case, the Rule would apply, and that profit would be held on trust for the client (or, more accurately, his share of the adjoining land would be held on trust)...

More recently, in 1993, in Attorney General for Hong Kong v Reid, the Privy Council concluded that bribes received by a corrupt policeman were held on trust for his principal, and so they could be traced into properties which he had acquired in New Zealand. In his judgment on behalf of the Board, Lord Templeman disapproved the reasoning in Heiron , and the reasoning and outcome in Lister , and he thought his conclusion inconsistent with only one of the opinions, that of Lord Chelmsford, in Tyrrell . In Daraydan Holdings Ltd v Solland International Ltd [2005] Ch 119 , paras 75ff, Lawrence Collins J indicated that he would follow Reid rather than Lister , as did Toulson J in Fyffes Group Ltd v Templeman [2000] 2 Lloyd's Rep 643 , 668–672. But in Sinclair Investments Ltd v Versailles Trade Finance Ltd [2012] Ch 453, in a judgment given by Lord Neuberger MR, the Court of Appeal decided that it should follow Heiron and Lister , and indeed Tyrrell , for a number of reasons set out in paras 77ff, although it accepted that this Court might follow the approach in Reid . In this case, Simon J considered that he was bound by Sinclair, whereas the Court of Appeal concluded that they could and should distinguish it.

As mentioned above, the issue raised on this appeal has stimulated a great deal of academic debate. The contents of the many articles on this issue provide an impressive demonstration of penetrating and stimulating legal analysis. One can find among those articles a powerful case for various different outcomes, based on analysing judicial decisions and reasoning, equitable and restitutionary principles, and practical and commercial realities. It is neither possible nor appropriate to do those articles justice individually in this judgment, but the court has referred to them for the purpose of extracting the principle upon which the Rule is said to be based…

The respondents' formulation of the Rule, namely that it applies to all benefits received by an agent in breach of his fiduciary duty to his principal, is explained on the basis that an agent ought to account in specie to his principal for any benefit he has obtained from his agency in breach of his fiduciary duty, as the benefit should be treated as the property of the principal, as supported by many judicial dicta including those in para 19 above, and can be seen to be reflected in Jonathan Parker LJ's observations in para 14 above. More subtly, it is justified on the basis that equity does not permit an agent to rely on his own wrong to justify retaining the benefit: in effect, he must accept that, as he received the benefit as a result of his agency, he acquired it for his principal. Support for that approach may be found in Mellish LJ's judgment in McKay's Case at p 6, and Bowen J's judgment in Whaley Bridge at p 113.

The appellant's formulation of the Rule, namely that it has a more limited reach, and does not apply to bribes and secret commissions, has, as mentioned in para 10 above, various different formulations and justifications. Thus, it is said that, given that it is a proprietary principle, the Rule should not apply to benefits which were not derived from assets which are or should be the property of the principal, a view supported by the reasoning of Lord Westbury in Tyrrell . It has also been suggested that the Rule should not apply to benefits which could not have been intended for the principal and were, rightly or wrongly, the property of the agent, which seems to have been the basis of Cotton LJ's judgment in Heiron at p 325 and Lister at p 12. In Sinclair , it was suggested that the effect of the authorities was that the Rule should not apply to a benefit which the agent had obtained by taking advantage of an opportunity which arose as a result of the agency, unless the opportunity "was properly that of the [principal]" – para 88…

Each of the formulations set out in paras 30 and 31 above have their supporters and detractors. In the end, it is not possible to identify any plainly right or plainly wrong answer to the issue of the extent of the Rule, as a matter of pure legal authority. There can clearly be different views as to what requirements have to be satisfied before a proprietary interest is created. More broadly, it is fair to say that the concept of equitable proprietary rights is in some respects somewhat paradoxical. Equity, unlike the common law, classically acts in personam (see e.g. Maitland, Equity , p 9); yet equity is far more ready to accord proprietary claims than common law. Further, two general rules which law students learn early on are that common law legal rights prevail over equitable rights, and that where there are competing equitable rights the first in time prevails; yet, given that equity is far more ready to recognise proprietary rights than common law, the effect of having an equitable right is often to give priority over common law claims – sometimes even those which may have preceded the equitable right. Given that equity developed at least in part to mitigate the rigours of the common law, this is perhaps scarcely surprising. However, it underlines the point that it would be unrealistic to expect complete consistency from the cases over the past 300 years. It is therefore appropriate to turn to the arguments based on principle and practicality, and then to address the issue, in the light of those arguments as well as the judicial decisions discussed above...

The notion that an agent should not hold a bribe or commission on trust because he could not have acquired it on behalf of his principal is somewhat inconsistent with the long-standing decision in Keech, the decision in Phipps approved by the House of Lords, and the Privy Council decision in Bowes. In each of those three cases, a person acquired property as a result of his fiduciary or quasi-fiduciary position, in circumstances in which the principal could not have acquired it: yet the court held that the property concerned was held on trust for the beneficiary. In Keech, the beneficiary could not acquire the new lease because the landlord was not prepared to let to him, and because he was an infant; in Boardman, the trust could not acquire the shares because they were not authorised investments; in Bowes, the city corporation would scarcely have been interested in buying the loan notes which it had just issued to raise money.

The respondents are also able to point to a paradox if the appellant is right and a principal has no proprietary right to his agent's bribe or secret commission. If the principal has a proprietary right, then he is better off, and the agent is worse off, than if the principal merely has a claim for equitable compensation. It would be curious...if a principal whose agent wrongly receives a bribe or secret commission is worse off than a principal whose agent obtains a benefit in far less opprobrious circumstances, e.g. the benefit obtained by the trustees' agents in Boardman. Yet that is the effect if the Rule does not apply to bribes or secret commissions.

Wider policy considerations also support the respondents' case that bribes and secret commissions received by an agent should be treated as the property of his principal, rather than merely giving rise to a claim for equitable compensation. As Lord Templeman said giving the decision of the Privy Council in Attorney General for Hong Kong v Reid [1994] 1 AC 324, 330H, "[b]ribery is an evil practice which threatens the foundations of any civilised society". Secret commissions are also objectionable as they inevitably tend to undermine trust in the commercial world. That has always been true, but concern about bribery and corruption generally has never been greater than it is now – see for instance, internationally, the OECD Convention on Combating Bribery of Foreign Public Officials in International Business Transactions 1999 and the United Nations Convention against Corruption 2003, and, nationally, the Bribery Acts 2010 and 2012. Accordingly, one would expect the law to be particularly stringent in relation to a claim against an agent who has received a bribe or secret commission...

Nonetheless, the appellant's argument based on potential prejudice to the agent's unsecured creditors has some force, but it is, as we see it, balanced by the fact that it appears to be just that a principal whose agent has obtained a bribe or secret commission should be able to trace the proceeds of the bribe or commission into other assets and to follow them into the hands of knowing recipients (as in Reid). Yet... tracing or following in equity would not be possible, at least as the law is currently understood, unless the person seeking to trace or follow can claim a proprietary interest. Common law tracing is, of course, possible without a proprietary interest, but it is much more limited than equitable tracing. Lindley LJ in Lister at p 15 appears to have found it offensive that a principal should be entitled to trace a bribe, but he did not explain why, and we prefer the reaction of Lord Templeman in Reid, namely that a principal ought to have the right to trace and to follow a bribe or secret commission.

Finally, on this aspect, it appears that other common law jurisdictions have adopted the view that the Rule applies to all benefits which are obtained by a fiduciary in breach of his duties...As overseas countries secede from the jurisdiction of the Privy Council, it is inevitable that inconsistencies in the common law will develop between different jurisdictions. However, it seems to us highly desirable for all those jurisdictions to learn from each other, and at least to lean in favour of harmonising the development of the common law round the world...

Were it not for the decision in Tyrrell, we consider that it would be plainly appropriate for this Court to conclude that the courts took a wrong turn in Heiron and Lister , and to restate the law as being as the respondents contend. Although the fact that the House of Lords decided Tyrrell in the way they did gives us pause for thought, we consider that it would be right to uphold the respondents' argument and disapprove the decision in Tyrrell. In the first place, Tyrrell is inconsistent with a wealth of cases decided before and after it was decided. Secondly, although Fawcett was cited in argument at p 38, it was not considered in any of the three opinions in Tyrrell; indeed, no previous decision was referred to in the opinions, and, although the opinions were expressed with a confidence familiar to those who read 19th century judgments, they contained no reasoning, merely assertion. Thirdly, the decision in Tyrrell may be explicable by reference to the fact that the solicitor was not actually acting for the client at the time when he acquired his interest in the adjoining land...in other words, it may be that their Lordships thought that the principal should not have a proprietary interest in circumstances where the benefit received by the agent was obtained before the agency began and did not relate to the property the subject of the agency.

Quite apart from these three points, we consider that, the many decisions and the practical and policy considerations which favour the wider application of the Rule and are discussed above justify our disapproving Tyrrell. In our judgment, therefore, the decision in Tyrrell should not stand in the way of the conclusion that the law took a wrong turn in Heiron and Lister, and that those decisions, and any subsequent decisions...at least in so far as they relied on or followed Heiron and Lister, should be treated as overruled.

In this case, the Court of Appeal rightly regarded themselves as bound by Sinclair, but they managed to distinguish it. Accordingly, the appeal is dismissed.

The Supreme Court was, therefore, unanimous that the appropriate remedy for property obtained as a bribe or secret commission was that of the constructive trust. It must be inferred, therefore, that the constructive trust will now *always* be the appropriate remedy with respect to property obtained through breach of fiduciary duty.

9

Trustee Duties

Introduction

Trustees have numerous duties with regard to how they deal with beneficiaries and trust property. A potential consequence of these duties existing is the possibility of a breach taking place. This possibility of a breach taking place is made more likely by the fact that a breach can be made inadvertently as well as deliberately. Furthermore, a breach of trust can take many forms and can lead to a variety of remedies to rectify the breach.

9.1 Causation

Due to the nature of how trust assets are used while the trust is up and running, it would be unfair to find a trustee liable for every single event that touches on the assets themselves. We therefore have to find a link between the trustee and what has happened to the asset to justify finding the trustee in breach of trust. The following two cases show the casual link to the breach that is required, firstly when the trustee does something they are not authorised to do with the trust property, and secondly where the trustee does something which they are authorised to do with the trust property.

***Target Holdings Ltd v Redferns (A Firm) and Another Appellants* [1996] AC 421**

Panel: Lord Keith of Kinkel, Lord Ackner, Lord Jauncey of Tilluchettle, Lord Browne-Wilkinson and Lord Lloyd of Berwick

Facts: Target Holdings was a finance company that entered into a mortgage arrangement for £1,525,000 with a company, Crowngate Ltd, for the acquisition of commercial property. Redferns was the firm of solicitors acting on the part of both Target Holdings and Crowngate Ltd, as well as Kohli Ltd and Panther Ltd, two sister companies to Crowngate, for the facilitation of the mortgage.

Unfortunately, Target Holdings was the victim of a cunning mortgage fraud. Target Holdings knew nothing of these events, and thought that it was providing a mortgage for a property worth more than the amount of money that was lent. The sum of £1,525,000 was duly transferred from Target Holdings to Redferns, who held the money on bare trust subject to instructions from Target Holdings. In breach of trust Redferns transferred the money to Crowngate Ltd one month before the charges were actually executed. Crowngate Ltd subsequently defaulted upon the mortgage and Target Holdings were only able to sell the commercial property at its true value of £500,000. Target Holdings sued Redferns for breach of trust

LORD BROWNE-WILKINSON

Before considering the technical issues of law which arise, it is appropriate to look at the case more generally. Target allege, and it is probably the case, that they were defrauded by third parties (Mr. Kohli and Mr. Musafir and possibly their associates) to advance money on the security of the property. If there had been no breach by Redferns of their instructions and the transaction had gone through, Target would have suffered a loss in round figures of £1.2m. (i.e. £1.7m. advanced less £500,000 recovered on the realisation of the security). Such loss would have been wholly caused by the fraud of the third parties. The breach of trust committed by Redferns left Target in exactly the same position as it would have been if there had been no such breach: Target advanced the same amount of money, obtained the same security and received the same amount on the realisation of that security. In any ordinary use of words, the breach of trust by Redferns cannot be said to have caused the actual loss ultimately suffered by Target unless it can be shown that, but for the breach of trust, the transaction would not have gone through, e.g. if Panther could not have obtained a conveyance from Mirage otherwise than by paying the purchase money to Mirage out of the moneys paid out, in breach of trust, by Redferns to Panther on 29 June. ...

The argument both before the Court of Appeal and your Lordships concentrated on the equitable rules establishing the extent and quantification of the compensation payable by a trustee who is in breach of trust. In my judgment this approach is liable to lead to the wrong conclusions in the present case because it ignores an earlier and crucial question, viz., is the trustee who has committed a breach under any liability at all to the beneficiary complaining of the breach? There can be cases where, although there is an undoubted breach of trust, the trustee is under no liability at all to a beneficiary. For example, if a trustee commits a breach of trust with the acquiescence of one beneficiary, that beneficiary has no right to complain and an action for breach of trust brought by him would fail completely. Again there may be cases where the breach gives rise to no right to compensation. Say, as often occurs, a trustee commits a judicious breach of trust by investing in an unauthorised investment which proves to be very profitable to the trust. A carping beneficiary could insist that the unauthorised investment be sold and the proceeds invested in authorised investments: but the trustee would be under no liability to pay compensation either to the trust fund or to the beneficiary because the breach has caused no loss to the trust fund. ...

The basic right of a beneficiary is to have the trust duly administered in accordance with the provisions of the trust instrument, if any, and the general law. Thus, in relation to a traditional trust where the fund is held in trust for a number of beneficiaries having different, usually successive, equitable interests, (e.g. A for life with remainder to B), the right of each beneficiary is to have the whole fund vested in the trustees so as to be available to satisfy his equitable interest when, and if, it falls into possession. Accordingly, in the case of a breach of such a trust involving the wrongful paying away of trust assets, the liability of the trustee is to restore to the trust fund, often called 'the trust estate,' what ought to have been there.

The equitable rules of compensation for breach of trust have been largely developed in relation to such traditional trusts, where the only way in which all the beneficiaries' rights can be protected is to restore to the trust fund what ought to be there. In such a case the basic rule is that a trustee in breach of trust must restore or pay to the trust estate either the assets which have been lost to the estate by reason of the breach or compensation for such loss. Courts of Equity did not award damages but, acting *in personam*, ordered the defaulting trustee to restore the trust estate... . If specific restitution of the trust property is not possible, then the liability of the trustee is to pay sufficient compensation to the trust estate to put it back to what it would have been had the breach not been committed... . Even if the immediate cause of the loss is the dishonesty or failure of a third party, the trustee is liable to make good that loss to the trust estate if, but for the breach, such loss would not have occurred...

[A]s I have sought to show a beneficiary becoming absolutely entitled to a trust fund has no automatic right to have the fund reconstituted in all circumstances. Thus, even applying the strict rules so developed in relation to traditional trusts, it seems to me very doubtful whether Target is now entitled to have the trust fund reconstituted. But in my judgment it is in any event wrong to lift wholesale the detailed rules developed in the context of traditional trusts and then seek to apply them to trusts of quite a different kind. In the modern world the trust has become a valuable device in commercial and financial dealings. The fundamental principles of equity apply as much to such trusts as they do to the traditional trusts in relation to which those principles were originally formulated. But in my judgment it is important, if the trust is not to be rendered commercially useless, to distinguish between the basic principles of trust law and those specialist rules developed in relation to traditional trusts which are applicable only to such trusts and the rationale of which has no application to trusts of quite a different kind.

...I have no doubt that, until the underlying commercial transaction has been completed, the solicitor can be required to restore to client account moneys wrongly paid away. But to import into such trust an obligation to restore the trust fund once the transaction has been completed would be entirely artificial. The obligation to reconstitute the trust fund applicable in the case of traditional trusts reflects the fact that no one beneficiary is entitled to the trust property and the need to compensate all beneficiaries for the breach. That rationale has no application to a case such as the present. ...

But the fact that there is an accrued cause of action as soon as the breach is committed does not in my judgment mean that the quantum of the compensation payable is ultimately fixed as at the date when the breach occurred. The quantum is fixed at the date of judgment at which date, according to the circumstances then pertaining, the compensation is assessed at the figure then necessary to put the trust estate or the beneficiary back into the position it would have been in had there been no breach. I can see no justification for 'stopping the clock' immediately in some cases but not in others: to do so may, as in this case, lead to compensating the trust estate or the beneficiary for a loss which, on the facts known at trial, it has never suffered.

For these reasons I reach the conclusion that, on the facts which must currently be assumed, Target has not demonstrated that it is entitled to any compensation for breach of trust. Assuming that moneys would have been forthcoming from some other source to complete the purchase from Mirage if the moneys had not been wrongly provided by Redferns in breach of trust, Target obtained exactly what it would have obtained had no breach occurred, i.e. a valid security for the sum advanced. ...

I would therefore allow the appeal, set aside the order of the Court of Appeal and restore the order of Warner J.

There are two important aspects to take from Lord Browne-Wilkinson's speech. First, whilst a breach of trust might exist, if it is rectified before the trust suffers any loss, then the trustees cannot be held liable for the subsequently corrected breach. Secondly, the quantification of liability with regard to the specific breach does not stop at the moment the breach takes place, but instead will be assessed at the date of the trial.

On both of these factors Redferns was therefore not liable for the losses Target Holdings suffered. They had ensured charges were executed over the commercial property and therefore Target Holdings was in exactly the same situation they would have been in had the charges been executed before the money was transferred to Crowngate Ltd. Secondly, whilst Redferns was liable for the whole sum of money at the moment it was paid to Crowngate Ltd in breach of trust, the obtaining of the charges executed over the property meant that the valid substitute for the money was obtained. From that stage onwards, Redferns' liability was reduced to nothing.

***Bartlett and Others v Barclays Bank Trust Co. Ltd. (Nos. 1 and 2)* [1980] Ch 515**

Panel: Brightman J

Statute: Trustee Act 1925 s61

Facts: Barclays Bank was trustee of a family trust that had a majority of shares in a private company, Bartlett Trust Ltd ('BTL'). BTL subsequently became a subsidiary of Bartlett Trust Holdings ('BTH'), in which the trust had 99.8% of the shareholding. Barclays Bank took no role in the management nor exercised any form of control of the company from 1960. During this time period BTH altered its investment programme to go into property development. Barclays Bank made no objection to this change.

BTH then embarked upon two hazardous property transactions without any consultation or interaction with Barclays Bank. Although the first project in Guildford was profitable, the second project at the Old Bailey in London involved the purchase of land for more than the market rate, with only a slight chance of obtaining planning permission on the land. Planning permission was subsequently not forthcoming and the land could not be developed. BTH subsequently suffered a loss of £500,000 from this transaction and the beneficiaries subsequently sued the trustees for failing to exercise proper supervision and management of BTH.

It was held that Barclays were in breach of their duties as trustee to manage BTH prudently. However, since the profit from the Guildford project and the loss from the Old Bailey project stemmed from the same breach, a set-off of the loss from the Old Bailey project against the profit from the Guildford project was allowed.

MR JUSTICE BRIGHTMAN

The situation may be summed up as follows. Bartlett Trust (Holdings) Ltd. (BTH) made a large loss as a result of the involvement of itself and BTL in the Old Bailey project. This loss reduced the value of the BTH shares and thereby caused a loss to the trust fund of the 1920 settlement. The bank, had it acted in time, could by reason of its shareholding have stopped the board of BTL embarking upon the Old Bailey project; and, had it acted in time, could have stopped the board of BTL and later the board of BTH (it is unnecessary to differentiate) from continuing with the project; and could, had it acted in time, have required BTH to sell its interest in Far Investments Ltd. (Far) to Stock Conversion on the no-loss or small-loss terms which (as I find) were available for the asking.

What, then, was the duty of the bank and did the bank fail in its duty? It does not follow that because a trustee could have prevented a loss it is therefore liable for the loss. The questions which I must ask myself are (1) What was the duty of the bank as the holder of 99.8 per cent of the shares in BTL and BTH? (2) Was the bank in breach of duty in any and if so what respect? (3) If so, did that breach of duty cause the loss which was suffered by the trust estate? (4) If so, to what extent is the bank liable to make good that loss? In approaching these questions, I bear in mind that the attack on the bank is based, not on wrongful acts, but on wrongful omissions, that is to say, non-feasance not misfeasance.

Alert

The cases establish that it is the duty of a trustee to conduct the business of the trust with the same care as an ordinary prudent man of business would extend towards his own affairs… .

If the trust had existed without the incorporation of BTL, so that the bank held the freehold and leasehold properties and other assets of BTL directly upon the trusts of the settlement, it would in my opinion have been a clear breach of trust for the bank to have hazarded trust money upon the Old Bailey development project in partnership with Stock Conversion. The Old Bailey project was a gamble, because it involved buying into the site at prices in excess of the investment values of the properties, with no certainty or probability, with no more than a chance, that planning permission could be obtained for a financially viable redevelopment, that the numerous proprietors would agree to sell out or join in the scheme, that finance would be available upon acceptable terms, and that the development would be completed, or at least become a marketable asset, before the time came to start winding up the trust. However one looks at it, the project was a hazardous speculation upon which no trustee could properly have ventured without explicit authority in the trust instrument. I therefore hold that the entire expenditure in the Old Bailey project would have been incurred in breach of trust, had the money been spent by the bank itself. The fact that it was a risk acceptable to the board of a wealthy company like Stock Conversion has little relevance.

I turn to the question, what was the duty of the bank as the holder of shares in BTL and BTH? I will first answer this question without regard to the position of the bank as a specialist trustee, to which I will advert later. The bank, as trustee, was bound to act in relation to the shares and to the controlling position which they conferred, in the same manner as a prudent man of business. The prudent man of business will act in such manner as is necessary to safeguard his investment. He will do this in two ways. If facts come to his knowledge which tell him that the company's affairs are not being conducted as they should be, or which put him on inquiry, he will take appropriate action. Appropriate action will no doubt consist in the first instance of inquiry of and consultation with the directors, and in the last but most unlikely resort, the convening of a general meeting to replace one or more directors. What the prudent man of business will *not* do is to content himself with the receipt of such information on the affairs of the company as a shareholder ordinarily receives at annual general meetings. Since he has the power to do so, he will go further and see that he has sufficient information to enable him to make a responsible decision from time to time either to let matters proceed as they are proceeding, or to intervene if he is dissatisfied. ...

Alert

So far, I have applied the test of the ordinary prudent man of business. ...I am of opinion that a higher duty of care is plainly due from someone like a trust corporation which carries on a specialised business of trust management. A trust corporation holds itself out in its advertising literature as being above ordinary mortals. With a specialist staff of trained trust officers and managers, with ready access to financial information and professional advice, dealing with and solving trust problems day after day, the trust corporation holds itself out, and rightly, as capable of providing an expertise which it would be unrealistic to expect and unjust to demand from the ordinary prudent man or woman who accepts, probably unpaid and sometimes reluctantly from a sense of family duty, the burdens of a trusteeship. Just as, under the law of contract, a professional person possessed of a particular skill is liable for breach of contract if he neglects to use the skill and experience which he professes, so I think that a professional corporate trustee is liable for breach of trust if loss is caused to the trust fund because it neglects to exercise the special care and skill which it professes to have. The advertising literature of the bank was not in evidence (other than the scale of fees) but counsel for the defendant did not dispute that trust corporations, including the bank, hold themselves out as possessing a superior ability for the conduct of trust business, and in any event I would take judicial notice of that fact. Having expressed my view of the higher duty required from a trust corporation, I should add that the bank's counsel did not dispute the proposition.

In my judgment the bank wrongfully and in breach of trust neglected to ensure that it received an adequate flow of information concerning the intentions and activities of the boards of BTL and BTH. It was not proper for the bank to confine itself to the receipt of the annual balance sheet and profit and loss account, detailed annual financial statements and the chairman's report and statement, and to attendance at the annual general meetings and the luncheons that followed, which were the limits of the bank's regular sources of information. Had the bank been in receipt of more frequent information it would have been able to step in and stop, and ought to have stopped, Mr Roberts and the board embarking on the Old Bailey project. That project was imprudent and hazardous and wholly unsuitable for a trust whether undertaken by the bank direct or through the medium of its wholly owned company. Even without the regular flow of information which the bank ought to have had, it knew enough to put it upon inquiry. There were enough obvious points at which the bank should have intervened and asked questions. Assuming, as I do, that the questions would have been answered truthfully, the bank would have discovered the gamble upon which Mr Roberts and his board were about to embark in relation to the Old Bailey site, and it could have, and should have, stopped the initial move towards disaster, and later on arrested further progress towards disaster. I have indicated in the course of this judgment a number of obvious points at which the bank should have intervened, and it would be repetitive to summarise them.

I hold that the bank failed in its duty whether it is judged by the standard of the prudent man of business or of the skilled trust corporation. The bank's breach of duty caused the loss which was suffered by the trust estate. If the bank had intervened as it could and should have that loss would not have been incurred. By "loss," I mean the depreciation which took place in the market value of the BT shares, by comparison with the value which the shares would have commanded if the loss on the Old Bailey project had not been incurred, and reduction of dividends through loss of income. The bank is liable for the loss so suffered by the trust estate, except to the extent that I shall hereafter indicate.

...There remains this defence, which I take from paragraph 26 of the amended pleading:

"In about 1963 [BTL] purchased a site at Woodbridge Road, Guildford, pursuant to the policy pleaded in paragraph 19 hereof, for the sum of £79,000, and re-sold the same for £350,000 to MEPC Ltd. in 1973. The net profit resulting from such sale was £271,000. If, which is denied, the defendant is liable for breach of trust whether as alleged in the amended statement of claim or otherwise, the defendant claims credit for such sum of £271,000 or other sum found to be gained in taking any accounts and inquiries."

The general rule as stated in all the textbooks, with some reservations, is that where a trustee is liable in respect of distinct breaches of trust, one of which has resulted in a loss and the other in a gain, he is not entitled to set off the gain against the loss, unless they arise in the same transaction: see Halsbury's Laws of England, 3rd ed., vol. 38 (1962), p. 1046; Snell's Principles of Equity ,

27th ed. (1973), p. 276; Lewin on the Law of Trusts, 16th ed. (1964), p. 670 and Underhill's Law of Trusts and Trustees, 12th ed. (1970), p. 634. The relevant cases are, however, not altogether easy to reconcile. All are centenarians and none is quite like the present. The Guildford development stemmed from exactly the same policy and (to a lesser degree because it proceeded less far) exemplified the same folly as the Old Bailey project. Part of the profit was in fact used to finance the Old Bailey disaster. By sheer luck the gamble paid off handsomely, on capital account. I think it would be unjust to deprive the bank of this element of salvage in the course of assessing the cost of the shipwreck. My order will therefore reflect the bank's right to an appropriate set-off.

This case is extremely useful in revealing the methodology judges use when ascertaining whether a breach of trust has occurred when trustees have dealt with trust property in a manner authorised by the trust instrument. Furthermore, quantification of loss in such circumstances will be quantified in relation to what the value of the trust fund would have been but for the breach taking place.

It is also important to realise Brightman J's judgment covers other important aspects of breach of trust. First, the duty of a trustee is to deal with the trust to the same standard as the ordinary prudent man of business. However, where the 'professional' trustee has specialist experience or skills that would go beyond that of the ordinary 'lay' trustee, then the duty of care should be of a higher standard than the ordinary prudent man of business. This higher standard also extends to the situations where the court can forgive a trustee for breach under the Trustee Act 1925 s61. Where a professional trustee is seeking relief from liability under s61, there is also a higher standard to pass before the court will excuse the breach than if a lay trustee was asking to be excused for the same breach.

Link
see "Defences to Breach of Trust" below.

The final point of interest is the set-off itself. It is submitted that Brightman J's statement of the principles for when a set-off should be allowed are correct. However, it is questionable whether these principles have been correctly applied to this case. It must be remembered that Barclays' course of dealings throughout was not to run the company, in other words to be passive instead of playing an active role. If Barclays had been active in running BTH then a set-off would be clearly justifiable. Yet, since Barclays in essence did nothing, it is submitted that this is different from pursuing a constant course of action; it is not pursuing a course of action at all. Therefore, a set-off should not have been allowed in this case.

9.2 Liability Between Trustees

As a general principle, trustees are jointly and severally liable for breach of trust. This means that a beneficiary can claim against any of the trustees in the event of a breach, and trustees share the liability between them. This is even the case where the breach has only been undertaken by one of the trustees.

***Bahin v Hughes* (1886) 31 Ch D 390**

Panel: Cotton, Bowen and Fry LJJ

Facts: A testator, Robert Hughes, bequeathed £2,000 to his daughters Eliza Hughes, Sarah Hughes (who subsequently became Sarah Burden) and Frances Hughes (who subsequently became Frances Edwards), to hold on trust to invest in specified securities in England and Wales. Mrs Bahin was the life tenant of this trust. It is important to note at the time of this case married women were not allowed to own property and therefore Mr Burden and Mr Edwards would have to perform trustee functions upon their behalf.

Eliza Hughes, being unmarried, was able to actively manage the trust with Mr Burden. They invested in unauthorised leasehold properties. Frances Edwards was informed of this at the time but subsequently agreed to investing in unauthorised assets. Mrs Bahin found out about the breach and sued the trustees. By this time Frances Edwards had died and Mr Edwards was sued instead. Mr Edwards claimed an indemnity from liability, as Frances Edwards was the trustee and any investments were made solely through the instigation or subsequent consent of Frances Edwards, not him.

It was held that, despite Mr Edwards being entirely passive and only having trustee duties as a consequence of his marriage to Frances Edwards, he was still liable for the breach of trust and could not claim an indemnity.

LORD JUSTICE COTTON

As regards this first question, namely, whether Mr Edwards is answerable for the default of his wife in committing such a breach of trust as this, as much as if she had misspent the money, in my opinion he is altogether answerable. It was an action brought for the loss of the fund, occasioned by a breach of trust, being negligence, on the part of the trustees. We feel no doubt that the *cestui que trust* is entitled to redress as against the trustees, and therefore consider both that the wife of Mr Edwards and himself, as well as Mr and Mrs Burden, were answerable. ...and in my opinion it would be wrong to raise a distinction as regards the liability of Mr Edwards. He is answerable for the same breach of trust, and is not to be differently treated from the other trustees in the matter. The husband is acting and administering on the part and in the right of his wife the duty of trusteeship, who cannot act in the matter without him; therefore he is liable for the breaches of trust committed by her, without drawing any minute distinctions, as might have been done if the case had come within a recent Act, the Married Women's Property Act. But that Act does not apply to this case.

But then we come to another and more difficult question, namely, how far Mr Edwards can, as against Miss Hughes, have indemnity for the loss, on the ground that she was the acting trustee, that she and Mrs Burden took upon themselves to invest this money, and that although both she and Mr Edwards are liable to the beneficiaries, she is liable to Mr Edwards, who left the matter in her hands. On going into the authorities, there are very few cases in which one trustee, who has been guilty with a co-trustee of breach of trust and held answerable, has successfully sought indemnity as against his co-trustee. ... Of course where one trustee has got the money into his own hands, and made use of it, he will be liable to his co-trustee to give him an indemnity. Now I think it wrong to lay down any limitation of the circumstances under which one trustee would be held liable to the other for indemnity, both having been held liable to the *cestui que trust*; but so far as cases have gone at present, relief has only been granted against a trustee who has himself got the benefit of the breach of trust, or between whom and his co-trustees there has existed a relation, which will justify the Court in treating him as solely liable for the breach of trust. Here, when Miss Hughes got the money, she handed it over to the mortgagor... The Appellant, Mr Edwards, relies on the fact that she sent him a letter with the cheque for him and his wife to indorse, saying that nothing should be done with the money without consulting him... Miss Hughes was the active trustee and Mr Edwards did nothing, and in my opinion it would be laying down a wrong rule to hold that where one trustee acts honestly, though erroneously, the other trustee is to be held entitled to indemnity who by doing nothing neglects his duty more than the acting trustee. That Miss Hughes made an improper investment is true, but she acted honestly, and intended to do the best she could, and believed that the property was sufficient security for the money, although she made no inquiries about their being leasehold houses. In my opinion the money was lost just as much by the default of Mr Edwards as by the innocent though erroneous action of his co-trustee, Miss Hughes. All the trustees were in the wrong, and everyone is equally liable to indemnify the beneficiaries.

Therefore, a trustee cannot escape liability by stepping back from the trust and letting other trustees breach their duties. Indeed, by doing so a trustee is breaching the duty to safeguard trust property. This case does show, however, that it is possible for a trustee to obtain an indemnity against the breach by another trustee.

***Head v Gould* [1898] 2 Ch 250**

Panel: Kekewich J

Facts: Robert Head created a marriage settlement for his wife and himself successively for life, remainder to their children. The original trustees were Mr Clapp and Mr Houlditch. After Robert Head died his widow obtained advances out of the capital of the fund up to her maximum share. Clapp and Houlditch were unwilling to advance any more capital. They wrote a letter to Mrs Head which contained the following phrase 'The only way we can assist you is by handing the trust over to others, as we are most desirous of doing.' Clapp and Houlditch were subsequently replaced with Mr Gould, a solicitor who was a family friend, and Miss Head, one of the children and a remainderman to the settlement.

The new trustees sold a house in breach of trust and surrendered some life insurance policies on the life of Mrs Head, with Mrs Head's agreement. The proceeds went to Mrs Head.

The trustees were sued for breach of trust by one of the children, whose share in the trust had been given to his mother, Mrs Head.

MR JUSTICE KEKEWICH

It will be convenient here at once to deal with the claim made by Miss Head against her co-trustee Gould. By her third-party notice she seeks to be indemnified by him against loss by reason of the breaches of trust, on the ground that the loss and misapplication (if any) of the trust funds, or any part thereof, were occasioned entirely by his acts or defaults, and that he assumed to act as solicitor to the trust estate and as sole trustee thereof, and exercised control of the administration of the trust funds, and that whatever was done by herself in connection with the trust was at his instigation and in reliance upon his advice.

This is a serious charge, and if it had been proved would have entitled her to the relief claimed according to well-known and well-recognised principles. … My conclusion from such evidence as there is before the Court is distinctly adverse to the claim. I know that, before the appointment of herself and Gould as trustees, Miss Head was an active party to the importunities of her mother which induced the former trustees to commit a breach of trust for their benefit, and that she looked to the change of trustees as a means of, in some way or other, obtaining further advances. I know further that she was well acquainted with the position of the trust, and that it was all-important to maintain the policies and to appropriate the rents of the house to that purpose. She now affects to ignore all that has been done since her appointment, and professes not to remember having executed the several instruments which must have been executed by her for the sale of the house and the surrender of the policies, or the receipt of moneys arising therefrom. With regret and under a painful sense of duty, I am bound to say that I do not credit her testimony. True it is that the defendant Gould is a solicitor, and that he was appointed a trustee for that very reason. True no doubt, also, that the legal business was managed by him, and I do not propose to absolve him from any responsibility attaching to him on that ground; but I do not myself think that … any other judge ever intended to hold that a man is bound to indemnify his co-trustee against loss merely because he was a solicitor, when that co-trustee was an active participator in the breach of trust complained of, and is not proved to have participated merely in consequence of the advice and control of the solicitor. …

Alert

A key issue is the fact that Miss Head was unable to obtain an indemnity merely because Mr Gould was a solicitor and handled the legal aspects of trusteeship. This reasoning is undoubtedly correct; even if the lay trustee does not understand all the legal consequences of administering the trust, it is always possible to run some rudimentary checks to ensure the expert trustee is doing what is supposed to be done.

This scenario can be distinguished from the situation where the expert trustee uses his/her influence to prevent the lay trustee from performing various trust duties. This can be seen from the case of *Re Partington* (1887) 57 LT 654. In this case the trustees, which included Mr Allen, a solicitor trustee, and Mrs Partington, the widow of the testator, were found liable for investing in an unauthorised mortgage. Mrs Partington subsequently applied for an indemnity against Mr Allen. In his judgment Stirling J held that when Mr Allen made the investment he did so in such a way that Mrs Partington was unable to exercise her judgment upon this investment. To make a judgment upon the mortgage Mrs Partington relied upon Mr Allen to give her information surrounding the transaction. On the evidence Stirling J held that Mr Allen neither communicated the real state of the property that was going to be subject to the mortgage nor that investing in such a mortgage would be an improper investment. This situation was distinguishable from *Bahin v Hughes* (1886) 31 Ch D 390 because Mrs Partington was not merely standing by whilst Mr Evans committed the breach, but instead had been actively misinformed by Mr Evans. In essence, her will to act properly as trustee had been overborne. Consequently, it was held that Mrs Partington was entitled to an indemnity and Mr Allen was primarily liable for this breach of trust.

9.3 Defences to Breach of Trust

With the wide range of possibilities in which a breach of trust can exist, it is unsurprising that there are circumstances where it is unsuitable to find a trustee liable. As such, a number of defences have been created, both judicially and through statute. The defences of consent, acquiescence, and the Trustee Act 1925 s61 were considered in *Re Pauling's Settlement Trusts* [1964] Ch 303.

***Re Pauling's Settlement Trusts* [1964] Ch 303**

Panel: Willmer, Harman and Upjohn LJJ

Statute: Trustee Act 1925 s61

Facts: The following extract focuses firstly upon the nature of undue influence, which was one of the factors relevant to the breaches of trust. The extract then considers the various defences to breach of trust.

LORD JUSTICE WILLMER delivering the judgment of the court

Where the presumption of undue influence exists, a gift by a child cannot be retained by a parent unless he or she can show, first, that the gift was the spontaneous act of the child, and, secondly, that the child knew what his rights were. Thirdly, it is desirable, though not essential, that a child should have independent, and, if possible, professional, advice before making a gift. "In such a case the court," said Cotton LJ in *Allcard v Skinner*, "sets aside the voluntary gift, unless it is proved that in fact the gift was the spontaneous act of the donor acting under circumstances which enabled him to exercise an independent will and which justifies the court in holding that the gift was the result of a free exercise of the donor's will." ...

The question of the duration of the presumption has also been much discussed. ... In our judgment the question is one of fact and degree. One begins with a strong presumption in the case of a child just 21 living at home, and this will grow less and less as the child goes out in the world and leaves the shelter of his home. Nevertheless, the presumption normally lasts only a "short" time after the child has attained 21 (see *Lancashire Loans Ltd v Black*, *per* Greer LJ, and it seems impossible and undesirable to define it further. A married daughter with a separate establishment of her own may be emancipated directly she attains 21, whereas a spinster who has never left home might be able to rely on the presumption for a longer period. We reject, however, Mr Bagnall's submission that this presumption continues indefinitely until it is proved that the undue influence has ceased to exist. That is to confuse a case of actual undue influence with the presumption. On the other hand, it may not be difficult for a spinster daughter living at home to prove a case of actual undue influence for many years after she has attained the age of 21. In the present case it is important to remember that only the presumption is relied on; no actual undue influence is alleged.

Then Sir Milner argued that trustees who have obtained no benefit from payments induced by undue influence could not be held liable, and that the only person who could be sued would be the parent presumed to have exercised the undue influence, or any person (short of a bona fide purchaser for value) who received the benefit of the payments. On the other hand, Mr Bagnall argued that the bank were in the position of volunteers, and therefore could not escape the consequences of dealing in breach of trust with a beneficiary presumed to have been actuated by the undue influence of a third party; they were at risk just as any other volunteer who takes the property acquired in breach of trust. In the circumstances of this case, we do not think it necessary to express a concluded opinion upon this matter except to say that we reject Sir Milner Holland's argument that the bank cannot be made liable unless they received some benefit from the breach of trust. It seems to us in principle that a trustee dealing in breach of trust with a beneficiary who has just attained the age of 21 years must realise the danger that such beneficiary may be acting under the influence of a parent. We do not see how a trustee can possibly escape the consequences of that knowledge. ... Without expressing a final opinion, we think that the true view may be that a trustee carrying out a transaction in breach of trust may be liable if he knew, or ought to have known, that the beneficiary was acting under the undue influence of another, or may be presumed to have done so, but will not be liable if it cannot be established that he so knew, or ought to have known.

Alert

That is sufficient for the purposes of the present case, for, of course, the bank knew very exactly the ages of each of the children, and they knew further that as each child attained 21, that child received advances from the bank which went straight into the banking account of the mother. Indeed, in Ann's case plans were made to effect this unhappy result even before the child attained 21. Accordingly, it seems to us clear that if it can be established that the presumption exists in any given case, the bank are fixed with notice of it and cannot rely on any consents given under such influence.

The bank also rely for relief from the consequences of any breach of trust upon section 61 of the Trustee Act 1925. At this stage all we propose to say is that it would be a misconstruction of the section to say that it does not apply to professional trustees, but, as was pointed out in the Judicial Committee of the Privy Council in National Trustees Company of Australasia Ltd v General Finance Company of Australasia Ltd., "... without saying that the remedial provisions of the section should never be applied to a trustee in the position of the appellants, their Lordships think it is a circumstance to be taken into account ..." Where a banker undertakes to act as a paid trustee of a settlement created by a customer, and so deliberately places itself in a position where its duty as trustee conflicts with its interest as a banker, we think that the court should be very slow to relieve such a trustee under the provisions of the section. ...

LORD JUSTICE UPJOHN

Continuing reading the judgment of the court: ...

It seems to us that the whole picture must be looked at, and it is from the documents that a fairly clear view can be had. It does not appear that the mother, the source of the money was more than a cypher willing to sign whatever her husband put before her. He controlled the family fortune by his right to draw on the family banking account, and he assumed throughout that what he said would go. As we have already said, he was the originator of all the transactions complained of here. His method was to cajole the bank into going as far as they thought they dared, and then to prepare what he called "chits" (or sometimes got them prepared by the bank) and send them to his wife or the child or children concerned for signature. So far this looks like a typical case where undue influence ought to be presumed, but the judge, who saw the witnesses, was chary of acting upon the presumption. The impression he got was of a united family determined to extract from the bank by hook or by crook the money necessary to continue its extravagant way of life. On this view of it, the passage we have quoted about the sons being willing to sign anything bears a less sinister aspect. At the time of this advance the son George was twenty-three years old. He had done his military service, and was up at Cambridge. The judge thought him an exceptionally able young man, well acquainted with his rights, and able to take care of himself. He had no separate advice about this £2,000 advance, but he had been advised about the Hodson loan transaction, and in the course of receiving the explanations then offered he must have realised what the power was which the trustees were purporting to exercise. ...

The case of the other son, Francis, is quite different. He was at this time 28 years old, and was apparently living for the most part with his grandmother, so that he was removed from immediate parental control. On the other hand, we now know that he was a schizophrenic. This diagnosis had been made in 1940 when he found one day of life in the Royal Air Force altogether too much for him, and was repeated by a doctor who saw him in 1951. He was not called by either side, it being agreed that his memory was not at all to be trusted. Consent to this, as to other transactions in which he was involved, was written out and sent to him by his father. There is no letter from him anywhere in the correspondence. No representative of the bank ever saw him. He was obviously left purposely in the background. On the other hand, he was capable of teaching in a boys school, which he did for two years towards the end of the war, and was accepted for entry to Edinburgh University after the war, where also he continued for two years as a student. Further, when he went with his brother to be advised over the Hodson loan, the partner in Farrer & Co who saw him thought him capable of understanding the transaction. Moreover, it has never been alleged that he was at any material time incapacitated from contracting or conducting business affairs by reason of his mental health, though we cannot think that if the bank had known of his history of ill-health they would have acted on the consents he returned signed to his father. But the bank did not know the facts. We have considered anxiously whether, before making an advance, they should have made some inquiry into his circumstances. ... On the whole, we do not feel able to say that the presumption of undue influence must be held to exist between Francis and his parents having regard to his age and his absence from home, and we conclude that the bank were not bound to make inquiries as to his state of mind or fitness as an object of the power they were affecting to exercise. Accordingly, though this was the plainest breach of trust, we agree with the judge that the bank have a good defence, for they obtained consents from the two children concerned, and they were emancipated. ...

Alert

The next victim on the list was the daughter Ann. ...

There is no doubt that Ann asked for each of these sums to be advanced, and it is clear that on each such occasion that Ann requested these advances she did so in writing, and represented that they were required for furniture, etc., well knowing in fact that only about £300 was expended on the purchase of furniture from start to finish. The rest went in the family living expenses through the mother's account. Of course, Ann appreciated that these representations were untrue; "silly lies," as she said in the witness-box. The judge refused to give relief to Ann in these respects. He carefully set out the details of the payments. We think it is to be inferred that he did not believe that Ann was so innocent as she pretended in the witness-box, saying that she always regarded the money as her mother's. Nevertheless, the judge was clearly of opinion that a presumption of undue influence applied in Ann's case because he stated it was essential that she should have independent advice on the transaction. Independent advice she did have on the purchase of the house, but none upon the expenditure on furniture, which was quite a separate matter, and this the judge overlooked. The judge says that the bank acted on the faith of untrue statements by Ann, and refused Ann relief on this ground. We cannot agree with this. If the judge meant no more than that the bank required some document signed by Ann stating that the money was required for furniture, we agree with him, but we do not think that the bank can have really acted on a sincere belief in the truth of the representations; their supine conduct shows that they really could have no more than a pious hope, which they did not dare to test by pressing to see receipts for the purchase of this vast quantity of furniture, that most of it was being invested in furniture. A moment's study of the mother's account at this time would have shown that even this was improbable. They merely wanted some document which, as they thought, would give legal justification for making the payments.

Further, it seems to us that these very untrue statements must be treated as issuing out of the presumed undue influence of her father, made, as they were, either to the bank in his presence, or by arrangement with him. Finally, we do not consider that these statements, if true, would, as the judge held, have justified the advances... . The bank at this stage ought to have had their eyes wide open to the situation and insisted on calling a halt to this reckless expenditure apparently for furniture. Ann by her counsel concedes that she must give credit for £300 of furniture actually purchased. Subject to that, we feel constrained to come to the conclusion that, without separate advice, the bank cannot rely on the assent of this young girl to gifts direct into her mother's and father's pockets, and we hold the bank liable in respect of advances numbered 8, 10, 12, 17, 18, half of 20 and 22 as set out in the statement of claim, and pro tanto allow the appeal accordingly. Having behaved unreasonably, the bank cannot rely on section 61.

Ann's portion had now been fully used, but there remained one chicken to be plucked, a younger brother, Anthony... . He attained 21 on June 15, 1951, and three days after that event there is recorded an interview with the father, the terms of which are too important to omit. "Date June 18, 1951. Interview with Commander Younghusband. They want £2,000 to be raised for the youngest son. Mr Burrell is to write to the boy explaining that the money will be his to do as he likes with and when that has been done and we receive Mrs Younghusband's formal request we are to raise the money and get the boy's directions for its disposal."

As the judge said, the process had become streamlined. So long as Burrell could write a letter telling the boy the money was his, all else would be automatic. This is exactly what happened. Burrell wrote a most perfunctory letter to the young man in Germany which he agreed in the witness-box could not constitute proper separate advice, and in fairness to him was not intended to be more than a pipe opener to a lawyer's relationship with a potential client, and between July 11, 1951, and February 7, 1952, £6,500 was paid straight into the mother's account. There is one payment which is characteristic. The father had succeeded to the tune of £1,000 in raising the wind by a charge on Ann's house, and half the first payment to Anthony was used to repay the bank this amount, thus robbing Anthony to pay Ann. There was not even a pretence in any instance of any countervailing benefit to Anthony except as mentioned later. We do not feel any doubt that the bank is liable on these payments, as the judge held. Relief under section 61 is out of the question.

> ... As to acquiescence, we think that this must be looked at rather broadly. ... In this case it would be wrong, we feel, to place any disability upon the beneficiaries because it so happened that George was a member of the bar, and had been in well-known chambers. He had not been in Chancery chambers where it may be said that these things are better understood; but the real truth of the matter is that a party cannot be held to have acquiesced unless he knew, or ought to have known, what his rights were. On the facts of this case we cannot criticise any of the plaintiffs for failing to appreciate their rights until another junior counsel, whom they consulted on a far-fetched and futile scheme of George's for avoiding estate duty on his mother's death, advised that the advances might be improper That was in 1954, and thereupon the family, headed, of course, by George, took immediate steps to explore this matter. This is a most complicated action, and many matters had to be explored before an action for breach of trust could properly be mounted. The writ was issued in 1958, and we do not think it right to hold that the plaintiffs were debarred by acquiescence from bringing an action which otherwise, to the extent we have indicated, is justified. ...
>
> In my judgment, therefore, the only question that arises is whether the bank should be relieved from the consequences of their breach of trust under section 61 of the Trustee Act 1925, to any, and if so, what extent. This, I think, is a very difficult question. The judgment of the court has already pointed out that the bank were personally innocent, but they were ill-advised by their own solicitors; but the bank must accept responsibility for such negligence, and section 61 cannot possibly be invoked to relieve them from its consequences without more. The circumstance that seems to me to make the application of the section possible is that the bank received the letter quoted in the judgment of the court written by Burrell on behalf of Francis and George saying that the matter was in a satisfactory state. Thereafter it would have been quite unreasonable for the bank to take any further step to assure themselves that the transaction had been properly carried out, and they were lulled into a false sense of security. Section 61 is purely discretionary, and its application necessarily depends on the particular facts of each case. I think, in the circumstances of this case, that I am prepared to hold that the bank acted honestly (that is not in dispute) and reasonably and ought fairly to be excused to the extent of the surrender value of the policies transferred to the boys at the date of the transaction, about £650, but no doubt the exact figure can be ascertained. I do not see how the bank can properly be relieved to any greater extent. ...

In this case there were numerous breaches that took place over an extended period, which means the full facts of the case are extremely complicated. However, the general principles applied to the case are clear.

First, where the trustee knows or ought to have known that the beneficiary was giving trust property to another as a consequence of undue influence, then the trustee will be in breach of trust. Furthermore, if the beneficiary is a child then undue influence from a parent can be rebuttably presumed where the child is not emancipated from parental control. When emancipation will take place will depend upon the facts of the case.

Secondly, the defence of consent from a beneficiary would appear to only be present where the beneficiary is *sui juris*, gives consent free of any external pressure or undue influence, and at least understands the nature of the proposed breach. Subsequent acquiescence to a breach can also only take place where the beneficiary knew or ought to have known their rights under the trust and the breach of these rights which the beneficiary has forgiven.

Thirdly, whilst the Trustee Act 1925 s61 was held to apply to both lay and professional trustees, the courts will look at the trustee's acts to see if the trustee has acted honestly, fairly, and ought reasonably to be excused from liability. If any of the criteria are missing, particularly acting in a reasonable way, then the court will not apply s61. It is important to also note that s61 is a last resort defence for a trustee and the general body of caselaw suggests it will only ever be applied by the court in extraordinary circumstances. The fact that the trustee breached the trust as a consequence of incorrect legal advice is not a sufficiently meritorious circumstance, as held in *Re Pauling's Settlement Trusts*.

***Dreamvar (UK) Limited v Mischon De Reya (a firm)* [2016] EWHC 3316 (Ch)**

Panel: Mr David Railton QC (sitting as a Deputy High Court Judge)

Statute: Trustee Act 1925 s61

Facts: The claimant instructed the defendant firm of solicitors to act on their behalf with respect to a purchase of land. Unknown to either the claimant or defendant, the vendor of the land was actually a fraudster posing as the true owner. The claimant's purchase monies, held by the defendant solicitor, were eventually paid to the fraudulent vendor, who promptly disappeared. The claimant sued the defendant solicitors for breach of trust in an attempt to recover their lost purchase monies, which were otherwise irrecoverable.

In defence of this claim, the defendant firm of solicitors raised (*inter alia*) the statutory defence of s61 TA 1925.

MR DAVID RAILTON QC (sitting as a Deputy High Court Judge)

... it is now appropriate to return to [Dreamvar's] claim against MdR, and MdR's application for relief from personal liability for breach of trust under s.61, Trustee Act, 1925 . That section provides as follows:

'If it appears to the court that a trustee, whether appointed by the court or otherwise, is or may be personally liable for any breach of trust ... but has acted honestly and reasonably and ought fairly to be excused for the breach of trust ... then the court may relieve him either wholly or partly from personal liability for the same.'

The principles to be applied in relation to s.61 in the context of conveyancing transactions have been discussed by the Court of Appeal in the three recent decisions of Markandan, Davisons and RA Legal. I gratefully adopt the summary of the applicable principles as set out by Mr Dicker QC in P&P, at [252]:

The relevant principles governing the application of section 61 , as they appear in particular from the three authorities referred to above, can be summarised for present purposes as follows:

(1) The section requires the solicitor to have acted reasonably. Section 61 must be interpreted consistently with equity's high expectations of a trustee discharging fiduciary obligations; [RA Legal] per Sir Terence Etherton C at [108]. It requires the trustee to have acted "... with exemplary professional care and efficiency" and to have been "careful, conscientious and thorough"; [Markandan] per Rimer LJ at [60]-[61]. This does not however predicate that he has necessarily complied with best practice in all respects and the requisite standard is that of reasonableness not perfection; Davisons per Sir Andrew Morritt C at [48] and [RA Legal] per Briggs LJ at [30].

(2) A strict causation test casts the net too narrowly for the purposes of identifying relevant conduct. It would not be appropriate to exclude as irrelevant conduct which consisted of a departure from best or reasonable practice which increased the risk of loss caused by fraud, even if the court concludes that the fraudster would nonetheless have achieved his goal if the solicitor had acted reasonably. On the other hand, the court's jurisdiction to grant relief is not precluded by conduct of the trustee which, although unreasonable, played absolutely no part in the occasioning of the loss; [RA Legal] per Briggs LJ at [25] and Sir Terence Etherton C at [109]-[110].

(3) The burden of proving that he acted reasonably lies squarely on the solicitor; [RA Legal] per Briggs LJ at [54]. The onus is on the trustee to place before the court a full account of his or her conduct leading to the breach of trust; per Sir Terence Etherton C at [111].

(4) Even if the trustee ought fairly to be excused, the court still retains a discretionary power to grant relief from liability, in whole or in part, or to refuse it. Much may depend at this discretionary stage upon the consequences for the beneficiary. An institutional lender may well be insured (or effectively self-insured) for the consequences of third party fraud. But an innocent purchaser may have contributed his life savings to the purchase and have no recourse at all other than against his insured solicitor where, for example, the fraudster is a pure interloper;[RA Legal] per Briggs LJ at [33].

The first stage of the s.61 analysis is that the trustee, MdR, must show (the onus being on it), that it has acted both honestly and reasonably. No question of dishonesty arises in the present proceedings...I have already found, on the balance of probabilities, that MdR was not negligent...In these circumstances MdR has discharged the onus on it, that its conduct was reasonable. It was not suggested that the standard by which reasonableness should be assessed in this context is any different to that applicable in considering the allegations of negligence against MdR.

The second stage of the s.61 analysis involves deciding two related discretionary matters. The first is whether MdR ought fairly to be excused for the breach of trust; the second is whether, even if MdR ought fairly to be excused, the court should in its discretion grant relief (in whole or in part) or refuse it.

... the effect of the breach of trust on Dreamvar has been disastrous. It has lost the purchase price, and in return received nothing. It did not have insurance, or any ability (or knowledge) to enable it to self-insure against the risk of fraud...As for MdR's position, it is common ground that it is insured for events such as this, and that its insurance cover is sufficient to cover in full the loss suffered, should it not be excused from liability. In terms of balancing the relative effects or consequences of the breach of trust, it is apparent that MdR (with or without insurance) is far better able to meet or absorb it than Dreamvar.

...For these reasons, I conclude that MdR ought not fairly to be excused for the breach of trust, and that I should in any event, in my discretion, decline the relief sought. I would however add that if, contrary to my conclusions above, MMS were liable to Dreamvar, I would have exercised my discretion to relieve MdR of its liability for breach of trust to the extent of the liability found against MMS.

Another statutory defence within the court's discretion is the ability to impound a beneficiary's interest to be used by the trustee as an indemnity to the extent that the beneficiary's interest can replace any loss suffered by the trust.

Re Pauling's Settlement Trusts (No 2) **[1963] Ch 576**

Panel: Wilberforce J

Statute: Trustee Act 1925 s62

Facts: After judgment was given in the High Court decision of *Re Pauling's Settlement Trusts*, the claimants took out a summons to appoint new trustees. The trustees, Coutts Bank, refused the new appointment on the ground that they were entitled to the interest of the life tenant, Mrs Younghusband, and that their removal as trustees would imperil their right to impound this interest. It was held that the trustees did not have a right to remain as trustees until they had impounded Mrs Younghusband's equitable interest, as s62 could be exercised by the court in favour of a former trustee. However, in the circumstance it was not suitable to appoint new trustees.

MR JUSTICE WILBERFORCE

... What is said by the defendants is that that right to impound would be prejudiced if new trustees were appointed now and the trust fund handed over to them. That involves a consideration as to what is the nature of the right to impound which exists in favour of a trustee who has committed a breach of trust at the instigation of a beneficiary. I have to consider both the ordinary right which exists in equity apart from statute and also the further statutory right which has been conferred by section 62 of the Trustee Act 1925, both of which are invoked by the defendants as plaintiffs in the Chancery action now pending. It seems to me that it is not possible to maintain, as is the defendants' contention here, that a trustee, having committed a breach of trust, is entitled to remain as a trustee until it has exercised its right to impound the income of the beneficiary in order to recoup itself. That seems to me an impossible proposition. It is quite true that, in the reported authorities, there is no case where the right to impound has been exercised by a former trustee as distinct from an existing trustee, but it seems to me in principle that it is impossible to contend that the right to impound is limited to the case where the trustee seeking the right is an actual trustee. The nature of the right to impound seems to me to turn on two things: first, that the money paid back to capital is in its origin the money of the trustee, and that when it comes to considering who should get the income of it, the trustee who has provided the money has a better right to it than the tenant for life who has instigated the breach of trust. The alternative way of putting the matter is that the trustee in breach of trust is in some way subrogated to the rights of the beneficiary. He stands in his position in order that he may be indemnified. ...

It is said that the defendants have a right to control the investment of the trust fund, so that it is not invested in such a way as to prejudice their right to recoup out of income. That point seems to me to be completely misconceived. It is, of course, the duty of any trustee to exercise his powers of investment in such a way as to hold the balance properly between capital and income. If the fund were transferred to new trustees they would be under that duty and it is to be observed... in place of the life tenant, and the plaintiffs who are in the position of those entitled to capital. The new trustees would be under the normal duty of preserving an equitable balance, and if at any time it was shown they were inclining one way or the other, it would not be a difficult matter to bring them to account.

It is clear from Wilberforce J's judgment that s62 is not meant to replace the court's inherent power to impound a beneficiary's interest under the trust but is in addition to this power. However it must be noted that defences under ss61 and 62 will only be allowed by the court in truly meritorious circumstances.

10

Investment

Introduction

Trustees must invest the trust fund during the lifetime of the trust for the benefit of the beneficiaries. The primary source of their obligations in this regard will be the trust instrument. However, regardless of whether or not the trust instrument contains express powers in relation to investment, both common law and statute (principally the Trustee Act 2000) also apply in relation to the trustees' duty to invest.

As is discussed in more detail below, the common law duty is one of 'prudence', whereas the 2000 Act s1 imposes a statutory duty of care. However, the statutory duty only relates to certain aspects of the trustees' obligations in relation to investment, so the common law duty of prudence remains relevant to those obligations to which the Act does not apply.

10.1 The Common Law Duty of Prudence

Speight v Gaunt (1883) 9 App Cas 1

Panel: Earl of Selborne LC, Lord Blackburn, Lord Watson and Lord Fitzgerald

Facts: A trustee gave a broker the entirety of a trust fund to invest in municipal stocks, which was an authorised investment under the trust deed. The broker failed to make the intended investment but instead used the money for his own purposes. He became insolvent, whereupon the beneficiaries brought proceedings against the trustee for breach of trust for having used the services of a broker rather than having made the investment himself. The House of Lords dismissed the claim.

LORD BLACKBURN

...The case is of importance to the parties as involving a very considerable sum of money. It is also of general importance, so far as the application of the principles, on which the Court acts in respect to the liability of trustees to make good losses of trust funds, to the facts disclosed by the evidence, will be an authority in future cases. After some consideration, and reading the evidence, I have come to the conclusion that the judgment appealed against is right, and should be affirmed. ...

 Alert

The authorities cited ... shew that as a general rule a trustee sufficiently discharges his duty if he takes in managing trust affairs all those precautions which an ordinary prudent man of business would take in managing similar affairs of his own. There is one exception to this: a trustee must not choose investments other than those which the terms of his trust permit, though they may be such as an ordinary prudent man of business would select for his own money; and it may be that however usual it may be for a person who wishes to invest his own money, and instructs an agent, such as an attorney, or a stockbroker, to seek an investment, to deposit the money at interest with the agent till the investment is found, that is in effect lending it on the agent's own personal security, and is a breach of trust. No question as to this arises here, for [the trustee] did nothing of that kind. Subject to this exception, as to which it is unnecessary to consider further, I think the case of *Ex parte Belchier* Amb 218 establishes the principle that where there is a usual course of business the trustee is justified in following it, though it may be such that there is some risk that the property may be lost by the dishonesty or insolvency of an agent employed.

The transactions of life could not be carried on without some confidence being bestowed. When the transaction consists in a sale where the vendor is entitled to keep his hold on the property till he receives the money, and the purchaser is entitled to keep his money till he gets the property, it would be in all cases inconvenient if the vendor and purchaser were required to meet and personally exchange the one for the other; when the parties are, as is very often the case, living remote from each other, it would be physically impossible. ...

Judges and lawyers who see brought before them the cases in which losses have been incurred, and do not see the infinitely more numerous cases in which expense and trouble and inconvenience are avoided, are apt to think men of business rash. I think that the principle ... is that, while the course is usual, a trustee is not to be blamed if he honestly, and without knowing anything that makes it exceptionally risky in his case, pursues that usual course. ... It would be both unreasonable and inexpedient to make a trustee responsible for not being more prudent than ordinary men of business are.

The House of Lords, therefore, held that a trustee did not breach his duty to exercise reasonable care and prudence in the performance of his duties as trustee if he employed an apparently reputable agent to carry out certain tasks. If those tasks were then apparently carried out in the usual way there would be no breach.

***Re Whiteley, Whiteley v Learoyd* (1886) 33 Ch D 347**

Panel: Lord Halsbury LC, Lord Watson and Lord Fitzgerald

Facts: The defendants were trustees under a will of a sum of £5,000, with power to invest in 'real securities' in England and Wales. They invested £3,000 on the mortgage of freehold brickworks, having first obtained a valuation that the property would be good security for £3,500 before certain projected improvements. In fact, the business failed and the security proved to be insufficient. The beneficiaries sought to hold the trustees liable in respect of the loss arising from that investment. The House of Lords held that the trustees had failed to invest the trust fund prudently and hence were liable to the beneficiaries.

LORD WATSON

My Lords: I also am of opinion that the order of the Court of Appeal must be affirmed. As a general rule, the law requires of a trustee no higher degree of diligence in the execution of his office than a man of ordinary prudence would exercise in the management of his own private affairs. Yet he is not allowed the same discretion, in investing the moneys of the trust, as if he were a person 'sui juris' dealing with his own estate. Business men of ordinary prudence may and frequently do select investments which are more or less of a speculative character; but it is the duty of a trustee to confine himself to the class of investments which are permitted by the trust, and likewise to avoid all investments of that class which are attended with hazard. So long as he acts in the honest observance of these limitations the general rule already stated will apply. The courts of equity in England have indicated and given effect to certain general principles for the guidance of trustees in lending money upon the security of real estate. Thus it has been laid down that, in the case of ordinary agricultural land, the margin ought not to be less than one-third of its value; whereas in cases where the subject of the security derives its value from buildings erected upon the land, or its use for trade purposes, the margin ought not to be less than one-half. I do not think these have been laid down as hard-and-fast limits up to which trustees would be invariably safe, and beyond which they could never be in safety to lend, but as indicating the lowest margins which, in ordinary circumstances, a careful investor of trust funds ought to accept. It is manifest that, in cases where the subject of the security is exclusively or mainly used for the purposes of trade, no prudent investor could be in a position to judge of the amount of margin necessary to make a loan for a term of years reasonably secure until he had ascertained, not only their present market price, but their intrinsic value, apart from those trading considerations which gave them a speculative, and, it might be, a temporary value. Upon the general law applicable to this case I have only to observe further that, while trustees cannot delegate the execution of the trust, they may, as was held by this House in *Speight v Gaunt* (1883) 9 App Cas 1), avail themselves of the services of others, wherever such employment is according to the usual course of business. If they employ a person of competent skill to value a real security, they may, so long as they act in good faith, safely rely upon the correctness of his valuation. But the ordinary course of business does not justify the employment of a valuator for any other purpose than obtaining the data necessary in order to enable the trustees to judge of the sufficiency of the security offered. They are not in safety to rely upon his bare assurance that the security was sufficient, in the absence of information which would enable them to form, and without forming, an opinion for themselves. At all events, if they chose to place reliance upon his opinion without the means of testing its soundness they could not, should the security prove defective, escape from personal liability, unless they proved that the security was such as would have been accepted by a trustee of ordinary prudence, fully informed of its character, and having in view the principles to which I have already adverted. ...

The trustees' fault, therefore, was in investing a significant sum of money on a parcel of land which depended ultimately upon the continuing success of the manufacturing business which was carried out upon it, as to which there could be no certainty. Whilst a commercial businessman might legitimately take the view that it constituted an acceptable risk for him to take with his own money, the House of Lords considered that the trustees should have been more prudent. They were not investing their own money on such a 'hazard', and so had a greater 'moral' obligation to be prudent.

It seems that the common law duty applies not only to the decision to make an investment, but also to the decision whether to retain an investment in its current form or to sell it and find an alternative form of investment. The decision to retain/sell is, therefore, predicated upon a duty to review the current state of the trust's investments periodically with a view to deciding whether retention constitutes the best investment decision at the relevant time.

***Nestle v National Westminster Bank plc* [1993] 1 WLR 1260**

Panel: Dillon, Staughton and Leggatt LJJ

Facts: Between 1922 and 1986 the defendant bank was the trustee of a trust fund, the substantial part of which was invested in bank and insurance company shares. On the death of the last surviving life tenant, the plaintiff became entitled to the entire fund absolutely. She complained that the fund, which was worth some £269,000, would have been worth over £1million if the bank had periodically reviewed the performance of the shares and had adopted a different investment strategy. It was common ground that the bank had erroneously believed that it was only entitled to invest in bank and insurance company shares under the terms of the trust instrument. The Court of Appeal held that the bank had not failed in its duty of prudence.

LORD JUSTICE LEGGATT

...There is no dispute about the nature of the bank's duty. It was, as Lindley LJ has expressed it, a duty 'to take such care as an ordinary prudent man would take if he were minded to make an investment for the benefit of other people for whom he felt morally bound to provide' (see *Re Whiteley, Whiteley v Learoyd* (1886) 33 Ch D 347 at 355). The trustee must have regard 'not only to the interests of those who are entitled to the income, but to the interests of those who will take in future' (at 350 per Cotton LJ). 'A trustee must not choose investments other than those which the terms of his trust permit' (see *Speight v Gaunt* (1883) 9 App Cas 1 at 19 per Lord Blackburn). So confined, the trustee must also 'avoid all investments of that class that are attended with hazard' (see *Learoyd v Whiteley* (1887) 12 App Cas 727 at 733 per Lord Watson). The power of investment-

'must be exercised so as to yield the best return for the beneficiaries, judged in relation to the risks of the investments in question; and the prospects of the yield of income and capital appreciation both have to be considered in judging the return from the investment.' (See *Cowan v Scargill* [1984] 2 All ER 750 at 760, [1985] Ch 270 at 287 per Megarry VC.)

Link
See *Cowan v Scargill* below

Since the Trustee Investments Act 1961 came into force a trustee has been required by s6(1)(a) to have regard in the exercise of his powers of investment-

'to the need for diversification of investments of the trust, in so far as is appropriate to the circumstances of the trust ...'

It is common ground that a trustee with a power of investment must undertake periodic reviews of the investments held by the trust. In relation to this trust, that would have meant a review carried out at least annually, and whenever else a reappraisal of the trust portfolio was requested or was otherwise requisite. ...

The appellant alleges that the bank is in breach of trust because over the years since her grandfather set up the trust the bank has supposed that its power of investment was more limited than it was, has failed to carry out periodic reviews of the portfolio and to maintain a proper balance between equities and gilts and to diversify the equity investments, and has unduly favoured the interests of her father and her uncle as life tenants at the expense of her own interest as remainderman. She says that in consequence the trust fund was worth less in 1986 than it should have been.

The essence of the bank's duty was to take such steps as a prudent businessman would have taken to maintain and increase the value of the trust fund. Unless it failed to do so, it was not in breach of trust. A breach of duty will not be actionable, and therefore will be immaterial, if it does not cause loss. In this context I would indorse the concession of Mr Nugee QC for the bank that 'loss' will be incurred by a trust fund when it makes a gain less than would have been made by a prudent businessman. A claimant will therefore fail who cannot prove a loss in this sense caused by breach of duty. So here, in order to make a case for an inquiry, the appellant must show that loss was caused by breach of duty on the part of the bank.

Alert

On the appellant's behalf Mr Lyndon-Stanford QC seeks to rely on a presumption against a wrongdoing trustee. He invokes Brightman LJ's dictum in *Bartlett v Barclays Bank Trust Co Ltd (No 2)* [1980] 2 All ER 92 at 96, [1980] Ch 515 at 545 that 'The trustee's obligation is to restore to the trust estate the assets of which he has deprived it'. But that presupposes deprivation.

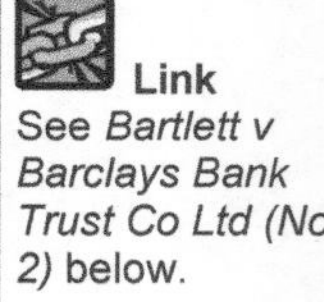
Link
See *Bartlett v Barclays Bank Trust Co Ltd (No 2)* below.

The appellant alleges, and I am content to assume, that the bank was at all material times under a misapprehension about the meaning of the investment clause in the will, with the result that the bank believed that the scope of its powers of investment was more confined than it was. I also regard it as unlikely that the bank conducted any reviews of the portfolio between 1922 and 1959. If any were conducted, they were unplanned, sporadic and indecisive. Mr Lyndon-Stanford argues that it should be presumed that, had there been a better balance between gilts and equities and had the equity investment been more diversified, the fund would ultimately have been worth more than it was. The fallacy is that it does not follow from the fact that a wider power of investment was available to the bank than it realised either that it would have been exercised or that, if it had been, the exercise of it would have produced a result more beneficial to the bank than actually was produced. Loss cannot be presumed if none would necessarily have resulted. Until it was proved that there was a loss, no attempt could be made to assess the amount of it. ...

In my judgment, either there was a loss in the present case or there was not. Unless there was a loss, there was no cause of action. It was for the appellant to prove on balance of probabilities that there was, or must have been, a loss. If proved, the court would then have had to assess the amount of it, and for the purpose of doing so might have had recourse to presumptions against the bank. In short, if it were shown that a loss was caused by breach of trust, such a presumption might avail the appellant in quantifying the loss. The appellant's difficulty is in reaching that stage.

The appellant therefore had to prove that a prudent trustee, knowing of the scope of the bank's investment power and conducting regular reviews, would so have invested the trust funds as to make it worth more than it was worth when the appellant inherited it. That was a matter for expert evidence. In the result, there was evidence which the judge was entitled to accept and did accept that the bank did no less than expected of it up to the death of the testator's widow in 1960. ...

After 1960 investment of the trust funds preponderantly in tax-exempt gilts for the benefit of life tenants resident abroad is not shown to have produced a less satisfactory result for the remainderman than an investment in equities after taking into account savings in estate duty and capital transfer tax, because this policy had the effect of preserving the capital. ...

No testator, in the light of this example, would choose this bank for the effective management of his investments. But the bank's engagement was as a trustee, and, as such, it is to be judged not so much by success as by absence of proven default. The importance of preservation of a trust fund will always outweigh success in its advancement. Inevitably, a trustee in the bank's position wears a complacent air, because the virtue of safety will in practice put a premium on inactivity. Until the 1950s active management of the portfolio might have been seen as speculative, and even in these days such dealing would have to be notably successful before the expense would be justified. The very process of attempting to achieve a balance, or (if that be old fashioned) fairness, as between the interests of life tenants and those of a remainderman inevitably means that each can complain of being less well served than he or she ought to have been. But by the undemanding standard of prudence the bank is not shown to have committed any breach of trust resulting in loss.

I am therefore constrained to agree that the appeal must be dismissed.

Lord Justice Leggatt, whose reasoning mirrored that of the other two members of the Court, was content to assume that one aspect of a trustee's duty in relation to investment was the obligation to review the state of the trust's investments. And yet, the outcome in this case is perhaps rather surprising. Although the trustee bank had manifestly failed to fulfil its duty to review, and had been wrong about the extent of its investment powers, it avoided liability to the plaintiff because she was unable to prove that the trustees had made decisions they should not have made or had failed to make decisions they should have made. This seems to set an extremely low bar for a trustee to overcome; or, as Leggatt LJ put it, the standard of prudence is 'undemanding'.

10.1.1 Investment criteria

There have been two cases of note as to the factors which the trustees must take into account and, equally, what factors they must ignore when deciding where to invest trust funds.

***Cowan and Others v Scargill and Others* [1985] Ch 270**

Panel: Sir Robert Megarry V-C

Facts: The five plaintiffs and the five defendants comprised all the trustee members of the management committee of the mineworkers' pension scheme. The defendants, all of whom had been appointed by the National Union of Mineworkers, objected to certain proposed investment decisions ('the 1982 plan') on the grounds that they conflicted with union policy. The management committee was therefore deadlocked and unable to implement the 1982 plan. On the application of the remaining (non-union) trustees, the court held that the interests of the pension scheme beneficiaries rather than those of the union were paramount, and that accordingly the union trustees were in breach of their duties as members of the management committee by refusing to concur in the adoption of the 1982 plan.

SIR ROBERT MEGARRY V-C

...The main issue (and I put it very shortly) is whether the defendants are in breach of their fiduciary duties in refusing approval of an investment plan for the [Mineworkers' Pension Scheme] unless it is amended so as to prohibit any increase in overseas investment, to provide for the withdrawal of existing overseas investments at the most opportune time, and to prohibit investment in energies which are in direct competition with coal ... which I shall call the "1982 plan". ...

[Having reviewed the evidence at length, the judge continued]

I turn to the law. The starting point is the duty of trustees to exercise their powers in the best interests of the present and future beneficiaries of the trust, holding the scales impartially between different classes of beneficiaries. This duty of the trustees towards their beneficiaries is paramount. They must, of course, obey the law; but subject to that, they must put the interests of their beneficiaries first. When the purpose of the trust is to provide financial benefits for the beneficiaries, as is usually the case, the best interests of the beneficiaries are normally their best financial interests. In the case of a power of investment, as in the present case, the power must be exercised so as to yield the best return for the beneficiaries, judged in relation to the risks of the investments in question; and the prospects of the yield of income and capital appreciation both have to be considered in judging the return from the investment. ...

Alert

In considering what investments to make trustees must put on one side their own personal interests and views. Trustees may have strongly held social or political views. They may be firmly opposed to any investment in South Africa or other countries, or they may object to any form of investment in companies concerned with alcohol, tobacco, armaments or many other things. In the conduct of their own affairs, of course, they are free to abstain from making any such investments. Yet under a trust, if investments of this type would be more beneficial to the beneficiaries than other investments, the trustees must not refrain from making the investments by reason of the views that they hold.

Trustees may even have to act dishonourably (though not illegally) if the interests of their beneficiaries require it. Thus where trustees for sale had struck a bargain for the sale of trust property but had not bound themselves by a legally enforceable contract, they were held to be under a duty to consider and explore a better offer that they received, and not to carry through the bargain to which they felt in honour bound: *Buttle v Saunders* [1950] 2 All ER 193. In other words, the duty of trustees to their beneficiaries may include a duty to "gazump," however honourable the trustees. As Wynn-Parry J said at p 195, trustees "have an overriding duty to obtain the best price which they can for their beneficiaries." ...

Third, by way of caveat I should say that I am not asserting that the benefit of the beneficiaries which a trustee must make his paramount concern inevitably and solely means their financial benefit, even if the only object of the trust is to provide financial benefits. Thus if the only actual or potential beneficiaries of a trust are all adults with very strict views on moral and social matters, condemning all forms of alcohol, tobacco and popular entertainment, as well as armaments, I can well understand that it might not be for the "benefit" of such beneficiaries to know that they are obtaining rather larger financial returns under the trust by reason of investments in those activities than they would have received if the trustees had invested the trust funds in other investments. The beneficiaries might well consider that it was far better to receive less than to receive more money from what they consider to be evil and tainted sources. "Benefit" is a word with a very wide meaning, and there are circumstances in which arrangements which work to the financial disadvantage of a beneficiary may yet be for his benefit: see, for example, *In re T's Settlement Trusts* [1964] Ch 158 and *In re CL* [1969] 1 Ch 587. But I would emphasise that such cases are likely to be very rare, and in any case I think that under a trust for the provision of financial benefits the burden would rest, and rest heavy, on him who asserts that it is for the benefit of the beneficiaries as a whole to receive less by reason of the exclusion of some of the possibly more profitable forms of investment. Plainly the present case is not one of this rare type of cases. ...

Fourth, the standard required of a trustee in exercising his powers of investment is that he must:

"take such care as an ordinary prudent man would take if he were minded to make an investment for the benefit of other people for whom he felt morally bound to provide:"

per Lindley LJ in *In re Whiteley* (1886) 33 Ch D 347, 355; see also at pp 350, 358; and see *Learoyd v Whiteley* (1887) 12 App Cas 727. That duty includes the duty to seek advice on matters which the trustee does not understand, such as the making of investments, and on receiving that advice to act with the same degree of prudence. This requirement is not discharged merely by showing that the trustee has acted in good faith and with sincerity. Honesty and sincerity are not the same as prudence and reasonableness. Some of the most sincere people are the most unreasonable; and Mr Scargill [for himself and the other defendants] told me that he had met quite a few of them. Accordingly, although a trustee who takes advice on investments is not bound to accept and act on that advice, he is not entitled to reject it merely because he sincerely disagrees with it, unless in addition to being sincere he is acting as an ordinary prudent man would act.

Fifth, trustees have a duty to consider the need for diversification of investments. By section 6(1) of the Trustee Investments Act 1961:

"In the exercise of his powers of investment a trustee shall have regard - (a) to the need for diversification of investments of the trust, in so far as is appropriate to the circumstances of the trust; (b) to the suitability to the trust of investments of the description of investment proposed and of the investment proposed as an investment of that description."

The reference to the "circumstances of the trust" plainly includes matters such as the size of the trust funds: the degree of diversification that is practicable and desirable for a large fund may plainly be impracticable or undesirable (or both) in the case of a small fund.

In the case before me, it is not in issue that there ought to be diversification of the investments held by the fund. The contention of the defendants, put very shortly, is that there can be a sufficient degree of diversification without any investment overseas or in oil, and that in any case there is no need to increase the level of overseas investments beyond the existing level. Other pension funds got on well enough without overseas investments, it was said, and in particular the NUM's own scheme had, in 1982, produced better results than the scheme here in question. ...

Even if other funds in one particular year, or in many years, had done better than the scheme which is before me, that does not begin to show that it is beneficial to this scheme to be shorn of the ability to invest overseas. ...

Sixth, there is the question whether the principles that I have been stating apply, with or without modification, to trusts of pension funds. Mr Stamler [for the plaintiffs] asserted that they applied without modification, and that it made no difference that some of the funds came from the members of the pension scheme, or that the funds were often of a very substantial size. Mr Scargill did not in terms assert the contrary. ...

I shall refer to the authorities in a moment, and consider the question of principle first. I can see no reason for holding that different principles apply to pension fund trusts from those which apply to other trusts. Of course, there are many provisions in pension schemes which are not to be found in private trusts, and to these the general law of trusts will be subordinated. But subject to that, I think that the trusts of pension funds are subject to the same rules as other trusts. The large size of pension funds emphasises the need for diversification, rather than lessening it, and the fact that much of the fund has been contributed by members of the scheme seems to me to make it even more important that the trustees should exercise their powers in the best interests of the beneficiaries. In a private trust, most, if not all, of the beneficiaries are the recipients of the bounty of the settlor, whereas under the trusts of a pension fund many (though not all) of the beneficiaries are those who, as members, contributed to the funds so that in due time they would receive pensions. It is thus all the more important that the interests of the beneficiaries should be paramount, so that they may receive the benefits which in part they have paid for. I can see no justification for holding that the benefits to them should run the risk of being lessened because the trustees were pursuing an investment policy intended to assist the industry that the pensioners have left, or their union.

I turn to the authorities. *Evans v London Co-operative Society Ltd* The Times, 6 July 1976 is a decision of Brightman J which has apparently achieved a considerable measure of renown among those concerned with pension funds as being the only English authority on the subject. I do not think that I need discuss the details of the case, because it seems to me to be perfectly clear that it is a decision upon a particular rule of the pension fund there in question, rule 7, and not upon the general law. ... I find it impossible to read pp 17-20 of the transcript without reaching the conclusion that the judge was deciding the case on the extent to which rule 7 took the case out of the ordinary law of trusts, and that but for rule 7 the ordinary law of trusts would have been applied to the case. In my judgment, the case does nothing to support the contentions of the defendants. Instead, I think it provides some support for the plaintiffs.

Blankenship v Boyle (1971) 329 F Supp 1089 was a case heard in the US District Court for the District of Columbia by Judge Gesell. The trustees of a pension fund had allowed large sums of money to remain in bank accounts bearing no interest at a bank controlled by the union. Over an 18-year period, varying sums between $14 million and $75 million, representing between 14 per cent and 44 per cent of the fund's total resources, had been left in this way. The fund was established for the benefit of employees of coal operators, their families and dependants, and over 95 per cent of the members of the fund were also members of the union. It was contended that the trustees could properly consider not only the interests of the beneficiaries but also collateral matters such as increasing the tonnage of union-mined coal; but this was rejected. The court re-affirmed the duty of undivided loyalty to the beneficiaries that a trustee owes, and did not accept that regard should also be paid to the union or its members who generated some of the income of the fund, or to the industry as a whole. That seems to me to be plainly right.

Withers v Teachers' Retirement System of the City of New York (1978) 447 F Supp 1248 arose out of the impending insolvency of the City of New York in 1975. The Teachers' Retirement System ("TRS") and four other New York pension funds agreed to purchase $2,530 million unmarketable and highly speculative New York City bonds over the next two and a half years in an attempt to stave off the imminent bankruptcy of the city; the share contributed by TRS was $860 million. TRS was an unfunded scheme, and the evidence was that if the city ceased to make its massive contributions to the scheme, the reserves would be exhausted in some 8 to 10 years, even if the contributions by employees continued and there was a constant rate of retirement of teachers. In the US District Court for the Southern District of New York, Judge Conner considered and accepted *Blankenship v Boyle* ... and the traditional rules of equity, but held that the trustees had been justified in purchasing the bonds since they had done so in the best interests of the beneficiaries, and not out of concern for the general public welfare or the protection of the jobs of city teachers. The object of the trustees, who had imposed stringent conditions in an attempt to protect the TRS, had been to ensure the continuance of the city's major contributions to the scheme, and preserve the city's position as the ultimate guarantor of the payment of pension benefits; and this was in the best interests of the beneficiaries. This differed from the position in *Blankenship v Boyle*, where

"the trustees pursued policies which may incidentally have aided the beneficiaries of the fund but which were intended, primarily, to enhance the position of the union and the welfare of its members, presumably, through the creation and/or preservation of jobs in the coal industry": p 1256.

Apart from the expression "and/or," I would agree.

The American cases do not, of course, bind me; but they seem, if I may say so, to be soundly based on equitable principles which are common to England and most jurisdictions in the United States, and they accord with the conclusion that I would have reached in the absence of authority. Accordingly, on principle, on the *Evans* case, and on the two American cases, I reach the unhesitating conclusion that the trusts of pension funds are in general governed by the ordinary law of trusts, subject to any contrary provision in the rules or other provisions which govern the trust. In particular, the trustees of a pension fund are subject to the overriding duty to do the best that they can for the beneficiaries, the duty that in the United States is known as "the duty of undivided loyalty to the beneficiaries": see *Blankenship v Boyle* ... .

In considering that duty, it must be remembered that very many of the beneficiaries will not in any way be directly affected by the prosperity of the mining industry or the union. Miners who have retired, and the widows and children of deceased miners, will continue to receive their benefits from the fund even if the mining industry shrinks: for the scheme is fully funded, and the fund does not depend on further contributions to it being made. If the board fell on hard times, it might be unable to continue its voluntary payments to meet cost-of-living increases ... [but] the impact of that remote possibility falls far short of the imminent disaster facing the City of New York and TRS in the *Withers* case ... ; and I cannot regard any policy designed to ensure the general prosperity of coal mining as being a policy which is directed to obtaining the best possible results for the beneficiaries, most of whom are no longer engaged in the industry, and some of whom never were. The connection is far too remote and insubstantial. Further, the assets of even so large a pension fund as this are nowhere near the size at which there could be expected to be any perceptible impact from the adoption of the policies for which Mr Scargill contends.

I turn to consider the grounds on which the prohibitions put forward by the defendants have been supported. First, there are the reasons put forward during the discussions by the trustees. ... Put shortly, these were that the prohibitions were NUM policy: the union, as a matter of principle, was totally and unequivocally opposed to investment overseas. These views were put forward in various ways on various occasions, but the substance was unvarying. However, ... [at] no stage did [Mr Scargill] explain how or why it was for the benefit of the beneficiaries to put union policy into force under the scheme by imposing the prohibitions. ...

I can see no escape from the conclusion that the NUM trustees were attempting to impose the prohibitions in order to carry out union policy; and mere assertions that their sole consideration was the benefit of the beneficiaries do not alter that conclusion. If the NUM trustees were thinking only of the benefit of the beneficiaries, why all the references to union policy instead of proper explanations of how and why the prohibitions would bring benefits to the beneficiaries? No doubt some trustees with strong feelings find it irksome to be forced to submerge those feelings and genuinely put the interests of the beneficiaries first. Indeed, there are some who are temperamentally unsuited to being trustees, and are more fitted for campaigning for changes in the law. This, of course, they are free to do; but if they choose to become trustees they must accept it that the rules of equity will bind them in all that they do as trustees. ...

I therefore reject any ... assertion that prior to the commencement of these proceedings the benefit of the beneficiaries was the sole consideration that the union trustees had: that ... is untrue. The union trustees were mainly, if not solely, actuated by a desire to pursue union policy, and they were not putting the interests of the beneficiaries first, as they ought to have done. ... They were adamant in their determination to impose the restrictions, whether or not they harmed their beneficiaries. ...

This conclusion, however, does not end the matter. If trustees make a decision upon wholly wrong grounds, and yet it subsequently appears, from matters which they did not express or refer to, that there are in fact good and sufficient reasons for supporting their decision, then I do not think that they would incur any liability for having decided the matter upon erroneous grounds; for the decision itself was right. ...

Some of the evidence filed by the defendants tended to show that the prohibitions would not be harmful to the beneficiaries, or jeopardise the aims of the fund, and that some pension funds got along well enough without any overseas investments. Such evidence misses the point. Trustees must do the best they can for the benefit of their beneficiaries, and not merely avoid harming them. I find it impossible to see how it will assist trustees to do the best they can for their beneficiaries by prohibiting a wide range of investments that are authorised by the terms of the trust. Whatever the position today, nobody can say that conditions tomorrow cannot possibly make it advantageous to invest in one of the prohibited investments. It is the duty of trustees, in the interests of their beneficiaries, to take advantage of the full range of investments authorised by the terms of the trust, instead of resolving to narrow that range.

There was other evidence filed by the defendants which was more to the point; and it was met by countervailing evidence of the plaintiffs. This evidence was directed to economics and investment strategy. At the outset I must say that I found the plaintiffs' evidence the more cogent and practical, and more directly related to what was in issue. The general thrust of the defendants' evidence in support of the restrictions that they seek to impose was along the following lines. Pensions funds in Britain have enormous assets. If all, or nearly all, of these assets were invested in Britain, and none, or few, were invested overseas, this would do much to revive this country's economy and so benefit all workers, especially if the investments were in the form not of purchasing established stocks and shares but of "real" investment in physical assets and new ventures. For the mineworkers' scheme, the prosperity of the coal industry would aid the prosperity of the scheme, and so lead to benefits for the beneficiaries under the scheme. This point was put in various ways, and a short summary necessarily omits many facets; but in the end the approach seems to me to have been along these general lines.

I readily accept that a case, and perhaps a strong case, can be made for legislation or other provisions that in the general public interest would restrict the outflow of large funds from this country and put the money to work here. ... But I am not concerned with changes in the law or in the scheme for any pension fund, whether this fund or any other. I have to deal with this fund under the scheme as it now stands. I am concerned with a fund under which there are many beneficiaries who no longer have any financial interest in the welfare of the coal industry. They may well be "interested" in it in the sense that they remember the years that they spent in it with affection or the reverse, and they may well find it "interesting" to know what is going on in it, in the sense of gratifying a natural curiosity and concern about the industry and the people in it. But apart from such matters, they are not affected by the industry and its success.

In my view, therefore, the broad economic arguments of the defendants provide no justification for the restrictions that they wish to impose. Any possible benefits from imposing the restrictions that would accrue to the beneficiaries under the scheme (as distinct from the general public) are far too speculative and remote. Large though the fund is, I cannot see how the adoption of the restrictions can make any material impact on the national economy, or bring any appreciable benefit to the beneficiaries under the scheme. There is nothing whatever to suggest that the board will be in any difficulty in making its payments under the scheme unless the restrictions are adopted. There is not a shred of evidence to suggest that the board is in a state of imminent disaster like that which faced the City of New York in the *Withers* case ... , or that even if it were the imposition of the restrictions would save it; and in any case the scheme, unlike that in the *Withers* case, is fully funded. As for diversification, I can see that the risks inherent in an individual investment can be met by a modest degree of diversification; but where the risks are not merely for one particular investment but for a whole sector of the market, such as mining or tea, a wider degree of diversification will be needed. In any case, the question is one of excluding a very large sector of the market, and preventing diversification into investments in other countries which may do well at a time when the whole British market is depressed; and I can see no possible benefit in such an exclusion, especially in the case of a very large fund with highly skilled investment expertise.

Accordingly, on the case as a whole, in my judgment the plaintiffs are right and the defendants are wrong. ... [Subject] to what may be said when I have concluded this judgment, I propose to make suitable declarations, and to give liberty to apply for directions or other appropriate relief if the declarations are not duly acted upon. ...

So, except in very rare circumstances, trustees must not allow political or economic considerations to influence their investment decision-making. Nor may they take account of ethical or moral considerations.

***Harries (Bishop of Oxford) and Others v The Church Commissioners for England and Another* [1992] 1 WLR 1241**

Panel: Sir Donald Nicholls V-C

Facts: The plaintiffs were concerned that the investment policy of the Church Commissioners in their administration of trust funds of the Church of England attached undue importance to financial considerations and failed to take into account the underlying purpose for which the assets were held. They therefore applied for declarations that in the management of their assets the Church Commissioners were obliged to have regard to the object of promoting the Christian faith through the established Church of England and might not act in a manner which would be incompatible with that object. The court declined to make those declarations.

SIR DONALD NICHOLLS V-C

The Church Commissioners for England administer vast estates and large funds. At the end of 1990 their holdings of land were valued at about £1.7bn, their mortgages and loans at about £165m, and their stock exchange investments at about £780m. In 1990 these items yielded altogether an investment income of £164m. The commissioners' income included also some £66m derived principally from parish and diocesan contributions to clergy stipends. So the commissioners' total income last year was £230m.

The needs which the commissioners seek to satisfy out of this income are daunting. In 1990 they provided almost one half of the costs of the stipends of the Church of England serving clergy, much of their housing costs, and almost all their pension costs. These items absorbed over 85 per cent of the commissioners' income: that is, a sum of almost £200m. Unfortunately, this does not mean that the clergy are well remunerated or that the retired clergy receive good pensions. Far from it. The commissioners' income has to be spread widely, and hence thinly, over 11,400 serving clergy and 10,100 clergy pensioners and widows. So, as is well known, the amount each receives is not generous. In 1990–1991 the national average stipend of incumbents was only £11,308. The full-service pension from April 1991 was £6,700 per year.

For some time there have been voices in the Church of England expressing disquiet at the investment policy of the commissioners. They do not question either the good faith or the investment expertise of the commissioners. Their concern is not that the commissioners have failed to get the best financial return from their property and investments. Their concern is that, in making investment decisions, the commissioners are guided too rigorously by purely financial considerations, and that the commissioners give insufficient weight to what are now called "ethical" considerations. They contend, moreover, that the commissioners have fallen into legal error. The commissioners attach overriding importance to financial considerations, and that is a misapprehension of the approach they ought property to adopt when making investment decisions. The commissioners ought to have in mind that the underlying purpose for which they hold their assets is the promotion of the Christian faith through the Church of England. The commissioners should not exercise their investment functions in a manner which would be incompatible with that purpose even if that involves a risk of incurring significant financial detriment. So these proceedings, seeking declaratory relief, were launched ... . I understand that by an ethical investment policy is meant an investment policy which is not guided solely by financial criteria but which takes into account non-financial considerations deduced from Christian morality. ...

Before going further into the criticism made of the commissioners I will consider the general principles applicable to the exercise of powers of investment by charity trustees. It is axiomatic that charity trustees, in common with all other trustees, are concerned to further the purposes of the trust of which they have accepted the office of trustee. That is their duty. To enable them the better to discharge that duty, trustees have powers vested in them. Those powers must be exercised for the purpose for which they have been given: to further the purposes of the trust. That is the guiding principle applicable to the issues in these proceedings. Everything which follows is no more than the reasoned application of that principle in particular contexts.

Broadly speaking, property held by charity trustees falls into two categories. First, there is property held by trustees for what may be called functional purposes. The National Trust owns historic houses and open spaces. The Salvation Army owns hostels for the destitute. And many charities need office accommodation in which to carry out essential administrative work. Second, there is property held by trustees for the purpose of generating money, whether from income or capital growth, with which to further the work of the trust. In other words, property held by trustees as an investment. Where property is so held, prima facie the purposes of the trust will be best served by the trustees seeking to obtain therefrom the maximum return, whether by way of income or capital growth, which is consistent with commercial prudence. That is the starting point for all charity trustees when considering the exercise of their investment powers. Most charities need money; and the more of it there is available, the more the trustees can seek to accomplish.

In most cases this prima facie position will govern the trustees' conduct. In most cases the best interests of the charity require that the trustees' choice of investments should be made solely on the basis of well-established investment criteria, having taken expert advice where appropriate and having due regard to such matters as the need to diversify, the need to balance income against capital growth, and the need to balance risk against return.

In a minority of cases the position will not be so straightforward. There will be some cases, I suspect comparatively rare, when the objects of the charity are such that investments of a particular type would conflict with the aims of the charity. Much-cited examples are those of cancer research companies and tobacco shares, trustees of temperance charities and brewery and distillery shares, and trustees of charities of the Society of Friends and shares in companies engaged in production of armaments. If, as would be likely in those examples, trustees were satisfied that investing in a company engaged in a particular type of business would conflict with the very objects their charity is seeking to achieve, they should not so invest. Carried to its logical conclusion the trustees should take this course even if it would be likely to result in significant financial detriment to the charity. The logical conclusion, whilst sound as a matter of legal analysis, is unlikely to arise in practice. It is not easy to think of an instance where in practice the exclusion for this reason of one or more companies or sectors from the whole range of investments open to trustees would be likely to leave them without an adequately wide range of investments from which to choose a properly diversified portfolio.

There will also be some cases, again I suspect comparatively rare, when trustees' holdings of particular investments might hamper a charity's work either by making potential recipients of aid unwilling to be helped because of the source of the charity's money, or by alienating some of those who support the charity financially. In these cases the trustees will need to balance the difficulties they would encounter, or likely financial loss they would sustain, if they were to hold the investments against the risk of financial detriment if those investments were excluded from their portfolio. The greater the risk of financial detriment, the more certain the trustees should be of countervailing disadvantages to the charity before they incur that risk. Another circumstance where trustees would be entitled, or even required, to take into account non-financial criteria would be where the trust deed so provides.

No doubt there will be other cases where trustees are justified in departing from what should always be their starting point. The instances I have given are not comprehensive. But I must emphasise that of their very nature, and by definition, investments are held by trustees to aid the work of the charity in a particular way: by generating money. That is the purpose for which they are held. That is their raison d'être. Trustees cannot properly use assets held as an investment for other, viz, non-investment, purposes. To the extent that they do they are not properly exercising their powers of investment. This is not to say that trustees who own land may not act as responsible landlords or those who own shares may not act as responsible shareholders. They may. The law is not so cynical as to require trustees to behave in a fashion which would bring them or their charity into disrepute (although their consciences must not be too tender: see *Buttle v Saunders* [1950] 2 All ER 193). On the other hand, trustees must act prudently. They must not use property held by them for investment purposes as a means for making moral statements at the expense of the charity of which they are trustees. Those who wish may do so with their own property, but that is not a proper function of trustees with trust assets held as an investment.

Alert

I should mention one other particular situation. There will be instances today when those who support or benefit from a charity take widely different views on a particular type of investment, some saying that on moral grounds it conflicts with the aims of the charity, others saying the opposite. One example is the holding of arms industry shares by a religious charity. There is a real difficulty here. To many questions raising moral issues there are no certain answers. On moral questions widely differing views are held by well-meaning, responsible people. This is not always so. But frequently, when questions of the morality of conduct are being canvassed, there is no identifiable yardstick which can be applied to a set of facts so as to yield one answer which can be seen to be "right" and the other "wrong." If that situation confronts trustees of a charity, the law does not require them to find an answer to the unanswerable. Trustees may, if they wish, accommodate the views of those who consider that on moral grounds a particular investment would be in conflict with the objects of the charity, so long as the trustees are satisfied that course would not involve a risk of significant financial detriment. But when they are not so satisfied trustees should not make investment decisions on the basis of preferring one view of whether on moral grounds in investment conflicts with the objects of the charity over another. This is so even when one view is more widely supported than the other.

I have sought above to consider charity trustees' duties in relation to investment as a matter of basic principle. I was referred to no authority bearing directly on these matters. My attention was drawn to *Cowan v Scargill* [1985] Ch 270, a case concerning a pension fund. I believe the views I have set out accord with those expressed by Sir Robert Megarry VC in that case, bearing in mind that he was considering trusts for the provision of financial benefits for individuals. In this case I am concerned with trusts of charities, whose purposes are multifarious. ...

The commissioners' investment policy is set out in their annual report for 1989 in terms I should quote in full:

"The primary aim in the management of our assets is to produce the best total return, that is capital and income growth combined. While financial responsibilities must remain of primary importance (given our position as trustees), as responsible investors we also continue to take proper account of social, ethical and environmental issues. As people became increasingly aware of the many factors which can adversely affect both their own and other people's lives, so we must be responsive to these areas of concern. As regards our Stock Exchange holdings this means that we do not invest in companies whose main business is armaments, gambling, alcohol, tobacco and newspapers: it also means that we must continue to be vigilant in our monitoring of the activities of those companies where we do have a shareholding. Our practice is to follow up with senior management any major criticisms of a particular company's activities through confidential correspondence and, where appropriate, direct discussions. Our aim is to establish facts, to see whether there is any basis for the criticism and to evaluate what action the company has taken or is prepared to take if the criticism is justified. Each case is considered on its merits. The ultimate pressure we can bring to bear is that of disinvestment. The paradox of doing so is that we then lose any opportunity to use our influence for good. Our policy with regard to investment and South Africa remains unchanged. We do not invest in any South African company nor in any other company where more than a small part of their business is in South Africa. Where we do invest in a company with a small stake in South Africa we try to ensure that it follows enlightened social and employment policies, so far as is possible within the system of apartheid of which we have repeatedly expressed our abhorrence. In common with the rest of the Church, we welcome the important political developments since the end of 1989 and hope that the momentum will be sustained. On the property side, although we shall continue to seek out development possibilities so as to discharge our duties as trustees, we are conscious of the effect of our actions upon local communities and their perceptions of the Church as a whole. We shall therefore continue to ensure that environmental considerations are properly taken into account when development schemes arise. In particular, during the year we have introduced new procedures for keeping bishops, incumbents and local church members informed whenever we are involved in a scheme affecting their community. We are also keen to find investments which respond positively to specific areas of concern in our society. We were glad therefore that our development of four small light industrial units at Walsall was completed during 1989. We believe that in direct property investments such as this we can set an example of what help can be given to small businesses wishing to expand, particularly in urban priority areas, although only a small proportion of our total funds can be invested in this way. However, if we can influence others to respond in a similar way it will do much to improve the quality of life of those living in areas of high unemployment."

It will be seen, therefore, that the commissioners do have an "ethical" investment policy. They have followed such a policy for many years. Indeed they have done so ever since they were constituted in 1948. Let me say at once that I can see nothing in this statement of policy which is inconsistent with the general principles I have sought to expound above.

The statement of policy records that the commissioners do not invest in companies whose main business is in armaments, gambling, alcohol, tobacco or newspapers. Of these, newspapers fall into a category of their own. The commissioners' policy regarding newspapers is based on the fact that many newspapers are associated, to a greater or lesser extent, with a particular political party or political view. Leaving aside newspapers, the underlying rationale of the commissioners' policy on these items is that there is a body of members of the Church of England opposed to the businesses in question on religious or moral grounds. There are members who believe these business activities are morally wrong, and that they are in conflict with Christian teaching and its moral values. But this list has only to be read for it to be obvious that many committed members of the Church of England take the contrary view. To say that not all members of the Church of England eschew gambling, alcohol or tobacco would be an understatement. As to armaments, the morality of war, and the concepts of a "just war," [these] are issues which have been debated for centuries. These are moral questions on which no single view can be shown to be "right" and the others "wrong." As I understand the position, the commissioners have felt able to exclude these items from their investments despite the conflicting views on the morality of holding these items as investments because there has remained open to the commissioners an adequate width of alternative investments.

I have already indicated that at the heart of the plaintiffs' case is a contention that the commissioners' policy is erroneous in law in that the commissioners are only prepared to take non-financial considerations into account to the extent that such considerations do not significantly jeopardise or interfere with accepted investment principles. I think it is implicit, if not explicit, in the commissioners' evidence that they do regard themselves as constrained in this way. So far as I have been able to see, this is the only issue identifiable as an issue of law raised in these proceedings. In my view this self-constraint applied by the commissioners is not one which in practice has led to any error of law on their part, nor is it likely to do so. I have already indicated that the circumstances in which charity trustees are bound or entitled to make a financially disadvantageous investment decision for ethical reasons are extremely limited. I have noted that it is not easy to think of a practical example

of such a circumstance. There is no evidence before me to suggest that any such circumstance exists here.

So the duty of trustees when exercising their powers of investment is, save in the very rare cases identified both by Sir Robert Megarry V-C and Sir Donald Nicholls V-C, to secure the maximum income and/or capital return, consistent with the exercise of prudence.

10.1.2 Controlling shareholdings

The trust fund may consist of shares which give the trustees a controlling interest over a company. In this situation, the common law duty of prudence in relation to such an investment requires the trustees to do more than simply keep themselves appraised of the company's affairs, e.g. by reading the material which is sent by the company to shareholders from time to time or by taking account of such information about the company as is in the public domain.

***In re Lucking's Will Trusts* [1968] 1 WLR 866**

Panel: Cross J

Facts: A trust held nearly 70 per cent of the shares in a small private company. There were two trustees of the fund (L and B). The remaining shares were owned or controlled by L. The directors were L, his wife and a third party (D), who was the manager of the business. D wrongfully withdrew some £15,000 from the company's bank account and later became bankrupt, as a result of which the money was lost. L had been aware of the unauthorised withdrawals but had accepted D's assurances that the money would be repaid. The beneficiaries brought proceedings for breach of trust, and Cross J held that L (but not B) was liable to make good the loss.

MR JUSTICE CROSS

... The conduct of the defendant trustees is, I think, to be judged by the standard applied in *Speight v Gaunt*, namely, that a trustee is only bound to conduct the business of the trust in such a way as an ordinary prudent man would conduct a business of his own.

Now what steps, if any, does a reasonably prudent man who finds himself a majority shareholder in a private company take with regard to the management of the company's affairs? He does not, I think, content himself with such information as to the management of the company's affairs as he is entitled to as shareholder, but ensures that he is represented on the board. He may be prepared to run the business himself as managing director or, at least, to become a non-executive director while having the business managed by someone else. Alternatively, he may find someone who will act as his nominee on the board and report to him from time to time as to the company's affairs. In the same way, as it seems to me, trustees holding a controlling interest ought to ensure so far as they can that they have such information as to the progress of the company's affairs as directors would have. If they sit back and allow the company to be run by the minority shareholder and receive no more information than shareholders are entitled to, they do so at their risk if things go wrong.

In this case, of course, the trust was represented on the board by [L]. But, as I see it, one ought not to regard him as performing a duty to the trust which it was incumbent on the trustees to perform personally, so that [B] became automatically responsible for any deficiencies in [L], as does a passive trustee who allows his co-trustee to exercise alone discretions which it is their duty to exercise jointly.

If these trustees had decided, as they might have done, to be represented on the board by a nominee they would have been entitled to rely on the information given them by that nominee as to the way in which the company's affairs were being managed even though such information was inaccurate or inadequate, unless they had some reason to suspect that it was inaccurate or inadequate. [B], as I see it, cannot have been in a worse position because his co-trustee was the trust's representative on the board than he would have been if their representative had not been a trustee at all. The position of [L], on the other hand, as I see it, was much different. He cannot say that what he knew, or ought to have known, about the company's affairs he knew, or ought to have known, simply as a director with a duty to the company and no one else. He was in the position he was partly as a representative of the trust and if and so far as he failed in his duty to the company he also failed in his duty to the trust. ...

Finally, I must ask myself how these principles are to be applied to the facts of this case. It is not suggested that it was not proper for the company to appoint [D] to be manager of its business on the terms contained in the service agreement, nor can it be suggested that [L] failed to follow the fortunes of the company under [D's] management. ... [But] this position changed altogether when [L] realised ... that [D] was overdrawing at a rate of some £1,400 a year on top of his salary and his expenses and travel allowance. I do not say that he ought to have leaped there and then to the conclusion that [D] was dishonest and that he would be unable to pay what he owed ... but [L] saw - or if he did not, ought to have seen - that [D] was very careless in matters of account, and in my judgment it was negligent of him to retain [him] as manager without imposing any check on his drawings. ... With his own property a man may well say: "I will trust my friend even though there are circumstances which might make some stranger suspicious of him. I would rather be cheated than spy on him." But a trustee cannot take that line ... . Although I have sympathy for [L], I feel bound to hold that he is liable to the other beneficiaries for such loss as was suffered by the trust shareholding for his falling adequately to supervise [D]'s drawings ... .

Bartlett and Others v Barclays Bank Trust Co. Ltd. (Nos. 1 and 2) [1980] Ch 515

Panel: Brightman J

Facts: The defendant bank was the trustee of a fund which held 99.8 per cent of the shares in a property company. The company's directors decided upon a change of investment policy, which led it to undertake various speculative property development projects with third parties, none of which was challenged or questioned by the bank. Ultimately, those projects brought about the company's insolvency, whereupon the beneficiaries brought proceedings against the bank to recover the losses which they had suffered. The bank was held liable.

MR JUSTICE BRIGHTMAN

...What, then, was the duty of the bank and did the bank fail in its duty? It does not follow that because a trustee could have prevented a loss it is therefore liable for the loss. The questions which I must ask myself are (1) What was the duty of the bank as the holder of 99.8 per cent of the shares ... ? (2) Was the bank in breach of duty in any and if so what respect? (3) If so, did that breach of duty cause the loss which was suffered by the trust estate? (4) If so, to what extent is the bank liable to make good that loss? ...

The cases establish that it is the duty of a trustee to conduct the business of the trust with the same care as an ordinary prudent man of business would extend towards his own affairs: *In re Speight* (1883) 22 Ch D 727, per Sir George Jessel MR at p 739 and Bowen LJ at p 762; affirmed on appeal, *Speight v Gaunt* (1883) 9 App Cas 1, and see Lord Blackburn at p 19. In applying this principle, Lindley LJ (who was the third member of the court in the *Speight* case) added in *In re Whiteley* (1886) 33 Ch D 347, 355:

"... care must be taken not to lose sight of the fact that the business of the trustee, and the business which the ordinary prudent man is supposed to be conducting for himself, is the business of investing money for the benefit of persons who are to enjoy it at some future time, and not for the sole benefit of the person entitled to the present income. The duty of a trustee is not to take such care only as a prudent man would take if he had only himself to consider; the duty rather is to take such care as an ordinary prudent man would take if he were minded to make an investment for the benefit of other people for whom he felt morally bound to provide. That is the kind of business the ordinary prudent man is supposed to be engaged in; and unless this is borne in mind the standard of a trustee's duty will be fixed too low; lower than it has ever yet been fixed, and lower certainly than the House of Lords or this Court endeavoured to fix it in *Speight v Gaunt*."

See on appeal *Learoyd v Whiteley* (1887) 12 App Cas 727, where Lord Watson added, at p 733:

"Business men of ordinary prudence may, and frequently do, select investments which are more or less of a speculative character; but it is the duty of a trustee to confine himself to the class of investments which are permitted by the trust, and likewise to avoid all investments of that class which are attended with hazard."

That does not mean that the trustee is bound to avoid all risk and in effect act as an insurer of the trust fund: see Bacon VC in *In re Godfrey* (1883) 23 Ch D 483, 493:

"No doubt it is the duty of a trustee, in administering the trusts of a will, to deal with property intrusted into his care exactly as any prudent man would deal with his own property. But the words in which the rule is expressed must not be strained beyond their meaning. Prudent businessmen in their dealings incur risk. That may and must happen in almost all human affairs."

The distinction is between a prudent degree of risk on the one hand, and hazard on the other. Nor must the court be astute to fix liability upon a trustee who has committed no more than an error of judgment, from which no business man, however prudent, can expect to be immune: see Lopes LJ in *In re Chapman* [1896] 2 Ch 763, 778:

"A trustee who is honest and reasonably competent is not to be held responsible for a mere error in judgment when the question which he has to consider is whether a security of a class authorized, but depreciated in value, should be retained or realized, provided he acts with reasonable care, prudence, and circumspection."

If the trust had existed ... [in such a way] ... that the bank held the freehold and leasehold properties and other assets [of the company] directly upon the trusts of the settlement, it would in my opinion have been a clear breach of trust for the bank to have hazarded trust money upon the Old Bailey development project with Stock Conversion. The Old Bailey project was a gamble, because it involved buying into the site at prices in excess of the investment values of the properties, with no certainty or probability, with no more than a chance, that planning permission could be obtained for a financially viable redevelopment, that the numerous proprietors would agree to sell out or join in the scheme, that finance would be available upon acceptable terms, and that the development would be completed, or at least become a marketable asset, before the time came to start winding up the trust. However one looks at it, the project was a hazardous speculation upon which no trustee could properly have ventured without explicit authority in the trust instrument. I therefore hold that the entire expenditure in the Old Bailey project would have been incurred in breach of trust, had the money been spent by the bank itself. The fact that it was a risk acceptable to the board of a wealthy company like Stock Conversion has little relevance.

I turn to the question, what was the duty of the bank as the holder of shares in [the company]? I will first answer this question without regard to the position of the bank as a specialist trustee, to which I will advert later. The bank, as trustee, was bound to act in relation to the shares and to the controlling position which they conferred, in the same manner as a prudent man of business. The prudent

Alert

man of business will act in such manner as is necessary to safeguard his investment. He will do this in two ways. If facts come to his knowledge which tell him that the company's affairs are not being conducted as they should be, or which put him on inquiry, he will take appropriate action. Appropriate action will no doubt consist in the first instance of inquiry of and consultation with the directors, and in the last but most unlikely resort, the convening of a general meeting to replace one or more directors. What the prudent man of business will not do is to content himself with the receipt of such information on the affairs of the company as a shareholder ordinarily receives at annual general meetings. Since he has the power to do so, he will go further and see that he has sufficient information to enable him to make a responsible decision from time to time either to let matters proceed as they are proceeding, or to intervene if he is dissatisfied. This topic was considered by Cross J in *In re Lucking's Will Trusts* [1968] 1 WLR 866 ...

I do not understand Cross J to have been saying that in every case where trustees have a controlling interest in a company it is their duty to ensure that one of their number is a director or that they have a nominee on the board who will report from time to time on the affairs of the company. He was merely outlining convenient methods by which a prudent man of business (as also a trustee) with a controlling interest in a private company, can place himself in a position to make an informed decision whether any action is appropriate to be taken for the protection of his asset. Other methods may be equally satisfactory and convenient, depending upon the circumstances of the individual case. Alternatives which spring to mind are the receipt of copies of the agenda and minutes of board meetings if regularly held, the receipt of monthly management accounts in the case of a trading concern, or quarterly reports. Every case will depend on its own facts. The possibilities are endless. It would be useless, indeed misleading, to seek to lay down a general rule. The purpose to be achieved is not that of monitoring every move of the directors, but of making it reasonably probable, so far as circumstances permit, that the trustee or (as in the *Lucking* case) one of them will receive an adequate flow of information in time to enable the trustees to make use of their controlling interest should this be necessary for the protection of their trust asset, namely, the shareholding. The obtaining of information is not an end in itself, but merely a means of enabling the trustees to safeguard the interests of their beneficiaries. ...

So far, I have applied the test of the ordinary prudent man of business. Although I am not aware that the point has previously been considered, except briefly in *In re Waterman's Will Trusts* [1952] 2 All ER 1054, I am of opinion that a higher duty of care is plainly due from someone like a trust corporation which carries on a specialised business of trust management. A trust corporation holds itself out in its advertising literature as being above ordinary mortals. With a specialist staff of trained trust officers and managers, with ready access to financial information and professional advice, dealing with and solving trust problems day after day, the trust corporation holds itself out, and rightly, as capable of providing an expertise which it would be unrealistic to expect and unjust to demand from the ordinary prudent man or woman who accepts, probably

Alert

unpaid and sometimes reluctantly from a sense of family duty, the burdens of a trusteeship. Just as, under the law of contract, a professional person possessed of a particular skill is liable for breach of contract if he neglects to use the skill and experience which he professes, so I think that a professional corporate trustee is liable for breach of trust if loss is caused to the trust fund because it neglects to exercise the special care and skill which it professes to have. The advertising literature of the bank was not in evidence (other than the scale of fees) but counsel for the defendant did not dispute that trust corporations, including the bank, hold themselves out as possessing a superior ability for the conduct of trust business, and in any event I would take judicial notice of that fact. Having expressed my view of the higher duty required from a trust corporation, I should add that the bank's counsel did not dispute the proposition.

In my judgment the bank wrongfully and in breach of trust neglected to ensure that it received an adequate flow of information concerning the intentions and activities of the boards of [the company]. It was not proper for the bank to confine itself to the receipt of the annual balance sheet and profit and loss account, detailed annual financial statements and the chairman's report and statement, and to attendance at the annual general meetings and the luncheons that followed, which were the limits of the bank's regular sources of information. Had the bank been in receipt of more frequent information it would have been able to step in and stop, and ought to have stopped [the company] embarking on the Old Bailey project. That project was imprudent and hazardous and wholly unsuitable for a trust whether undertaken by the bank direct or through the medium of its wholly owned company. Even without the regular flow of information which the bank ought to have had, it knew enough to put it upon inquiry. There were enough obvious points at which the bank should have intervened and asked questions. Assuming, as I do, that the questions would have been answered truthfully, the bank would have discovered the gamble upon which [the company was] about to embark in relation to the Old Bailey site, and it could have, and should have, stopped the initial move towards disaster, and later on arrested further progress towards disaster. I have indicated in the course of this judgment a number of obvious points at which the bank should have intervened, and it would be repetitive to summarise them.

I hold that the bank failed in its duty whether it is judged by the standard of the prudent man of business or of the skilled trust corporation. The bank's breach of duty caused the loss which was suffered by the trust estate. If the bank had intervened as it could and should have that loss would not have been incurred. By "loss," I mean the depreciation which took place in the market value of the ... shares, by comparison with the value which the shares would have commanded if the loss on the Old Bailey project had not been incurred, and reduction of dividends through loss of income. The bank is liable for the loss so suffered by the trust estate ... .

10.2 The Statutory Duty of Care

Section 3 of the Trustee Act 2000 vests in a trustee broad investment powers to 'make any kind of investment that he could make if he were absolutely entitled to the assets of the trust'. This is known as the 'general power of investment'. This power applies to all trusts, whenever created (section 7(1) of the Act) unless it is excluded by the trust document (section 6(1)(b) of the Act). This power does not apply to pension trusts, authorised unit trusts or certain common investment schemes for charities (sections 36 to 38 of the Act).

To prevent abuse, these powers are, necessarily, subject to standards imposed by the statutory duty (unless excluded) contained in s1 Trustee Act 2000. This requires trustees to exercise such care and skill as is reasonable in the circumstances, having regard in particular —

(a) to any special knowledge or experience that he has or holds himself out as having [this subjective standard imposes a higher standard for professional trustees] , and

(b) if he acts as trustee in the course of a business or profession, to any special knowledge or experience that it is reasonable to expect of a person acting in the course of that kind of business or profession [a minimum objective standard for all who act as a trustee].

The statutory duty of care applies to the specified functions whether they are conferred upon the trustees expressly by the terms of the trust instrument or by implication under the Act. They apply regardless of whether the trust was created before or after the Act came into effect.

By paragraph 1 of Schedule 1 to the Act, this statutory duty of care is applied to trustees whenever exercising their powers of investment under section 3 of the Act. This includes, first, considering the standard investment criteria in section 4 of the Act trustees must have regard to: that the type of investment is suitable; to periodically review the performance of the investments; and the need to sufficiently diversify the portfolio of investment assets to hedge against risk. Second, the section 5 obligation for trustees to consider if advice is required before investing trust funds. This should be sought from a "proper" advisor with sufficient experience and qualifications to advise on the risk of investing in a certain asset unless the trustee himself has sufficient expertise in investing in that field.

Paragraph 2 of Schedule 1 applies the statutory duty of care to trustees when acquiring land. Section 8(1) of the Act permits trustees to use their investment powers to acquire land in the UK for the purpose of 'investment'; for 'occupation by a beneficiary'; or 'for any other reason'. When compared to the 1947 decision in Re Power's Will Trusts [1947] Ch. 572, it can be seen that the modern powers of trustees to invest in land are now much broader. The will in Re Power stated, 'all moneys requiring to be invested under this my will may be invested by the trustee in any manner in which he may in his absolute discretion think fit in all respects as if he were the sole beneficial owner of such moneys including the purchase of freehold property in England or Wales'. Despite this seemingly wide power, Jenkins J held that the trustee was not authorised to apply the trust fund to buy freehold property for the deceased's widow and his minor children to live in as this purpose was akin to 'use', as opposed to an 'investment', so would be a misapplication of trust funds.

The statutory duty of care also determines the trustee's liability for delegating functions to agents (paragraph 3 of Schedule 1). This comprises selecting the agent and the terms by which they are to act. In relation to these matters, a trustee will not be liable for any act or default of the agent unless he fails to act in accordance with the duty of care (section 23 of the Act).

Pursuant to paragraph 7 of Schedule 1 to the Act, it should be noted that the statutory duty of care may be excluded in the trust document.

11

Tracing

Introduction

Tracing is used as a generic term to describe two processes: following and tracing. Following is the process of identifying the same asset as it moves from person to person. Tracing is the term used when one asset is exchanged for another and is the process of identifying the new asset as a substitute for the original. Lord Millett outlined the nature of tracing very clearly in the House of Lords decision below.

***Foskett v McKeown and Others* [2001] 1 AC 102**

Panel: Lord Browne-Wilkinson, Lord Steyn, Lord Hoffmann, Lord Hope of Craighead and Lord Millett

Facts: The appellants had entered into contracts with a Mr Murphy to purchase land in Portugal. It was agreed that Murphy would hold the appellants' money on trust until the land was developed and transferred. Murphy used the money to pay some annual premiums on his life insurance policy. He held this policy for the benefit of the defendants. Murphy then committed suicide and the policy paid out £1 million. The appellants sought to trace their money into the money paid out on Murphy's death. At first instance they were held to be entitled to 53.46%, being the proportion of the premiums paid with their money. The Court of Appeal held that they were merely entitled to a charge over the proceeds of the policy to recover their money, together with interest thereon. A further appeal was successful and the House of Lords held them to be entitled to the same proportion of the payment as the proportion of the premiums which had been paid with their money.

LORD MILLETT

My Lords, this is a textbook example of tracing through mixed substitutions. At the beginning of the story the plaintiffs were beneficially entitled under an express trust to a sum standing in the name of Mr Murphy in a bank account. From there the money moved into and out of various bank accounts where in breach of trust it was inextricably mixed by Mr Murphy with his own money. After each transaction was completed the plaintiffs' money formed an indistinguishable part of the balance standing to Mr Murphy's credit in his bank account. The amount of that balance represented a debt due from the bank to Mr Murphy, that is to say a chose in action. At the penultimate stage the plaintiffs' money was represented by an indistinguishable part of a different chose in action, *viz*, the debt prospectively and contingently due from an insurance company to its policyholders, being the trustees of a settlement made by Mr Murphy for the benefit of his children. At the present and final stage it forms an indistinguishable part of the balance standing to the credit of the respondent trustees in their bank account.

Tracing and following

The process of ascertaining what happened to the plaintiffs' money involves both tracing and following. These are both exercises in locating assets which are or may be taken to represent an asset belonging to the plaintiffs and to which they assert ownership. The processes of following and tracing are, however, distinct.

Following is the process of following the same asset as it moves from hand to hand. Tracing is the process of identifying a new asset as the substitute for the old. Where one asset is exchanged for another, a claimant can elect whether to follow the original asset into the hands of the new owner or to trace its value into the new asset in the hands of the same owner. In practice his choice is often dictated by the circumstances. In the present case the plaintiffs do not seek to follow the money any further once it reached the bank or insurance company, since its identity was lost in the hands of the recipient (which in any case obtained an unassailable title as a bona fide purchaser for value without notice of the plaintiffs' beneficial interest). Instead the plaintiffs have chosen at each stage to trace the money into its proceeds, viz, the debt presently due from the bank to the account holder or the debt prospectively and contingently due from the insurance company to the policy holders.

Having completed this exercise, the plaintiffs claim a continuing beneficial interest in the insurance money. Since this represents the product of Mr Murphy's own money as well as theirs, which Mr Murphy mingled indistinguishably in a single chose in action, they claim a beneficial interest in a proportionate part of the money only. The transmission of a claimant's property rights from one asset to its traceable proceeds is part of our law of property, not of the law of unjust enrichment. There is no "unjust factor" to justify restitution (unless "want of title" be one, which makes the point). The claimant succeeds if at all by virtue of his own title, not to reverse unjust enrichment. Property rights are determined by fixed rules and settled principles. They are not discretionary. They do not depend upon ideas of what is "fair, just and reasonable". Such concepts, which in reality mask decisions of legal policy, have no place in the law of property.

A beneficiary of a trust is entitled to a continuing beneficial interest not merely in the trust property but in its traceable proceeds also, and his interest binds every one who takes the property or its traceable proceeds except a bona fide purchaser for value without notice. In the present case the plaintiffs' beneficial interest plainly bound Mr Murphy, a trustee who wrongfully mixed the trust money with his own and whose every dealing with the money (including the payment of the premiums) was in breach of trust. It similarly binds his successors, the trustees of the children's settlement, who claim no beneficial interest of their own, and Mr Murphy's children, who are volunteers. They gave no value for what they received and derive their interest from Mr Murphy by way of gift.

Tracing

We speak of money at the bank, and of money passing into and out of a bank account. But of course the account holder has no money at the bank. Money paid into a bank account belongs legally and beneficially to the bank and not to the account holder. The bank gives value for it, and it is accordingly not usually possible to make the money itself the subject of an adverse claim. Instead a claimant normally sues the account holder rather than the bank and lays claim to the proceeds of the money in his hands. These consist of the debt or part of the debt due to him from the bank. We speak of tracing money into and out of the account, but there is no money in the account. There is merely a single debt of an amount equal to the final balance standing to the credit of the account holder. No money passes from paying bank to receiving bank or through the clearing system (where the money flows may be in the opposite direction). There is simply a series of debits and credits which are causally and transactionally linked. We also speak of tracing one asset into another, but this too is inaccurate. The original asset still exists in the hands of the new owner, or it may have become untraceable. The claimant claims the new asset because it was acquired in whole or in part with the original asset. What he traces, therefore, is not the physical asset itself but the value inherent in it.

Tracing is thus neither a claim nor a remedy. It is merely the process by which a claimant demonstrates what has happened to his property, identifies its proceeds and the persons who have handled or received them, and justifies his claim that the proceeds can properly be regarded as representing his property. Tracing is also distinct from claiming. It identifies the traceable proceeds of the claimant's property. It enables the claimant to substitute the traceable proceeds for the original asset as the subject matter of his claim. But it does not affect or establish his claim. That will depend on a number of factors including the nature of his interest in the original asset. He will normally be able to maintain the same claim to the substituted asset as he could have maintained to the original asset. If he held only a security interest in the original asset, he cannot claim more than a security interest in its proceeds. But his claim may also be exposed to potential defences as a result of intervening transactions. Even if the plaintiffs could demonstrate what the bank had done with their money, for example, and could thus identify its traceable proceeds in the hands of the bank, any claim by them to assert ownership of those proceeds would be defeated by the bona fide purchaser defence. The successful completion of a tracing exercise may be preliminary to a personal claim (as in *El Ajou v Dollar Land Holdings plc* [1993] 3 All ER 717) or a proprietary one, to the enforcement of a legal right (as in *Trustees of the Property of F C Jones & Sons v Jones* [1997] Ch 159) or an equitable one.

11.1 When is Tracing Possible?

***Re Diplock* [1948] Ch 465**

Panel: Lord Greene MR, Wrottesley and Evershed LJJ

Facts: Caleb Diplock had left the residue of his estate, 'for such charitable institution or institutions or other charitable or benevolent object or objects in England as my acting executors or executor may in their or his absolute discretion select'. His executors had paid out a large amount of the residue to various charities before his next-of-kin challenged the validity of the clause. The House of Lords held the gift to be void as it was not for exclusively charitable purposes. This case concerned the next of kin's claims to recover the money wrongly paid out to the charities.

11.1.1 Into whose hands can property be traced?

Property cannot be traced into the hands of a bone fide purchaser for value without notice. It can, however, be traced into the hands of the innocent volunteer.

LORD GREENE MR

Alert

Where the moneys are handed by way of transfer to a person who takes for value without notice, the claim of the owner of the moneys is extinguished just as all other equitable estates or interests are extinguished by a purchase for value without notice.

In the case, however, of a volunteer who takes without notice, e.g., by way of gift from the fiduciary agent, if there is no question of mixing, he holds the money on behalf of the true owner whose equitable right to the money still persists as against him. On the other hand, if the volunteer mixes the money with money of his own, or receives it mixed from the fiduciary agent, he must admit the claim of the true owner, but is not precluded from setting up his own claim in respect of the moneys of his own which have been contributed to the mixed fund. The result is that they share pari passu. It would be inequitable for the volunteer to claim priority for the reason that he is a volunteer: it would be equally inequitable for the true owner of the money to claim priority over the volunteer for the reason that the volunteer is innocent and cannot be said to act unconscionably if he claims equal treatment for himself. The mutual recognition of one another's rights is what equity insists upon as a condition of giving relief

Lord Greene MR also cited the situation where a fiduciary mixes property acquired from two different funds, and noted Lord Parker's conclusions on this in *Sinclair v Brougham* [1914] AC 398.

The first of Lord Parker's own two illustrations is the case where a person standing in a fiduciary relation to two different persons acquires property by means of a mixed fund of money part of which had belonged to one and part to the other. In such a case each has an equal equity. Each is entitled to a charge and neither is entitled to priority over the other. The explanation of this result lies in the fact that each has an equitable right of property and that right of property can be traced by each into the asset purchased. Equity gives effect to this right by means of the equitable remedy of a declaration of charge.

11.1.2 Property cannot be traced if it has been dissipated

Much of the wrongly paid out money had been spent on unsecured debts or to pay general expenses. Lord Greene MR held that this money could not be traced.

> The equitable remedies pre-suppose the continued existence of the money either as a separate fund or as part of a mixed fund or as latent in property acquired by means of such a fund. If, on the facts of any individual case, such continued existence is not established, equity is as helpless as the common law itself. If the fund, mixed or unmixed, is spent upon a dinner, equity, which dealt only in specific relief and not in damages, could do nothing.
>
> It is, therefore, a necessary matter for consideration in each case where it is sought to trace money in equity, whether it has such a continued existence, actual or notional, as will enable equity to grant specific relief.

He considered the specific case of money spent on a pre-owned asset by an innocent volunteer.

> In the present cases, however, the charities have used the Diplock money, not in combination with money of their own to acquire new assets, but in the alteration and improvement of assets which they already owned. The altered and improved asset owes its existence, therefore, to a combination of land belonging to the charity and money belonging to the Diplock estate. The question whether tracing is possible and if so to what extent, and also the question whether an effective remedy by way of declaration of charge can be granted consistently with an equitable treatment of the charity as an innocent volunteer, present quite different problems from those arising in the simple case above stated. [...] The result may add not one penny to the value of the house. Indeed, the alteration may well lower its value; for the alteration, though convenient to the owner, may be highly inconvenient in the eyes of a purchaser. Can it be said in such cases that the trust money can be traced and extracted from the altered asset? Clearly not, for the money will have disappeared leaving no monetary trace behind: the asset will not have increased (or may even have depreciated) in value through its use.
>
> But the matter does not end here. What, for the purposes of the inquiry, is to be treated as "the charity property"? Is it to be the whole of the land belonging to the charity? or is it to be only that part of it which was altered or reconstructed or on which a building has been erected by means of Diplock money? If the latter, the result may well be that the property, both in its original state and as altered or improved, will, when taken in isolation, have little or no value. What would be the value of a building in the middle of Guy's hospital without any means of access through other parts of the hospital property? If, on the other hand, the charge is to be on the whole of the charity land, it might well be thought an extravagant result if the Diplock estate, because Diplock money had been used to reconstruct a corner of it, were to be entitled to a charge on the entirety.

11.1.2.1 The Remedies Available as a Result of Tracing

***Foskett v McKeown and Others* [2001] 1 AC 102**

Panel: Lord Browne-Wilkinson, Lord Steyn, Lord Hoffmann, Lord Hope of Craighead and Lord Millett

Having described tracing as a process (see the nature of tracing, above) Lord Millett then identified the remedies available as a result of tracing. He noted that any remedy would depend on property rights rather than unjust enrichment.

LORD MILLETT

A plaintiff who brings an action in unjust enrichment must show that the defendant has been enriched at the plaintiff's expense, for he cannot have been unjustly enriched if he has not been enriched at all. But the plaintiff is not concerned to show that the defendant is in receipt of property belonging beneficially to the plaintiff or its traceable proceeds. The fact that the beneficial ownership of the property has passed to the defendant provides no defence; indeed, it is usually the very fact which founds the claim. Conversely, a plaintiff who brings an action like the present must show that the defendant is in receipt of property which belongs beneficially to him or its traceable proceeds, but he need not show that the defendant has been enriched by its receipt. He may, for example, have paid full value for the property, but he is still required to disgorge it if he received it with notice of the plaintiff's interest.

11.1.3 A straightforward substitution

Here, the beneficiary can chose between claiming the property or a lien or charge on the property.

The simplest case is where a trustee wrongfully misappropriates trust property and uses it exclusively to acquire other property for his own benefit. In such a case the beneficiary is entitled at his option either to assert his beneficial ownership of the proceeds or to bring a personal claim against the trustee for breach of trust and enforce an equitable lien or charge on the proceeds to secure restoration of the trust fund. He will normally exercise the option in the way most advantageous to himself. If the traceable proceeds have increased in value and are worth more than the original asset, he will assert his beneficial ownership and obtain the profit for himself. There is nothing unfair in this. The trustee cannot be permitted to keep any profit resulting from his misappropriation for himself, and his donees cannot obtain a better title than their donor. If the traceable proceeds are worth less than the original asset, it does not usually matter how the beneficiary exercises his option. He will take the whole of the proceeds on either basis. This is why it is not possible to identify the basis on which the claim succeeded in some of the cases.

Both remedies are proprietary and depend on successfully tracing the trust property into its proceeds. A beneficiary's claim against a trustee for breach of trust is a personal claim. It does not entitle him to priority over the trustee's general creditors unless he can trace the trust property into its product and establish a proprietary interest in the proceeds. If the beneficiary is unable to trace the trust property into its proceeds, he still has a personal claim against the trustee, but his claim will be unsecured. The beneficiary's proprietary claims to the trust property or its traceable proceeds can be maintained against the wrongdoer and anyone who derives title from him except a bona fide purchaser for value without notice of the breach of trust. The same rules apply even where there have been numerous successive transactions, so long as the tracing exercise is successful and no bona fide purchaser for value without notice has intervened.

11.1.4 The property being traced has been mixed with other property

The beneficiary can choose between claiming a proportion of the property equivalent to the proportion their contribution bore to the purchase price or a lien or charge on the property for the amount of his contribution. Alternatively, they would have a personal claim against the wrongdoer.

A more complicated case is where there is a mixed substitution. This occurs where the trust money represents only part of the cost of acquiring the new asset. As James Barr Ames pointed out in "Following Misappropriated Property into its Product" (1906) 19 HarvLRev 511, consistency requires that, if a trustee buys property partly with his own money and partly with trust money, the beneficiary should have the option of taking a proportionate part of the new property or a lien upon it, as may be most for his advantage. In principle it should not matter (and it has never previously been suggested that it does) whether the trustee mixes the trust money with his own and buys the new asset with the mixed fund or makes separate payments of the purchase price (whether simultaneously or sequentially) out of the different funds. In every case the value formerly inherent in the trust property has become located within the value inherent in the new asset.

[...]

In *In re Hallett's Estate; Knatchbull v Hallett* (1880) 13 ChD 696, 709 Sir George Jessel MR acknowledged that where an asset was acquired exclusively with trust money, the beneficiary could either assert equitable ownership of the asset or enforce a lien or charge over it to recover the trust money. But he appeared to suggest that in the case of a mixed substitution the beneficiary is confined to a lien. Any authority that this dictum might otherwise have is weakened by the fact that Sir George Jessel MR gave no reason for the existence of any such rule, and none is readily apparent. The dictum was plainly obiter, for the fund was deficient and the plaintiff was only claiming a lien. It has usually been cited only to be explained away [...]

In my view the time has come to state unequivocally that English law has no such rule. It conflicts with the rule that a trustee must not benefit from his trust. I agree with Burrows that the beneficiary's right to elect to have a proportionate share of a mixed substitution necessarily follows once one accepts, as English law does, (i) that a claimant can trace in equity into a mixed fund and (ii) that he can trace unmixed money into its proceeds and assert ownership of the proceeds.

Accordingly, I would state the basic rule as follows. Where a trustee wrongfully uses trust money to provide part of the cost of acquiring an asset, the beneficiary is entitled at his option either to claim a proportionate share of the asset or to enforce a lien upon it to secure his personal claim against the trustee for the amount of the misapplied money. It does not matter whether the trustee mixed the trust money with his own in a single fund before using it to acquire the asset, or made separate payments (whether simultaneously or sequentially) out of the differently owned funds to acquire a single asset.

Two observations are necessary at this point. First, there is a mixed substitution (with the results already described) whenever the claimant's property has contributed in part only towards the acquisition of the new asset. It is not necessary for the claimant to show in addition that his property has contributed to any increase in the value of the new asset. This is because, as I have already pointed out, this branch of the law is concerned with vindicating rights of property and not with reversing unjust enrichment. Secondly, the beneficiary's right to claim a lien is available only against a wrongdoer and those deriving title under him otherwise than for value. It is not available against competing contributors who are innocent of any wrongdoing. The tracing rules are not the result of any presumption or principle peculiar to equity. They correspond to the common law rules for following into physical mixtures (though the consequences may not be identical). Common to both is the principle that the interests of the wrongdoer who was responsible for the mixing and those who derive title under him otherwise than for value are subordinated to those of innocent contributors. As against the wrongdoer and his successors, the beneficiary is entitled to locate his contribution in any part of the mixture and to subordinate their claims to share in the mixture until his own contribution has been satisfied. This has the effect of giving the beneficiary a lien for his contribution if the mixture is deficient.

11.1.5 The property has been mixed with property of innocent contributors

Where the beneficiary's property is mixed with that of an innocent contributor, a lien will not be available. The property must be shared rateably, i.e. proportionately.

Innocent contributors, however, must be treated equally inter se. Where the beneficiary's claim is in competition with the claims of other innocent contributors, there is no basis upon which any of the claims can be

subordinated to any of the others. Where the fund is deficient, the beneficiary is not entitled to enforce a lien for his contributions; all must share rateably in the fund.

The primary rule in regard to a mixed fund, therefore, is that gains and losses are borne by the contributors rateably. The beneficiary's right to elect instead to enforce a lien to obtain repayment is an exception to the primary rule, exercisable where the fund is deficient and the claim is made against the wrongdoer and those claiming through him. It is not necessary to consider whether there are any circumstances in which the beneficiary is confined to a lien in cases where the fund is more than sufficient to repay the contributions of all parties. It is sufficient to say that he is not so confined in a case like the present.

11.1.6 Innocent volunteers who are not contributors

[...]There are relatively few cases which deal with the position of the innocent recipient from the wrongdoer, but *Jones v De Marchant* (1916) 28 DLR 561 may be cited as an example. A husband wrongfully used 18 beaver skins belonging to his wife and used them,(sic) together with four skins of his own, to have a fur coat made up which he then gave to his mistress. Unsurprisingly the wife was held entitled to recover the coat. The mistress knew nothing of the true ownership of the skins, but her innocence was held to be immaterial. She was a gratuitous donee and could stand in no better position than the husband. The coat was a new asset manufactured from the skins and not merely the product of intermingling them. The problem could not be solved by a sale of the coat in order to reduce the disputed property to a divisible fund, since (as we shall see) the realisation of an asset does not affect its ownership. It would hardly have been appropriate to require the two ladies to share the coat between them. Accordingly it was an all or nothing case in which the ownership of the coat must be assigned to one or other of the parties. The determinative factor was that the mixing was the act of the wrongdoer through whom the mistress acquired the coat otherwise than for value.

The rule in equity is to the same effect, as Sir William Page Wood V-C observed in *Frith v Cartland* (1865) 2 H & M 417 ,420: "if a man mixes trust funds with his own, the whole will be treated as the trust property, except so far as he may be able to distinguish what is his own". This does not, in my opinion, exclude a pro rata division where this is appropriate, as in the case of money and other fungibles like grain, oil or wine. But it is to be observed that a pro rata division is the best that the wrongdoer and his donees can hope for. If a pro rata division is excluded, the beneficiary takes the whole; there is no question of confining him to a lien. *Jones v De Marchant* 28 DLR 561 is a useful illustration of the principles shared by the common law and equity alike that an innocent recipient who receives misappropriated property by way of gift obtains no better title than his donor, and that if a proportionate sharing is inappropriate the wrongdoer and those who derive title under him take nothing.

Alert

11.1.7 The beneficiary's money is spent by a volunteer on a pre-owned asset

This situation was considered by Lord Browne Wilkinson, who stated that the only remedy available would be a lien.

LORD BROWNE-WILKINSON

The question of tracing which does arise is whether the rules of tracing are those regulating tracing through a mixed fund or those regulating the position when moneys of one person have been innocently expended on the property of another. In the former case (mixing of funds) it is established law that the mixed fund belongs proportionately to those whose moneys were mixed. In the latter case it is equally clear that money expended on maintaining or improving the property of another normally gives rise, at the most, to a proprietary lien to recover the moneys so expended. In certain cases the rules of tracing in such a case may give rise to no proprietary interest at all if to give such interest would be unfair: see *In re Diplock; Diplock v Wintle* [1948] Ch 465 , 548.

Lord Browne-Wilkinson then noted that the Court of Appeal considered what had happened in this case as being akin to an innocent volunteer spending trust money on pre-owned land.

Cases where the money of one person has been expended on improving or maintaining the physical property of another raise special problems. The property left at the end of the day is incapable of being physically divided into its separate constituent assets, i.e. the land and the money spent on it. Nor can the rules for tracing moneys through a mixed fund apply: the essence of tracing through a mixed fund is the ability to re-divide the mixed fund into its constituent parts pro rata according to the value of the contributions made to it.

11.1.8 Money is spent paying secured debts

Where the claimant's money is spent to pay off secured debts, the remedy available to him is called subrogation. This allows him to step into the creditor's shoes and become a secured creditor. The rule on subrogation was dealt with in *Bowcawen v Bajwa* [1996] 1WLR 328.

***Boscawen v Bajwa* [1996] 1 WLR 328**

Panel: Stuart-Smith, Waite and Millett LJJ

Facts: Abbey National, one of the defendants, had advanced money to purchase a house. They were to receive the first legal charge on that house. Before the sale was completed, the money was paid to the vendors and used to discharge the existing mortgage with the Halifax Building Society. The purchase then fell through. The plaintiffs were the vendor's creditors, who claimed the house. Abbey National claimed to be subrogated to the position of the Halifax Building Society and thereby to have a charge over the house, which took priority over the claims of the vendor's other creditors. The judge held this to be the case. The Court of Appeal dismissed an appeal, holding that Abbey National's money had been held on trust, first by the purchaser's solicitors and then the vendor's solicitors, pending completion. The Abbey National therefore had an equitable interest in the money which paid off the Halifax mortgage.

LORD JUSTICE MILLETT

If the plaintiff succeeds in tracing his property, whether in its original or in some changed form, into the hands of the defendant, and overcomes any defences which are put forward on the defendant's behalf, he is entitled to a remedy. The remedy will be fashioned to the circumstances. The plaintiff will generally be entitled to a personal remedy; if he seeks a proprietary remedy he must usually prove that the property to which he lays claim is still in the ownership of the defendant. If he succeeds in doing this the court will treat the defendant as holding the property on a constructive trust for the plaintiff and will order the defendant to transfer it in specie to the plaintiff. But this is only one of the proprietary remedies which are available to a court of equity. If the plaintiff's money has been applied by the defendant, for example, not in the acquisition of a landed property but in its improvement, then the court may treat the land as charged with the payment to the plaintiff of a sum representing the amount by which the value of the defendant's land has been enhanced by the use of the plaintiff's money. And if the plaintiff's money has been used to discharge a mortgage on the defendant's land, then the court may achieve a similar result by treating the land as subject to a charge by way of subrogation in favour of the plaintiff.

Subrogation, therefore, is a remedy, not a cause of action: see Goff & Jones, Law of Restitution, 4th ed. (1993), pp. 589 et seq.; *Orakpo v Manson Investments Ltd* [1978] AC 95,104, per Lord Diplock and *In re T. H. Knitwear (Wholesale) Ltd* [1988] Ch 275,284.

11.2 Payments In and Out of Bank Accounts Representing Mixed Funds

Rules have been developed concerning payments in and out of bank accounts containing mixed funds.

11.2.1 The Claimant and the wrongdoer

Very often a claimant's money will have been paid into the wrongdoer's own bank account. As seen above, the claimant will then have a charge over the wrongdoer's bank account for the value of that money.

11.2.2 Payments out

The general rule is that the first payments out of such a mixed fund are deemed to be of the wrongdoer's own money. This arises from a presumption of honesty. The wrongdoer is deemed to intend to spend their own money before that of the trust.

***In re Hallett's Estate, Knatchbull v Hallett* (1879-80) LR 13 Ch D 696**

Panel: Sir George Jessel MR, Baggallay and Thesiger LJJ

Facts: Hallett was a solicitor who looked after some Russian bonds for his client, Mrs Cotterill. He sold the bonds and paid the proceeds into his bank account, which contained some of his own money. He then withdrew money from his account and used it for his own purposes. The Court held that this money was Hallett's and Mrs Cotterill's money was left in the account. There was enough money in the account for her claim to be met in full.

SIR GEORGE JESSEL MR

Now, first upon principle, nothing can be better settled, either in our own law, or, I suppose, the law of all civilised countries, than this, that where a man does an act which may be rightfully performed, he cannot say that that act was intentionally and in fact done wrongly. A man who has a right of entry cannot say he committed a trespass in entering. A man who sells the goods of another as agent for the owner cannot prevent the owner adopting the sale, and deny that he acted as agent for the owner. It runs throughout our law, and we are familiar with numerous instances in the law of real property. A man who grants a lease believing he has sufficient estate to grant it, although it turns out that he has not, but has a power which enables him to grant it, is not allowed to say he did not grant it under the power. Where ever it can be done rightfully, he is not allowed to say, against the person entitled to the property or the right, that he has done it wrongfully. That is the universal law.

When we come to apply that principle to the case of a trustee who has blended trust moneys with his own, it seems to me perfectly plain that he cannot be heard to say that he took away the trust money when he had a right to take away his own money. The simplest case put is the mingling of trust moneys in a bag with money of the trustee's own. Suppose he has a hundred sovereigns in a bag, and he adds to them another hundred sovereigns of his own, so that they are commingled in such a way that they cannot be distinguished, and the next day he draws out for his own purposes £100, is it tolerable for anybody to allege that what he drew out was the first £100, the trust money, and that he misappropriated it, and left his own £100 in the bag? It is obvious he must have taken away that which he had a right to take away, his own £100. What difference does it make if, instead of being in a bag, he deposits it with his banker, and then pays in other money of his own, and draws out some money for his own purposes? Could he say that he had actually drawn out anything but his own money? His money was there, and he had a right to draw it out, and why should the natural act of simply drawing out the money be attributed to anything except to his ownership of money which was at his bankers.

The presumption that the first payment out is of the wrongdoer's money does not apply when there is no money left in the account to represent the claimant's money. This was held in the case below.

***In re Oatway, Hertslet v Oatway* [1903] 2 Ch 356**

Panel: Joyce J

Facts: Oatway received £7,000 in breach of trust which he paid into his own bank account. He paid out about £5,000 for his own purposes and then paid in £3,000 of his own money. He then bought some shares in the Oceana Company for approximately £2,000. Later, the rest of the money in the account was dissipated, but he owned the shares on his death. It was held that the trust could claim the proceeds of the shares.

MR JUSTICE JOYCE

...[I]f money held by any person in a fiduciary capacity be paid into his own banking account, it may be followed by the equitable owner, who, as against the trustee, will have a charge for what belongs to him upon the balance to the credit of the account. If, then, the trustee pays in further sums, and from time to time draws out money by cheques, but leaves a balance to the credit of the account, it is settled that he is not entitled to have the rule in *Clayton's Case* applied so as to maintain that the sums which have been drawn out and paid away so as to be incapable of being recovered represented *pro tanto* the trust money, and that the balance remaining is not trust money, but represents only his own moneys paid into the account. *Brown v Adams* to the contrary ought not to be followed since the decision in *In re Hallett's Estate.* It is, in my opinion, equally clear that when any of the money drawn out has been invested, and the investment remains in the name or under the control of the trustee, the rest of the balance having been afterwards dissipated by him, he cannot maintain that the investment which remains represents his own money alone, and that what has been spent and can no longer be traced and recovered was the money belonging to the trust. In other words, when the private money of the trustee and that which he held in a fiduciary capacity have been mixed in the same banking account, from which various payments have from time to time been made, then, in order to determine to whom any remaining balance or any investment that may have been paid for out of the account ought to be deemed to belong, the trustee must be debited with all the sums that have been withdrawn and applied to his own use so as to be no longer recoverable, and the trust money in like manner be debited with any sums taken out and duly invested in the names of the proper trustees. The order of priority in which the various withdrawals and investments may have been respectively made is wholly immaterial. I have been referring, of course, to cases where there is only one fiduciary owner or set of *cestuis que trust* claiming whatever may be left as against the trustee. In the present case there is no balance left. The only investment or property remaining which represents any part of the mixed moneys paid into the banking account is the Oceana shares purchased for 2137l. Upon these, therefore, the trust had a charge for the 3000l. trust money paid into the account. That is to say, those shares and the proceeds thereof belong to the trust.

It was objected that the investment in the Oceana shares was made at a time when Oatway's own share of the balance to the credit of the account (if the whole had been then justly distributed) would have exceeded 2137l., the price of the shares; that he was therefore entitled to withdraw that sum, and might rightly apply it for his own purposes; and that consequently the shares should be held to belong to his estate. To this I answer that he never was entitled to withdraw the 2137l. from the account, or, at all events, that he could not be entitled to take that sum from the account and hold it or the investment made therewith, freed from the charge in favour of the trust, unless or until the trust money paid into the account had been first restored, and the trust fund reinstated by due investment of the money in the joint names of the proper trustees, which never was done.

The investment by Oatway, in his own name, of the 2137l. in Oceana shares no more got rid of the claim or charge of the trust upon the money so invested, than would have been the case if he had drawn a cheque for 2137l. and simply placed and retained the amount in a drawer without further disposing of the money in any way. The proceeds of the Oceana shares must be held to belong to the trust funds under the will of which Oatway and Maxwell Skipper were the trustees

The question remains whether a claimant can claim property bought with an earlier payment out of the account when there is enough money left in the account to satisfy their claim. This has been referred to as 'cherry picking'. Mr Justice Joyce in *Re Oatway* saw the claimant's charge on the whole account lasting only until the trust money had been restored. Lord Millett in *Foskett v McKeown* reiterated this but later left the matter open.

The High Court in *Shalson v Russo* suggested, obiter, that cherry picking might be allowed against the wrongdoer regardless of whether the balance in the mixed fund would cover their losses.

***Shalson and Others v Russo and Others (Mimran and Another, Part 20 Claimants)* [2003] EWHC 1637 [2005] Ch 281**

Panel: Rimer J

Facts: This case arose from the business dealings of Russo, an Italian, who had fraudulently obtained money from the claimants and several others, including Mimran, one of the defendants. Mimran was attempting to trace his money into a yacht owned jointly by Shalson and Russo. The court held he was unable to do so, but Mr Justice Rimer stated the following, obiter.

MR JUSTICE RIMER

This method is a "cherry-picking" exercise, as Mr Smith recognised. But in a case in which the only contest is between the claimant seeking to trace (Mr Mimran) and the wrongdoer (WIB/Mr Russo), there is, he says, every reason why the latter's interests should be subordinated to the claimant's. Normally, it is presumed that if a trustee uses money from a fund in which he has mixed trust money with his own, he uses his own money first: *In re Hallett's Estate* (1880) 13 Ch D 696. But Mr Smith submits that this is not an inflexible rule and that if the trustee can be shown to have made an early application of the mixed fund into an investment, the beneficiary is entitled to claim that for himself. He says, and I agree, that this is supported by *In re Oatway* [1903] 2 Ch 356. The justice of this is that, if the beneficiary is not entitled to do this, the wrongdoing trustee may be left with all the cherries and the victim with nothing. The limitation referred to in the penultimate sentence of the previous paragraph is the "lowest intermediate balance" rule, illustrated by *James Roscoe (Bolton) Ltd v Winder* [1915] 1 Ch 62.

***FHR European Ventures LLP and others v Mankarious and others* [2016] EWHC 359 (Ch)**

Panel: Master Clark

Facts: This case arises out of the litigation *FHR European Ventures LLP and others v Cedar Capital Partners LLC* [2014] UKSC 45 (see Chapter 8 on Fiduciary Duties). The commission was paid into a Jersey bank account in euros. Some of it was transferred to a sterling account with the same bank, where it was mixed with the fiduciary's own money. Subsequently, £180,000, which included £78,982 of the commission, was paid from the sterling account as a deposit for a freehold property in London. The question arose as to the proportionate share which the claimants could claim in the London the property. The claimants relied on *Re Oatway* to argue that the full amount of £180,000 should be treated as being paid from money derived from the commission, rather than £79,982. The court rejected the claimants' argument.

MASTER CLARK

The claimants' counsel relied upon *Re Oatway* as authority for the proposition that the defendants, as fiduciaries, are not entitled to claim to be able to withdraw any sum from *any account* without having first restored the trust money to its rightful owners, the claimants. I consider that, by this submission, he invited me to treat all 3 of Cedar LLC's accounts as effectively one mixed fund, so that the monies derived from the Savoy payment should be treated as having been spent on Cedar LLC's own purposes, and the equivalent amount treated as derived from the Fee held in the euro account. He submitted that while there were funds in the 3 accounts as a whole, it was not open to the first defendant to say that he used his own monies in relation to the Property.

[...]One way of testing the claimants' counsel's submissions is to consider the following

scenarios where money from the Fee and the defendants' money are both used to purchase an asset:

(1) the Fee is retained in cash (not paid into an account) and the defendants' money is in an account;

(2) the Fee is paid into an account and the defendants' money is retained as cash;

(3) the Fee is paid into an account with one bank and the defendants' money is paid into an account with a different bank.

(4) the Fee is paid into an account with one bank and the defendants' money is paid into another account with the same bank - as in this case.

In the first 3 cases it cannot be said that the Fee has been paid into a mixed account and Re Oatway would not apply. In my judgment, there is no distinction in principle to be drawn between these cases and the fourth case even though the accounts are at the same bank - as a matter of fact, the funds are not mixed. As the defendants' counsel submitted, tracing is a matter of "hard-nosed property rights", not on whether it is fair, just and reasonable to treat the claimants as entitled to the entirety of the deposit (see *Foskett v McKeown* at pl09C-D).

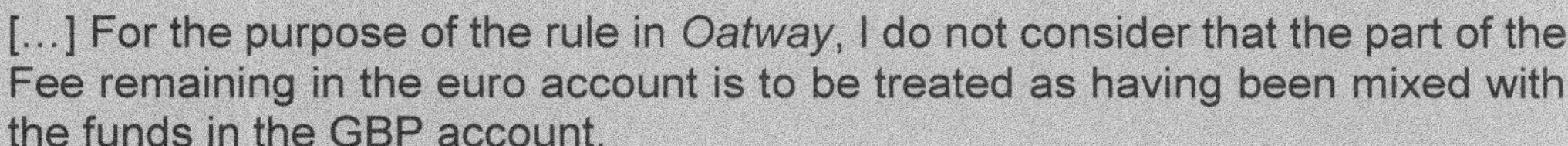

[...] For the purpose of the rule in *Oatway*, I do not consider that the part of the Fee remaining in the euro account is to be treated as having been mixed with the funds in the GBP account.

I therefore accept the defendants' counsel's submission. *Oatway* was concerned with a single account in which monies belonging to the trustee and to the beneficiary were mixed. In support of the claimants' counsel's submission that it should be of broader application, he did not refer me to any statements of principle in the reported cases on this topic. To accept his submissions would be to extend the application of Oatway, but the only basis put forward for doing so was that the defendants' position was as unattractive as that of the trustee in *Oatway*.

11.2.3 Payments in – the lowest intermediate balance rule

Once the claimant's money has been paid out of the wrongdoer's bank account, it is not replaced by money subsequently paid in by the wrongdoer. This later money will only be subject to a trust if the wrongdoer shows an intention that it should replace the earlier money.

***James Roscoe (Bolton), Limited v Winder* [1915] 1 Ch 62**

Panel: Sargant J

Facts: The plaintiff company was in voluntary liquidation and the defendant was the trustee in bankruptcy of William Wigham (W). The company had been sold to W and it had been agreed that W would collect the existing debts and pay them to the company. He collected over £6,000 in existing debts, but paid it into his own bank account. The court decided that he was thus holding this money on trust for the company. W spent all but £25 18s of the money. He later paid money into his account. The Court held that the later money did not replace the company's money. It would only have done so if W had shown a clear intention that he was to hold the later money on trust for the company and he had not done this.

MR JUSTICE SARGANT

Practically, what Mr. Martelli and Mr. Hansell have been asking me to do – although I think Mr. Hansell in particular rather disguised the claim by the phraseology he used – is to say that the debtor, by paying further moneys after May 21 into this common account, was impressing upon those further moneys so paid in the like trust or obligation, or charge of the nature of a trust, which had formerly been impressed upon the previous balances to the credit of that account. No doubt, Mr. Hansell did say "No. I am only asking you to treat the account as a whole, and to consider the balance from time to time standing to the credit of that account as subject to one continual charge or trust." But I think that really is using words which are not appropriate to the facts. You must, for the purpose of tracing, which was the process adopted in In re Hallett's Estate, put your finger on some definite fund which either remains in its original state or can be found in another shape. That is tracing, and tracing, by the very facts of this case, seems to be absolutely excluded except as to the 25l. 18s.

Alert

Then, apart from tracing, it seems to me possible to establish this claim against the ultimate balance of 358l. 5s. 5d. only by saying that something was done, with regard to the additional moneys which are needed to make up that balance, by the person to whom those moneys belonged, the debtor, to substitute those moneys for the purpose of, or to impose upon those moneys a trust equivalent to, the trust which rested on the previous balance. Of course, if there was anything like a separate trust account, the payment of the further moneys into that account would, in itself, have been quite a sufficient indication of the intention of the debtor to substitute those additional moneys for the original trust moneys, and accordingly to impose, by way of substitution, the old trusts upon those additional moneys. But, in a case where the account into which the moneys are paid is the general trading account of the debtor on which he has been accustomed to draw both in the ordinary course and in breach of trust when there were trust funds standing to the credit of that account which were convenient for that purpose, I think it is impossible to attribute to him that by the mere payment into the account of further moneys, which to a large extent he subsequently used for purposes of his own, he intended to clothe those moneys with a trust in favour of the plaintiffs.

Certainly, after having heard In re Hallett's Estate stated over and over again, I should have thought that the general view of that decision was that it only applied to such an amount of the balance ultimately standing to the credit of the trustee as did not exceed the lowest balance of the account during the intervening period. That view has practically been taken, as far as I can make out, in the cases which have dealt with *In re Hallett's Estate. In re Oatway* , a decision of Joyce J., was cited to me in support of the plaintiffs' case, but I do not find anything in it to help them. All that Joyce J. did in that case was to say that, if part of the mixed moneys can be traced into a definite security, that security will not become freed from the charge in favour of the trust, but will, together with any residue of the mixed moneys, remain subject to that charge. I am sure that nothing which he said was intended to mean that the trust was imposed upon any property into which the original fund could not be traced. The head-note to the decision of North J. in *In re Stenning* (which accurately represents the effect of the case) is stated in such terms as to indicate that the application of the doctrine in *In re Hallett's Estate* implied that there should be a continuous balance standing to the credit of the account equal to the balance against which the charge is sought to be enforced. And certainly in the recent case of *Sinclair v Brougham* I can see nothing in any way to impeach the doctrine as to tracing laid down in *In re Hallett's Estate.*

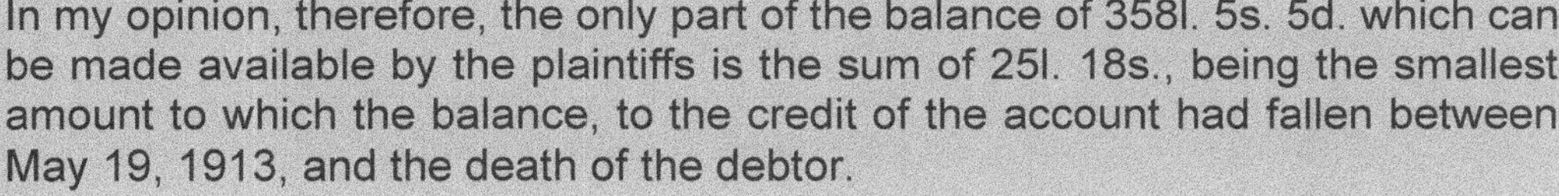

In my opinion, therefore, the only part of the balance of 358l. 5s. 5d. which can be made available by the plaintiffs is the sum of 25l. 18s., being the smallest amount to which the balance, to the credit of the account had fallen between May 19, 1913, and the death of the debtor.

***Bishopsgate Investment Management Limited (In Liquidation) v Homan* [1995] Ch 211**

Panel: Dillon, Leggatt and Henry LJJ

Facts: Bishopsgate Investment Management Ltd (BIM) was the trustee of pension funds for employees of the Maxwell group of companies. Money was fraudulently paid from BIM's pension funds into the accounts of Maxwell Communication Corporation plc (MCC). Those accounts were either overdrawn at the time of the payments in, or became overdrawn later. BIM went into liquidation and the liquidators claimed an equitable charge over the assets of MCC to the amount of the misapplied pension money, thus giving the pensioners priority over other creditors.

The Court of Appeal agreed with the judge at first instance and acknowledged the possibility that 'backwards tracing' might be available in certain circumstances.

> **DILLON LJ**
>
> The judge gave as an instance of such a case what he called "backward tracing" - where an asset was acquired by M.C.C. with moneys borrowed from an overdrawn or loan account and there was an inference that when the borrowing was incurred it was the intention that it should be repaid by misappropriations of B.I.M.'s moneys. Another possibility was that moneys misappropriated from B.I.M. were paid into an overdrawn account of M.C.C. in order to reduce the overdraft and so make finance available within the overdraft limits for M.C.C. to purchase some particular asset.

However, the court said that the circumstances of this case were different. Here, the liquidators for BIM had argued for an equitable charge over other accounts of MCC, which were in credit. Applying the 'lowest intermediate balance rule' (see above), however, Dillon LJ rejected this argument.

> [...] the National Westminster Bank account into which the misappropriated B.I.M. trust moneys were paid happened to be in credit when the administrators were appointed. B.I.M. therefore claims a lien on that credit balance in the National Westminster Bank account for the amount of the misappropriated trust moneys.[...] But in the absence of clear evidence of intention to make good the depredations on B.I.M. it is not possible to assume that the credit balance has been clothed with a trust in favour of B.I.M. and its beneficiaries: see *James Roscoe (Bolton) Ltd. v. Winder [1915] 1 Ch. 62* .
>
> It is not open to us to say that because the moneys were trust moneys the fact that they were paid into an overdrawn account or have otherwise been dissipated presents no difficulty to raising an equitable charge on assets of M.C.C. for their amount in favour of B.I.M.

11.2.4 Payments out – Two claimants or a claimant and an Innocent Volunteer

Where the money of one claimant is mixed in a bank account with the money of another claimant, or that of an innocent volunteer, they share the mixture rateably. The general rule is that payments out of the account will be in proportion to their share of the mixed fund. However, a special rule was developed for active current accounts in *Re Clayton's Case* (1816) 1 Mer 572. This rule states that payments out of the account will be made in the same order that they were made into the account, so the first payment in will be the first payment out. This rule has been heavily criticised. The Court of Appeal has confirmed that the rule is still good law, but may be displaced by evidence of contrary intention.

***Barlow Clowes International Ltd (in liq) and others v Vaughan and others* [1992] 4 All ER 22**

Panel: Dillon, Woolf and Leggatt LJJ

Facts: Barlow Clowes International had fraudulently acquired money from numerous investors, which it was supposed to invest on their behalf. Instead, the directors appropriated and spent most of the money on themselves. This case concerned the method of distribution amongst the creditors of the money which remained in the Company's bank accounts after it went into liquidation. The judge appointed a defendant to represent the early investors and another defendant to represent the later investors. At first instance the rule in *Re Clayton's Case* was applied. The defendant representing the earlier investors appealed.

LORD JUSTICE WOOLF

...[T]he rule in *Clayton's Case, Devaynes v Noble* (1816) 1 Mer 572, [1814–23] All ER Rep 1. That case was authority for the principle that, when sums are mixed in a bank account as a result of a series of deposits, withdrawals are treated as withdrawing the money in the same order as the money was deposited.

Lord Justice Woolf then noted the alternative ways in which it had been suggested the money could be allocated and continued:

...[I]t is settled law that the rule in *Clayton's Case* can be applied to determine the extent to which, as between each other, equally innocent claimants are entitled in equity to moneys which have been paid into a bank account and then subject to the movements within that account. However, it does not, having regard to the passages from the judgments in the other authorities cited, follow that the rule has always to be applied for this purpose. In a number of different circumstances the rule has not been applied. The rule need only be applied when it is convenient to do so and when its application can be said to do broad justice having regard to the nature of the competing claims. *Re Hallett's Estate* shows that the rule is displaced where its application would unjustly assist the trustee to the disadvantage of the beneficiaries. In *Re Diplock's Estate* the rule would have been displaced by the trustee subsequently earmarking the beneficiary's funds. It is not applied if this is the intention or presumed intention of the beneficiaries. The rule is sensibly not applied when the cost of applying it is likely to exhaust the fund available for the beneficiaries.

Lord Justice Woolf then noted other instances in which the rule was not applied, and concluded:

For the reasons I have expressed, the approach, in summary, which I would adopt to resolving the issues raised by this appeal are as follows.

(1) While the rule in *Clayton's Case* is prima facie available to determine the interests of investors in a fund into which their investments have been

paid, the use of the rule is a matter of convenience and if its application in particular circumstances would be impracticable or result in injustice between the investors it will not be applied if there is a preferable alternative.

(2) Here the rule will not be applied because this would be contrary to either the express or inferred or presumed intention of the investors. If the investments were required by the terms of the investment contract to be paid into a common pool this indicates that the investors did not intend to apply the rule. If the investments were intended to be separately invested, as a result of the investments being collectively misapplied by BCI a common pool of the investments was created. Because of their shared misfortune, the investors will be presumed to have intended the rule not to apply.15.2.4.1 Defences

11.2.5 Inequitability

The Court of Appeal in *Re Diplock* allowed the defence of inequitability to many of the claims against the charities. However, later cases suggest that this defence should be used sparingly. In *Re Diplock,* two of the charities had used money from the Diplock estate to redeem mortgages on their properties, but it was said to be inequitable to allow a claim of subrogation.

***Re Diplock* [1948] Ch 465**

LORD GREENE MR

If equity is now to create a charge (and we say "create" because there is no survival of the original charge) in favour of the judicial trustee, it will be placing him in a position to insist upon a sale of what was contributed by the charity. The case, as it appears to us, is in effect analogous to the cases where Diplock money is expended on improvements on charity land. The money was in this case used to remove a blot on the title; to give the judicial trustee a charge in respect of the money so used would, we think, be equally unjust to the charity who, as the result of such a charge, would have to submit to a sale of the interest in the property which it brought in. We may point out that if the relief claimed were to be accepted as a correct application of the equitable principle, insoluble problems might arise in a case where in the meanwhile fresh charges on the property had been created or money had been expended upon it.

Link
see Martin in 'Hanbury & Martin Modern Equity', Further Reading.

The use of the defence in such circumstances has attracted criticism, both academic and judicial.

***Boscawen and Others v Bajwa and Another* [1996] 1 WLR 328**

Panel: Stuart-Smith, Waite and Millett LJJ

LORD JUSTICE MILLETT

Taken as a whole, however, the passage cited [from Re Diplock , see above] is an explanation of the reasons why, in the particular circumstances of that case, it was considered unjust to grant the remedy of subrogation. The hospital had changed its position to its detriment. It had in all innocence used the money to redeem a mortgage held by its bank, which, no doubt, was willing to allow its advance to remain outstanding indefinitely so long as it was well secured and the interest was paid punctually. The next of kin were seeking to be subrogated to the bank's security in order to enforce it and enable a proper distribution of the estate to be made. This would have been unjust to the hospital. It may be doubted whether in its anxiety to avoid injustice to the hospital the court may not have done an even greater injustice to the next of kin, who were denied even the interest on their money. Justice did not require the withholding of any remedy, but only that the charge by subrogation should not be enforceable until the hospital had had a reasonable opportunity to obtain a fresh advance on suitable terms from a willing lender, perhaps from the bank which had held the original security.

The House of Lords decision in *Foskett v McKeown* casts further doubt on inequitability being a defence to subrogation.

***Foskett v McKeown and Others* [2001] 1 AC 102**

Panel: Lord Browne-Wilkinson, Lord Steyn, Lord Hoffmann, Lord Hope of Craighead and Lord Millett

LORD BROWNE-WILKINSON

If, as a result of tracing, it can be said that certain of the policy moneys are what now represent part of the assets subject to the trusts of the purchasers trust deed, then as a matter of English property law the purchasers have an absolute interest in such moneys. There is no discretion vested in the court. There is no room for any consideration whether, in the circumstances of this particular case, it is in a moral sense "equitable" for the purchasers to be so entitled. The rules establishing equitable proprietary interests and their enforceability against certain parties have been developed over the centuries and are an integral part of the property law of England. It is a fundamental error to think that, because certain property rights are equitable rather than legal, such rights are in some way discretionary. This case does not depend on whether it is fair, just and reasonable to give the purchasers an interest as a result of which the court in its discretion provides a remedy. It is a case of hard-nosed property rights

LORD MILLETT

Property rights are determined by fixed rules and settled principles. They are not discretionary. They do not depend upon ideas of what is "fair, just and reasonable". Such concepts, which in reality mask decisions of legal policy, have no place in the law of property.

Despite the above, the House of Lords recognised two occasions when it would be inequitable to allow a remedy as a result of tracing. The first of these was the bone fide purchaser for value without notice.

LORD MILLETT

A beneficiary of a trust is entitled to a continuing beneficial interest not merely in the trust property but in its traceable proceeds also, and his interest binds everyone who takes the property or its traceable proceeds except a bona fide purchaser for value without notice.

The second was an innocent volunteer who has spent money on a pre-owned asset

LORD BROWNE -WILKINSON

In certain cases the rules of tracing in such a case may give rise to no proprietary interest at all if to give such interest would be unfair: see *In re Diplock; Diplock v Wintle* [1948] Ch 465, 548.

11.2.6 Change of position

The House of Lords introduced the defence of change of position in *Lipkin Gorman v Karpnale* [1991] 2 AC 548 (see below) and suggested that it could apply to both personal and proprietary claims in equity. In the light of *Foskett v McKeown*, it looks unlikely that this is available as a defence to an equitable *proprietary* claim. This is implied in this extract from that case.

LORD MILLETT

Furthermore, a claim in unjust enrichment is subject to a change of position defence, which usually operates by reducing or extinguishing the element of enrichment. An action like the present [an equitable proprietary claim] is subject to the bona fide purchaser for value defence, which operates to clear the defendant's title.

Further, Lord Millett, having stated in *Boscawen v Bajwa*, when he was Millett LJ, that change of position could be a defence to a proprietary claim, has now stated expressly, extra-judicially in 'Equity in Commercial Law' eds S.Degeling and J. Edelman, that this is not so.

11.3 Personal Claims in Equity

There will be personal claims against recipients of trust property whose knowledge makes it unconscionable for them to receive the property free of trust (see Chapter 16). However there is no general claim in equity against innocent recipients: *Re Montagu's Settlement* [1987] 1 Ch 264. An exception is where money is wrongly paid out in the administration of an estate, rather than from a trust.

***Ministry of Health v Simpson and Others* [1951] AC 251**

Panel: Lord Simonds, Lord Normand, Lord Oaksey, Lord Morton of Henryton and Lord Macdermott

Facts: This was an appeal from the case of *Re Diplock.* The only issue was whether there was a personal claim against the charities.

LORD SIMONDS

I think that it is important in the discussion of this question to remember that the particular branch of the jurisdiction of the Court of Chancery with which we are concerned relates to the administration of assets of a deceased person. While in the development of this jurisdiction certain principles were established which were common to it and to the comparable jurisdiction in the execution of trusts, I do not find in history or in logic any justification for an argument which denies the possibility of an equitable right in the administration of assets because, as it is alleged, no comparable right existed in the execution of trusts. I prefer to look solely at the authorities which are strictly germane to the present question: it is from them alone that the nature and extent of the equity are to be ascertained.

Before I turn back to the 17th century when the Court of Chancery was gradually wresting from the Spiritual Courts the jurisdiction in administering the assets of deceased persons and framing apt rules to that end, I will first refer to a statement made by Lord Davey early in this century, which, as I think, illuminates the position. In *Harrison v Kirk*. Lord Davey says this: "But the Court of Chancery, in order to do justice and to avoid the evil of allowing one man to retain what is really and legally applicable to the payment of another man, devised a remedy by which, where the estate had been distributed either out of court or in court without regard to the rights of a creditor, it has allowed the creditor to recover back what has been paid to the beneficiaries or the next of kin who derive title from the deceased testator or intestate".

The importance of this statement is manifold. It explains the basis of the jurisdiction, the evil to be avoided and its remedy: its clear implication is that no such remedy existed at common law: it does not suggest that it is relevant whether the wrong payment was made under error of law or of fact: it is immaterial whether those who have been wrongly paid are beneficiaries under the will or next of kin, it is sufficient that they derive title from the deceased. It is true that Lord Davey expressly dealt with the case of a claimant creditor not a beneficiary or next of kin. I shall show your Lordships that what he said of the one might equally well be said of the other. It would be strange if a court of equity, whose self-sought duty it was to see that the assets of a deceased person were duly administered and came into the right hands and not into the wrong hands, devised a remedy for the protection of the unpaid creditor but left the unpaid legatee or next of kin unprotected

Alert

The judgment of the Court of Appeal was therefore upheld. The Court of Appeal had allowed the remedy subject to two limitations. The claim was limited to the amount the beneficiaries could not recover from the personal representatives and it was for the principal sum only, no interest being payable.

The charities had no defence to this claim, but since then the defence of change of position has emerged and it is generally accepted that this will apply to such a personal claim.

***Lipkin Gorman (A Firm) v Karpnale Ltd* [1991] 2 AC 548**

Panel: Lord Bridge of Harwich, Lord Templeman, Lord Griffiths, Lord Ackner and Lord Goff of Chieveley

Facts: Cass was a partner in Lipkin Gorman, a firm of solicitors. He was also a compulsive gambler. He took cheques belonging to the firm and used them to get chips at The Playboy Club, the defendant's casino. It was held that, because gaming contracts were unenforceable, the casino had not given consideration, so was not a bone fide purchaser for value without notice. Therefore a claim was available against it for money had and received. A defence of change of position was allowed for the amount it had paid out in winnings.

LORD GOFF OF CHIEVELY

Whether change of position is, or should be, recognised as a defence to claims in restitution is a subject which has been much debated in the books. It is however a matter on which there is a remarkable unanimity of view, the consensus being to the effect that such a defence should be recognised in English law. I myself am under no doubt that this is right.

In these circumstances, it is right that we should ask ourselves: why do we feel that it would be unjust to allow restitution in cases such as these? The answer must be that, where an innocent defendant's position is so changed that he will suffer an injustice if called upon to repay or to repay in full, the injustice of requiring him so to repay outweighs the injustice of denying the plaintiff restitution. If the plaintiff pays money to the defendant under a mistake of fact, and the defendant then, acting in good faith, pays the money or part of it to charity, it is unjust to require the defendant to make restitution to the extent that he has so changed his position. Likewise, on facts such as those in the present case, if a thief steals my money and pays it to a third party who gives it away to charity, that third party should have a good defence to an action for money had and received. In other words, bona fide change of position should of itself be a good defence in such cases as these.

[...]

The time for its recognition in this country is, in my opinion, long overdue.

I am most anxious that, in recognising this defence to actions of restitution, nothing should be said at this stage to inhibit the development of the defence on a case by case basis, in the usual way. It is, of course, plain that the defence is not open to one who has changed his position in bad faith, as where the defendant has paid away the money with knowledge of the facts entitling the plaintiff to restitution; and it is commonly accepted that the defence should not be open to a wrongdoer. These are matters which can, in due course, be considered in depth in cases where they arise for consideration. They do not arise in the present case. Here there is no doubt that the respondents have acted in good faith throughout, and the action is not founded upon any wrongdoing of the respondents. It is not however appropriate in the present case to attempt to identify all those actions in restitution to which change of position may be a defence. A prominent example will, no doubt, be found in those cases where the plaintiff is seeking repayment of money paid under a mistake of fact; but I can see no reason why the defence should not also be available in principle in a case such as the present, where the plaintiff's money has been paid by a thief to an innocent donee, and the plaintiff then seeks repayment from the donee in an action for money had and received. At present I do not wish to state the principle any less broadly than this: that the defence is available to a person whose position has so changed that it would be inequitable in all the circumstances to require him to make restitution, or alternatively to make restitution in full. I wish to stress however that the mere fact that the defendant has spent the money, in whole or in part, does not of itself render it inequitable that he should be called upon to repay, because the expenditure might in any event have been incurred by him in the ordinary course of things. I fear that the mistaken assumption that mere expenditure of money may be regarded as amounting to a change of position for present purposes has led in the past to opposition by some to recognition of a defence which in fact is likely to be available only on comparatively rare occasions. In this connection I have particularly in mind the speech of Lord Simonds in *Ministry of Health v Simpson* [1951] AC 251, 276.

Alert

I wish to add two further footnotes. The defence of change of position is akin to the defence of bona fide purchase; but we cannot simply say that bona fide purchase is a species of change of position. This is because change of position will only avail a defendant to the extent that his position has been changed; whereas, where bona fide purchase is invoked, no inquiry is made (in most cases) into the adequacy of the consideration. Even so, the recognition of change of position as a defence should be doubly beneficial. It will enable a more generous approach to be taken to the recognition of the right to restitution, in the knowledge that the defence is, in appropriate cases, available; and while recognising the different functions of property at law and in equity, there may also in due course develop a more consistent approach to tracing claims, in which common defences are recognised as available to such claims, whether advanced at law or in equity.

Alert

Lord Goff concluded that the casino should have the defence to prevent restitution of the amount it had paid out on winning bets.

The nature and extent of the 'extraordinary expenditure' necessary for the change of position defence was addressed in the next case.

***Phillip Collins Limited v Davis and another* [2000] 3 AER 818**

Panel: Jonathan Parker J

Facts: Two backing musicians to Phil Collins were paid royalties periodically, over several years, for tracks on a live album on which they had performed. When it transpired that they had mistakenly been paid for several tracks on which they had not in fact played, Phil Collins sought to recoup the overpayments. The musicians raised the change of position defence as they had incurred expenditure on the basis of the payments.

The judge identified four principles relating to the defence which were significant in the case. Applying them, he found that the musicians had adjusted their lifestyle and expenditure in accordance with the level of royalty payments, which were their principle source of income. There was no one item of expenditure attributable to the overpayments, but he nonetheless allowed the defence as to one half of the overpayments.

JONATHAN PARKER J

Alert

In the first place, the evidential burden is on the defendant to make good the defence of change of position. However, in applying this principle it seems to me that the court should beware of applying too strict a standard. Depending on the circumstances, it may well be unrealistic to expect a defendant to produce conclusive evidence of change of position, given that when he changed his position he can have had no expectation that he might thereafter have to prove that he did so, and the reason why he did so, in a court of law (see the observations of Slade LJ in *Avon CC v Howlett* [1983] 1 All ER 1073 at 1085-1086, [1983] 1 WLR 605 at 621-622, and Goff and Jones at p 827). In the second place, as Lord Goff stressed in the passage from his speech in the *Lipkin Gorman* case quoted above, to amount to a change of position there must be something more than mere expenditure of the money sought to be recovered, 'because the expenditure might in any event have been incurred in the ordinary course of things'. In the third place, there must be a causal link between the change of position and the overpayment. In *South Tyneside Metropolitan BC v Svenska International plc* [1995] 1 All ER 545, Clarke J, following Hobhouse J in *Kleinwort Benson Ltd v South Tyneside Metropolitan BC* [1994] 4 All ER 972, held that, as a general principle, the change of position must have occurred after receipt of the overpayment, although in Goff & Jones the correctness of this decision is doubted (see pp 822-3). But whether or not a change of position may be anticipatory, it must (as I see it) have been made as a consequence of the receipt of, or (it may be) the prospect of receiving, the money sought to be recovered: in other words it must, on the evidence, be referable in some way to the payment of that money. In the fourth place, as Lord Goff also made clear in his speech in the *Lipkin Gorman* case, in contrast to the defence of estoppel the defence of change of position is not an 'all or nothing' defence: it is available only to the extent that the change of position renders recovery unjust.

[...]

On the basis of the defendants' oral evidence, coupled with such documentary evidence as they were able to produce, I am unable to find that any particular item of expenditure was directly referable to the overpayments of royalties. Their evidence was simply too vague and unspecific to justify such a finding. On the other hand, in the particular circumstances of the instant case the absence of such a finding is not, in my judgment, fatal to the defence of the change of position. Given that the approach of the defendants to their respective financial affairs was, essentially, to gear their outgoings to their income from time to time (usually, it would seem, spending somewhat more than they received), and bearing in mind that the instant case involves not a single overpayment but a series of overpayments at periodic intervals over some six years, it is in my judgment open to the court to find, and I do find, that the overpayments caused a general change of position by the defendants in that they increased their level of outgoing by reference to the sums so paid. In particular, the fact that in the instant case the overpayments took the form of a series of periodical payments over an extended period seems to me to be significant in the context of a defence of change of position, in that it places the defendants in a stronger position to establish a general change of position such as I have described, consequent upon such overpayments.

12

Liability of Strangers

Introduction

This topic concerns third parties (i.e. non-trustees or fiduciaries) who are somehow implicated in a breach of trust or fiduciary duty and so become personally liable for any loss caused by the breach. There are two main heads of liability, 'dishonest assistance' (in older cases referred to as 'knowing assistance') and 'knowing receipt', sometimes referred to as 'unconscionable receipt'.

A knowing recipient is someone who has held trust or principal property for their own benefit, rather than merely as an agent. To the extent that they still hold it or its traceable proceeds, a proprietary claim can be made (see Chapter 11 on Tracing). To the extent that they no longer hold it or its traceable proceeds, the liability is personal, for knowing receipt. A dishonest assistant, however, can be personally liable even if they never held trust or principal property.

It is sometimes said that third parties become liable as 'constructive trustees', although this terminology is not really apt in relation to third parties who never held trust property. What it really means is that they are liable to the beneficiaries in the same way *as if they had been* trustees.

There has been much judicial and academic debate about the basis of liability under either head. This has centred around the kind of knowledge necessary to make the third party personally liable, and whether the requirements for the two heads of liability are the same.

Many of the older cases refer to a five-scale categorisation of knowledge to establish liability from *Baden v Société Générale pour Favoriser le Développement du Commerce et de l'Industrie en France SA* [1993] 1 WLR 509 (the *Baden* scale of knowledge).

***Baden v Société Générale pour Favoriser le Développement du Commerce et de l'Industrie en France SA* [1993] 1 WLR 509**

Panel: Gibson J

Facts: This case concerns financial transactions involving IOS, a large financial complex, which was involved in dishonestly misapplying trust money. The defendant bank received money into trust accounts and, acting on instructions, transferred money from the trust accounts to a Panamanian bank. After the companies involved in the scheme went into liquidation, the defendant was sued. It was held not liable to the beneficiaries as it did not have knowledge at the time that it was assisting a fraudulent scheme. The judge set out five states of knowledge, which have become known as the *Baden* scale, and explained which states will give rise to personal liability.

GIBSON J

...What types of knowledge are relevant for the purposes of constructive trusteeship? Mr. Price submits that knowledge can comprise any one of five different mental states which he described as follows: (i) actual knowledge; (ii) wilfully shutting one's eyes to the obvious; (iii) wilfully and recklessly failing to make such inquiries as an honest and reasonable man would make; (iv) knowledge of circumstances which would indicate the facts to an honest and reasonable man; (v) knowledge of circumstances which would put an honest and reasonable man on inquiry. More accurately, apart from actual knowledge they are formulations of the circumstances which may lead the court to impute knowledge of the facts to the alleged constructive trustee even though he lacked actual knowledge of those facts. Thus the court will treat a person as having constructive knowledge of the facts if he wilfully shuts his eyes to the relevant facts which would be obvious if he opened his eyes, such constructive knowledge being usually termed (though by a metaphor of historical inaccuracy) "Nelsonian knowledge." Similarly the court may treat a person as having constructive knowledge of the facts — "type (iv) knowledge" — if he has actual knowledge of circumstances which would indicate the facts to an honest and reasonable man...

...One logical basis for allowing, as relevant to constructive trusteeship types of constructive knowledge, would be to allow only those types arising from circumstances in which the conscience of the alleged constructive trustee was affected. This would accord with the equitable basis of constructive trusteeship. Thus if a person shuts his eyes to the obvious, or if he wilfully and recklessly fails to make obvious inquiries, that person is guilty of unconscionable behaviour such that a court of equity might wish to impute to him the knowledge that he would have gained by opening his eyes or making the obvious inquiries. To extend the categories of knowledge relevant for the purposes of constructive trusteeship beyond actual knowledge to Nelsonian knowledge, as well as to type (iii) knowledge but no further, accords with the provisional views expressed by Buckley L.J. in *Belmont Finance Corporation Ltd. v. Williams Furniture Ltd.* [1979] Ch. 250, 267. Goff L.J. expressed similar views at p. 275.

The judge then reviewed the cases on whether knowledge of types (iv) and (v) would give rise to liability and concluded:

It is plainly right that a person with Nelsonian knowledge or type (iii) knowledge should be treated as having knowledge for the purpose of constructive trusteeship. It seems to me... that there is a sufficient line of authorities to justify treating a person with type (iv) or type (v) knowledge as having knowledge for that purpose. It is little short of common sense that a person who actually knows all the circumstances from which the honest and reasonable man would have knowledge of the relevant facts should also be treated as having knowledge of the facts. The dividing line between Nelsonian and type (iv) knowledge may often be difficult to discern. If an objective test is appropriate to let in type (iv) knowledge, it would be illogical not to apply a similar objective test in circumstances where the honest and reasonable man would be put on inquiry (type (v) knowledge).

But in my judgment the court should not be astute to impute knowledge where no actual knowledge exists. In particular, it is only in exceptional circumstances that the court should impute type (v) knowledge to an agent like a bank acting honestly on the instructions of its principal but alleged to have provided knowing assistance in a dishonest and fraudulent design. It is not every inquiry that might be made that the court will treat the agent as having been under a duty to make inquiry even though the omitted inquiry would, if made, have led to the agent having knowledge of the facts. If an explanation is offered, the presumption of honesty is strong and the court will not require the agent to be hypercritical in examining that explanation.

12.1 Dishonest Assistance

***Royal Brunei Airlines Sdn. Bhd. v Philip Tan Kok Ming* [1995] 2 AC 378**

Panel: Lord Goff of Chieveley, Lord Ackner, Lord Nicholls of Birkenhead, Lord Steyn and Sir John May

Facts: The plaintiff airline appointed a travel agent, Borneo Leisure Travel (BLT), to sell airline tickets. The agreement expressly provided that the ticket money would be held on trust for the airline until accounted for, although BLT could deduct its commission. BLT paid the ticket money into its ordinary account, not a separate one, and used it for ordinary business purposes, in breach of trust. It fell behind with payments to the airline and became insolvent. The airline brought an action for unpaid money against Tan, the managing director and principal shareholder of BLT. The judge upheld the claim against Tan for knowingly assisting a breach of trust. Tan appealed to the Court of Appeal of Brunei Darussalam, which allowed the appeal on the basis that dishonesty by the trustee BLT had not been established. The airline appealed to the Privy Council, which advised that Tan had acted dishonestly in causing or permitting BLT to commit a breach of trust and so was liable.

LORD NICHOLLS OF BIRKENHEAD delivering the advice of the Board

The proper role of equity in commercial transactions is a topical question. Increasingly plaintiffs have recourse to equity for an effective remedy when the person in default, typically a company, is insolvent. Plaintiffs seek to obtain relief from others who were involved in the transaction, such as directors of the company, or its bankers, or its legal or other advisers. They seek to fasten fiduciary obligations directly onto the company's officers or agents or advisers, or to have them held personally liable for assisting the company in breaches of trust or fiduciary obligations.

This is such a case. An insolvent travel agent company owed money to an airline. The airline seeks a remedy against the travel agent's principal director and shareholder. Its claim is based on the much-quoted dictum of Lord Selborne L.C., sitting in the Court of Appeal in Chancery, in *Barnes v Addy* (1874) LR 9 Ch App 244, 251-252:

"[The responsibility of a trustee] may no doubt be extended in equity to others who are not properly trustees, if they are found ... actually participating in any fraudulent conduct of the trustee to the injury of the *cestui que trust*. But ... strangers are not to be made constructive trustees merely because they act as the agents of trustees in transactions within their legal powers, transactions, perhaps of which a court of equity may disapprove, unless those agents receive and become chargeable with some part of the trust property, or unless they assist with knowledge in a dishonest and fraudulent design on the part of the trustees."

In the conventional shorthand, the first of these two circumstances in which third parties (non-trustees) may become liable to account in equity is "knowing receipt," as distinct from the second, where liability arises from "knowing assistance." ...[T]he first limb ... is concerned with the liability of a person as a recipient of trust property or its traceable proceeds. The second limb is concerned with what ... can be called the liability of an accessory to a trustee's breach of trust. Liability as an accessory is not dependent upon receipt of trust property. ...It is a form of secondary liability... . In the present case the plaintiff airline relies on the accessory limb. ...

[T]he issue on this appeal is whether the breach of trust which is a prerequisite to accessory liability must itself be a dishonest and fraudulent breach of trust by the trustee.

The honest trustee and the dishonest third party

...Take a case where a dishonest solicitor persuades a trustee to apply trust property in a way the trustee honestly believes is permissible but which the solicitor knows full well is a clear breach of trust. The solicitor deliberately conceals this from the trustee. ...[T]he case for liability of the dishonest third party seems stronger where the trustee is innocent, because in such a case the third party alone was dishonest and that was the cause of the ... misapplication of the trust property. ...

[W]hat matters is the state of mind of the third party..., not the state of mind of the trustee. The trustee will be liable in any event for the breach of trust, even if he acted innocently, unless excused by an exemption clause ... or relieved by the court. ...

If the liability of the third party is fault-based, what matters is the nature of his fault, not that of the trustee. ...[D]ishonesty on the part of the third party would seem to be a sufficient basis for his liability, irrespective of the state of mind of the trustee who is in breach of trust. ...The alternative view would mean that ... if the trustee did not act dishonestly that ... would excuse a dishonest third party from liability. That would make no sense.

[...]

No liability

The starting point for any analysis must be to consider the extreme possibility: that a third party who does not receive trust property ought never to be liable directly to the beneficiaries merely because he assisted the trustee to commit a breach of trust or procured him to do so. This possibility can be dismissed summarily. ...[T]he beneficiary should be able to look for recompense to the third party as well as the trustee. Affording the beneficiary a remedy against the third party serves the dual purpose of making good the beneficiary's loss should the trustee lack financial means and imposing a liability which will discourage others from behaving in a similar fashion. ...

Strict liability

The other extreme possibility can also be rejected out of hand. This is the case where a third party deals with a trustee without knowing, or having any reason to suspect, that he is a trustee. Or the case where a third party is aware he is dealing with a trustee but has no reason to know or suspect that their transaction is inconsistent with the terms of the trust. The law has never gone so far as to give ... a remedy against a non-recipient third party in such circumstances. Within defined limits, proprietary rights ... endure against third parties who were unaware of their existence. But accessory liability is concerned with the liability of a person who has not received any property. ...Beneficiaries could not reasonably expect that third parties should deal with trustees at their peril, to the extent that they should become liable ... even when they received no trust property and even when they were unaware and had no reason to suppose that they were dealing with trustees.

Fault-based liability

...[T]he next step is to seek to identify the touchstone of liability. By common accord dishonesty fulfils this role. Whether, in addition, negligence will suffice is an issue on which there has been a well-known difference of judicial opinion. ...[His Lordship cited a number of cases and continued:]

[T]he tide in England has flowed strongly in favour of the test being one of dishonesty... Most, but not all, commentators prefer the test of dishonesty...

Dishonesty

...[I]t will be helpful to define the terms being used by looking more closely at what dishonesty means in this context. Whatever may be the position in some criminal or other contexts (see, for instance, Reg. v Ghosh [1982] QB 1053), in the context of the accessory liability principle acting dishonestly, or with a lack of probity, which is synonymous, means simply not acting as an honest person would in the circumstances. This is an objective standard. At first sight this may seem surprising. Honesty has a connotation of subjectivity, as distinct from the objectivity of negligence. Honesty, indeed, does have a strong subjective element in that it is a description of a type of conduct assessed in the light of what a person actually knew at the time, as distinct from what a reasonable person would have known or appreciated. Further, honesty and its counterpart dishonesty are mostly concerned with advertent conduct, not inadvertent conduct. Carelessness is not dishonesty. Thus for the most part dishonesty is to be equated with conscious impropriety. However, these subjective characteristics of honesty do not mean that individuals are free to set their own

Alert

standards of honesty in particular circumstances. The standard of what constitutes honest conduct is not subjective. ...If a person knowingly appropriates another's property, he will not escape a finding of dishonesty simply because he sees nothing wrong in such behaviour.

In most situations there is little difficulty in identifying how an honest person would behave. Honest people do not intentionally deceive others to their detriment. Honest people do not knowingly take others' property. Unless there is a very good and compelling reason, an honest person does not participate in a transaction if he knows it involves a misapplication of trust assets to the detriment of the beneficiaries. Nor does an honest person in such a case deliberately close his eyes and ears, or deliberately not ask questions, lest he learn something he would rather not know, and then proceed regardless. ...

Taking risks

...Imprudence is not dishonesty, although imprudence may be carried recklessly to lengths which call into question the honesty of the person making the decision. This is especially so if the transaction serves another purpose in which that person has an interest of his own. ...

The individual is expected to attain the standard which would be observed by an honest person placed in those circumstances. It is impossible to be more specific. ...Acting in reckless disregard of others' rights or possible rights can be a tell-tale sign of dishonesty. ...Ultimately, in most cases, an honest person should have little difficulty in knowing whether a proposed transaction, or his participation in it, would offend the normally accepted standards of honest conduct.

Alert

Likewise, when called upon to decide whether a person was acting honestly, a court will look at all the circumstances known to the third party at the time. The court will also have regard to personal attributes of the third party, such as his experience and intelligence, and the reason why he acted as he did.

...To inquire ... whether a person dishonestly assisted in ... a breach of trust is to ask a meaningful question... . This is not always so if the question is posed in terms of "knowingly" assisted. Framing the question in the latter form all too often leads one into tortuous convolutions about the "sort" of knowledge required, when the truth is that "knowingly" is inapt as a criterion when applied to the gradually darkening spectrum where the differences are of degree and not kind.

Negligence

It is against this background that the question of negligence is to be addressed. This question ... is directed at whether an honest third party who receives no trust property should be liable if he procures or assists in a breach of trust of which he would have become aware had he exercised reasonable diligence. Should he be liable to the beneficiaries for the loss they suffer... ?

...[T]heir Lordships consider that dishonesty is an essential ingredient here. ...As a general proposition, ... beneficiaries cannot reasonably expect that all the world dealing with their trustees should owe them a duty to take care lest the trustees are behaving dishonestly.

Unconscionable conduct

Mention, finally, must be made of the suggestion that the test for liability is that of unconscionable conduct. Unconscionable is a word of immediate appeal to an equity lawyer. ...It must be recognised, however, that unconscionable is not a word in everyday use by non-lawyers. If ... it is to be the touchstone for liability as an accessory, it is essential to be clear on what, *in this context*, unconscionable *means*. If unconscionable means no more than dishonesty, then dishonesty is the preferable label. If unconscionable means something different, it must be said that it is not clear what that something different is. Either way, therefore, the term is better avoided in this context.

Link

Note the adoption of 'unconscionability' as the basis of liability for knowing receipt in *BCCI v Akindele.*

The accessory liability principle

Drawing the threads together, their Lordships' overall conclusion is that dishonesty is a necessary ingredient of accessory liability. It is also a sufficient ingredient. A liability in equity to make good resulting loss attaches to a person who dishonestly procures or assists in a breach of trust or fiduciary obligation. It is not necessary that, in addition, the trustee or fiduciary was acting dishonestly, although this will usually be so where the third party who is assisting him is acting dishonestly. "Knowingly" is better avoided as a defining ingredient of the principle, and in the context of this principle the Baden [1993] 1 W.L.R. 509 scale of knowledge is best forgotten.

Link

For further discussion of the relevance of the Baden scale, see per Nourse LJ in *BCCI v Akindele.*

Conclusion

From this statement of the principle it follows that this appeal succeeds. [...]

Although only of persuasive authority, the Privy Council's decision in *Tan* was generally seen as bringing clarity in relation to this head of liability. For that reason, the majority in the House of Lords in the next case purported to adopt the reasoning from *Tan*. However, they appeared to give a different interpretation to the subjective element of dishonesty.

***Twinsectra Ltd v Yardley and others* [2002] 2 AC 164**

Panel: Lord Slynn of Hadley, Lord Steyn, Lord Hoffmann, Lord Hutton and Lord Millett

Facts: Twinsectra lent money to Yardley and received an undertaking from Yardley's solicitor, Sims, that the money would be used solely for the acquisition of property on Yardley's behalf and for no other purpose and would be retained by Sims until so applied. In breach of the undertaking, Sims transferred the money to Leach, another solicitor acting for Yardley. Leach was aware of the terms of the undertaking but paid the money out on Yardley's instructions without ensuring that it would be used for acquiring property. Some of the money was used for other purposes. When the loan was not repaid,

Twinsectra brought a number of claims, including a claim against Leach for dishonestly assisting in a breach of trust. The judge held that the money was not subject to a trust and that Leach was not dishonest. The Court of Appeal allowed Twinsectra's appeal, holding that the terms of the undertaking created a trust for Twinsectra and that Leach was dishonest and therefore liable. Leach appealed to the House of Lords, which held unanimously that the money was subject to a trust but, Lord Millett dissenting, that Leach was not liable for dishonest assistance.

LORD HOFFMANN

...The terms of the trust upon which Sims held the money must be found in the undertaking which ... made it clear that the money was not to be at the free disposal of Mr Yardley. ...

Link
For the meaning of 'the combined test' see the speech of Lord Hutton.

The ... question is whether Mr Leach, in receiving the money and paying it to Mr Yardley without concerning himself about its application, could be said to have acted dishonestly. The judge found that in so doing he was "misguided" but not dishonest. He had "shut his eyes" to some of the problems but thought he held the money to the order of Mr Yardley without restriction. The Court of Appeal reversed this finding and held that he had been dishonest.

...Lord Millett considers that the Court of Appeal was justified in taking this view because liability as an accessory to a breach of trust does not depend upon dishonesty in the normal sense of that expression. It is sufficient that the defendant knew all the facts which made it wrongful for him to participate in the way in which he did. In this case, Mr Leach knew ... all the facts... .

I do not think that it is fairly open to your Lordships to take this view of the law without departing from the principles laid down by the Privy Council in *Royal Brunei*... . For the reasons given by ... Lord Hutton, I consider that those principles require more than knowledge of the facts which make the conduct wrongful. They require a dishonest state of mind, that is to say, consciousness that one is transgressing ordinary standards of honest behaviour. I also agree ... that the Court of Appeal was not entitled ... to make a finding of dishonesty which the judge ... did not.

Alert

...I do respectfully think it was unfortunate that the judge three times used the expression "shut his eyes" to "the details", or "the problems", or "the implications". The expression produces in judges a reflex image of Admiral Nelson at Copenhagen and the common use of this image by lawyers to signify a deliberate abstinence from inquiry in order to avoid certain knowledge of what one suspects to be the case... . But ... there were in this case no relevant facts of which Mr Leach was unaware. What I think the judge meant was that he took a blinkered approach to his professional duties as a solicitor, or buried his head in the sand... . But neither of those would be dishonest.

Mr Leach believed that the money was at the disposal of Mr Yardley. He thought that whether Mr Yardley's use of the money would be contrary to the assurance he had given Mr Sims or put Mr Sims in breach of his undertaking

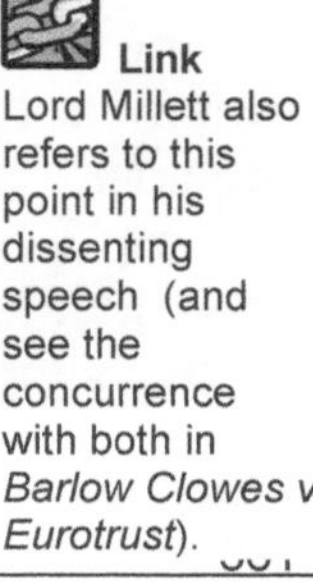

Link
Lord Millett also refers to this point in his dissenting speech (and see the concurrence with both in *Barlow Clowes v Eurotrust*).

was a matter between those two gentlemen. Such a state of mind may have been wrong. It may have been, as the judge said, misguided. But if he honestly believed, as the judge found, that the money was at Mr Yardley's disposal, he was not dishonest. ...

A person may dishonestly assist in ... a breach of trust without any idea of what a trust means. The necessary dishonest state of mind may be found to exist simply on the fact that he knew perfectly well that he was helping to pay away money to which the recipient was not entitled. But that was not the case here. I would therefore allow the appeal... .

LORD HUTTON

...I agree that the undertaking ... created a trust...

[W]hether the Court of Appeal was right to hold that Mr Leach had acted dishonestly depends on the meaning to be given to that term in the judgment ... in *Royal Brunei Airlines Snd Bhd v Tan...*

[T]here are three possible standards which can be applied to determine whether a person has acted dishonestly. There is a purely subjective standard, whereby a person is only regarded as dishonest if he transgresses his own standard of honesty, even if that standard is contrary to that of reasonable and honest people. This has been termed the "Robin Hood test" and has been rejected... .

Secondly, there is a purely objective standard whereby a person acts dishonestly if his conduct is dishonest by the ordinary standards of reasonable and honest people, even if he does not realise this. Thirdly, there is a standard which combines an objective test and a subjective test, and ... requires that before there can be a finding of dishonesty it must be established that the defendant's conduct was dishonest by the ordinary standards of reasonable and honest people and that he himself realised that by those standards his conduct was dishonest. I will term this "the combined test".

See the speech of Lord Steyn who accepted this as the correct test.

There is a passage in ... the judgment in *Royal Brunei* which suggests that Lord Nicholls considered that dishonesty has a subjective element. Thus in discussing the honest trustee and the dishonest third party ... he stated: " ...[W]hat matters is the state of mind of the third party... ."

[...] Lord Nicholls stated the general principle that dishonesty is a necessary ingredient of accessory liability and that knowledge is not an appropriate test...

There is, in my opinion, a further consideration which supports the view that ... the defendant must himself appreciate that what he was doing was dishonest by the standards of honest and reasonable men. A finding by a judge that a defendant has been dishonest is a grave finding, and it is particularly grave against a professional man, such as a solicitor. Notwithstanding that the issue arises in equity law and not in a criminal context, I think that it would be less than just for the law to permit a finding that a defendant had been "dishonest" in assisting in a breach of trust where he knew of the facts which created the trust and its breach but had not been aware that what he was doing would be regarded by honest men as being dishonest.

It would be open to your Lordships to depart from the principle stated by Lord Nicholls that dishonesty is a necessary ingredient ... and to hold that knowledge is a sufficient ingredient. But the statement of that principle by Lord Nicholls has been widely regarded as clarifying this area of the law and, as he observed, the tide of authority in England has flowed strongly in favour of the test of dishonesty. Therefore I consider that the courts should continue to apply that test and that your Lordships should state that dishonesty requires knowledge by the defendant that what he was doing would be regarded as dishonest by honest people, although he should not escape a finding of dishonesty because he sets his own standards of honesty and does not regard as dishonest what he knows would offend the normally accepted standards of honest conduct. ...

Alert

At the trial Mr Leach was cross-examined very closely and at length about his state of mind when he paid to Mr Yardley the moneys transferred to him by Mr Sims. The tenor of his replies was that he paid the moneys to his client because his client instructed him to do so. [...]

It would have been open to the judge to hold that Mr Leach was dishonest... . But the experienced judge who was observing Mr Leach being cross-examined at length found that Mr Leach, although misguided, was not dishonest in carrying out his client's instructions.

The judge did not give reasons for this finding or state what test he applied to determine dishonesty, but I think it probable that he applied the combined test and I infer that he considered that Mr Leach did not realise that in acting on his client's instructions in relation to the moneys he was acting in a way which a responsible and honest solicitor would regard as dishonest. ...

It is only in exceptional circumstances that an appellate court should reverse a finding by a trial judge on a question of fact (and particularly on the state of mind of a party)... . Therefore I do not think that it would have been right for the Court of Appeal in this case to have come to a different conclusion from the judge and to have held that Mr Leach was dishonest in that ... he knew that his conduct was dishonest by the standards of responsible and honest solicitors. ...

I agree ... that it is unfortunate that Carnwath J referred to Mr Leach deliberately shutting his eyes... but like Lord Hoffmann I do not think it probable that having cited the passage from the judgment of Lord Nicholls ... the judge then overlooked the issue of Nelsonian dishonesty in finding that Mr Leach was not dishonest. ...[T]his was not a case where Mr Leach deliberately closed his eyes and ears, or deliberately did not ask questions ... - he already knew all the facts, but the judge concluded that nevertheless he had not been dishonest. I also think that Potter LJ applied too strict a test when he stated... : "It seems to me that, save perhaps in the most exceptional circumstances, it is not the action of an honest solicitor knowingly to assist or encourage another solicitor in a deliberate breach of his undertaking." This test does not address the vital point whether Mr Leach realised that his action was dishonest by the standards of responsible and honest solicitors. ...

I would allow Mr Leach's appeal and set aside the judgment of the Court of Appeal.

LORD MILLETT

My Lords, there are two issues in this appeal. The first is concerned with the nature of the so-called "Quistclose trust" and the requirements for its creation. The second ... is whether his [the appellant's] conduct rendered him liable for having assisted in a breach of trust. This raises two questions of some importance. One concerns the extent of the knowledge of the existence of a trust which is required before a person can be found civilly liable for having assisted in its breach. ...The other, which has led to a division of opinion among your Lordships, is whether, in addition to knowledge, dishonesty is required and, if so, the meaning of dishonesty in this context. ...

Link
For more detail on this, see Chapter 9 on Resulting Trusts.

[His Lordship concluded that the undertaking created a *Quistclose* trust. He continued:] Twinsectra parted with the money to Mr Sims, relying on him to ensure that the money was properly applied or returned to it. Mr Sims' act in paying the money over to Mr Leach was a breach of trust... .

Knowing (or dishonest) assistance

...Liability for "knowing receipt" is receipt-based. ...There is no basis for requiring actual knowledge of the breach of trust, let alone dishonesty, as a condition of liability. Constructive notice is sufficient, and may not even be necessary. There is powerful academic support for the proposition that the liability of the recipient is the same as in other cases of restitution, that is to say strict but subject to a change of position defence.

Link
See the discussion of this point in *BCCI v Akindele*.

Mr Leach received sums totalling £22,000 in payment of his costs for his own use and benefit, and Twinsectra seek their repayment on the ground of knowing receipt. But he did not receive the rest of the money for his own benefit at all. He never regarded himself as beneficially entitled to the money. He held it to Mr Yardley's order... . Twinsectra cannot and does not base its claim in respect of these moneys in knowing receipt, not for want of knowledge, but for want of the necessary receipt. It sues in respect of knowing (or dishonest) assistance.

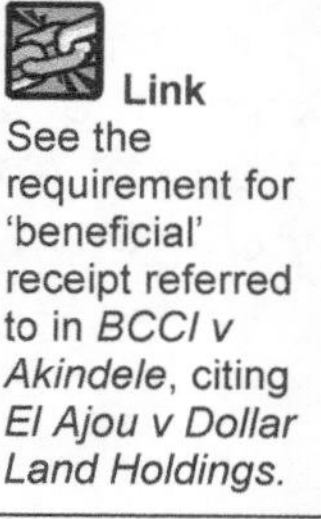

Link
See the requirement for 'beneficial' receipt referred to in *BCCI v Akindele*, citing *El Ajou v Dollar Land Holdings*.

The accessory's liability for having assisted in a breach of trust is quite different. It is fault-based, not receipt-based. ..[T]he claimant seeks compensation for wrongdoing. ...Liability is not restricted to the person whose breach of trust or fiduciary duty caused [the] original diversion [of funds]. His liability is strict. Nor is it limited to those who assist him in the original breach. It extends to everyone who consciously assists in the continuing diversion of the money. Most of the cases have been concerned, not with assisting in the original breach, but in covering it up afterwards by helping to launder the money. Mr Leach's wrongdoing is not confined to the assistance he gave Mr Sims to commit a breach of trust by receiving the money from him knowing that Mr Sims should not have paid it to him (though this is sufficient to render him liable for any resulting loss); it extends to the assistance he gave in the subsequent misdirection of the money by paying it out to Mr Yardley's order without seeing to its proper application.

The ingredients of accessory liability

...Since ...[*Royal Brunei Airlines Sdn Bhd v Tan*] it has been clear that actual knowledge is necessary; the question is whether it is sufficient, or whether there is an additional requirement of dishonesty in the subjective sense in which that term is used in criminal cases.[...]

The meaning of dishonesty in this context

In taking dishonesty to be the condition of liability, however, Lord Nicholls used the word in an objective sense. He did not employ the concept of dishonesty as it is understood in criminal cases. ... [His Lordship cited the passage beginning "Whatever may be the position in some criminal or other contexts" and ending "and then proceed regardless." Extracted above and continued:]

Dishonesty as a state of mind or as a course of conduct?

In *R v Ghosh* [1982] QB 1053, Lord Lane CJ drew a distinction between dishonesty as a state of mind and dishonesty as a course of conduct, and held that dishonesty in section 1 of the Theft Act 1968 referred to dishonesty as a state of mind. The question was not whether the accused had in fact acted dishonestly but whether he was aware that he was acting dishonestly. ...

The same test of dishonesty is applicable in civil cases where, for example, liability depends upon intent to defraud, for this connotes a dishonest state of mind. ...But it is not generally an appropriate condition of civil liability, which does not ordinarily require a guilty mind. Civil liability is usually predicated on the defendant's conduct rather than his state of mind; it results from his negligent or unreasonable behaviour or, where this is not sufficient, from intentional wrongdoing. ...

Lord Nicholls rejected a dishonest state of mind as an appropriate condition of liability. This is evident from the opening sentence of the passage cited above, from his repeated references ... to the defendant's conduct in "acting dishonestly" and "advertent conduct", and from his statement that "for the most part" (i.e. not always) it involves "conscious impropriety". "Honesty," he said, "is a description of a type of conduct assessed in the light of what a person actually knew at the time." Usually ("for the most part"), no doubt, the defendant will have been guilty of "conscious impropriety"; but this is not a condition of liability. ...There is no trace in Lord Nicholls' opinion that the defendant should have been aware that he was acting contrary to objective standards of dishonesty. In my opinion, in rejecting the test of dishonesty adopted in *R v Ghosh* ... Lord Nicholls was using the word to characterise the defendant's conduct, not his state of mind.

...[H]is approach to dishonesty is premised on the belief that it is dishonest for a man consciously to participate in the misapplication of money. This is ... most clearly evident in the way in which Lord Nicholls described the conduct of the defendant in the case under appeal. ...:

" ...[H]e caused or permitted his company to apply the money in a way he knew was not authorised by the trust... . Set out in these bald terms, the defendant's conduct was dishonest."

There was no evidence and Lord Nicholls did not suggest that the defendant realised that honest people would regard his conduct as dishonest. ...

In my opinion Lord Nicholls was adopting an objective standard of dishonesty by which the defendant is expected to attain the standard which would be observed by an honest person placed in similar circumstances. Account must be taken of subjective considerations such as the defendant's experience and intelligence and his actual state of knowledge at the relevant time. But it is not necessary that he should actually have appreciated that he was acting dishonestly...

Alert

The only subjective elements are those relating to the defendant's knowledge, experience and attributes. ...The question is whether an honest person would appreciate that what he was doing was wrong or improper, not whether the defendant himself actually appreciated this. The third limb of the test established for criminal cases in *R v Ghosh* ... is conspicuously absent. ...

The modern tendency is to deprecate the use of words like "fraud" and "dishonesty"... . There is much to be said for ... changing the language while retaining the incidents of equitable liability; but there is nothing to be said for retaining the language and giving it the meaning it has in criminal cases so as to alter the incidents of equitable liability.

Should subjective dishonesty be required?

The question for your Lordships is ... whether a plaintiff should be required to establish that an accessory to a breach of trust had a dishonest state of mind (so that he was subjectively dishonest in the *R v Ghosh* sense); or whether it should be sufficient to establish that he acted with the requisite knowledge (so that his conduct was objectively dishonest). ...[W]e are free to resolve it either way.

I would resolve it by adopting the objective approach. I would do so because:

(1) Consciousness of wrongdoing is an aspect of mens rea and an appropriate condition of criminal liability: it is not an appropriate condition of civil liability. ...For ... civil liability, it should not be necessary that the defendant realised that his conduct was dishonest; it should be sufficient that it constituted intentional wrongdoing.

Link
See the similar view expressed by Arden LJ in *Abou-Rahmah v Abac*.

(2) The objective test is in accordance with Lord Selborne's statement in *Barnes v Addy*... and traditional doctrine. This taught that a person who knowingly participates in the misdirection of money is liable to compensate the injured party. While negligence is not a sufficient condition of liability, intentional wrongdoing is. Such conduct is culpable

> and falls below the objective standards of honesty adopted by ordinary people. ...

If we were to reject subjective dishonesty as a requirement of civil liability in this branch of the law, the remaining question is merely a semantic one. Should we return to the traditional description of the claim as "knowing assistance", reminding ourselves that nothing less than actual knowledge is sufficient; or should we adopt Lord Nicholls' description of the claim as "dishonest assistance", reminding ourselves that the test is an objective one?

For my own part, I have no difficulty in equating the knowing mishandling of money with dishonest conduct. But the introduction of dishonesty is ... conducive to error. Many judges would be reluctant to brand a professional man as dishonest where he was unaware that honest people would consider his conduct to be so. If the condition of liability is intentional wrongdoing and not conscious dishonesty as understood in the criminal courts, I think that we should return to the traditional description of this head of equitable liability as arising from "knowing assistance".

Alert

Knowledge

...It is sufficient that he knows that the money is not at the free disposal of the principal. In some circumstances it may not even be necessary that his knowledge should extend this far. It may be sufficient that he knows that he is assisting in a dishonest scheme.

...[K]nowledge of the arrangements which constitute the trust is sufficient; it is not necessary that the defendant should appreciate that they do so. Of course, if they do not create a trust, then he will not be liable for having assisted in a breach of trust. But he takes the risk that they do.

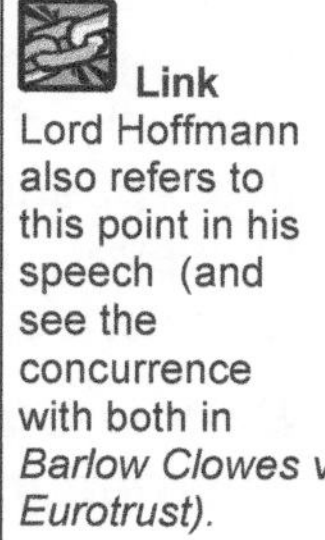
Link
Lord Hoffmann also refers to this point in his speech (and see the concurrence with both in *Barlow Clowes v Eurotrust*).

...[T]he accessory is ... assisting a person ... entrusted with the control of a fund to dispose of the fund in an unauthorised manner. He should be liable if he knows of the arrangements by which that person obtained control of the money and that his authority to deal with the money was limited, and participates in a dealing with the money in a manner which he knows is unauthorised. I do not believe that the man in the street would have any doubt that such conduct was culpable. ...

Conclusion

I do not think that this was a case of wilful blindness, or that the judge overlooked the possibility of imputed knowledge. There was no need to impute knowledge to Mr Leach, for there was no relevant fact of which he was unaware. ...He knew of the terms of the undertaking, that the money was not to be at Mr Yardley's free disposal. ...There were no enquiries which Mr Leach needed to make to satisfy himself that the money could properly be put at Mr Yardley's free disposal. He knew it could not. The only thing that he did not know was that the terms of the undertaking created a trust...

> Yet ... he treated it as held to Mr Yardley's order and at Mr Yardley's free disposition. He did not shut his eyes to the facts, but to ... the impropriety of putting the money at Mr Yardley's disposal. His explanation was that this was Mr Sims' problem, not his.
>
> Mr Leach knew that Twinsectra had entrusted the money to Mr Sims with only limited authority to dispose of it; that Twinsectra trusted Mr Sims to ensure that the money was not used except for the acquisition of property; that Mr Sims had betrayed the confidence placed in him by paying the money to him (Mr Leach) without seeing to its further application; and that by putting it at Mr Yardley's free disposal he took the risk that the money would be applied for an unauthorised purpose and place Mr Sims in breach of his undertaking. But all that was Mr Sims's responsibility.
>
> In my opinion this is enough to make Mr Leach civilly liable as an accessory ... for assisting in a breach of trust. It is unnecessary to consider whether Mr Leach realised that honest people would regard his conduct as dishonest. His knowledge that he was assisting Mr Sims to default in his undertaking to Twinsectra is sufficient.

The general view of this decision was that the majority had misinterpreted the subjective element of dishonesty as set out in *Tan* and had introduced an additional requirement that the defendant must realise that his conduct would be regarded as dishonest by ordinary people. Lord Millett was viewed as correctly interpreting the meaning given to dishonesty in *Tan* and his view on this appears to have been vindicated in subsequent decisions (see below). However, his suggestion that the terminology should revert to 'knowing' assistance, and the label of dishonesty be dropped, has not been adopted.

***Barlow Clowes International Ltd (in liquidation) and others v Eurotrust International Ltd and others* [2006] 1 WLR 1476**

Panel: Lord Nicholls of Birkenhead, Lord Steyn, Lord Hoffmann, Lord Walker of Gestingthorpe and Lord Carswell

Facts: Barlow Clowes Ltd (a company in Gibraltar) fraudulently promised UK investors high returns from investments in UK gilt-edged securities. In fact, the money was mainly spent by Peter Clowes and his associate, Cramer, on speculative personal investments and extravagant living. Some of the investors' money was paid through bank accounts of companies administered by ITC, an Isle of Man company. The principal directors of ITC, including Mr Henwood, were sued (in the Isle of Man High Court) by Barlow Clowes Ltd (in administration) for dishonestly assisting Mr Clowes. They were found liable by the Acting Deemster (Isle of Man equivalent of High Court judge). Mr Henwood's appeal to the Staff of Government Division of the High Court (Isle of Man appeal court) was allowed. Barlow Clowes then appealed to the Judicial Committee of the Privy Council, which held that the Acting Deemster's decision should be restored.

LORD HOFFMANN delivering the advice of the Board

...The judge stated the law in terms largely derived from the advice of the Board ... in *Royal Brunei Airlines Sdn Bhd v Tan*... . In summary, she said that liability for dishonest assistance requires a dishonest state of mind on the part of the person who assists in a breach of trust. Such a state of mind may consist in knowledge that the transaction is one in which he cannot honestly participate (for example, a misappropriation of other people's money), or it may consist in suspicion combined with a conscious decision not to make inquiries which might result in knowledge... . Although a dishonest state of mind is a subjective mental state, the standard by which the law determines whether it is dishonest is objective. If by ordinary standards a defendant's mental state would be characterised as dishonest, it is irrelevant that the defendant judges by different standards. The Court of Appeal held this to be a correct statement of the law and their Lordships agree.

Alert

The judge found that during and after June 1987 Mr Henwood strongly suspected that the funds passing through his hands were moneys which Barlow Clowes had received from members of the public who thought that they were subscribing to a scheme of investment in gilt-edged securities. If those suspicions were correct, no honest person could have assisted Mr Clowes and Mr Cramer to dispose of the funds for their personal use. But Mr Henwood consciously decided not to make inquiries because he preferred in his own interest not to run the risk of discovering the truth.

Their Lordships consider that by ordinary standards such a state of mind is dishonest. The judge found that Mr Henwood may well have lived by different standards and seen nothing wrong in what he was doing. He had an: 'exaggerated notion of dutiful service to clients, which produced a warped moral approach that it was not improper to treat carrying out clients' instructions as being all important. Mr Henwood may well have thought this to be an honest attitude, but, if so, he was wrong.'

Lord Neill of Bladen QC, who appeared for Mr Henwood, submitted to their Lordships that such a state of mind was not dishonest unless Mr Henwood was aware that it would by ordinary standards be regarded as dishonest. Only in such a case could he be said to be consciously dishonest. But the judge made no finding about Mr Henwood's opinions about normal standards of honesty. The only finding was that by normal standards he had been dishonest but that his own standard was different.

...Lord Neill relied upon a statement by Lord Hutton in *Twinsectra Ltd v Yardley*... , with which the majority of their Lordships agreed... .

Their Lordships accept that there is an element of ambiguity in these remarks which may have encouraged a belief, expressed in some academic writing, that the *Twinsectra* case had departed from the law as previously understood and invited inquiry not merely into the defendant's mental state about the nature of the transaction in which he was participating but also into his views about generally acceptable standards of honesty. But they do not consider that this is what Lord Hutton meant.

The reference to 'what he knows would offend normally accepted standards of honest conduct' meant only that his knowledge of the transaction had to be such as to render his participation contrary to normally acceptable standards of honest conduct. It did not require that he should have had reflections about what those normally acceptable standards were.

Similarly in the speech of Lord Hoffmann, the statement ... that a dishonest state of mind meant 'consciousness that one is transgressing ordinary standards of honest behaviour' was in their Lordships' view intended to require consciousness of those elements of the transaction which make participation transgress ordinary standards of honest behaviour. It did not also require him to have thought about what those standards were.

On the facts of the *Twinsectra* case, neither the judge who acquitted Mr Leach of dishonesty nor the House undertook any inquiry into the views of ... Mr Leach about ordinary standards of honest behaviour. ...The judge found that he was not dishonest because he honestly believed that the undertaking did not, so to speak, run with the money and that, as between him and his client, he held it for his client unconditionally. He was therefore bound to pay it upon his client's instructions without restriction on its use. The majority in the House of Lords considered that a solicitor who held this view of the law, even though he knew all the facts, was not by normal standards dishonest.

Their Lordships therefore reject Lord Neill's submission that the judge failed to apply the principles of liability for dishonest assistance which had been laid down in the Twinsectra case. In their opinion they were no different from the principles stated in Royal Brunei Airlines Sdn Bhd v Tan ... which were correctly summarised by the judge. ...

Their Lordships consider that ... it was not necessary ... that Mr Henwood should have concluded that the disposals were of moneys held in trust. It was sufficient that he should have entertained a clear suspicion that this was the case. ...[I]t is quite unreal to suppose that Mr Henwood needed to know all the details ... before he had grounds to suspect that Mr Clowes and Mr Cramer were misappropriating their investors' money. The money in Barlow Clowes was either held on trust for the investors or else belonged to the company and was subject to fiduciary duties on the part of the directors. In either case, Mr Clowes and Mr Cramer could not have been entitled to make free with it as they pleased. In *Brinks Ltd v Abu-Saleh (No 3)* [1996] CLC 133 at 151 Rimer J expressed the opinion that a person cannot be liable for dishonest assistance in a breach of trust unless he knows of the existence of the trust or at least the facts giving rise to the trust. But their Lordships do not agree. Someone can know, and can certainly suspect, that he is assisting in a misappropriation of money without knowing that the money is held on trust or what a trust means: see Twinsectra Ltd v Yardley ... (Lord Hoffmann) and ... (Lord Millett). And it was not necessary to know the 'precise involvement' of Mr Cramer in the

group's affairs in order to suspect that neither he nor anyone else had the right to use Barlow Clowes money for speculative investments of their own.

...[T]here was abundant evidence on which the judge was entitled to make the findings of fact which she did... . The Staff of Government Division should not have set them aside.

This case returned to the meaning of dishonesty set out in *Tan*. However, like *Tan*, it is only of persuasive authority, whereas the decision of the House of Lords in *Twinsectra* is binding. In the next case, Arden LJ, in the Court of Appeal, took the view that the decision of the Privy Council in *Barlow Clowes v Eurotrust* should be followed. The other two Lord Justices preferred not to commit themselves on the subject of the relationship between that case and the case of *Twinsectra*.

***Abou-Ramah and another v Abacha and others* [2007] 1 All ER (Comm) 827**

Panel: Pill, Rix and Arden LJJ

Facts: Abou-Rahmah (a lawyer in Kuwait) was asked by fraudsters to assist in investing a large sum in an Arab country. He was told that it was money from a trust but that the money was in Benin and could only be transferred out if certain payments were made. On the fraudsters' instructions, he made payments to a London-based account of City Express Bank, a Nigerian bank. The Bank transferred it to the account in Nigeria of Trusty International, a company run by Ibrahim and Saminu, who were accomplices in the fraud. The fraudsters disappeared. Abou-Rahmah sued City Express Bank for dishonest assistance in a breach of trust. The judge found that the fraud amounted to a breach of trust and that the Bank's local manager, Mr Farobi, who dealt with the opening of the Trusty International account, had suspected that Ibrahim and Saminu might sometimes assist corrupt politicians to launder money, but did not have any particular suspicions about the transactions involved in the case. The judge found that the bank did not act dishonestly, so the claim failed. The claimant appealed to the Court of Appeal which upheld the judge's decision.

LORD JUSTICE RIX

...Knowing/dishonest assistance

The Privy Council's decision in Barlow Clowes emerged only after trial, pending judgment. The judge invited, and received, further written submissions in the light of that decision. ...

It would seem that a claimant in this area needs to show three things: first, that a defendant has the requisite knowledge; secondly, that, given that knowledge, the defendant acts in a way which is contrary to normally acceptable standards of honest conduct (the objective test of honesty or dishonesty); and thirdly, possibly, that the defendant must in some sense be dishonest himself (a subjective test of dishonesty which might, on analysis, add little or nothing to knowledge of the facts which, objectively, would make his conduct dishonest).

It is the third element which raises a problem of definition in the light of Twinsectra and Barlow Clowes. In commenting on Twinsectra before Barlow Clowes, Snell's Equity, 31st ed, 2005, at 692/3 (para 28-46) put the matter in this way:

"The Defendant must be proved to have been dishonest in giving his assistance to the trustee's breach. In applying this standard the Defendant is not free to be judged according to his standards of dishonesty. Nor is he to be judged by a purely objective standard of whether an ordinary honest person in his position would regard his conduct as dishonest. Rather, it must be established that he knew that ordinary honest people would regard his assistance as dishonest in all the circumstances."

In commenting on the subject-matter after Barlow Clowes, however, Snell ... has replaced the above paragraph with the following:

"The Defendant must be proved to have been dishonest in giving his assistance to the trustee's breach. In applying this standard, it is clear that the Defendant is not free to be judged according to his own standards of honesty. He is judged according [to] the standard of ordinary honest people (Royal Brunei Airlines Sdn Bhd v Tan...). The authorities have in the past been uncertain about whether the trustee [sic] also needs to be aware that his conduct would be regarded as dishonest by this standard. The better view is that it is unnecessary for the Defendant to take a view on the propriety of his conduct. (Compare Twinsectra Ltd v Yardley ... with Barlow Clowes v Eurotrust International Ltd...). A finding that the Defendant was dishonest need only involve an assessment of his participation in the light of his knowledge of the facts of the transaction."

In Twinsectra the House of Lords split ... on the question whether the dishonesty spoken of in Tan was objective or subjective. The majority ... were in favour of a subjective test. ...

Lord Millett, however, was for adopting an objective approach as being more apposite to civil as distinct from criminal liability... . He would therefore have placed particular weight on the requirement of knowledge...

In Barlow Clowes ... [t]he single judgment was delivered by Lord Hoffmann. There are passages in the judgment which have raised academic controversy (see for instance LQR 2006 171, JIBLR 2006 377) as to whether the Privy Council has in Barlow Clowes rowed back towards Lord Millett's views in Twinsectra... . [His Lordship cited the passage where Lord Hoffmann commented on his own speech in Twinsectra and continued:]

I do not need to enter into that controversy for the purposes of this appeal. It is sufficient to concentrate on what was said in Barlow Clowes about the element of knowledge required to set up an investigation of the subsequent element of dishonesty. For in this respect, the Privy Council underlined that there may be sufficient knowledge (a) in suspicion and (b) despite ignorance that money is held on trust at all. ...

[O]nce Mr Faronbi suspected Trusty International's directors of participating in money laundering, ... the distinction which the judge then drew between Mr Faronbi's suspicions of the business in general and his ignorance about the particular transactions in question ... becomes a thin line... . It is one thing to be negligent in failing to spot a possible money launderer, providing the negligence does not extend to shutting one's eyes to the truth. It is another thing ... to have good grounds for suspecting money laundering and then to proceed as though one did not. ...I do not see why a bank which has, through its managers, a clear suspicion that a prospective client indulges in money laundering, can be said to lack that knowledge...

However, ...where the trial judge has nevertheless acquitted Mr Faronbi of any dishonesty ... I do not consider it ... possible to reverse the judge's finding on appeal so as to conclude that Mr Faronbi or the bank was dishonest in the Twinsectra sense, even as clarified in Barlow Clowes. ...

LADY JUSTICE ARDEN

...The dishonest assistance issue

I agree with Rix LJ that the appeal on this issue fails. In Barlow Clowes International Ltd (in liquidation) v Eurotrust International Ltd... , the Privy Council considered the case law of England and Wales on the issue of the element of dishonesty necessary for liability under this head. Its interpretation of that case law was that it is unnecessary to show subjective dishonesty in the sense of consciousness that the transaction is dishonest. It is sufficient if the defendant knows of the elements of the transaction which make it dishonest according to normally accepted standards of behaviour. ...[I]n my judgment this court should follow the decision of the Privy Council. ...

The decision of the Privy Council in Royal Brunei Airlines Sdn Bhd v Tan ... had been taken to establish for the purposes of English law that dishonesty was required before liability for assisting in a breach of trust could be imposed... . Indeed, in the Twinsectra case, Lord Hutton accepted that the House should follow ... the Royal Brunei case... . Lord Nicholls ... [in Royal Brunei] held that "the standard of what constitutes honest conduct is not subjective" ... and gave other indications that consciousness of wrongdoing was not required for accessory liability for breach of trust.

The subsequent decision of the House of Lords in Twinsectra Ltd v Yardley ... was widely interpreted as requiring both an objective and subjective test to be applied... . In the case of the subjective test, that would mean that the Defendant would not be guilty of dishonesty unless he was conscious that the transaction fell below normally acceptable standards of conduct. The Privy Council in the Barlow Clowes case has now clarified that this is a wrong interpretation of the Twinsectra decision. It is not a requirement of the standard of dishonesty that the defendant should be conscious of his wrongdoing. Snell's Equity now refers to this as the "better view"... .

On the basis of this interpretation, the test of dishonesty is predominantly objective: did the conduct of the defendant fall below the normally acceptable standard? But there are also subjective aspects of dishonesty. As Lord Nicholls said in the Royal Brunei case, honesty has:

"a strong subjective element in that it is a description of a type of conduct assessed in the light of what a person actually knew at the time, as distinct from what a reasonable person would have known or appreciated"... .

In this case, the judge applied the Barlow Clowes decision without asking himself, on the basis that Twinsectra was binding on him under the doctrine of precedent and the Barlow Clowes case ... was only persuasive authority, whether the interpretation in that case was one he would himself have come to... . Adherence to the doctrine of precedent is important... . On the other hand special factors can arise with respect to decisions of the Privy Council...

[B]efore this court ... decides to follow a decision of the Privy Council in place of a decision of the House of Lords the circumstances must be quite exceptional and the court must be satisfied that in practice the result would be a foregone conclusion. In my judgment, the circumstances of this case are ... exceptional and justify the course which the judge took for the following reasons:

i. The decision in Twinsectra is of course binding on this court and the judge. But the Barlow Clowes decision does not involve a departure from, or refusal to follow, the Twinsectra case. Rather, the Barlow Clowes case gives guidance as to the proper interpretation to be placed on it as a matter of English law. It shows how the Royal Brunei case and the Twinsectra case can be read together to form a consistent corpus of law.

Alert

ii. The meaning of dishonesty in the Twinsectra case appeared to involve an additional subjective element, namely an awareness on the part of the accessory that his conduct was dishonest. ...The approach of the Privy Council [in Barlow Clowes] was both striking and bold: one writer has referred to it as taking judicial re-interpretation "to new heights" (Virgo, Mapping the Law, Essays in memory of Peter Birks, ed Burrows and Rodger (2006)(Oxford) ch 5 p 86). The decision in the Barlow Clowes case could probably have been reached without consideration of the Twinsectra decision... , and it is significant that the Privy Council took another course.

iii. ...[T]he approach in Barlow Clowes was to clarify the meaning of the speeches of Lord Hutton and Lord Hoffmann in the Twinsectra case. The view expressed by Lord Hutton represented the view of the majority. Two members of the constitution of the Appellate Committee which sat in Twinsectra (Lord Steyn and Lord Hoffmann) were parties to the decision in Barlow Clowes. It is difficult to see that another constitution of the Appellate Committee would itself come to a different view as to what the majority in Twinsectra had meant. ...I do not see how in these particular circumstances this court could be criticised for adopting the interpretation of the Twinsectra decision unanimously adopted by the Privy Council... .

Link

See the similar view expressed by Lord Millett in his dissenting speech in *Twinsectra v Yardley*.

iv. There is no overriding reason why in respect of dishonesty in the context of civil liability ... the law should take account of the Defendant's views as to the morality of his actions.

For all the above reasons, I consider that the judge was right to proceed on the basis that the law as laid down in the Twinsectra case, as interpreted ... in Barlow Clowes, represented the law... .

In considering the decision in the Barlow Clowes case, I would acknowledge in addition to the articles to which Rix LJ referred in para 22 of his judgment the case note entitled Dishonesty in the Context of Assistance – again [2006] 65 CLJ 18 by Conaglen & Goymour.

I now turn to consider the application of the test of dishonesty as established in the Barlow Clowes case to the present case. ...The highest that it can be put is that the bank had suspicions about TI's possible involvement in the money-laundering of money at the instance of corrupt politicians. But it had no knowledge of any specific act of dishonesty by TI and it had no grounds for believing that the Appellants were, or were associates of, politicians and it had no particular suspicions about the transactions in question. There was no finding that in those circumstances a bank would normally raise additional inquiries ... or decline to act. Thus, the lack of particular suspicions about the transactions in question ... diminished Mr Faronbi's general suspicions ... to an extent that it was no longer commercially unacceptable for the bank to implement the instructions that [it] had received.

...I would thus dismiss the appeal on the dishonest assistance issue. ...

It seems likely from Arden LJ's judgment that the courts will adopt the interpretation of *Twinsectra* given in *Barlow Clowes v Eurotrust* but the matter cannot be regarded as settled beyond doubt.

***Ultraframe (UK) Ltd v Fielding* [2005] EWCH 1638**

Panel: Lewison J

Facts: Ultraframe claimed that Fielding dishonestly assisted the commission of breaches of fiduciary duty by two of Ultraframe's subsidiary companies. The judge stated the elements which were needed for liability for dishonest assistance, explaining what the defendant must know about the breach of trust.

LEWISON J

What must a dishonest assistant know? In Brink's Ltd v. Abu-Saleh [1999] CLC 133 Mrs Elcombe accompanied her husband on a number of trips to Switzerland. Mr Elcombe was carrying money which was part of the proceeds of the Brinks-Mat gold bullion robbery. However, Mrs Elcombe did not know that. She thought that the money was the subject of a tax evasion exercise. Brink's claimed against her that she was liable as a dishonest assistant in a breach of trust. Rimer J held (obiter) that although Mrs Elcombe knew that her husband was engaged in a dishonest scheme (i.e. tax evasion) that was not enough. It had to be proved that she knew of the existence of the trust or, at least of the facts giving rise to the trust. Mance J revisited this question in Grupo Torras SA v. Al-Sabah [1999] CLC 1469 , 1665–6. He said that he had difficulty in accepting Rimer J's formulation of the requisite knowledge. He concluded, however, that: "... the answer to this problem seems to lie in recognising that, for dishonest assistance, the defendant's dishonesty must have been towards the plaintiff in relation to property held or potentially held on trust or constructive trust, rather than the introduction of a separate criterion of knowledge of any such trust."

If and in so far as there is a difference of opinion between Rimer J and Mance J, I respectfully prefer the opinion of Mance J.

It is not necessary for a dishonest assistant to know all the details of the dishonest scheme. As Peter Gibson J said in Baden v. Société Générale etc [1993] 1 WLR 509 , 575: "Again, however, I do not think it need be knowledge of the whole design: that would be an impossibly high requirement in most cases. What is crucial is that the alleged constructive trustee should know that a design having the character of being fraudulent and dishonest was being perpetrated. Further he must know that his act assisted in the implementation of such design."

[...]

The essence of the requisite knowledge, in this context, is that the assistant knows that the person being assisted is doing something he is not entitled to do. In the case of the proceeds of a bullion robbery, or the payment away of monies held on express trusts, this may not be difficult to establish. But as Twinsectra itself shows, a mistaken appreciation of the legal effect of the relevant documentation is (or can be) critical. Where, as here, the liability for dishonest assistance takes as its foundation a breach of the fiduciary duties owed to a company by one who is not a de jure director of it, establishing the requisite knowledge may be a much more difficult task.

Although it is not necessary for the dishonest assistant to know all the details of the whole design, he must, I think, know in broad terms what the design is. Liability as a dishonest assistant, as the law has developed, is a secondary liability akin to the criminal liability of one who aids and abets the commission of a criminal offence...

Finally, on this point the test of knowledge is subjective. The question is not: what did the assistant suspect; nor what ought he as a reasonable person to have appreciated? Liability will only be established if the assistant actually knew that the property in question was not at the disposal of the fiduciary; or (perhaps) he shut his eyes to that possibility...

***Statek Corp v Alford* [2008] EWHC 32 (Ch)**

Panel: Evans-Lombe J

Facts: Statek Corp had been bought by a company owned by Alford and two others, J and S. Alford did not become a director of Statek, but left the running of the company to J and S. They fraudulently misappropriated USD $19.8 million from Statek, passing some of the money through Alford's account. Alford was held liable to Statek for dishonestly assisting the breach by J and S by receiving money into his bank account and paying it out in accordance with their instructions.

EVANS-LOMBE J

At para.226 of his written closing submissions Mr Miles made the following submissions as to Mr Alford's state of mind when receiving the payments from Statek sources into his joint sterling account and his dollar account and thereafter disbursing that money on the instructions of Johnston and Spillane.

a) Mr Alford knew that the moneys were Statek's property. These moneys were therefore trust property.

b) He knew that Statek was a successful manufacturing company with its own employees and creditors.

c) He was asked to allow his own personal bank accounts to be used to receive and disburse Statek's corporate funds.

d) He knew there was no good reason for his own accounts being used to receive and disburse moneys. Statek had its own bank accounts in the UK.

e) He also knew, in respect of many of the receipts that the moneys were actually received from a UK bank account of Statek.

f) He did receive an explanation for the payments to him, that it was for acquisitions in Europe, but the explanation was nonsensical and he believed it to be illogical at the time.

g) He knew that many of the payments were to Johnston or his entities.

h) He knew that the payments into and out of his bank accounts were of very large amounts of money, were generally for short periods, and were for no apparent commercial purpose. Certainly the moneys were not being held for "acquisitions" and he knew this.

i) So not only had he received an "illogical" explanation-the pattern of payments was actually inconsistent with what had been explained.

j) He was also told that the reason for paying Statek's money to his accounts was to remove it from the normal banking system. This can only have meant putting moneys of Statek out of its name into that of Mr Alford, i.e. to conceal the moneys. Mr Alford was pressed about this on day 4. He agreed that the purpose must have been to move the money out of Statek's name into his own name so that someone would not know that Statek had the money, but said that he did not think about it at the time. He said that he made no inquiries about it and that he treated it as an entirely normal transaction. He still asked no questions when the moneys were paid to Johnston. When he was asked why Johnston could not get the money direct from Statek he said "I can't answer that question."

I accept Mr Miles' submissions and find that Mr Alford's state of mind was as he submits it to have been when each of the large transactions complained of were being handled by him. Like the Deputy Deemster in relation to the second respondent in the Barlow Clowes case, which has some factual similarity to the present case, I find that Mr Alford rendered his assistance to carrying out the transactions complained of dishonestly.

***Starglade Properties Ltd v Nash* [2010] EWCA Civ 1314**

Panel: Sir Andrew Morritt C, Hughes and Leveson LJJ

Facts: Nash was a director of a company, Larkstore. Larkstore agreed to hold approximately £154,500 received in litigation for itself and Starglade. By the time the money was paid to Larkstore it was insolvent. Nash distributed the money to various other creditors in order to frustrate Starglade. Starglade sued Nash personally for dishonestly assisting Larkstore to breach trust. The judge at first instance dismissed the claim on the basis that Nash was not dishonest. He said that dishonesty is conduct which *all* normal people consider to be wrong. The Court of Appeal held that the wrong test had been applied. The Chancellor reviewed *RBA v Tan, Twinsectra Ltd v Yardley, Barlow Clowes Ltd v Eurotrust Ltd* and *Abu Rahman v Abacha* extracted above, and stated that the test was whether Nash had been dishonest by the standard of ordinary commercial behaviour.

SIR ANDREW MORRITT, CHANCELLOR

Having referred to the relevant authorities at some length I return to the rival submissions I summarised in paragraphs 21 and 22 above. It is convenient to start with the second submission of counsel for Starglade. He contends that the statement of the deputy judge in paragraph 51 of his judgment, quoted in paragraph 19 above, that the appropriate standard is "what all [as opposed to some only] normal people would regard as dishonest" is wrong in law. He contends that it is not supported by any of the cases to which I have referred and is contrary to principle in that it is ultimately a question of law for the court.

For my part, I consider that the deputy judge's comments are apt to mislead. The relevant standard, described variously in the statements I have quoted, is the ordinary standard of honest behaviour. Just as the subjective understanding of the person concerned as to whether his conduct is dishonest is irrelevant so also is it irrelevant that there may be a body of opinion which

 Alert

regards the ordinary standard of honest behaviour as being set too high. Ultimately, in civil proceedings, it is for the court to determine what that standard is and to apply it to the facts of the case.

That is my conclusion. As I have already said, the question was whether the relevant conduct of Mr Nash in seeking to frustrate Starglade, given that he knew that Larkstore was insolvent but otherwise had sufficient assets to pay a dividend to its creditors, was dishonest. The deputy judge never looked at that issue. He concentrated on whether payments to or security given to Glancestyle might be set aside in due course by a liquidator of Larkstore. No advice was sought or given on what Mr Nash proposed to do or did or his reasons for doing so. The deliberate removal of the assets of an insolvent company so as entirely to defeat the just claim of a creditor is, in my view, not in accordance with the ordinary standards of honest commercial behaviour, however much it may occur. Nor could a person in the position of Mr Nash have thought otherwise notwithstanding a lack of understanding as to the legal position.

For all these reasons I would accept the first submission of counsel for Starglade and, notwithstanding those of counsel for Mr Nash, recognise the conduct of Mr Nash in assisting the undoubted breach of trust in favour of Starglade as dishonest by the ordinary standards of honest commercial behaviour. I would allow this appeal. ...

12.2 Knowing Receipt

Prior to the case extracted below, there had been conflicting case law on the level of knowledge required. In *Akindele,* the court focused on *Belmont Finance Corp v Williams Furniture Limited* [1979] Ch 250 in deciding that although a knowing recipient will often be found to have acted dishonestly, dishonesty is not an essential ingredient of liability.

***Bank of Credit and Commerce International (Overseas) Ltd and another v Akindele* [2001] Ch 437**

Panel: Nourse, Ward and Sedley LJJ

Facts: Akindele, a Nigerian businessman, entered into an agreement in 1985 with ICIC, a Cayman Islands company controlled by BCCI. Under this agreement, Akindele was to buy BCCI shares and hold them for at least two years. If he decided to sell them after two years, but before five years had elapsed, he would be guaranteed a return of 15% per annum on his investment. The shares would not actually be transferred to his name unless he held them for more than five years. The agreement was part of a fraudulent scheme devised by BCCI directors who were acting in breach of their fiduciary duties. By late 1987, there were press rumours of irregularities within BCCI and, in 1988, the defendant found out that certain BCCI officials had been arrested in connection with money laundering. He decided to end his agreement and received his money back, with the agreed interest, under a divestiture agreement. BCCI went into liquidation and the liquidators, in an attempt to recover the amount of the interest paid, sued Akindele for knowing assistance (now known as dishonest assistance) and knowing receipt. The judge held that Akindele was unaware of the fraud and had not acted dishonestly. The liquidators appealed and the Court of Appeal upheld the judge's decision. The significance of this case is the clarification by Nourse LJ of the test for liability for knowing receipt.

LORD JUSTICE NOURSE

Knowing Receipt

The essential requirements of knowing receipt were stated by Hoffmann LJ in *El Ajou v Dollar Land Holdings plc* [1994] 2 All ER 685, 700:

"For this purpose the plaintiff must show, first, a disposal of his assets in breach of fiduciary duty; secondly, the beneficial receipt by the defendant of assets which are traceable as representing the assets of the plaintiff; and thirdly, knowledge on the part of the defendant that the assets he received are traceable to a breach of fiduciary duty."

Link on the need for 'beneficial' receipt, see the discussion by Lord Millett in *Twinsectra v Yardley*.

In the present case the first two requirements were satisfied in relation to the defendant's receipt of the US$16.679m paid to him pursuant to the divestiture agreement. But the satisfaction of the third requirement ... is problematical.

So far as the law is concerned, ... there are two questions which, though closely related, are distinct: first, what, in this context, is meant by knowledge; second, is it necessary for the recipient to act dishonestly? [T]he convenient course is to deal with the second of those questions first.

Knowing receipt-dishonesty

...Carnwath J proceeded on an assumption that dishonesty in one form or another was the essential foundation of the claimants' case, whether in knowing assistance or knowing receipt. That was no doubt caused by the acceptance before him (though not at any higher level) ... that the thrust of the recent authorities at first instance was that the recipient's state of knowledge must fall into one of the first three categories listed by Peter Gibson J in *Baden v Société Générale pour Favoriser le Développement du Commerce et de l'Industrie en France SA* [1993] 1 WLR 509, 575-576, on which basis, said Carnwath J, it was doubtful whether the test differed materially in practice from that for knowing assistance. However, the assumption on which the judge proceeded, derived as I believe from an omission to distinguish between the questions of knowledge and dishonesty, was incorrect in law. While a knowing recipient will often be found to have acted dishonestly, it has never been a prerequisite of the liability that he should.

Alert

An authoritative decision on this question ... is *Belmont Finance Corpn Ltd v Williams Furniture Ltd (No 2)* [1980] 1 All ER 393... . [T]hough the claim in knowing assistance failed because the directors of Belmont did not act dishonestly, the claim in knowing receipt succeeded. ...

Belmont Finance Corporation Ltd v Williams Furniture Ltd (No 2) [1980] 1 All ER 393 is clear authority for the proposition that dishonesty is not a necessary ingredient of liability in knowing receipt. There have been other, more recent, judicial pronouncements to the same effect. ...

Knowing receipt--the authorities on knowledge

...[T]here has been a sustained judicial and extrajudicial debate as to the knowledge on the part of the recipient which is required in order to found liability in knowing receipt. Expressed in its simplest terms, the question is whether the recipient must have actual knowledge (or the equivalent) that the assets received are traceable to a breach of trust or whether constructive knowledge is enough. The instinctive approach of most equity judges, especially in this court, has been to assume that constructive knowledge is enough. But there is now a series of decisions of eminent first instance judges who, after considering the question in greater depth, have come to the contrary conclusion, at all events when commercial transactions are in point. In the Commonwealth, on the other hand, the preponderance of authority has been in favour of the view that constructive knowledge is enough. ...

In *Belmont Finance Corporation Ltd v Williams Furniture Ltd (No 2)* [1980] 1 All ER 393, 405 Buckley LJ ... [said]:

"So, if the directors of a company in breach of their fiduciary duties misapply the funds of their company so that they come into the hands of some stranger to the trust who receives them with knowledge (actual or constructive) of the breach, he cannot conscientiously retain those funds ... . He becomes a constructive trustee for the company of the misapplied funds." ...

Sir Robert Megarry V-C in *In re Montagu's Settlement Trusts* [1987] Ch 264 ... first plumbed the distinction between notice and knowledge. It was he who, building on a passage in the judgment of this court in *In re Diplock* [1948] Ch 465, 478-479, first emphasised the fundamental difference between the questions which arise in respect of the doctrine of purchaser without notice on the one hand and the doctrine of constructive trusts on the other. Reading from his earlier judgment in the same case, ... he said:

"The former is concerned with the question whether a person takes property subject to or free from some equity. The latter is concerned with whether or not a person is to have imposed upon him the personal burdens and obligations of trusteeship. I do not see why one of the touchstones for determining the burdens on property should be the same as that for deciding whether to impose a personal obligation on a [person]. The cold calculus of constructive and imputed notice does not seem to me to be an appropriate instrument for deciding whether a [person's] conscience is sufficiently affected for it to be right to bind him by the obligations of a constructive trustee." ...

Sir Robert Megarry V-C summarised his conclusions in eight subparagraphs... . I read the first three:

"(1) The equitable doctrine of tracing and the imposition of a constructive trust by reason of the knowing receipt of trust property are governed by different rules and must be kept distinct. Tracing is primarily a means of determining the rights of property, whereas the imposition of a constructive trust creates personal obligations that go beyond mere property rights. (2) In considering whether a constructive trust has arisen in a case of the knowing receipt of trust property, the basic question is whether the conscience of the recipient is sufficiently affected to justify the imposition of such a trust. (3) Whether a constructive trust arises in such a case primarily depends on the knowledge of the recipient, and not on notice to him; and for clarity it is desirable to use the word 'knowledge' and avoid the word 'notice' in such cases."

The effect of Sir Robert Megarry V-C's decision, broadly stated, was that, in order to establish liability in knowing receipt, the recipient must have actual knowledge (or the equivalent) that the assets received are traceable to a breach of trust and that constructive knowledge is not enough. ...

[His Lordship referred to three decisions in New Zealand and one in Canada, all cases of commercial transactions, where the view was that constructive knowledge was enough. He cited a passage from the judgment in *Westpac Banking Corporation v Savin* [1985] 2 NZLR 41 in which Richardson J, having expressed a provisional preference for the view that constructive knowledge was enough, said that "courts would not readily import a duty to inquire in the case of commercial transactions" and continued:]

The *Baden* case

It will have been observed that up to this stage I have made no more than a passing reference to the fivefold categorisation of knowledge accepted by Peter Gibson J in *Baden v Société Générale pour Favoriser le Développement du Commerce et de l'Industrie en France SA* [1993] 1 WLR 509, 575-576: (i) actual knowledge; (ii) wilfully shutting one's eyes to the obvious; (iii) wilfully and recklessly failing to make such inquiries as an honest and reasonable man would make; (iv) knowledge of circumstances which would indicate the facts to an honest and reasonable man; (v) knowledge of circumstances which will put an honest and reasonable man on inquiry. Reference to the categorisation has been made in most of the knowing receipt cases to which I have referred from *In re Montagu's Settlement Trusts* [1987] Ch 264 onwards. In many of them it has been influential in the decision. In general, the first three categories have been taken to constitute actual knowledge (or its equivalent) and the last two constructive knowledge.

Two important points must be made about the *Baden* categorisation. First, it appears to have been propounded by counsel for the plaintiffs, accepted by counsel for the defendant and then put to the judge on an agreed basis. Secondly, though both counsel accepted that all five categories of knowledge were relevant and neither sought to submit that there was any distinction for that purpose between knowing receipt and knowing assistance (a view with which the judge expressed his agreement...), the claim in constructive trust was based squarely on knowing assistance and not on knowing receipt... . In the circumstances ... it is natural to assume that the categorisation was not formulated with knowing receipt primarily in mind. ...

Knowing receipt--the recipient's state of knowledge

In *Royal Brunei Airlines Sdn Bhd v Tan...* , which is now the leading authority on knowing assistance, Lord Nicholls ... said ... that "knowingly" was better avoided as a defining ingredient of the liability, and that in that context the *Baden* categorisation was best forgotten. Although my own view is that the categorisation is often helpful in identifying different states of knowledge which may or may not result in a finding of dishonesty for the purposes of knowing assistance, I have grave doubts about its utility in cases of knowing receipt. Quite apart from its origins in a context of knowing assistance ... any categorisation is of little value unless the purpose it is to serve is adequately defined, whether it be fivefold, as in the *Baden* case... , or twofold, as in the classical division between actual and constructive knowledge, a division which has itself become blurred... .

Link
Compare this with the view expressed in *Royal Brunei Airlines v Tan.*

What then, in the context of knowing receipt, is the purpose to be served by a categorisation of knowledge? It can only be to enable the court to determine whether, in the words of Buckley LJ in *Belmont Finance Corpn Ltd v Williams Furniture Ltd (No 2)* ... the recipient can "conscientiously retain [the] funds against the company" or, in the words of Sir Robert Megarry V-C in *In re Montagu's Settlement Trusts...* , "[the recipient's] conscience is sufficiently affected for it to be right to bind him by the obligations of a constructive trustee". But, if that is the purpose, there is no need for categorisation. All that is necessary is that the recipient's state of knowledge should be such as to make it unconscionable for him to retain the benefit of the receipt.

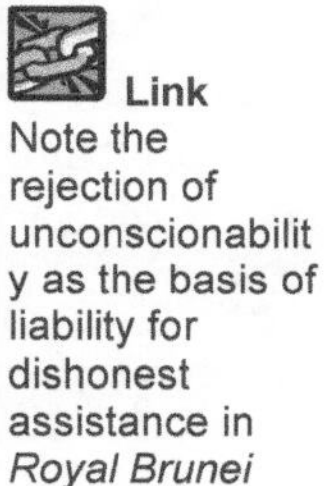

Link
Note the rejection of unconscionability as the basis of liability for dishonest assistance in *Royal Brunei Airlines v Tan.*

For these reasons I have come to the view that, just as there is now a single test of dishonesty for knowing assistance, so ought there to be a single test of knowledge for knowing receipt. The recipient's state of knowledge must be such as to make it unconscionable for him to retain the benefit of the receipt. A test in that form, though it cannot, any more than any other, avoid difficulties of application, ought to avoid those of definition and allocation to which the previous categorisations have led. Moreover, it should better enable the courts to give commonsense decisions in the commercial context in which claims in knowing receipt are now frequently made...

Alert

Knowing receipt--a footnote

We were referred in argument to "Knowing Receipt: The Need for a New Landmark", an essay by Lord Nicholls of Birkenhead in *Restitution Past, Present and Future* (1998) p 231, a work of insight and scholarship... . Most pertinent for present purposes is the suggestion ... at p 238, in reference to the decision of the House of Lords in *Lipkin Gorman v Karpnale Ltd* [1991] 2 AC 548:

"In this respect equity should now follow the law. Restitutionary liability, applicable regardless of fault but subject to a defence of change of position, would be a better-tailored response to the underlying mischief of misapplied property than personal liability which is exclusively fault-based. Personal liability would flow from having received the property of another, from having been unjustly enriched at the expense of another. It would be triggered by the mere fact of receipt, thus recognising the endurance of property rights. But fairness would be ensured by the need to identify a gain, and by making change of position available as a defence in suitable cases when, for instance, the recipient had changed his position in reliance on the receipt."

See the brief *obiter* comment on recipient liability made by Lord Nicholls in *Royal Brunei Airlines v Tan* and the view on this expressed *obiter* by Lord Millett in *Twinsectra v Yardley*.

Lord Nicholls goes on to examine the *In re Diplock* [1948] Ch 465 principle, suggesting, at p 241, that it could be reshaped by being extended to all trusts but in a form modified to take proper account of the decision in *Lipkin Gorman v Karpnale Ltd* [1991] 2 AC 548.

No argument before us was based on the suggestions made in Lord Nicholls's essay. Indeed, at this level of decision, it would have been a fruitless exercise. ...While in general it may be possible to sympathise with a tendency to subsume a further part of our law of restitution under the principles of unjust enrichment, I beg leave to doubt whether strict liability coupled with a change of position defence would be preferable to fault-based liability in many commercial transactions, for example where, as here, the receipt is of a company's funds which have been misapplied by its directors. Without having heard argument it is unwise to be dogmatic, but in such a case it would appear to be commercially unworkable ... that, simply on proof of an internal misapplication of the company's funds, the burden should shift to the recipient to defend the receipt either by a change of position or perhaps in some other way. ...

Knowing receipt – the facts of the present case

I return to the facts of the present case, in order to determine whether the defendant is liable in knowing receipt to repay (together with interest) US$6.679m of the sum received by him pursuant to the divestiture agreement, being the excess over the US$10m he paid to ICIC Overseas pursuant to the 1985 agreement. ...

I start with the defendant's state of knowledge at the date of the 1985 agreement. As to that, the judge found that there was no evidence that anyone outside BCCI had reason to doubt the integrity of its management at that time. More specifically, it is clear that the judge was of the view that the defendant had no knowledge of the underlying frauds within the BCCI group either in general or in relation to the 1985 agreement. ...Moreover, he was not prepared to draw the conclusion that the high rate of interest and the artificial nature of the agreement were sufficient to put an honest person in the defendant's position on notice that some fraud or breach of trust was being perpetrated. He said that the defendant would have had no reason to question the form of the transaction.

Those findings, expressed in language equally appropriate to an inquiry as to constructive notice, appear to me to be consistent only with the view that the defendant's state of knowledge at the date of the 1985 agreement was not such as to make it unconscionable for him to enter into it. However, ...[w]e have also to consider the defendant's state of knowledge at the date of the divestiture agreement, by which time ... he did have suspicions as to the conduct of BCCI's affairs. ...

There having been no evidence that the defendant was aware of the internal arrangements within BCCI which led to the payment to him of the US$16.679m pursuant to the divestiture agreement, did the additional knowledge which he acquired between July 1985 and December 1988 make it unconscionable for him to retain the benefit of the receipt? In my judgment it did not. The additional knowledge went to the general reputation of the BCCI group from late 1987 onwards. It was not a sufficient reason for questioning the propriety of a particular transaction entered into more than two years earlier, at a time when no one outside BCCI had reason to doubt the integrity of its management and in a form which the defendant had no reason to question. The judge said that the defendant was entitled to take steps to protect his own interest, and that there was nothing dishonest in his seeking to enforce the 1985 agreement. Nor was there anything unconscionable in his seeking to do so. Equally, had I thought that that was still the appropriate test, I would have held that the defendant did not have actual or constructive knowledge that his receipt of the US$6.79m was traceable to a breach or breaches of fiduciary duty... .

Conclusion

For these reasons, though by a different route in relation to knowing receipt, I have come to the conclusion that Carnwath J's decision to dismiss the action was correct. I would affirm it and dismiss the claimants' appeal.

The *Akindele* test for liability for knowing receipt set out above was applied in the next case, but was expressed in '*Baden*-like' language.

***Armstrong DLW GmbH v Winnington Networks Ltd* [2012] EWCH 10 (Ch)**

Panel: Stephen Morris QC sitting as Deputy High Court Judge

Facts: Winnington Networks Ltd was a company which traded in carbon emission allowances. It bought some allowances from an intermediary. These had been fraudulently obtained from the claimant by the intermediary. Winnington Networks Ltd was liable for knowing receipt of the claimant's property.

STEPHEN MORRIS QC

The current position as to the circumstances in which receipt of trust property by a defendant will render that person liable to the owners of the beneficial interests is now to be found in the Court of Appeal's decision in *Bank of Credit and Commerce International (Overseas) Ltd v Akindele [2001] Ch 437* where, after concluding that there was no need for the Baden categorisation, Nourse LJ said, at p 455:

"All that is necessary is that the recipient's state of knowledge should be such as to make it unconscionable for him to retain the benefit of the receipt ... I have come to the view that, just as there is now a single test of dishonesty for knowing assistance, so ought there to be a single test of knowledge for knowing receipt. The recipient's state of knowledge must be such as to make it unconscionable for him to retain the benefit of the receipt. A test in that form, though it cannot, any more than any other, avoid difficulties of application, ought to avoid those of definition and allocation to which the previous categorisations have led. Moreover, it should better enable the courts to give common sense decisions in the commercial context in which claims in knowing receipt are now frequently made ..."

Lewin, at para 42-49, (and others— Goff & Jones , para 33-029) comment that, despite what the Court of Appeal said in the *Akindele* case, the *Baden* classification of knowledge is still useful in distinguishing different types of knowledge for the purpose of determining what kind of knowledge makes it unconscionable for the defendant to retain the trust property. Both parties agreed that it was thus helpful (and indeed necessary) to consider which types of *Baden* "knowledge" would render receipt of trust property "unconscionable" and then each made arguments in line with their arguments on the issue of "notice" for the bona fide purchaser defence, suggesting that the tests for knowledge and for notice overlap considerably. I agree. Lewin suggests that this is the case (by its express cross-reference between the two issues in the commercial context, see paras 115 and 116 above).

Alert

In my judgment, the position, in a commercial context, can be summarised as follows: (1) Baden types (1) to (3) knowledge on the part of a defendant render receipt of trust property "unconscionable". It is not necessary to show that the defendant realised that the transaction was "obviously" or "probably" in breach of trust or fraudulent; the possibility of impropriety or the claimant's interest is sufficient. (2) Further Baden types (4) and (5) knowledge also render receipt "unconscionable" but only if, on the facts actually known to this defendant, a reasonable person would either have appreciated that the transfer was probably in breach of trust or would have made inquiries or sought advice which would have revealed the probability of the breach of trust.

... Indeed this was not just a case where the defendant failed to make inquiries that should have been made, but rather was a case where the relevant inquiries were made, but not followed through by awaiting a response to those inquiries. Winnington deliberately and consciously chose to take the risk that the EUAs did not belong to Armstrong. Mr Pursell raised the question in the first place because he had doubts and then wilfully closed his eyes to the risk to which those doubts gave rise. What Winnington did was to fail, wilfully and recklessly, to pursue the inquiries which not only an honest and reasonable man would have made, but which it had in fact made.

In this way, by not awaiting an answer to the inquiries, Winnington was either "wilfully shutting one's eyes to the obvious" or at the very least "wilfully and recklessly failing to make such inquiries as an honest and reasonable man would make".

Put another way, Winnington's knowledge fell within, at least, Baden type (3), because Winnington wilfully and reckless failed to make *such further* inquiries as an honest and reasonable man would have made in the circumstances then pertaining.

These facts constitute knowledge within the band of Baden types (2) and (3) and in any event are such as to render Winnington's receipt of the EUAs unconscionable.

13

Implied Trusts

Introduction

Unlike express trusts, which arise as a consequence of the settlor's express intention for property to be held on trust, resulting and constructive trusts arise by operation of law. What this essentially means is that despite a lack of adherence to the rules regarding formalities and constitution, the courts will imply a trust to come into existence in various situations.

As the noted academic Birks clarified in his work on English Private Law, the word 'resulting' in the context of resulting trusts derives from the Latin word *resilare*, which means 'to jump back'. A resulting trust therefore describes the situation where beneficial interest in the property jumps back to the person who was absolute owner of the property immediately before legal title was transferred to the trustee.

13.1 Types of Resulting Trust

An attempt to categorise the situations in which a resulting trust comes in to existence was made by Megarry J in *Re Vandervell's Trusts (No 2)* [1974] Ch 269.

***Re Vandervell's Trusts (No 2)* [1974] Ch 269**

Panel: Megarry J

Statute: Law of Property Act 1925 s53(1)(c)

The relevant part of this High Court judgment discusses how resulting trusts can be categorised, which received no adverse comment from the Court of Appeal.

MR JUSTICE MEGARRY

... It seems to me that the relevant points on resulting trusts may be put in a series of propositions which, so far as not directly supported, appear at least to be consistent with Lord Wilberforce's speech, and reconcilable with the true intent of Lord Upjohn's speech, though it may not be with all his words on a literal reading. The propositions are the broadest of generalisations, and do not purport to cover the exceptions and qualifications that doubtless exist. Nevertheless, these generalisations at least provide a starting point for the classification of a corner of equity which might benefit from some attempt at classification. The propositions are as follows.

(1) If a transaction fails to make any effective disposition of any interest it does nothing. This is so at law and in equity, and has nothing to do with resulting trusts.

(2) Normally the mere existence of some unexpressed intention in the breast of the owner of the property does nothing: there must at least be some expression of that intention before it can effect any result. To yearn is not to transfer.

> (3) Before any doctrine of resulting trust can come into play, there must at least be some effective transaction which transfers or creates some interest in property.
>
> (4) Where A effectually transfers to B (or creates in his favour) any interest in any property, whether legal or equitable, a resulting trust for A may arise in two distinct classes of case. For simplicity, I shall confine my statement to cases in which the transfer or creation is made without B providing any valuable consideration, and where no presumption of advancement can arise; and I shall state the position for transfers without specific mention of the creation of new interests.
>
> (a) The first class of case is where the transfer to B is not made on any trust. If, of course, it appears from the transfer that B is intended to hold on certain trusts, that will be decisive, and the case is not within this category; and similarly if it appears that B is intended to take beneficially. But in other cases there is the rebuttable presumption that B holds on a resulting trust for A, The question is not one of the automatic consequences of a dispositive failure by A, but one of presumption: the property has been carried to B, and from the absence of consideration and any presumption of advancement B is presumed not only to hold the entire interest on trust, but also to hold the beneficial interest for A absolutely. The presumption thus establishes both that A is to take on trust and also what that trust is. Such resulting trusts may be called "presumed resulting trusts."
>
> (b) The second class of case is where the transfer to B is made on trusts which leave some or all of the beneficial interest undisposed of. Here B automatically holds on a resulting trust for A to the extent that the beneficial interest has not been carried to him or others. The resulting trust here does not depend on any intentions or presumptions, but is the automatic consequence of A's failure to dispose of what is vested in him. Since *ex hypothesi* the transfer is on trust, the resulting trust does not establish the trust but merely carries back to A the beneficial interest that has not been disposed of. Such resulting trusts may be called "automatic resulting trusts."
>
> (5) Where trustees hold property in trust for A, and it is they who, at A's direction, make the transfer to B, similar principles apply, even though on the face of the transaction the transferor appears to be the trustee and not A. If the transfer to B is on trust, B will hold any beneficial interest that has not been effectually disposed of on an automatic resulting trust for the true transferor, A. If the transfer to B is not on trust, there will be a rebuttable presumption that B holds on a resulting trust for A.

In essence, Megarry J held that resulting trusts arose in two different scenarios. The first scenario can be categorized as 'presumed' resulting trusts. In this type of resulting trust there is a rebuttable presumption that where property is placed in the name of another person, that person will hold it on trust for the original owner. The second scenario can be categorized as 'automatic' resulting trusts. This type of resulting trust arises where there is a failure to dispose of the beneficial interest, either when the trust has been constituted but equitable title has not passed from the original absolute owner, or when there are assets remaining when the trust has come to an end.

This categorisation was doubted, however, in *Westdeutsche Landesbank Girozentrale v Islington LBC* [1996] AC 669.

***Westdeutsche Landesbank Girozentrale v Islington LBC* [1996] AC 669**

Panel: Lord Goff of Chieveley, Lord Browne-Wilkinson, Lord Slynn of Hadley, Lord Woolf and Lord Lloyd of Berwick

Statute: Senior Courts Act 1981 s35A

Facts: The local authority was one of many that borrowed money from a bank to supplement what it had received from central government funding in a complex transaction known as a credit swap agreement. These agreements were subsequently found to be void as local authorities did not have the powers to enter into them. The bank attempted to recover the sum of £1,145,525 from the local authority. The Court of Appeal held the bank was entitled to the money plus compound interest. The local authority appealed this on the ground that compound interest was only payable if there was a trust relationship between the bank and the local authority.

It was held that there was no trust relationship and, therefore, the bank only had a personal claim to the money. Consequently, only simple interest was payable on the sum lent to the local authority.

LORD BROWNE-WILKINSON

This is not a case where the bank had any equitable interest which pre-dated receipt by the local authority of the upfront payment. Therefore, in order to show that the local authority became a trustee, the bank must demonstrate circumstances which raised a trust for the first time either at the date on which the local authority received the money or at the date on which payment into the mixed account was made. Counsel for the bank specifically disavowed any claim based on a constructive trust. This was plainly right because the local authority had no relevant knowledge sufficient to raise a constructive trust at any time before the moneys, upon the bank account going into overdraft, became untraceable. ... Therefore, as the argument for the bank recognised, the only possible trust which could be established was a resulting trust arising from the circumstances in which the local authority received the upfront payment.

Under existing law a resulting trust arises in two sets of circumstances: (A) where A makes a voluntary payment to B or pays (wholly or in part) for the purchase of property which is vested either in B alone or in the joint names of A and B, there is a presumption that A did not intend to make a gift to B: the money or property is held on trust for A (if he is the sole provider of the money) or in the case of a joint purchase by A and B in shares proportionate to their contributions. It is important to stress that this is only a *presumption*, which presumption is easily rebutted either by the counter-presumption of advancement or by direct evidence of A's intention to make an outright transfer... . (B) Where A transfers property to B *on express trusts*, but the trusts declared do not exhaust the whole beneficial interest... . Both types of resulting trust are traditionally regarded as examples of trusts giving effect to the common intention of the parties. A resulting trust is not imposed by law against the intentions of the trustee (as is a constructive trust) but gives effect to his presumed intention. Megarry J in Re Vandervell's Trusts (No. 2) suggests that a resulting trust of type (B) does not depend on intention but operates automatically. I am not convinced that this is right. If the settlor has expressly, or by necessary implication, abandoned any beneficial interest in the trust property, there is in my view no resulting trust: the undisposed-of equitable interest vests in the Crown as bona vacantia...

Applying these conventional principles of resulting trust to the present case, the bank's claim must fail. There was no transfer of money to the local authority on express trusts: therefore a resulting trust of type (B) above could not arise. As to type (A) above, any presumption of resulting trust is rebutted since it is demonstrated that the bank paid, and the local authority received, the upfront payment with the intention that the moneys so paid should become the absolute property of the local authority. It is true that the parties were under a misapprehension that the payment was made in pursuance of a valid contract. But that does not alter the actual intentions of the parties at the date the payment was made or the moneys were mixed in the bank account.

As no trust was found, these statements are strictly *obiter*. Furthermore, the statement on resulting trusts made by Lord Browne-Wilkinson can be criticised as being conceptually wrong. These criticisms can be split into two categories.

First, Lord Browne-Wilkinson has suggested that where there are undisposed of assets that would come within an 'automatic' resulting trust under Megarry J's classification, these would go as *bona vacantia* to the Crown. Whilst there is some High Court authority that agrees with this, such as *Re West Sussex Constabulary's Widows, Children and Benevolent (1930) Fund Trusts* [1971] Ch 1, there is House of lords authority in *Vandervell v Inland Revenue Commissioners* that property will be found to go on resulting trust to the original owner rather than to the Crown *bona vacantia*. Indeed, on the facts Vandervell wanted anybody but himself to be the beneficial owner of the shares, yet the House of Lords held that he would be the beneficiary of a resulting trust.

The second point of criticism of Lord Browne-Wilkinson's judgment is his statement that resulting trusts give effect to the common intention of the parties. With respect, this must be wrong. There is House of Lords authority, such as *McPhail v Doulton* [1971] AC 424, that states the overriding considerations of the Court are to give effect to the intentions of the settlor. Therefore only the settlor's intentions are relevant.

It is therefore submitted that the classification given by Megarry J in *Re Vandervell's Trusts (No 2)* is to be preferred over Lord Browne-Wilkinson's *obiter* comments.

13.2 'Presumed' Resulting Trusts

The first category of resulting trusts described by Lord Browne-Wilkinson in *Westdeutche Landesbank Girozentrale* arises where a person voluntarily transfers the legal title in property to someone else. In that situation, equity will presume that the recipient will hold the property under a resulting trust. An example of when the presumption will arise in the case of personalty is *Re Vinogradoff* [1935] WN 68, where a grandmother transferred war stock into the joint names of herself and her four year old granddaughter. It was held that the presumption of a resulting trust applied so the granddaughter held the stock on trust.

In the case of land, s60(3) Law of Property Act 1925 appears to remove the presumption of a resulting trust, a point discussed in *Lohia v Lohia.*

***Lohia v Lohia* Ch 1987 L No 988**

Panel: Strauss J

Facts: In 1955 the defendant and his father purchased the property at 41 Aberdeen Road, London and they both agreed that they would each own a half share. Ten years later, the father was registered as the sole owner of the property and the defendant sought a declaration that a share of the property was being held on trust for him.

MR JUSTICE STRAUSS

It is therefore necessary to consider first whether a resulting trust is to be presumed from the undoubted fact that the transfer was for no value. Such a presumption would have arisen before 1925: see Dyer v Dyer (1788) 2 Cox Eq. 92, 93 per Eyre CB. It still would apply (in the absence of evidence to the contrary) in the case of chattels or other personal property: see Fowkes v Pascoe (1875) 10 Ch. App. 343, 345, 348; *Tinsley v Milligan* [1994] 1 A.C. 340, 371 per Lord Browne-Wilkinson. The question is whether, in the case of land, the presumption has been abolished by section 60 of the Law of Property Act 1925.

.....

I agree with Mr. Chambers' view that, on a plain reading of section 60, the presumption has been abolished. It seems to me that section 60(1) establishes a general rule that a conveyance should be construed according to the words it uses, so that is possible to tell from it who holds the legal and beneficial estate in the land. Consistently with this, section 60(3) provides in effect that a voluntary conveyance means what it says; it is not necessary to use additional words to make it effective. It is likely that by 1925 the suspicion with which gifts of land were formerly viewed, which was at least one of the underlying reasons for the presumption, would no longer have been regarded as material, and that the purpose of section 60(3) was accordingly to do away with the presumption of a resulting trust in the cases of voluntary conveyance and to make it necessary for the person seeking to establish a resulting trust to prove it. Another consideration is that section 60(3), unless so construed, would be something of a trap for the unwary conveyancer, since the suggestion implicit in its wording that it is no longer necessary to use the old formula would be misleading, except in cases in which the presumption of advancement applied.

As against all this, the countervailing consideration that section 60(3) on this view would change the law with regard to real property alone and therefore would lead to different conclusions in relation to real and personal property in the same situation, does not seem to me to be a factor of sufficient potency to displace the natural construction of the section.

Accordingly, I hold that a voluntary conveyance does not give rise to a presumption of a resulting trust. This view appears to be supported by the weight of academic opinion, albeit without any such detailed analysis as to be found in Mr. Chambers' work: see Snell's Equity 30th ed. para. 9.20; Halsbury's Laws of England vol. 48 para. 613; Riddall 'The Law of Trusts' 5th ed. 1996 p.224; Maudsley and Burn 'Trusts and Trustees' 8th ed. 1996 pp.215–6; Keeton and Sheridan 'The Comparative Law of Trusts in the Commonwealth and the Irish Republic' 1976 p.262; Hayton and Marsh 'Commentary and Cases on the Law of Trusts and Equitable Remedies' 10th ed. 1996 p.307; Williams on Title 4th ed. p.644. I have not been referred to, nor have I been able to find, any textbook or academic article which supports the contrary view.

The Court, therefore, confirmed that the effect of section 60(3) of the Law of Property Act 1925 is to abolish the presumption of a resulting trust when land is voluntarily transferred to another person. On appeal, two of the Lord Justices of the Court of Appeal preferred to express no view as to the effect of section 60(3) as they were able to deal with the matter on other grounds. The point was discussed again by the Court of Appeal in *Ali v Khan.*

***Ali v Khan and Others* [2002] EWCA Civ 974**

Panel: The Vice Chancellor, Rix LJ, Sir Swinton Thomas

Facts: The fourth defendant was the father of six children and in 1986 he bought the freehold to a property in Sparkhill, Birmingham as a family home. In 1997, the father transferred the title to two of his daughters. Following a dispute one of the daughters became the sole legal owner and she tried to evict her father from the property.

THE VICE CHANCELLOR

I should also refer to *Lohia v Lohia [2001] WTLR 101* , 113. This case establishes that the presumption of a resulting trust on a voluntary conveyance of land has been abolished by s.60(3) Law of Property Act 1925 . It was not suggested that this proposition precludes a party to the conveyance from relying on evidence from which a resulting trust may be inferred. Accordingly there is nothing in this case to inhibit the Father from relying on the extrinsic evidence the judge accepted.

The Court of Appeal, therefore, appeared to approve of the High Court decision in *Lohia* but decided the case on its specific facts.

The second category of cases mentioned by Lord Browne-Wilkinson in *Westdeutsche* arises where one person contributes towards the purchase of property and the property is registered in someone else's name or in the joint names of the contributor and a third party. In that situation the legal owner holds the property on resulting trust for the contributor, as illustrated in *Bull v Bull.*

***Bull v Bull* [1955] 1 QB 234**

Panel: Denning, Hodson and Parker LJJ

Facts: A son bought a property with his mother for them both to live in, and the son contributed most of the purchase price. The court noted that the mother did not intend to gift the balance of the purchase price to her son. Following a dispute the son attempted to evict his mother from the property.

LORD JUSTICE DENNING

The son is of course the legal owner of the house; but the mother and son are, I think, equitable tenants in common. Each is entitled in equity to an undivided share in the house, the share of each being in proportion to his or her respective contribution. The rights of equitable tenants in common as between themselves have never, so far as I know, been defined; but there is plenty of authority about the rights of legal owners in common. Each of them is entitled to the possession of the land and to the use and enjoyment of it in a proper manner. Neither can turn out the other; but if one of them should take more than his proper share the injured party can bring an action for an account.

Bull v Bull is, therefore, a clear example of how someone can acquire rights in property through making a contribution towards the purchase price.

The presumption of a resulting trust has to be considered in conjunction with the presumption of advancement, which presumes that in certain situations the transferee is presumed to be making an outright gift. An illustration of how the presumption of advancement operates as between a husband and wife can be seen in *Abrahams v Trustee in Bankruptcy of Abrahams.*

***Abrahams v Trustee in bankruptcy of Abrahams* [2000] WTLR 593**

Panel: Lindsay J

Facts: A husband and wife participated in a lottery syndicate organised by their local pub landlord. Following the couple's separation the husband refused to pay his ongoing contributions, although the wife continued to pay for her husband's place in the syndicate. After the syndicate won a large prize the husband's trustee in bankruptcy argued that a share of the proceeds formed part of the husband's estate.

MR JUSTICE LINDSAY

In some cases a presumption will arise, the presumption of advancement, such that it will be taken, unless proved otherwise, that the true purchaser was making a gift to the person in whose name the acquisition is put. Thus if a man buys property and has it conveyed to his wife, it will, absent contrary evidence, be taken to have been intended to be a gift to her. In such a way the presumption of resulting trust can be undone leaving the acquisition to be beneficially held for the person into whose name it was put. However — see Snell's Equity page 179 — "no such presumption of advancement arises when a wife buys property and puts it in her husband's name; prima facie he holds as trustee for her."

[Counsel] says that this is just such a case. She accepts the husband is entitled to rebut the presumption of resulting trust by evidence, but where there is no relevant evidence of sufficient weight to show that the purchaser's real intention was not that there should be a resulting trust in her favour, then the presumption of resulting trust prevails. It is not all evidence that is, for these purposes, admissible.

The court accepted the wife's submissions and held that there was no evidence rebutting the presumption of a resulting trust. Furthermore, the presumption of advancement did not apply in relation to a transfer from a wife to her husband. However, the result of the case might have been different had the husband paid for his wife's ticket as the presumption of advancement would then apply and the wife would be presumed to be making an outright gift to her husband.

The principles relating to the establishment of a resulting trust were also helpfully set out in the case of *Aroso v Coutts.*

***Aroso v Coutts [2002]* 1 All ER (Comm) 241**

Panel: Collins J

Facts: The deceased had transferred substantial amounts of money into an account held jointly with a nephew. When the money passed by survivorship to the nephew, the deceased's family argued that the money should be held on resulting trust.

MR JUSTICE LAWRENCE COLLINS

The starting point is that where a person transfers property, or directs a trustee for him to transfer property, otherwise than for valuable consideration, and where the presumption of advancement does not apply, it is a question of the intention of the transferor in making the transfer whether the transferee was to take beneficially or on trust, and if on trust, what trusts: *Vandervell v. IRC* [1967] 2 AC 291, at 312, *per* Lord Hodson. If, as a matter of construction of the document making or directing the transfer, it is possible to discern the intentions of the transferor, that is an end of the matter and no extraneous evidence is admissible to correct and qualify his intentions so ascertained, but if the document is silent, then a resulting trust arises in favour of the transferor, but this is only a presumption and is easily rebutted. All the relevant facts and circumstances can be considered in order to ascertain the intentions of the transferor with a view to rebutting the presumption. Ibid. See also Westdeutsche *Landesbank v. Islington LBC* [1996] AC 669, 708: "It is important to stress that this only a presumption , which presumption is easily rebutted either by the counter-presumption of advancement or by direct evidence of ... intention to make an outright transfer."

....

A resulting trust will not arise where the relationship between the transferor and the transferee is such as to raise a presumption that a gift was intended and where the presumption is not rebutted, but in this case the relationship between the deceased and [the nephew] was not such as to raise a presumption of advancement. In this case [the nephew] gave no consideration for the transfer to him (and the deceased) of the interests of the deceased in the property standing to the credit of [the account]. The question therefore is whether there is evidence of the intention of the deceased. That question has been considered in a number of cases relating to property, including bank accounts, in joint names, of which the most relevant for the purposes of this case are the decisions of Rome J. in *Young v. Sealey* [1949] Ch. 278, Megarry J. *in Re Figgis* [1969] 1 Ch. 123, and of the High Court of Australia in Russell v. Scott (1936) 55 CLR 440.

This is a useful restatement of the relevant principles and the court confirmed that the presumption of a resulting trust can easily be rebutted. On the evidence presented in the case the court rejected the argument in favour of a resulting trust, principally because the terms of the bank mandate were very clear and the deceased had been made aware of the consequences.

A difficult case addressing the presumed intention resulting trust is *Hodgson v Marks.*

***Hodgson v Marks* [1971] Ch 892**

Panel: Russell, Buckley and Cairns LJJ

Facts: Mrs Hodgson was an elderly widow who took in a lodger. The lodger persuaded Mrs Hodgson to transfer the legal title to the property into his name to prevent him from being evicted by Mrs Hodgson's nephew. Once the legal title had been transferred, the lodger sold the property to Mr Marks.

LORD JUSTICE RUSSELL

I turn next to the question whether section 53(1) of the Law of Property Act 1925 prevents the assertion by the plaintiff of her entitlement in equity to the house. Let me first assume that, contrary to the view expressed by the judge, Mr. Marks is not debarred from relying upon the section, and the express oral

> arrangement or declaration of trust between the plaintiff and Mr. Evans found by the judge was not effective as such. Nevertheless, the evidence is clear that the transfer was not intended to operate as a gift, and, in those circumstances, I do not see why there was not a resulting trust of the beneficial interest to the plaintiff, which would not, of course, be affected by section 53 (1). It was argued that a resulting trust is based upon implied intention, and that where there is an express trust for the transferor intended and declared – albeit ineffectively – there is no room for such an implication. I do not accept that. If an attempted express trust fails, that seems to me just the occasion for implication of a resulting trust, whether the failure be due to uncertainty, or perpetuity, or lack of form. It would be a strange outcome if the plaintiff were to lose her beneficial interest because her evidence had not been confined to negativing a gift but had additionally moved into a field forbidden by section 53 (1) for lack of writing. I remark in this connection that we are not concerned with the debatable question whether on a voluntary transfer of land by A to stranger B there is a presumption of a resulting trust. The accepted evidence is that this was not intended as a gift, notwithstanding the reference to love and affection in the transfer, and section 53 (1) does not exclude that evidence.

This is a difficult decision as it is not entirely certain why a resulting trust was found in this case. The court accepted that Mrs Hodgson did not intend to make a gift of the property to her lodger, and we would therefore expect the resulting trust to be based upon the presumed intention of the parties. However, Lord Justice Russell also seemed to find that the trust was based upon the failure of the express trust, which looks like an automatic resulting trust, as seen below.

13.3 'Automatic' Resulting Trusts

A clear example of how 'automatic' resulting trusts work can be seen in *Vandervell v Inland Revenue Commissioners.* In this case, due to the fact there was no specified beneficiary of the shares, there was no valid declaration of trust due to a lack of certainty of object. However, another example of when an 'automatic' resulting trust will be found is in commercial practice, following a line of cases starting with *Barclays Bank v Quistclose Investments Ltd* [1970] AC 567.

***Barclays Bank v Quistclose Investments Ltd* [1970] AC 567**

Panel: Lord Reid, Lord Morris of Borth-Y-Gest, Lord Guest, Lord Pearce and Lord Wilberforce

Facts: Rolls Razor was a company that was in serious financial difficulties. It had an overdraft with Barclays Bank of about £484,000. Rolls Razor negotiated with the financier Sir Isaac Woolfson for a loan of £1,000,000. The financier was willing to lend the money as long as Rolls Razor was able to source money for a dividend it had declared as a means of inspiring investor confidence. Rolls Razor procured a loan for £209,719 8s 3d from Quistclose on the condition the money was to be paid into a separate bank account and was only to be used for the purpose of paying the dividend.

The money was duly paid into a separate bank account set up by Barclays. After the account was created, Rolls Razor sent a letter to Barclays recording the agreement between Rolls Razor and Barclays Bank that the money was to be used solely to pay the dividend. Subsequently, the cheque from Quistclose was paid into the account and cleared.

Before the dividend could be paid, Rolls Razors went into voluntary liquidation. Barclays claimed the money in the account for the dividend to pay off part of the dividend. Quistclose went to court claiming that, since the dividend could no longer be paid, the money should return to Quistclose under a resulting trust.

It was held that there was a trust of the money given to pay the dividend. Since Rolls Razor was now in voluntary liquidation the money was now on trust for Quistclose instead of being available to pay Rolls Razor's debts.

LORD WILBERFORCE

Two questions arise, both of which must be answered favourably to the respondents if they are to recover the money from the bank. The first is whether as between the respondents and Rolls Razor Ltd. the terms upon which the loan was made were such as to impress upon the sum of £209,719 8s. 6d. a trust in their favour in the event of the dividend not being paid. The second is whether, in that event, the bank had such notice of the trust or of the circumstances giving rise to it as to make the trust binding upon them.

It is not difficult to establish precisely upon what terms the money was advanced by the respondents to Rolls Razor Ltd There is no doubt that the loan was made specifically in order to enable Rolls Razor Ltd to pay the dividend. There is equally, in my opinion, no doubt that the loan was made only so as to enable Rolls Razor Ltd to pay the dividend and for no other purpose. This follows quite clearly from the terms of the letter of Rolls Razor Ltd to the bank of July 15, 1964, which letter, before transmission to the bank, was sent to the respondents under open cover in order that the cheque might be (as it was) enclosed in it. The mutual intention of the respondents and of Rolls Razor Ltd, and the essence of the bargain, was that the sum advanced should not become part of the assets of Rolls Razor Ltd, but should be used exclusively for payment of a particular class of its creditors, namely, those entitled to the dividend. A necessary consequence from this, by process simply of interpretation, must be that if, for any reason, the dividend could not be paid, the money was to be returned to the respondents: the word "only" or "exclusively" can have no other meaning or effect.

That arrangements of this character for the payment of a person's creditors by a third person, give rise to a relationship of a fiduciary character or trust, in favour, as a primary trust, of the creditors, and secondarily, if the primary trust fails, of the third person, has been recognised in a series of cases over some 150 years. ...

The second, and main, argument for the appellant was of a more sophisticated character. The transaction, it was said, between the respondents and Rolls Razor Ltd, was one of loan, giving rise to a legal action of debt. This necessarily excluded the implication of any trust, enforceable in equity, in the respondents' favour: a transaction may attract one action or the other, it could not admit of both.

My Lords, I must say that I find this argument unattractive. Let us see what it involves. It means that the law does not permit an arrangement to be made by which one person agrees to advance money to another, on terms that the money is to be used exclusively to pay debts of the latter, and if, and so far as not so used, rather than becoming a general asset of the latter available to his creditors at large, is to be returned to the lender. The lender is obliged, in such a case, because he is a lender, to accept, whatever the mutual wishes of lender and borrower may be, that the money he was willing to make available for one purpose only shall be freely available for others of the borrower's creditors for whom he has not the slightest desire to provide.

I should be surprised if an argument of this kind – so conceptualist in character - had ever been accepted. In truth it has plainly been rejected by the eminent judges who from 1819 onwards have permitted arrangements of this type to be enforced, and have approved them as being for the benefit of creditors and all concerned. There is surely no difficulty in recognising the co-existence in one transaction of legal and equitable rights and remedies: when the money is advanced, the lender acquires an equitable right to see that it is applied for the primary designated purpose... if the primary purpose cannot be carried out, the question arises if a secondary purpose (i.e., repayment to the lender) has been agreed, expressly or by implication: if it has, the remedies of equity may be invoked to give effect to it, if it has not (and the money is intended to fall within the general fund of the debtor's assets) then there is the appropriate remedy for recovery of a loan. I can appreciate no reason why the flexible interplay of law and equity cannot let in these practical arrangements, and other variations if desired: it would be to the discredit of both systems if they could not. In the present case the intention to create a secondary trust for the benefit of the lender, to arise if the primary trust, to pay the dividend, could not be carried out, is clear and I can find no reason why the law should not give effect to it.

I pass to the second question, that of notice. ... It is common ground, and I think right, that a mere request to put the money into a separate account is not sufficient to constitute notice. But on July 15, 1964, the bank, when it received the cheque, also received the covering letter of that date which I have set out above: previously there had been the telephone conversation between Mr Goldbart and Mr Parker, to which I have also referred. From these there is no doubt that the bank was told that the money had been provided on loan by a third person and was to be used only for the purpose of paying the dividend. This was sufficient to give them notice that it was trust money and not assets of Rolls Razor Ltd.

Quistclose was, therefore, able to claim the money as beneficiaries of a resulting trust and the case established that where money has been lent for a specific purpose and the money was paid into a separate bank account, then if some or all of the money was not used for the specified purpose it was held on resulting trust for the lender. If the money *was* used for a specified purpose, however, the trust relationship came to an end and the relationship between the lender and the debtor was that of an ordinary unsecured loan.

This has the important consequence of affecting the ability of the lender to get the money back. Once the money has been used as specified, the lender no longer has the advantage of a proprietary claim against the money. The lender will not be able to take priority over the ordinary unsecured creditors of the debtor. Instead, the lender must share what assets are available with all of the debtor's other creditors if the debtor becomes insolvent. The harsh practicality of this is that an unsecured creditor sees little, if any, return for the money that was originally lent if the debtor becomes insolvent.

Whilst the finding of the existence of this type of trust has clear commercial advantages to those wanting to engage in credit relationships, there are elements of uncertainty as to how these types of trust apply. This first major issue is how Lord Wilberforce described the *Quistclose* trust mechanism. If we accept his belief that *Quistclose* trusts start as a primary trust, then we have to accept that the primary trust could possibly be to fulfil a purpose, such as the paying off of a dividend in *Quistclose* itself. This is inherently problematic as it would allow private purpose trusts to exist outside of the limitations described in *Re Endacott* [1960] Ch 232. The courts have therefore tried to find alternative interpretations for how *Quistclose* trusts operate.

Link
See Chapter 6

***Twinsectra v Yardley and Others* [2002] 2 AC 164**

Panel: Lord Slynn of Hadley, Lord Steyn, Lord Hoffmann, Lord Hutton and Lord Millett

Facts: Mr Yardley wanted to obtain a loan of £1,000,000 to purchase some land. Both Mr Yardley and his solicitor Mr Leach made applications for loans to various parties. Eventually they were successful in that Twinsectra was willing to lend the entire sum. However, Twinsectra wanted a solicitor's personal undertaking from Mr Leach to protect Twinsectra in the event of Yardley defaulting on the loan. Mr Leach was unwilling to agree to such an undertaking so Mr Yardley contacted a second solicitor, Mr Sims. Mr Sims was willing to provide an undertaking, as he had worked with Mr Yardley in the past and owed Mr Yardley about $1,500,000. The loan was agreed with the agreement that the money was to be used for the sole purpose of acquiring property and that the money was to be retained by Mr Sims until Mr Yardley acquired the property.

The money was consequently paid to Mr Sims, who in breach of his undertaking transferred the money to Mr Leach. Mr Sims faxed a copy of the undertaking to Mr Leach, but since the undertaking had no reference to Mr Leach at all he felt he was not bound by what it said. Mr Leach therefore felt he was merely holding

Link
See Chapter 16

the money subject to Mr Yardley's instruction, and when Mr Yardley asked for the money, Mr Leach transferred it to him. Mr Yardley then began to spend some of the money contrary to the instructions in the undertaking. Mr Yardley defaulted on the loan and Twinsectra tried to claim their money back, firstly through a proprietary claim for whatever money remained in Mr Yardley's account and secondly against Mr Leach for assisting a breach of trust.

It was held that there was a *Quistclose* trust of the money and, therefore, whatever money was left in Mr Yardley's account that was identifiable as belonging to Twinsectra was subject to a resulting trust. Twinsectra were therefore able to take priority over Mr Yardley's unsecured creditors in claiming this part of the loan money back.

LORD MILLETT

My Lords, there are two issues in this appeal. The first is concerned with the nature of the so-called "Quistclose trust" and the requirements for its creation. The second arises only if the first is answered adversely to the appellant. It is whether his conduct rendered him liable for having assisted in a breach of trust. …

Money advanced by way of loan normally becomes the property of the borrower. He is free to apply the money as he chooses, and save to the extent to which he may have taken security for repayment the lender takes the risk of the borrower's insolvency. But it is well established that a loan to a borrower for a specific purpose where the borrower is not free to apply the money for any other purpose gives rise to fiduciary obligations on the part of the borrower which a court of equity will enforce. In the earlier cases the purpose was to enable the borrower to pay his creditors or some of them, but the principle is not limited to such cases.

Such arrangements are commonly described as creating "a Quistclose trust", after the well known decision of the House in Quistclose Investments Ltd v Rolls Razor Ltd [1970] AC 567 in which Lord Wilberforce confirmed the validity of such arrangements and explained their legal consequences. When the money is advanced, the lender acquires a right, enforceable in equity, to see that it is applied for the stated purpose, or more accurately to prevent its application for any other purpose. This prevents the borrower from obtaining any beneficial interest in the money, at least while the designated purpose is still capable of being carried out. Once the purpose has been carried out, the lender has his normal remedy in debt. If for any reason the purpose cannot be carried out, the question arises whether the money falls within the general fund of the borrower's assets, in which case it passes to his trustee in bankruptcy in the event of his insolvency and the lender is merely a loan creditor; or whether it is held on a resulting trust for the lender. This depends on the intention of the parties collected from the terms of the arrangement and the circumstances of the case.

In the present case Twinsectra contends that paragraphs 1 and 2 of the undertaking which Mr Sims signed on 24 December created a Quistclose trust. Mr Leach denies this and advances a number of objections to the existence of a trust. He says that Twinsectra lacked the necessary intention to create a trust, and relies on evidence that Twinsectra looked exclusively to Mr Sims' personal undertaking to repay the loan as its security for repayment. He says that commercial life would be impossible if trusts were lightly inferred from slight material, and that it is not enough to agree that a loan is to be made for a particular purpose. There must be something more, for example, a requirement that the money be paid into a segregated account, before it is appropriate to infer that a trust has been created. In the present case the money was paid into Mr Sims' client account, but that is sufficiently explained by the fact that it was not Mr Sims' money but his client's; it provides no basis for an inference that the money was held in trust for anyone other than Mr Yardley. Then it is said that a trust requires certainty of objects and this was lacking, for the stated purpose "to be applied in the purchase of property" is too uncertain to be enforced. Finally it is said that no trust in favour of Twinsectra could arise prior to the failure of the stated purpose, and this did not occur until the money was misapplied by Mr Yardley's companies.

Intention

The first two objections are soon disposed of. A settlor must, of course, possess the necessary intention to create a trust, but his subjective intentions are irrelevant. If he enters into arrangements which have the effect of creating a trust, it is not necessary that he should appreciate that they do so; it is sufficient that he intends to enter into them. Whether paragraphs 1 and 2 of the undertaking created a *Quistclose* trust turns on the true construction of those paragraphs.

The fact that Twinsectra relied for its security exclusively on Mr Sims's personal liability to repay goes to Twinsectra's subjective intention and is not relevant to the construction of the undertaking, but it is in any case not inconsistent with the trust alleged. Arrangements of this kind are not intended to provide security for repayment of the loan, but to prevent the money from being applied otherwise than in accordance with the lender's wishes. If the money is properly applied the loan is unsecured. This was true of all the decided cases, including the *Quistclose* case itself.

The effect of the undertaking

A Quistclose trust does not necessarily arise merely because money is paid for a particular purpose. A lender will often inquire into the purpose for which a loan is sought in order to decide whether he would be justified in making it. He may be said to lend the money for the purpose in question, but this is not enough to create a trust; once lent the money is at the free disposal of the borrower. Similarly payments in advance for goods or services are paid for a particular purpose, but such payments do not ordinarily create a trust. The money is intended to be at the free disposal of the supplier and may be used as part of his cashflow. Commercial life would be impossible if this were not the case.

The question in every case is whether the parties intended the money to be at the free disposal of the recipient. ...

Alert

In the present case paragraphs 1 and 2 of the undertaking are crystal clear. Mr Sims undertook that the money would be used solely for the acquisition of property and for no other purpose; and was to be retained by his firm until so applied. It would not be held by Mr Sims simply to Mr Yardley's order; and it would not be at Mr Yardley's free disposition. Any payment by Mr Sims of the money, whether to Mr Yardley or anyone else, otherwise than for the acquisition of property would constitute a breach of trust. ...

The nature of the trust

...They call for an exploration of the true nature of the *Quistclose* trust, and in particular the location of the beneficial interest while the purpose is still capable of being carried out.

This has been the subject of much academic debate. The starting point is provided by two passages in Lord Wilberforce's speech in the *Quistclose* case [1970] AC 567. ...

... [T]here are two successive trusts, a primary trust for payment to identifiable beneficiaries, such as creditors or shareholders, and a secondary trust in favour of the lender arising on the failure of the primary trust. But there are formidable difficulties in this analysis, which has little academic support. What if the primary trust is not for identifiable persons, but as in the present case to carry out an abstract purpose? Where in such a case is the beneficial interest pending the application of the money for the stated purpose or the failure of the purpose? There are four possibilities: (i) in the lender; (ii) in the borrower; (iii) in the contemplated beneficiary; or (iv) in suspense.

(i) *The lender.* In "The *Quistclose* Trust: Who Can Enforce It?" (1985) 101 LQR, 269, I argued that the beneficial interest remained throughout in the lender. This analysis has received considerable though not universal academic support... .

On this analysis, the *Quistclose* trust is a simple commercial arrangement akin (as Professor Bridge observes) to a retention of title clause (though with a different object) which enables the borrower to have recourse to the lender's money for a particular purpose without entrenching on the lender's property rights more than necessary to enable the purpose to be achieved. The money remains the property of the lender unless and until it is applied in accordance with his directions, and insofar as it is not so applied it must be returned to him. I am disposed, perhaps pre-disposed, to think that this is the only analysis which is consistent both with orthodox trust law and with commercial reality. Before reaching a concluded view that it should be adopted, however, I must consider the alternatives.

(ii) *The borrower*. It is plain that the beneficial interest is not vested unconditionally in the borrower so as to leave the money at his free disposal. That would defeat the whole purpose of the arrangements, which is to prevent the money from passing to the borrower's trustee in bankruptcy in the event of his insolvency. It would also be inconsistent with all the decided cases where the contest was between the lender and the borrower's trustee in bankruptcy, as well as with the *Quistclose* case itself... .

(iii) In the contemplated beneficiary. In the *Quistclose* case itself [1970] AC 567, as in all the reported cases which preceded it, either the primary purpose had been carried out and the contest was between the borrower's trustee in bankruptcy or liquidator and the person or persons to whom the borrower had paid the money; or it was treated as having failed, and the contest was between the borrower's trustee-in-bankruptcy and the lender. It was not necessary to explore the position while the primary purpose was still capable of being carried out and Lord Wilberforce's observations must be read in that light. ...

There are several difficulties with this analysis. In the first place, Lord Wilberforce's reference to *Re Rogers* 8 Morr 243 makes it plain that the equitable right he had in mind was not a mandatory order to compel performance, but a negative injunction to restrain improper application of the money; for neither Lindley LJ nor Kay LJ recognised more than this. In the second place, the object of the arrangements was to enable the subsidiary to continue trading, and this would necessarily involve it in incurring further liabilities to trade creditors. Accordingly the application of the fund was not confined to existing creditors at the date when the fund was established. The company secretary was given to understand that the purpose of the arrangements was to keep the subsidiary trading, and that the fund was "as good as share capital". Thus the purpose of the arrangements was not, as in other cases, to enable the debtor to avoid bankruptcy by paying off existing creditors, but to enable the debtor to continue trading by providing it with working capital with which to incur fresh liabilities. There is a powerful argument for saying that the result of the arrangements was to vest a beneficial interest in the subsidiary from the start. If so, then this was not a *Quistclose* trust at all.

In the third place, it seems unlikely that the banks' object was to benefit the creditors (who included the Inland Revenue) except indirectly. The banks had their own commercial interests to protect by enabling the subsidiary to trade out of its difficulties. If so, then the primary trust cannot be supported as a valid non- charitable purpose trust: see *Re Grant's Will Trusts, Harris v Anderson* [1980] 1 WLR 360 and cf. *Re Denley's Trust Deed* [1969] 1 Ch 373.

Link
see Chapter 6

The most serious objection to this approach is exemplified by the facts of the present case. In several of the cases the primary trust was for an abstract purpose with no one but the lender to enforce performance or restrain misapplication of the money. In *Edwards v Glyn* (1859) 2 E & E 29 the money was advanced to a bank to enable the bank to meet a run. In *Re EVTR, Gilbert v Barber* [1987] BCLC 646 it was advanced "for the sole purpose of buying new equipment". ... The present case is another example. It is simply not possible to hold money on trust to acquire unspecified property from an unspecified vendor at an unspecified time. There is no reason to make an arbitrary distinction between money paid for an abstract purpose and money paid for a purpose which can be said to benefit an ascertained class of beneficiaries, and the cases rightly draw no such distinction. Any analysis of the *Quistclose* trust must be able to accommodate gifts and loans for an abstract purpose.

(iv) *In suspense.* As Peter Gibson J pointed out in *Carreras Rothmans Ltd v Freeman Matthews Treasure Ltd* [1985] Ch 207, 223 the effect of adopting Sir Robert Megarry V-C's analysis is to leave the beneficial interest in suspense until the stated purpose is carried out or fails. The difficulty with this (apart from its unorthodoxy) is that it fails to have regard to the role which the resulting trust plays in equity's scheme of things, or to explain why the money is not simply held on a resulting trust for the lender. ...

(v) The Court of Appeal's analysis. The Court of Appeal were content to treat the beneficial interest as in suspense, or (following Dr Chambers's analysis) to hold that it was in the borrower, the lender having merely a contractual right enforceable by injunction to prevent misapplication. Potter LJ put it in these terms [1999] Lloyd's Rep Bank 438, 456, para 75:

> "The purpose imposed at the time of the advance creates an enforceable restriction on the borrower's use of the money. Although the lender's right to enforce the restriction is treated as arising on the basis of a 'trust', the use of that word does not enlarge the lender's interest in the fund. The borrower is entitled to the beneficial use of the money, subject to the lender's right to prevent its misuse; the lender's limited interest in the fund is sufficient to prevent its use for other than the special purpose for which it was advanced."

This analysis, with respect, is difficult to reconcile with the court's actual decision in so far as it granted Twinsectra a proprietary remedy against Mr Yardley's companies as recipients of the misapplied funds. Unless the money belonged to Twinsectra immediately before its misapplication, there is no basis on which a proprietary remedy against third party recipients can be justified.

Dr Chambers's "novel view" (as it has been described) is that the arrangements do not create a trust at all; the borrower receives the entire beneficial ownership in the money subject only to a contractual right in the lender to prevent the money being used otherwise than for the stated purpose. If the purpose fails, a resulting trust in the lender springs into being. In fact, he argues for a kind of restrictive covenant enforceable by negative injunction yet creating property rights in the money. But restrictive covenants, which began life as negative easements, are part of our land law. Contractual obligations do not run with money or a chose in action like money in a bank account.

Dr Chambers's analysis has attracted academic comment, both favourable and unfavourable. For my own part, I do not think that it can survive the criticism levelled against it... . It provides no solution to cases of non-contractual payment; is inconsistent with Lord Wilberforce's description of the borrower's obligation as fiduciary and not merely contractual; fails to explain the evidential significance of a requirement that the money should be kept in a separate account; cannot easily be reconciled with the availability of proprietary remedies against third parties; and while the existence of a mere equity to prevent misapplication would be sufficient to prevent the money from being available for distribution to the creditors on the borrower's insolvency (because the trustee in bankruptcy has no greater rights than his bankrupt) it would not prevail over secured creditors. If the bank in the *Quistclose* case [1970] AC 567 had held a floating charge (as it probably did) and had appointed a receiver, the adoption of Dr Chambers's analysis should have led to a different outcome.

Thus all the alternative solutions have their difficulties. But there are two problems which they fail to solve, but which are easily solved if the beneficial interest remains throughout in the lender. One arises from the fact, well established by the authorities, that the primary trust is enforceable by the lender. But on what basis can he enforce it? He cannot do so as the beneficiary under the secondary trust, for if the primary purpose is fulfilled there is no secondary trust... . He cannot do so as settlor, for a settlor who retains no beneficial interest cannot enforce the trust which he has created.

Dr Chambers insists that the lender has merely a right to prevent the misapplication of the money, and attributes this to his contractual right to specific performance of a condition of the contract of loan. As I have already pointed out, this provides no solution where the arrangement is non-contractual. But Lord Wilberforce clearly based the borrower's obligation on an equitable or fiduciary basis and not a contractual one. He was concerned to justify the co-existence of equity's exclusive jurisdiction with the common law action for debt. Basing equity's intervention on its auxiliary jurisdiction to restrain a breach of contract would not have enabled the lender to succeed against the bank, which was a third party to the contract. There is only one explanation of the lender's fiduciary right to enforce the primary trust which can be reconciled with basic principle: he can do so because he is the beneficiary.

The other problem is concerned with the basis on which the primary trust is said to have failed in several of the cases ... and the *Quistclose* case itself [1970] AC 567. Given that the money did not belong to the borrower in either case, the borrower's insolvency should not have prevented the money from being paid in the manner contemplated. A man cannot pay some only of his creditors once he has been adjudicated bankrupt, but a third party can. A company cannot pay a dividend once it has gone into liquidation, but there is nothing to stop a third party from paying the disappointed shareholders. The reason why the purpose failed in each case must be because the lender's object in making the money available was to save the borrower from bankruptcy in the one case and collapse in the other. But this in itself is not enough. A trust does not fail merely because the settlor's purpose in creating it has been frustrated: the trust must become illegal or impossible to perform. The settlor's motives must not be confused with the purpose of the trust; the frustration of the former does not by itself cause the failure of the latter. But if the borrower is treated as holding the money on a resulting trust for the lender but with power (or in some cases a duty) to carry out the lender's revocable mandate, and the lender's object in giving the mandate is frustrated, he is entitled to revoke the mandate and demand the return of money which never ceased to be his beneficially. ...

Alert

... I do not think that subtle distinctions should be made between "true" Quistclose trusts and trusts which are merely analogous to them. It depends on how widely or narrowly you choose to define the Quistclose trust. There is clearly a wide range of situations in which the parties enter into a commercial arrangement which permits one party to have a limited use of the other's money for a stated purpose, is not free to apply it for any other purpose, and must return it if for any reason the purpose cannot be carried out. The arrangement between the purchaser's solicitor and the purchaser's mortgagee is an example of just such an arrangement. All such arrangements should if possible be susceptible to the same analysis.

As Sherlock Holmes reminded Dr Watson, when you have eliminated the impossible, whatever remains, however improbable, must be the truth. I would reject all the alternative analyses, which I find unconvincing for the reasons I have endeavoured to explain, and hold the *Quistclose* trust to be an entirely orthodox example of the kind of default trust known as a resulting trust. The lender pays the money to the borrower by way of loan, but he does not part with the entire beneficial interest in the money, and in so far as he does not it is held on a resulting trust for the lender from the outset. Contrary to the opinion of the Court of Appeal, it is the borrower who has a very limited use of the money, being obliged to apply it for the stated purpose or return it. He has no beneficial interest in the money, which remains throughout in the lender subject only to the borrower's power or duty to apply the money in accordance with the lender's instructions. When the purpose fails, the money is returnable to the lender, not under some new trust in his favour which only comes into being on the failure of the purpose, but because the resulting trust in his favour is no longer subject to any power on the part of the borrower to make use of the money. Whether the borrower is obliged to apply the money for the stated purpose or merely at liberty to do so, and whether the lender can countermand the borrower's mandate while it is still capable of being carried out, must depend on the circumstances of the particular case.

Certainty

After this over-long exposition, it is possible to dispose of the remaining objections to the creation of a *Quistclose* trust very shortly. A trust must have certainty of objects. But the only trust is the resulting trust for the lender. The borrower is authorised (or directed) to apply the money for a stated purpose, but this is a mere power and does not constitute a purpose trust. Provided the power is stated with sufficient clarity for the court to be able to determine whether it is still capable of being carried out or whether the money has been misapplied, it is sufficiently certain to be enforced. ...

Conclusion

In my opinion the Court of Appeal were correct to find that the terms of paragraphs 1 and 2 of the undertaking created a *Quistclose* trust. The money was never at Mr Yardley's free disposal. It was never held to his order by Mr Sims. The money belonged throughout to Twinsectra, subject only to Mr Yardley's right to apply it for the acquisition of property. Twinsectra parted with the money to Mr Sims, relying on him to ensure that the money was properly applied or returned to it. Mr Sims act in paying the money over to Mr Leach was a breach of trust, but it did not in itself render the money incapable of being applied for the stated purpose. In so far as Mr Leach applied the money in the acquisition of property, the purpose was achieved.

Lord Millett's analysis is undeniably deeply impressive for its level of detail and consideration of a wide range of possible interpretations of how *Quistclose* trusts operate. Furthermore, from a pragmatic perspective it is *ratio* for how to interpret *Quistclose* trusts and the basis for discussing *Quistclose* trusts in this chapter.

However, this analysis has not been universally accepted as properly explaining why *Quistclose* trusts work.

The second issue with *Quistclose* trusts, as highlighted by *Twinsectra v Yardley*, is that such trusts have been found in situations that do not exactly correspond to the scenario of *Quistclose* itself. *Twinsectra v Yardley* and the following three cases show how the limits of *Quistclose* trusts have been teased out by the subsequent caselaw.

***Re Chelsea Cloisters Ltd (In liquidation)* (1981) 41 P & CR 98**

Panel: Lord Denning MR, Bridge and Oliver LJJ

Facts: The landlords of a block of flats granted an underlease to a company, Chelsea Cloisters, who subsequently managed the block. Part of these managerial responsibilities entailed granting furnished and unfurnished tenancies. Under clause 1 of a tenancy agreement between the company and a tenant, the tenant had to pay a deposit to cover any damages or compensation to the company. If the deposit was not required at the end of the tenancy it was to be paid back to the former tenant.

Initially, there was no formal arrangement for how these tenancy moneys were managed, but in 1974 the company fell into financial difficulty and a chartered accountant was employed to supervise how the company was run. The accountant subsequently opened a separate bank account that was designated specifically for the tenant deposit moneys. All deposits made from June 1974 were paid into this account.

In November 1974, the underlease expired and the landlords took over the block of flats. The company subsequently went into liquidation. The liquidator went to court to find out whether the money in the tenant deposit account belonged to the landlords to hold on trust for the tenants or the creditors of the company.

It was held that in the beginning there was merely a contractual relationship between the company and the tenants. However, from the moment moneys were paid into the separate bank account, combined with the nature of clause 1 of the tenancy agreement, there was a trust for the tenants. The landlords were therefore entitled to the money to hold on trust, together with any interest accrued upon it.

LORD DENNING MR

Alert

Mr Parker first suggested that these sums paid by way of a deposit were impressed with a trust from the very beginning. He said that they were deposited as a security with the tenants having an equity to the return of any balance. I do not think that is correct. I think these deposits were made contractually with an obligation to repay the whole or some lesser sum. There was no trust at the beginning... .

The second way in which Mr Parker put it was on the special conduct of Mr Iredale in setting up the tenants' deposit account when he took over. The question to be answered is, what is the proper inference to be drawn from the nature of the transaction? It does not matter what the transaction was called. The question is what was the nature of it. ...

It is important to have regard to Mr Iredale's affidavit when he says what the nature of this transaction was. It is given in paragraphs 12 and 13:

> On August 14, 1974, I arranged for the company to open a separate bank account designated "tenants' deposit account," and gave instructions that all future deposits were to be paid into that account. This was a practical step, designed to ensure that the deposits would not be spent as part of the company's general cash flow, as had happened in the past. I was also concerned that I and my firm could be open to criticism if deposits were spent in this way and the company was then unable to make refunds to tenants. Nothing was said to the tenants about the new account.
>
> I regarded the tenants' deposit account as available only for repaying the deposit of any tenant who had paid a deposit on or after June 18, 1974. For about a fortnight after June 18, I continued to repay the deposits of earlier tenants out of the general funds of the company. But I had to stop this soon after the receiver was appointed, because the company was receiving no income.

To my mind it is as plain as can be that Mr Iredale realised that the company was in a hopeless position: it had no money to pay anybody: and there was a danger that these deposits might fall into the hands of the other creditors of the company, contrary to the justice of the case. So, he thought that all these deposits, which the tenants had paid, and which they were entitled to have back under the terms of their agreements, ought to be kept as a separate fund to be secure against other creditors, and to be made available only to the tenants.

On the principles I have stated, it seems to me that the nature of this transaction was inevitably such as to create a trust of those moneys—from June 18 to November 16—on the terms of the original arrangements. They were to be held until the end of each tenancy. At the end of each tenancy, the dilapidations were to be calculated. If there were no dilapidations, the whole deposit was to go back to the tenants. If there were dilapidations, there were to be deductions accordingly. That seems to me to be the nature of the trust. That being the nature of the trust, it seems to me that there is nothing to go to the general body of creditors here.

LORD JUSTICE BRIDGE

"This"—that is to say, the opening of a separate bank account—"was a practical step, designed to ensure that the deposits would not be spent as part of the company's general cash flow." That is entirely consistent with an intention to keep these funds from the general funds of the company in order that they should not be swallowed up by the general funds of the company. The second critical statement was this: "I was also concerned that I and my firm could be open to criticism if deposits were spent in this way"—that is to say, if they were absorbed in the general funds of the company and spent as if they were available to be treated as part of the general funds of the company. Why was Mr Iredale apprehensive of criticism of himself and his firm? It surely can only have been that he at that time regarded the company, whose affairs he was managing, as being either under a moral or perhaps a legal duty to treat the tenants' deposits as impressed with some sort of beneficial interest in favour of the tenants and to ensure that sufficient funds were available to meet the tenants' claims to recover the deposits as and when those claims were made. It may even be that Mr Iredale supposed that the terms of clause 1 of the tenancy agreement had in fact impressed these deposits with a trust. That would have left unresolved the question arising out of the terms of that agreement. But, if he was mistaken in that belief, it would not—as Mr Parker has satisfied me in his reply—have prevented his intention from being effective, if his intention in setting aside what he believed to be trust moneys was to ensure that they were available for what he believed to be the trust purposes.

LORD JUSTICE OLIVER

I should add this, that I was bothered at one time by this point, that, when the account was opened on August 14, 1974, there was paid into it the sum of £11,000, being the amount which had been received by Mr Iredale since June 18 when he became a signatory on the company's account in respect of deposits by tenants. The argument presented by Mr Unwin as regards this was that, if a trust was created, would this not in fact involve that Mr Iredale had in mind the possibility that the company would be unable to meet its obligations and thus constitute a refund to the tenants a fraudulent preference? It is suggested that that is an unlikely intention to ascribe to a chartered accountant of Mr Iredale's experience. It seems to me that the answer is that it is not suggested that there was an express trust here in the sense that Mr Iredale consciously said "I am going to create a trust." The question is, what is the result of what was done in the light of what Mr Iredale has said was his intention? He told the court in his affidavit what his intention was, and the funds paid in on August 14, 1974, cannot, I think, have been paid in with any different intention from the intention in respect of the funds subsequently paid in.

This case is important, as a *Quistclose* trust was found despite there being no instruction by the original owner of the money, i.e. the tenants. For this reason the concerns as highlighted by Bridge and Oliver LJJ are extremely pertinent. Every time a *Quistclose* trust is found it means that the beneficiaries of such a trust have *proprietary* rights to the money. It could be argued that such persons are only entitled to rights as strong as these if they intended themselves to have them; whether a trust is found or not should depend upon the intention of the original absolute owner of the property as to what should be done with regard to rights in the property.

***Carreras Rothmans Ltd v Freeman Mathews Treasure Ltd and Another* [1985] Ch 207**

Panel: Peter Gibson J

Facts: Carreras Rothmans produced cigarettes and tobacco, which they extensively advertised. They employed Freeman Matthews Treasure as their advertising agents. As part of the advertising plan, the agents acquired advertising space in publications and on bill boards. They negotiated favourable rates for this advertising space and incurred debts in acquiring it. Carreras Rothmans then paid the advertising agents in time so that they could pay off the debts incurred for acquiring the advertising space.

In 1982, the advertising company fell into financial difficulty and, at Carreras Rothman's suggestion, the money for acquiring the advertising space was paid into a separate bank account from July 1983. Pursuant to this, Carreras Rothmans made a payment of £597,128.72 to cover the cost for the June advertising but the advertising agent went into voluntary liquidation before the advertising space was paid for. The liquidator froze all of the advertising agency's bank accounts and the third party publishers reacted by refusing to publish the adverts for Carreras Rothmans until the June advertising had been paid for. Carreras Rothmans paid off the June advertising and claimed the money in the segregated bank account from the liquidator.

It was held that Carreras Rothmans was entitled to the money in the account under a *Quistclose* trust.

MR JUSTICE PETER GIBSON

The July agreement was plainly intended to vary the contractual position of the parties as to how, as the contract letter put it, payments made by the plaintiff to the defendant for purely onwards transmission, in effect, to the third party creditors, would be dealt with. If one looks objectively at the genesis of the variation, the plaintiff was concerned about the adverse effect on it if the defendant, which the plaintiff knew to have financial problems, ceased trading and the third party creditors of the defendant were not paid at a time when the defendant had been put in funds by the plaintiff. The objective was accurately described by Mr. Higgs in his informal letter of 19 July as to protect the interests of the plaintiff and the third parties. For this purpose a special account was to be set up with a special designation. The moneys payable by the plaintiff were to be paid not to the defendant beneficially but directly into that account so that the defendant was never free to deal as it pleased with the moneys so paid. The moneys were to be used only for the specific purpose of paying the third parties and as the cheque letter indicated, the amount paid matched the specific invoices presented by the defendant to the plaintiff. The account was intended to be little more than a conduit pipe, but the intention was plain that whilst in the conduit pipe the moneys should be protected. There was even a provision covering the possibility (though what actual situation it was intended to meet it is hard to conceive) that there might be a balance left after payment and in that event the balance was to be paid to the plaintiff and not kept by the defendant. It was thus clearly intended that the moneys once paid would never become the property of the defendant. That was the last thing the plaintiff wanted in view of its concern about the defendant's financial position. As a further precaution the bank was to be put on notice of the conditions and purpose of the account. I infer that this was to prevent the bank attempting to exercise any rights of set off against the moneys in the account.

Only two matters were relied on as indicating that no trust was intended. One was the consideration fee; but the presence of consideration does not negative a trust. The other was the express reference in the penultimate paragraph in relation to placements and forward media options with which was contrasted the absence of the word "trust" in relation to the moneys in the account. But I regard that as of minimal significance when I consider all the other indications as to the capacity in which the defendant was to hold any moneys in the account. In my judgment even in the absence of authority it is manifest that the defendant was intended to act in relation to those moneys in a fiduciary capacity only.

There is of course ample authority that moneys paid by A to B for a specific purpose which has been made known to B are clothed with a trust. In the *Quistclose* case [1970] AC 567, 580 Lord Wilberforce referred to the recognition, in a series of cases over some 150 years, that arrangements for the payment of a person's creditors by a third person gives rise to

> "a relationship of a fiduciary character or trust, in favour, as a primary trust, of the creditors, and secondarily, if the primary trust fails, of the third person ..."

Alert

Lord Wilberforce in describing the facts of the Quistclose case said a little earlier on p. 580 that the mutual intention of the provider of the moneys and of the recipient of the moneys and the essence of the bargain was that the moneys should not become part of the assets of the recipient but should be used exclusively for payment of a particular class of its creditors. That description seems to me to be apt in relation to the facts of the present case too. ...

It is of course true that there are factual differences between the *Quistclose* case and the present case. The transaction there was one of loan with no contractual obligation on the part of the lender to make payment prior to the agreement for the loan. In the present case there is no loan but there is an antecedent debt owed by the plaintiff. I doubt if it is helpful to analyse the *Quistclose* type of case in terms of the constituent parts of a conventional settlement, though it may of course be crucial to ascertain in whose favour the secondary trust operates (as in the *Quistclose* case itself) and who has an enforceable right. In my judgment the principle in all these cases is that equity fastens on the conscience of the person who receives from another property transferred for a specific purpose only and not therefore for the recipient's own purposes, so that such person will not be permitted to treat the property as his own or to use it for other than the stated purpose. Most of the cases in this line are cases where there has been an agreement for consideration so that in one sense each party has contributed to providing the property. But if the common intention is that property is transferred for a specific purpose and not so as to become the property of the transferee, the transferee cannot keep the property if for any reason that purpose cannot be fulfilled. I am left in no doubt that the provider of the moneys in the present case was the plaintiff. True it is that its own witnesses said that if the defendant had not agreed to the terms of the contract letter, the plaintiff would not have broken its contract but would have paid its debt to the defendant, but the fact remains that the plaintiff made its payment on the terms of that letter and the defendant received the moneys only for the stipulated purpose. That purpose was expressed to relate only to the moneys in the account. In my judgment therefore the plaintiff can be equated with the lender in Quistclose as having an enforceable right to compel the carrying out of the primary trust. ...

Alert

In my judgment therefore a trust was created by the July agreement, the trust was completely constituted by the payment of moneys into the special account and the plaintiff as the provider of the moneys has an equitable right to an order for the carrying out by the defendant of the trust.

Two of the key issues in Peter Gibson J's judgment are first, that it was vital in finding a *Quistclose* trust that the money was paid into a separate bank account. However, in *Re EVTR Ltd* (1987) 3 BCC 389 the fact the money was paid into the company's general bank account was not fatal to finding a *Quistclose* trust. Secondly, it was also reported that a specific purpose had been stated for how the money was used. However, it is important to note that this has not been found to be essential in every *Quistclose* trusts case. Please refer to *Re Chelsea Cloisters Ltd (In liquidation)* (1981) 41 P & CR 98 above and see also *Cooper v PRG Powerhouse Ltd* [2008] 2 All ER (Comm) 964.

Re EVTR Ltd (1987) 3 BCC 389

Panel: Dillon, Woolf and Bingham LJJ

Facts: Mr Barber, a former employee of EVTR, won nearly £250,000 on a premium bonds win. He wanted to help his former company, which was in financial difficulty. He lent £60,000 to EVTR for the purpose of acquiring equipment from a manufacturer, Quantel. Since this sum was insufficient to purchase the equipment outright, EVTR agreed to lease the equipment from a leasing company, Concord. The new equipment would take seven months to arrive. In the meantime, some temporary equipment was leased to EVTR through Concord. The £60,000 was paid by EVTR as a deposit against the cost of the permanent equipment, in order to get the temporary equipment on loan.

Before the new equipment was delivered, receivers were appointed to administer EVTR. EVTR ceased trading and the leasing company took the temporary equipment back. Since EVTR never received the new equipment, the leasing company returned the £60,000, with a reduction for an agreed sum for EVTR's breach of contract and loss of interest.

The issue before the Court was whether the money was a company asset and, therefore, should be used to meet the claims of EVTR's creditors, or whether the money was held under a *Quistclose* trust for Mr Barber.

Despite the money being used to hire equipment, it was held that the fact the permanent equipment had never arrived meant that there was a *Quistclose* trust of the money.

LORD JUSTICE DILLON

In the present case the £60,000 was released by Knapp-Fishers to the company on the appellant's instructions for a specific purpose only, namely the sole purpose of buying new equipment. Accordingly, I have no doubt, in the light of *Quistclose*, that, if the company had gone into liquidation, or the receivers had been appointed, and the scheme had become abortive before the £60,000 had been disbursed by the company, the appellant would have been entitled to recover his full £60,000, as between himself and the company, on the footing that it was impliedly held by the company on a resulting trust for him as the particular purpose of the loan had failed.

At the other end of the spectrum, if after the £60,000 had been expended by the company as it was, the Encore system had been duly delivered to, and accepted by, the company, there could be no doubt that the appellant's only right would have been as an unsecured creditor of the company for the £60,000. There would have been no question of the Encore system, or any interest in it, being held on any sort of trust for the appellant, and if, after it had been delivered and installed, the company had sold the system, the appellant could have had no claim whatsoever to the proceeds of sale as trust moneys held in trust for him.

The present case lies on its facts between those two extremes of the spectrum. Other scenarios between the extremes could equally be written, e.g. if, after the £60,000 had been paid by the company, Quantel had been enjoined by a third party from supplying the Encore system on the ground that the Encore system infringed patent rights or copyright of the third party and Quantel had thereupon refunded the £60,000, or if the Encore system was supplied but proved totally useless for its purpose and was therefore rejected and the money was returned.

The deputy judge took the view that the trust concept was spent when the £60,000 was paid out by the company. But he considered that the correctness of that view could be tested by an analogy which, with all respect to him, was false. He considered – rightly on the facts – that, had Concord or Quantel gone into liquidation after cashing the cheque or bankers' draft issued by the company, it could not have been argued that the proceeds of the cheque or bankers' draft were other than part of their general assets; but that is a false analogy, in that Concord and Quantel had no notice of any trust in favour of the appellant, whereas the company did have notice, and it was the company and not Concord or Quantel which was bound as to the manner in which the £60,000 could be used. ...

On *Quistclose* principles, a resulting trust in favour of the provider of the money arises when money is provided for a particular purpose only, and that purpose fails. In the present case, the purpose for which the £60,000 was provided by the appellant to the company was, as appears from the authority to Knapp-Fishers, the purpose of the company's buying new equipment. But in any realistic sense of the words that purpose has failed in that the company has never acquired any new equipment, whether the Encore system which was then in mind or anything else. True it is that the £60,000 was paid out by the company with a view to the acquisition of new equipment, but that was only at half-time, and I do not see why the final whistle should be blown at half-time. The proposed acquisition proved abortive and a large part of the £60,000 has therefore been repaid by the payees. The repayments were made because of, or on account of, the payments which made up the £60,000 and those were payments of trust moneys. It is a long established principle of equity that, if a person who is a trustee receives money or property because of, or in respect of, trust property, he will hold what he receives as a constructive trustee on the trusts of the original trust property. ... It follows, in my judgment, that the repayments made to the receivers are subject to the same trusts as the original £60,000 in the hands of the company. There is now, of course, no question of the £48,536 being applied in the purchase of new equipment for the company, and accordingly, in my judgment, it is now held on a resulting trust for the appellant. ...

The company did of course have the benefit for some months of the loan of the temporary equipment. Therefore, at any rate as between the company and Quantel, there was not a total failure of consideration so far as the company was concerned. But, even assuming (contrary to submissions made by counsel for the appellant) that the appellant was at the material times aware of the loan of the temporary equipment, the loan of the temporary equipment was merely ancillary to the purchase of the Encore system to cover the gap until the Encore system was available to be delivered to the company. On the way matters developed, it was the Encore system, and not the temporary system, that the company was to purchase, and the company never got the Encore system.

LORD JUSTICE BINGHAM

Alert

It would, I think, strike most people as very hard if Mr Barber were in this situation to be confined to a claim as an unsecured creditor of the company. While it is literally true that the fund which he provided was applied to the stipulated purpose, the object of the payment was not achieved and that was why the balance was repaid to the receivers. My doubt has been whether the law as it stands enables effect to be given to what I can see as the common fairness of the situation. Our attention has not, I think, been drawn to any case closely analogous to the present. But the company certainly held the fund on trust in the first instance.

An example of where a *Quistclose* trust was found not to apply is *Re Farepak*, as the business model was inconsistent with the trust analysis.

***In the matter of Farepak Food and Gifts Limited (in administration)* [2006] EWHC 3272**

Panel: Mann J

Facts: Farepak Food and Gifts Ltd ran a Christmas savings scheme whereby customers spread their Christmas savings over a year. Contributions were generally made on a monthly basis so that sufficient savings had accumulated by the end of the year to buy a hamper or vouchers. The customers paid their money to various representatives, but the company went into administration in October 2006. In the High Court the customers argued, among other claims, that the savings money was held on a *Quistclose* trust.

MR JUSTICE MANN

[Counsel] ……argued that an analysis of the facts and the customer conditions showed that there was a payment for a specific purpose, and that since that purpose had not been fulfilled the customer money was held on resulting trust. The purpose in question was the provision of vouchers (or other products elected by the customer). So far as the customer conditions are concerned he relied on a term which provided that payments must be “completed in full” before any entitlement arose, and that as between categories of goods ordered the payment would be allocated in a given priority — first vouchers, the frozen hampers, then grocery hampers and so on down the line. He pointed out that if the price were altered the customer has the right to the return of the contributions in full, and the same was true if there were a substitution.

This argument, if good, would work to the theoretical of all customers of Farepak in the 2006 Farepak year, and not just those whose payments were received at the time under consideration in this application (though there is no practical benefit to most of them because most of the money has gone anyway). Unfortunately, on the material that I have had the argument fails. I have already held that the money is taken by the Agents as agent for Farepak. That of itself does not militate against the existence of a Quistclose trust. However, there is no suggestion that the Agent was expected to keep the money separate from other money (or indeed his or her own), and it is indeed known that it was mixed with the money of others and paid over to Farepak with the money of others. Again, that of itself it not inconsistent with a Quistclose trust, but it does not help. But crucially, there is no suggestion that the money ought to have been put on one side by Farepak pending the transmutation from credited money to goods or vouchers. If there were a Quistclose trust then that obligation would have been inherent in it, but the business model would have made no sense. It would have required Farepak to have kept all the customer moneys in a separate account from January until November, untouched until the time when the goods or vouchers were acquired and then sent out. That is completely implausible. It would turn Farepak into a very odd savings organisation. Even banks do not have to do that. Mr Trace urged on me that the description of this as a savings scheme (which is how it was described in some publicity) indicated that there was a trust until the vouchers/goods were provided, and pointed to an OED definition which he said supported him. I am afraid it gives him no support at all. The concept of a trust is not inherent in the use of the word “savings”; indeed, most savings organisations do not operate via a trust at all. They operate at the level of contract and debt.

On analysis it is apparent enough that what the customer was making was advance payments towards the purchase price of goods or vouchers. The payments were noted on the relevant cards. When the price had been paid the customer was entitled to the chosen goods or vouchers. That describes, and is, a contractual relationship. The provision for the return of money if the price went up, or if acceptable goods were not provided, are contractual terms for the return of an equivalent amount of money, not money held on trust.

This argument therefore fails.

The Court in this decision was influenced by the fact that Farepak was able to use the customer receipts during the year as part of its working capital and it would have been contrary to the firm’s business model to keep the receipts separate.

A *Quistclose* trust was also found not to exist in the case of *Bieber v Teathers*.

Raymond Bieber and Others v Teathers Limited (in liquidation) [2012] EWHC 190

Panel: Norris J

Facts: Teathers promoted an unregulated collective investment scheme for investors, with the objective of obtaining specific tax relief. Investors were given an Information Memorandum explaining the scheme but the scheme was ultimately unsuccessful. The investors argued that the funds should have only been applied in investments meeting certain criteria set out in the Information Memorandum and that there had been a breach of trust where this had occurred. In his judgment, Norris J set out some principles for establishing when a Quistclose trust will arise.

MR JUSTICE NORRIS

Following the decisions in *Barclays Bank v Quistclose Investments* [1970] AC 567 and Twinsectra Ltd v Yardley [2002] AC 164 the underlying principles by reference to which such a trust will arise are clear. I would summarise them as follows.

First, the question in every case is whether the payer and the recipient intended that the money passing between them was to be at the free disposal of the recipient: *Re Goldcorp Exchange* [1995] 1 AC 74 and *Twinsectra* at [74].

Second, the mere fact that the payer has paid the money to the recipient for the recipient to use it in a particular way is not of itself enough. The recipient may have represented or warranted that he intends to use it in a particular way or have promised to use it in a particular way. Such an arrangement would give rise to personal obligations but would not of itself necessarily create fiduciary obligations or a trust: *Twinsectra* at [73].

So, thirdly, it must be clear from the express terms of the transaction (properly construed) or must be objectively ascertained from the circumstances of the transaction that the mutual intention of payer and recipient (and the essence of their bargain) is that the funds transferred should not be part of the general assets of the recipient but should be used exclusively to effect particular identified payments, so that if the money cannot be so used then it is to be returned to the payer: *Toovey v Milne* (1819) 2 B&A 683 and *Quistclose Investments* at 580B.

Fourth, the mechanism by which this is achieved is a trust giving rise to fiduciary obligations on the part of the recipient which a court of equity will enforce: Twinsectra at [69]. Equity intervenes because it is unconscionable for the recipient to obtain money on terms as to its application and then to disregard the terms on which he received it from a payer who had placed trust and confidence in the recipient to ensure the proper application of the money paid: *Twinsectra* at [76].

Fifth, such a trust is akin to a "retention of title" clause, enabling the recipient to have recourse to the payer's money for the particular purpose specified but without entrenching on the payer's property rights more than necessary to enable the purpose to be achieved. It is not as such a "purpose" trust of which the recipient is a trustee, the beneficial interest in the money reverting to the payer if the purpose is incapable of achievement. It is a resulting trust in favour of the payer with a mandate granted to the recipient to apply the money paid for the purpose stated. The key feature of the arrangement is that the recipient is precluded from misapplying the money paid to him. The recipient has no beneficial interest in the money: generally the beneficial interest remains vested in the payer subject only to the recipient's power to apply the money in accordance with the stated purpose. If the stated purpose cannot be achieved then the mandate ceases to be effective, the recipient simply holds the money paid on resulting trust for the payer, and the recipient must repay it: *Twinsectra* at [81], [87], [92] and [100].

Sixth, the subjective intentions of payer and recipient as to the creation of a trust are irrelevant. If the properly construed terms upon which (or the objectively ascertained circumstances in which) payer and recipient enter into an arrangement have the effect of creating a trust, then it is not necessary that either payer or recipient should intend to create a trust: it is sufficient that they intend to enter into the relevant arrangement: *Twinsectra* at [71].

Seventh, the particular purpose must be specified in terms which enable a court to say whether a given application of the money does or does not fall within its terms: *Twinsectra* at [16].

It is in my judgment implicit in the doctrine so described in the authorities that the specified purpose is fulfilled by and at the time of the application of the money. The payer, the recipient and the ultimate beneficiary of the payment (that is, the person who benefits from the application by the recipient of the money for the particular purpose) need to know whether property has passed.

Although the court accepted that the investment monies were not at the free disposal of Teathers at the time the monies were paid across, it was held that there was no *Quistclose* trust. The court noted that where money is applied for a specific purpose, the purpose must be defined with clarity to the extent that it could be ascertained objectively whether the purpose is being fulfilled. Furthermore, it was noted that the investment criteria were too loosely expressed to qualify as directions. The court finally held that a trust was inconsistent with the documentation, which set out that the investment money should form part of the general assets of Teathers. The decision was upheld on appeal, with the Court of Appeal confirming that for a trust to exist it was essential that the relevant money should not be at the free disposal of the recipient but also that the money should continue to belong to the payer unless and until any conditions are complied with.

13.4 Conclusion on *Quistclose* Trusts

The cases post-*Quistclose* show that *Quistclose* trusts have been found in a far wider range of scenarios than would have been suggested by reading Lord

Wilberforce's judgment in *Quistclose* alone. Sadly, however, these cases do not all speak with one voice and the only certainty we do have is that some deviation from the original *Quistclose* requirements will not be fatal to finding a trust, but ignoring those requirements to too great a degree will preclude the existence of a trust. This lack of clarity leads to a great deal of uncertainty as to how far the envelope can be pushed and it appears that currently much depends upon the facts of each case and how they are presented in court. The problem with this is that whilst the beneficiaries of a *Quistclose* trust have a proprietary right to the money and are therefore 'winners' every time such a trust is found, it leads to the inevitable consequence of the unsecured creditors always losing out.

If the law is to allow this to happen it must be able to justify when *Quistclose* trusts can be found and why they exist. Otherwise there is always the risk of this area of law becoming unprincipled, impracticable and unfair. To ensure we reach this happy state, a considered analysis of the cases will be required in future decisions.

14

Implied Trusts of the Home

14.1 Introduction

The law of trusts has proven to be of particular importance when dealing with cases regarding the home. It is uncommon for those living together to expressly declare that the home is to be held on trust for one or both of the parties in compliance with the Law of Property Act (LPA) 1925 s53(1)(b). It has instead been left to the courts to use their powers under the LPA 1925 s53(2) to imply a trust in favour of the party claiming a beneficial interest.

While the trust has been used in the case of spouses or civil partners, legislation provides a discretion to *adjust* property rights on the breakdown of these types of relationship. There is no such discretion for unmarried cohabitants. Increasingly, cohabitants have applied to the courts claiming beneficial interests in the home and it is in this field particularly that implied trusts have adapted to changing social and economic conditions. In the absence of an express declaration of trust, the courts have looked to implied trusts for a possible solution.

Gissing v Gissing [1971] AC 886

House of Lords: Lord Reid, Lord Morris of Borth-y-Gest, Viscount Dilhorne, Lord Pearson, and Lord Diplock

The claimant and defendant had married while both were in employment and a house was subsequently purchased as the matrimonial home in the name of the defendant alone. While the claimant had not financially contributed to the purchase, she did spend her own money on family clothes, furniture, and the garden. Following a number of years of marriage, the defendant left the claimant, who subsequently sued for a share in the matrimonial home. The issue was whether she could claim a beneficial interest under an implied trust.

It was held that despite expenditures of her own money on the house and family, the claimant was unable to establish a common intention to share the house with her husband. She had not contributed to the purchase price either initially or through mortgage payments and there was no evidence of any express discussions between the parties relating to beneficial ownership.

LORD DIPLOCK:

> ... I did, however, differ from the majority of the members of your Lordships' House who were parties to the decision in *Pettitt v Pettitt* in that I saw no reason in law why the fact that the spouses had not applied their minds at all to the question of how the beneficial interest in a family asset should be held at the time when it was acquired should prevent the court from giving effect to a common intention on this matter which it was satisfied that they would have formed as reasonable persons if they had actually thought about it at that time. I must now accept the majority decision that, put in this form at any rate, this is not the law.
>
> In all the previous cases about the beneficial interests of spouses in the matrimonial home the arguments and judgments have been directed to the

question whether or not an agreement between the parties as to their respective interests can be established on the available evidence. This approach to the legal problem involved is in most cases adequate, but it passes over the first stage in the analysis of the problem, viz, the role of the agreement itself in the creation of an equitable estate in real property. In the instant appeal, I think it is desirable to start at the first stage.

Any claim to a beneficial interest in land by a person, whether spouse or stranger, in whom the legal estate in the land is not vested must be based upon the proposition that the person in whom the legal estate is vested holds it as trustee upon trust to give effect to the beneficial interest of the claimant as *cestui que trust*. The legal principles applicable to the claim are those of the English law of trusts and in particular, in the kind of dispute between spouses that comes before the courts, the law relating to the creation and operation of 'resulting, implied or constructive trusts.' Where the trust is expressly declared in the instrument by which the legal estate is transferred to the trustee or by a written declaration of trust by the trustee, the court must give effect to it. But to constitute a valid declaration of trust by way of gift of a beneficial interest in land to a *cestui que trust* the declaration is required by s53 (1)(b) of the Law of Property Act, 1925, to be in writing. If it is not in writing it can only take effect as a resulting, implied or constructive trust to which that section has no application.

A resulting, implied or constructive trust – and it is unnecessary for present purposes to distinguish between these three classes of trust – is created by a transaction between the trustee and the *cestui que trust* in connection with the acquisition by the trustee of a legal estate in land, whenever the trustee has so conducted himself that it would be inequitable to allow him to deny to the *cestui que trust* a beneficial interest in the land acquired, and he will be held so to have conducted himself if by his words or conduct he has induced the *cestui que trust* to act to his own detriment in the reasonable belief that by so acting he was acquiring a beneficial interest in the land.

This is why it has been repeatedly said in the context of disputes between spouses as to their respective beneficial interests in the matrimonial home, that if at the time of its acquisition and transfer of the legal estate into the name of one or other of them an express agreement has been made between them as to the way in which the beneficial interest shall be held, the court will give effect to it - notwithstanding the absence of any written declaration of trust. Strictly speaking this states the principle too widely, for if the agreement did not provide for anything to be done by the spouse in whom the legal estate was not to be vested, it would be a merely voluntary declaration of trust and unenforceable for want of writing. But in the express oral agreements contemplated by these *dicta* it has been assumed *sub silentio* that they provide for the spouse in whom the legal estate in the matrimonial home is not vested to do something to facilitate its acquisition, by contributing to the purchase price or to the deposit or the mortgage instalments when it is purchased upon mortgage or to make some other material sacrifice by way of contribution to or economy in the general family expenditure. What the court gives effect to is the trust resulting or implied from the common intention expressed in the oral agreement between the spouses that if each acts in the manner provided for in the agreement the beneficial interests in the matrimonial home shall be held as they have agreed.

An express agreement between spouses as to their respective beneficial interests in land conveyed into the name of one of them obviates the need for showing that the conduct of the spouse into whose name the land was conveyed was intended to induce the other spouse to act to his or her detriment upon the faith of the promise of a specified beneficial interest in the land and that the other spouse so acted with the intention of acquiring that beneficial interest. The agreement itself discloses the common intention required to create a resulting, implied or constructive trust.

But parties to a transaction in connection with the acquisition of land may well have formed a common intention that the beneficial interest in the land shall be vested in them jointly without having used express words to communicate this intention to one another; or their recollections of the words used may be imperfect or conflicting by the time any dispute arises. In such a case – a common one where the parties are spouses whose marriage has broken down – it may be possible to infer their common intention from their conduct.

Alert

As in so many branches of English law in which legal rights and obligations depend upon the intentions of the parties to a transaction, the relevant intention of each party is the intention which was reasonably understood by the other party to be manifested by that party's words or conduct notwithstanding that he did not consciously formulate that intention in his own mind or even acted with some different intention which he did not communicate to the other party. On the other hand, he is not bound by any inference which the other party draws as to his intention unless that inference is one which can reasonably be drawn from his words or conduct. It is in this sense that in the branch of English law relating to constructive, implied or resulting trusts effect is given to the inferences as to the intentions of parties to a transaction which a reasonable man would draw from their words or conduct and not to any subjective intention or absence of intention which was not made manifest at the time of the transaction itself. It is for the court to determine what those inferences are. [...]

Where in any of the circumstances described above contributions, direct or indirect, have been made to the mortgage instalments by the spouse into whose name the matrimonial home has not been conveyed, and the court can infer from their conduct a common intention that the contributing spouse should be entitled to some beneficial interest in the matrimonial home, what effect is to be given to that intention if there is no evidence that they in fact reached any express agreement as to what the respective share of each spouse should be?

Alert

I take it to be clear that if the court is satisfied that it was the common intention of both spouses that the contributing wife should have a share in the beneficial interest and that her contributions were made upon this understanding, the court in the exercise of its equitable jurisdiction would not permit the husband in whom the legal estate was vested and who had accepted the benefit of the contributions to take the whole beneficial interest merely because at the time the wife made her contributions there had been no express agreement as to how her share in it was to be quantified.

In such a case the court must first do its best to discover from the conduct of the spouses whether any inference can reasonably be drawn as to the probable common understanding about the amount of the share of the contributing spouse upon which each must have acted in doing what each did, even though that understanding was never expressly stated by one spouse to the other or even consciously formulated in words by either of them independently. It is only if no such inference can be drawn that the court is driven to apply as a rule of law, and not as an inference of fact, the maxim 'equality is equity,' and to hold that the beneficial interest belongs to the spouses in equal shares.

The same result however may often be reached as an inference of fact. The instalments of a mortgage to a building society are generally repayable over a period of many years. During that period, as both must be aware, the ability of each spouse to contribute to the instalments out of their separate earning is likely to alter, particularly in the case of the wife if any children are born of the marriage. If the contribution of the wife in the early part of the period of repayment is substantial but is not an identifiable and uniform proportion of each instalment, because her contributions are indirect or, if direct, are made irregularly, it may be a reasonable inference that their common intention at the time of acquisition of the matrimonial home was that the beneficial interest should be held by them in equal shares and that each should contribute to the cost of its acquisition whatever amounts each could afford in the varying exigencies of family life to be expected during the period of repayment. In the social conditions of today this would be a natural enough common intention of a young couple who were both earning when the house was acquired but who contemplated having children whose birth and rearing in their infancy would necessarily affect the future earning capacity of the wife.

The relative size of their respective contributions to the instalments in the early part of the period of repayment, or later if a subsequent reduction in the wife's contribution is not to be accounted for by a reduction in her earnings due to motherhood or some other cause from which the husband benefits as well, may make it a more probable inference that the wife's share in the beneficial interest was intended to be in some proportion other than one-half. And there is nothing inherently improbable in their acting on the understanding that the wife should be entitled to a share which was not to be quantified immediately upon the acquisition of the home but should be left to be determined when the mortgage was repaid or the property disposed of, on the basis of what would be fair having regard to the total contributions, direct or indirect, which each spouse had made by that date. Where this was the most likely inference from their conduct it would be for the court to give effect to that common intention of the parties by determining what in all the circumstances was a fair share.

Alert

Difficult as they are to solve, however, these problems as to the amount of the share of a spouse in the beneficial interest in a matrimonial home where the legal estate is vested solely in the other spouse, only arise in cases where the court is satisfied by the words or conduct of the parties that it was their common intention that the beneficial interest was not to belong solely to the spouse in whom the legal estate was vested but was to be shared between them in some proportion or other. [...]

On what then is the wife's claim based? In 1951 when the house was purchased she spent about £190 on buying furniture and a cooker and refrigerator for it. She also paid about £30 for improving the lawn. As furniture and household doorbells are depreciating assets whereas houses have turned out to be appreciating assets it may be that she would have been wise to have devoted her savings to acquiring an interest in the freehold; but this may not have been so apparent in 1951 as it has now become. The court is not entitled to infer a common intention to this effect from the mere fact that she provided chattels for joint use in the new matrimonial home; and there is nothing else in the conduct of the parties at the time of the purchase or thereafter which supports such an inference. There is no suggestion that the wife's efforts or her earnings made it possible for the husband to raise the initial loan or the mortgage or that her relieving her husband from the expense of buying clothing for herself and for their son was undertaken in order to enable him the better to meet the mortgage instalments or to repay the loan. The picture presented by the evidence is one of husband and wife retaining their separate proprietary interests in property whether real or personal purchased with their separate savings and is inconsistent with any common intention at the time of the purchase of the matrimonial home that the wife, who neither then nor thereafter contributed anything to its purchase price or assumed any liability for it, should nevertheless be entitled to a beneficial interest in it.

Both Buckley J and Edmund Davies LJ in his dissenting judgment in the Court of Appeal felt unable on this evidence to draw an inference that there was any common intention that the wife should have any beneficial interest in the house. I think that they were right. Like them I, too, come to this conclusion with regret, because it may well be that had husband and wife discussed the matter in 1951 when the house was bought he would have been willing for her to have a share in it if she wanted to. But this is speculation, and if such an arrangement had been made between them there might well have also been a different allocation of the household expenses between them in the ensuing years.

Gissing v Gissing establishes that implied trusts may be used with regard to beneficial interests in the absence of any express declaration to satisfy LPA 1925 s53(1)(b). It is also a good example of the presumption that, where legal title is in one name only, the beneficial ownership belongs to that person alone and the other party is required to show a common intention that they should have a beneficial interest. While it was dealing with a matrimonial case, subsequent authorities expanded upon *Gissing,* and carried forward its observations regarding use of the implied trust. The common intention constructive trust has acquired prominence in this context. The operation of the constructive trust differs according to whether the legal title is held in joint names or one name.

14.2 Legal title held in joint names

Stack v Dowden [2007] UKHL 17, [2007] 2 AC 432

House of Lords: Lord Hoffmann, Lord Hope of Craighead, Lord Walker of Gestingthorpe, Baroness Hale of Richmond, and Lord Neuberger of Abbotsbury

A home was purchased in the sole name of the respondent (D). She earned substantially more money than the appellant (S) and, as such, paid all of the mortgage payments together with a large proportion of the household bills. A great number of improvements were also made to the house and it eventually sold for three times its original purchase price. A new home was purchased in the names of both parties but over two thirds was provided by way of a bank account in the respondent's sole name including the equity from the sale of their first home. Mortgage repayments for the balance were paid by both parties but approximately 60% were provided by the respondent. For the entirety of this period the appellant and respondent kept separate bank accounts and made separate transactions with regard to savings and investments. Upon separation the appellant claimed an interest in the house.

It was held that because both parties were on the legal title the presumption was that it was to be held in equal beneficial shares. This could be rebutted by the party claiming unequal shares, however. The respondent was able to do so because she had provided a larger amount of the purchase price and had also kept her financial assets, investments, and interests separate from the appellant. This was enough to indicate that an unequal distribution of assets was intended and the respondent was given a higher share.

LORD HOPE OF CRAIGHEAD:

The cases can be broken down into those where there is a single legal ownership and those where there is joint legal ownership. There must be consistency of approach between these two cases, a point to which my noble and learned friend, Lord Neuberger of Abbotsbury, has drawn our attention. I think that consistency is to be found by deciding where the onus lies if a party wishes to show that the beneficial ownership is different from the legal ownership. I agree with Baroness Hale that this is achieved by taking sole beneficial ownership as the starting point in the first case and by taking joint beneficial ownership as the starting point in the other. In this context joint beneficial ownership means property is assumed to be held by the beneficial owners equally. So in a case of sole legal ownership the onus is on the party who wishes to show that he has any beneficial interest at all, and if so what that interest is. In a case of joint legal ownership it is on the party who wishes to show that the beneficial interests are divided other than equally. [...]

In a case such as this, where the parties had already been living together for about 18 years and had four children when 114 Chatsworth Road was purchased in joint names and payments on the mortgage secured on that property were in effect contributed to by each of them equally, there would have been much to be said for adhering to the presumption of English law that the beneficial interests were divided between them equally. But I do not think that it is possible to ignore the fact that the contributions which they made to the purchase of that property were not equal. The relative extent of those contributions provides the best guide as to where their beneficial interests lay, in the absence of compelling evidence that by the end of their relationship they did indeed intend to share the beneficial interests equally. The evidence does not go that far. On the contrary, while they pooled their resources in the running of the household, in larger matters they maintained their financial independence from each other throughout their relationship.

The result might have been different if greater weight could have been given to the inclusion in the transfer of the standard-form receipt clause. But English property law does not permit this, for the reasons explained in *Mortgage Corpn v Shaire* [2001] Ch 743, 753. I think that indirect contributions, such as making improvements which added significant value to the property, or a complete pooling of resources in both time and money so that it did not matter who paid for what during their relationship, ought to be taken into account as well as financial contributions made directly towards the purchase of the property. I would endorse Chadwick LJ's view in *Oxley v Hiscock* [2005] Fam 211, para 69 that regard should be had to the whole course of dealing between them in relation to the property. But the evidence in this case shows that there never was a stage when both parties intended that their beneficial interests in the property should be shared equally. Taking a broad view of the matter, therefore, I agree that the order that the Court of Appeal made provides the fairest result that can be achieved in the circumstances.

LORD WALKER OF GESTINGTHORPE:

[In *Lloyds Bank plc v Rosset*] Lord Bridge then asked himself whether it was worthwhile to add any general remarks by way of illumination of the law. He limited himself to drawing attention to one 'critical distinction.' If, at p 132E-G, there is to be a finding of an actual 'agreement, arrangement, or understanding' between the parties it must 'be based on evidence of express discussions between the partners, however imperfectly remembered and however imprecise their terms may have been.' Lord Bridge continued, at pp 132–133:

'In sharp contrast with this situation is the very different one where there is no evidence to support a finding of an agreement or arrangement to share, however reasonable it might have been for the parties to reach such an arrangement if they had applied their minds to the question, and where the court must rely entirely on the conduct of the parties both as to the basis from which to infer a common intention to share the property beneficially and as the conduct relied on to give rise to a constructive trust. In this situation direct contributions to the purchase price by the partner who is not the legal owner, whether initially or by payment of mortgage instalments, will readily justify the inference necessary to the creation of a constructive trust. But, as I read the authorities, it is at least extremely doubtful whether anything less will do.'

In concurring in this passage the House was unanimously, if unostentatiously, agreeing that a 'common intention' trust could be inferred even when there was no evidence of an actual agreement. Apart from two bare references, at p 132G and p 133F, to 'a constructive trust or a proprietary estoppel' Lord Bridge did not refer to the elaborate arguments of counsel, at pp 110–125, addressed to him as to the varieties and interaction of these two concepts.

Lord Bridge's extreme doubt 'whether anything less will do' was certainly consistent with many first-instance and Court of Appeal decisions, but I respectfully doubt whether it took full account of the views (conflicting though they were) expressed in Gissing v Gissing [1971] AC 886 (see especially Lord Reid, at pp 896G –897B, and Lord Diplock, at p 909D-H). It has attracted some trenchant criticism from scholars as potentially productive of injustice: see Gray & Gray, Elements of Land Law, 4th ed, paras 10.132–10.137, the last paragraph being headed 'A More Optimistic Future.' Whether or not Lord Bridge's observation was justified in 1990, in my opinion the law has moved on, and your Lordships should move it a little more in the same direction, while bearing in mind that the Law Commission may soon come forward with proposals which, if enacted by Parliament, may recast the law in this area. [...]

In the ordinary domestic case where there are joint legal owners there will be a heavy burden in establishing to the court's satisfaction that an intention to keep a sort of balance-sheet of contributions actually existed, or should be inferred, or imputed to the parties. The presumption will be that equity follows the law. In such cases the court should not readily embark on the sort of detailed examination of the parties' relationship and finances that was attempted (with limited success) in this case. I agree with Lady Hale that this is, on its facts, an exceptional case.

In those cases (it is to be hoped, a diminishing number) in which such an examination is required the court should in my opinion take a broad view of what contributions are to be taken into account. In *Gissing v Gissing* [1971] AC 886, 909G, Lord Diplock referred to an adjustment of expenditure 'referable to the acquisition of the house.' 'Referable' is a word of wide and uncertain meaning. It would not assist the development of the law to go back to the sort of difficulties that arose in connection with the doctrine of part performance, where the act of part performance relied on had to be 'uniquely referable' to a contract of the sort alleged: see *Steadman v Steadman* [1976] AC 536. Now that almost all houses and flats are bought with mortgage finance, and the average period of ownership of a residence is a great deal shorter than the contractual term of the mortgage secured on it, the process of buying a house does very often continue, in a real sense, throughout the period of its ownership. The law should recognise that by taking a wide view of what is capable of counting as a contribution towards the acquisition of a residence, while remaining sceptical of the value of alleged improvements that are really insignificant, or elaborate arguments (suggestive of creative accounting) as to how the family finances were arranged.

That is in my view the way in which the law can be seen developing through a considerable number of decisions of the Court of Appeal, of which I would single out *Grant v Edwards* [1986] Ch 638 (before *Lloyds Bank plc v Rosset* [1991] 1 AC 107) and then *Stokes v Anderson* [1991] 1 FLR 391, *Midland Bank plc v Cooke* [1995] 2 All ER 562 and *Oxley v Hiscock* [2005] Fam 211. In the last-mentioned case Chadwick LJ summarized the law as follows, at para 69, Lord Bridge's 'second category' cases):

'But, in a case where there is no evidence of any discussion between them as to the amount of the share which each was to have – and even in a case where the evidence is that there was no discussion on that point – the question still requires an answer. It must now be accepted that (at least in this court and below) the answer is that each is entitled to that share which the court considers fair having regard to the whole course of dealing between them in relation to the property. And, in that context, "the whole course of dealing between them in relation to the property" includes the arrangements which they make from time to time in order to meet the outgoings (for example, mortgage contributions, council tax and utilities, repairs, insurance and housekeeping) which have to be met if they are to live in the property as their home.'

That summary was directed at cases where there is a single legal owner. In relation to such cases the summary, with its wide reference to 'the whole course of dealing between them in relation to the property,' is in my opinion a correct statement of the law, subject to the qualifications in paras 61 *et seq* of Lady Hale's opinion. I would only add that Chadwick LJ did not refer to contributions in kind in the form of manual labour on improvements, possibly because that was not an issue in that case. For reasons already mentioned, I would include contributions in kind by way of manual labour, provided that they are significant.

BARONESS HALE OF RICHMOND:

Alert

Just as the starting point where there is sole legal ownership is sole beneficial ownership, the starting point where there is joint legal ownership is joint beneficial ownership. The onus is upon the person seeking to show that the beneficial ownership is different from the legal ownership. So in sole ownership cases it is upon the non-owner to show that he has any interest at all. In joint ownership cases, it is upon the joint owner who claims to have other than a joint beneficial interest. [...]

The issue as it has been framed before us is whether a conveyance into joint names indicates only that each party is intended to have some beneficial interest but says nothing about the nature and extent of that beneficial interest, or whether a conveyance into joint names establishes a *prime facie* case of joint and equal beneficial interests until the contrary is shown. For the reasons already stated, at least in the domestic consumer context, a conveyance into

Alert

joint names indicates both legal and beneficial joint tenancy, unless and until the contrary is proved.

The question is, how, if at all, is the contrary to be proved? Is the starting point the presumption of resulting trust, under which shares are held in proportion to the parties' financial contributions to the acquisition of the property, unless the contributor or contributors can be shown to have had a contrary intention? Or is it that the contrary can be proved by looking at all the relevant circumstances in order to discern the parties' common intention? [...]

The burden will therefore be on the person seeking to show that the parties did intend their beneficial interests to be different from their legal interests, and in what way. [...]

In law, 'context is everything' and the domestic context is very different from the commercial world. Each case will turn on its own facts. Many more factors than financial contributions may be relevant to divining the parties' true intentions. These include: any advice or discussions at the time of the transfer which cast light upon their intentions then; the reasons why the home was acquired in their joint names; the reasons why (if it be the case) the survivor was authorised to give a receipt for the capital moneys; the purpose for which the home was acquired; the nature of the parties' relationship; whether they had children for whom they both had responsibility to provide a home; how the purchase was financed, both initially and subsequently; how the parties arranged their finances, whether separately or together or a bit of both; how they discharged the outgoings on the property and their other household expenses. When a couple are joint owners of the home and jointly liable for the mortgage, the inferences to be drawn from who pays for what may be very different from the inferences to be drawn when only one is owner of the home. The arithmetical calculation of how much was paid by each is also likely to be less important. It will be easier to draw the inference that they intended that each should contribute as much to the household as they reasonably could and that they would share the eventual benefit or burden equally. The parties' individual characters and personalities may also be a factor in deciding where their true intentions lay. In the cohabitation context, mercenary considerations may be more to the fore than they would be in marriage, but it should not be assumed that they always take pride of place over natural love and affection. At the end of the day, having taken all this into account, cases in which the joint legal owners are to be taken to have intended that their beneficial interests should be different from their legal interests will be very unusual.

This is not, of course, an exhaustive list. There may also be reason to conclude that, whatever the parties' intentions at the outset, these have now changed. An example might be where one party has financed (or constructed himself) an extension or substantial improvement to the property, so that what they have now is significantly different from what they had then. [...]

Applying the law to the facts

The starting point is that it is for Ms Dowden to show that the common intention, when taking a conveyance of the house into their joint names or thereafter, was that they should hold the property otherwise than as beneficial joint tenants. Unfortunately, we lack precise findings on many of the factors relevant to answering that question, because the judge addressed himself to 'looking at the parties' entire course of conduct together.' He looked at their relationship rather than the matters which were particularly relevant to their intentions about this property. He founded his conclusion on the length and nature of their relationship, which he repeatedly referred to as a partnership, despite the fact that they had maintained separate finances throughout their time together. With the best will in the world, and acknowledging the problems of making more precise findings on many issues after this length of time, this is not an adequate answer to the question. It amounts to little more than saying that these people were in a relationship for 27 years and had four children together. During this time Mr Stack made unquantifiable indirect contributions to the acquisition and improvement of one house and quantifiable direct contributions to the acquisition of another. Both co-operated in looking after the home and bringing up their children. [...]

This is, therefore, a very unusual case. There cannot be many unmarried couples who have lived together for as long as this, who have had four children together, and whose affairs have been kept as rigidly separate as this couple's affairs were kept. This is all strongly indicative that they did not intend their shares, even in the property which was put into both their names, to be equal (still less that they intended a beneficial joint tenancy with the right of survivorship should one of them die before it was severed). Before the Court of Appeal, Ms Dowden contended for a 65% share and in my view she has made good her case for that. [...]

Despite the eloquent view espoused by Baroness Hale, Lord Neuberger was less impressed with the logic that had been applied to both the present case and the law of implied trusts of the home in general. Dissenting, he went on to give his own opinion regarding the facts in issue.

LORD NEUBERGER OF ABBOTSBURY:

In the present type of case, while the number of unmarried cohabitants has increased very substantially over the past 50 (and even more over the past 20) years, the change has been one of degree, and does not, in my view, justify a departure from established legal principles. I agree with Griffiths LJ (see *Bernard v Josephs* [1982] Ch 391, 402) that the applicable principles are the same whether the parties are married or not, although the nature of the relationship will bear on the inferences to be drawn from their discussions and actions. [...]

Beneficial ownership on acquisition: where there is no evidence [...]

In the absence of any relevant evidence other than the fact that the property, whether a house or a flat, acquired as a home for the legal co-owners is in joint names, the beneficial ownership will also be joint, so that it is held in equal shares. This can be said to result from the maxims that equity follows the law and equality is equity. On a less technical, and some might say more practical, approach, it can also be justified on the basis that any other solution would be arbitrary or capricious.

Where the only additional relevant evidence to the fact that the property has been acquired in joint names is the extent of each party's contribution to the purchase price, the beneficial ownership at the time of acquisition will be held, in my view, in the same proportions as the contributions to the purchase price. That is the resulting trust solution. The only realistic alternative in such a case would be to adhere to the joint ownership solution. There is an argument to support the view that equal shares should still be the rule in cohabitation cases, on the basis that it may be what many parties may expect if they purchase a home in joint names, even with different contributions. However, I consider that the resulting trust solution is correct in such circumstances. [...]

There are also practical reasons for rejecting equality and supporting the resulting trust solution. The property may be bought in joint names for reasons which cast no light on the parties' intentions with regard to beneficial ownership. It may be the solicitor's decision or assumption, the lender's preference for the security of two borrowers, or the happenstance of how the initial contact with the solicitor was made. [...]

In other words, where the resulting trust presumption (or indeed any other basis of apportionment) applies at the date of acquisition, I am unpersuaded that (save perhaps in a most unusual case) anything other than subsequent discussions, statements or actions, which can fairly be said to imply a positive intention to depart from that apportionment, will do to justify a change in the way in which the beneficial interest is owned. To say that factors such as a long relationship, children, a joint bank account, and sharing daily outgoings of themselves are enough, or even of potential central importance, appears to me not merely wrong in principle, but a recipe for uncertainty, subjectivity, and a long and expensive examination of facts.

Fowler v Barron [2008] EWCA Civ 377, [2008] 2 FLR 831

Court of Appeal: Waller VPCA, Arden LJ, and Toulson LJ

Miss Fowler and Mr Barron formed a relationship in 1983. In 1988, they acquired a house in their joint names. Mr Barron paid the deposit from his available funds, and the balance was raised by a joint mortgage. Mr Barron and Miss Fowler did not obtain advice as to the consequences of the property being held in their joint names, nor did they discuss the beneficial ownership of the property. Mr Barron's uncommunicated intention was that, provided he and Miss Fowler continued their relationship, the house would become her sole property on his death. Shortly after the property was acquired, Mr Barron and Miss Fowler executed mutual wills in which they each left their interest in the house to the other.

Mr Barron and Miss Fowler had a son in 1987 and a daughter in 1994. They never had a joint bank account.

During the they lived together, Mr Barron paid all mortgage instalments, council tax charges and utility bills. He also paid for the weekly groceries. Miss Fowler was employed for most of the period they lived together. She used her income to purchase additional food, clothing for herself and the children, and seasonal gifts. She also paid for school clubs and trips and for family holidays. Mr Barron and Miss Fowler separated in 2005.

The trial judge held that, as Miss Fowler had not contributed to the acquisition of the house, she was not entitled to an equitable interest in the property. Miss Fowler successfully appealed to the Court of Appeal.

ARDEN LJ, with whom **WALLER VPCA** and **TOULSON LJ** agreed:

The issues raised in the parties' submissions may be grouped into the following issues:

(i) Was the judge in error in seeking to determine the parties' intentions with respect to the shares in which they owned the property by concentrating on the parties' financial contributions? I answer this question below in the affirmative. This was an error of principle on the part of the judge which entitles and requires this court to intervene and reach its own conclusion as to whether Miss Fowler had a beneficial interest.

(ii) Has Mr Barron discharged the onus on him of showing that it was not the parties' shared intention that Miss Fowler should have a one half-share in the property? I answer this question below in the negative.

I will take each of those issues in turn.

Issue (i) Was the judge in error in seeking to determine the parties' intentions with respect to the shares in which they owned the property by concentrating on the parties' financial contributions?

30. In my judgment, the answer to this is yes. In *Stack*, the view of the majority was that, in the absence of an express agreement, '[t]he search is to ascertain the parties' shared intentions, actual, inferred or imputed, with respect to the property in the light of their whole course of conduct in relation to it' (*per* Baroness Hale of Richmond at para 60). The judge for his part concentrated on the parties' financial contributions: see the passages in paras 22 to 30 of his judgment which I have italicised at para 13 of this judgment.

This was an error of principle on the part of the judge that entitles and requires this court to intervene and reach its own conclusion as to whether Miss Fowler had a beneficial interest.*Issue (ii) Has Mr Barron discharged the onus on him of showing that it was not the parties' shared intention that Miss Fowler should have a one half-share in the property?*For the purpose of determining the parties' shared intentions about the beneficial ownership of the property, the court must consider the whole of the parties' relationship so far it illumines their shared intentions about the ownership of the property and the court must draw any appropriate inferences.

The starting point is of course that the transfer of the property was into the joint names of Mr Barron and Miss Fowler. Whatever Mr Barron's motive was for doing this, it was a deliberate choice. As a matter of law, a presumption of joint beneficial ownership arose from the fact that they were joint legal owners: see *Stack* at para 58 *per* Baroness Hale of Richmond. It was open to Mr Barron to rebut this presumption. There was no direct evidence of the parties' intentions, and accordingly the only evidence was circumstantial.

At this point it may be appropriate to make some observations about the effect of the presumption. It provides a default rule that, unless and until the contrary is proved, joint tenants in this context are treated as joint legal and beneficial owners. If the contrary were not proved, the mere fact that the property was transferred into their joint names would be enough to give both parties an equal beneficial share.

In determining whether the presumption is rebutted, the court must in particular consider whether the facts as found are inconsistent with the inference of a common intention to share the property in equal shares to an extent sufficient to discharge the civil standard of proof on the person seeking to displace the presumption arising from a transfer into joint names.

The emphasis is on the parties' shared intentions. As Lord Diplock said in *Gissing v Gissing* [1971] AC 886, at 906B-C, '... the relevant intention of each party is the intention which was reasonably understood by the other party to be manifested by that party's words or conduct notwithstanding that he did not consciously formulate that intention in his own mind or even acted with some different intention which he did not communicate to the other party'. This would be broadly consistent with the principles applicable to the interpretation of a written document, if that had set out their intention.

Alert

Thus any secret intention of Mr Barron, that Miss Fowler should only benefit in the event of his death and on the basis that they were then still living together, does not provide the evidential basis for rebutting the presumption, since it is not evidence of the parties' shared intention. (Moreover, there was nothing on the face of the document to prevent Miss Fowler from severing her interest before the date of his death.) For the same reason, the fact that Mr Barron was mistaken as to the effect of putting the property into joint names, and did not appreciate that that would give Miss Fowler an immediate and absolute entitlement to a beneficial interest is of no materiality. He did not communicate his belief to Miss Fowler, and there is no basis for saying that it should have been apparent to her.

On this point, I would add that the judge did not have the benefit of the warning given by Baroness Hale of Richmond about the potential unreliability of evidence given about beneficial interests after the event. She said:

'In family disputes, strong feelings are aroused when couples split up. This often leads the parties, honestly but mistakenly, to reinterpret the past in self-exculpatory or vengeful terms. They also lead people to spend far more on the legal battle and is warranted by the sums actually at stake. A full examination of the facts is likely to involve disproportionate costs. In joint names cases it is also unlikely to lead a different result, unless the facts are very unusual.' (Paragraph 68)

Had the judge had in mind a warning that in this situation former cohabitees may (consciously or subconsciously) reinterpret the past, the judge might possibly have been more sceptical of Mr Barron's evidence. We have not been asked, however, to go behind his finding as to Mr Barron's secret intention that Miss Fowler should only have a beneficial interest if he pre-deceased her and the relationship subsisted at the date of death. It is not appropriate that this court go behind a finding that is based on the way in which he gave his evidence. However, I note that the judge does not refer to another claim which Mr Barron made, namely that he was the primary carer for the two children. Miss Fowler hotly disputed this claim. In future cases, the warning given by Baroness Hale of Richmond should be borne in mind.

Miss Fowler signed the mortgage, although she was not expected to make any payment towards the discharge of the mortgage debt. It is said on Mr Barron's behalf that her involvement in the mortgage was purely nominal, as in *Carlton v Goodman* [2002] EWCA Civ 545, [2002] 2 FLR 259. The significant point however is that the fact that she signed the mortgage is not inconsistent with the shared intention that she should be a joint beneficial owner. Signature of the mortgage cannot therefore of itself assist Mr Barron on his case that the presumption is rebutted.

Alert

Mr Barron also places reliance on the fact that Miss Fowler made no contribution to the cost of acquiring the property (whether directly or by paying off the mortgage). But the decision in Stack shows that the critical factor is not necessarily the amount of the parties' contributions: the court has to have regard to all the circumstances which may throw light on the parties' intentions as respects ownership of the property. In this case, the judge found that Miss Fowler paid a number of expenses: see the extract from para 11 of his judgment set out above. He went on to hold that 'it was completely understood and accepted [by Miss Fowler] that her money was hers to spend as she chose when she wanted.' With respect to the judge, this makes it sound as if her income was no more than old-fashioned 'pin money'. The reality was that she spent much of her income and the child benefits principally on herself and her children and meeting what the judge termed 'optional expenditure' such as gifts, school clubs and trips, personal clothing, holidays and special occasions. In my judgment, the proper inference is that, with the exception of clothing for herself, these payments were her contributions to household expenses for which both parties were responsible. As I see it, the correct finding is that Mr Barron paid some items properly described as household expenses, such as the council tax and the utilities bills, whereas she paid other such items. The

Alert

division was perfectly logical if, as I assume, she did most of the shopping for the children. The further inference that, in my judgment, it is appropriate to draw is that the parties intended that it should make no difference to their interests in the property which party paid for what expense. Those payments also throw light on their intentions in this respect. There was no prior agreement as to who would pay what. The inference from this, especially when taken with the evidence as to mutual wills referred to below, was that the parties simply did not care about the respective size of each other's contributions.

The evidence about mutual wills came from Mr Barron and on the judge's approach it was not necessary to deal with it and he did not deal with it. However, if regard is had to the totality of the parties' conduct, it illumines their intentions about the beneficial ownership of the property. The parties would not need to have made mutual wills unless they thought that each had a beneficial interest to convey and that the execution of a will was necessary to vest the deceased partner's interest in the other. There is no evidence that the wills were revoked before the parties' relationship broke down. Accordingly, in my judgment, the proper inference from the execution of mutual wills is that they intended each to have an interest. Mr Barron of course says that this evidence is consistent with his case that Miss Fowler was only to have an interest if they stayed together and he pre-deceased her but I have already dealt with that point above.

That brings me to the submission by Mr Living, for Mr Barron, on the quantification of any interest on the part of Miss Fowler. Mr Living submits that this is one of the exceptional cases identified by Baroness Hale of Richmond in *Stack* simply because the parties had never pooled their resources. He submits that the parties cannot have intended that she should have had as great an interest as 50%. He submits that her maximum share should be 25%, representing a one half-share of the contribution to the purchase price made by the mortgage to which she was a party.

This requires some analysis as to the basis on which Ms Dowden was able to rebut the presumption of equal shares in *Stack* and successfully assert that the parties' shares in the property should reflect their contributions to the purchase price in cash payments towards the price or the mortgage payments made in respect of it or the premiums on the endowment policies supporting the mortgage. At paras 87 to 92, Baroness Hale of Richmond identified a number of points arising out of the facts in that case: the fact that Ms Dowden paid much more of the purchase price, the fact that she paid the greater part of the lump sums required to redeem the mortgage, the fact that Mr Stack's payments in respect of the mortgage were to service the interest payments due and to pay premiums on one of the endowment polices supporting it, the fact that the parties intended to reduce the mortgage as soon as they could, the fact that the parties kept their financial affairs 'rigidly separate' and did not pool their resources 'even notionally' for the common good, and the fact that Ms Dowden paid all the other household expenses. Baroness Hale of Richmond considered that the case was very unusual with regard to the way the parties maintained their affairs separately.

In a case where the parties have made unequal contributions to the cost of acquiring their home, it is obvious that in some cases there may be a thin dividing line between the case where the parties' shared intention is properly inferred to be ownership of the home in equal shares, and the case where the parties' shared intention is properly inferred to be that the party who has contributed less should have a smaller interest than the other. The resolution of such cases must however all depend on the facts. In my judgment, it is important to return to the *ratio* in *Stack*. The essential reasoning of the House was: (1) that, where parties put their home into joint names, the burden is on the one asserting that they own the property other than in equal shares to rebut the presumption of joint beneficial ownership that arises from their legal co-ownership; and (2) that the court must have regard to all the circumstances which would throw light on their shared intentions and not just their financial contributions to the cost of acquiring the property. It is necessary to consider the resolution of the facts in *Stack* with these principles in mind. In other words, it was not the fact that the parties made unequal contributions to the cost of acquiring their property in Chatsworth Road that mattered so much as the inferences as to their shared intentions to be gleaned from the evidence overall.

The facts in this case are different in many respects. For instance, the evidence as to mutual wills is not replicated in *Stack*. Moreover, unlike the parties in *Stack*, there is no evidence that Mr Barron and Miss Fowler had any substantial assets apart from their income and their interest if any in the property, and Miss Fowler made no direct contribution to paying for the property. I do not think that it is reasonable to infer that the parties intended that Miss Fowler should have no share of the house if the relationship broke down. That might leave Miss Fowler dependent on State benefits and housing for support. The way that she used her own income indicates that the parties largely treated their incomes and assets as one pool from which household expenses will be paid. There is also important evidence about their wills. Moreover, there is no logical reason why Miss Fowler's interest should be equal to a one half-share of the proportion that the mortgage loan bore to the total acquisition cost to the property since the parties cannot have expected her actually to contribute to that amount. In those circumstances, I do not consider that the presumption of equal beneficial interests can be successfully rebutted.

This result can be criticised because it may leave Miss Fowler better off than the case of a cohabitee who contributes (say) 20% of the purchase price. But that would only be the case where the court found that the parties' shared intention was that they should share the beneficial interest in their home in proportion to the amount of their financial contributions to the cost. But the reason why the result in that case may be different is because that is what the court infers to be the parties' intention. It would have been open to them to agree to divide the ownership in any other way. The basis, on which *Stack* proceeds, is that the court's jurisdiction is based on the parties' common intention, expressed or inferred. The parties' autonomy to devise a solution suitable for their circumstances is preserved. Accordingly, subject always to the strength of the presumption arising from legal ownership in joint names, the result may depending on the facts be different in different cases.

Disposition

In my judgment, for the reasons given above, this appeal should be allowed. There will be a declaration that Miss Fowler is entitled to a half-share in the property.

Jones v Kernott [2011] UKSC 53, [2012] 1 AC 776

Supreme Court: Lord Walker of Gestingthorpe JSC, Baroness Hale of Richmond JSC, Lord Kerr of Tonaghmore JSC, Lord Wilson JSC, and Lord Collins of Mapesbury

The appellant (J) and respondent (K) met in 1980. Both worked and their incomes were similar. J bought a mobile home in her sole name in 1981 and K moved in with her in 1983. In 1985, J sold the mobile home and the couple bought a property in their joint names for £30,000. The £6,000 deposit was paid from the sale proceeds of the mobile home and the balance came from a mortgage in their joint names. K paid £100 a week towards household expenses and J paid the mortgage and other household bills out of their joint resources. In 1986, they took out a joint loan of £2,000 to build an extension and K did some of the work and paid friends and relatives to do other work on it. The trial judge found that the extension probably increased the value of the property from £30,000 to £44,000. K moved out in 1993 and J continued to live there with their two children and paid all the outgoings. The parties tried unsuccessfully to sell the property in 1995. At some point, they agreed to cash in a joint life insurance policy and they divided the proceeds, so that K could use his share as a deposit on a home. The judge found that K was able to afford his home because he had not contributed to the joint property or made any significant contribution to the support of his children for the past 14½ years. The judge held that the parties' intentions as to their beneficial interests had changed after they separated and ordered that the joint property be divided as to 90% for J and 10% for K. K appealed to the High Court, where Mr Nicholas Strauss QC held that the change in intention could readily be inferred or imputed from the parties' conduct and that, in the absence of words or conduct indicating how their shares should alter, the appropriate criterion was what he considered fair and just. The judge's assessment could be justified as such. K then appealed to the Court of Appeal, which allowed the appeal, holding that there was nothing to indicate that the parties' intentions had changed and that they owned the property as tenants in common in equal shares. J then appealed to the Supreme Court, which reversed the decision of the Court of Appeal and restored the order made by the judge.

LORD WALKER OF GESTINGTHORPE JSC and **BARONESS HALE OF RICHMOND JSC:**

The decision in *Stack v Dowden* has [...] attracted a good deal of comment. [...] This appeal provides an opportunity for some clarification.

Stack v Dowden [2007] 2 AC 432 [...]

The curious feature of the decided cases up until then had been that, once an intention to share ownership had been established, the courts had tended to adopt a more flexible and 'holistic' approach to the quantification of the parties' shares in cases of sole legal ownership than they had in cases of joint legal ownership. In the former, they had adopted a concept of the 'common intention' constructive trust which depends upon the shared intentions of the parties. In the latter, they had tended to analyse the matter in terms of a resulting trust, which depends upon the law's presumption as to the intention of the party who makes a financial contribution to the purchase. [...]

The leading opinion in the House of Lords was that of Lady Hale. [...]

[... In] the case of a house transferred into [...] joint names [...] she held that there is a presumption that the beneficial interests coincide with the legal estate. [...]

[...] if the task [of seeking to show that the parties intended their beneficial interests to be different from their legal interests] is embarked upon, it is to ascertain the parties' common intentions as to what their shares in the property would be, in the light of their whole course of conduct in relation to it: Lady Hale, at para 60. It is the way in which this point was made which seems to have caused the most difficulty in the lower courts. The difficulty is well illustrated in Lord Wilson JSC's judgment, at paras 85-87, which read the judgment in a way which we would not read it. It matters not which reading is correct. It does matter that any confusion is resolved.

Link
See Lord Wilson's judgment below

It was also accepted that the parties' common intentions might change over time [...]

At its simplest the principle in *Stack v Dowden* is that a 'common intention' trust, for the cohabitants' home to belong to them jointly in equity as well as on the proprietorship register, is the default option in joint names cases. The trust can be classified as a constructive trust, but it is not at odds with the parties' legal ownership. [...]

A single regime?

[...] we recognize that a 'common intention' trust is of central importance to 'joint names' as well as 'single names' cases [...] Nevertheless it is important to point out that the starting point for analysis is different in the two situations. That is so even though it may be necessary to enquire into the varied circumstances and reasons why a house or flat has been acquired in a single name or in joint names [...]

The starting point is different because the claimant whose name is not on the proprietorship register has the burden of establishing some sort of implied trust, normally what is now termed a 'common intention' constructive trust. The claimant whose name is on the register starts (in the absence of an express declaration of trust in different terms [...]) with the presumption (or assumption) of a beneficial joint tenancy. [...]

The competing presumption: a resulting trust? [...]

The time has come to make it clear, in line with *Stack v Dowden* [2007] 2 AC 432 (see also *Abbott v Abbott* [2008] 1 FLR 1451), that in the case of the purchase of a house or flat in joint names for joint occupation by a married or unmarried couple, where both are responsible for any mortgage, there is no presumption of a resulting trust arising from their having contributed to the deposit (or indeed the rest of the purchase) in unequal shares. The presumption is that the parties intended a joint tenancy both in law and in equity. But that presumption can of course be rebutted by evidence of a contrary intention, which may more readily be shown where the parties did not share their financial resources.

Alert

Inference or imputation?

In *Stack v Dowden* [2007] 2 AC 432 Lord Neuberger observed, at paras 125-126:

'While an intention may be inferred as well as express, it may not, at least in my opinion, be imputed. [...]

An inferred intention is one which is objectively deduced to be the subjective actual intention of the parties, in the light of their actions and statements. An imputed intention is one which is attributed to the parties, even though no such actual intention can be deduced from their actions and statements, and even though they had no such intention. Imputation involves concluding what the parties would have intended, whereas inference involves concluding what they did intend.'

Alert

Rimer LJ made some similar observations in the Court of Appeal in this case [...]

In deference to the comments of Lord Neuberger and Rimer LJ, we accept that the search is primarily to ascertain the parties' actual shared intentions, whether expressed or to be inferred from their conduct. However, there are at least two exceptions. The first, which is not this case, is where the classic resulting trust presumption applies. Indeed, this would be rare in a domestic context, but might perhaps arise where domestic partners were also business partners: see *Stack v Dowden*, para 32. The second, which for reasons which will appear later is in our view also not this case but will arise much more frequently, is where it is clear that the beneficial interests are to be shared, but it is impossible to divine a common intention as to the proportions in which they are to be shared. In those two situations, the court is driven to impute an intention to the parties which they may never have had.

Alert

> Lord Diplock, in *Gissing v Gissing* [1971] AC 886, 909, pointed out that, once the court was satisfied that it was the parties' common intention that the beneficial interest was to be shared in some proportion or other, the court might have to give effect to that common intention by determining what in all the circumstances was a fair share. And it is that thought which is picked up in the subsequent cases, culminating in the judgment of Chadwick LJ in *Oxley v Hiscock* [2005] Fam 211, paras 65, 66 and 69, and in particular the passage in para 69 which was given qualified approval in *Stack v Dowden*: 'the answer is that each is entitled to that share which the court considers fair having regard to the whole course of dealing between them in relation to the property.'
>
> Chadwick LJ was not there saying that fairness was the criterion for determining whether or not the property should be shared, but he was saying that the court might have to impute an intention to the parties as to the proportions in which the property would be shared. [...]
>
> However, while the conceptual difference between inferring and imputing is clear, the difference in practice may not be so great. [...] The law recognizes that a legitimate inference may not correspond to an individual's subjective state of mind. [...]

Lord Walker and Baroness Hale summarized the facts and proceedings in the lower courts. In referring to the decision of the Court of Appeal, they stated:

> Rimer LJ, in the majority, held that there was nothing to indicate that the parties' intentions had changed after their separation. A crucial part of his reasoning was his interpretation of the decision in *Stack v Dowden*: that it did not 'enable courts to find, by way of the imputation route, an intention where none was expressly uttered nor inferentially formed:' para 77. Wall LJ also concluded that he could not infer an intention to change the beneficial interests from the parties' conduct: paras 57, 58.
>
> *Discussion*
>
> It is always salutary to be confronted with the ambiguities which later emerge in what seemed at the time to be comparatively clear language. The primary search must always be for what the parties actually intended, to be deduced objectively from their words and their actions. If that can be discovered, then, as Mr Nicholas Strauss QC pointed out in the High Court, it is not open to a court to impose a solution upon them in contradiction to those intentions, merely because the court thinks it fair to do so.

> [...] where the parties already share the beneficial interest, and the question is what their interests are and whether their interests have changed, the court will try to deduce what their actual intentions were at the relevant time. [...] But if it cannot deduce exactly what shares were intended, it may have no alternative but to ask what their intentions as reasonable and just people would have been had they thought about it at the time. This is a fallback position which some courts may not welcome, but the court has a duty to come to a conclusion on the dispute put before it.

In this case, there is no need to impute an intention that the parties' beneficial interests would change, because the judge made a finding that the intentions of the parties did in fact change. At the outset, their intention was to provide a home for themselves and their progeny. But thereafter their intentions did change significantly. He did not go into detail, but the inferences are not difficult to draw. They separated in October 1993. No doubt in many such cases, there is a period of uncertainty about where the parties will live and what they will do about the home which they used to share. This home was put on the market in late 1995 but failed to sell. Around that time a new plan was formed. The life insurance policy was cashed in and Mr Kernott was able to buy a new home for himself. He would not have been able to do this had he still had to contribute towards the mortgage, endowment policy and other outgoings on 39 Badger Hall Avenue. The logical inference is that they intended that his interest in Badger Hall Avenue should crystallise then. Just as he would have the sole benefit of any capital gain in his own home, Ms Jones would have the sole benefit of any capital gain in Badger Hall Avenue. In so far as the judge did not in so many words infer that this was their intention, it is clearly the intention which reasonable people would have had had they thought about it at the time. But in our view it is an intention which he both could and should have inferred from their conduct.

Link
Contrast the views of Lord Kerr at para 77 and Lord Wilson at para 89

A rough calculation on this basis produces a result so close to that which the judge produced that it would be wrong for an appellate court to interfere. [...]

Conclusion

Alert

In summary, therefore, the following are the principles applicable in a case such as this, where a family home is bought in the joint names of a cohabiting couple who are both responsible for any mortgage, but without any express declaration of their beneficial interests. (1) The starting point is that equity follows the law and they are joint tenants both in law and in equity. (2) That presumption can be displaced by showing (a) that the parties had a different common intention at the time when they acquired the home, or (b) that they later formed the common intention that their respective shares would change. (3) Their common intention is to be deduced objectively from their conduct [...] Examples of the sort of evidence which might be relevant to drawing such inferences are given in Stack v Dowden [2007] 2 AC 432, para 69. (4) In those cases where it is clear either (a) that the parties did not intend joint tenancy at the outset, or (b) had changed their original intention, but it is not possible to ascertain by direct evidence or by inference what their actual intention was as to the shares in which they would own the property, 'the answer is that each is entitled to that share which the court considers fair having regard to the whole course of dealing between them in relation to the property:' Chadwick LJ in Oxley v Hiscock [2005] Fam 211, para 69. In our judgment, 'the whole course of dealing ... in relation to the property' should be given a broad meaning, enabling a similar range of factors to be taken into account as may be relevant to ascertaining the parties' actual intentions. (5) Each case will turn on its own facts. Financial contributions are relevant but there are many other factors which may enable the court to decide what shares were either intended (as in case (3)) or fair (as in case (4)).

This case is not concerned with a family home which is put into the name of one party only. The starting point is different. The first issue is whether it was intended that the other party have any beneficial interest in the property at all. If he does, the second issue is what that interest is. There is no presumption of joint beneficial ownership. But their common intention has once again to be deduced objectively from their conduct. If the evidence shows a common intention to share beneficial ownership but does not show what shares were intended, the court will have to proceed as at para 51(4) and (5) above.

The assumptions as to human motivation, which led the courts to impute particular intentions by way of the resulting trust, are not appropriate to the ascertainment of beneficial interests in a family home. Whether they remain appropriate in other contexts is not the issue in this case.

It follows that we would allow this appeal and restore the order of the judge.

LORD COLLINS OF MAPESBURY:

I agree that the appeal should be allowed for the reasons given in the joint judgment of Lord Walker of Gestingthorpe and Baroness Hale of Richmond JJSC [...]

The absence of legislative intervention [...] made it necessary for the judiciary to respond by adapting old principles to new situations. That has not been an easy task. [...]

I agree [...] that authority justifies the conceptual approach of Lord Walker and Baroness Hale JJSC that, in joint names cases, the common intention to displace the presumption of equality can, in the absence of express agreement, be inferred (rather than imputed: see para 31 of the joint judgment) from their conduct, and where, in such a case, it is not possible to ascertain or infer what share was intended, each will be entitled to a fair share in the light of the whole course of dealing between them in relation to the property.

That said, it is my view that in the present context the difference between inference and imputation will hardly ever matter (as Lord Walker and Baroness Hale JJSC recognize at para 34), and that what is one person's inference will be another person's imputation. [...]

LORD KERR OF TONAGHMORE JSC:

I agree that this appeal should be allowed. There are differences of some significance in the reasoning that underlies the joint judgment of Lord Walker of Gestingthorpe and Baroness Hale of Richmond JJSC and that contained in Lord Wilson JSC's judgment. I agree with Lord Collins of Mapesbury that these are both terminological and conceptual. I am less inclined to agree, however, that the divergence in reasoning is unlikely to make a difference in practice. While it may well be that the outcome in many cases will be the same, whether one infers an intention or imputes it, that does not mean that the process by which the result is arrived at is more or less the same. Indeed, it seems to me that a markedly and obviously different mode of analysis will generally be required. [...]

The following appear to be the areas of agreement. (i) In joint names' cases, the starting point is [...] the presumption that the parties are joint tenants and are thus entitled to equal shares. (ii) That presumption can be displaced by showing (a) that the parties had a different common intention at the time when they acquired the home or (b) that they later formed the common intention that their respective shares would change. (iii) The common intention, if it can be inferred, is to be deduced objectively from the parties' conduct. (iv) Where the intention as to the division of the property cannot be inferred, each is entitled to that share which the court considers fair. In considering the question of what is fair the court should have regard to the whole course of dealing between the parties.

The areas of disagreement appear to be these: (a) is there sufficient evidence in the present case from which the parties' intentions can be inferred? (b) is the difference between inferring and imputing an intention likely to be great as a matter of general practice?

How far should the court go in seeking to infer actual intention as to shares?

At para 32 above Lord Walker and Baroness Hale JJSC have quoted the important judgment of Chadwick LJ in *Oxley v Hiscock* [2005] Fam 211 and at para 51(4) have said that, on the authority of what was said in para 69 of *Oxley's* case, where it is not possible to ascertain what the actual intention of the parties was as to the shares in which they would own the property, each is entitled to the share which the court considers fair having regard to the whole course of dealing between them in relation to the property. This, I believe, casts the test somewhat differently from the way that it was formulated by Chadwick LJ. [...]

Chadwick LJ did not confine the circumstances in which an intention is to be imputed to those where it was impossible to infer an intention. Rather, he considered that it was proper- - and necessary – to impute it when there had been no discussion about the amounts of the shares that each was to have or where there was no evidence of such a discussion. Lord Walker and Baroness Hale JJSC have pointed out that *Oxley v Hiscock* received qualified approval in *Stack v Dowden* [2007] 2 AC 432. It seems clear, however, that there was no approval of the notion that an intention should be imputed where there had been no discussion between the parties [...]

It is hardly controversial to suggest that the parties' intention should be given effect to where it can be ascertained and that, although discussions between them will always be the most reliable basis on which to draw an inference as to that intention, these are not the only circumstances in which that exercise will be possible. There is a natural inclination to prefer inferring an intention to imputing one. If the parties' intention can be inferred, the court is not imposing a solution. [...] I believe that the court should anxiously examine the circumstances in order, where possible, to ascertain the parties' intention but it should not be reluctant to recognise, when it is appropriate to do so, that inference of an intention is not possible and that imputation of an intention is the only course to follow.

[...] There are reasons to question the appropriateness of the notion of imputation in this area but, if it is correct to use this as a concept, I strongly favour the way in which it was described by Lord Neuberger in Stack v Dowden [...]

Link
see para 26 where this is quoted

[...] In many ways, it would be preferable to have a stark choice between deciding whether it is possible to deduce what their intention was and, where it is not, deciding what is fair, without elliptical references to what their intention might have – or should have – been. But imputing intention has entered the lexicon of this area of law and it is probably impossible to discard it now.

[...] As soon as it is clear that inferring an intention is not possible, the focus of the court's attention should be squarely on what is fair [...]

Is there sufficient evidence in the present case from which the parties' intentions can be inferred?

Lord Walker and Baroness Hale JJSC have concluded that the failure of the parties to sell their home in Badger Hall Avenue in late 1995, leading as it did to the cashing in of the life insurance policy, meant that Mr Kernott intended that his interest in the Badger Hall Avenue property should crystallise then. That may indeed have been his intention but, for my part, I would find it difficult to *infer* that it actually was what he then intended. [...] the bare facts of his departure from the family home and acquisition of another property are a slender foundation on which to conclude that he had entirely abandoned whatever stake he had in the previously shared property.

On the other hand, I would have no difficulty in concluding [...] that it was eminently fair that the property should be divided between the parties in the shares decreed by Judge Dedman. Like Lord Wilson JSC, therefore, I would prefer to allow this appeal on the basis that it is impossible to infer that the parties intended that their shares in the property be apportioned as the judge considered they should be but that such an intention should be imputed to them.

Link
See Lord Wilson at para 89 and contrast the view of Lord Walker and Baroness Hale at para 48

LORD WILSON JSC:

[...] I warmly applaud the development of the law of equity, spear-headed by Baroness Hale of Richmond and Lord Walker of Gestingthorpe in their speeches in *Stack v Dowden* [2007] 2 AC 432, and reiterated in their judgment in the present appeal, that the common intention which impresses a constructive trust upon the legal ownership of the family home can be *imputed* to the parties to the relationship. [...]

In *Oxley v Hiscock* [... the] home had been held in Mr Hiscock's sole name so, for Chadwick LJ, the first question was whether Mrs Oxley could establish that they had nevertheless had a common intention that she should have some beneficial share in it. In the present case, however, the home is held in the joint names of the parties so, for us, the first question is whether Ms Jones can establish that they nevertheless had (albeit not necessarily at the outset) a common intention that the beneficial shares of herself and Mr Kernott should be in some proportions other than joint and equal. The second question, which arises in the event only of an affirmative answer to the first, is to determine the proportions in which the beneficial shares are held.

In relation to the second question Chadwick LJ concluded, in his summary at para 69, that, where there was no evidence of any discussion between the parties as to the proportions in which their beneficial shares in the family home were to be held, each was 'entitled to that share which the court considers fair having regard to the whole course of dealing between them in relation to the property;' ... because 'what the court is doing, in cases of this nature, is to supply or impute a common intention as to the parties' respective shares (in circumstances in which there was, in fact, no common intention) on the basis of that which ... is shown to be fair.' Emboldened by developments in the case law [...] Chadwick LJ thus saw fit to reassert the power to impute [...]

The analysis by Chadwick LJ of the proper approach to the second question was correct. In paras 31 and 51(4) above Lord Walker and Baroness Hale JJSC reiterate that, although its preference is always to collect from the evidence an expressed or inferred intention, common to the parties, about the proportions in which their shares are to be held, equity will, if collection of it proves impossible, impute to them the requisite intention. Before us is a case in which Judge Dedman, the trial judge, found – and, was entitled on the evidence to find – that the common intention required by the first question could be inferred. Thus the case does not require us to consider whether modern equity allows the intention required by the first question also to be imputed if it is not otherwise identifiable. That question will merit careful thought.

Alert

In para 61 of her ground-breaking speech in *Stack v Dowden* Lady Hale quoted, with emphasis, the words of Chadwick LJ in para 69 of *Oxley v Hiscock*, which I have quoted in para 83 above. Then she quoted a passage from a Discussion Paper published by the Law Commission in July 2002 and entitled *Sharing Homes* about the proper approach to identifying the proportions which 'were intended.' Finally she added four sentences to each of which, in quoting them as follows, I take the liberty of attributing a number:

'[1] That may be the preferable way of expressing what is essentially the same thought, for two reasons. [2] First, it emphasises that the search is still for the result which reflects what the parties must, in the light of their conduct, be taken to have intended. [3] Second, therefore, it does not enable the court to abandon that search in favour of the result which the court itself considers fair. [4] For the court to impose its own view of what is fair upon the situation in which the parties find themselves would be to return to the days before *Pettitt v Pettitt* [1970] AC 777 ... '

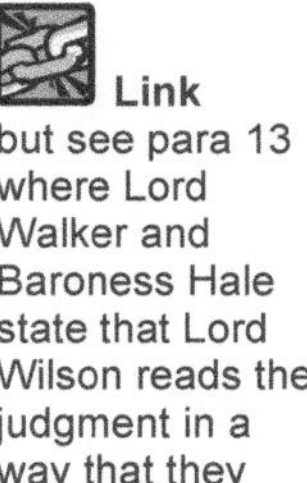
Link
but see para 13 where Lord Walker and Baroness Hale state that Lord Wilson reads the judgment in a way that they would not

I leave on one side Lady Hale's first sentence although, whereas Chadwick LJ was identifying the criterion for imputing the common intention, the context of the passage in the Discussion Paper suggests that the Law Commission was postulating a criterion for inferring it. On any view Lady Hale's second sentence is helpful; and, by her reference to what the parties must, in the light of their conduct, be taken to have intended (as opposed to what they did intend), Lady Hale made clear that, by then, she was addressing the power to resort to imputation. Lady Hale's fourth sentence has been neatly explained – by Mr Nicholas Strauss QC [...] who determined the first appeal in these proceedings [...] – as being that, in the event that the evidence were to suggest that, whether by expression or by inference, the parties intended that the beneficial interests in the home should be held in certain proportions, equity would not 'impose' different proportions upon them; and, at para 46 above, Lord Walker and Baroness Hale JJSC endorse Mr Strauss QC's explanation.

The problem has lain in Lady Hale's third sentence. Where equity is driven to impute the common intention, how can it do so other than by search for the result which the court itself considers fair? The sentence was not *obiter dictum* so rightly, under our system, judges below the level of this court have been unable to ignore it. Even in these proceedings judges in the courts below have wrestled with it. [...] In his judgment on the second appeal Rimer LJ went so far as to suggest, at para 77, that Lady Hale's third sentence must have meant that, contrary to appearances, she had not intended to recognise a power to impute a common intention at all.

I respectfully disagree with Lady Hale's third sentence.

Lord Walker and Baroness Hale JJSC observe, at para 34 above, that in practice the difference between inferring and imputing a common intention to the parties may not be great. I consider that, as a generalisation, their observation goes too far – at least if the court is to take (as in my view it should) an ordinarily rigorous approach to the task of inference. Indeed in the present case they conclude, at paras 48 and 49, that, in relation to Chadwick LJ's second question the proper inference from the evidence, which, if he did not draw, the trial judge should have drawn, was that the parties came to intend that the proportions of the beneficial interests in the home should be held on a basis which in effect equates to 90% to Ms Jones and to 10% to Mr Kernott [...] As it happens, reflective perhaps of the more rigorous approach to the task of inference which I prefer, **I regard it, as did Mr Strauss QC [...] as more realistic, in the light of the evidence before the judge, to conclude that inference is impossible but to proceed to impute to the parties the intention that it should be held on a basis which equates to those proportions.** At all events I readily concur in the result which Lord Walker and Baroness Hale JJSC propose.

Link
See also Lord Kerr at para 77 and contrast Lord Walker and Baroness Hale at para 48

Barnes v Phillips [2015] EWCA Civ 1056, [2016] HLR 3 (p 24)

Court of Appeal: Longmore LJ, Lloyd Jones LJ, and Hayden J

Mr Barnes and Ms Phillips formed a relationship in 1983 and started living together in 1989. The had two daughters, one born in 1993 and the other in 2000. In January 1996, Mr Barnes and Ms Phillips bought a house in their joint names. The purchase price was £135,000. They paid the deposit from their savings and financed the balance with the assistance of a joint mortgage. From January 1996 to May 2005, Mr Barnes paid all the mortgage instalments and Ms Phillips paid the council tax charges. They both contributed to utility bills and the costs of improving the property.

In May 2005, Mr Barnes and Ms Phillips re-mortgaged the house in order to discharge Mr Barnes' debts. They borrowed £145,000. £79,000 of this money was applied to discharge the acquisition mortgage and the balance – approximately £65,000 – was paid to Mr Barnes' creditors. The value of the equity in the house, after the acquisition mortgage had been discharged, was £275,000.

In June 2005, Mr Barnes and Ms Phillips separated. Mr Barnes moved out of the house. Mr Barnes agreed to pay Ms Phillips £250 per month to help with the care of their daughters, but he made these payments on very few occasions. From June 2005 to April 2008, Mr Barnes paid approximately £22,100, and Ms Phillips approximately £12,500, towards the mortgage instalments. From January 2008 to the date of the proceedings (March 2014), Ms Phillips paid all mortgage instalments and other costs connected with the house. She also had sole financial responsibility for the children.

During the course of their relationship, Mr Barnes bought three properties in his sole name as personal business investments.

The Court of Appeal held that there was sufficient evidence to rebut the presumption of an equitable joint tenancy, and that the judge had correctly imputed to Mr Barnes and Ms Phillips an intention that Ms Phillips should own 85%, and Mr Barnes 15%, of the equitable interest in the house.

LLOYD JONES LJ, with whom **LONGMORE LJ** and **HAYDEN J** agreed:

If I am correct in my reading of paras 37 and 38 of the judgment, the judge has moved directly from considering whether there was an express common intention to vary shares in the property to considering in what shares the parties now hold the property, from concluding that there was 'no specific agreement' to considering what intention must be imputed as to the shares. A critical step in the process is simply not addressed in the judgment. As we have seen, the judge was well aware of the structure laid down in *Jones v Kernott* within which the issues should be addressed; he had just set it out in great detail in his judgment. He cannot be taken to have departed from it in the radical manner submitted by the appellant. Moreover, he must have appreciated that there would be no point in discussing the shares in which the property is held following variation if no common intention to vary had been established. In these circumstances, it is at the very least strongly arguable that the judge must be taken to have concluded that there was such a common intention. Nevertheless, this stage of the reasoning is totally absent from his judgment.

In these circumstances it is open to this court to consider whether a common intention to vary shares should be inferred in the circumstances of this case. It is clear from the judgments of the majority in *Jones v Kernott* that the scope for inference in this context is very extensive indeed. (See in particular Lord Walker and Baroness Hale at para 34: 'In this area, as in many others, the scope for inference is wide.') It is also significant that the majority in *Jones v Kernott* felt able to drawn an inference as to the shares in which the property should be held after the variation.

In the present case the weight of the evidence supports an inference that the parties intended to alter their shares in the property. Throughout the relationship the appellant was carrying on business activities. The property at 7 Stoke Newington Road, which he had owned since 1988 was owned by him in his sole name and was rented out. It was the respondent's evidence that this was 'in order to supplement his income.' In addition, during their relationship the appellant purchased two more properties at Otter Close where he installed tenants. These were owned by the appellant in his sole name. It was the respondent's evidence that the appellant had told her at the time he acquired them that he considered the properties as a business investment for himself. The re-mortgage of the property in May 2005 was entered into for the sole benefit of the appellant, in order to pay off debts which he had incurred in his personal capacity. After the repayment of the original mortgage this made available £65,600.13. Virtually all of this money went to the appellant for his personal use. In particular, the judge found that the respondent did not receive £10,000 from the proceeds of the re-mortgage. The judge accepted the submission of Mr Jones that the appellant received between 24% and 25% of the net equity, which was approximately £275,000, for his sole benefit. [...] A month later, in June 2005 their relationship came to an end and the appellant left the property. I consider that in those circumstances, where nearly 25% of the equity in the property had been paid to the appellant for his own purposes and the relationship ended almost immediately thereafter, there is to be inferred a common intention at that point to vary their interests in the property.

Between June 2005 and January 2008 both the appellant and the respondent contributed to the mortgage repayments. It was the respondent's evidence that at first the appellant continued to pay the mortgage and she made some payments to him to support this initially. However, the appellant only paid the mortgage without problem for about eight months and then his direct debit payments ceased. In total, over that period the appellant paid £22,077.12 and the respondent paid £12,552.27. After January 2008 the appellant made no further contribution to the mortgage repayments which were paid by the respondent alone. It was his evidence that prior to ceasing to pay any contribution to the mortgage he informed the respondent that the strain of paying two mortgages, one on the flat he was occupying and the other on the property, plus child care, was proving difficult and he would have to cease paying for the mortgage on the property. It was the respondent's evidence that he simply stopped paying the mortgage. These further matters support an inference that there was a common intention in June 2005 to vary their beneficial interests in the property. The appellant could only legitimately have taken this stance and acted in this way if there had been a change in the beneficial interests in the property. [...]

For these reasons, I consider that a common intention should be inferred to the parties at June 2005 to vary their beneficial interests in the property. [...]

For reasons set out above, I consider that the judge did not infer that the parties had formed a common intention to hold the property in shares of 85% to the respondent and 15% to the appellant. On the contrary, having inferred a common intention to vary their interests in the property he imputed an intention to them as to their respective shares.

Mr Horton submits on behalf of the appellant that it is wholly wrong to impute a change to the shares of 75% to the respondent and 25% to the appellant in May 2005 when over the next thirty-four months the appellant contributed approximately 64% of the mortgage repayments on a property in which he was not living. However, to my mind the judge's conclusion as to the intention to be imputed at that point is entirely appropriate. The appellant had received almost 25% of the equity in the property for his own use very shortly before the parties split up in 2005. This entirely warranted an adjustment of the beneficial shares in the property which reflected that change of position. Furthermore the judge was clearly correct in his conclusion that subsequent events require a further adjustment in the intention to be imputed to the parties. Here, the judge properly took account of the respective positions of the parties and, in particular, the payments made in respect of the mortgage and in respect of repairs. For reasons set out below in relation to ground 3, I also consider that he acted correctly in taking account of payments made (or not made) in respect of the children. In this regard the contributions to the mortgage after June 2005 are particularly important. In the period from June 2005 to January 2008 the appellant paid approximately two-thirds of the mortgage contributions and the respondent one-third. However thereafter the appellant failed to contribute towards the mortgage repayments for a period of six years up to trial. In these circumstances it was clearly necessary to vary the intention to be imputed to the parties as to their respective interests in the property. The further adjustment of 10 per cent in the respondent's favour was entirely justified by these changed circumstances. [...]

On behalf of the appellant it is submitted that the judge, when imputing an intention to the parties as to the shares in which the beneficial interests in the property should be held, erred in law in taking account of the failures of the appellant to make maintenance payments for the children. Mr Horton submits that this is not a matter which is relevant to the quantification of the parties' beneficial interests and that bringing child support issues into the process of quantification is liable to result in double counting. In particular, he submits that any monies which are owed by the appellant to the Child Support Agency (CSA) will remain owing to the CSA notwithstanding their inclusion in the judge's assessment of the appropriate shares in the property.

In *Stack v Dowden* [2007] UKHL 17, [2007] 2 AC 432, Baroness Hale (at para 69) emphasized the importance of the domestic context and contemplated that a very wide range of circumstances, including responsibility for children, would be relevant. Similarly in *Jones v Kernott* Lord Walker and Baroness Hale considered that, when imputing intention as to the shares in which property was held, the whole course of dealing in relation to the property would be relevant. They emphasized (at para 51) that this concept should be given a broad meaning, enabling a similar range of factors to be taken into account as may be relevant to ascertaining the parties' actual intentions. (In this regard, see also *Fowler v Barron* [2008] EWCA Civ 377, [2008] 2 FLR 831, *per* Arden LJ at para 32.)

I note that in *Jones v Kernott* the deputy High Court Judge (Mr Nicholas Strauss QC) who heard the first appeal expressed the view, *obiter*, that failure to contribute to the maintenance of children was a factor which could legitimately be taken into account. In doing so he referred to the speech of Baroness Hale in *Stack v Dowden* at paras 69 and 91. However, on appeal to this court, Wall LJ (at para 51) left to one side the defendant's failure to maintain the children on the ground that the claimant in that case had a remedy in this regard which she had chosen not to exercise. However, he observed that the defendant's failure to maintain the children might well be relevant were he to seek to charge the claimant for her occupation of the property and were the process of equitable accounting applied between them.

In view of the very wide terms in which the House of Lords in *Stack v Dowden* and the Supreme Court in *Jones v Kernott* described the relevant context, I consider that, in principle, it should be open to a court to take account of financial contributions to the maintenance of children (or lack of them) as part of the financial history of the parties save in circumstances where it is clear that to do so would result in double liability. However, there seems to be no danger of that in the present case. Mr Horton pointed to the fact that monies are owed by Mr Barnes to the Child Support Agency and makes the point that such monies will remain owing notwithstanding the fact that they have been taken into account in the assessments of the parties' fair shares in the property. However, the respondent only referred the matter to the CSA in 2013 when only their second daughter was under the age of 18. By February 2014 when the judge delivered his judgment the appellant's liability to the CSA would be limited to that single year. In the context of the case as a whole such liability is of very limited significance.

14.3 Legal title held in one name

14.3.1 Express common intention constructive trusts

Grant v Edwards [1986] Ch 638

Court of Appeal: Sir Nicolas Browne-Wilkinson VC, Mustill LJ, and Nourse LJ

The defendant purchased a house in the names of himself and his brother, in which both he and the claimant resided. The brother had no beneficial interest in the home but was included for the purpose of securing a mortgage. The claimant made no contribution to either the purchase price or mortgage instalments, which were paid by the defendant. She was informed, however, that her name had not been put on the legal title as it would have adversely affected her current divorce proceedings. Substantial outgoings and expenses were paid by the claimant and an insurance payout on the home was paid into their joint account. Upon separation the claimant claimed a share in the home. It was held that she was entitled to a 50% share in the house through her beneficial interest under a trust.

NOURSE LJ:

In most of these cases the fundamental, and invariably the most difficult, question is to decide whether there was the necessary common intention, being something which can only be inferred from the conduct of the parties, almost always from the expenditure incurred by them respectively. In this regard the court has to look for expenditure which is referable to the acquisition of the house: see *per* Fox LJ in *Burns v Burns* [1984] Ch 317, 328H-329C. If it is found to have been incurred, such expenditure will perform the twofold function of establishing the common intention and showing that the claimant has acted upon it.

There is another and rarer class of case, of which the present may be one, where, although there has been no writing, the parties have orally declared themselves in such a way as to make their common intention plain. Here the court does not have to look for conduct from which the intention can be inferred, but only for conduct which amounts to an acting upon it by the claimant. And although that conduct can undoubtedly be the incurring of expenditure which is referable to the acquisition of the house, it need not necessarily be so.

The clearest example of this rarer class of case is *Eves v Eves* [1975] 1 WLR 1338. That was a case of an unmarried couple where the conveyance of the house was taken in the name of the man alone. At the time of the purchase he told the woman that if she had been 21 years of age, he would have put the house into their joint names, because it was to be their joint home. He admitted in evidence that that was an excuse for not putting the house into their joint names, and this court inferred that there was an understanding between them, or a common intention, that the woman was to have some sort of proprietary interest in it; otherwise no excuse would have been needed. After they had moved in, the woman did extensive decorative work to the downstairs rooms and generally cleaned the whole house. She painted the brickwork of the front of the house. She also broke up with a 14-lb sledgehammer the concrete surface which covered the whole of the front garden and disposed of the rubble into a skip, worked in the back garden and, together with the man, demolished a shed there and put up a new shed. She also prepared the front garden for turfing. Pennycuick VC at first instance, being unable to find any link between the common intention and the woman's activities after the purchase, held that she had not acquired a beneficial interest in the house. On an appeal to this court the decision was unanimously reversed, by Lord Denning MR on a ground which I respectfully think was at variance with the principles stated in *Gissing v Gissing* [1971] AC 886 and by Browne LJ and Brightman J on a ground which was stated by Brightman J [1975] 1 WLR 1338, 1345:

'The defendant clearly led the plaintiff to believe that she was to have some undefined interest in the property, and that her name was only omitted from the conveyance because of her age. This, of course, is not enough by itself to create a beneficial interest in her favour; there would at best be a mere "voluntary declaration of trust" which would be "unenforceable for want of writing:" *per* Lord Diplock in *Gissing v Gissing* [1971] AC 886, 905. If, however, it was part of the bargain between the parties, expressed or to be implied, that the plaintiff should contribute her labour towards the reparation of a house in which she was to have some beneficial interest, then I think that the arrangement becomes one to which the law can give effect. This seems to be consistent with the reasoning of the speeches in *Gissing v Gissing*." [...]

So what sort of conduct is required? In my judgment it must be conduct on which the woman could not reasonably have been expected to embark unless she was to have an interest in the house. If she was not to have such an interest, she could reasonably be expected to go and live with her lover, but not, for example, to wield a 14-lb. sledge hammer in the front garden. In adopting the latter kind of conduct she is seen to act to her detriment on the faith of the common intention. [...]

Alert

From the above facts and figures it is in my view an inevitable inference that the very substantial contribution which the plaintiff made out of her earnings after August 1972 to the housekeeping and to the feeding and to the bringing up of the children enabled the defendant to keep down the instalments payable under both mortgages out of his own income and, moreover, that he could not have done that if he had had to bear the whole of the other expenses as well. [...]

Was the conduct of the plaintiff in making substantial indirect contributions to the instalments payable under both mortgages conduct upon which she could not reasonably have been expected to embark unless she was to have an interest in the house? I answer that question in the affirmative. I cannot see upon what other basis she could reasonably have been expected to give the defendant such substantial assistance in paying off mortgages on his house. I therefore conclude that the plaintiff did act to her detriment on the faith of the

Alert

common intention between her and the defendant that she was to have some sort of proprietary interest in the house.

MUSTILL LJ:

Turning to the facts, the first question is whether there was an explicit bargain or a common intention at the moment of acquisition to the effect that the plaintiff should have a beneficial interest in the house. Strictly speaking, there was not. There was no discussion as to the *quid pro quo*, if any, which the plaintiff was to provide. Nor was there any common intention, for it is found that the defendant never intended the plaintiff to have a share. The reason given for placing the brother's name on the title was simply an untruthful excuse for not doing at once what he never meant to do at all.

This is not, however, fatal to the claim. Whatever the defendant's actual intention, the nature of the excuse which he gave must have led the plaintiff to believe that she would in the future have her name on the title, and this in turn would justify her in concluding that she had from the outset some kind of right to the house. The [...] defendant's conduct must now preclude him from denying that it is sufficiently analogous to these categories to make the relevant principles apply. [...]

Finally, there remains the question whether the conduct of the plaintiff can be regarded as referable to the bargain or intention thus construed. On the facts as analysed by Nourse LJ I consider that it can. Accordingly, the conditions are satisfied for the creation of an interest, and for the reasons given by Nourse LJ I agree that the interest should be quantified at 50%.

BROWNE-WILKINSON VC:

I agree. In my judgment, there has been a tendency over the years to distort the principles as laid down in the speech of Lord Diplock in *Gissing v Gissing* [1971] AC 886 by concentrating on only part of his reasoning. For present purposes, his speech can be treated as falling into three sections: the first deals with the nature of the substantive right; the second with the proof of the existence of that right; the third with the quantification of that right.

1. The nature of the substantive right: [1971] AC 886, 905B-G

If the legal estate in the joint home is vested in only one of the parties ('the legal owner') the other party ('the claimant'), in order to establish a beneficial interest, has to establish a constructive trust by showing that it would be inequitable for the legal owner to claim sole beneficial ownership. This requires two matters to be demonstrated: (a) that there was a common intention that both should have a beneficial interest; (b) that the claimant has acted to his or her detriment on the basis of that common intention.

2. The proof of the common intention

(a) Direct evidence (p 905H). It is clear that mere agreement between the parties that both are to have beneficial interests is sufficient to prove the necessary common intention. Other passages in the speech point to the admissibility and relevance of other possible forms of direct evidence of such intention: see pp 907C and 908C.

(b) Inferred common intention (pp 906A-908D). Lord Diplock points out that, even where parties have not used express words to communicate their intention (and therefore there is no direct evidence), the court can infer from their actions an intention that they shall both have an interest in the house. This part of his speech concentrates on the types of evidence from which the courts are most often asked to infer such intention *viz* contributions (direct and indirect) to the deposit, the mortgage instalments or general housekeeping expenses. In this section of the speech, he analyses what types of expenditure are capable of constituting evidence of such common intention: he does not say that if the intention is proved in some other way such contributions are essential to establish the trust.

3. The quantification of the right (pp 908D-909)

Once it has been established that the parties had a common intention that both should have a beneficial interest and that the claimant has acted to his detriment, the question may still remain 'what is the extent of the claimant's beneficial interest?' This last section of Lord Diplock's speech shows that here again the direct and indirect contributions made by the parties to the cost of acquisition may be crucially important.

If this analysis is correct, contributions made by the claimant may be relevant for four different purposes, *viz*: (1) in the absence of direct evidence of intention, as evidence from which the parties' intentions can be inferred; (2) as corroboration of direct evidence of intention; (3) to show that the claimant has acted to his or her detriment in reliance on the common intention: Lord Diplock's speech does not deal directly with the nature of the detriment to be shown; (4) to quantify the extent of the beneficial interest. [...]

But as Lord Diplock's speech in *Gissing v Gissing* [1971] AC 886, 905D and the decision in *Midland Bank Plc v Dobson* (unreported) make clear, mere common intention by itself is not enough: the claimant has also to prove that she has acted to her detriment in the reasonable belief that by so acting she was acquiring a beneficial interest.

There is little guidance in the authorities on constructive trusts as to what is necessary to prove that the claimant so acted to her detriment. What 'link' has to be shown between the common intention and the actions relied on? Does there have to be positive evidence that the claimant did the acts in conscious reliance on the common intention? Does the court have to be satisfied that she would not have done the acts relied on but for the common intention, *e.g.* would not the claimant have contributed to household expenses out of affection for the legal owner and as part of their joint life together even if she had no interest in the house? Do the acts relied on as a detriment have to be inherently referable to the house, *e.g.* contribution to the purchase or physical labour on the house?

I do not think it is necessary to express any concluded view on these questions in order to decide this case. *Eves v Eves* [1975] 1 WLR 1338 indicates that there has to be some 'link' between the common intention and the acts relied on as a detriment. In that case the acts relied on did inherently relate to the house (*viz* the work the claimant did to the house) and from this the Court of Appeal felt able to infer that the acts were done in reliance on the common intention. So, in this case, as the analysis of Nourse LJ makes clear, the plaintiff's contributions to the household expenses were essentially linked to the payment of the mortgage instalments by the defendant: without the plaintiff's contributions, the defendant's means were insufficient to keep up the mortgage payments. In my judgment where the claimant has made payments which, whether directly or indirectly, have been used to discharge the mortgage instalments, this is a sufficient link between the detriment suffered by the claimant and the common intention. The court can infer that she would not have made such payments were it not for her belief that she had an interest in the house. On this ground therefore I find that the plaintiff has acted to her detriment in reliance on the common intention that she had a beneficial interest in the house and accordingly that she has established such beneficial interest. [...]

In many cases of the present sort, it is impossible to say whether or not the claimant would have done the acts relied on as a detriment even if she thought she had no interest in the house. Setting up house together, having a baby, making payments to general housekeeping expenses (not strictly necessary to enable the mortgage to be paid) may all be referable to the mutual love and affection of the parties and not specifically referable to the claimant's belief that she has an interest in the house. As at present advised, once it has been shown that there was a common intention that the claimant should have an interest in the house, any act done by her to her detriment relating to the joint lives of the parties is, in my judgment, sufficient detriment to qualify. The acts do not have to be inherently referable to the house: see *Jones (A.E) v Jones (FW)* and *Pascoe v Turner* [1979] 1 WLR 431. The holding out to the claimant that she had a beneficial interest in the house is an act of such a nature as to be part of the inducement to her to do the acts relied on. Accordingly, in the absence of evidence to the contrary, the right inference is that the claimant acted in reliance on such holding out and the burden lies on the legal owner to show that she did not do so: see *Greasley v Cooke* [1980] 1 WLR 1306 . [...]

Taking into account the fact that the house was intended to be the joint property, the contributions to the common expenditure and the payment of the fire insurance moneys into the joint account, I agree that the plaintiff is entitled to a half interest in the house.

Curran v Collins [2015] EWCA Civ 404, [2016] 1 FLR 505

Court of Appeal: Arden LJ, Davis LJ, and Lewison LJ

Ms Curran and Mr Collins formed a relationship in 1977, but did not start living together until 2002. In 1986, Mr Collins contracted to buy a house in Feltham. Ms Curran asked Mr Collins about ownership of the house, and, in particular, whether she was to have a share in the property. Mr Collins told Ms Curran it would be too expensive to acquire the property in their joint names because it would require payment of *premia* on two life assurance policies. In the event, the house was acquired in Mr Collins' sole name. Ms Curran made no financial contribution to the acquisition of the house or its associated costs; Ms Curran and Mr Collins were not living together when it was acquired, nor was there any expectation that they would do so. Ms Curran and Mr Collins separated in 2010.

Ms Curran initiated proceedings in which she claimed an equitable interest in the Feltham house by way of express common intention constructive trust. The trial judge rejected Ms Curran's claim. In particular, he rejected her argument that Mr Collins' 'excuse' was evidence of a common intention to share beneficial ownership of the house. The Court of Appeal dismissed Ms Curran's appeal.

ARDEN LJ, with whom **DAVIS LJ** agreed:

Ms Crowther contends that the judge wrongly applied a subjective test to the excuse. It is well established that the meaning of words in the context of shared intention is to be deduced objectively, see for example *Jones v Kernott* [2012] 1 AC 766, paras 46 and 51, *per* Lord Walker, citing Lord Diplock in *Gissing v Gissing* [1977] AC 886, 906. Ms Crowther submits that the judge failed to consider what the reasonable person in Ms Curran's situation would have understood from the excuse. [...]

On Ms Crowther's submission, the excuse was a classic example of a statement from which the court will infer that the parties intended that they should each have a beneficial share in property, as it did in *Grant v Edwards* [1986] Ch 638 and *Eves v Eves* [1975] 1 WLR 1338. [...]

The judge's interpretation of events surrounding the excuse was an evaluation by her of all the relevant facts and circumstances. This court could only properly interfere if the judge were wrong: see generally *Assicurazioni Generali Spa v Arab Insurance Group (BSC)* [2003] 1 WLR 577, para 16, *per* Clarke LJ. The parties were not living together when the excuse was given, and did not do so until many years later. That is not conclusive but taken with the absence of significant contribution it constitutes material which supports the judge's finding. [...]

Given that the parties were not living together and the absence of significant contribution by Ms Curran, it is clear that the judge in my judgment applied the objective test in her interpretation of the excuse.

LEWISON LJ, with whom **DAVIS LJ** agreed:

[…] [The trial judge] made her more detailed finding at para 100:

'I believe Miss Curran that something was said in the context of the acquisition of the Feltham house, at least with regard to the costs of an insurance policy as a reason for her not being 'on the title' but I am equally satisfied that this was said to forestall what Mr Collins would quite reasonably have seen as Miss Curran's getting what he would have regarded as the wrong end of the stick about the acquisition of the property. In other words I am satisfied that this was not an excuse made in the context of a pre-existing agreement arrangement or understanding that this was to be a joint purchase, of which Mr Collins was fully aware, but made in order to prevent evidence of that being recorded, but was an excuse made to forestall a confrontation arising from Miss Curran making an unjustifiable assumption as to his intention. Any such assumption would, I am satisfied, have been just such an unjustifiable assumption; I am satisfied that Mr Collins did not represent to Miss Curran that she was to have an interest in the property he was buying nor say or do anything which she could reasonably have interpreted as being intended to assure her that she did.'

In this passage the judge has clearly rejected Ms Curran's evidence that there had been an agreement or understanding that she had a joint equal interest in the property. Although she was not in a position to make a finding about exactly what it was that Mr Collins said, it cannot be right that the giving of a reason why someone is not on the title deeds inevitably leads to the inference that it must have been agreed that they would have an interest in the property. If one who is not versed in the difference between legal and beneficial ownership asks to be on the deeds and is told 'No,' the more usual inference would be that they would have understood that they were not to become owners or part owners of the property. I cannot see that the result is very different if the reason given is that it is too expensive. There are, however, two cases in which a specious excuse has been held to give rise to the inference of a constructive trust. However, these cases are fact-sensitive and need to be carefully examined.

In *Eves v Eves* [1975] 1 WLR 1338 Janet and Stuart Eves were already cohabiting and had a daughter together. They were looking for a family home. It was in that context that Stuart Eves made the representation:

'He told her that it was to be their house and a home for themselves and their children. He said that, as she was under 21, it could not be in joint names and had to be in his name alone; and that, but for her age, it would have been purchased in joint names. She accepted his explanation: but he admitted in the witness-box that it was simply an 'excuse.' He all along was determined that it was to be in his name alone.'

There are two important parts to this representation, neither of which is present in our case. First, Stuart Eves told Janet Eves that the house was to be a home for both of them and their children. In our case Ms Curran had no intention of moving into the Feltham house at the time it was acquired. Second, Stuart Eves told Janet Eves that the house would have been bought in both names but for her age. It is that positive assertion that it would have been bought in joint names that was capable of giving rise to an expectation that Janet Eves would acquire an interest in the house. In our case nothing of the sort was said to Ms Curran. She was simply told that she could not be on the deeds because it was too expensive.

The second case is *Grant v Edwards* [1986] Ch 638. Once again the parties were living together at the time of the purchase, and had had a child together. The exact representation that was made to Mrs Grant is not set out *verbatim*, but Browne-Wilkinson V-C described it thus:

' ... the representation made by the defendant to the plaintiff [was] that the house would have been in joint names but for the plaintiff's matrimonial disputes ... '

Again there are two factors present in that case which are absent from ours. First, in that case (but not in ours) the house being acquired was acquired as a family home. Second, in that case (but not in ours) there was a positive representation that Mrs Grant would have been a joint owner but for her matrimonial dispute.

These cases do not establish the proposition that the mere giving of a 'specious excuse' necessarily or even usually leads to an inference that the person to whom the excuse is given can reasonably regard herself as having an immediate entitlement to an interest in the property in question.

Alert

14.3.2 Inferred common intention constructive trusts

In the absence of express agreement between the parties regarding beneficial interests in the home, the courts may infer an intention to share based purely on the conduct of the parties. The inferred common intention constructive trust may arise, traditionally, if one pays substantial mortgage repayments: *Lloyds Bank v Rosset*. However, over recent years, cases have developed whereby other contributing factors may be taken into account in order to allow the courts to infer a common intention to share the home beneficially between the parties. The common intention can only be inferred; it cannot be imputed.

***Capehorn v Harris* [2015] EWCA Civ 955, [2016] HLR 1 (p 1)**

Court of Appeal: Leveson PQBD, Sharp LJ, and Sales LJ

The trial judge *imputed* to cohabitants a common intention that one should have an equitable interest in the property of the other. The Court of Appeal held that this approach was wrong in principle.

SALES LJ, with whom **LEVESON PQBD** and **SHARP LJ** agreed:

The legal framework was common ground between the parties at trial and again before us on appeal. In relation to assets acquired by unmarried cohabitees or partners, where an asset is owned in law by one person but another claims to

share a beneficial interest in it a two-stage analysis is called for to determine whether a common intention constructive trust arises. First, the person claiming the beneficial interest must show that there was an agreement that he should have a beneficial interest in the property owned by his partner even if there was no agreement as to the precise extent of that interest. Secondly, if such an agreement can be shown to have been made, then absent agreement on the extent of the interest, the court may impute an intention that the person was to have a fair beneficial share in the asset and may assess the quantum of the fair share in the light of all the circumstances: see *Oxley v Hiscock* [2005] Fam 211; *Stack v Dowden* [2007] AC 432; *Jones v Kernott* [2011] UKSC 53.

There is an important difference between the approach applicable at each stage. At the first stage, an actual agreement has to be found to have been made, which may be inferred from conduct in an appropriate case. At the second stage, the court is entitled to impute an intention that each person is entitled to the share which the court considers fair having regard to the whole course of dealing between them in relation to the property. A court is not entitled to impute an intention to the parties at the first stage in the analysis.

Unfortunately, in this case in the critical part of her judgment, at paras 152 and 153, the judge erroneously elided these two stages. [...]

In my judgment, the judge erred in this paragraph of the judgment. She imputed an intention to the parties for the first stage of the two-stage analysis rather than identifying an actual agreement made by them that Mr Harris should have any beneficial interest in Sunnyside Farm. No actual agreement to that effect was ever made by Mrs Capehorn and Mr Harris, as the judge's findings elsewhere in the judgment made clear. [...]

[...] there never was an agreement that Mr Harris should have a beneficial interest in Sunnyside Farm. Therefore the judge should have found that his claim to have such an interest must fail.

Note: In addition to the agreement mentioned by Sales LJ the extract above, it is also necessary for the claimant to demonstrate that she acted to her detriment in reliance on the agreement: see *Grant v Edwards* (above) and *James v Thomas* (below).

***Abbott v Abbott* [2007] UKPC 53, [2008] 1 FLR 1451**

Judicial Committee of the Privy Council: Lord Bingham of Cornhill, Lord Walker of Gestingthorpe, Baroness Hale of Richmond, Lord Carswell, and Lord Neuberger of Abbotsbury

The parties were given a piece of land in Antigua by the defendant's mother for the purpose of building their matrimonial home. This was conveyed into the defendant's name alone. The money to build the house was secured by gifts and a series of loans, which were subsequently turned into mortgages. These were secured by the defendant in his sole name but the claimant was also jointly and severally liable for the sums. Income was paid into a joint account, from which the mortgage repayments were made. Upon dissolution of the marriage the claimant claimed a beneficial share in the home. It was held that the land provided by the defendant's mother was to be considered as a gift to both parties rather than just to the defendant. Since the mortgage taken out over the house was in both names there was also a clear intention to share the house beneficially. Furthermore, the factors to be taken into consideration regarding quantification of beneficial shares in the land had moved on since *Lloyds Bank v Rosset*, which had been given too much weight by the Court of Appeal. As the parties had made mortgage repayments out of their joint account and had shared liability for the mortgage equally it was appropriate to award equal division of the house.

BARONESS HALE OF RICHMOND:

There are, of course, two separate questions: first, was it intended that the parties should share the beneficial interest in a property conveyed to one of them only; and second, if it was so intended, in what proportions was it intended that they share the beneficial interest? There are two separate concepts which may help in answering those questions, explained by Peter Gibson LJ in *Drake v Whipp* [1996] 1 FLR 826, 827:

'A potent source of confusion, to my mind, has been suggestions that it matters not whether the terminology used is that of the constructive trust, to which the intention, actual or imputed, of the parties is crucial, or that of the resulting trust which operates as a presumed intention of the contributing party in the absence of rebutting evidence of actual intention.'

It is now clear that the constructive trust is generally the more appropriate tool of analysis in most matrimonial cases. [...]

[...] Lord Walker pointed out [in *Stack v Dowden*], at para 25, that although Lord Bridge had drawn a sharp contrast between cases in which there had been some prior agreement to share and those where there had not, he and all the other members of the House were 'unanimously, if unostentatiously, agreeing that a "common intention" trust could be inferred even when there was no evidence of an actual agreement.' Lord Walker went on to comment, in para 26:

'Lord Bridge's extreme doubt "whether anything less will do" was certainly consistent with many first-instance and Court of Appeal decisions, but I respectfully doubt whether it took full account of the views (conflicting though they were) expressed in *Gissing v Gissing* (see especially Lord Reid [1971] AC 886 at pp 896G-897B and Lord Diplock at p 909D-H). It has attracted some trenchant criticism from scholars as potentially productive of injustice (see Gray & Gray, *Elements of Land Law*, 4th ed, paras 10.132 to 10.137, the last paragraph being headed "A More Optimistic Future"). Whether or not Lord Bridge's observation was justified in 1990, in my opinion the law has moved on, and your Lordships should move it a little more in the same direction ... '

Lord Walker, Lord Hoffmann and Lord Hope of Craighead all agreed with my own opinion, in which I summed the matter up thus at para 60:

'The law has indeed moved on in response to changing social and economic conditions. The search is to ascertain the parties' shared intentions, actual, inferred or imputed, with respect to the property in the light of their whole course of conduct in relation to it.'

The House also approved a passage from the Law Commission's discussion paper on *Sharing Homes* (2002, Law Com No 278, para 4.27):

'If the question really is one of the parties' "common intention," we believe that there is much to be said for adopting what has been called a "holistic approach" to quantification, undertaking a survey of the whole course of dealing between the parties and taking account of all conduct which throws light on the question what shares were intended.' [...]

The matrimonial home: applying the law to the facts [...]

Alert

It has been said more than once in the English courts that if a parent gives financial assistance to a newly married couple to acquire their matrimonial home, the usual inference is that it was intended as a gift to both of them rather than to one alone: see McHardy & Sons (A Firm) v Warren [1994] 2 FLR 338, at 340; Midland Bank plc v Cooke [1995] 4 All ER 562, at 570. It might be doubted whether such an inference could so readily be drawn in other countries where the culture may be different. But this was a Caribbean judge, albeit from a different small Caribbean island, and it is certainly not for us to say that it was an inference which he was not entitled to draw.

Furthermore, it was supported by the behaviour of both parties throughout the marriage until it broke down. Not only did they organize their finances entirely jointly, having only a joint bank account into which everything was paid and from which everything was paid. They also undertook joint liability for the repayment of the mortgage loan and interest. This has always been regarded as a significant factor: see *Hyett v Stanley* [2003] EWCA Civ 942, [2004] 1 FLR 394. Yet the Court of Appeal appear to have attached no weight to it at all.

Alert

Finally, it must be borne in mind that the husband accepted in the course of his evidence that the wife did have a beneficial interest in the home, although he disputed the amount. The Court of Appeal appears to have attached undue significance to the dictum of Lord Bridge in Lloyd's Bank plc v Rosset, in particular as to what conduct is to be taken into account in quantifying an acknowledged beneficial interest. The law has indeed moved on since then. The parties' whole course of conduct in relation to the property must be taken into account in determining their shared intentions as to its ownership.

For all those reasons, the Board is of the view that the Court of Appeal should not have interfered with the findings of the learned trial judge on the beneficial ownership of the matrimonial home. [...]

The Board will therefore humbly advise Her Majesty that the appeal should be allowed in respect of the house and the furniture. There should be a declaration that the husband holds the house in trust for them both in equal shares. There should also be an order that the house be sold and the proceeds divided equally, subject to an adjustment in favour of the wife for 20% of the costs of acquiring the furniture.

It seems clear, therefore, that Baroness Hale intended the factors discussed in *Stack v Dowden* to apply to inferred common intention constructive trusts where legal title is in one name only. Subsequent cases have asserted that, since *Stack v Dowden*, a common intention to share ownership in a sole name case can be inferred from the whole course of conduct. However, in most cases, the court has held that the particular conduct of the claimant on the facts did not suffice for this purpose. It is arguably a pity that, in *Jones v Kernott*, the Supreme Court did not take the opportunity to offer more *obiter* guidance on the kind of conduct needed to infer an intention for the non-legal owner to have an interest. The court did, however, make clear its view that the same principles apply to *quantifying* interests in all cases of common intention trusts, whether the legal title is in sole or joint names. Although this is *obiter dicta* in relation to sole name cases, it is at the top end of the persuasive scale.

***James v Thomas* [2007] EWCA Civ 1212, [2007] 3 FCR 696**

Court of Appeal: Smith LJ, Wilson LJ, and Sir John Chadwick

Mr Thomas carried on business as an agricultural builder and drainage contractor. He held a current account at Barclays Bank which he used as his personal and business account. In 1986, Mr Thomas acquired a property, 'The Cottage,' with the assistance of a mortgage.

In May 1989, Mr Thomas formed a relationship with Miss James, who moved into The Cottage. In 1990, Miss James started assisting Mr Thomas in his business: she drove a tipper, dug trenches, picked up materials, laid concrete, tarmac and gravel and generally undertook the manual work associated with the business. She was not paid for this work. In 1999, Mr Thomas and Miss James started to carry on the business as a partnership. By this time, Miss James only assisted in the business on a part-time basis, focussing on book-keeping and paperwork.

In 1991, Mr Thomas acquired – in his sole name – a small parcel of land adjoining The Cottage. Mr Thomas was not required to pay any money for the land: the consideration for the transfer was the provision of building and drainage services to the transferor. These services were provided by Mr Thomas and Miss James, working together in the course of Mr Thomas' business.

During the period Miss James lived in The Cottage, extensive renovation works were carried out at the property. Miss James contributed – 'on a hands-on basis' – to these works; and they were funded from the profits of the business. Mr Thomas told Miss James the improvements to The Cottage would benefit them both. However, on occasions when Miss James suggested to Mr Thomas that The Cottage should be transferred into their joint names, Mr Thomas was evasive or unwilling.

All household, living and personal expenses of Mr Thomas and Miss James were paid out of Mr Thomas' current account. In February 2002, that account was re-designated as Mr Thomas and Miss James' joint account.

Mr Thomas and Miss James separated in 2004; Miss James moved out of The Cottage. In June 2005, they dissolved their business partnership.

The trial judge held that Miss James was not entitled to an equitable interest in the Cottage. The Court of Appeal affirmed his decision.

SIR JOHN CHADWICK, with whom **SMITH LJ** and **WILSON LJ** agreed:

The judge found that there was no sufficient evidence to support a claim based on a common understanding or common intention. At paras 53 and 54 of his judgment he said this:

'The difficulty with [the submissions made on behalf of the claimant], as it seems to me, is that a constructive trust can only arise when land is purchased for the use of two or more persons, only one of whom is registered as the legal owner. It does not seem to me that the claimant can rely on later indirect contributions to the mortgage by her labour as constituting in some way the acquisition of the property for these purposes.

[...] The claimant and the defendant did not know each other at the time the defendant acquired the property in 1986. As such, the property was not acquired for joint use. There cannot have been any common intention, whether actual or presumed, that the claimant should have any beneficial interest in the property. Moreover, it is not alleged by the claimant that there were any discussions between the parties either at the time of the acquisition or subsequently to the effect that they had an agreement or an understanding that the property would be shared. On the contrary, when, on the claimant's evidence, she raised the issue of putting the property in joint names, the defendant was evasive and, she accepted, unwilling.'

Insofar as para 54 contains findings of fact, those findings are not challenged in the grounds of appeal. [...]

[...] It is said [...] that the judge erred in holding (at paras 53 and 54 of his judgment) that 'a common intention constructive trust can only arise where the relevant common intention is formed at the time the property which is alleged to be subject to the trust is acquired'; and [...] that he erred in holding (in para 54) that 'a common intention constructive trust can only come into existence when there is evidence of discussions between the parties to the effect that they had an agreement or understanding that the property would be shared.' It is said that, as a matter of law, the common intention may be formed at any time before, during or after the acquisition of the property; and that the common intention may be inferred from evidence of the parties' conduct during the whole course of their dealings in relation to the property. For my part, I would accept each of those propositions of law. The relevant question is whether, on a true analysis of his judgment as a whole, the judge did (as contended) fail to recognise and give effect to those propositions. [...]

Alert

Did the judge err in law?

Taken out of context, the judge's observation (at para 53 of his judgment) that 'a constructive trust can only arise when land is purchased for the use of two or more persons, only one of whom is registered as the legal owner' provides powerful support for the submission that he misunderstood the law in this field. In the first place, the observation (as a generality) is plainly incorrect: a constructive trust can arise in circumstances where two parties become joint registered proprietors. But that, of course, is not this case. More pertinently, if the circumstances so demand, a constructive trust can arise some years after the property has been acquired by, and registered in the sole name of, one party who (at the time of the acquisition) was, beyond dispute, the sole beneficial owner: *Gissing v Gissing* [1971] AC 886, 901D-E, *Bernard v Josephs* [1982] Ch 391, 404E–F. But, as those cases show, in the absence of an express post-acquisition agreement, a court will be slow to infer from conduct alone that parties intended to vary existing beneficial interests established at the time of acquisition.

Alert

The judge was plainly correct, on the facts in this case, to hold that there was no common intention, at or before the acquisition of the property by Mr Thomas in 1985 or 1986, that Miss James should have some beneficial share: as he found, the parties had not then met. It follows that, unless the judge is to be taken to have accepted (notwithstanding his apparent rejection of that proposition in the observation at para 53 to which I have just referred) that, as a matter of law, it would be sufficient to establish that such an intention arose in or after 1989, there would have been no purpose in going on to consider whether the evidence did establish a common intention that Miss James should have a share. But, plainly, he did consider that question. He referred, in terms (at para 54), to the absence of an allegation by Miss James that 'there were any discussions between the parties *either at the time of the acquisition or subsequently* to the effect that they had an agreement or an understanding that the property would be shared' (emphasis added). To my mind, notwithstanding the observation in para 53 which (taken alone) suggests otherwise, the better view (when the judgment is read as a whole) is that the judge did recognise that there was a need to consider (in relation to constructive trust as well as in relation to proprietary estoppel) whether the parties formed a common intention, in or after 1989, that Miss James should have a beneficial share in the property. Accordingly – although not without hesitation – I reject the submission that the judge erred in law in the first of the three respects summarised in para 23(1) above.

There is force, also, in the submission that the judge failed to recognise that, as a matter of law, a common intention that Miss James should be entitled to a beneficial share in the property might be inferred from evidence of the parties' conduct during the whole course of their dealings in relation to the property. Powerful support for that submission is found in the second sentence of para 53 of the judgment: where the judge observed that Miss James could not rely on later indirect contributions to the mortgage (from the fruits of her labour in the business) 'as constituting in some way the acquisition of the property.' The real question, in this context, was whether Miss James could rely on the use of partnership moneys (or, perhaps, receipts of the business at a time when she was not a partner) to fund payment of instalments due under the mortgage as evidence of an agreement, understanding or intention (made or reached after 1989) that she should have a beneficial share in the property. The judge did not ask himself the question in those terms. But if he had asked himself that question he would have been bound to conclude, on the facts in this case, that the answer must be 'No'.

Alert

Although it is possible to envisage circumstances in which the fact that one party began to make contributions to capital repayments due under a mortgage might evidence an agreement that that party was to have a share in the property, the circumstances of this case are not of that nature. On the facts found by the judge, the only source of funds to meet Mr Thomas' commitments under the mortgage, as well as all other household and personal expenses, was the receipts of the business. While the parties were living together they were dependent on the success of the business to meet their outgoings. It was not at all surprising that, in the early days of their relationship, Miss James should do what she could to ensure that the business prospered. That is not to undervalue her contribution; which, as Mr Thomas recognised, was substantial. But it is to recognise that what she was doing gives rise to no inference that the parties had agreed (or had reached a common understanding) that she was to have a share in the property: what she was doing was wholly explicable on other grounds.

For those reasons, although I find it impossible to be confident that the judge did appreciate that he had to consider whether any (and if so what) inferences as to common intention should be drawn from the parties' conduct in relation to the property – and so impossible to be confident that the judge did not err in law in that respect – I am not persuaded that his error (if he were indeed in error) in the second of the three respects summarised in 23(1) above was material in the circumstances of this case. [...]

Should the judge have held that the assurances given by Mr Thomas (taken with other evidence) were sufficiently specific to found proprietary estoppel or a constructive trust?

The first of the assurances said to have been relied upon – as pleaded at para 15 of the particulars of claim – is that 'whenever the parties discussed carrying out improvements to the property and matters relating to the business, the defendant would say to the claimant 'this will benefit us both.' It must be kept in mind that that was said by Mr Thomas at a time when he and Miss James were living together at the property as man and wife; and in circumstances in which (on the evidence) there was no reason for either of them to doubt that they would continue to do so for the foreseeable future. In that context it is, to my mind, at least as likely that the observation 'this will benefit us both' (in relation to improvements to the property) was intended to mean – and was understood at the time to mean – that the improvements would have the effect

Alert

that the property in which they were living as their home would be more comfortable and more convenient: or, to put the point another way, that the improvements to the property would be reflected in an improvement to the quality of their life together. It is, I think, unreal to suggest that an observation in those terms, made in that context, was intended or understood to be a promise of some property interest, either present or in the future. Confirmation that it was not so intended – and was not understood to be so intended – is found in the judge's observation (in the final sentence at para 54 of his judgment) that 'when, on the claimant's evidence, she raised the issue of putting the property in joint names, the defendant was evasive and, she accepted, unwilling.'

Nor, as it seems to me, can it be said that the observation 'this will benefit us both', when made in the context of a discussion of matters relating to the business, was intended or understood to be a promise of some property interest in The Cottage. Given that the outgoings of both parties were funded by the receipts of the business – and that, from about 1999, the business was carried on in partnership – there is no reason to think that the observation 'this will benefit us both' (in relation to the business) was more than a statement of the obvious: what was of benefit to the business was of benefit to both Mr Thomas and Miss James, for whom the business was their livelihood. [...]

The judge did not find it necessary to address the question whether Miss James acted upon the assurances to her detriment. That is understandable, given that he held that the assurances were not sufficiently specific to found proprietary estoppel or a constructive trust. In the circumstances that I share that view, I, too, find it unnecessary to address the question of reliance. But, for completeness, I should add that the factors which lead to the conclusion that the assurances were not intended or understood as a promise of some property interest lead, also, to the conclusion that it would be unreal to think that Miss James did what she did in reliance on such a promise. The true position, as it seems to me, is that she worked in the business, and contributed her labour to the improvements to the property, because she and Mr Thomas were making their life together as man and wife. The Cottage was their home: the business was their livelihood. It is a mistake to think that the motives which lead parties in such a relationship to act as they do are necessarily attributable to pecuniary self-interest. [...]

Alert

[...] Her interest in the property (if any) must be determined by applying principles of law and equity which (however inadequate to meet the circumstances in which parties live together in the 21st century) must now be taken as well established. Unless she can bring herself within those principles, her claim in the present case must fail. As Baroness Hale of Richmond observed in *Stack v Dowden* [2007] UKHL 17, [2007] 2 AC 432, at para 61, it is not for the court to abandon the search for the result which reflects what the parties must, in the light of their conduct, be taken to have intended in favour of the result which the court itself considers fair.

Geary v Rankine [2012] EWCA Civ 555, [2012] 2 FLR 1409

Court of Appeal: Thorpe LJ, Etherton LJ, and Lewison LJ

Mrs Geary was married, but separated from her husband. In 1990, she formed a relationship with Mr Rankine. They started living together and, in 1992, they had a son.

In 1996, Mr Rankine purchased a guest house – 'Castle View' – in Hastings. He paid the purchase price from his savings. He bought the property as a commercial investment, to be run by a manager. Mr Rankine and Mrs Geary had no intention of living in Castle View or running its business. However, the manager of the business proved unsatisfactory, and Mr Rankine decided to run the business himself. Mr Rankine moved to Castle View, but he was unable to run the business alone. Consequently, Mrs Geary quit her job as a receptionist and moved to Castle View to assist Mr Rankine. Mrs Geary was heavily involved in the business: she helped with the cleaning, she prepared three meals a day for the guests, and she assisted Mr Rankine with the paperwork and banking. She was not paid for these services.

Mrs Geary and Mr Rankine separated in 2009. During their relationship, Mr Rankine told Mrs Geary that he would not 'recognize her' or make a will in her favour until she divorced her husband. When Mrs Geary asked what security she had for herself and their son, Mr Rankine would ignore her or make a non-committal response. Mrs Geary was not divorced from her husband until 2002.

The trial judge dismissed Mrs Geary's claim to an equitable interest in Castle View. The Court of Appeal dismissed her appeal.

LEWISON LJ, with whom **THORPE LJ** and **ETHERTON LJ** agreed:

The second way in which Mrs Geary put her case was that there was a 'common intention' constructive trust. The judge's crucial finding was that Castle View was bought by Mr Rankine entirely with his own money and that at the time of the purchase it was intended to be an investment rather than a home. It was not even intended at that time that Mrs Geary should play any part in the running of the business. The judge accepted Mr Rankine's evidence that at the time of the purchase:

'... the intention was that we would continue to live in London and I would arrange for someone to manage the business in Hastings. There was never an intention that the property would be purchased jointly, nor was there any discussion to that effect. It was not even going to be our home.'

The judge recorded that counsel then appearing for Mrs Geary accepted that the claim to a beneficial interest based on a common intention at the time of the purchase could not be sustained. Mr Broatch did not challenge that conclusion. Rather, he argued that there had been a subsequent change in the common intention such as to give Mrs Geary an interest in the property, even if she was not Mr Rankine's business partner. The applicable principles had been settled at the highest level in *Stack v Dowden* [2007] UKHL 17, [2007] 2 WLR 831 and *Jones v Kernott* [2011] UKSC 53, [2011] 2 WLR 1121. The starting point is the legal title. In this case legal title was in Mr Rankine's name alone. Thus Mrs Geary has the burden of establishing some sort of implied trust; normally what is now termed a 'common intention' constructive trust. The burden is all the more difficult to discharge where, as here, the property was bought as an investment rather than as a home. The search is to ascertain the parties' actual shared intentions, whether express or to be inferred from their conduct. In *Jones v Kernott* it was pointed out that there are at least two exceptions. The first is where there is a presumption of a resulting trust. That presumption may arise where the partners are business partners as well as domestic partners. In the present case, if it applies, that exception would work in Mr Rankine's favour since he provided all the money.

The second is where it is clear that the beneficial interests are to be shared but it is impossible to divine a common intention as to the proportions in which they are to be shared. Whether the beneficial interests are to be shared at all is still a question of a party's actual shared intentions. An imputed intention only arises where the court is satisfied that the parties' actual common intention, express or inferred, was that the beneficial interest would be shared, but cannot make a finding about the proportions in which they were to be shared. The relevant principles are summarized in paras 51 and 52 of *Jones v Kernott* [...]

In a single name case of which this is one, the first issue is whether it was intended that the claimant should have any beneficial interest in the property at all. If that issue is determined in the claimant's favour, the second issue is what that interest is. There is no presumption of joint beneficial ownership. But the common intention has to be deduced objectively from their conduct.

Having rejected the claim Mrs Geary and Mr Rankine had a common intention at the time of the purchase that Mrs Geary should have a beneficial interest in Castle View, the judge went on to consider whether that common intention subsequently changed. It is important to stress that the object of the search is a common intention; that is, an intention common to both parties. So Mrs Geary had to establish that despite the fact that the legal title to the property remained in Mr Rankine's sole name, he actually intended that she should have a beneficial interest in it. As I have said that actual intention may have been expressly manifested, or may be inferred from conduct; but actual intention it remains. The judge found that there was no change in Mr Rankine's intention. He also said that there was no evidence that Mrs Geary had taken any steps to change her own position in reliance on any assertion by Mr Rankine that she would have an interest in the property or in reliance on any steps taken by Mr Rankine from which she could have inferred that his intention had changed. Mr Broatch challenges that finding of fact. He points to a passage in Mrs Geary's evidence to the following effect:

'The manager called Tony (who the defendant had put in to the property to run it) turned out to be a disaster. Events moved quickly. The defendant required me to give up my job in London and move down to Hastings to manage 7

Devonshire Road. The timescale was immediate so that I did not have an opportunity to give proper notice to my employers. The defendant moved our belongings from London to Hastings and within a short time we had both moved to Hastings and relinquished the London property. No matter that the business was purchased in the defendant's sole name, the common intention was that the business would be our joint venture, which we would run together.'

I do not consider that this passage in the evidence supports that claim. What Mrs Geary was saying was that the common intention was that she and Mr Rankine would run the business together, but in my judgment it is an impermissible leap to go from a common intention that the parties would run a business together to a conclusion that it was their common intention that the property in which the business was run, and which was bought entirely with money provided by one of them, would belong to both of them. In addition, Mrs Geary's own evidence makes it clear to my mind that Mr Rankine had no intention that she should have an interest in the property itself. First, as I have said, her evidence was, as was his, that he would refuse to recognize her unless she got divorced. She did not get divorced until 2002, some 6 years after the acquisition. That refusal to recognize her is, in my judgment, inconsistent with an intention on his part that she should have a beneficial interest in the property. I might add that his given reason, namely that he feared that her husband might make a claim on the property, is a perfectly rational reason even if it might not have been given effect. Secondly, Mrs Geary's evidence was that as the years went by she asked what security she had for her and her son and that Mr Rankine either said that the business should remain in his sole name, or was non-committal. Those passages are also, in my judgment, inconsistent with an intention on Mr Rankine's part that Mrs Geary should have a beneficial interest in the freehold of Castle View.

***Thompson v Hurst* [2012] EWCA Civ 1752, [2014] 1 FLR 238**

Court of Appeal: Thorpe LJ, Etherton LJ, and Lewison LJ

In 1983, Miss Hurst was granted a tenancy of a house by a local authority. Miss Hurst formed a relationship with Mr Thompson and he moved into the house in 1985. They had two children. In 2001, Miss Hurst and Mr Thompson agreed to buy the house from the local authority. Their intention was to purchase the house in joint names. However, they were advised by a mortgage broker that Mr Thompson would be an unacceptable risk to lenders. Consequently, the house was purchased in Miss Hurst's name with the assistance of a mortgage for which she was solely responsible. The purchase price (discounted under the right-to-buy scheme) was £15,000.

During the period they were a couple, Mr Thompson and Miss Hurst kept their finances separate. Miss Hurst had two jobs. She paid the rent when the house was rented and the mortgage instalments after it was purchased. She also paid the utility bills. Mr Thompson helped with the council tax charge from 2003. Mr Thompson worked in various jobs throughout the relationship, but there were also periods of unemployment. When he was working, Mr Thompson contributed £100 per week to the household; he contributed less when he was unemployed. Mr Thompson's contribution to the household was used for housekeeping, maintaining and treating the children, and occasional extras. Mr Thompson made no financial contributions after 2005. Mr Thompson did some manual work about the house: he and a friend divided a bedroom into two rooms, he levelled the garden, he painted and decorated.

The relationship between Miss Hurst and Mr Thompson broke down in 2005. Mr Thompson moved out of the house in 2009.

The trial judge held that, as the parties' original intention was to purchase the house in their joint names, there was a common intention that Mr Thompson was to have a beneficial interest in the house. The judge quantified Mr Thompson's share of the equitable interest at 10%. The Court of Appeal dismissed Mr Thompson's appeal.

ETHERTON LJ, with whom **THORPE LJ** and **LEWISON LJ** agreed:

In deciding what beneficial interest should be attributed to the appellant, the district judge took her guidance from the principles in *Oxley v Hiscock*. In particular, she considered that her task was to attribute to the appellant a beneficial interest that was fair, having regard to the whole history of the parties' relationship. In reaching her conclusion that a 10% beneficial interest to the appellant would be fair, the district judge was guided by the following matters. First, she found (at para 18) that '... the only person who brought any financial contribution to the table of the purchase was [the respondent].' She said that the respondent had brought the discount by virtue of her occupation and consistent payment of rent since before the appellant took up occupation at the property. As a result of the discount the property was purchased for £15,000, even though it was valued at £28,000. The mortgage was arranged by the respondent, who spoke to different potential lenders and worked out how much she could afford as the only reliable earner in the household. She alone paid the mortgage.

Secondly, the only subsequent major capital contribution throughout the rest of the time when they were both together in the property was £8,000, which the respondent had received from an equal pay award, and which was largely applied in improvements to the property. It had been applied in alterations to the kitchen, for a fire, for guttering, fascia boards, French windows, a front door and a garden wall.

Thirdly, so far as concerned household contributions, the district judge described (at para 21) the appellant's contributions towards housekeeping of £100 or less per week, depending on his employment situation, as 'perfectly reasonable amounts.' The appellant also contributed to the council tax from 2003. The district judge said (at para 22) that '... the reality is that the basics and the ability to keep their house and live in their house, was provided by [the respondent's] jobs and her financial discipline and order.'

Fourthly, both the appellant and the respondent were responsible for improvements, repairs and renewals. The district judge took into account three specific items on which the appellant relied. They were: helping a tradesman friend to divide a bedroom into two, at a time when the property was still rented; taking the lead within the family in levelling out the garden, including the rockery area; and some painting and decorating in addition to that done by the respondent, and some which was paid for.

The district judge found (at para 29) that the appellant did not really mind that his name was not on the deeds, and that, once the property had been purchased, it was never discussed and was never seriously taken as something that would happen by the respondent.

The appellant made no contribution after 2005. The district judge summarized (at para 35) a 10% beneficial interest to the appellant as reflecting:

'... in fairness, the overwhelming responsibility and contribution which [the respondent] made, both in terms of being the only capital contributor, and also being the major outgoings contributor.'

The appeal

The grounds of appeal fall into two parts and can be simply summarized as follows. First, it is said that, if parties intend to purchase a property in joint names for their occupation as a couple, but fail to do so only as a result of 'external factors,' then the court should proceed on the basis of what would have occurred if the parties had succeeded in that intention. Mr William Josling QC, who appears today as counsel for the appellant, described the intervention of the mortgage adviser in this case as 'a random intervening event.' It is said by Mr Josling that as a matter of common sense, on the facts of this case, the court should proceed on the hypothesis that the joint intention of the parties is reflected in their intention that, subject to the advice of a mortgage adviser, they would wish to take and would have taken the purchase of the property in joint names. If, in the present case, there had been a transfer of the property into the joint names of the appellant and respondent, with no express declaration as to their respective beneficial interests, then, Mr Josling submits, on the basis of *Stack v Dowden* and *Jones v Kernott*, there would have been a presumption that they were beneficially entitled in equal shares and the burden of showing the contrary would have been on the respondent. Mr Josling submits that, in view of the district judge's finding (at para 16) of a common intention about purchasing the property in joint names, there was plainly no contrary intention at the time of purchase. He further submits that, bearing in mind that matters continued after 2001 as they had beforehand, there is nothing to show that the parties' intention, actual, inferred or imputed, changed after the property was purchased.

The second ground for the appeal is that, in any event, the district judge's apportionment of the beneficial interest as to 90% to the respondent and only 10% to the appellant was plainly wrong. It was not fair, Mr Josling submits, having regard to the parties' whole course of dealing between them. The respondent may have paid a greater share of the household expenses, but the parties lived together as equals for 20 years, some 16 of them before the purchase of the property. They raised their children together in the property. The appellant made a perfectly reasonable contribution towards the household expenditure, with he and the respondent contributing such amounts as they were able towards the family pot.

Discussion and conclusion

Mr Josling has argued the appeal valiantly, and with skill, but in my judgment it quite plainly cannot succeed.

The appellant's starting point is that the court should analyse the appellant's entitlement to a beneficial interest in the property as if the transfer actually had been in the joint names of himself and the respondent. There is no doubt that, if the legal title to the property had been transferred into their joint names, then pursuant to *Stack v Dowden* and *Jones v Kernott* the presumption would have been that they intended a joint tenancy both in law and equity. The presumption that they intended their equitable interest to be equal could be rebutted only by evidence of their intention, actual or inferred, objectively ascertained. If there were such evidence, but it was not possible to say what their actual intention was as to the shares in which they were to own the property, they would each be entitled to that share which the court considered fair, having regard to the whole course of dealing in relation to the property.

I do not accept, however, the appellant's starting point. The transfer was not in fact into the joint names of the appellant and the respondent. There is, therefore, no scope for a legal presumption that the parties intended a joint tenancy both in law and equity. Mr Josling's argument amounts to a submission that there should be a legal presumption of joint beneficial ownership, not merely where the parties are indeed the joint legal owners, but where there is evidence that they would have liked to be joint legal owners but for one reason or another that was not practical or desirable. Neither Stack v Dowden nor Jones v Kernott, nor any other case, is authority for such a proposition. Indeed, the proposition is neither consistent with principle nor sound policy.

In any event, it is unrealistic to make the assumption that, had matters proceeded as the parties intended, inevitably they would have been joint legal owners of the property but without any express declaration as to the trusts on which they held it. If they had proceeded to take legal advice, their legal adviser would have been bound to advise them that they should make an express declaration as to the trusts on which they were to hold the property. They would have explained to the legal adviser that their primary purpose was to ensure something for the children. If the legal adviser had explored what was to happen before their deaths while still owning the property, for example if, as happened, the parties were to split up and end their relationship, it is quite impossible to say what the reaction of the parties would have been. It certainly cannot be assumed that they would have agreed that they were to be joint beneficial owners as well as joint legal owners, bearing in mind the facts of this particular case as found by the district judge. Moreover, as Lewison LJ pointed out in the course of argument, the matter could only have proceeded towards a joint purchase in joint names if the appellant had been willing and able to assume a liability as a mortgagor; but he could not and he did not.

Accordingly, I do not accept Mr Josling's submission that it is a matter of common sense that, merely because prior to receiving the advice from the mortgage adviser the parties intended that the purchase should be in joint names, the court should proceed on the hypothetical basis that that is what took place for the purpose of analysing the appellant's equitable interest, even though the actual transfer was into the respondent's name alone. As Lewison LJ has recently emphasized in *Chapman v Jaume* [2012] EWCA Civ 476, [2012] 2 FLR 830, both *Stack v Dowden* and *Jones v Kernott* make clear that, in the case of a transfer into the name of only one of the cohabiting parties, the starting point is quite different from the joint legal owner case. In the case of joint legal ownership, the property is necessarily held on trust and the only question is as to the size of the respective beneficial interests of the parties. In the case of a single legal owner, such as the present, where there is no express declaration of a trust, the claimant has first to establish some sort of implied trust, normally what is now termed a common intention constructive trust: *Jones v Kernott* at para 17 and para 52. The claimant must show that it was intended that he or she was to have a beneficial interest at all. That can only be achieved by evidence of the parties' actual intentions, express or inferred, objectively ascertained. If such evidence does show a common intention to share beneficial ownership, but does not show what shares were intended, then each of them is to have that share which the court considers fair, having regard to the whole of dealing in relation to the property: *Jones v Kernott* at paras 51 and 52).

In the present case, the district judge considered (at para 16) that a common intention that the appellant was to have a beneficial interest in the property was to be inferred from the common intention, prior to the advice of the mortgage adviser, that they would buy the property jointly. I have some difficulty in understanding why the district judge reached that conclusion in the light of all her other findings, including that neither the appellant nor the respondent gave any thought as to how the beneficial interest should fall if it did not go to the children. There is, however, no cross-appeal against the district judge's finding on that aspect.

Having reached her conclusion that there was a common intention that the appellant should have a beneficial interest in the property, but that there was no common intention, express or inferred, about what the respective beneficial interests of the appellant and the respondent should be, the district judge quite correctly then embarked on the task of determining what would be fair having regard to the whole course of dealing between them in relation to the property. She carried out that task in a careful and exemplary fashion. Mr Josling accepts that her decision on that aspect can only be overturned if she made an error of principle or was plainly wrong. It is quite impossible, in my view, to say that any such error of principle was made, or that the district judge was plainly wrong.

***Aspden v Elvy* [2012] EWHC 1387 (Ch), [2012] 2 FCR 435**

Chancery Division: Judge Behrens (sitting as a judge of the High Court)

Mr Aspden and Ms Elvy formed a relationship in 1985 and started living together in 1986. They had two children. The relationship did not last and they separated in 1996.

In 2006, Ms Elvy acquired Outlaithe Barn. Mr Aspden helped Ms Elvy convert the barn into a house. He did much of the manual labour himself and allowed Ms Elvy the use of his JCB, saving Ms Elvy 'substantial' labour and hiring costs. Mr Aspden also contributed between £65,000 and £70,000 to the costs of the conversion.

In these circumstances, Judge Behrens inferred an intention on the part of Mr Aspden and Ms Elvy that Mr Aspden should have a beneficial interest in Outlaithe Barn.

JUDGE BEHRENS:

This is not a case where there were any express discussions that Mr Aspden should obtain an interest in Outlaithe Barn. Thus in order to succeed in establishing an implied trust Mr Aspden must establish that the common intention of the parties (objectively ascertained) was that he should have an interest as a result of the substantial contributions both in financial and physical terms that he made to the works. Mr Aspden's case is that he was because he was expecting to be able (at some time in the future) to move back in to Outlaithe Barn. Ms Elvy's case is that the contributions were simply gifts to her made no doubt in recognition of the relationship, and the fact that she was the mother of his two children.

I have not found the resolution of this question easy. In the end I cannot accept that the proper inference is that the contributions were intended to be gifts. The moneys involved represented a very substantial part of Mr Aspden's assets after he had paid off his creditors. If they were intended as gifts he would in effect leave himself with nowhere to live except the caravan. I think that Mr Aspden did hope and expect to be able to live in and have an interest in Outlaithe Barn when it was complete and that Ms Elvy was fully aware of it.

I think that the proper inference from the whole course of dealing is that there was a common intention that Mr Aspden should have some interest in Outlaithe Barn as a result of the very substantial contributions made to the conversion works. I am fortified in this by observations of Griffiths LJ in *Bernard v Joseph* [1982] 3 AER 162, 171:

Alert

'It might in exceptional circumstances be inferred that the parties agreed to alter their beneficial interests after the house was bought; an example would be if the man bought the house in the first place and the woman years later used a legacy to build an extra floor to make more room for the children. In such circumstances the obvious inference would be that the parties agreed that the woman should acquire a share in the greatly increased value of the house produced by her money ...'

It seems to me that the contributions made by Mr Aspden are akin to the case envisaged by Griffiths LJ.

Valuation of Mr Aspden's interest is also difficult. There were no express discussions and the only valuation I have is that the current value of Outlaithe Barn is of the order of £400,000. In those circumstances I have to impute an intention by reference to what is fair having regard to the whole course of dealing between the parties. The submissions of counsel suggested wildly different results. Miss Darlington suggested that the interest should be limited to the expenditure itself or at most be 10%. Miss Greenan suggested (probably on the basis of the primary case) that it should be 75%.

In the end I have decided that the appropriate fair assessment of the interest is 25%. To my mind that represents a fair return for the investment of £65,000 to £70,000 and the work carried out by Mr Aspden in a property now worth £400,000. The figure is somewhat arbitrary but it is the best I can do with the available material.

14.4 Quantification

Where a cohabitant in a joint names case establishes a common intention that the equitable title should be held other than jointly, or where the non-legal owner in a sole name case establishes a common intention that she was to have an equitable interest coupled with detrimental reliance on that common intention, the court will have to quantify the parties' shares in the property. If the parties' expressed their intention in relation to their shares, or it can be inferred from their conduct, the court will give effect to that intention. In other cases the court will impute an intention to the parties as to their respective shares. Many of the cases above discuss this issue. One other case is worth noting here.

Graham-York v York **[2015] EWCA Civ 72, [2015] HLR 26 (p 532)**

Court of Appeal: Moore-Bick VPCA, Tomlinson LJ, and King LJ

Miss Graham-York lived with Mr York from 1976 until Mr York's death in 2009. Their relationship was dysfunctional: Mr York had a controlling nature and a proclivity for violence. Miss Graham-York and Mr York had two children, a son and a daughter. Their son was raised by his grandmother.

In 1983, Mr York acquired a house with the assistance of a mortgage. Miss Graham-York and Mr York moved into the house in 1985. Mr York paid the mortgage instalments and other outgoings.

In 1983-1985, Miss Graham-York worked as a singer. She contributed her earnings to the household: they materially assisted the purchase of the house. After 1985, Miss Graham-York earned £30,000 from various business activities. The judge did not make any specific finding as to how much of this money (if any) was contributed to the household. But the judge did hold that Miss Graham-York's financial contributions to the household, during the 33 years she lived with Mr York, did 'not amount to much.' Miss Graham-York cooked all the family meals and cared for their daughter.

The trial judge held that Miss Graham-York was entitled to 25% of the equity in the house. The Court of Appeal rejected Miss Graham-York's argument that her interest should have been quantified at 50%.

TOMLINSON LJ, with whom **MOORE-BICK VPCA** and **KING LJ** agreed:

[...] It is essential, in my judgment, to bear in mind that, in deciding in such a case what shares are fair, the court is not concerned with some form of redistributive justice. Thus it is irrelevant that it may be thought a 'fair' outcome for a woman who has endured years of abusive conduct by her partner to be allotted a substantial interest in his property on his death. The plight of Miss Graham-York attracts sympathy, but it does not enable the court to redistribute property interests in a manner which right-minded people might think amounts to appropriate compensation. Miss Graham-York is 'entitled to that share which the court considers fair having regard to the whole course of dealing between them in relation to the property.' It is these last words, which I have emphasized, which supply the confines of the enquiry as to fairness.

The judge can perhaps be criticized for omitting these qualifying words from her formulation at her para 42, set out at para 13 above. But to my mind it is clear from the balance of that paragraph, and from her para 43, that the judge focused on the relevant consideration, which was the extent of Miss Graham-York's contribution, both financial and non-financial, in relation to the property which was their family home for many years.

In this regard I do not consider that reference to the evaluations made by judges in other cases of particular assistance. Reference was made on the appeal to *Webster v Webster* [2008] EWHC (Ch) 31, [2009] 1 FLR 1240, a decision of Judge Behrens. That was a case of sole legal ownership by the male partner and cohabitation for twenty seven years. Both partners worked although the male partner had the greater income. There was much better evidence than here of the woman's regular contribution, which was significantly less than that of her partner. Judge Behrens did not in the event have to assess the extent of the woman's interest, because that issue had become academic in the light of his intended disposition under the Inheritance (Provision for Family and Dependants) Act 1975, which was that the property in question should be transferred to her outright. He did however indicate that having regard to the whole history of the dealings between them it was unlikely that he would have assessed it at 50 per cent and probable that he would have assessed it at between 33 per cent and 40 per cent. [...]

Reference to that case does however, I consider, throw into sharp focus three features of the debate. First, as established in *Oxley v Hiscock* itself, at para 39 of the judgment of Chadwick LJ, in the case of a property purchased in the

name of one party only, even with the aid of a substantial contribution from the other, there is no presumed starting point of equality of interests. *Oxley* was a case of sole ownership by the man with considerable financial contribution from the woman. It led only to a 40 per cent share being regarded as her fair entitlement. Secondly, therefore, the suggestion in the present case that equality of interests is the only fair solution is quite hopeless. Third, the judicial evaluation of the fair share is not one in respect of which there is only one right answer. It is an exercise the outcome of which should only be disturbed by an appellate court if it falls outside the ambit of reasonable decision-making.

It is also I think possible to be led astray by the length of the cohabitation. It is obviously true that in the normal case the non-financial contribution is likely to be proportionately greater the longer the cohabitation. But to be set against that in the present case is the judge's damning finding at para 23 of her judgment that 'even if she were telling the truth about her financial contribution during the 33 years of cohabitation it does not amount to much.'

The woman's financial contribution in *Webster v Webster* was very significantly greater than that which the judge found here, and that combined with a cohabitation of 27 years might apparently have led the judge to find as fair an entitlement in the range of 33 per cent to 40 per cent.

The judge in the present case, with the advantage of having heard argument and evidence over five days, regarded her evaluation of a 25 per cent interest as 'generous.' The judge directed herself properly as to the approach which she should take to the evaluative exercise. She fell into no legal or analytical error, certainly neither of those identified at para 15 above. I can discern no principled basis upon which this court can regard her evaluation as falling outside the ambit of reasonable decision-making. Had the judge evaluated Miss Graham-York's interest at, say, 33 per cent, her decision would I consider have been equally unassailable, but for this court now to evaluate the interest in that way would be unprincipled, would rightly be castigated as what is in another context described as 'tinkering,' and would simply encourage appeals, raising false expectations and leading to further erosion of modest estates.